PRA

"In writing his parents, novelist Gus Lee perforce weaves a tapestry of Chinese history that went on before them, behind them, and around them. It's a huge tapestry, parti-colored, spanning a busy century that included the Taiping Rebellion, Chiang Kai-shek, Mao Zedong, the Rape of Nanking, and *Gone with the Wind*. Fashioning a panorama of such dimensions is no easy task." —*San Francisco Chronicle*

"Lee . . . has created a gripping and beautiful portrait of his ancestors and their powerful legacy. He calls *Chasing Hepburn* nonfiction, but it reads just as richly as any novel . . . [a] powerful brew of historical detail and a mélange of Western and Eastern images." —*Boston Globe*

"Laced with physical peril, political intrigue, and a host of key historical figures . . . [*Chasing Hepburn*] is at once a gripping adventure and a tender recreation of the author's parents' young lives and their elegant ancestral traditions." —*Colorado Springs Independent*

"*Chasing Hepburn* will surely find its audience. Students of Chinese history, and especially those curious about Shanghai in the first three decades of the twentieth century (possibly the most fascinating metropolis ever), will find a book filled with detail and information." —*The Washington Post Book World*

"[F]illed with heartbreak, regret, and remorse."
—*The New York Times Book Review*

"*Chasing Hepburn* is a memoir of staggering richness . . . [a] marvelous account of a Chinese family in a startling historical context."
—*Richmond Times-Dispatch*

"[R]ich in detail: a uniquely personal perspective on one of the most fascinating and tumultuous periods in history." —*Kirkus Reviews*

"Lee's writing is a constant pleasure of vibrant detail and effective dialogue . . . Lee's most remarkable skill, however, is his ability to deftly move between the personalities of his family's intimate moments, and his observations of Chinese cultural history." —*Publishers Weekly*

"Gus Lee brings to his first work of nonfiction the consummate storytelling skills which have always delighted us in his critically acclaimed novels. I promise that you will be captivated by this epic story of two families who epitomize all that is rich and varied in Chinese culture."
—Ron Bass, screenwriter of *The Joy Luck Club* and *Rain Man*

Chasing Hepburn

A Memoir of Shanghai,
Hollywood, and a Chinese
Family's Fight for
Freedom WITHDRAWN

GUS LEE

 THREE RIVERS PRESS • NEW YORK

Frontispiece photograph: Zee Zee, Da-tsien, Elinor. *Hongchiao Airport, Shanghai, 1930. Da-tsien has again refused to fly.*

Published by Three Rivers Press, New York, New York.
Member of the Crown Publishing Group, a division of Random House, Inc.
www.randomhouse.com

THREE RIVERS PRESS and the Tugboat design are registered trademarks of Random House, Inc.

Originally published in hardcover by Harmony Books, a division of Random House, Inc., in 2003

Printed in the United States of America

Design by Lauren Dong

Library of Congress Cataloging-in-Publication Data
Lee, Gus.
  Chasing Hepburn : a memoir of Shanghai, Hollywood, and a Chinese family's fight for freedom / by Gus Lee.
  1. Lee, Gus. 2. Novelists, American—20th century—Biography. 3. Hollywood (Los Angeles, Calif.)—Biography. 4. Chinese American—Biography. 5. Shanghai (China)—Biography. 6. Family—China—Shanghai. I. Title.
PS3562.E3524 Z465   2002
813'.54—dc21   [B] 2002017285

ISBN 1-4000-5155-X

10 9 8 7 6 5 4 3 2 1

First Paperback Edition

To Mah-mee,
with love and faith and hope.

Acknowledgments

I BOW TO my mother, Tzu Da-tsien of Soochow, and to my father, Tsung-chi Lee of Yangchow.

I extend loving appreciation to my wonderful sisters—Elinor Lee Hause, Ying Lee and Dr. Ming Tzu. Thank you for raising me and for inspiring me with your strength and courage. My love to our family—Lars, Cece and Jasmine Ai-wen Stenberg, Max and Sallie Kelley, Sara Ying Kelley and Dr. Mark Rounsaville, Anna Lagios and Eva Chrysanthe, and Robert and Maralyn Elliott, parents-in-law.

I offer deepest appreciation to our brave Shanghai cousins—Li Huo-son, Li Chin, and Li Lulu and our wonderful family—Yuan Chung, Chen, Wang, Chien, Chan, Ying, Hai Peng, Shiao Peng and Chieh. Thank you for sharing your precious lives and priceless memories.

Heartfelt thanks go to Joe and Su-mi Tu, who shared their Shanghai memories as if I were one of their fortunate children. With deepest thanks to my siblings-of-the-heart, David Kai Tu and Kristl Tu, with appreciation for David letting me use his middle name in my books.

Writing is collaborative. I would have no career without my dear friend and agent, Jane Dystel, and the brilliant Miriam Goderich, of Jane Dystel Literary Management. I would have no final manuscript without Shaye Areheart, my incredible and insightful editor. I would have missed these writing opportunities without the historic and groundbreaking art of my beloved sister-in-heart, Amy Tan. I owe much to my other editors—Gary Luke, Arnold Dolin, Ash Green and Leona Nevler. Thanks to Teryn Johnson and Lauren Dong for your help and your art.

As always, I salute from the heart the West Point Class of 1968 and members of Company A, Third Regiment, USCC.

I thank my Endur colleagues, who in many ways were part of this book: Frank Ramirez, Chris Kay, John Whitcomb, Rufus Nagel, Bob Skaggs, Alec Wynne, Adrian Foley, Skip Spensley, Buz Barclay, Mike Minor, Lt. Gen. Jim Ellis, Ret., and my mentors, Gen. H. Norman Schwarzkopf, Ret., and Col. Charlie Murray, Ret., and John Prosser.

For historical texture, I owe deep gratitude to my graduate advisor, Professor Emeritus Kwang-ching Liu, University of California at Davis, for his teaching, counsel and friendship. I relied upon his revelatory books and other wonderful authors: Jonathan Spence, Harrison E. Salisbury, John King Fairbank, Frederick Wakeman, Jr., Harriet Sergeant, Graham Peck, Anne Edwards, Stephen Becker and fine writers who still serve West Point—Ed Ruggero, Tom Carhart and Len Marella.

Thank you to Lee Mendelson of Mendelson Pictures, my film partner.

I owe gratitude to the First Presbyterian Churches of Colorado Springs and Burlingame. I thank my covenant brothers, with singular appreciation to Frank Ramirez. Your broad shoulders have guarded families and clans against wolves. Deep thanks to my first friend, Dr. Toussaint Streat, and to brethren Barry Shiller, Eric Becker, Bob Batchelder, Robin Dailey, Bill Helwig, Rob Dougherty, Bob Laird, David Croslin, Tom Baker, Ike Elliott, Steve Schibsted, Paul Benchener and Paul Watermulder, who, as I, know where all thanks are due.

Life is even more collaborative than writing. I am blessed in Diane and in our wonderful children, Jena, Eric and Jessica. You are my *shinkan*, heart and liver, and you are my loves. Is life not wonderful?

Contents

I was raised on fractured clan stories and have chased their missing parts all my life. After four autobiographical novels, this work, *Chasing Hepburn*, represents the essence of the effort.

This is a work of memory and storytelling. It is the sum of many recollections of those who suffered Chinese history. The story began a century ago when my parents were born to tung oil lamps in the spring and winter of 1906. For half a century, their pasts remained in shadow.

In his ninety-first year, Dad began to tell me his stories. Yet, despite incredible disclosures in the autumn of his life, many of Dad's accounts lacked endings. When I asked for them, he said he had already told me.

Dad passed away on March 6, 1998. Later, I moved his many papers into my study. In 2000, while clearing space to research this book, I came across an old manila file of Dad's labeled "My Story." This was eight pages of his autobiography, written in the 1980s and never finished. Behind them were hundreds of handwritten letters scribed in fading pencil. They began on February 5, 1970, and continued into the late Eighties. They were addressed to me; he had never mailed them. In these letters were many of the missing parts of his stories.

On a linguistic note, I have used Dad's traditional Wade-Giles Romanization of Chinese words. Dad was nothing if not stubborn, and he refused to learn modern Pinyin with its formidable X's, Q's and Z's. This is a story of the Twentieth Century, and the older spelling fits that time.

On a storytelling note, I make a prosecutor's observation that eyewitnesses to common events can disagree on identities, dates and locations. This story is no different. In criminal law, the focus is upon provable facts. Because this story is morally my mother's, the focus is upon relationships, where she believed the truth lived.

As a deputy district attorney preparing a murder case, I would ask relatives of the victim for small, personal details of the deceased's life. *What awakened her in the morning? Was she a morning person? Was she a reader? Was she funny? Who was her best friend? Her soul mate? Who were her enemies? Was she a reader? Could she see herself with insight?* Did she meet Kierkegaard's definition of a self-aware person who can resist the seduction of bad habits?

I put those questions to my sisters, to our Shanghai cousins, to our father. The answers dwelled on character, relationships and setting.

The facts are that our father died virtually alone and that I still miss my mother. It is also a fact that I created bridges between missing story elements, particularly for scenes set in the Nineteenth Century. I filled in imagined details and added weight to the known spines of dialogue and setting.

It is a truth that we are an American family, typical in many ways and common in many habits. We are blessed with legal rights, moral opportunities and material advantages, and our children have access to liberties that would shock an emperor. Loving America, I miss the Chinese relational roots that were the cost of acquiring freedom.

I have used my Chinese roots and my American legal education to argue the story of my mother.

My mother was a woman of faith and relationship. I pray that this story is worthy of her.

She was a storyteller and I am her son, a minor tale-spinner in a fine and ancient parade of rubber-faced Yangtze River storytellers. Each of our predecessors told and retold histories to preserve meaning, to advance honor, to tell truth and to entertain anyone who paused in a busy marketplace to hear a tale about courage and beauty.

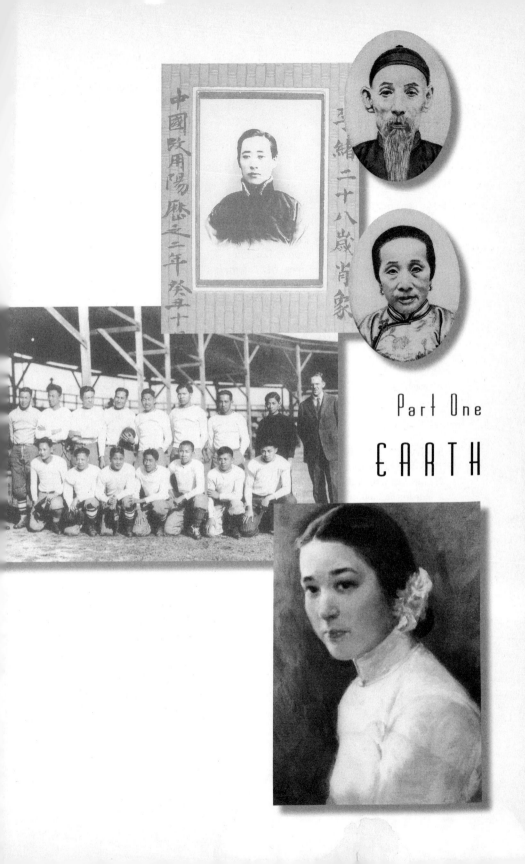

中國改用陽歷之二年癸丑十

光緒二十八歲肖象

Part One

EARTH

LEE SHUI-FENG, Great-grandfather and the husband of the Bravest Wife, wearing the fine long scholar's beard that elevated him above common men of the earth.

LEE KUNG-DOO, son of Lee Shui-feng. My paternal grandfather, Master Lee, and Zee Zee's father, before the opium poppy ravaged him.

LEE SHUI-FENG'S SECOND WIFE, whom he married after being freed from Nanking following his second captivity. Lee Kung-doo, Master Lee, was not born to her, but to Shui-feng's second concubine, who had no portrait.

ST. JOHN'S FOOTBALL TEAM, Shanghai 1923. Zee Zee is fifth from left, first row. He has just returned from being sick after a year in the Gobi with the German Army, where a fever nearly killed him.

DA-TSIEN, Shanghai c. 1925. Criticized by her mother, loved by her father, hopeful that her husband will give her a son and never leave her.

Who Will Marry You Now?

THE FUTURE SHIFTED when the clan ladies failed to break my mother's tiny feet. From then on, her life was guided by the good and the bad of that day. She would grow up to be a dreamer who married a rogue, a woman who laughed easily whenever she thought of how her big, unbound feet had saved four females and caused us to become Americans.

The story begins when she is three. She is the Only Daughter of the House of Tzu. Cherished by all, she loves easily. Servants pamper her to chase away the tiniest frown, tickling her toes to hear her sweet laughter. All of heaven, from Lei Tsu, the three-eyed father of thunder, to T'u Ti, the dwarfed, puckish local deity, honor this sweet child. She is Little Missy Da-tsien, granddaughter of a great man, and she smiles at all people and loves all gods. Surely she will win a rich husband and make fruitful sons, multiplying clan wealth and making everyone except herself crazy with happiness.

If I look into the distance of my family's past, I see fireflies flitting in the fields as low angles of soft afternoon sunlight fill the upper rooms of the great house. It is the hour of late tea in the pleasant autumn of 1909, just before the entire world will change.

Da-tsien has been denied her nap to make her slow and pliable, so now, instead, she's quick and cranky. Lao Chu, the burly chef, and his robust white-jacketed cooks bang hot black iron woks in clouds of sizzling steam to produce a sumptuous second meal of the day for forty mouths and eighty chopsticks. The neatly dressed house staff anticipate the good dishes, enjoying the textured scents that promise a satisfying meal.

Rich homes of this era have housemasters, majordomos. In the crossings of oceans and the tides of time, our domo's name has been lost. He's remembered as a blunt man with keen eyes, a harsh voice and a neat mustache that would bristle for dramatic emphasis. He had little to do since the Tzu *jia*— the clan of the Tzus—stopped doing trade and making money.

The basic social unit in China is the family. Chinese families are not nuclear with parents at the center—they are vertical and horizontal, with ruling elders and the dead ancestors earnestly watching from above and, not infrequently, from below. These are the *jia*, the clans—lacking in privacy, prosperous in community, robust in support and rich in conflict.

The Tzu *jia* was once part of the bustling pharmaceutical Yangtze River herb trade. It was like being in medicine before managed care. Business was so good that the majordomo bragged about it. But gods listen and punish pride. The big words floated upward to heaven with the kitchen-stove smoke, drying up rain clouds and creating droughts that killed Tzu-land crops and caused starving pirates to raid their herbal boats for the last vestiges of the produce.

Now, instead of making business, the clan cruises on old profits and the domo gambles with Ah Tsui, my mother's amah, a personal maid who will attend her until one of them dies. Ah Tsui is a round and full country girl who is quick to criticize imperfection and to remember cards. When cards run towards her luck, she snorts through her nose like a young mare in spring; when they don't, she grinds her molars.

Later, Amah will comfort her little girl. Amah's the laziest and most superstitious member of the nonworking house. She's been eating Lao Chu's cooking since Da-tsien's birth, but her sudden, bloodcurdling midnap howls at invisible spirits still make the others jump as if T'sao T'sao, the devil, had stuck a kitchen knife into their bottoms. Ah Tsui is plagued by spirits that try to dig their way into her clothing to find secret hidden coins and old, sequestered food.

She heats a tub of warming and healing mineral waters to soothe her baby girl. Anxious servants watch the majordomo and the amah play cards as the mineral waters cool, dishes sizzle and hot spicy aromas lace the air. Soon it will happen. Screams will fill the house, chasing away all good thoughts. Pain for the sweet little girl, their precious Da-tsien, the one with the laughter of heaven. Some will cry; most will lower their heads. Hot food will help. They wait uneasily, cleaning their teeth and nails. The frowning men are more nervous than the women, who are unusually quiet.

The gentry ladies have been preparing all day, complimenting one another loudly, laughing abruptly, eating too much, joking about wine-drinking men and slow servants. They are steeling themselves. They look at Taitai, my maternal grandmother, my mother's mah-mee, the conductor of the house's feelings, for guidance.

Taitai is a short, fine-featured woman in a comfortable silk cheongsam, loose enough for doing work. She has so much burning clarity in her left eye that tricky merchants lower their heads, not crazy enough to bargain with so much heat. Today her eye is sharp and feral.

Finally, Taitai nods and the household ladies take her little daughter upstairs. She'll be a famous beauty, they remind one another—a fabled bride who'll make sons with long luck, old money, perfect faces and big male organs. They encourage one another because hurting this child will be hard, harder than any other in their long experience.

They close the doors and windows, locking out a sun fatigued by its hot work for Mr. and Mrs. Tu-di, the Chinese gods of the earth. The mister and missus are heavenly white-haired elders who manage agriculture for the best farmers of the earth. The missus is careful, ensuring that the soil is fertile, but the old man can be forgetful, allowing torrential floods or accidentally kicking away the clouds of rain from sun-parched fields. Some of the women will later recall that they glimpsed ominous shadows of evil fox spirits dancing on the waters by the house, and that the outside air seemed tomblike, leaving a bad weight on the heart.

On the canal, a lonely dirt farmer on a bony raft calls out his last wares with hopeful notes—cheap, half a copper for all that's left! But none of the pretty ladies in swishing high-necked silk gowns appear on their balcony of Shi Shr er, Lucky Seventy Two Way, to clack their long nails on the mahogany railing. He calls again, mournfully.

The women take deep breaths. They softly caress the little girl's cheeks, brush her dark hair, gaze into her immense round eyes and soothe her with cooing words, "Shiaobaobee, Shiaobaobee, Little Precious," while removing her tiny silk slippers.

Kind Auntie Gao reclines the child on the padded tabletop. She caresses the girl's feet, warming the ligaments. The girl smiles, then jerks as Auntie bends the four smallest toes, stretching the joints, leaving the largest to stand like a lonely sentinel, watching the fate of the others.

There are many methods for binding feet. In the backcountry, toes can be bent with increasing pressure for months. But this is Soochow, the city of elegant women, and the technique is brutal. When joints are loosened and warm, Auntie will nod and one of the ladies will sharply pinch the girl's ear to distract her as Auntie snaps the toes, making the sound of fried grasshoppers in a sizzling-hot wok. As the girl shrieks, Auntie will send her soft thoughts, then break the big toe and, with steady pressure, tightly bind all five to the body of the foot with a pure white bandage, fifteen palms long. This will bend the foot under itself. Her little niece will scream and fight as pain fills every nerve in her body. The pain will ebb as she gasps for air, recovering some *chi*, her inner strength, and then Auntie Gao will break the toes of the other foot.

The pain will persist through adolescence, ebbing and cresting while other bones fail and the foot dies and the skin with it as the girl matures into womanhood. Of course, some girls will perish from infections, and others will be crippled. It is the Soochow way. The canals that grace the city replaced arable soil, and now beautiful feet replace country feet. This is life and the commandment of beauty. It's a blessing for wellborn girls to be groomed for rich men, their tiny, inviting feet held by diminutive shoes.

In other times and lands, alternative parts of the female body will be emphasized or encased in other challenging interventions. This is the era of crippling feet, of hamstringing the liberty of girls for the pleasure of male eyes. It is a time of strengthening gentry clans by producing sons, for sons determine a clan's destiny and ensure survival for five thousand years. Sons serve elders in this world and care for the dead in the next life. Only sons warrant clan memory tablets and are able to survive against capricious gods who control weather, fertility and fortune.

When Auntie Gao was little, her clan women botched the binding, breaking the wrong bones and inducing a purple fever that stunted her growth and cost cash in doctoring and remedial fortune-telling. Her right foot grew at a bad-luck angle, ruining her future as a bride and cloaking her house with a spiritual darkness. Because the women had *tsa guo*, "dropped the pots" with her, Auntie grew into a small, limping woman who deserved her angry husband with the sour heart. But her victimization as a wife made her sensitive to the needs of others. She became a top foot-binder in Soochow, the city of picturesque canals and lovely ladies. Wearing Taoist black and a kind look, she calmed the unhappiest girl and quickly and neatly broke toes to create beauty and to help clans.

Auntie has a small face framed by tightly coiled black hair. She looks older than her twenty-six years. She dearly loves her three-year-old niece, taking her time, warming up the precious foot as she breathes deeply to collect strength for the snapping of bones. She says a quick prayer to Guan Yin, the female goddess of mercy and male children. *May good luck and healthy sons come from this hard day!*

Da-tsien cries under the cresting pain, calls out to young Auntie Gao— *Please stop!* She begs for Ah Tsui, her amah, but *Amah's gone!* She reaches for Mother—*Mah-mee helps them!* She can't hear Mah-mee's encouragements, her justifications, her descriptions of fine young men with old money who will be pleased with the results of today's tears. The girl squirms to fight free, but she's pinned to the table by a phalanx of women, and she screams pitifully, her cries echoing through the three floors of the Chinese mansion. She weeps to heaven, and some women bite their lips as others show teeth and blink back tears. The house's gray mouser cats perk pointed ears and sedately take cover.

Downstairs, Ah Tsui freezes, her round face wrenching in pain. She prays to Guan Yin, apologizing for her laziness, her weaknesses. Since birth, Da-tsien has been taught all about the goddess of mercy. *Guan Yin is strong and heals all hurts*, Ah Tsui promised my mother.

Da-tsien, a child who has never known hardship or privation in a household of kind women, begs Guan Yin to come as a bright-winged phoenix from the sky to rescue her. She cries needfully at the ceiling, but no one comes. Desperately, she screams for Baba, her father.

They smile tightly. Her mother breathes, "Ssss, be strong." Auntie straightens the foot, the toes protesting, bending them.

Da-tsien's baba, my maternal grandfather, is a silly man given to reading foreign books, catching unneeded fish and babbling foreign thoughts in his sleep. It's a fact, they say, that if he keeps dozing with foreign books in his lap, he'll absorb the White Devil tongue and become a follower of the Christian god who smacks his lips as he devours children. The women make fun of Baba, but they like his kind heart and quiet voice. They appreciate these qualities more than beauty. In China, a woman's freedom from total male dominion of her words and actions comes only from kind men.

Baba loves his library. Books, unlike his wife, are open and shut and susceptible to being read at a gentlemanly pace. Peace, unlike criticism, invites sleep, so he naps in a room lined with quiet texts. His favorite spot is a kind French chair that replaced an unforgiving, hardwood cherry Kiangsu seat that was designed by the enemy of happy backs. Perhaps he dreams that his little daughter has caught a fish.

Her screams cascade down the grand staircase to bounce off the domed ceiling and he jerks awake, his book—Balzac?—tumbling onto a thick Tehrani carpet.

He is tall with a full head of jet-black hair, a long, straight nose, a handsome, rectangular face, large eyes, thick hands and broad shoulders rounded by years of good reading and zealous fishing. His thoughts resemble the movements of his bearlike body—slow, hesitant, reflective.

Little Missy! Foggy from sleep and foreign thoughts, he finds himself bounding up the stairs, abandoning his well-earned reputation for inaction and caution, a reputation that allows him to avoid family squabbles and the tiring monetary frictions of gentry clan management. He moves well for a big man, but his sprint up the stairs alarms the servants—only the uneducated are authorized to exert physical effort.

Panting, he enters an upper room. The women are dressed up with red cheeks, fine clothes and coiffed hair in a riot of shining peach, azure, burgundy and sea-green silks. Black-gowned Auntie Gao is at the center of the group, her hair fallen over an eye. He thinks: *A party!* The household ladies in one place, closely packed, looking so young. They gawk as if *they* were men and *he* were a woman who had stumbled into the strictly male-only ancestral hall. Unknowingly, he has crossed a closed border few men have seen. His daughter is struggling on the table.

So, this is how they do it. She's scared . . . this is wrong, very wrong. . . . He fumbles for a word, any word. "No?" he tries.

This is new for them, Old Father giving orders, even orders that come like questions, so they shrug and go back to work. The girl cries furiously and tries to twist free as her toes are bent farther and farther.

Baba hisses and thinks, shaking his right hand as if a bee had stung him. They are not obeying him. *Think!* He's not a physical man. He slams the door, hard, roars, "STOP!" Everyone jumps, including him.

One woman falls on her bottom. A man yelling in this house of women is unheard of! They're panicked, especially Auntie Gao, who knows the warning signs of male rage. She winces, her tender heart stopped, ready for hard blows.

"Ayy! Keep going, Sister!" shouts Da-tsien's mother, holding her heart. "Sahhhhh, Husband! You scared us! Why do you say stop?" she asks with her great frown of many wrinkles and her one ferocious eye.

"Because I say so!" says Baba. "I can't stand her crying."

"Tsa! We've cried for centuries," she says. "No one ever listens."

Da-tsien takes her cue and howls from the bottom of her lungs, trying again to twist away. The little girl of sweet smiles is surprising everyone with her strength.

"Then one more reason to stop," Baba says. Her screams hurt his ears, so he covers them, providing little help. "Two reasons?" he suggests.

"Lo Fa," says Miao-miao, a teenage kinswoman with a high voice and no cheekbones, using his nickname. "Lo Fa, this is women's work. Go catch a fish, okay?" She's encouraged his lazy ways; his indolence allows her to hide in his home when her husband drinks. Strong men cause pain, and strong men who drink gulp women's lives like typhoons taking boats. Weak men are treasures. Lo Fa might be the only man in Soochow who could comfort a little girl after her feet were broken. Miao-miao doesn't believe in gods or good luck; her flat face is proof of the power of bad fortune. She pulls up the sleeves of her floor-length silk dress and tightly covers the girl's mouth. The silence is sudden. Her eyes say, *Control yourself, now.*

"Lo Fa, go read a foreign-country-person book, then come back later, yes? Then you talk to your daughter. She'll need you then."

"Good idea!" he says brightly, moving forward. "I'll take her now."

"No no no!" they cry, but again Auntie Gao has paused from an overripe imagination borne by experience. *What's wrong with Brother-in-Law? He's crazy! Why's he here? Why ruin his daughter's future? Is he drunk? Is he now a demon like my husband who will knock me out with a stick and have sex on me while he bites my skin?*

Da-tsien struggles against an octopus of soft hands. She reaches for her baba, knowing that time is running out. These women are strong, their hearts are hardening and her mother is getting testy, pointing her sharp finger like a dagger.

"Ai-yaa! If we don't bind them, they'll grow like carp and flap like fish, no end in sight! They'll be the first part of her to enter a room! *Here's our daugh-*

ter, *excuse her huge feet! Who'll marry her? Feet from here to Vietnam!* You ruin her! Make her marry a beast who'll send her to hell, and they'll laugh and shame us! She'll have no sons, and we'll have no outside grandsons! *We won't be able to show our faces! It'll destroy us!*"

Baba wonders, *All this from her feet?* "Hey, see here, she doesn't even have to marry! I read a new book, and it says—"

His wife tries to remain sane. *No marriage! No sons! No purpose in life!* "No no no! Aiyaa, no! No French books! Sister, ignore him! Do it now!"

Baba always denied pushing his way through the women; he said he only had to place his hand on his heart and speak resonantly like a scholar, and they honored him as the learned patriarch, a man of books, rectitude and thunder as they instantly parted for him, bowing low with a thousand apologies, their foreheads banging nine times on the floor like Tibetan drumsticks.

But Miao-miao said Baba was like a drunk Australian sailor in a good-time house on payday as he rudely shoved everyone aside.

My mother held on to her father's neck as he thumped down the stairs, his sleep-wrinkled *ma-gua* navy blue gown flapping like the wings of a great bird. She was thrilled with the speed, the urgency, the frenetic bouncing of this wild carnival ride, his strong arms, a faint musky hint of old books, shocked by his physical closeness. She closed her eyes, not breathing, certain they would fall and die. He had never moved so quickly. He never would again, even when the Japanese came for him.

He turned back, panting, to grab his best fishing pole and tackle box from the closet. He paused to nudge Deaf Man Fu, his manservant, who snored on a pallet on the parquet floor. Old Lao Fu grunted, fell silent and resumed snoring. Deaf Man Fu was supposed to escort Baba wherever he went, but he would usually awaken to the closing of the front door, alertly look about, then fall back to sleep.

The women couldn't pursue him—their feet were bound, and running on broken bones made tortured and long-traumatized sciatic nerves scream for days of acupuncture. They gathered in a knot at the top of the stairs and wailed and cried at the destruction of Da-tsien's future. *A beautiful little girl, totally ruined by her feet! Now no sons! No future! Because of that double-stupid, double-weak, double-lazy man, that demon! Who will marry her now?*

The mustache-bristling majordomo, the amah, the house servants, the cook's white-jacketed family had crowded at the bottom of the stairs during the argument. They fled as the master of the house came pounding down as if every hatchet-bearing warlord in China were chasing him. The front door slammed, and they ran back to the staircase as the outside servants peered through the windows. All were trying to divine the cause of the weeping that they knew would, in time, impact them.

Those loyal to Taitai—all of them—wailed with her, for her happiness was their joy and her grief was their loss. She was a woman of judgment, a manager of many skills and tougher than a one-armed Yangtze River mule driver. Ignorant of the trouble but understanding the emotion, they cried for her and waited for the consequences.

And as for Master, her husband—well, he fished.

Auntie Gao was the last to limp to the railing, trembling on her good foot, the bad one pointing at its foul-luck angle. She wasn't a true aunt, but a cousin on Baba's side who visited the Tzus to avoid her abusive husband. She was an animistic Taoist who wore optimistic black to fend off scary, ghostlike white colors. Now she cried, apologizing to the brooding female spirits of the good house and the whispering *yin* deities of the picturesque canal. She had inadvertently passed her tragedy of broken feet to a golden girl, ruining her life as well and inviting the anger of the girl's hard mother. *Why this precious girl? She doesn't deserve my fate.*

Thus my mah-mee's feet were left unbound. She was grateful to her baba for the rescue from pain. But a distance grew between her and her mother the way a stitch, once loosened, widens under the pressure of wear.

My grandmother was responsible for sending her daughter to a good marriage that promised sons and a household secure from hard times. But with Da-tsien's feet allowed to grow amok, Taitai couldn't fulfill the primary maternal duty of matchmaking her daughter upward into a family of wealth. Da-tsien could no longer be her true child. Her big feet had eaten the beauty of her face and disturbed the rituals of parental duty, the harmony of the house and the promise of educated males.

Her social and psychological health, as with many Chinese children, would depend less on the affections of her mother and more upon the kindnesses of her relatives in the *jia*. To her benefit, she would have her father on her side, and her father was a kind man who would help as Da-tsien's feet grew and consumed the goodwill of her aristocratic mother. In those days, a few peasant children were raised as entertainers. Entertainment was beneath manual labor, but it brought a few coppers. A country mother would tie pink string around her daughter's multiple pigtails, rouge the cheeks and paint the eyebrows, dressing her in bright colors. The girl would learn to sing *hwagushi*, flower drum songs, tossing and catching the drumsticks, hitting the little drum and singing as her brother struck a brass gong. Down the river in Shanghai, flower drums were used by famous prostitutes to beguile their customers.

The child entertainers of Soochow sang songs of social commentary. The song that remained with Da-tsien was called the *Feng-yang*, based on the place where famine strikes and emperors are born.

The little girl would sing that she had a maligned fate: While other husbands became officials, her spouse only played the flower drum.

Her brother would sing that he too possessed a foul fortune, for while other men married beautiful girls, his spouse had huge, ugly feet. It was a lovely song with a sad message of old Chinese laments.

Taitai couldn't stand *hwagushi*. But Da-tsien would close her eyes as the music wafted to her window, where she often sat alone.

two

The Bravest Wife

THE RUBBER-FACED STORYTELLER waves his arms as he beats drums and brass gongs and cries in the voices of demons and lords to shoppers at a crowded market, "HEY YOU! *Kai t'ien pi di!* When the heavens separated from the earth! Once upon a time . . . friends and sisters, listen to my story!"

My father used to wave his arms as he told stories with extravagant gestures. His tales had no genesis, middle or end. He pitched an orphaned shard of a story the way the sea gives up fragments of wrecked ships. But he had a favorite, disconnected finale, his lonely line of words. Each time he said it, he nearly cried.

"Ah, *the Bravest Wife!* She killed herself to save her husband, so sad." Dad had dreamed of being an orator, but his voice was like a steel shovel in a gravel pit. "She die." His voice choked, then he laughed. Bitter laughter was a cleansing coda. He used a false laugh to erase memories of pain. I hoped he was enjoying the misery of others, which is human, but he was engaging in other people's memories, which is Chinese.

As a victim of Asian history, Dad relied heavily on his American future. As a Chinese soldier trained by sergeants of the Kaiser's German army, he liked the value of shock. For fifty years, this dapper man in a bow tie surprised me with unlinked morsels of family secrets, but there was always one story that he worried like a dog with a tough bone.

"Why did she kill herself?" I was on my footstool, its red leather striated and faded, a place where the sun warmed me and made me brave enough to ask Saturday questions of my angry, weekday-driven father.

In those days, my mah-mee said misty, magical prayers to keep us safe from American street demons and night devils that hungered for our unsettled souls. Some evenings, as she tucked me in my bed, she looked into my eyes and kissed my nose, saying that it was a good nose, and that I would be smart and rich. Later, I learned that she was afraid I'd have a big nose like my father's and become a man who sniffed for distant winds that would carry me far away. Her kiss was a prayer to keep it small.

Asking Dad about family history was like asking the IRS for advice. If an answer came, it could be unrelated to the inquiry. Worse, it resulted in being noticed, which inevitably bore its own costs.

When he was in his nineties, Dad began to tell the stories of our clan, of my mother's life, of their adventures together in times of prosperity and pain. He told me the full story of the Bravest Wife, a kaleidoscopic tale painted in Yangchow poetry and Shanghai hardness with his tough, German-toned English. Always an actor, Dad played the roles of the central characters, using voices of dragons and lords to tell truths he had withheld all his life. If I looked above his head, I could see a rubber-faced storyteller by a busy market stall, waving his arms and hitting a drum.

The refugee mob runs, shedding the weak to the shoulders of the road. They ignore dropped clothing, food and valuables, and can't hear the wailing of abandoned baby girls crying for their mothers. Bathed in the flickering heat of a burning sky, the refugees press doggedly onward, driven by the beat of drums and the tramp of a fast-approaching army.

The panicked refugees jostle the young girl with tiny bound feet as she struggles through the detritus on the margins of the road. Her husband keeps elbowing the crowd away from his young wife.

She was a poor city girl from Ji'an, and we are in central China. She probably has been crying all day. Her delicate hands bleed on the canes that help her inch forward. She burns with fatigue, but the central agony is in her feet. Broken and bent under the heel when she was small, bound with cloths fifteen hands long into lovely golden lilies, they drew the admiration of her low-ranking clan and the passions of matchmakers. They distinguished her from mere country girls and won her a literate husband. From pain came endurance. From endurance came good luck. From good luck would come many sons.

Now the broken bones in her young feet grind against one another. There is not one small corner in her body where she can hide from pain. Her glorious feet now promise her death; worse, they will kill her husband. Perhaps, as she tries to flee from the yellow-headbanded men who beat drums and carry blood-wetted swords and spears, she wishes for the strong feet of a peasant, for legs that can squat in rice fields for days and trek water-heavy produce to market in a monsoon storm.

I can picture this young girl, but without an outward sign of care. This was Dad's way. It pains me that I don't know her name and that I may be behaving like my father. The girl was my great-grandfather's wife. Great-grandfather brought so much good luck to our family that it nearly destroyed everyone.

I am at my desk with Pookie, a small and loyal Chinese dog curled up at my feet, telling you I should know the girl's name so I can honor her in the *li*, the rituals that mark Confucian families. But my father deliberately left the rites and their road signs behind when he came to America, and we lost our Chinese way. I have been awkward in all hereditary customs ever since. Even if I knew this fabled woman's name, I would struggle to honor her seamlessly, as if I were an extension of ancient Chinese custom, instead of the American *wang ben* rock on which tradition broke and was forgotten.

I remember that my mah-mee's courage, and this unnamed girl's bravery, saved the clan and created an American family.

"What was the Bravest Wife's name, Dad?" I asked in 1998, when his health began to fail.

"Her name was Lee," he said.

"I knew that part."

He says nothing, his face an old and familiar stone, and then he begins to tell me the story in the rich detail I had longed to hear since I was a boy.

What comes through my father's story is that this young girl had vision, that she was, in important ways, smarter than her husband, and that most importantly, she had guts.

Chinese stories have two themes. One is beauty. The other is courage. Both are the outcomes of prayer and good fortune. When the Lee clan was rich, beauty came first, but before prosperity, it was courage.

SHE HAS LARGE, bright eyes spaced as widely as burners in a rich man's stove. Everyone says that she was polite and respectful, but that is obligatorily said of all our Before Borns.

It is 1853, and money has no meaning as she struggles on a hard road along the cold waters of the Gan River in Kiangsi Province. She's fleeing the Taiping rebels, the Heavenly Peace warriors, who actually are not that interested in her, a Chinese woman. The Taipings are Chinese men who are hunting Manchu horsemen and rulers, the Manchurian conquerors from the far north.

Two centuries earlier, in 1644, Manchu Bannermen cavalry crossed the Great Wall to defeat the tottering Ming Dynasty. The Manchus enslaved the Chinese, the old masters of subjugation. The victorious Manchus made vanquished Chinese men wear queues so they resembled horses, to be ridden and corralled, sold and bartered. The pigtail became the symbol of slavery, of a lowered face.

Now, after two hundred years, the Chinese Taipings are rebelling. They want to kill all the Manchus and create a native regime with a new twist. The Taipings had emerged from the Guest People, the *Hakka*, Central Chinese who had migrated to southern China centuries before. The *Hakka* Taipings are now in open revolt against the Manchus and they are being joined by charcoal burners, landless root-eating peasants, deserters, blackened river pullers, bent-back miners and hordes of starving *yaofan*, want-rice beggars. They are the disenchanted, the feudal serfs, the abused ejecta from rich landlords, foreigners and officials. As America nears its Civil War, these brave, landless poor—the very heart of China—are initiating the largest and longest revolution in human history. The revolution will change every member of every clan in the biggest country in the world. It is a revolution whose final chapter is yet to be written.

Hong Hsiu-ch'uän, the Taiping leader, is a handsome, charismatic visionary with a deep voice and an iron will. He had a fever once, awakening with the belief that he was the younger brother of Jesus Christ, a realization that made him the Chinese son of the Christian God. He says now that Jesus talks to him, directing the Chinese to rise up and kill the devil Manchus and to accept the Kingdom of God. Hong and his Taipings have cut off their degrading slave braids, which is a capital offense under Manchu laws. Even in America, Chinese gold miners and laundrymen driven by the horrors of the Taiping Rebellion to seek any kind of work would rather die than lose their queues.

Free of slave markings, the Taiping rebels take up arms and dissect Manchu soldiers, mounting their heads atop red spears. Hundreds of thousands of Chinese join the inspirational Hong and his Soldiers of Heavenly Peace, to violently overthrow their Manchu masters, to regain freedom and to seek a better life. Farmers who have the strength to work sixteen hours a day, every day of the year, learn that they can also fight a terrifying army across an entire continent.

The Taipings are political radicals who hold property in common, who free women from servitude to men, who end foot binding, who practice temperance and who honor peasants. They fight as regiments. They do not loot or rape as they execute Manchu devils and Chinese loyalists. They plan to take the Forbidden City in Peking and to behead the Manchu emperor and all his devils. Then they will found a half-Christian Taiping state, bringing with it the kingdom to come.

China is overwhelmed by confusion and terror as the civil war spreads, killing thousands, then millions who are caught in epic, rolling campaigns. *Who is right? What can we do?* My great-grandfather was confused. In the absence of clear answers came a great fear.

He was of medium height with wide shoulders and a kind face, thick legs and strong wrists. He had a big brain and bad eyes from years of candlelight reading, and worked hard as a paddy-rice farmer in a family line that had gone five centuries without one note of scholastic distinction. He studied hard to become a scholar of literature, for such men were at the absolute apex of Chinese social achievement. As all men, he wanted to be tall, thin and learned with a fine scholar's beard. His name was Lee Shui-feng. His name is pronounced "Shwee Fung," but Confucian sons can never say aloud the names of their fathers. It would be too disrespectful.

In the spring of 1853, Lee Shui-feng was looking to the west where Taiping braves were sounding war drums and chopping off the heads of Manchus and Chinese traitors. Tramping regiments shook the earth, slaying Buddhist monks and burning temples that defied the True God. Fear made his stomach hurt and thinned his breath—what if they couldn't tell you were Chinese? If you looked Manchu, pro-Manchu, rich, Buddhist or hostile, they impaled you and your family. The Taipings are changing China the way a millennial Yellow River flood changes crops.

Great-grandfather thinks about running. He thinks about it every day. Life has become confusing. The rebels who threaten you are Chinese, like yourself, but they're also wild killers. If you ran, you'd run to the Manchus—the foreigners who enslaved you, took the best land and made you wear a queue. There is nowhere else to go.

In his home, Lo Chuen, Snail Creek village, people argue, packing, then unpacking, children crying at the chaos, fishnets and crops ignored. They are communal Chinese; when danger comes, the dismay is openly shared, nothing hidden, nothing held back. What to do with first sons, our elders, seed grain, spirit tablets and ancestors' graves? The Taipings will burn our fishing boats and tear our nets! At night the villagers are scared out of their sleep, praying in hot whispers to the white-haired earth gods, Mr. and Mrs. Tu-di.

Word comes: Taiping scouts are in the passes of the western Wugong Mountains. Wearing their yellow headbands and carrying sharp pennoned spears, riding black fire-snorting horses, they shout that only devil Manchus, their lackeys, Buddhist monks, pimps and gamblers will lose property. If you stay inside with the character *shun*—obedient—on your door, you and your property will be safe. Hong, the Taiping leader, has read foreign missionary tracts and knows the Book of Exodus. The word passes up and down the Gan River like a hot wind. It is a Chinese Passover.

There are two choices. Ask a literate man to write *shun*—a tough, eleven-stroke character—on your door and pray to all the gods you know. Or run like a wild crazy person to Ji'an's walls and its Manchu garrison. Or, if you're really scared, sail all the way to great Nanking.

Lee Shui-feng doesn't know what to do. Maybe the Taipings will miss their village completely. They live on a west-bank crook where trees grow tall and floods stall at good-luck orchards and strong rock walls. Cod fill nets that are thrown into the Gan River three times a day. Snails work the soil, feed pigs and catch groupers, which are best when quickly seared. In winter, farming stops and small-framed men make wood toys while the big ones work as porters for merchants who ply the Gan. People rest against ginkgo trees next to blazing fires and tell wine-warmed stories about silly or stupid people while children rub their aching backs. The soil is good and the clan dead are with them, giving good luck to bad seasons and significance to a confusing world. It is a pleasant village, watched over by many fathers. You cannot leave to become a wanderer, detached from life.

Great-grandfather curses his bad luck. He had just changed his fortune by becoming a Ji'an pawnshop manager, a commoner's banker who uses relationships and numerical agility to set his rates. He can read the wind, appraise the seller, establish trust, move the abacus beads, set a true price and lend no more than half the resale value. This isn't as good as being a scholar, not nearly, but it's far better than being a farmer. His new luck has lifted him from the fields of the *di-ren*, the people of the earth—dirt peasants with black soil in their skin. He manages three brokerages in a big city of colors and foods while winning a smart wife with small feet and a sweet dowry. At twenty, he is a person of incredible good fortune who can pay his salt and tea tax and use a brush. But at heart, he's still a farmer. As his clerks lend, buy and make business, he spends more time in Snail Creek, near the ducks and the graves of his fathers. Quietly, he gardens. After work, he sits by the Gan River and by candlelight practices calligraphy, the gentleman's art. He listens to lovesick cicadas and croaking frogs, all of which like the tasty snails. He uses good parchment to ensure that each stroke is sincere and precise, worthy of posterity. When he's tired, his wife rubs his back, telling him not to worry that his eyes are growing weaker as his penmanship improves.

But now the Taipings are coming. They honor the *di-ren*, and they kill the people of incredible good fortune. *Aiya, this is the wrong time to succeed and to improve your station!*

He can write "obedient" on his door and the door of his *jia*, his clan, and his young wife urges him to do so. She also has him write many of these characters on pieces of wood, which she gives to the villagers who want them. She also tells her husband to wear simpler clothes, to conceal his small-landowner status, to use his big brains. She sews tiny silver ingots into the lining of his simple jackets.

Hide that which is obvious, she says.

Great-grandfather looks west to see if the Taiping rebels are burning up what is left of his good luck. His parents are dead, so he's not bound to the village by *gang*, the magical unbreakable Confucian bond to parents, which is far stronger than his mere wedding pledge to a wife. He would owe her more if she had borne him sons, but they remain childless.

She reminds him that the smart clans are quiet in their huts, avoiding trouble, pitifully trying to copy *shun* again and again with chicken blood onto clothing and walls. It is peasant custom to smear cock's blood on door lintels in a universal act of atonement. The blood wards off the demons of cosmic misfortune, which pours from a place farmers call the Mouth of the Tiger. Sadly, many in the village now superstitiously kill their fine roosters.

The stupid, she says, left earlier. The really stupid left yesterday, risking all to hike Gan River roads towards Ji'an or the great sanctuary of Nanking, fifteen hundred *li* away. Only the *incredibly* stupid would run now, when it is too late; the Taipings are coming like a Hwang Ho flood. She can taste their drums in her mouth. She has been raised to be a wife and mother, not a refugee, and her husband's village is her home.

Snow still sits on far hills when Great-grandfather sees the pillars of smoke. His ear to the ground, he feels the tramp of a fast army. Mountains are moving; the value of the world is shifting. What's the price to stay, to go, to resell? How do you pawn safety? *Run, or don't run?*

His wife urges no action; the Taiping are like Shensi hunting dogs—if you don't run, they ignore you. Still, he owns property and has no dirt in his pores. He looks like a devil official. When the fires are two hills away, lighting up the night sky in ghostly reds, when they can feel the drums in their bed and undisciplined children cry, he picks up his abacus, dons his jackets with secret linings and decides they must run.

She is a girl of house duties and handwork who prays to Guan Yin for sons. Now she struggles like a newborn kitten up a rocky, rutted path under moonlight in the middle of a Chinese nightmare. With two canes, she moves efficiently, but bound feet do not allow anything resembling speed.

"Running is like moving over broken glass on bare knuckles," says Dad. "Bound feet are broken feet."

Great-grandmother is a hard worker. Legend says that she had good judgment, vision, a kind mouth. But I imagine her complaining to her husband as they trudged forty *li*—fourteen miles—to the fortified city of Ji'an with its thirty-foot walls and a Bannermen army, red armor-plated Manchu troops united under the flags of the northern steppe tribes. She endures pain. To encourage her, her husband tells her again and again, "It's impossible for the Taipings and their fires to take Ji'an!"

A villager can tote a full load of produce to Ji'an in half a dry day. Her husband has done the trip hundreds of times in less. On tiny, bound feet, if the journey doesn't kill her, it will take a week. Does he feel guilty for not having the wisdom to stay? Running has made them look like devil lovers, dog turtles, enemies of the Kingdom of Heavenly Peace. Only such people would risk running in front of the Taiping army.

Her delicate lotus feet helped find her a husband with advantages, and now they, and his decision to run, will be the death of them.

It has been three or four days on the up-and-down road, a blur of gravel, rocks and forests, of endless crowds of refugees passing them and treasures left behind. Great-grandmother's distress knows no borders. The pain in her feet has grown into her back and shoulders. She had a bag of millet and corn but lost it, she has no idea where. The bones in her feet have ground against one another from the first step. It is as if the Taipings, who burn the sky and the earth, have set fire to her body. Fever clouds her once great vision. The running mob jostles them. This is true misery. Villagers who know everything about one another now do not even risk eye contact, much less nod and ask *"Chur gwo fan le ma?" Have you eaten? Can I feed you? May I offer you comfort?* There is no culture, no politeness, no pleasure. The quest for the common good has been lost as surely as Great-grandmother's sack of grain. They have become individualized.

In the West, people ignore one another in good times and help strangers in a disaster. In China, people share everything in good times, but no people are more practical in an emergency run than the Chinese. At times like that, the bonds that connect them to the earth, to the dirt, to the past and to the future, have been severed. They are floating souls, the running dead, fleeing the land and duties that make people true and real. Survivors must protect what they can for the later survival of clans.

To the beat of distant drums and strangled cries, she falls, shaking like an old willow in a night wind. She sees a forgotten well in a copse of trees and, with his help, pulls herself away from the crush of panicking, running refugees, the road littered with cast-off clothing, food, lucky red-spotted memory tablets, favorite teacups and screaming baby girls. Her body quivers in pain and agony. Her stomach is probably aching, and she is distressed to see her own blood-soaked feet. She is fourteen years old.

Her husband has tried for years to be a Confucian gentleman of accounting and fine manners, a man of great moral rectitude and emotional restraint. But his heritage is of the soil, so he probably holds her in his arms the way a peasant would, trying to warm her, to comfort her. Perhaps he caresses her face and her hair, allowing himself to feel affection for her. He doesn't apologize for the decision that is killing her.

It was a man's call, and no woman can question it, and no man can know fate. He had felt something irresistible the night that he heard the drums. Something made him leave his warm bed and his good village. It wasn't fear. It was something else. Something secret and unknown.

He presses her ear against his shoulder and covers her face, but she cries when she hears drums and gunfire. They stare at the sky behind them and shudder at the violent and vivid reds.

"Run, Husband! They'll ignore me, a stupid girl." A lie, for her feet reveal her as a woman of class, a high-class traitor running for the devil city of Ji'an. She'll be killed. Or worse: Taipings have suffered high combat losses against Manchu armies; they've enlisted deserters and raw men from broken clans to fill the bloodied ranks. These new men lack discipline and do not pretend to respect law, property or women.

Shui-feng has a peasant's thick legs and feet that can take a thousand miles of bad road, but he won't leave her. He can carry her. . . .

With frantic, fever-strained eyes, she looks about. "Water," she says. "No, not the old. Fresh and cold! Husband, please, I'm on fire. Go! Fast, very fast! Then we go to my clan in Ji'an! We're so close!"

Reluctantly, Great-grandfather leaves to refill the clay water pot in a distant stream. His wife crawls toward the abandoned well, a shattering of ancient broken stones without bucket or rope. China is an ancient land of tired hardscrabble dirt and dry wells. Into such structures have fallen thousands of infant girls, dropped from painful sight by starving families during famines, floods and droughts, a place of sad endings and new hope for the survivors and precious sons.

Great-grandfather returns—she's gone. He rushes about, calling her name, her nickname, endearments unknown to descendants. He hears Taipings in the trees and whispers for her. Dying Manchu Bannermen scream, and Chinese refugees cry, as the Taipings divide them into two groups: porters and the dead. He sees an old well, rushes to it and looks down, dropping his jug, shattering it. *Tsa guo, I dropped pots—my mistake.* Below, in the light of fires, he can see his wife, her earthly pains ended.

He calls to her. She is silent. He covers his face in pain.

Go fast, she had said. *Go very fast!* She had spoken in a secret code. *With me, you could never make it. Without me, live to raise sons.*

Does he weep for her sacrifice? Does he apologize? Perhaps he promises to return to bury her in a fine, expensive five-hundred-silver *tael* red *nai moh*

Yunnanese casket, for this way a loved one's spirit can reach the next world. A *tael* was a thirty-eight-gram silver ingot, the root of the Chinese treasury, and five hundred ingots paved the road to harmony after death; no underworld demon could overcome the nobility of a garnet hardwood casket. Certainly, Great-grandfather promises to remember her on an ancestor tablet of the best stone in the best calligraphy with the costliest, longest-life ink. Tired, thirsty and scared, he cries and kicks the well with his big feet and curses his stupidity in leaving her.

We know that he stacks boulders in the pattern of a snail and memorizes the spot for another day. Then he runs, pacing himself as a *di-ren*, a man of the earth. Free of her damning tiny feet, he runs all night until he outdistances the Taiping advance cavalry. He knows how to suck morning dew from high branches and to stay off ridgelines during the false dawn. He reaches the walled city of Ji'an with a great wailing mob of refugees who scream and tear their hair, but the Manchu garrison has shut the gates. A single Taiping rebel soldier entering Ji'an disguised as a peasant could set fires, assassinate officers, blow up powder stores and open the gates to hell itself.

Lee Shui-feng cries out his wife's family name and the names of his pawnshop staff to the thousands of onlookers on the walls, but no one hears. Some throw coins up to the gawkers, begging for water. Some food is thrown down, and rioting results. He jogs away from the madness.

Great-grandfather strides around the walls. He writes his name and *Lo Chuen village* in the sand before East Gate, which is so high that refugees avoid it. His calligraphy allows him to be recognized as a man of incredible good fortune. He doesn't look like a charcoal burner or a miner, and his accent reveals him to be a Gan River man and not a *Hakka*. Guards check him and feel the silver ingots. They rip apart his jackets and take the silver. He doesn't protest, and they allow him to enter the city. For the first time, he appreciates Manchus with hungry swords. He offers to work for the Manchurian government. His calligraphy and counting skills are admired, and he's assigned to a Manchu taxman. He thanks Mr. and Mrs. Tu-di for work. He tries not to think about anything else but fails. His mind is too rich, too fertile, too stimulated by learning, and so he uses his intellect to plumb the depths of his sadness, his depression, his longing for his sweet, courageous wife who had given him a debt of honor that few men carry for any women.

three

Hide That Which Is Obvious

OT LONG THEREAFTER, smoke plumes darken skies that lighten into violent reds. The earth shakes. The Taipings have arrived. The rebel armies unfold across the Gan River to surround the city walls. Cannon fire erupts into the city, and death and screaming become the music of every day. Tough Shanhwaikan miners tunnel and blow great holes in the walls as massed Taiping riflemen blast Bannermen from the towers. The rice stores are depleted, and Ji'an's water supply is contaminated. Soldiers will be tortured for further resistance, so finally, the exhausted garrison surrenders to be executed. The Taipings line up the devils and Bannermen and all who appear pro-Manchu, and behead them.

The others are beaten and divided into two camps—those with peasant bodies capable of bitter labor, and those with thin scholar's bodies. The scholars are tortured and killed; the peasants have their queues chopped. Shui-feng keeps touching the emptiness on his neck where his pigtail had hung since childhood. He's shipped five hundred miles up the Yangtze River on a filthy prison barge. He bails water, chanting to the river god with other slaves en route to the southern capital of Nanking. He tries not to think of his fate, but he has seen too much horror.

In Nanking, he and tens of thousands of other slaves carry and dig for the Taiping armies as they besiege the great Manchu walled city in a horrific campaign. It is Joshua taking Jericho—cannons roar, cascades of burning arrows fall like typhoon storms, fires eat the sky, mines explode and the massive walls fall. Great-grandfather leans tiredly on his shovel and closes his eyes as the rebels execute hundreds of thousands of Manchus and Chinese and then cut the rich survivors with methodical slices so the victims will reveal caches of gold, silver and jade. Blood runs like Great Sea tides, and Great-grandfather's mind finally goes into shock.

Great-grandfather and the other *k'u-li* captives are herded into the burning city and ordered to clean up the carnage; the great Taiping lord, Jesus' younger brother, the *Hakka* Hong Hsiu-ch'uän, is coming. Nanking must be godly clean! Shui-feng prays to heaven that when they're done, they'll be beheaded and not shredded into red pieces. They work all day and sleep a few fitful hours in rotting Nanking jails to the sounds of torture and torment.

Preceded by tall mounted women warriors in yellow tunics, the Taiping lord Hong and his armies enter Nanking in a grand procession. Great-grandfather doesn't see because slaves kneel and bow, heads pressed hard to the reddened dirt. One day he is pulled from the slave mass and thrown in with other abacus men.

"You see why, right?" Dad asks me. "Taipings take so much loot, they need thousands of accountants! But kill so many, only a few abacus men left in central China! Grandfather now very important—had to count the treasury for the Taiping kingdom. Millions die, but Grandfather knew numbers. So he lived—and got paid! You surprised, yes?"

Great-grandfather works hard, day and night, while the Taiping rebellion rages through China. Nanking becomes the Taiping capital. Inside the rich city, Taiping combat leaders grow soft and corrupt. At night, Shui-feng closes his books, blows out candles and thinks. He imagines fishing in Snail Creek, watching the ducks. Perhaps he remembers a favorite tree, his wife rubbing his shoulders after a long day of work and calligraphy. He remembers writing *shun*, obedience, over and over again back in their village, and he closes his eyes when he remembers her body in the well.

Eleven years pass as China suffers bloody war. Now the great Chinese general Tseng Kuo-fan and his Chinese provincial army sortie against the Taipings. Their main target is the Taiping capital. They set siege to Nanking. The sky turns red again, and Hong dies of a strange and unknown disease. Perhaps it is a fever similar to the one that induced his vision of a murderous Jesus and the Kingdom of Heavenly Peace.

Why would a Chinese army help the Manchus suppress a Chinese revolt? Because the Taipings espoused the missionary disease of Christianity. China had absorbed the world's religions like the desert taking sand. Buddhism arrived from India in the body of humble monks, and Taoism came through Lao-tzu's gentle writings, but Christianity came with foreign armies, opium importation, small-business-killing foreign industries and the devil warships of the foreign white powers. Christianity was so intrinsically associated with fear that it made Manchu rule look desirable. Most Chinese preferred Manchu slave queues to the cross, which to them symbolized economic subjugation instead of transformation.

Tseng Kuo-fan's sappers demolish the huge East Gate. His armies engage a furious Taiping defense as Chinese kill Chinese. Nanking falls. Taipings are executed by the hundreds of thousands. There is no mercy in a sea of slaughter, for the Empire hates these rebels as none other, marked as they are by a mass swallowing of the foreign-god religion.

The Chinese army finds the Taiping treasury's ledgers and line up the surviving accountants. Those who can explain the most are saved; those who know less are beheaded. An old set of ledgers is in code.

"Who can explain these secret marks?" asks an imperial officer.

A man lowers his head. The officer looks at Great-grandfather, Lee Shui-feng. Every day that he translates the books, he's told, is a day of life.

Great-grandfather has done as his wife directed—to hide that which is obvious. For eleven years, he has made his journal entries in his own secret code. Most Taipings are illiterate swordfighters who have no idea that Shui-feng has been making codified entries. For the next two years, as the last rebels are hunted down throughout China and beheaded, Great-grandfather sits by candlelight in a cell of a familiar city jail and translates the part of the Taiping treasury he helped to record. It is a precise record of the plunder from a hundred cities and from thousands of landowning clans. Night and day, he identifies the hiding places of Tang vases, gold pieces, silver ingots, jade earrings, magical, singing Sung swords, crowns of ancient dead kings and the deep green jade armor of past emperors.

When he finally finishes in 1866, he's happy because he's worked hard and has received a mean rice *konji* gruel on many days. He and two surviving accountants, men named Shen and Shim, who also made coded entries, look forward to being killed with the sharp, considerate fall of an executioner's finely sharpened ax. Every day, other men who had been captured and therefore tainted by the Taipings are cruelly beheaded with dull swords.

One morning a bearded officer with a torch enters his cell. He questions a rail-thin Shui-feng. Later, Tseng Kuo-ch'uan, the younger brother of General Tseng Kuo-fan, enters the jail with an entourage of battle-hardened soldiers. They inspect the three dirty, half-blind abacus men. Tseng Kuo-ch'uan says,

China's tax infrastructure has been wiped out by the war—our administrators and everyone who could write were killed by the Taipings. If you could, how would you three poor souls rebuild the tax base of the Empire of China?

The three accountants hurriedly devise a plan. Trembling, they submit it. Nothing happens. They are returned to lesser accounting duties, and now they feel fear. One day Great-grandfather is given water to bathe, clean clothes and the best food he has smelled in thirteen years. Famished, he eats slowly, believing that he's being watched, hiding that which is obvious. He's brought into a courtyard. It's summer, and his eyes can't take the light. A magistrate hands him something that he recognizes as his death certificate, but Shui-feng can't read in the blast of the sun. He prepares himself. Sun, the daytime lantern of Mr. Tu-di, is a good sign for farmers. Shen and Shim are next to him, trying to be respectful without opening their blinded eyes. Great-grandfather licks his salty lips, sampling his last taste of life, hoping for a quick, sharp blade.

A magistrate makes solemn announcements at the top of his lungs. It goes on too long. Shui-feng looks down at the paper in his hand; it's made of mulberry wood, with woodblock characters. Mulberry wood is the best—a symbol of China's creation of the silk trade. He's never seen, much less held, an Official Certificate of Title of Office before.

He hears cries of *Hao, hao*, good, good, and servants are ordered to bow. An unseen crowd murmurs in awe. The accountants knit their brows; they think the crowd is cheering the approach of their executioner, but they are wrong. The words sink in. They are not going to die. Shui-feng tries to speak but can't.

Great-grandfather and his two peers have been appointed salt tax administrators. Lee Shui-feng of Snail Creek has been given a region centered at Yangchow, an idyllic, tree-lined city of poets and writers on the confluence of the Yangtze and the Grand Tribute Canal to Peking. He must regrow his queue. When this is understood, the former prisoners can only bow on rickety knees, again and again, lower and lower until they face the emperor in Peking and kowtow, their foreheads striking the ground nine times in a moment of unforgettable grace. Lee Shui-feng is grateful. He is also sad, for salvation has come to a lonely widower.

He is now a magistrate. With help, he stands. Lee, Shen and Shim regard one another and bow, right fists sitting in left palms. How can they forget this day? Each is given horses and a carriage; a permanent guard of mounted Manchu officers and soldiers to protect their treasuries; an imperial seal that reflects the personal favor of Shian-feng, emperor of China; a priceless, ceremonial rabbit-hair brush to commend character; and a heavy bag of gold coins to reestablish the rebellion-ravaged salt industry. The coins will buy salt farmers and administrators. Franchisers will provide the salt, all Chinese will buy it to preserve and season food, and Shui-feng will send taxes to Peking to pay for this costly war. As Great-grandfather's entourage passes, beggars scoop up sand in their trail and laugh, rubbing the granules into their palms and putting them in their mouths for luck.

Great-grandfather has moved from death to paradise. For returning wealth to the Empire, and for suggesting a workable tax-plan draft, he has become a man of unimaginable station, an administrator who will have an army and the income of four provinces.

He envisions a mansion rich in food and servants. A private garden to shade the sun, a moon gate round with good luck, a stream of fat carp and a bridge arched like a snail's back. He will grow orchards of bamboo, whose character means solitude. A monkish, emaciated, nearsighted, lonely man for thirteen years, he imagines marrying again and having strong sons who can fish from the bridge and watch ducklings swim after their mothers. Remembering his former physical strength, now long gone, he cries.

Dad grew up in Yangchow and Shanghai. The Yangchow mansion was rich in servants and food. As a boy, Dad raced in a garden with shading bamboo and a twelve-foot-high moon gate. He played in a carp-filled stream as panting servants crossed a bridge to follow him and keep him from harm. Later, the family moved to Shanghai, where my father lived in a European mansion with a courtyard filled with fruit trees.

In both homes, he ate beneath a marble memory tablet. It belonged in the shrine of ancestor tablets. But this particular one lived in the most social room in the house. It depicted neither a patriarch nor a couple.

From that tablet stared a girl with bright widely spaced eyes, her face wise and calm. Anyone who knew of her said she had been polite and respectful, but that is said of all ancestors. Though few ancestors are invited to every meal.

Long after the Taiping wars, Lee Shui-feng led an expedition into Kiangsi Province, returning to the place where he had buried his parents, become literate, learned to farm and loved to fish, where he had run pawnshops, where he had married his first wife. Dutifully, as the villagers knelt and kept their eyes on the fish-enriched soil, he wrote the names of his sons on the Lee memory tablets of Lo Chuen, Snail Creek village, where good-luck orchards stall Gan River floods.

Trailed by aides and obedient sons and small grandsons in sun-shaded carriages, he tried to walk the forty *li* between shaded Snail Creek village and Ji'an city, but he was unable. The years of captivity, beatings and malnutrition had left him painfully thin. He now looked quite intellectual, and had grown a long scholar's beard.

He stepped stiffly from his carriage to study the landscape. The Taiping wars had been fought here for ten years. Forests and orchards had burned, paddies were ruined, crops flooded, the land ravaged into debris fields without end. He found a hundred dry wells, not one of which reminded him of the grave of his first wife. The boulders he had stacked to mark the place of her death during the years of mad slaughter had been moved long ago. Now he made a decision. My father, a very small child, was lifted from the carriage by his tall amah. His wet nurse knelt next to him. Peering upward, my father saw his grandfather kneeling in a field, surrounded by salt-tax soldiers on their knees, their faces and lances lowered. He recalled women weeping as a ritual grave was dug and a marble marker was planted deep in the earth. The party marched on for a distance and waited as the sun set. Lee Shui-feng remained alone in that unknown field for a while, covering his face and honoring the memory of his first wife.

First Wife's name was etched deeply in boldest black, long-life ink on a brilliant white stone of pure marble, a lavishly expensive spirit tablet that was meant to transcend space and time and spirit, an Egyptian icon placed for all time amid the happy sounds of a prosperous Chinese clan. It was an outlandishly expensive, outsize spirit tablet, heavy and permanent.

Every person from Master Lee to the servant who emptied night soil came to light incense and pray to her. On memory day in the spring, the household gathered at the family graves near the Yangtze River, where her imaginary body had been buried in a thousand-*tael* garnet casket made from the best *nai moh* hardwood coffin trees from the western mountains of Yunnan. As incense smoke writhed to heaven, the family left oranges and food and reported on the status of the *jia*, lying about the weak and exaggerating the strong. Later, each reverently asked for money, for husbands, for sons, for good salt-tax revenues. Eyes scrunched, they asked for sons, again.

Dad, who would later become a violent iconoclast, prayed to her in his early Yangchow days. He shut his eyes and sent his secret thoughts to heaven. It is a Chinese habit to deify the dead, to pray to people of history for help in the present. Old warriors of legend, like Guan Yu of the *chuan kuo*, the Warring States, become gods to the Chinese people, as if Achilles and Ajax could help the Greeks of today.

No Chinese youth could say the name of any of the Before Borns. Her name, etched in black on white, remained an unspoken secret even to an honoring grandson in the days when he believed in gods.

This girl, his ancestor by clan, became known as the Bravest Wife. Her death had made life possible. All knew that courage was something that came from good ancestors and from hard prayer.

Courage was something that my father, and my mother, would someday need in great abundance.

Glimpsing Shanghai

SERVANTS CHERISHED MY father because he was male, and they liked him because he was cute. They admired him when he slept, which he did well, but loathed him when he ran, which he did often.

"Chase me!" he would cry, pigtail bouncing as he accelerated, his feet barely touching the earth. He ran happily through the packed crowd just beyond the reach of grasping hands, the servants' fingers so deliciously close. He arched his back and raced away laughing and skipping, making wild bird-calls as he flew into the freedom of the marketplace mob.

For this was Shanghai, far from their Yangchow estate and the bamboo garden with the moon gate and the curved bridge over a quiet, carp-filled stream. There life was poetry. Here life was for sale.

Shanghai is a city of the Whangpu and Yangtze Rivers. It is like a big eyeball above the nose-shaped Whangpu, which flows downward from the Yangtze. In 1920, the original, Old Chinese City of Shanghai was the lower part of the eyeball. Surrounding the Old City was the International Concession, filled with Englishmen and Americans.

In 1842, after the British defeated the Chinese Empire in the Opium War,

London won the right to directly sell illicit drugs to the Chinese people as it took Chinese cities for its own territory—its "concessions." Other foreign nations demanded equal treaty rights: What England had taken from China would have to be matched in compelled concessions to the other powers. Fair was fair.

When my father was a boy, the British and Americans shared the International Concession. To the west of the Chinese City was the French Concession. The Japanese were above the Old City in Chapei. The Germans were to the far north, in Shantung, the home province of Confucius. Missionaries who, as everyone knows, take eyeballs from the dead for magic incantations, were everywhere, guarded by foreign gunboats. Armed foreigners camped on the coast of China in heavy numbers.

Here in Shanghai, the boy giggled as his speed made the servants' faces turn red. He was flattered when one stopped, bending over and pretending to make gagging sounds.

Lee Zeu-zee raced through orchards of legs, dodging women in pants lugging heavy groceries; men in blue gowns attended by facedown slaves; high-voiced hawkers pitching oysters and cod; bearded men displaying whale-tusk mahjong pieces; white-ducked European sailors groping thin, adolescent singsong girl prostitutes. He raced around crickets in fine bamboo cages and pitiful, suppurating, wailing beggars in tattered rags; he saw bare-armed musicians clanging gongs and muscular martial artists turning cartwheels and breaking boards, and heard guttural arguments and hot cries for money and mercy. It all resembled the high whining orchestra of the summer locusts on the Yangtze, the discordance creating a background of human nature pushed to extremes of competition.

"*Yi bao char dar, lo yu dar!*" cried a bun merchant, his musically throaty calls—common to his guild—matching desert tambourines of Gobi storytellers hungry for listeners and the mournful chants of thin, otherworldly saffron-robed monks seeking private roads to paradise.

The boy ran across a sidewalk chalked with calligraphy, drawing wails from a thin intellectual whose life story the boy's small feet had just smudged. In hard times, teachers scratched their biographies on the street to draw sympathetic coppers from the literate, and a dragon coin—one-four-hundredth of a dollar—from those who only pretended they could read.

This was Shanghai, the city above the sea, the metropolis of profits, the hub of leaping foreign evils, the teeming port that led to the great oceans to the east and to a hundred thousand *li* of Yangtze River waterways to the west. Its commerce fed 10 percent of the Chinese people.

Millions of people floated on its money, drowned in its poverty and flooded its packed streets from a crumbling Chinese Empire. Inertia and corruption had collided with Western industrialism. It was the end of time—barbarians were inside the gates. Everyone waited for the fall of an ax from grasping foreigners or angry gods, and probably both.

The boy loved sailing from the family home in Yangchow down the Yangtze and Whangpu to the foreign-country town of Shanghai. For almost two days, he ran the deck and climbed the swaying rigging of the great red batwing sail while the servant women screamed for him to come down.

The boy didn't know that Shanghai was run by foreign-country people; he judged people by their shoes and legs. He laughed because his amah was pretending to be scared by his running away—so he ran faster.

The new cook, the cook's assistant and Amah panted after him. The new cook was Wong Mah-tze, meaning "sesame face," indicating that he had suffered from smallpox but survived. Wong had been ordered on the trip because he had to judge Shanghai produce, and because he was tall, fat and had a white crew cut that would scare away devils.

Tall Amah had been my father's servant since birth. She lost sight of him, and a sting of panic consumed her. They were moving slower since Sesame Face Wong's assistant had become ill from the running. The boy was buoyed by the excitement.

"At our home market," gasped the nauseated lesser cook, "everyone would gather around me if I got sick. Showing concern—"

"Showing disgust," said Sesame Face. Yangchow elders would gather around an ill one, arguing causes, offering remedies. A kind mother would bring a cold, wet cloth. All would complain about the weather while gossiping about infidelities, food and red-eyed foreigners.

Tall Amah had to agree. Here a hundred Manchus with hatchets could cut out and eat their hearts, and some Shanghai bastard would yell at them to clean up after themselves. Tall Amah liked Shanghai about as much as she would have liked her face chewed on by a wild dog.

The boy was somewhere ahead. Zeu-zee was Master's second son. His tendency to fly like a bird was making their brains and hearts leap from their bodies. Why couldn't he be like Older Brother, an earthbound little boy who lived the word *shun*, obedience?

Lee Gee-zee the Firstborn, Zeu-zee's older brother, was a self-contained, square-faced nine-year-old with a loud stomach. He sat at his desk like a frog awaiting a fly, while his younger brother was as kinetic as a grasshopper with a burning tail.

In the quiet family gardens in Yangchow, Zeu-zee ran all day. When not running, he climbed trees in an attempt to reach for birds. Below, in a rain of leaves and snapped branches, women wailed and men covered their eyes. But the boy was charming and laughed quickly and infectiously, and no one punished him. When little Zee Zee—as he was called—held his knees and laughed for no reason at all, even Skinny Wu, a somber, stone-faced seamstress with dead sons and no daughters, guffawed, covering her gap-toothed mouth with old, needle-pricked hands.

"Stop, *Saoyeh*, Young Master!" she'd beg. "Aiy, strong emotions hurt digestion!"

Besides, to whom could the servants report the boy's naughtiness except his beloved wet nurse? The Master, who was the boy's baba and the son of Shui-feng the Yangchow salt-tax lord, was indifferent to his children. Master's father had been an abacus man who had survived both sieges of Nanking during the Taiping Wars; he had enjoyed his newfound riches by intentionally spoiling his sons and unintentionally making them hostile to their own children. Shui-feng's sons discovered that children interfered with pleasure. Nor could the servants tell Lee Taitai, Master's wife, because she'd hysterically fire them before experiencing regret and rehiring them. Then she'd make all the women kneel and pray to her Christian God: *Make the master stop smoking opium. Make Second Son stop running.*

The household had been alarmed when Lee Taitai ate the foreign-god religion. They harbored superstitious fears that vast armies would appear to behead her and all those who lived with her. Superstitiously, Sesame Face Wong had killed roosters, writing *shun* on the barn lintels in their blood. The memory of the Taiping was yet fresh in a land that knew its history.

Lee Taitai had declared that henceforth, no one could pray to Taoist gods and household deities without first bowing to the Jesu God, and Father God, and a scary devil called the Holy Ghost. *At least ten kowtows for each! I'll be listening!* The servants nodded energetically and immediately ignored the edict; it was happening to the best families—troubled wives of addicts were turning to a dead Jewish rabbi named Jesu for relief from Indian opium, and now no one could be safe from the future. Everyone knew that the Christian God was trouble.

Nor could the servants report Zee Zee to Gee. That would be like throwing a torch into a dry field, for the older brother resented Second Son and needed no excuse to torture him. All day, Gee quietly studied with his tutor, pausing only to scream as Zee Zee ran by. His baby brother was supposed to study the trimetrical classics four hours a day with his tutor and always got away with less. When no one was watching, Gee would pinch Zee Zee's private parts, making the little boy scream. After dark, an angry Gee curled into a knot and tossed like a boat on sour seas, crying pitifully to the dead and the unseen. The servants could find no way to calm him.

Gee's amah never said aloud the damning words that other servants whispered in the great house: When Gee was born, his father, swimming in pride, had moved his Firstborn Son into his private rooms, where the tiny infant inhaled opium smoke for the first six months of life. When the Master tired of having the boy in his room, he evicted him and his wet nurse, but the boy never seemed thereafter to be able to sleep through the night. Because of her six months with Gee's father, the wet nurse had become an opium addict and had been fired long ago.

Gee's opposite was, of course, Zee Zee, who ate fast and raced through prayers in the dark ancestral prayer hall. "Honored Before Borns, I'm nothing. I'll please you with work," he lied to the watching dead. Then he would run to his room, making faces at his older brother, Tall Amah chasing him, and dive into his small bed. Na-ma, the soft-eyed wet nurse, would let him suckle her as she sang him to sleep with her beautiful voice, and he would sleep all night without moving.

Zee Zee would race back and forth in the Yangchow garden, making sharp butterfly turns as if escaping devils—whom everyone knew could march only in straight lines—unlike his maids, who could only throw up. In the dense garden, he was a rabbit searching for a way to jump the wall into the outer world, leaping at birds, chasing clouds, laughing at ghosts as he left behind him the exhausted, the panting and the nauseated.

"There!" he'd say as they caught him. "Bird spirits up high!"

They would look up at an empty sky, and he would sprint away.

Now, unaccustomed to crowds, the servants cried out each time the hard shoulder of a Shanghainese struck them. They cursed an endless mob in which everyone was a faceless stranger, where all had forgotten how to nod or smile at visitors.

The servants wailed, for Zee Zee was running farther from them than ever before. At home in Yangchow, they could cry for Na-ma. One word from the pretty wet nurse in her Chekiang accent, and the boy would stop like a plum hitting earth. The challenge was finding her, for she was always talking to the cooks, rickshaw pullers, seamstresses, stable coolies and salt-tax soldiers, chatting with visitors, cleaning the scraped knee of a household child, talking to the horses or the chickens or the pigs. But Na-ma had been ordered to stay behind in Yangchow, and now Zee Zee was losing his *chigong*, his inner essence, in his little-boy perspiration. He was losing his life in evil Shanghai, and it was all their fault!

Even more than sweat, they feared ghosts and their slimy grip on your face, their fetid breath as you turned in to a dark alley. Every shadowed window, hidden door and sinister building could hide a crafty devil and this city of ghosts leered at them from evil, unfriendly angles that made their stomachs hurt. Ghosts kidnapped children and took them into the lower levels and made them suffer the ten woeful courts of Buddhist torture. Men and women disappeared in Shanghai every day. At dawn, hundreds of corpses were retrieved from the streets and canals by the Dong Jen Fu An Tong, a benevolent Buddhist sect whose yellow-robed members prayed over the daily harvest of the dead, those reaped from murder, disease, greed, drugs and modern industry. Sesame Face hawked and spat ferociously to keep evil at bay.

"Leave the boy alone, sodding spirits!" hissed the assistant cook at a long, dark alley that swallowed words and ate the moment of courage.

The Lee cooks worried about ghosts while Tall Amah worried about bad men. Shanghai was home to *pigun*, villains, and the *Chingbang*, the Green Gang—*pigun* with guns and sharp knives who dealt in money and blood. She knew that inside their chests, they had no hearts. If a *Chingbang* gangster saw the well-dressed Zee Zee, he'd spy a son of good fortune and would take him for ransom—a ransom to be paid out of the servants' blood. She saw a shadowy man looking—

"*Zee Zee, stop!*" she cried.

Mah-mee provided the womb for his first months and Na-ma provided the milk for his first years, but Tall Amah was responsible for him every hour of the day. She was a tall woman, like the boy's mother.

Zee Zee's mah-mee was nearly six feet tall—taller than most foreign men. Wanting a commanding amah for Zee Zee, Lee Taitai had hired a Shantung woman of nearly equal height. Second Son was cute and good-natured and was, against all customs, her favorite child. Choosing a servant from Shantung would bring good luck: Two millennia earlier, it had been the birthplace of Confucius. Tall Amah had gladly joined the House of Lee because she feared the red-faced, beefy Beer Makers, the Germans, who had forced their way into her home province and now owned that part of China. Her stomach had performed acrobatics when she heard they were moving to Shanghai, the foreign-country town that was full of Germans.

Tall Amah approached the boy, looking away as if approaching a wary squirrel, and played her best card. "Zee Zee, come now or I'll tell Na-ma!"

The crushing roar of Shanghai seemed to subside. Zee Zee, age five, appeared out of the thick crowd, his head down. Tall Amah offered her hand; he reached high. With one hand, Tall Amah untied her hair bun and wrapped the cord around his wrist and hers, the tightness a security against his flight and a punishment for her negligence. The boy scowled. He hated the cord.

The cooks followed, coughing and gasping, warding off unseen evil spirits and spitting out bad luck, walking deeper into the bowels of the terrible, hooting, chomping, carnivorous city.

Sesame Face Wong had never been this worried, and he didn't like it. Behind lay costly lost groceries that had been savaged instantly by the crowds. Shaking with the penalty they would have received had they actually lost Second Son—death—they were torn between slapping the boy silly and thanking the gods for his return.

In Shanghai, foreigners ruled, and foreign law protected white superiority and crushed the values that preserved family relationships and Confucian rules. White police wore guns, drove farting cars and treated people like bugs. Small country girls were tied together by the neck and sold like fruit to rapacious men. Armies of raggedy sunburned beggars died of starvation, exposure and disease. Shanghai stank of the dominion of evil spirits and the ghosts of the hungry, unsatisfied dead.

"We're of a Yangchow house of learning. Our master is a scholar," Tall Amah said to each passerby whose elbow or shoulder struck her. She bit her lip to avoid shouting at the stupid new cooks. There they were, haggling for produce before they even found 30 Burkill Road in the International Settlement, one of two neighboring houses the Master had just bought on credit. *Idiots!* They were supposed to build relationships with the markets and shops that the family would need, establish face connections, *guan shi*, near the Burkill houses so the Lee household could survive, even thrive, in Shanghai's sea of strangers and white devils and evil spirits. *Foreigners. They will be the end of us.*

Master had wanted to buy houses in the French Concession, where there were even fewer social rules than in the wide-open English- and American-dominated International Settlement, but thankfully, he could no longer afford it. Two Shanghai English houses were cheaper than one French one, but none were worth the move from Yangchow.

What was I thinking, bringing the boy here! He has the energy of a man on his wedding night! You stupid woman! Did I just yell that aloud? In this noisy hell of twelve layers, no one could tell. The boy was looking up at her.

"It's okay, I just miss the Hus." The fine cooks had left and were allowed to take their good pots and seasonings. Now everything tastes like poor country food. Tall Amah remembered famine in Shantung; peasants ate roots and bark, and then dirt. Anything to fill the stomach and ease the waves of pain.

The Hus would joke with Taitai, Zee Zee's mother. *Ah, she gave good times, gossiping, shelling peas, telling country jokes and stories of the river, of days of wealth and fun and river men, making laughter! Now she swallows foreign ways and gives cash to Big Nose temples to buy off Master's opium habit. Creditors hound the mansion and harass us at market. Next we'll lose the horse master and the grooms. Horses are the mark of gentlemen, from when horsemen ruled China. And not even a stable in the new Shanghai home! First Son is more sullen. Second Son runs!* She squeezed his hand hard and he yelped.

It was because of the Indian poppy; Master had found Cloud Biting Mountain, Lotus Land, the kingdom of dreams, the Country of Cannot Do, as in Cannot Sleep, Cannot Remember, Cannot Work, Cannot Get Well. There were five others, but Tall Amah couldn't remember them. Master had become a slave to opium, to *ta-yen*, the Big Smoke.

Shanghai burst with warehouses of top-quality, brain-cooking Indian Malwa, opium that was far superior to the grainy water-compromised Kiangsi *ta-yen* that flooded the market up and down the Yangtze River. Shanghai opium sold at a huge discount from the inland premium rate, so here they were closer to the source. Soon, they would move here.

Below her, in Shanghai's French Concession, a Marseilles police chief ran the opium cartel as though selling crêpes suzette. Guests in the Grand or the Cathay Hotel on the Bund could order Indian opium or Turkish heroin through room service. For five dollars, you could have a clean and pretty ten-year-old girl. For ten dollars, you could keep her.

Shanghai was beyond sin; its vices had guilds guarded by the cops. Shanghai annually smoked $40 million U.S. in fifteen hundred dank, acrid, business-booming opium dens. Zee Zee's father was selling the Yangchow family estate to be closer to what soothed his pain.

Tall Amah looked down at little Zee Zee, who tilted his head up and smiled at her, and her heart broke. Shanghai would swallow a sweet boy without a guiding father like a cruel sea dragon taking a small fish.

"Why are you sad, Amah?" he asked.

"Don't let Shanghai eat you!" she cried.

five

Goodbye, Soochow

EVERYONE HAD LOVED Little Missy Da-tsien. If they had the rank and the right, they'd touch her silken face. Low-rankers cooed at her as if she were a bejeweled Peking diva. But in the wake of the foot-binding crisis, when household members passed the once favored girl, their faces fell. To lessen interaction with her and to avoid displeasing her mother, they stopped breathing so they wouldn't inhale the girl's bad luck, grimacing when she stumbled on her expanding feet. In time, it was noticed that the now isolated child had developed the penetrating look of an older person.

Ah Tsui, her round amah with the appetite of ten Mongols, became subdued, imitating the defeat of the girl's mother, the Taitai, the head female. Lao

Chu, the burly chef, had cooked best when Taitai was happy. Now morose, he let Fatty Soo, an assistant with five thumbs and no imagination, do the cooking. It was household science—if Taitai sneezed, all caught the flu.

The exceptions to the communal sadness were Auntie Gao and excitable Miao-miao, who still visited, gay refugees from bad husbands. They gushed over Da-tsien, showering her with gifts and pampering her with the attention they would've given to their daughters had they not been barren and therefore deserving of their husbands' malice. Miao-miao incessantly talked about new silks, for Soochow was China's silk capital, and it was well known that excellent silks compensated for a lack of physical beauty. Auntie Gao offered *I Ching* prophecies, both women talking so rapidly that Da-tsien had trouble remembering it all. Auntie Gao later joined servants in the kitchen to compete with fast-shoveling Ah Tsui for leftovers. Both women raced to reach the best dishes, one eye on plates and the other on her rival. Ah Tsui was faster, for she used oversize Hunan *kwaidz*, chopsticks. Hunan was the province of robust appetites, spicy cuisine, big dishes and big bellies.

Taitai couldn't stop these visits to her daughter. But knowing that both women lived on thin allowances from fat husbands, she banned the gifts. In the wake of growing disfavor, Da-tsien's younger brother, Da-shing, benefited, for he was cute, smart, uncontroversial and male.

"Everyone hates me," said Da-tsien, crying.

"No tears, Little Missy," said Baba. "Our people love you. But your feet confuse them. No crying! Tears block vision and cloud memory."

"Mah-mee hates me."

"Please do not speak this way. It hurts my digestion. You're her only daughter. Her heart is full of care for you."

"She likes everyone else, even Old Deaf Man Fu. Everyone loves Da-shing more than me!"

"Daughter, he's my Only Son. He'll carry the family name. Don't resent him, please. That would hurt my heart."

"Oh, Baba, I'm sorry!"

"You must love your brother, agreed?"

"Yes, Baba. But I'm so clumsy at everything I do!"

"No, no, you're graceful as—as a swan."

"But I walk like a duck!"

"Oh, well, that's okay, too, isn't it?"

But Soochow was the visionary city of eight fabled water gates, the home of beautiful and graceful ladies, with soft, sensual voices, none of whom walked like ducks.

Baba set aside his translated foreign books to read Da-tsien tales of dragons, phoenixes and women warriors. "See, she jumped high—she *had* to have big feet! And a heart for so much courage, like you." He encouraged reading and imagination—the two magic carpets he rode to escape an increasingly unhappy wife and a dying treasury.

He also used fishing. It took cajoling and a bucket of luck to get his son to join him and Da-tsien for a day of fishing on the canals. It was also a day of decision.

Scars from the old Taiping rebellion against the Manchus were still evident. This year a revolution had started in Wuhan and had spread to Peking, resulting in the surprisingly total and final defeat of the Manchurians. After three centuries of harsh rule and intermarriage, the Manchus had faded like an old bruise. The revolution was under way, and changes beyond imagination were coming, but learning remained the key to culture.

Baba had found two tutors for his children, which would have made sense if he had two sons. One tutor was excellent, and one was not.

"Son, would you like a new tutor? It's time you had— *Aha!* You got a fish! Set the hook! Pull him in! Yes, *banjila!* You're better than Chiang Tzu-ya!" Chiang was his hero; according to legend, fish jumped out of the water to impale themselves on his spear.

The boy shut his eyes, praying the fish would see that being hooked was unhealthy and do something to free itself. But Baba helped him land it. The boy burst into tears as the beautiful fish flopped unhappily on the pier.

"No, no, don't cry!" said Baba. "Put him in the tub! Later we'll return him and his brothers to the river, okay?"

But Da-shing cried bitterly for the sad fish, so Baba quickly freed it and dropped it in the canal. He asked his son if he wanted a Grown-up Tutor, but the boy wandered away without answering, his amah waddling after him.

Rubbing his scalp as if to warm up his brain, Baba thought about matters for a while. "Daughter, would you like a tutor for yourself?"

"Baba, really? To be smart, like a boy?"

"I met a Hanlin named Magistrate Chen. He's not very nice, but he's very, very smart. That's good, isn't it?"

Hanlins were the Fulbrights of Imperial China, the top brains in a culture that worshiped intellect. In Old China, the scholars ruled.

"Chen was with the Board of Rites. The officials have been unemployed since Dr. Sun Yat-sen made the boy emperor step down. We have a new Chinese government. So Magistrate Chen has become Teacher Chen."

"But Brother needs a new tutor—"

"I have one for him, too."

"Another Hanlin?"

"Not exactly. He's a rural teacher. He has long hair that falls across his face. Luckily, he's not expensive."

"Baba, is he as smart as Teacher Chen?"

He was as smart as a rock pile, but Baba said, "Oh, quite!"

Yet hiring anyone strained the budget. When Taitai, Da-tsien's mother, complained about the cost, the country tutor complained about his small rice bowl and asked for a raise. This made Teacher Chen, the Hanlin scholar, scowl until Taitai ordered everyone to change their faces, right now! Taitai, however, did not change hers.

If assets and affection were in short supply, there remained at least austerity and high parental expectations. As Chinese students know, these are the standard ingredients for scholarship.

Teacher Chen was a scholar, so naturally, Da-tsien admired him. If Chen reciprocated the feeling towards his girl pupil, he concealed it. Before coming to Soochow, he had been a yellow-robed minister who rose each dawn to the chants of monks in the Forbidden City to serve the child emperor Pu-yi. It had been a corrupt and arrogant government, but the rank was high, the food was good and the comforts incomparable.

In 1911, when Da-tsien was five, the Chinese Revolution began a bloody fifty-year campaign against China's storied past. When her baba told her that the world had changed, she asked, "Does that mean we can't fish?"

The Empire had been failing for two centuries. Now it was as dead as the last chicken in the Han Dynasty. Sun Yat-sen, a revolutionary thinker with American medical training, had founded the new Republic of China. But in Peking and in the villages, ex-imperial generals and their regional armies were contending for true control of China.

China would come to know these men as the *jun fa*, the warlords.

The mandarin scholars who had managed the Empire of China for three thousand years had been discarded like stockbrokers after a crash. The rich hired these confused intellectuals as tutors. It was as if today's wealthy could buy the chairman of the Federal Reserve Board and a few undersecretaries of state to coach their kids in economics and social studies. Teacher Chen once outranked everyone in Soochow. Now he was a simple teacher in a house with questionable finances. Worse, he filled his rice bowl by teaching an upstart girl who tripped over her big feet and liked to fish. Da-tsien was the first female with whom he had ever worked. He did not consider this a precedent worth comment.

In late afternoon, after lessons, Baba and his little daughter sat on the stairs of their home and watched the canal traffic, waving to water taxis, merchants and neighbors who were being ferried to one of the eight water gates. They bought sweets and mandarin oranges from floating vendors and threw crumbs at surfacing fish as the sun turned the water crimson.

Behind them sat Ah Tsui with a parasol to guard Da-tsien's face, and the unhappy Teacher Chen, his nose in a book. As father and daughter chattered, Da-tsien angled closer to him. She looked up for his reactions, occasionally glancing over her shoulder to tease her amah or gaze at her tutor. She didn't blush; once seated, she never tripped or experienced surprising collisions. She wanted to hold her baba's hand, but fathers and daughters couldn't touch. Even in the most loving family relationship, such closeness could not be tolerated. The only close contact she would ever have with her baba was that one exciting escape down the staircase in their flight from tradition.

Relatives laughed for fifty years about the bookish patriarch picking up his little girl from the binding table and running from a horde of screaming women as if the Taipings were hunting the heads of the rich and burning homes without *shun* painted on their doors. Baba, our maternal grandfather, never joined in the laughter, for it was that fall afternoon when he ran away with his daughter that his marriage began to fail. After that his wife began to view her husband not so much as a lazy gentryman who liked to fish but as a dangerous mental defective who, to save a few tears, had pissed away the future of the *jia*.

Taitai had top blood—a line of superior scholars and Hanlins, the peak of Chinese aristocracy. Her father had been viceroy of the maritime provinces of Kwangtung and Fukien and the cities of Canton and Hong Kong, a position not unlike being the governor of Oregon, California and Washington. He once had a dozen Chens reporting to him every dawn. A model governor, he retired with honors, declining the greasy wealth that came with high office. He had moral rectitude. Nothing was worth more. But times were changing. Now you could be moral if you could afford it.

Taitai watched her husband fish while foreigners gave China a new greed that rotted away tradition and let bad ideas fester in the moldering wood. The foreigners brought plagues of troops, machines, child prostitution, opium and a nation of missionaries who wanted your soul, who hungered to eat your eyeballs.

Even Taitai's brother, a kind, walleyed widower, was losing his house staff of over twenty generations to higher-paying foreign jobs in Shanghai. Working for the white devils cost you your customs, but it paid more cash, which let you buy things to replace the needs of the heart.

"We need money. Lots of money," Taitai said, pounding her fist into an open palm. A good husband would not be at home at noon, dozing with a foreign book and hiring a pricey Hanlin scholar for a big-footed daughter. He'd be making money from the foreign-country people while letting the women maintain intricate relationships, manage the future of the clan, shop, cook and break the feet of its daughters. Even his useless *nu li* slave—Deaf Man Fu—slept all day. It was all so unacceptable!

She became increasingly sharp-tongued. At dinner she recited the Master's wrongs as he nodded and their children remained silent and the servants hissed. Stomachs grew sour and dishes grew cold. *You're lazy. You won't support us. We grow weak and poor and disrespected. Our reputation evaporates, and you dishonor us, and you catch fish we don't need! Where will we get our grandsons, our future, our destiny?*

When she couldn't stand it, she took independent action. She made her clumsy daughter sit beside her. As no right-thinking man would marry a girl with monstrous lower appendages that stretched to the Yellow River and the Always Snow Mountains, the girl would have to learn to make business. Making business meant making money, a hateful, disgusting thing for a woman with royal blood. But money now trumped honor.

Taitai had her handsome son, Da-shing, attend as well. If he failed to marry money, business knowledge would be helpful. But before long he'd pat his gown and wander away to find forgotten things and never return. He was trying to read foreign books about fisheries and machinery, as if to impress his father. Taitai had no choice but to teach her daughter.

"This steward who sat in our room and talked about the *likin*, the road tax," Taitai would say to her unworthy child, "what's he want?"

Da-tsien would carefully answer, identifying relationship, position, information, money, access, leverage, *guan shi* connections or goods, or some heady combination of these interests.

"What truly drives him to our door?" asked the mother.

Da-tsien would identify hope, greed, need or fear.

"What is his nature? To control or to be loved? To be an exterior person, of relationships, or to be interior, connected to private thoughts?"

Da-tsien liked these questions; they were easy to answer.

"To approach this particular clan, do you use *guan shi*, face relationship? Or top-floor, *sa-mien*? Or back-door connections, *ho-men*?"

"They are salt-tax people, so it must be back-door, out of sight, but we always rely on *guan shi* if we don't have stronger connections. Mah-mee, everything is relationships."

"Excellent, Daughter! Where did you learn to listen so well?"

"I think Baba taught me."

"No, no, can't be. Don't use that answer. Now, did the man's words show his true intent, or was there a purpose buried beneath the words?"

Da-tsien would answer, giving true reasons born from a gift of sight.

"Good. Can you see beyond the man who sat in this room? Do you see the clan he represents? The needs that push on him, that create his fear or his hope, over the horizon? Can you see what can't be seen?"

And the girl would close her eyes and tell her mah-mee what she saw.

"Yes, yes, good, you got it," said Taitai. "Now, what about this morning's merchant? A sweet, kind man, yes? But was he *huatou*, slippery? *Biesan*, hustler? *Wen ren*, celebrity, or *mentu*, disciple to his boss; or did you see a *gaodeng huaren*, upper-class man? Or was he *shimen*, a died-in-the-wool Shanghainese businessman who will try to outbargain us for our blood?"

Da-tsien might say, "He's *mentu* of a *gaodeng biesan*, with Songhai instincts. He'll try to take everything to fill his bags for ten generations."

"Yes, yes, I think so, too. You're good. Too bad your feet are so big."

In came a rickshaw puller, all muscle, ribs and sinew, feet hard and reptilian. He had bathed in the horse stall but still stank from running fifteen hours a day only to sink deeper in debt. He slurped the hot tea and hungrily inhaled the cakes, making a huge mess, grunting answers to the cool matriarch and the soft girl who saw his scrapes and wounds. "Yes, Lady, I carry English Number Three white devil to Lloyds Bank every Friday morning, no fail," he said, picking up crumbs from the sleek hardwood floor and licking callused fingers.

Taitai's hard left eye saw the smears of his fingerprints on the floor; her daughter saw the poor man's pleasure to eat crumbs.

Later came porters who carried valuable crates to hotels; hotel clerks who gave rooms; Chinese secretaries who took notes in important meetings; and then well-dressed Chinese businessmen who offered counsel and knew to sip tea and bypass the cakes because money was at hand. Normally, they wouldn't listen to a woman with an evil, bargaining eye and her big-footed daughter. But they remembered the woman's honorable father, the great viceroy, who had been a man of virtue.

Da-tsien listened, smoothing the interviews, her un-Chinese enjoyment of strangers balancing her mother's insistent, no-nonsense tones. The girl knew which men smiled with their teeth and which ones smiled from their stomachs.

Grandmother was cashing in social chits earned by her father's integrity in a distinguished civil life. It was not what was supposed to be, but it answered to what was needed. Later, armed with information, she met the sons of her father's ministers, officers, magistrates, clerks. They made introductions to white-demon men. As a lady, she could not put her eyes on a foreign white devil who liked to touch your hands and look at you. Even the rudest rickshaw puller had better manners.

The white demon spoke in a voice full of flame and smoke.

The Chinese translator said, "Can he speak English?"

"Yes, of course," replied Taitai.

Miles away, closer to the sea, money was exchanged, debts of honor were settled, papers were signed. It was done.

"He'll be another Master Hsu Jun!" Hsu Jun had worked for Dent, a major foreign China *taipan* trader, and had prospered fabulously.

Lo Fa, Taitai's husband, the quiet, bearlike reader of books who licked his lips and smiled as he turned the pages, now had a job. Befitting the son-in-law of a viceroy of the Empire of China, he had been named a senior deputy comprador for Jardine Matheson, the global mercantile enterprise that inspired the tales of the *taipans*. Its offices were at 27 The Bund, and it was one of history's greatest opium dealers.

Compradors were the middlemen who worked the Chinese side of the port for the Portuguese, Dutch, British, Americans, Italians, Germans and French, and could dance tax minuets with the Customs Service. The world had come to Chinese shores to take what they could with both hands, and compradors, from the Portuguese word involving "buyers," bridged the east-west gap for cash. Compradors arranged secure berths for Indian opium, competent harbormasters, strong-backed porters for fragile porcelain, honest *hoppo*, port supervisors who saw a two-*picul* error in a tea sampan at midnight, high-integrity godown warehouses for Chinese silver and gold. Compradors handled security, peculation, bribes, nepotism, customs, road tariffs, tugs, lights, duties, portage and, if necessary, salvage. They negotiated squeeze — tips for good service in redundant tasks. For this, they became rich. Unloved because they made money from exploitation, they were respected, for they filled rice bowls and made business.

For this job, the elegant Tzu clan, descendants of scholars, would move from the beautiful crimson canals of Soochow to grimy, pestilential, foreign-run Shanghai.

"Don't go!" cried Auntie Gao, her bad-luck foot angling outward as she hugged her favorite niece. "Stay here with us. You're my daughter, too!"

Da-tsien kept saying, "Dama, Auntie, come with us!" But Auntie Gao's husband was in Soochow, and he was her life anchor. Da-tsien loved Auntie's thin, off-balance form, her small, pinched face and thinning hair, the warmth and intelligence within. Knowing the parting was inevitable, Auntie Gao gave her niece her best advice about life, warning her about handsome boys and the needs of men.

Miao-miao whimpered, jumping up and down to stanch her sharp inner pains. Other women of the clan had already been shed by the failing economics of a nonworking father. This petite inner community wept as the Tzus left their pretty mansion on the canal. Taitai was embarrassed by the small farewell. Da-tsien feared that Auntie Gao and Miao-miao would now die. So she kept her eyes dry and clear as she memorized their faces and their voices and their richly spilled emotions.

Teacher Chen did not weep, but he managed a frown when Da-tsien tripped on his toes as she bowed. Would he miss his student? He would have to miss the great house, the banquets, the majestic trees and drunken poets who sang under moonlit skies. In Shanghai, a comprador's income would make his tutoring fee look like buying a peanut. But Shanghai was barbarian, and old mandarins had standards. He would rather starve in Soochow than read fine books by the stink of foreign waters. Teacher Chen's empire had been upended less by revolutionaries and more by foreign ideas that had been derived from American democratic operating principles.

Da-tsien cried as she said goodbye to the florid, fat-faced horse master and the other servants who couldn't follow because they were outside the budget or because they had family obligations in Soochow. Taitai had found other jobs for them, but once Da-tsien began to cry, the dam broke; she cried so hard that she had no memory of the 150-kilometer trip east to Shanghai and the sea.

We'll be rich, just like the old days, thought Taitai. *No more sleepless nights, fretting. God, my bloodless feet hurt, but I tell you this: I will never miss that house! It cost so much money! Who said "Beauty before life"? Bah! Nonsense! Money first!*

Taitai

AITAI HAD FOUND a foreign house in Shanghai's American and English International Settlement, but she was lucky to be renting from a Chinese family from Yangchow. The International Settlement sat between Soochow Creek and the wide-open French Concession. The creek was named for the beautiful city they had left behind, but it was filled with waste. If she shuttered her eyes, she could imagine that it was their home canal. But Shanghai, the city of cash, welcomed the Tzus like any big city—with deadly indifference.

Baba went to work in the Jardine offices and the Shanghai docks the way Huckleberry Finn attended school. Both looked dreamily out the window, thinking of warm days and fat worms instead of focusing on hard work; in time, both wandered away from their desks to go fishing. Even Taitai's hot advocacy couldn't save him; Baba was soon fired from the only employment of his life.

With expenses exceeding revenue, Taitai had to release more house staff and pay for their return to Soochow. The shame of breaking moral contracts with multigenerational lines of servants, of breaching ancient relational duties to so many, of failing her father's fine reputation so acutely, while owing the people who helped procure her husband's job, cracked her heart. In the crevices grew bitterness.

My grandmother couldn't fire her own amah—her maid since birth. Nor could she release her son's slow country tutor, or his waddling amah, or Da-tsien's round one. Big Chef Chu and his family, including his cousin Fatty Soo, were the third generation to serve the Tzus, and who could live without their summer long beans, even if Chu had lost his will to cook? And she couldn't free Deaf Man Fu—he was a slave, his status imprinted in his hunched posture.

Near the new Shanghai ancestral hall, with good-luck banners appropriately removed and candles snuffed, Taitai bowed to the staff she could no longer afford. Servants wept, children cried and the household shrank, shaming its Before Borns. The servants might have been relieved—it hadn't been a happy home, and the meals had lost volume and taste. But they cried, for they loved Taitai and admired Old Dead Master, Taitai's father, the honored viceroy, the great man of rectitude. This was China, a land of relationships. If you cannot cry for others, you do not need eyes.

Females cannot enter the family ancestral hall. So when the house was silent, Taitai knelt at the door and sobbed out her failures to her father and his fathers before him, loud enough for her husband to hear, her cries bouncing off the spirit tablets of the dead and echoing in the quiet house. Silently, she apologized for her deficiencies to the women of the *jia*, asking the one thing that is so hard to find in China—forgiveness. Her ancient amah hobbled over to stand by her weeping mistress and to cry with her, adding her pain so the mistress's misery would not be lonely and un-Chinese, and now Taitai could not remain quiet.

"Forgive my failure with my lazy husband. Forgive my stupid, clumsy daughter. Looking at her feet makes me sick! Heaven, return to us the Empire of China, and even the Manchus and their horse culture. Give us back obedient daughters and virtuous men!" She pounds the floor with her tiny fists, pulling at her hair, wailing.

"Forgive me! I have to fire people pledged to our house, *but must keep my worthless, ungraceful daughter!*"

She doesn't know that Da-tsien, kneeling at the other corner of the hallway to say her female prayers, hears her mah-mee's petitions.

In SHANGHAI, DA-TSIEN yearns for good feelings to fill the corners of the new, quiet house. She and Amah feel evil spirits lurking in the roof and in the coal cellar waiting to steal joy, but a disheartened Baba isn't interested in scaring them away by using his deep *yang* voice. Although she hates striking matches—she knows the sparks could be sent by the devil to kill her—she bares her teeth and lights them in empty rooms to scare the weaker *yin* ghosts. At night, after reading with Baba and receiving Amah's one hundred brush strokes to her long hair, she thinks of Miao-miao's irrepressible demonstrations of raw emotion. She misses servants, calligraphy lessons, the frowning of her Hanlin tutor, the red waters of Soochow at dusk, the calls of floating merchants.

She misses black-gowned Auntie Gao and her brave limp. Unsuccessfully, she tries to remember Auntie's warnings, something about handsome boys.

So it was a fateful day when she chased her brother out of the house. Da-shing had discovered the pleasure of sharply yanking on her hair and then gleefully fleeing as she chased him with dark violence in her heart. Taitai heard the commotion and threatened her daughter.

"You run and torment your brother? May your hair fall out!"

When her mother left, Da-tsien, holding on to her hair to keep it from falling out, chased her brother out the door, which she promptly locked. Avoiding the sleeping Old Fu, she tripped upstairs on her big feet to read a book about noble bandits who hid in marshes, fighting evil officials. It was dark when she heard her brother's amah calling for him. She jerked up. *Aiyaa! I locked him outside! Oh no! He's dead by now! Mah-mee will kill me!* Sobbing, she ran downstairs, her heart pounding, and saw him standing in the living room by the open window.

"There you are! Thank Amitabha!" she cried, grabbing him to celebrate his survival, but then recoiled—she was touching a stranger she had never seen in her life—and before she could ask who he was, he jumped out the window. She ran to the window, but the boy was gone, moving faster than she had ever seen anyone move. *Was he a ghost? But I felt him!* Her brother was still missing—and probably dead—

"Did you chase him away?" Her brother's voice.

He's alive! Mah-mee's not going to kill me! She turned—he was alive and dirty. "Da-shing! You're alive and dirty! Who was that boy?"

"My *pungyoh*, my friend. I think he likes me."

"Why'd he jump out the window?"

"It's how he comes and goes."

"That's pretty strange, don't you think? What's his family name? Are they good and well educated?"

Her brother shrugged. "His name's Zee Zee. Rich family, I think."

AT THIS TIME, hundreds of Chinese work battalions were in the trenches on the side of the Allies in the first world war against Germany. To the Chinese, there was little to differentiate the conduct of foreigners in China—it was all uniformly bad. But if the Chinese helped defeat Germany, the Allies promised to make the Germans return Shantung Province. So a budding Chinese republic joined the Allies in France to win back the land of Confucius, hoping that the Allies would then return the larger parts of China that they themselves held.

Da-tsien was ten when the Chinese government levied *k'u-li* workers, including some Tzu house staff, on steamships to the European war. The house staff now included four family members; the mustached, gravel-throated majordomo; three amahs; the hairy, complaining tutor; two cooks and their families; the deaf slave who slept all day; and a dwindling number of chickens and pigs. Separated by different jobs and unified by austerity, they wailed in unison when Da-tsien's mother did the unthinkable.

Taitai left her husband and moved out of her own home. Her walleyed brother had offered her space in his big, empty house in the French Concession. Grandmother left the failing finances to her worthless husband who read books all day but never seemed to notice the bills.

"Okay, Husband. Sit and read. But now, you are dead to me."

Grandfather liked his wife but hated conflict. As she walked painfully out the door on her tiny feet, a string of hired porters bearing her wardrobe, collectibles, handwork and favorite plants—things she could pawn—he was fishing on the Whangpu. Fishing as modern foreign ships unloaded cargo worth millions of *taels* of silver, a percentage of which had been earmarked for him. The slaughter in the European war had improved business in Asia. Taitai thought of the good people she had been forced to fire and shook her head so she wouldn't go crazy.

No Chinese woman could walk out on her husband, who could beat her in public, sell her in private, kill her in front of her father and sons and burn her bones in the public square. She would be expected to take her punishment in stoic silence, head bowed in shame. She was his property, and property does not walk away, especially on delicate bound feet. Besides, she owed the rest of her life to her son, Da-shing, whom she was to follow and obey after Baba died. Such rules had allowed China to last five millennia.

Taitai's decision was scandalous to all, confusing to her son and hard on her. She was the daughter of a viceroy, but even with her brains and inspiration, her husband couldn't overcome a pathetic mediocrity. So she slapped the face of Confucian custom and abandoned him. She did it because she could—Baba was soft and a stranger to violence—and this was Shanghai, where her face would burn less brightly with shame. Shanghai, she quickly learned, had no shame whatsoever.

Da-tsien cried inconsolably over the loss of her mother, certain that it was her willfulness, her superior Soochow tutor and her big feet that were squeezing her good and noble mah-mee from the house. How she yearned for her mother's kind word.

She threw herself at her mother's tiny satin shoes. "I'll be the comprador for Baba, and we'll hire back Teacher Chen and Tailor Wong and Horse Master Yip!" Touching her mother's small feet, she begged her to stay, to let her work. "You can bind my big feet!"

This stopped her mother. "You are so *stupid*! The new republic banned foot binding five years ago when they banished the boy emperor, Pu-yi! If we made you beautiful now, I could be arrested! Let go of me!"

The staff lowered its faces. Deaf Man Fu stood at the door, conforming his feelings to the facial expressions of the others. Porters waited patiently in the street with Taitai's possessions. The gruff-voiced majordomo stood sternly. When they reached the house of Taitai's brother, the majordomo would be released, unemployed. Da-tsien closed her eyes, grateful that he was a strong and resourceful man. The house seemed empty and forlorn. Publicly, Taitai spoke to her son, giving him her blessings and her wishes for him to focus on his studies.

"Da-shing, I will work with the matchmaker for you from my brother's home. My son, honor the Sage and remember your mother."

Da-shing bowed to her, steeling his face, holding his tears.

She spoke to her daughter. "Stand up! Why are you embarrassing me by groveling like a peasant? Can you think of only your own needs? Lift your chin! You're the granddaughter of a great man, and you shame him! He was honorable! You must be the same! Now listen: Care for your brother. He must win top grades. Make him Top Number One! And stop his friend from jumping in and out of the window like we live in a barn.

"It's a fact, Daughter: Your father loves you more than he honors me. So you be the wife. You care for him. I taught you to do business; deal with the landlord. Get a reduction on the rent, get discounts on the debts. Do something about the bills, or the few servants who are left will be thrown into the street. And this is Shanghai, the most dangerous city in the world! Don't touch me again, or I'll fall. No! Hush! Can you give me no peace at all? Take your eyes off me, and kneel as I leave this bad-luck place! I want no weight from you on my back as I walk away from what's made me miserable!"

seven

Marrow and Bone

A DAUGHTER WHO IS not close to her mother risks disgrace and death or, even worse, a bad marriage. Only a Chinese mother can guide an ignorant girl through the hard shoals of childhood and the strict protocols of Confucian conduct. Only a Chinese mother can bring a daughter to the safe harbor of a solid marriage that will produce sons.

In times of sadness, bad-luck daughters are left by the side of the road or sold to good-time madams to get cash, even murdered to avoid the trouble of finding halfway measures. Chinese mothers love their girls, but they can't risk being too close, because when they give their daughters to marriage brokers, the girls leave forever, bound to new clans as servants. In the new homes, the true mother, prone to sentimentality, is never welcome. To love a daughter is to eat sadness and loss. It's wiser to keep a distance and think with your head, and far better to have sons, who marry girls and bring them into your home to do your bidding and support the clan. Sons are wonderful! Daughters cause pain.

Da-tsien had begun well, faltered badly and was a bad-luck girl whose big feet always seemed to dance with catastrophe. Now she was simply trying to survive adolescence. She would later say that Baba and her mother were as alike as fire and water and that Baba and her brother were as far apart as head and toes, while she and her father were as close as bone and marrow.

After her mah-mee left their Shanghai home, Da-tsien ran, crying, to the river to find her father. Blinded by tears and chased by her overweight amah, Da-tsien tripped on something unseen and fell, scraping her knees badly. A sweaty puller stopped and lifted the crying girl into his sedan, yelling angrily at the amah.

"Yuuu! Watch her better! A high-class girl like this! So what if everything under heaven's screwed up? You should respect her future!"

"Aiya!" her amah said in disgust. "She's no fine girl! You see her feet? You see what she was doing? *Running in public!* What do you think she is, a *bao tze k'u-li* rickshaw puller? She's not supposed to run!" To release her tension, she screamed, and the puller picked up his poles and began to flee. Remembering he had the girl in his sedan, he stopped, helped Da-tsien down, and then ran.

IN HER MOTHER'S absence, the house was so quiet that Da-tsien could hear the caged nightingales shift their weight. In a similar stillness, her father sat on the porch in a soft European chair, watching the slow and noxious motor traffic on Burkill Road's tree-shaded lanes. Perhaps he remembered Soochow's poetic canals and the waves of neighbors, and the angry voice of his absent wife.

In her room, Da-tsien could feel the unhappy memories of the foreigners who had lived here before them. She realized that they, like she, would be homesick for their own places of birth. Sadly, she remembered her mother's hurtful prayers in the hallway of ancestors and thought about her profound lack of worth. Her mother had cursed her. It was not unlike what everyone was saying about China.

One night Da-tsien joined her baba on the porch to ask him a long-pent-up question. "Baba, why don't you fix China?"

"Hoh! What if China's problems exceed the ability of one person?"

"But, Baba, you'll fix whatever you can fix, right?"

"Little Precious, things are so bad, some scholars wish they weren't Chinese. They wish they were foreign-country people, with new ideas."

Not be Chinese? It was so inconceivable that she laughed, stopping when he turned his back. Suddenly he laughed, too, and quickly told a funny story about Old Fu. It was years before Da-tsien learned that her father, like the man she would later marry, laughed when he was sad.

"Old Fu and I," he said, "were on the Third Soochow canal, by the city pagoda of eighty-eight lights, talking about the great poet Li Po. Drunk, Li Po was admiring his reflection in the water when he fell out of his boat and drowned. Old Fu imitated Li Po, looking over the gunnel, just like this. Then he saw his own reflection and he jerked—lost his balance—and fell in the water!" It was an old story she never tired of hearing. She liked her father's animation, his imitation of Old Fu's loss of balance, their joined laughter. Even though the story was funny, she saw the thinness of his smile as it faded into the night.

"Doesn't fishing make you happy anymore?" she asked.

"I'll tell you something. Fishing never made me happy. It's true! I loved the canals and the poets and the trees. When I was a boy, I saw the circles that fish make when they break the surface. I wanted to be with them, so I jumped in. My mother scolded me so hard! She withheld my food. She had a cook teach me how to use a rod and how to sit for hours on the shore, which she said was the correct relationship between men and fish. I didn't like it, didn't want to hurt the fish, just like Da-shing that day when we made the decision about the tutors. But as a kid, I liked water, the sounds of life, the sun on the canals, the sounds of the gods."

"Baba, you miss Soochow, don't you?"

"Oh, yes, Little Missy. Down to my old bones. It's the world's most beautiful place. It was quiet. It sounded the way a good book reads."

As Soochow people, father and daughter had tried to ignore the din of Shanghai. On the Nantao docks below the Bund, amid the bellows of foghorns, tugboat whistles, police sirens, the hoarse chants of thousands of half-naked *k'u-li* porters, the cries of competing pullers, the angry cadences of foreign-devil troops and the heartbreaking wails of starving beggars, a metropolis was dying and birthing and doing business.

Da-tsien knew that Baba would never return to the city he loved. Going to the canals of Soochow would take lots of money, and money was the one thing her father could not find in Shanghai.

She almost touched his hand, before he withdrew his own. The two sat in their chairs until the sooty heat from Shanghai's factories cooled.

He was reading her an adventure story on the porch, their chairs side by side, the crickets calling, when he told her that the foreign people had two new ideas.

"One idea is about work—by men or by machines. This is called modernization. The second idea is about living—by orders from others or with harmony. This is called the freedom and democracy idea. There are other ideas, too, but they're not so good."

"Baba . . . could you please get me a job as a comprador?"

"Hoyy! Why would you want *that*?"

"To earn money. So we can put *ho-chi*, harmony, in Mah-mee's heart. And send you back to Soochow to put comfort in your bones."

"Young Missy, such sweet ideas! You want to hire back our staff."

"I miss everyone. Don't you?"

"You said they all hated you," he teased.

"Not now they don't. Baba, can you do this for me? Could you get me the job?" She wondered why he didn't say anything for a long time.

"Little One, why do you think I left the Jardine company?"

"You needed time to read. And to fish. To be a gentleman."

He reflected as the evening began to come alive with the whirring of insects and the tiny-paw steps of hungry cats.

"Da-tsien. For ten thousand years, *Chung-guo*, the Middle Kingdom, China, ruled the world. We were cruel. We killed people who weren't Han, like us. Vietnamese, Tibetans, Mongols, Manchus, Muslims—all died in great numbers under our swords and spears. We just wiped out the Taipings, who were Han but had swallowed the foreign religion, which we said could not be forgiven. We killed them, down to the last child of the last son. This was our rule of ten thousand years.

"Now, most strangely, we are weak and incompetent, and the white man is here to do to us what we did to others. The influence of the foreigners, and their cruelty, may last even hundreds of years, but not thousands. Do you understand?"

She nodded. He loved her quick mind, her grasp of the sine wave of Chinese history, the cyclic nature of the world that baffled the best thinkers in the land. It never bothered him that she was slow to embrace the etiquette of rich families, even though these customs would dictate the quality of her life.

He looked at her, face-to-face, and she sat up, her eyes bright.

"Daughter, Jardine is a big *taipan* company. They import opium. And tobacco and alcohol, Western clothes, English cotton, American toys. Jardine ships out Chinese silks and teas and porcelain and gold to foreigners. Western women like silk, and the English love tea even more than we do! I have heard it said that every English person drinks tea several times a day, just like us, but they add cow's milk and sugar." He shuddered.

"Jardine is a big, hungry business that eats Chinese firms. I worked only a few days. But those days I helped kill a small Hwang Ho silk firm, ten or twelve Hongkew-clan tailor families and, on that last day, a whole Yangtze farming village outside Changshu that made toys in winter. They paid me to wipe out small family businesses.

"Meanwhile, their opium kills clans and families. It does this by wiping out fathers." He shook his head. "You cannot believe how destructive, how evil, how un-Confucian it is to wipe out a father. It means morally killing sons and risking daughters. Or how wrong it is to be a comprador." He chuckled sadly. "In this way, despite my foreign reading, I am very traditional to old ways.

"You know, I was just a reader of books, a man who decided that anger was wrong. But it turns out I'm more like your mother. When she sees something wrong, she corrects it, *pao!* Like a cannon, right away!

"My earning Jardine's money would have put our beds together, a thing any man misses. A husband should sleep with his wife. It extends his life and makes him pleasant and humorous with people. And earning cash would save our *mian*, our face, and let us keep our servants."

He showed teeth. "Your mother! Did you know that she was the funniest girl I ever knew? Oh, she made me laugh so hard! Oh yes, it's very true! She could make me slap my knees until they ached for mercy!" He cleared his throat. "My ways have killed her laughter.

"But see here! Earning opium money would mean feeding you the blood of our small people. This is another new modernization idea, thinking like this. We're Tzus first. Second we're Soochow people. Now, I think, we're Chinese. Like a nation, what do you think?"

"I don't know," she said softly.

"Little Missy, a gentleman does not cannibalize others to live. I could not do it! What I did, without rudeness, was leave Jardine, and their opium ships, to fish. But I hurt your mother. I made her fire our staff. We have big money trouble . . . I wonder now if you can forgive me."

Da-tsien barely touched her head to his big shoulder. Words passed without sound. She felt that his bones were at peace, and she was happy. Motor cars passed, headlights illuminating the wide street, tall trees and big houses. Lights were on in the House of Silk Merchants, but the windows were dark in the House of Secret Neighbors.

"It was wrong of Mah-mee to criticize you, Baba," she said quietly.

He straightened. "You cannot criticize your mother! Taitai's *responsible* for all our people, for filling rice bowls. *I'd do what she did.*"

Hurt by his tone, Da-tsien began to cry, but he didn't comfort her.

"Daughter," he said tightly. "I did a foreign thing. I put my individual and personal standards above the ethics of the clan, the needs of the *jia*. The clan must survive at all costs. I should have worked for the great *taipan* company to support my son, who is the lifeblood for the rest of you. And Da-shing must make more sons, or we die out. If you learn nothing else from your father, learn this! Tell me you understand this."

"I understand, Baba," she cried, her cheeks wet. But she didn't believe it. She cared little for the clan and everything for her father.

"Little One, I'm the patriarch, the Responsible One. I'm letting the *jia* and the House of Tzu die in this new world, along with part of the House of Wong, your mother's proud family. This is very un-Confucian. Don't hug me, child. People will think I'm dying, and I hope I have some years remaining. Now, dry your tears." He lifted her chin and looked into her eyes. "You are so bright, so smart! You understand everything. Little One, your brains honor me! How did I ever deserve such a smart daughter, a girl with so much love in her heart for a silly old father, a father who can't fill rice bowls in this mysterious world?"

eight

The Milk Maiden

THE LEE FAMILY group returned to Yangchow from its Shanghai expedition exhausted and dusty. Sesame Face Wong fell asleep; his assistant with the weak stomach became ill; and Tall Amah took a bath. The welcome-home tea went cold.

Na-ma, Zee Zee's Chekiang wet nurse, embraced the little boy, caressing him with words. "Oh, Young Lord, your face makes me smile and cry for happiness." He glowed in her affection, then he ran off.

His father, Master Lee, was my paternal grandfather and the Patriarch. Master Lee was a quiet, cinema-handsome man who would rather be skinned by a *jinboi*-drunk Manchurian bandit than run about like an animal. Perhaps Second Son entertained him; perhaps he did not.

The wet nurse had learned to lengthen her country-girl stride to keep up with the boy, trusting in her bones that she would be forever bound to him. He had grown strong on her love and her lovely voice. She loved him as if he were truly her flesh and blood, her Only Son. But wasn't he, really? Hadn't she nursed him for five years, so now they were one? To the Chinese world, the boy was six, for who but barbarians would fail to count that critical near-year in the womb? To her, he was five. Five years before, after giving up her newborn daughter, she had been sold by her father as a wet nurse to the new-money Lee family of Yangchow.

She was young and talkative, popular with the house staff and local poets. She said little about her home village or family and, of course, following custom, never spoke of her own child. She was from the Chekiang coast below Shanghai. Thus Lee Taitai, Master Lee's wife and the boy's womb mother, decided that her son's wet nurse should not accompany him on the Shanghai visit. Being near the Great Sea and Chekiang's old tidal currents might confuse her loyalty; the country-girl wet nurse might feel like going home. But Madame Lee had underestimated the girl's love for her son.

Madame Lee had let Zee Zee go to Shanghai because her personal *ba-kua* seer, a good upriver *sven ming* fortune-teller, had read the mystical *I Ching* sticks: Travel was indicated for her favorite son. With the boy in Shanghai, Madame Lee might spend more cash on prophecy.

Night fell, and the wet nurse watched the boy playing in a tree. During the day, he wanted to be a bird or a butterfly and would chase them until the garden was empty. Now, at night, he was Pan Ku, creator of the world and resident of heaven. He liked to look up, laughing as he tried to touch the moon, the stars and wispy, half-visible clouds.

Gee, Zee Zee's older brother and the Firstborn, saw what was happening. Master K'ung Fu-tzu, known in the west by the Latin name of Confucius, had declared that firstborn sons were princes and secondborn sons were dog-boys. But Zee Zee, the brat, was overturning the world like it was a two-legged banquet table. Cooks gave *him* the best fish and meat! Horse Master smiled at Zee Zee and caught him as he jumped from trees! Ladies touched him with affection while ignoring the Firstborn! And Zee Zee still had a wet nurse! Deep inside, while his tall mother prayed and his father smoked opium, Gee stoked his anger. He began hitting his amah and his servants and crying at his fate.

Gee had tried to speak to Father about his baby brother's sins, but the Patriarch had been uncaring about his children long before he gave his life to the opium poppy. Gee's amah was a small, serious, hangdog woman who couldn't sleep because her boy was an insomniac. Not long after Gee was moved into his father's opium-saturated room, Master Lee had told Mother Lee, his wife, that it was time for Gee's wet nurse to stop giving milk to the infant.

Tall Amah, Sesame Face Wong and his queasy assistant cook recovered from the trauma of Shanghai by leaning against great sycamores by the quiet river. They closed their eyes and listened to the call of thrushes and cicadas as stars slowly appeared in a velvet sky. When they cared to speak, they did so softly; Yangchow poets sat nearby, enjoying sweet buns and cups of rice wine as their brushes stroked thin rice paper under flickering candlelight. Upstream, their servants floated toy bamboo rafts bearing more heated wine cups down to the poets, who laughed as they scooped them up with flowing sleeves and emptied them. They recited sonnets to the glittering stars and the spellbound servants, their voices floating to the demigods of the heavens. From across the river came a sentimental tune on a country lute. In the interludes between poems, farmers softly sang to the earth gods, wishing Mr. and Mrs. Tu-di an equally pleasant evening in heaven.

The great poet Li Po loved this place; for him there were no limits; there was no pain and no fear, only the sounds of the earth, sky and water, composed in effortless rhyme and meter, lubricated by cups of warm yellow rice wine. Here by this river, China, usually thought of as the muscular peasant with a conical sun hat, transformed into a lighter-hearted fellow with a good lute and a full cup. This was Yangchow, famous for wild parties, hot libations, lovely *changsan* courtesans and erotic poetry. An evening here was worth a return voyage to hell. The servants tried to commit each moment to memory, because they were moving to Shanghai and would need images of heaven for comfort.

IN 1839 THE Chinese were on heaven's side. They were the greatest people in a universe littered with lesser states. By 1842 the British, using technology whose development China had abandoned long before, destroyed a decrepit and obsolete Chinese junk fleet and took control of the Chinese coast, owning the cities and their people. They took fine Chinese goods, silver and gold in exchange for raw opium that they were stealing from India. In a moment, that which was known had changed forever. Millions of Chinese could not accept the new truth and argued hotly with heaven's turning of history.

One day in 1912, Lee Zeu-zee was a playful child at the center of a loving world. By dawn, he was in trauma. My father had undergone a modern Chinese moment, where truth invites profound self-doubt.

MASTER LEE ENJOYED looking out on his beautiful garden almost as much as he enjoyed observing the women who tended its plants. The garden had been designed by his illustrious father, Lee Shui-feng, the abacus man who became a salt-tax lord. Perhaps, as he considered leaving Yangchow forever for a future in Shanghai, he thought about the wet nurse with the long stride, the Chekiang country girl with the pretty voice who had been in their house since the birth of Second Son. As the Master's strength dissipated into clouds of sticky opium and he found new things he could no longer do, he could not have missed her energy, her passion for life, her habit of laughter, her lilting voice.

Zee Zee and his wet nurse played games with dice, ivory tiles and cards, the bone icons hitting hard wood, the cards riffling, the boy laughing when he won and clapping happily for her occasional victories. An old retired salt-tax soldier with a bad leg fanned Zee Zee's room in the summer and fed the floor coal heaters in winter. *Soohsh, soohsh, soohsh, soohsh* was the sound of the summer fan; *hssssssss*, said winter coals as they sparked magically. In either season, hooded nightingales warbled to each other from adjoining bamboo cages, urging the boy to his winnings.

How the Chekiang wet nurse must have loved the sounds of wealth, of prosperity, of security. Soon she would dismiss the old soldier, then nurse the boy, giving him comfort to fill the absence of his tall mother, who spent her days praying to the Christian god while her husband dissolved the family treasury with concubines in clouds of Indian Malwa poppy-seed smoke.

She cooed to Zee Zee, her son, reciting hopes for his future as he slept on her breast. She prayed for his *shigong*—his vital internal energy—all the while repeating her constant prayer, stated so many times that the boy could never forget. Later, as a man, in moments of danger, the old words would haunt him not like lyrics from a childhood song but as prophecies and promises, reminders of an unwanted past.

Zee Zee, you love life and are brave! Grow up, Son! Outweigh ten great men! Then you'll find my daughter for me . . . and marry her to a kind man . . . you'll take care of me when I'm an old woman. Yes, Young Lord, remember me, for we are one, for we are one, for we are one. . . .

And so the connection between them grew like heaven embracing earth. They looked forward to the New Year, the Year of the Rat, when good-luck coins, banquets and gifts would shower upon them. The previous year's celebration had been shrouded in doubt and fear—the Empire had collapsed, a republic had been declared, and everything under heaven was thrown up in the air. Now the Year of the Rat was welcomed with a spectacular absence of restraint, for the astrological rat was the first creature of the Chinese zodiac, and the symbol of clever survival.

Servants cleaned with extra energy, and scholars painted new inscriptions in gold ink on red silk banners, showing their faith in the gods. Elders were overly generous with gifts and hot yellow wine, telling stories at the tops of their voices as if tomorrow were already lost.

The New Year is a time to mend broken relationships, to pay old debts, to sweep out old corners. It is a time of renewal, of repair, of hope. Bonds are strengthened and connections healed. Elders celebrate everyone's birthday at once, giving the yearly allowance to the children in red good-luck *hong fung tao* envelopes. Brandy is exchanged under the guise of medical remedies and new winter clothes and thick shoes are exchanged with warm smiles. Women wear new red, peach and azure silk padded cheongsams. To the sounds of stringed *ch'in* zithers, *p'i-p'a* lutes and *di* flutes, Zee Zee ate dried glutinous rice cakes to prime his tummy for the great banquet, which would be rich with good-fortune foods. He also received wonderful gifts. Later, he could remember none of them.

Before the dawn of the new year 1912, when winter cicadas had been silent for hours, and catfish lay with eerie stillness in the stream and the boy was deep asleep, Master's body servant awoke the Chekiang wet nurse and led her out of the boy's room.

It was cold as she was taken to Master Lee's small house, where they climbed a staircase under the soft light of muted tung oil lamps. She wasn't used to the cold—rich households protected wet nurses from severe weather to safeguard the *nuna*, the precious milk, the builder of strong sons. A salt-tax soldier in a pressed khaki uniform slept across the Master's doorway. The floorboards had been shimmed so that footsteps made them squeak, but Master was probably awake. He let the wet nurse with the lovely voice enter.

The Master's room was dark and deep with a high ceiling, saturated in the odors of sweet Fukien incense and heavy American cigarettes. The wet nurse probably recoiled from smelling *ya-pien*, the black peace—the stench of bitter Indian opium residue. His great *kang*, the red contoured hardwood bed where he smoked his pleasure, sat solidly with its paraphernalia of opium balls, gum burners, heating bowls and pipes. The bed was in the corner of the room, but it was the spiritual center. Everything in China was supposed to be balanced, so this room made the unique visitor dizzy with its imbalance. Perhaps some early light came through the windows where the Master had stood and studied his garden.

Master was waiting for her.

ZEE ZEE AWOKE because he was cold and the bed was empty and she was not there. He knew something was wrong. Was she sick? He ran to see, but she wasn't in the toilets or the kitchen, where the coal fires had been stoked by tired servants anticipating the household's breakfast needs after an all-night celebration. The boy ran through the quiet house. "Where's Na-ma?" he asked the hungover servants, who didn't know and probably had trouble even shrugging.

They had a morning routine. Na-ma would nurse him. Then Tall Amah would wash his face, mouth and feet. Na-ma would tell his favorite stories about tigers and eagles, using a fast voice that raced like his legs. Then breakfast of *tsueh*, rice porridge, with minced pork and greens, and the best southern black teas. Afterwards Na-ma rubbed his back.

Zee Zee returned to his dark room, knowing Na-ma would be there. She wasn't. She couldn't be hiding—she'd never played tricks or done anything to shake his trust in her. He had trouble breathing. Was this a tradition of the new Rat Year? Where was she? He searched the room as if he had misplaced her, looking inside closets and chests.

Tall Amah was awakened by the child's cries; she found Zee Zee in the hallway, babbling and sobbing incomprehensibly, panting in short, tight wheezes—something had taken his *chi*. She kept trying to hug him, to comfort him, but without success.

"Where is she?" he cried. "Where's Na-ma?" His panic, his dismay, filled the hallways, and the servants stirred from their headaches and celebratory excesses to begin peeking blearily around corners. Sesame Face Wong, the new cook with the white crew cut, showed up with an enormous hatchet—he wasn't as good as Old Hu in the kitchen, and he had done poorly in Shanghai, so this was a chance to prove himself. The outside staff lit lanterns attached to light poles, grabbed bamboo fighting staffs and checked gates, walls, low roofs and the paths for disturbed stones. The domo, with a rusted Ming Dynasty sword, planked a bamboo pole to the roof, scrambled up and walked the green-tiled roofs. Uncle Chu Lin-da, a young relative on Madame Lee's side who was visiting from Yangchow, left the guest cottage to help search for the missing woman. Being younger, he looked under things while the adults looked upward.

Madame Lee, Zee Zee's tall mother, asked for a report.

"Young Lord was crying," said the majordomo. "Gates and walls are secure—nothing's disturbed on the perimeter, and the horses are safe."

"Food's okay, nothing disturbed," said Sesame Face Wong, feeling the need to say something.

"Na-ma is missing," said Tall Amah, putting her arms around the sobbing boy to muffle his crying. To answer Madame Lee's suspicion, she added, "Her side of the bed is cold, but none of her things are gone. I don't think she's run away."

"Hush, my son," said Madame Lee to the boy in her small voice. "You awaken ancestors." She wasn't one to talk a great deal. "Domo, check Master's apartment."

Zee Zee stopped his noises, but tears continued to stream down his small face. He breathed raggedly. "Na-ma," he whispered again and again. "Na-ma."

"Go back to sleep," said Tall Amah. "We'll look for her, okay?"

Zee Zee shook his head sadly. "I can't sleep without my na-ma."

"Go to bed," said Madame Lee to the household. Tall Amah took the boy to his room, and the cooks and servants slowly padded to their beds. When Zee Zee kept trying to go out the door to find his wet nurse, Amah bound his wrist to hers. Silently, he tugged on her body until her wrists were chafed. They exited the main house, walking quickly through the forest of the garden under fading night. She untied the boy's wrist and knocked on the guest-cottage door. Uncle Chu answered, holding a candle.

Tall Amah begged his forgiveness, asking if he would take the boy to the male-only ancestral hall to pray for guidance, with, of course, a stop in the dining room to pray for courage.

Uncle Chu, wearing his nightgown and carrying his candle, walked with great dignity to the memory tablet of the Bravest Wife. He was twelve years old. Below the wide-eyed gaze of the teenage girl who had died in a well, he directed his little nephew to kneel and pray.

Meanwhile, the domo returned and whispered in Madame Lee's ear. She nodded.

IN THE YEAR of the Rat, Master Lee, paternal grandfather, directed his family to conduct an exodus from idyllic Yangchow to foreign Shanghai, from poetry to grime, from old wealth to fresh opium. Some days later, he appeared in the new house in the International Settlement. In Shanghai he grew fond of a Swiss coffee shop, the Spinoza, which sat next to a cigar shop and the headquarters of the Second Battalion, Fourth U.S. Marines, a busy corner where Bubbling Well meets Chengtu Road.

Master Lee's walk to the Spinoza, named for the excommunicated philosopher who advocated the suppression of passion, resembled a papal parade. As he passed down the hallways of his European house for his Viennese coffee in a Swiss establishment, his two Chinese sons—Gee and Zee Zee—the relatives and the house staff silently kowtowed from their knees, foreheads to the floor.

Only Master's wife Madame Lee, a daughter of the House of Han who was now a tall, hard-praying Christian woman, stood. She had decided when her husband had become an opium eater that she would give money to the true church each time he smoked. She would kneel to the One God now, and to the Jesus God when He returned to judge the quick and the dead. She prayed for relief, for justice, for vengeance, and invited Armageddon to cure the anger in her heart and the sickness in her husband. She never considered retribution against her weak spouse, but she prayed for it.

If little Zee Zee had looked up in the months following that terrible first night of the Rat Year, he would have seen his wet nurse walking behind his father's first mistress, biting her lip to hold her tears as she waved secretly at her Only Son, the boy she could no longer greet, or hug, or kiss or bathe with song.

Perhaps, before Master Lee smoked the wealth out of the hereditary Yang-chow mansion, Dad looked up and saw a rustling behind French curtains in his father's apartment and thought of his wet nurse, who lived in a space so high that it defeated his climbing aptitude.

In the new Shanghai residence, the family lived on the bottom floors while Master Lee lived on the top with his concubines. There were only Two Great Rules. One: No one goes upstairs without express permission from Master Lee himself. Regarding this, no one even dared ask, for the Second Great Rule was: No discussion whatsoever of Master's life or private affairs, and certainly no speaking to him directly, for he had become hard of tongue, saying *"digga, digga, digga,"* which meant nothing except that he was out of words.

Everyone noticed how quiet Zee Zee had grown in the five years since Na-ma had left his life. His laugh could still make Skinny Wu the seamstress giggle, but no one could remember the last time that had happened. In time, he found the courage to write a note to his wet nurse; Tall Amah delivered it for him.

Weeks later, the note came back. Across it, in his father's once fine but now sadly distorted and shaky calligraphy, were the words:

Your na-ma was a milk cow. You were then a boy. Now be a man.

When Zee Zee was eleven years old, he broke the One Great Rule. His father was at the Spinoza with his first concubine and his rickshaw puller, a part-time Lee household member. The boy climbed the orange tree that flanked an upstairs window. He wanted to see his na-ma.

For the first time in his life, he entered his father's dark and oily rooms. He smelled the *ya-pien*, the opium, and discovered that his baba had only one concubine—his first Syau Taitai, Small Wife.

Na-ma, the Chekiang country girl who had raised him, was gone.

Zee Zee broke the second rule, asking his mother where Na-ma was.

Most Chinese women live for conversation. When her husband became an addict, Madame Lee could find little pleasure in dialogue. At first she said, "Who do you mean?" When Zee Zee persisted, she gave in.

"Ah, Young Lord, my son, you ask about your na-ma? Oh, she was married to a distant cousin of hers. Maybe five years ago. Right after we moved here to Shanghai. The cousin lives in British town, Hong Kong. A terrible place for a country girl, don't you think? So sad. No one told you? You still remember her from so long ago? Oh, too bad! You know, I think I'll get you a fine tutor, okay? To keep your mind in the right place! Oh, you look so somber, so sad!

"Here, Son, kneel, kneel with me, and pray that the Christian God makes you forget that day! Pray a hundred times to the Jesu God, okay? Here, I'll give you paper spirit money to offer to him. Yes, take it in your hand . . . no, no! Don't wipe tears with it, that's so much bad luck!"

Zee Zee couldn't stop crying, but she went on, "You were too old for a wet nurse anyway! Isn't it much better, growing up to become a man?"

For the rest of his life, Dad shunned the Chinese New Year and cursed those who celebrated it. In all seasons, he looked upward where birds flew and heaven seemed unlimited. He would point out high-flying aircraft, and we would silently observe the plane drawing a chalky contrail across a slate-blue sky. Both of us, for long periods, preferred the space above earth to the spaces upon it, and I knew that once, long ago, my father had lived in the sky and loved it far more than existence on cold soil.

n i n e

The Landlord's Son

THE NIGHT THAT her mother left their Shanghai home was the worst of young Da-tsien's life. When the house was silent, she buried herself in her bedding and cried until her back hurt. No books, hair brushing or old country lullabies could calm the pain in her skinned knees or in her heart.

She imagined running across the city of Shanghai to see her mother in Uncle's great French Concession house, but then she realized that the very act of running would further humiliate her mother and all her lady friends. She imagined her mother's excoriating scolding that would curl the skin of bystanders and make Da-tsien's eyeballs shrink. Besides, she had not the faintest idea as to the location of her uncle's house. It was in a place she couldn't see from her bedroom window, the porch or the fishing pier.

Meals became desultory without the bustle of the house staff and the majordomo's card games with her amah. Everyone missed Taitai, her insights, her stories, her business gossip, her bitter haranguing of her husband. They ate steaming dishes because there were no arguments to cool them. Unaccustomed to the heat, they burned their tongues.

To raise moods, Da-tsien invited the cooks to eat with them. This offended the amah Ah Tsui, because Fatty Soo made loud smacking noises that were normally concealed by the din of the kitchen. Big Chef Chu, unaccustomed to eating at a table with his employers and trying to be garrulous, talked with a full mouth, spewing morsels while smiling ferociously and causing others to grimace with all their teeth.

Unhappy with hot plates and cold rooms, Da-tsien induced her brother, Da-shing, and his waddling amah to travel all the way to Uncle's French Concession home to ask Mother to return, but he forgot what to say when he got there, while his amah lacked the authority to speak. Da-tsien wanted to ask Baba to try, but she knew better.

She had to deal with rent, food costs, maintaining the household and debt repayment. She asked Baba for the rent rate and the savings balance. He shrugged, which she took to mean all manner of bad news.

Mother had taught her to never do business directly. Instead, she'd said, use intermediaries so there's no *shi miantsi*—losing face. Anyone can say no to a go-between, for such people carry only messages, not emotions or clan. Da-tsien kept counting noses in the house, finding no intermediaries.

Da-tsien was so nervous leaving her house that she trembled. She had been out once since her mother left, and she had tripped and hurt herself. She had never traveled far since the move from Soochow, and then only with her mahmee or her baba. Taking only her brother and her amah, she felt naked and alone. Shaking, she bent over to hide her eyes and ears from the sight of so many people—not to mention the attempted grasping of pickpockets and slicky boys and her amah's blood-curdling shrieks to deflect them—when all of this threatened to overwhelm her resolve. Great Shanghai rang with the endless din of hell and suffering. She had feared leaving the International Settlement for the great unknown, and now she was entering the Old Chinese City.

Taking a deep breath, as if her mother were beside her and they were speaking inside their Soochow mansion, Da-tsien smiled and made appropriate eye contact. Answers to her questions began to flow.

By noon, they had found the clan of their old majordomo and arranged a meeting. He was delighted to see the Young Missy, smiling freely as if still under her roof, eyes moist, gruffness softened, face unshaved and clothes kept simple to reflect the grief of failing his employers and losing his job. He was a bachelor who had lived to serve the honorable Tzus. He smiled at the sun umbrella that Ah Tsui kept over the girl's head to prevent her aristocratic skin from becoming dark and peasantlike. Da-tsien and the domo exchanged long and sincere greetings, and then she asked her questions.

"Young Missy, the landlords are Yangchow people with good luck," he barked. "House of Lee family, salt merchants, I think." Salt people were fabulously rich and extremely dishonest. They were relegated to *ho-men*, back-door relationships, which began when salt deliveries went to the rear of the house to protect hardwood floors. "Your honorable mother negotiated a thousand dollars Shanghai. That's all I know, Young Missy."

"*Lao toutsi*, Old Boss, is that a lot, or is that cheap?"

"Oh, it's top rent for a top property. Your honorable house could hold a dozen families and has good *feng shui* and southern sun without stink from Soochow Creek, bad traffic or Whangpu River noise."

"Dear Old Boss, I need to cut the rent. Do the landlords, the Lees, live in the Settlement? Are they in Shanghai or Yangchow? Who exactly did Mah-mee pay every month? Who can I talk to?"

"Young Missy, I am so sorry, I do not know. I had no real job, you know. Not for years. I was for show. I know the Taitai was embarrassed that she was renting our home. She had secrets. I wish I knew more. But ever since your honorable father chose not to be a pharmacist or a comprador, I had little to do and nothing to know."

"Baba a pharmacist?" she asked. Children, particularly daughters, were not entitled to know private information about their parents, such as their names and their occupations. The only jobs that were announced publicly involved scholarship.

The domo covered his face. "A thousand pardons! I have no right to gossip on business. So wrong of me." But she needed knowledge, and he had always loved her. Ignoring the amah, he spoke in a low voice.

"Your baba's father was a pharmacist. I worked for him as a boy. One winter day, when winds from Taihu were very hard, the retired viceroy of Guangtung and Kiangsi, a man of virtue, beckoned him. You see, the viceroy had retired in Soochow but now was bitterly ill.

"Your father's own father administered the famous formula that I still remember. Yes, a fifth *shih fen* of *Monkujen* Mongol antler root with a thousandth of a *tan* of *Hanguo* Korean ginseng, heated in the right progressive amounts, to stop the fever that was going to kill this great man. The viceroy recovered. He was very grateful.

"So he promised one of his daughters in marriage to the son of the pharmacist. The Tzu son was tall and strong and read many books, a boy with a fine face. That son is your honorable father, who still reads like a scholar; the viceroy's daughter was a very pretty girl with small features and a sunny laugh. She, of course, is your honorable mah-mee, who always understood business and used to laugh a lot when she was young. That's how royal blood came to course in your clan."

Mah-mee was the payoff for saving a life, and Baba always loved books. She thanked the domo for this gift of knowledge and for the past kindnesses he had shown her and her family.

The domo pressed his head to her hand and said *tsai jen,* see you soon, not *tsai hui,* goodbye. He bowed to Round Amah, who had given him pleasure at cards when he had no true job, even if she had brayed like a donkey when she won.

Amah hid her face and tears for his lost company and her anger at his disclosures. She had heard a version of this story, but it was just servant gossip, not for the household's children. Not for her little girl, not for Da-tsien. She was supposed to be shielded from life, but she had skinned her knees and now, aiyaa!—she knew the occupation of her paternal grandfather. If that's what he really did. She knew a different story.

At home, the sun setting, exhausted by running the gauntlet through the treacheries of Shanghai with her umbrella held high, the amah paid the sweaty puller after nasty bargaining over a few coppers. For money, lazy Round Amah would have argued that night was day.

Over Amah's objections, Da-tsien asked the wiry, dripping rickshaw man which Burkill Road families were renters. He shrugged, so she fired an arrow at the moon. "Who are the landlords?" she asked.

The puller tiredly pointed to the huge house across the street. The place she and Da-shing called the House of Secret Neighbors. They had visitors, but few people had seen the occupants, and it was often dark at night, as if they couldn't afford electricity. Their three-story Euro-mansion had been built by a Liverpool drug dealer and silk trader named McBean. Tired of Asia's strange ways, he, an intimate of the Jardines and the Sassoons—the top opium merchants—had sold to the top bidder, who happened to be a rich Chinese man. Money had trumped social classes.

"What's their name?" Da-tsien asked the puller.

"Their honorable name is Lee," he said. "A Yangchow clan. Came here to Shanghai just before your good family came here from Soochow."

"What business, if you know?"

"I believe their honorable business is salt," he said.

"Sir, thank you very much." She gave him more coins. He bowed.

"Amah," she said, looking at the house across the street. "I think *they're* our landlords! Across the street! What do you know about them?"

The amah waved a hand, wanting to go inside. "A *ta-yen*, big smoke, opium house. Two sons, I think. Indian guards with rifles. Good cooks, I hear, with good deals at market. Their cook is named Sesame Face Wong, not as good as Lao Chu. Big money. No virtue."

Big money, no virtue. What happened to big virtue, big money? "Amah, I need to see their house boss."

But Amah was a mere woman, so Da-tsien got Baba to write a letter to Mr. Lee. From a window, she watched her brother amble across the street with the letter. He entered the Lee mansion but didn't come out. She waited. *He's forgotten to give the letter to anyone.* She gave up when her brother and his friend appeared. The weird jumping boy vaulted in the window like a ghost.

"You can't do that anymore," she said, using all of her willpower to not cover her eyes, marveling at how smoothly he moved.

"Want me to go?" he asked. She nodded.

He jumped out. The loud, intrusive European doorbell rang, making her jump. The small god of that doorbell was too powerful! She went to the door and bravely opened it. Her brother entered as the boy again vaulted in through the same window.

"What do you want with us?" asked the boy.

She spun around, almost falling. "Who *are* you?" she demanded, remembering to hold her chin high.

The boy remembered—there was no Taitai here. Really weird! So the girl was acting Taitai. The house was better furnished than his, so she was pretty good in holding on. He held up his hand, stepped back and bowed with the grace of an opera star performing for an emperor.

"I am the unworthy Lee Zeu-zee. Worthless second son of a great man. I showed no politeness and no learning. From my small position, I apologize. Do I have the honor of addressing Young Missy Tzu?"

"I am that unworthy one," she tried, using the male formula. *Frogs in the bath! He's the son of the landlord.*

"Your judgment," recited the boy, his eyes still lowered, "is a model for all of us. I know your brother and call him friend. Presumptuous to ask, but how may the House of Lee assist the House of Tzu?"

"I need to talk to your house boss. Is he kind, with a soft heart?"

The boy straightened. "If you don't work for him. Or want money."

She frowned. "I want money."

He made a face that made her smile. "Then I guess he won't be kind."

"Who *would* be kind to me?" she asked.

The boy couldn't think of anyone. "It's a tough house," he said.

Despite the peasantlike clothes, he had wonderfully bright eyes and was tall. She liked looking at him, so she looked away. He waited for her words.

"Would you carry a message to your house boss for me?" she asked. She looked at him as her mah-mee would, trying to see who he was beneath his rough ways. His speech showed that he had been tutored with some sensitivity. But he was a barbarian who jumped and grinned and moved like a monkey. She decided that she didn't like him. But she sensed his honesty, one of the three cardinal rules of doing business. Was he also smart? Was his family strong and good? A smart boy would use the door. And his family was hidden in opium smoke. What was his motive here? *Playfulness*, she thought. What unseen forces drove him? *I have no idea. I can't read him; he's too young. No, he's too disrespectful.* Ho-men, *a back-door salt boy who uses windows.*

Keeping her chin high against an internal gravity that had been tugging it downward, she said, "We would like to pay less rent."

"How much less?" he asked.

"Lots less. Lots and lots less."

"Uh-oh," he said, smiling. "That might be too much."

"Well, to us, anything . . . would help."

The boy looked around. The house boss had quit, and the father spent his time fishing. The girl had guts, telling truth to a young stranger, taking chances, showing big heart, standing up for the clan.

"Okay if I jump in the window when I want?" he asked.

She thought of her mother's orders. "Okay."

"Good," he said, vaulting through the window.

She replayed his magical leap. *So fast, like Sun Wu-gong.* Wu-gong was the legendary monkey who helped bring the Buddhist scriptures to the Chinese people. Monkeys represented human failing and the possibility of human redemption. The Lee boy was clearly a monkey.

The next day, the Lee headman, who proudly displayed his big appetite in his forward-looking belly, and a tall, severe-looking woman with her hair in a bun called on the master of the Tzu house. The Lee headman hit the door with a crashing, military rap appropriate to salt businessmen, who conventionally had to beat on the back door. The door opened cautiously—a bad-luck sign for the caller. A rumpled man gawked at his visitors. The man with the aggressive belly wore short sleeves like a boatman, and the woman frowned, looking like Mrs. Death.

The Lee domo recited that the honorable Mr. Tzu was renowned throughout the Su-Sungtai region as a cunning Jardine comprador, no less a *taipan* than the fabled Hsu Jun, maker of business, producer of wealth and shaker of the soil. The majordomo left out the parts about Mr. Tzu working two weeks before being fired, and being a weak man who hadn't beaten a wife who had left him, and having Little Missy do his business. Could the Lee headman and the Lee sons' female tutor, Miss Wong Fu-lu, speak to the great master?

Old Deaf Man Fu smiled blankly, then closed the door.

The headman knocked again, louder.

This time, Ah Tsui, Da-tsien's portly maid, appeared. The Lee house boss repeated his greeting while Ah Tsui trembled before the solemn woman in black. Ah Tsui managed to say that Mr. Tzu was doing big business on the docks (he was fishing) and that Honorable Son was deep in learning (he was asleep). Would the boss and tutor of the renowned House of Lee be willing to talk to the lowly Tzu daughter (who had been waiting in agony for them)?

They would, bowing politely.

Ah Tsui bowed as they entered. She escorted them to the sitting room, bowed to them again, stepped gingerly to the stairs and screamed "DA-TSIEN!" There was a great pounding on the stairs, a small cry, a loud crash, and the blushing girl limped into the room.

Da-tsien was surprised by the woman. What was she doing here?

The Lee domo bowed courteously to Tzu Da-tsien. Miss Wong lowered her head without removing her eyes from the girl's intelligent gaze. It was a gaze that triumphed over her brightly flushed cheeks and recent embarrassment. The Lee domo felt sorry for her—an unemployed baba, no mother, big clumsy feet—until she smiled warmly. Unable to not smile back, he decided to deal with her with his face square to hers.

"Young Missy, together we can admire the moon, but I say that we Lees are servants to all. We are reducing rents on all properties and can reduce your rent by half." Of course, a full inventory of the Lees' extensive properties would reveal that the Tzus were their only tenants.

"Sir," said Da-tsien, her eyes bright and deep, "your kindness sets an example for all. Such generosity for a poor and unworthy tenant! Being unworthy, we ask for reduction of another half, and will pay you the balance of the missing fourth when we are able. Sir, we are an honorable clan and have known much scholastic honor in the past, having one *jen-shih* scholar and two Han-lin, although one was a tutor. Who knows when a member of this small *jia* may be able to assist your honorable clan in an inconsequential way for a debt of honor that we can never repay?"

"*Banjila!* Wonderful!" he cried, despite his desire to be restrained. "Well said! Young Missy, we're new money from Yangchow salt. We have salt in our ears and our pockets and aren't half worthy. I'm the new domo. The old one left along with Chef Wu when the house swayed with shifting ballast. Missy, the Lee family doesn't have scholars like your *jia*! We profit by your very nearness. Done!"

"Oh, I thank you, sir. I thank you and Miss Wong and Landlord Master Lee!"

"Perhaps some thanks is due to the landlord's worthless second son, the Young Lord Lee Zeu-zee," the house boss said, smiling at her gratitude.

"Of course. Our respects to the honorable Young Lord Second Son, who is so fortunate to have a tutor of your stature, Miss Wong."

"You mean, how sad of the House of Lee to employ a mere female to teach a pair of sons?" Having a female tutor was a demonstration of weak judgment, opium addiction or growing poverty. For the Lees, it was all three.

"No, Miss, I meant how brilliant. Your teaching shows in Second Son's cultured speech."

Miss Wong laughed. "But not in anything else! He's a rogue! I look as if I've hit my second-life birthday, but in truth, I am still young! Ah, but I complain. I am proud of my station. I am the third tutor, having taught both Lee sons since they were in pigtails. Young Missy, I will tell you that I already know your brother, Da-shing. He is clever but forgetful." The second-life birthday was sixty years. Miss Wong was perhaps half that.

"I wanted to see you," she went on. "I will tell you why: Zee Zee pretends to study, but he draws pictures. He's quite good. It is too bad that sketching is not only useless but inappropriate and coarse. You see, lately, he mostly draws pictures of a particular girl. And now I have seen her."

THEY HAD BEEN in Shanghai for under a year when Da-tsien's now silent amah cried out with one of those yelps that means great pain or high surprise or both. Racing for the door, Da-tsien made the pounding sounds of a peasant going to market. There stood a short, plump woman with a small face, wearing funeral white.

Da-tsien squealed, jumping up and down and banging on the door-jamb as they stood facing each other, their cheeks coloring brightly. It was Little Auntie Gao with all of her luggage, next to a sweaty, tongue-dragging rickshaw puller.

"Little Missy, your face makes me show all my teeth! How do I look? I'm fatter! With Husband gone, I eat what he hogged! I brought his many clothes to sell for big cash so you can rehire some of the old Soochow staff! And now I eat beef, pork, chicken and prawns and the finest white rice for my round tummy! Best of all, no more old smelly fish!"

"Oh, Auntie Gao! I *love* how you look! So healthy, so round, so full of luck! It's heaven to see you! Oh, we can talk and talk and gossip and you can tell me *everything* about Soochow! Aiya! Can we really hire back our staff? Have you heard from Horse Man Yip? And Tailor Wen? But Auntie, where's your honorable—where's your husband?"

"He died," Auntie said brightly. "I have no son to follow. I'm here to be your little mother. If you and your father and brother will have me."

"Oh, Damama! Auntie! Oh yes, oh yes! We'll talk every meal and retell old Soochow family stories and recite poetry and have warm stomachs and good luck, and I'll be all ears for every story that you can tell me! Brother and Baba will be so happy!"

They clasped hands and hugged as daughters and mothers could not; for this and other crucial, spiritual reasons, aunties existed in Chinese networks. Parents could afford to be relentlessly stern for all the days of their lives, because in an extended, multigenerational *jia*, every person older than the child became a *Da-ma*, or a *Da-ba*, a Big Mother, a Big Father—an aunt or an uncle. They were small in status and power but large in heart and affection.

The Chinese ability to work came from demanding parents, but laughter was generated by loving relatives who could break the confining rules of Confucius. They gave sweets, comfort and a wondrous physical affection to replace the early care of a juvenile wet nurse and the parents' steely remoteness.

After a few moments of joyous hugging, Auntie pushed the girl away, making a dismissive gesture. The hug was for their relationship; the dismissal was for the neo-Confucians, who knew hugging was excessively emotional and perverted.

"Has your mother retained a matchmaker for you yet?"

Da-tsien, her face bright with happiness, said no, it was too early.

"Never too early to have sons! Your purpose in life, Little Missy! From now on, we pray to Ho Hsien-ku every morning!" Ho was the bald patroness of unmarried girls who used a magic lotus to find husbands for the unluckiest girls, such as those who stepped on their own feet.

The girl nodded at the truth and its probable difficulties.

Happy to greet the brother, Da-shing, Auntie Gao easily praised how he had grown tall, loving his handsomeness, his intelligence, his charm. She clapped her hands when he said that he was a friend of the landlord's second son. She hid her dismay when she learned that the landlord was a kind old opium smoker whom no one had ever seen. Auntie Gao remembered the oracles.

"Little Missy, is he cute? The Second Son."

"In some ways," said Da-tsien.

"Little One, we have to talk. I have serious warn—"

"Oh, no, Auntie! Nothing serious! Only gossip and news."

Have to tell her the dangerous future. "Missy, I threw the *I Ching* for you at dawn on the holiest day. You must watch out for a man—"

Baba trundled home alone and saw Auntie Gao. "Hey, hey, Auntie Gao! Hey, hey, you look so round and full!" His smile was like a room of fresh candles, "*Chr gwo fan le ma?* Have you eaten? Can we feed you?"

She rose, warmed by his politeness. She bowed deeply. He opened his old, smelly catch basket. "Say, Auntie, look what I caught for you!"

Auntie Gao smiled and bowed. Face lowered, she made teeth while nearly gagging at the smell. But the House of Tzu was still her sanctuary, and she felt as if she had come home.

Listen to the Taitai

THE ROUND AMAH stood in the warm, heavy rain from the Great Sea. Ah Tsui, like many amahs, saw Da-tsien as her actual child, so it was natural to spend days waiting outside her school, rubbing her hands together when it was cold and shaking rain from her hair in the spring. Getting soaked proved her love. Working in the house and the kitchen was too much for her lazy bones; standing outside in the rain to show respect—this was her skill.

She stared through the foreign school's windows until she saw her girl's big rabbit feet hurrying down the hall. Da-tsien sat on a bench and made noises on a tall black foreign box with a lid. Amah held the collapsed umbrella, unwilling to raise it for herself; it was for her daughter, not for a lowly woman with no status in a bad-luck house.

IN THE EARLY afternoon, dripping from the long rickshaw ride to the French Concession, Ah Tsui knocked on the door of the girl's true mother. Taitai, her small sharp features looking both grave and relaxed, gave her a towel, dry clothes, steaming hot tea with *chun-ya* seasonings and a hard look. Once dry, the amah took the offered chair and spoke. Taitai listened with a frown, then asked questions.

"She plays the piano box well?"

"With incredible, terrific skill. All recognize this."

"She is round and well fed with your meals. No foreign food?"

"No, Lady, none. She carries rice, vegetables and pork to school." The amah trembled under her mistress's hard gaze. "Yes, it's possible she eats some of their porridge. Lady, I'm sorry, but she says it tastes good. I know. Nothing could be more ridiculous." She licked her lips, hoping that no residual oatmeal was on them.

Taitai sighed. "No one hits her or speaks angrily at her?"

"Not that I see. I hear no screams, not even crying. No students sit in the rain, locked out of class. Foreign school is softer than ours, very lax, no standards. Taitai, your brother is speaking."

Taitai turned around. She often didn't hear her soft-spoken brother.

"Ask if our niece has dry socks," he said, hidden in his newspaper. He was too shy to face people with his walleye or to ask direct questions.

"Does she have dry socks?" asked Taitai.

"Yes, Taitai," Ah Tsui assured them. "And I brush her hair and rub her back and check all of her organs. All working fine," she added.

"Good. See you next week." Taitai gave her cash and dismissed her in time to return to St. Mary's, where the amah's umbrella would cover Da-tsien's precious face every day from rain and sun on the way home.

Taitai spoke to her brother. Uncle agreed pleasantly while turning the pages of the daily *Shenbao*, which he held to his ear so he could read it with his walleye. The paper was dark with criminal and political news. Green Gangsters had kidnapped more Chinese businessmen. The *pigun* grabbed them like chickens. Meanwhile, Europeans, Americans and the Japanese were carving up China like a *ya*, a duck. Bonnie Prince, a yearling, had won at the Shanghai racecourse by a length. Silk bolts of first quality were on sale from the interior due to last season's slow buying. American ladies were "flapping" with new short hems.

He read with difficulty, for his wayward eye kept trying to look out the window. He was a rich man who loved the printed word, and a practical man who liked austerity. At night he read by the light of a streetlamp that came free through a high window. He read week-old newspapers, which he got without charge from the butcher who supplied the household meats. Occasionally, red fluids dripped from them onto his lap, and he would cry out, thinking that the reading of bad news had actually wounded him.

"My daughter spends too much time on a foreign music box! If she keeps it up, she'll lose her essence. People will look at her feet and hear her make those strange music noises and think she's a faint-eyed stinky white devil!" Taitai shifted restlessly in her chair.

"Hm, yes," her brother said. "Aiyaa! We fought for the Allies and Americans in the world war. Helped beat Germany, so the Allies promised to kick out the Germans and give Shantung Province back to us. But at Versailles, they gave Shantung—the home of Confucius!—to *Japan*! It's so, so utterly shameless! *We're humiliated before the world!* Now students revolt all over

China, cursing the foreigners and smashing their goods. But this is also wrong. Something must done, don't you think?"

"What can we do? Take her out of St. Mary's? Why aren't there any good Chinese schools left? And they serve foreign food! *That's* shameless!"

"See here," said her brother, "we Chinese got rid of the Manchus and our slave braids!" He touched the space where his queue had hung all the years of his life. Even now he could feel it, and would awaken at night, terrified by its absence, convinced a screaming Bannerman would come through the door with an ax and ask him where his queue was, instantly beheading him for the offense of its removal.

The world wig market had taken an unprecedented harvest when a hundred million Chinese had cut off their braids. He hadn't wanted to—what if the Manchus came back and chopped everyone who lacked them? But the revolutionary government made him. He had cried as the weight of the queue fell from his head in a disgraceful mass hair-chopping by Nationalist students in the center of Avenue de Roi. It was as if he had lost his manhood. "Then we can get rid of the white devils, right?"

"But if we remove her, she loses her status. All eligible rich males attend that white-devil school. Then who will marry her? Who'd have her? How will we continue our blood? She's the one with the brains!" Taitai shook her head. "Shouldn't have said that," she breathed to the gods. She said, "My son, Da-shing, is brighter than she."

"See here," said her brother. "We have the world's best memory for things, the best thinking. How can the devils beat us? I dislike them now, so much!" He shook his head. "I show anger openly. Please forgive me."

"No, no, anger's good! It helps the appetite! Makes me feel alive!" Taitai laughed bitterly. "All the gods damn my stupid lazy husband, and all his stupid foreign books, and keep all fish away from his fishing spot!"

Her brother appreciated her company. Her criticism of the world, coming incessantly from every corner of the house, was like music to his lonely ears. She knew what to do, what to say. Her passionate opinions reminded him of their father. The great viceroy had shown a warm, generalized approval in his accidental contacts with his children, but the brother knew that he had deeply disappointed his father. The father could speak like thunder, while his son had the voice of a barn mouse. Great men had no time, so they raised lesser sons who would spend their lives wondering about the gap that separated them. His sister was talking again. Their baba had loved her the most because she was so pretty and so smart, not like him, slow and strange with a bad-luck eye. As a girl, his sister had been the funniest person in the world. But marriage, even to a kind man, had been hard on her.

"She's twelve with the brains of a child. Her grades are bad, and she eats foreign-devil porridge that make her feet bigger and wider, and she has no prospects at all for a good marriage, and I grow older as she grows more stupid. I shouldn't have left! What a mistake. I think I have to eat my pride and go back and recover her soul and find her a husband."

He put down his paper. "Not a good idea. Lo Fa is a good man, but he makes you crazy with money worries. You have better health here."

"I know, I know, but I have to arrange a match for my son or he'll forget, and at forty years he'll pat his clothes and look up and down and ask, *Where are my wife and sons? Did I forget them somewhere?* And Lo Fa's no good with matchmakers. I tell you, he's not good at much!"

"He's good at being kind. No small thing, I hope."

"There's good kindness and there's stupid kindness. He has the stupid type."

In the silence, she scratched her hands. "Do you think Da-tsien will obey me and respect me? Oh, she'd better! She's been with Auntie Gao. You remember her—the barren little foot-binder widow with the bad-luck foot who made the big mistake of delaying when she should've broken my daughter's toes. Oh, what a dark day that was! She put a curse on our house! Bad feet make bad *yeh*, karma. I like Gao, she's clever, though I'm convinced it was her line of bad luck that ruined my daughter's life. But she had a bad husband, and she's a relative. I had to guard her, to help her. Now she represents too many mouths to feed."

He nodded. "You'll need money. You know, the foreigners made me rich." He tried to laugh, knowing he wasn't good at it because usually the sound made people jump. "They'd say part of my money is yours. In France, you see, women can inherit. Besides, you sold my Soochow parcels very smartly, for much more than they're worth. Why don't you take the profits? Truly, I can't spend it."

She was silent, her face down, an aristocratic woman of means who needed help. She had eaten the bitterness of ten hard years and given up the beautiful Soochow estate on the canal rather than borrow. Borrowing cast shadows on her dear father, her silly husband, her only son. Borrowing troubled ancestors down to their old toes and was a painful snare to the next generation. Interest could kill a clan like a poison. Borrowing had to be reported to the clan and the dead, a bad thing. But Shanghai was so dangerous, and she was so exposed.

"You need more than that? I have plenty—"

"I need your permission to hire back some Soochow house staff," she said.

He brushed away her comment: No need.

"No, no, this is more than a formality. I want Singh the guard. Who watched over Father in his last years. *Chingbang* are kidnapping people from the good houses. Those businessmen they just took, one had his ear cut off! The last thing I need is to borrow ransom money from you to buy back Lo Fa or my son, part by part, from a bloody gangster." So many angry thoughts made her frown and look at her hands.

Older Brother disliked the idea of guards. "I'll find Singh for you."

"And I'll need his big gun, too," she said.

"Uuuh, of course." He shuddered.

"Good, thank you, Brother. Very good." She looked at him for a small moment. "You know, you've been a comfort. I don't deserve you. Forgive me, Brother, for leaving you now?"

"Nothing to forgive, Younger Sister," he said softly, as if the house were already silent, his walleye wandering sadly to the window. "Maybe you'll visit me and talk about what I should do," but she didn't hear him.

Her quiet brother locked his doors and left the house about as often as the dogs invited cats to meals. When he did leave, he walked like a commoner, too shy to have a bodyguard, walking erratically as he carried bundles of old, stained newspapers.

"SILENCE!" ROARED THE well-shaven domo, mustache bristling, chest puffed, face red, shaking with ancient drama that would have honored a Peking opera star. It was as if he were announcing the emperor with the old shout of *Lin tsun!* Tremblingly obey! The excited hubbub simmered into a hush.

"*Listen to the Taitai.*"

Standing next to the domo, Baba violated several Confucian edicts by holding a foreign book while shaking hands with Horseman Yip. All eyes were on Taitai. Old Deaf Man Fu stood straight for the house matriarch. She was seated in the hallway in a high hardwood Chinese chair. She was going to speak to them—a female speaking publicly, openly showing mouth and teeth! Most people held their breath.

This was unprecedented, the Taitai giving instructions to them as a group. The proper way to give directions was one to one. Then no one was embarrassed by inequality of treatment or reprimands, and special relationships based on rank, seniority, age and relationship could be protected as each deserved to be. In private, you could be scorched by authority, but you could preserve your face as you kept your eyes down. In public, all was at risk.

So they wondered if she would use many voices like a storyteller, or fly around in magic gong-fu circles, flapping her arms like Pi-hsia the Cloud Princess and leaping over chandeliers with a flashing of steel spears. They thought of Tzu Hsi, the last empress of China, the pretty concubine who became ruler. She had stored up her yin power and could kill people with a glance, poison young emperors, strangle disfavored eunuchs and then have sex with you or castrate you, taking your essence without your knowing it.

No one breathed as Taitai coughed, ready to use the verbs of men.

"We owe our good luck to my honored Older Brother," she said clearly, strongly. "His generosity exceeds our value. But our luck has weak legs, so we must make business. All of us." She didn't look at her husband. "Therefore I speak in public, so my meaning is clear to all.

"Majordomo, you must set aside courtesy. Cover your face and collect old loans to our house, with interest, no matter what it costs us in relationships."

"Yes, Taitai," he barked, bowing, reddening. He had been a fair cardplayer and a good Chinese man, allowing connections to trump debts. He was glad to be employed again, shaving off his whiskers of mourning, but cash was changing the world, and this made him sad.

"Lao Chu, everyone says that Old Sesame Face Wong across the street can stretch one meal to two days. Our meals must now stretch for three days, and when we have good rice, four." In other words, not even cooks could eat leftovers as snacks. Food was for meals, period. Also unspoken but implicit: You will eat in the kitchen, as is proper, and not at my table, as my stupid daughter has allowed.

"Amahs will sew—we can't afford Tailor Wen and the open mouths of his family, so I left them in Soochow to serve the county magistrate. At night, sew by the north window—there's a big free streetlight there, and you won't have to use candles." The amahs bowed.

"Horse Master Yip, we have no *ma*, no horses. Live with us and help Guard Man Singh look out for kidnappers and thieves, but I ask you to sell your services as a groom at the foreigners' gambling racetrack, where beggars spill more cash than we make in a year. Agreed? Good!

"Da-shing and Da-tsien will work at St. Mary's to reduce tuition. We can't afford to rehire Teacher Chen, so my worthless daughter will have no private tutor. It doesn't matter anyway, as all the education in the world won't match her big feet to a good husband." The message to her staff: *If I criticize my own daughter this freely in front of you—imagine my wrath if any of you fail.*

Da-tsien, face down and blushing hotly, had combed out her long thick hair and worn her best good-luck red dress for her mother.

"Anything to be sold, bring to me. I will pawn it. Auntie Gao, any food, clothing or services you can get from foot binding will be welcome. There are still some underground imperialists trying to bring back the boy emperor, and they need daughters with golden lilies. I hear they're hiding in Chapei and Hongkew." Auntie Gao trembled down to her bones; she had never gone to either of those horrible foreign districts.

"I will pay for your rickshaw fares.

"We have to save money, so if you gamble more than a copper or buy one cheap pipe of the opium flower or drink Western alcohol, you must leave." Taitai waited until all had nodded or bowed in assent.

"I see candles everywhere. Good. No one is to use this new foreign excitement called power of electricity. We fight the poverty demon that tries to eat us. Now, go thank our ancestors for watching over us in these hard times, and change all bad ways to make them proud of us."

The household reeled. Happy to be rejoined with the rehired Soochow staff, sobered by a woman's words that were a declaration of war. They lowered their eyes, as glancing at each other would be disrespectful. Some wondered if Taitai had just taken their manhood. Deaf Man Fu had no idea what had been said, but he saw some men surreptitiously opening their pants to inspect their privates. He remembered the legends of powerful women that he had heard in the days when he had ears, so he checked his equipment. Ah, all was in place.

The domo clapped his hands, and they began to shuffle away. Taking big steps, particularly during a personal inventory, would also be impolite.

With a look, Taitai froze her daughter in place. When everyone else had left, Taitai gestured. Da-tsien approached slowly, knelt and pressed her forehead deeply into a hardwood floor scuffed and marred by its prior history of porters freighting loads of opium in rough shoes.

She wanted to hear "Oh my daughter, you look so round and good."

But her mother asked, "How much is our rent?"

"Two-fifty," she said. "I apologize . . . it was the best—"

"Not bad. *So why are your grades bad?*"

"I have no excuse, Mother." She didn't say, *I spend my study time tutoring my brother, as you instructed me. I also run the house, pay the bills, feed the chickens and pigs and eight human mouths on twenty coppers a month. I utilize four-day-old produce and pawnshops without selling anything of clan value, without using electricity, while looking for a matchmaker for Da-shing. But thank Guan Yin that you've brought the domo back! Now Big Chef Chu will do better and help out poor Fatty Soo in the kitchen, and I won't have to shell peas all day or worry about burglars and kidnappers and chicken feed.*

"Improve your grades or I'll remove you from St. Mary's."

"Yes, Mother."

"And remember—focus on reading and English. Ignore the god-pig-slop that the foreign *laoshr* give with their lessons. Only people with no brains listen to talk of the foreign god. You know what swallowing foreign religions did to the Taipings, right?"

"Yes, Mother."

"Look at me." Taitai studied her daughter's face as Da-tsien studied hers. Even with her mother's harsh words hanging in the space between them, Da-tsien thought, *Mah-mee's so pretty. Such a good, gentle face with big eyes, perfect nose. A perfect mouth. And so smart!*

Her mother looked at Da-tsien's feet. "You're almost pretty, in a coarse, peasant way. I must make arrangements to marry you off. Will you cooperate, or will you make my life miserable and make me leave you and your brother and your father again? You are such a worthless daughter! You cause me so much pain! Just to *look* at you!"

Da-tsien burst into tears, then kowtowed nine times, saying to the scarred floor, with as much control as she could find, "I have *shiao*, filial piety, Mother, in my heart. I will practice obedience." *Shun. And I will hope for forgiveness. I will win good grades, and I will make a son for you, and he will love you and comfort you to make up for my badness, and he will take care of you in your old age, even before he cares for me, just like Chiang Keh, the best of all filial sons of all time, and he'll bring comfort to your bones for eternity, follow-ing you wherever you go, like Ruth followed Naomi, I promise!*

Da-tsien silently prayed to the Christian God and Jesus, who promised to love everyone, even women. A hymn ran through her mind, and she sat up. Later, she would hum it for her teachers.

They would tell her that it had been written by John Newton, an English slave trader who later became a minister opposed to slavery. Late in life, Newton would go blind.

The hymn was called "Amazing Grace," and it was for people who were lost.

The Matchmaker

THE *CHIH HUO ch'ai che,* matchmaker, was short, stout, steely-eyed and expensive. She was conditioned to persuade and trained to ferret out imperfection. Persuasion meant profits. Imperfections lowered a prospect's market value and paradoxically raised the commission, just as a lack of imper-fections raised a prospect's market value and also raised the commission. She naturally made sacrifices to Nu Kua, Goddess of All Matchmakers, but her beliefs were not wholly true, because she gave Nu Kua only fake paper money, which she burned quickly at the altar. The *chih huo* had to look rich to reflect success, optimistic to assure good matches and imperious to discourage bick-ering.

The matchmaker wore long dangling platinum earrings and heavy red rouge over white-rice face powder: She looked supernatural while advertising supernatural results. On every finger glittered beautiful gold rings, making her look like a short Buddhist god figurine from Siam. Her hair was slick and greasy, proof that bad fortune could find no grip on her, slipping off to latch on to people of lesser luck. She wore a tight red silk cheongsam to reveal small, pleasant, round rolls of prosperity. She drew a flower-perfumed hand-kerchief from her sleeve to press it against tiny flaring nostrils as she sniffed at Da-tsien, making judgments and subtracting points.

Da-tsien's brother, Da-shing, had already been sized up and found want-ing only in big money. He was kind, handsome, pleasant and smart, and the Tzus would have many attractive options from which to pick a worthy daugh-ter-in-law of good clan.

Da-tsien was another matter. Whereas Taitai had sat confidently during the premarital examination of her son, she now stood taller, forcing herself to breathe slowly as she asked Guan Yin to overcome her raging pessimism. Her daughter was a *da-jiao*, a big-footed maiden, and Taitai couldn't expect a reverse dowry to be given for their royal blood. The matchmaker, however, was still calculating.

Da-tsien, like all child brides of that time, demonstrated the female attrib-utes of steady silence, understated charm and wild obsequiousness as she was casually prodded like a sow on market day.

The small woman pointed. Taitai closed the doors to their most private room, her husband's study. Baba was somewhere pissing away time and chas-ing fish. Taitai lit candles that reflected brightly on the burnished, sepia-hued wall mirrors, making the room feel as if it were being prepared for a séance. Superstitiously, Taitai did not sit in her husband's French chair, as it con-tained too many terrifying thoughts left by dead foreign writers.

The matchmaker's hunt for defects began by an examination of Da-tsien's scalp for nits, which had appeared in Shanghai when foreign sailors arrived in force in late 1843. "Good hair," she said reluctantly.

She inspected the girl's unmade-up face and complexion. "Fine color, no sun, soft, firm." Every day, to and from school, Ah Tsui carried the umbrella above Da-tsien's head, whether the sun was shining or not.

Next the *chih huo* searched for crossed eyes, walleyes, drooping eyes, lop eyes, weeping eyes, pink eyes, glass eyes and acute myopia. "Okay, open your mouth." The woman stuck a hand inside Da-tsien's mouth and tugged hard on her teeth, baring her own as she prepared to find rot. She wiped her hands on her handkerchief. "Okay. Stand still. . . ."

Taitai nodded approvingly as the woman put her hands on her daughter. Such a good inspection, just like in *goo dai*, the old imperial days, well worth the added cost. But damn those big feet!

"Hm, good. Arms supple, not too soft, not too hard. Ten fingers . . .

good . . . breasts firm, won't be too big like a cow . . . good tummy, won't swell like a melon . . . no pain, huh, as I squeeze? Good. Hips fine for childbearing. Any female problems with this girl, Tzu Taitai? No? Okay. Legs fine, good shape . . . tsk, tsk, yes, yes, the feet, I know, I know, say no more."

She inspected hands and fingertips carefully, shaking her head as she checked the sworls. She rechecked, held them up to candlelight, rubbed them, frowned, reinspected, then sighed dramatically. This was the *chih huo's* special gift for which Taitai had paid extra.

Taitai waited breathlessly. "Yes, yes? What do you see? I expire from waiting!"

"I am sorry, Madame. Too much *yin*. She'll make daughters."

"How can you say this? Please, madam, look again—"

"No use, Lady. It says what it says. I am sorry."

"I insist! My own *sven ming* fortuneteller didn't say this!"

Reluctantly, the woman checked again, with the same results. Taitai hid her face in her hands and wept bitterly, stamping her feet as if her unborn grandsons had just died in front of her.

Da-tsien looked stricken; her life was over. A *chih huo* would never sour a deal by predicting an absence of sons. Years later, my father guessed that the matchmaker said these cruel words because she sensed Da-tsien's great *chi*, her life force and her vision, and was jealous, even frightened, of the young girl.

The matchmaker bowed to her respectfully, then continued. "Now, girl, walk as if to market. Hmm. She's done *that* before. Now walk to greet your *p'o-p'o*, your mother-in-law, good. Now walk behind your husband . . . aiyaa! Lower your face! Smaller steps! Don't swing your arms!"

Da-tsien didn't know what the matchmaker could have said to her mother in private that would have been worse than what she had said in public. But it couldn't have been good, because after the *chih huo* left, Taitai turned to her quailing daughter with a narrowed, reddened eye and flaring nostrils, looking like the ghost catcher Chong Kui who hid under the bed and scared the hair off the head of every kid in China.

"We'll be lucky to find a curly-tailed pig who'll marry you—after paying big cash! And you'll have only *daughters*! This is all so unacceptable! We're ruined! No! Don't kowtow in that dress or you'll tear it, you stupid, stupid girl! You humiliate me! And *you* cry and whimper and stamp your ugly feet!" Taitai burst into tears.

"Don't you know that I have to negotiate for a dowry for your body, you stupid thing. You with royal blood! And you'll bring us *nothing*! And you eat our family food and breathe our air! You break my heart, you awful, worthless thing! And if you run to your useless father and complain to him, you'll shame him, and me, and our Before Borns. *Stop crying!*"

Her daughter was in agony, unable to expend her pent-up energy by bowing or running away. She used all her strength to stop her tears. She felt ugly and stupid, and she wailed inside. She wanted to be so far away that Taitai's disapproval couldn't touch her. She knew that she could never please her mother, that she was doomed by a terrible *yeh* to always disappoint the woman who had brought her into this world of tears.

Now came the iron voice. "You will practice walking with small steps, as if you had golden lilies instead of huge shit-kickers. You will restrain the swinging of your arms, as if you had none. A man will come, a stranger. You will allow him to put your face into a foreign picture box. You will look at peace. That's for the matchmaker. She will show your picture around." Her mother restrained a shudder of disgust at modern times. "You *will* raise your grades and not disgrace us by getting anything other than top marks! You're not totally stupid, are you? Well, *are you?*"

Da-tsien shuddered, shaking her head. "No, I don't think so. . . ."

"*You don't think so,*" Taitai mimicked. "Ah, who cares! It doesn't matter what *you* think! Just *do*! Remember, foreign people are savages! They rape China and throw opium at us like we are turtle dogs! You are in a foreign-country school because that is where the gentry rich also send their sons in this terrible, upside-down city that we came to so your father would work. You are there to qualify for a match to someone of *my* father's class. We can't afford any of this for such a bad-luck girl, but your uncle is paying for it. Practice your walk! Raise your grades!"

Ladies never used coarse terms. That Taitai cursed and spoke of turtle dogs—combining phallic profanity and bestial servility—reflected her fear of foreigners, whom, she felt, now had direct access to her girl.

Da-tsien waited, facedown, until her mother called for Big Chef Chu, who appeared in a stained apron to help her stand and walk with a new, slow regal posture to the staircase. Taitai's ancient amah seldom left her room anymore, and it was a big step, my grandmother letting a man help her.

Alone in her room, panting from the weight of sorrow, Da-tsien tried to stop crying, but her mah-mee's words kept squeezing into her heart. She needed to talk to Baba. Not about her mother's harsh criticism, which would make things worse, but about fat fish and old books and monkey kings and ghosts and good, brave girls. She found her amah.

"Ah Tsui, walk with me to the river."

Her amah shook her head. "Your mother forbids it. You can't go anywhere until your grades go up. Sorry I'm the one to have to say this."

"I'M GOING WITH *lao-shr* to a foreign-god house. Don't be afraid." The *lao-shr* was a young female foreign-person teacher from America named Missy Roberts. She had old-person hair and colorless ghost eyes and was known to pluck eyeballs from babies, coveting their dark brown eyes.

Ah Tsui managed to close her jaw. "No! Can't do this! Taitai will flay my skin! And foreign-god devils will make you a Taiping—crazy, violent, no judgment, no *shiao*, no piety! They'll strip away what makes you a person!" *They'll take your eyeballs! Then how will you see, heh?*

"Amah. My mother won't hurt you. If she finds out, she'll just punish me. You know it's true. You don't have to listen to the foreign-country people. You can stay safe outside. No foreign words to go in your brain."

"Young Missy, your mother is going crazy looking for your husband. Not easy with your flapping feet. Now, you want to lose yourself in foreign thoughts, full of danger, knowing Mother would forbid it?"

"Yes, Amah, I think I do. It's okay. I can go without you if you like."

"Tsa! Not possible," muttered Ah Tsui. She glowered, her left eye almost shuttered, just like the Taitai's. "Do you know how many candles this will take, how many deep wishes to Buddha on painted lanterns on his birthday, how many prayers to the bodhisattvas, how many offerings to Taoist monks and Confucius temples and the ancestors and the kitchen gods and the city god and the gods of the sea? You make me spend my entire life in prayer for you!"

"I'm not that bad. You exaggerate. I'm not that bad."

Amah took a deep breath, fiercely shaking her umbrella. "But if they try to take your mind, you scream, and I'll hit them with this so hard it'll knock the organs from males and make women sing in deep voices!"

twelve

Mr. Tung

HE HAD A gentle face shaped by ample meals served by cooks with good *ho*, harmony, and a kind disposition formed by generations of pleasant table conversation. Good sense let him bargain for more in situations where others might expect less. He wanted a wife because trading leather goods now permitted him to have wealthy sons. Mr. Tung was in a hurry because his *yang* force might soon decline, and, according to his mother, he had already waited too long.

His French Concession mansion spanned five floors, counting a frequently flooded, inadvisable basement perilously close to the Whangpu River water table. The house staff was large because greater numbers compensated in part for a recent and precipitous drop in competence. Well-trained but underpaid Shanghai domestics were leaving for better pay in the more promising fields of foreign employment, smuggling, prostitution and violent crime. The rich did not know that these were signs of a coming revolution.

Mr. Tung was a fine catch. The matchmaker was smitten by his height, which made her look up; his good smell, which made her dizzy; the heft of his fee, which raised her pulse; and the speed with which he paid down the advance, which proved his innate goodness.

These were the details. The central fact was that Mr. Tung was a kind man. Finding him a wife would be as easy as finding gulls by the sea. So the matchmaker, wearing her best, had quickly interviewed his nose-up mother, who provided a fine spread of the usual lies.

"My honorable son is a scholar," she said, not mentioning that he had purchased his degrees and that his favorite reading was ledger books.

"The gods blessed his face." This was code for *Yes, he has a huge black mole on his cheek, but who's perfect nowadays?*

"His house staff loves him so much that they wash in his old bathwater to absorb his *chi* and his luck." In other words, *He saves money by recycling every-*

thing, including used water. The *chih huo* knew Taitai's family saved money by not using electricity. It would be a perfect match.

"I'M JUST AN average person," said Mr. Tung, "who wants beauty before life. My ideal wife? Of course. She thinks beautifully and has a harmonious spirit. She has a perfectly shaped face with widely spaced eyes, small nose, good mouth, smooth skin. A pleasing form. A kind person. She knows the classics and can handle cash but isn't pushy about her brains. She has a learned and graceful brush hand. Naturally, she can save money." His soft voice could smooth tough negotiations. This one was easy.

"Naturally," said the short, bejeweled *chih huo*, her nose aimed at the center of the earth. "But please tell more. Your sagacity warms my heart. Your knowledge makes me small, your—"

"My fee makes you rich," he said with a smile. "Her personality would calm a Tartar. She makes me kinder. She will give me sons upon sons, and we will all honor her as she sings to us on the *p'i-p'a* and arranges family feasts and honors my Before Borns and hosts and manages the house."

"I think I have just the girl, Master. Please describe her feet, her age."

"Golden lilies," he said automatically. "Say, fourteen years old."

"Are you ready for photos, Master?" She fanned them before him. He looked at them studiously. Pretending to look away, she peripherally gauged his reaction to each candidate based on the opening of his eyes, the time he took, his affirming grunts, the depth of his sighs.

He looked up. "I want to see *all* the pictures. You hold some back." Unspoken: *You are being rude.* Chinese hosts offer everything to their guests, and professionals hold nothing back from their clients. Accordingly, Chinese chefs present full fish and fowl dishes, with the heads, tails, gills and feet still attached. It means *I offer you everything.*

"They are unworthy of you. They are not as beautiful in face or figure, or they're too old for your requirements."

He gestured impatiently. She gave him the remaining pictures. It didn't take long. "I like this one, very much." He held up the photo.

The matchmaker bowed in deference to his keen judgment and insight but probably thought, *Aiyaa, what an idiot! Not her!*

"Ah, Master, your wisdom puts Wenlin Pen Forest Hanlins to shame." The

Forest of Pens was the great academy, the legendary Lyceum of the Empire of China. "Such discernment, sir! She is an historic catch! This is her biography . . .

"Her honorable name is Tzu. She is the maternal granddaughter of Viceroy Tzu of Kwangtung and Kwangsi, the famous model governor. Her father was a principal Jardine Matheson comprador, earning great cash as if he were another Hsu Jun. The girl is exceptionally bright and speaks a foreign-country tongue better than the white devils. She has a beautiful singing voice, well-spaced eyes, a good nose, a good figure, a sweet disposition, unbound feet, knows business, handles money sagely and has some moral courage to accompany her beauty."

"Huh! Did you say *unbound feet?*"

"Yes, it's true. She's *da-jiao*, a big-feet maiden. That is why I withheld her photograph."

"Oh, that's too bad . . . but fourteen years old?"

"Fifteen now, Master. In the spring, I think." Matchmakers knew true birth months. This was special knowledge since everyone celebrated their birthdays at the same time on the lunar New Year.

"Any other deficiencies? Rotting teeth? Bitter gas? Christian?"

"Oh, no, Master. Excellent teeth, fine stomach. Delicate girl. Smells like gardenias. She has the heart of a Buddhist and the luck of a Taoist."

"Okay, but a *da-jiao* should cost me less," he said almost to himself. "She has less market value."

And as if to herself, she replied, "Sadly, a *da-jiao* costs more. The mother is always unhappy and requires more work. The bride's big feet call for better actors in the wedding chorus for applause and stronger bearers for the palanquin, to carry her feet . . . and, I must tell you, sir—prepare yourself—this *huaren* woman expects a dowry to be given to her. It's because of her father the viceroy. You can acquire royal blood for royal sons!"

In northern cities, unlike other regions, nouveau-rich grooms sometimes found themselves buying aristocratic brides. Crazy modern times, but the matchmaker took a healthy cut either way.

"Tung *syensheng*," she went on, "a dowry in this case is acceptable. Ah, so, the mother knows business and the value of her *jia*! She's shrewd like a scholar!" The *chih huo* lowered her face to lessen the pain of bad news and waited, knowing that Mr. Tung had more money than she had discounts, and that she had more patience than he had time. Tung was fifty-five, and she had all day.

He sighed. "I'd like to see her. How much for a one-way viewing?"

"For you, sir, no extra charge. It is my honor."

He detected her tone. "Ah, so. Tell me what you dislike in her."

"I like her very much. But I honor you more. Shall we speak of the dowry? I cannot easily face Tzu Taitai without some sense of the offer. Asking for a one-way viewing must mean that you have doubts."

Mr. Tung put the photograph on his lap. "I have no doubts. I trust you totally. I merely need to see what she looks like in the flesh. When she's natural. Before the pressure of the clans and the ladies in power pinch her face and make her behave unnaturally. Of course, I want to see how a royal *da-jiao* walks. And I still need to know your concerns about this girl."

"Aiy, you're fire burning down my door!" She shook her head. "Mr. Tung, the girl is clumsy. It's her big feet. Please, give us a small delay. Besides . . ."

"Yes? What else?"

"The girl has a critical mother. I see it all the time—the mother wanted the girl's feet bound, but the revolutionary committees stopped it. Mr. Tung, the girl will respond to your kindness. The longer you wait, the more ready she will be. Can you be kind to her in this way? In patience?" The longer she waited, the more Tung would be willing to pay.

He looked at the photo. "I will try. But I feel the breath of my mother on my neck. While I am patient, you must hurry."

DA-TSIEN NEVER KNEW when her betrothed saw her for the first time. Years later, she learned that the *chih huo* had put off Mr. Tung again and again, in the hopes that before such a pivotal encounter, the big-footed Tzu girl would learn how to walk like a lady. The matchmaker had cringed too many times watching Da-tsien slip down stairs and jettison her books after catching a tiny crack with a big toe. All Da-tsien knew was that the pressure for her to improve her coordination increased while Mr. Tung relentlessly sought a viewing.

"Like I said, I want to just see her on the street, no words, just to see her eyes up close," said Mr. Tung.

"Not a good idea. I think she would recognize me."

"Well, yes. I could see her without you."

"That would be unusual." Code for *That would be scandalous.*

"You could sit in my car, hidden from sight. I could sit on a bench on the street she walks. I could read a newspaper. Madam, I can be discreet, I promise. I won't jump out at her and steal her books."

"Sir, I arrange high marriages. I do not put my body inside gas vehicles where my virtue and reputation could be polluted!" She shuddered, patting her hot forehead with a perfumed handkerchief.

"I'm so sorry, madam. Please, forgive me." He bowed.

"No, no apologies. It is my weakness, nothing else. I will arrange it," which meant *Patience, Mr. Tung. The girl's not ready.*

IF DA-TSIEN'S FEET had been bound, Taitai never would have felt the need to teach her to do business, to look over the horizon. Without those lessons about people and dreams, Da-tsien would have been more classically a little rich girl of two houses—her clan and her husband's—with no bridge to the outside world.

If her feet had been bound, it's doubtful that Taitai would have left her husband, despite the cost of electricity. Taitai would have treated a *syau-jiao* small-footed daughter more generously. While a Confucian mother could never show open approval, it could appear in small ways—in a kind look at New Year's, by offering choice pieces of the best dishes, by rare recognitions shared with relatives within earshot of the child.

Daughters, who lost their mothers forever upon marriage and were then ruled until death by dictatorial mothers-in-law, wildly missed their dear mah-mees, thinking of isolated moments of kindness for the rest of their lives.

Mothers most articulately expressed their affection by preparing their daughters for marriage. A girl might know that her mah-mee cared by the quality of the Shantung silk used for her bridal gown, the food that was ordered for the visit of the matchmaker, the choice morsels plucked from the hottest dishes for the plates of the daughter's friends. Da-tsien always hoped for these clear indications of love but never got them.

The dainty, tiny-footed Da-tsien whom Taitai had dreamed of would have obeyed her mother's most internal wishes. She would have seen a mother's caring wisdom in her choice of kind, rich Mr. Tung and would have agreed to marry him before the question was posed.

Da-tsien of the Small Feet would have helped Tung afford many sons. He had enough years to be wise and gentle with a young and pretty wife. He would be a comfort on hard days, which history seemed to be preparing for the Chinese people.

But Taitai did not have a perfect, delicate girl—hers was a clumsy shadow-stumbler who read newspapers about foreign movie actresses and told make-believe stories to the female household staff about unbound girls who fought with swords, jumped over rooftops with monkeys and laughed at mortal danger.

Taitai knew that her daughter would do something stupendously stupid—such as running away to a Small Mountain Buddhist nunnery—if she learned about her upcoming betrothal. This would be bad for the girl's future and bad for the household's immediate cash needs.

"Da-tsien! Come here! Ayy! Don't trip! Time to practice. Walk more slowly. Less arms! Head still—don't move it like a chicken! No, no, don't worry about your feet. Don't look down! Pretend to be one of those stupid fighting princesses you tell stories about. Graceful, contained. . . ."

One time, after these lessons, Da-tsien summoned Ah Tsui and whispered, "Amah, you have to find out what's happening."

"We know what's happening. Taitai is finding you a husband."

"But *who*? Is he nice? Is he handsome and tall? Oh, please find out!"

"But Missy, how? Matchmakers guard their client secrets deeper than the tomb of Chin Shih Huang-ti!" Chin was the first emperor of China, the builder of the Great Wall. "If I even *asked* questions of her household staff, Taitai would have my skin! And yours!"

"But there must be a way." Da-tsien wondered how her mother would proceed. Her mah-mee did business the traditional way—through a maze of intricate human relationships, saving face while inching her way to the center. There she found the relationship payoff—information.

Da-tsien knew the best source was the gruff majordomo. He worked for her baba but reported to her mother, so no help there. She went to Horse Master Yip after he returned from the foreign racetrack, where he groomed racing ponies and collected big tips for the household account.

"Ah, Young Missy," he said in a lovely deep voice, which rolled out her name like a summer storm. "Always a pleasure to hear your warm greeting. You want the name of the photographer who took your picture for the *chih huo?*" asked Yip. "I remember the man and his box. I have a second cousin who captures people's faces on paper, too. I'll ask him." In time, the answer filtered back: It was a high-priced portrait photographer named Wong with a shop on Nanking Road.

"Wong *syensheng*, how are you?" asked Da-tsien, bowing as a girl should. "I come with deep thanks. Your picture of me was so kind that I am now betrothed! My husband sends me because he wants another print of my picture. To send to his relatives so they can see my unworthy face. I wonder, sir, if you are so discerning, you can tell which man selected me."

"Ah!" he said. "Tung *syensheng*, the leather-goods trader, so round with cash, right? Tan *syensheng*, the Whangpu ship owner? Not young Mr. Guan, director of Delano's? Aiy, you won't say? You are such a clever young wife, and I am deeply perplexed. So, Tung Taitai, I have extra prints ready. No charge! A gift from a grateful tradesman, happy for business! No, please, I must refuse. No *k'u chi*, don't treat me like a guest, Young Miss, I mean, Taitai! I send blessings on your blessed wedding, which I'd be honored to shoot!"

Riding home in a rickshaw, Da-tsien kept a tight hold of her photograph. She did not like the idea of a strange man possessing it. "Amah, take my picture to each of these men. Say Photographer Wong asks if he ordered additional pictures of me. Then memorize each man. Tell me which one wants it. That would be the one Mah-mee and the *chih huo*—who stuck her hand in my mouth!—have picked."

"Young Missy, this is very bad luck. All this secrecy."

"I'm just using my mother's secret ways for us. Who's going to live with this man for the rest of her life—me or Mah-mee? Me! Amah, I *deserve* to know. Come on! Help me."

With little enthusiasm and less skill, Amah did as she was instructed. The suitor was Mr. Tung.

"Is he tall?" asked Da-tsien breathlessly, holding her throat.

"Yes."

"Slender?"

"Well, yes, except for excess weight and some big roundness."

"Oh. But is he handsome?"

Amah elevated a hand and moved it from side to side. "Not bad. Pleasant-looking. Except for a big mole on his face."

Da-tsien screamed.

"Hush! He's rich."

"I don't care!"

"He seemed very kind."

"Unimportant!"

"He seems to care about you."

"He shouldn't!"

"But the matchmaker picked him for you!"

"A mistake! A horrible mistake! An incredibly horrible mistake!"

"Stop jumping up and down or your mother will hear you!"

"I don't care! Let her kill me and end this! Oh, Amah, how awful!"

With fading interest, Da-tsien practiced walking. Meanwhile, Mr. Tung asked questions and discovered where Miss Tzu attended school. He began following Da-tsien home from St. Mary's. He did so using a car, and he did so without informing the matchmaker or revealing himself to his betrothed, acts that reflected modernity, recklessness and caution.

Tung's driver wore a European coat and a taxi driver's cap and handled a vehicle the way a mule would pour tea. Whatever he had done to earn his way before the invention of motor vehicles had not prepared him. He could manage thirty miles an hour on a macadam surface, but at slow speeds on ancient cobbled roads, the bricks would catch the narrow, underinflated tires and he would curse and bump onto curbs on both sides of the street, scraping trees and sideswiping innocent bystanders. When he tried to follow Da-tsien, other drivers became nervous, horses neighed and pedestrians fled.

To soothe her stomach en route to the foreign-god mission, Ah Tsui walked slowly with her head down while exhaling as if about to deliver an uncooperative baby. This was testimony to the effort required to walk with an upper-class *huaren* girl who strode like a farmer, washed dishes at school and now flirted with foreign gods. Amah carried an eight-trigrammed *ba-kua* mirror that she had bought at a discount, pointing it at anything that worried her. With great animation, she'd wave it at the one thing that absolutely terrified her—airplanes. She knew if she reflected their horrific bad luck back at them, they'd leave and, in recognition of her strength and courage, would never follow her again with their devilish, mosquitolike whining. The moment she saw one, she pushed the absentminded Da-tsien behind thick foliage, hissed at her to be absolutely silent and bravely held the mirror up to the plane until it left. Ah Tsui's fears made Da-tsien close her eyes at the sound of airplane engines, trembling as she shrank into herself.

Sometimes Amah flashed the mirror at groups of people if they were gathered in the unlucky number of four. *Ssu*, four, sounds like the word for death. Or she used the mirror on *hautou ren*, the slippery people in Western hats who wanted wallets and your body.

Ah Tsui disliked hard work and feared the world, so her only hope was to capture as much good luck every day as she could. She did this by observing propitious events, hearing good-luck sounds, offering warm toothy smiles to monks, never stepping on bugs and avoiding bad fortune in its many forms. It was a full-time job, because she also had to create an aura of good *foo chi* for her big-footed girl, whose *chi* was being diminished by daily association with foreigners and her weak *gang* with her mother.

Ah Tsui occasionally heard screams and crying horses behind her, but shrugged when she realized that people were only complaining about an unhappy *chi tz*, a gas vehicle, that kept fleeing its master. There were hordes of simple countryside refugees in Shanghai who could not understand how motorcars worked. After her third collision with a *chi tz*, Ah Tsui learned the ways of the gas vehicles: They often made a honking noise before they decided to hit you. The horn was like a warning but it didn't tell you if the *Chi tzs* would merely break bones or kill you outright. She also understood that drivers could not control these machines, which had their own spirits and their own problems—evidenced by the fact that they expelled such powerful farts with their effort, particularly up hills. *Chi tzs* were angry, having so much work.

Her last collision with a foreign machine had been her fault. A ghost was on her tail, trying to enter her clothing. Da-tsien had seen the small cyclone of evil spirits dancing on the ground like an angry devil, chasing the amah, making both of them scream. Da-tsien had closed her eyes—*do not look at evil*—but Ah Tsui had glanced at the traffic, timed her move and dashed into the street in front of a moving *chi tz*, hoping to scrape the ghost off on its bumper. The vehicle misunderstood her purpose and honked and swerved to hit her. The pain had not been as bad as she expected, and she went to bed and let a tearful Da-tsien tend to her for two months. She was proud that she had not only escaped the devil but had killed him with a modern foreign gas vehicle. The servants still oohed and ahhed about her power.

Once again Amah heard people cursing and running behind them. Turning, she saw a car bumping onto the sidewalk. Minutes later, she turned to see a repetition of the commotion without recognizing that it was the same machine. Nor did she see the connection between her turning to shine the good-luck mirror in the eyes of the capped, sweating driver and the car's sudden and painful collision with a large camphor tree.

On these walks home, Da-tsien recited English lessons. She liked poetry and disliked plays, which were largely incomprehensible. But top grades would please Mah-mee, so she tried to understand Shakespeare, which could lead to better marriage prospects than obese Mr. Tung. Good marriage prospects would put a smile on her mah-mee's face and restore to them the relationship that Confucius, Jesus Christ and Guan Yin had ordained. Good grades for Mah-mee and a handsome son for the clan. *But not with Mr. Tung with the mole. If they force me, I'll go to a nunnery. Or kill myself. Or I'll become a businesswoman.*

She was thinking about a handsome husband when Ah Tsui said, "If Mah-mee says marry Mr. Tung, you marry! If she says smile as he lifts your wedding veil to see you for the first time, you do it, showing all your teeth, nothing held back! No delays. No going to Taishan in Shantung, looking for nunneries and monkeys. Understand, Young Missy?"

Da-tsien nodded. It was fate. But how she wanted a young, handsome husband, someone with spirit and courage.

"Say you understand."

"Aiy! You talk like my mother."

"How you talk to me! I *am* your mother. Now say it."

"Oh, Amah, I understand. Now leave me alone so I can cry."

Da-tsien didn't see the portly man in the dented black Chrysler sedan. Nor did she see the person who was following the black car.

thirteen

Western Torture

LEE ZEE LEANED in to the microphone as it honked feedback through the auditorium. *"Long live China!"* he cried. Blue-uniformed boys cheered wildly and drummed their feet. Those who were truly talented in the ways of adolescence made screeching animal sounds and piercing whistles. Some stood on folding chairs and tore off their Western blazers, whipping them in circles over their heads. Zee Zee imagined he was a hero in a movie, leading his men to victory!

"Lee Zeu-zee, off the stage, right now!" yelled the American principal, but the lad shouted, "China for the Chinese!" followed by another roar. The principal pulled the plug, and Zee Zee crowed into a dead mike.

Lee Zeu-zee, winner of the gold medal in the oratorical contest (English-language round, freshmen), was supposed to close the day's assembly with a reflective English prayer thanking the Almighty for His Grace and His instruction, not with an hysterical Songhai cry for nationalism.

"I will inform your father forthwith!" cried the principal, who was slow to expel rebels; inflation made him welcome all the tuition money he could find. "Then woe betide you and your utter lack of judgment!"

Zee Zee shrugged; his dad would be too deeply in the arms of opium smoke to care.

St. John's was the typical 1920s Shanghai crossroads. At the edge of the International Settlement, it bordered the western badlands where crime was so heavy that cops refused to patrol. Encircling it like a horseshoe was Soochow Creek, filled with lotus plants, ducks, geese and corpses from among the eleven hundred dead the police pulled every month from Shanghai waters. Across the street was Jessfield Park, where opium importers and businessmen could promenade with their wives and children. Chinese and dogs were prohibited on these pastoral paths. The next avenue, Bubbling Well Road, held an array of fine English estates and Mexican and Chinese-run roulette establishments where the middle class gambled away pricey tuitions for their sons and mortgages for their homes. From there it was a short hop to the French Concession's Avenue Foch. Here chronic losers wandered east until it became Avenue Edward VII and they *huahui*, jumped into the Whangpu to repent Shanghai's one unforgivable moral offense—financial failure.

A few kilometers to the north sat the waiting warlord army of General Lu Yung-shian. His artillery and troops gave him the leverage to create an opium monopoly that made him and the city's leadership the wealthiest men in Shanghai. Only 450 nautical miles to the east was the expanding Japanese empire that had already swallowed Korea and the port of Darien. In Tokyo a peace faction argued with the war party that screamed for military expansion into Manchuria and China, which was already the unwilling host to six foreign armies and navies, jostling for more business.

The faculty at St. John's was mixed. The Chinese teachers were of the new mercantile class. Protected from physical activity all their lives and educated in the United States, they were now concerned about the political future of China. The Americans came from the Midwest and the East after graduating from some of the best colleges. They had been trained in physical education and were committed to saving souls for Christ.

The students were upper-class *gaodeng huaren* Chinese sons trying to escape the death grip of Confucian thinking and the heavy control of their fathers. Most were from Shanghai, and they were as interested in following a new lord named Jesus as they were in catching syphilis.

Like most young men, Zee Zee wanted adventure: to fight and fly and kill the enemies of his country, which, at the moment, seemed to be most of the world. It frustrated and depressed him that the West was robust while China was not. The antidote was yelling at the top of his lungs into a modern microphone. He thought heaven was preparing him to be an orator, and he had imaginary victorious debates with St. John's angry principal.

To prepare for saving his country, he boxed with associates of his best friend, Pooh Pan, in a makeshift, run-down Hongkew factory where the process was smuggling, the workers were crooks, the products they were handling depended on what came in that day and the permanent residents were insects. There young rowdies who wanted to become hoodlums studied *wushu*, martial arts, and there Zee Zee had met Pan. Their teacher was Barrel

Man Him Yao. He had changed his name to reflect the objects he threw for exercise. He was known for a big, unclassical gut; angry, porcupinelike black whiskers; and a ferocious stink. Yao saw himself as a master who taught violence with artistry; liking garlic and liking to sweat were extras. His hoodlums called him Bad Smell Man Yao. For Zee Zee, learning from Bad Smell meant being hit frequently by older street boys and by his enormous teacher, a condition to which, by living with his angry older brother and the St. John's upper classmen, he had become accustomed.

Zee Zee followed Bad Smell Yao because he was a second son from an unremarkable nouveau-riche clan, and because Yao was a famous fighter who regaled his students with stories of history, martial arts and sex. Yao's favorite stories involved the classical fighters of the fabled Boxer Rebellion who had been wiped out by foreign troops sixteen years ago in Peking.

"The Boxers of the *I Wor Kuen*, boy, they were the best! They killed with both hands. Not like me, good only with my right. They did everything! Cook like heaven, play music like gods, please educated girls all night and train hard all day. No, I can't do that. Too old, too fat, and I play the *p'i-p'a* like a camel frigging a water bag. Educated women don't like my stink. And they think I'm too heavy." He shrugged. "Maybe I am. See here, the worst of the Boxers could've flattened my ass with a single punch without distracting the girl or putting down the mandolin."

"But the Boxers lost," said Zee Zee, trying to understand the described geometry. "They lost to *chi kuan ch'iang*, machine guns, and *pao*, cannon."

"No! We Boxers had magic incantations so bullets couldn't hurt us. But the tricky Manchu dogs gave the reverse incantations to the white-devil soldiers. They used it in battle. Boxers were slaughtered, saving the Manchus *and* the white devils."

"Incantations?"

"Magic words! Don't you know anything? Words so secret even my teacher didn't say them." Like saying your father's name. Zee Zee's father was Lee Kung-doo. Yao flexed his trunklike arm. "All they wanted was what we want— freedom from the sogging, sucking foreigners!"

"China for the Chinese," said Zee Zee. "Are you a radical?"

"Farting mice, do I look like a politician or a college student?"

Zee Zee considered the question. "I don't think so."

"In *goo dai*, in the old days, someone with your brains and birth could open a silkworm factory, an herb shop, a letter-writing office, a manure collectors' guild, a rickshaw firm. Or follow a *wu-shu* fighting master and, in forty, fifty years, become a *lao-shr* yourself." He showed his best teeth. "Open your own school. Make business. After that you could get your son a tutor and your kid would become a great man.

"But the Manchus invaded and frigged it all up. Made us wear slave queues. Took all businesses, the good homes, our blue-water ships. Burned them. Sodding desert people—for them it was horses or nothing. Shut down our *wu-shu* schools so we couldn't fight their pig-breath Bannermen. After three hundred years, the Manchus screwed us so much they got their blood intermixed with ours, so we start to open up the fighting schools.

"Then the damn white devils come! *They* bring *real* big business. It kills all our family companies, fire in hay. No worms, no silks, no grain, no rice, no tea, no porcelain, no *crap* unless it goes through the white devils. They get big rich. We get small poor. See? You're not learning how to fight. You're learning how to defend China."

Bad Smell Him Man Yao also told Zee Zee that acrobatics were important to fighting and even more important in winning. "Speed. Balance. Agility."

"I take gymnastics at St. John's."

Yao narrowed his eyes. "Yuuuu! You go to that horseshit place?"

Zee Zee nodded.

Yao pointed a thick digit at the boy, making Zee Zee cross his eyes. "When the sodding white devils and the sodding Japanese burned the Forbidden City and the Summer Palace and the ancient texts, they beheaded the surviving Boxers to stamp out our art. You know that, right? White devils made *wu-shu* illegal! In China! *Our ancient art*!"

Yes. All Chinese kids knew that.

"Boy, there's more. Foreign devils made *us* pay *them* for losing! Said it cost them for their troops to kill us. Said the Boxers killed two hundred missionaries, but the devils killed *hundreds of thousands of us*, so that's pigshit. They just wanted our silver and gold. With a knife to our throat, we pay millions of *taels* every year to the bastards who ship in opium and force-feed us dog-crap Christianity and buy little girls to diddle. We have to pay *them* for *their burning our books of Confucius*!" He spat ferociously.

St. John's had not mentioned China having to pay its invaders.

"Listen, this is about you: The *Meigworen*, the Americans, took our indemnity cash and used it to kidnap our smartest boys to their country and pay tuition for them to *become* American. They said this was out of generosity, but it was to change our true and ethical natures."

Zee Zee shuddered.

"Where the crap do you think those asshole Chinese students went after spending ten years in America?"

Zee Zee knew the silent movies with Lillian Gish and Mary Pickford and Theda Bara. "New York?" he said. "San Francisco? Hollywood? Paris?"

"No, mulehead. *They shipped them back to us.* Now they teach at St. John's. The Chinese faculty are Boxer-payment bastards."

"Aiya!"

"Don't trust 'em, boy. They're not our countrymen, not anymore."

"Okay, I won't. But what about gymnastics?"

Yao shrugged. "Gymnastics, okay, learn that. But nothing else." Without changing his voice, he calmly said, "You get hit from behind—*kyaaaa!* What do you do to counter?"

Zee Zee found himself in the dirt, stunned and gasping for air. "Avoid the punch. If you can't, go with the punch. Recover your feet."

"Good! You went with the punch. Get up!"

To be better in acrobatics, Zee Zee installed Roman rings—the most diffi-cult of all the gymnastics apparatuses—in his room at home. Standing on a swaying ladder, he screwed heavy bolts into the beams in his bedroom and installed the rings into his ceiling. Below, Tall Amah, Sesame Face Wong and Skinny Woo wrung their hands. Later, they bit their fingers as he practiced pull-ups, handstands, semicrosses, vaults and dismounts above a floor strategi-cally covered with mattresses and quilts. When they couldn't watch anymore, they went to the kitchen and busily overate and argued over which demon possessed Second Son—the anger devil, the fear demon or the devil of the below. Clearly, he was possessed, trying to fend off internal pressures.

Tall Amah must have been glad for one thing—she no longer had to chase Zee Zee. But now there was a new torture.

St. John's ninth grade was notorious for Scriptural memorization and for a grueling track program with a highlighted one-mile run. For students raised on eight daily hours of calligraphy and Confucius' *Lun-yu*, memorizing the Bible was easy. For sheltered upper-class boys, running a mile was like being caught in an iron trap and having to gnaw off your own foot.

Out of duty, the mothers and amahs of these treasured sons would ride rickshaws to Jessfield Road to witness the death of their clans. In the bleachers, the more fragile would wail and pull their hair in lamentation as the precious essence of their offspring was lost by their running four cruel, endless laps around a cinder oval of torment.

"I can't look," sobbed Madame Lee, Zee Zee's mother. She pushed at Tall Amah. "Look for me. Tell me what happens. Don't scare me!"

"It's too painful," observed Tall Amah, peeking through her fingers.

"Is he dead already?" asked his mother. "Has he fallen? Does he spit up blood? Wang, can you do *nothing*?"

The herbalist had been hired by several mothers to accompany them during the torture of their doomed sons. He patted Madame Lee's shoulder. "See here, sweating doesn't cause death. Not in this season."

"Ay, stupid doctor! You know nothing! This is my *son*! His older brother, Gee, was smart enough to see that running was unhealthy, and he found a pain that kept him from it! Why doesn't Zee Zee do the same?"

Towering over the Chinese boys was a tall foreign white person in a suit. In his hand was a murderous-looking gun. *Aiyaaa!* cried some of the women. *Westerners are unspeakably cruel! They shoot students who refuse to run!*

"Oh, oh, he's dead, isn't he? Oh, Amah, is it over yet?"

"I don't think so, Taitai . . . I can't tell—"

"Ohhhh, I think I hear screaming—"

"Ladies, they haven't even started yet," said the doctor, sighing.

"Then stop him!" Madame Lee exclaimed.

"Not wise," offered the doctor, looking at the black pistol, "when you weigh one consequence against another. Besides, your son is healthy and strong. He has run many times before. He has good knowledge of it."

"Doesn't he see his mother up here, distraught, ready to tear my face?"

"I don't think so."

"Wave to him, Doctor! Stop him from doing this!"

"Lady, he is a strong boy and actually has an aptitude for the physical sciences. Besides, physically, he's done far worse!" The doctor didn't notice the amah's wild gestures for silence behind her mistress's back. "After all, he's been doing *wu-shu* and *gong-fu* for—"

"*Gong-fu?* What do you *mean, gong-fu?*" Lee Taitai stood, towering over the diminutive physician as he grimaced from his error. Some mothers crowded forward to hear of a wonderful disaster that could overshadow their own. Others showed teeth and shuffled away with small steps, leaving behind blankets, daughters and hot-tea bottles.

"The boy is learning some *wu-shu* moves. Nothing too terrible. I've only had to fix a dislocated shoul—"

Tall Amah elbowed the doctor, who took a painful breath and shut his mouth. He quailed below Lee Taitai's commanding height.

"How long has my son been doing *gong-fu* and *wu-shu*?" It was a simple question, but its complex consequences shrank his testicles.

A helpless shrug. "Five years? Certainly no more than that. I'm certain that's when I fixed his— Aiyaaa!" Amah, smiling, had stomped the doctor's foot, and he cleared his throat and quickly changed the subject. "Now, madam, don't vex yourself. Take slow breaths and don't look at what upsets you. Here, take some royal jelly to detoxify yourself."

Madame Lee swallowed the jelly with effort, glaring evilly at the herbalist. "It couldn't be five years," she said.

He searched his memory. "He was ten when I fixed his collapsed lung." He tried a smile as Lee Taitai fainted into Amah's arms. Amah sagged with the weight of her boss, but the doctor alertly caught them both.

"Aha, I have you," he said, and then all three fell into the stands.

The collapse was propitious because Lee Taitai missed the trauma of the starting gun's report, which inspired other women to faint, cry out or fall from the wooden bleachers.

Zee Zee, who had been running since he saw his first bird, won the race easily, but his sweaty effort caused Tall Amah to lose her lunch. The doctor treated Madame Lee for shock and the amah for indigestion, and left the stadium before his small role in this dark day could be remembered.

fourteen

The Rescue

T. A. SOONG AND Zee Zee Lee walked away from the cinder track after the race. T.A. was one of several pupils who had deduced that poor runners were never executed by the menacing starter pistol. Accordingly, he simply walked the mile Zee Zee ran, while others who had reached the same conclusion developed severe limps and shocking headaches and never reached the finish line.

Chinese students who despised physical exercise—which was most of them—shunned the sweaty Zee Zee and bowed to his best friend, the elegant and dry T. A. Soong. St. John's Chinese teachers nodded uncomfortably at Zee Zee while young American teachers hit him on the back, which was paradoxically intended to condone rather than discourage his labors. Chinese gentlemen knew physical contact to be wholly inappropriate.

"Zee Zee," said T.A., "you are a *wen ren*." A celebrity.

T.A. was brainy and studious and always spoke with the formality of a magistrate reciting before the Yellow Emperor. This was appropriate; T.A.'s older siblings had won incredible good fortune, and his father had helped finance and plot the Revolution that had unseated the Empire of China. Mr. Soong had not reshaped history so his sons could irrationally run in public and gasp like river coolies hauling barges in a dead wind.

"I'm no celebrity," said Zee Zee. "I have bad grades."

"That is because you do not study. Please do not walk so quickly."

"I study plenty," Zee Zee said, slowing down.

"Hanging from ropes and rings and boxing Hongkew thugs are not academic subjects. How are you going to help China without good grades? Graduates with top grades will get the best opportunities."

Zee Zee sighed. "T.A., I told you, I don't like school."

"If you study hard, my family can help you. Everyone remembers that Father liked you."

"Aw, come on. He didn't even know me."

"Father knew people quickly. It helped him succeed."

"So why don't you run, or at least walk faster on the track?"

"Running has nothing to do with success. It has everything to do with becoming too tired to execute top calligraphy."

"Hey, your dad worked hard."

"I also work hard. It is better to work with the mind and not the feet. Confucius knew this. I do not understand why you do not."

Mr. Soong had sold Bibles and was sent to study with the Methodists in the American Carolinas. He had become a Christian missionary and a publisher, and then a major industrial comprador and a shoulder-to-shoulder friend of Sun Yat-sen.

Sun Yat-sen was China's great revolutionary and the president of the Republic, known by the Western press as "the George Washington of China." Sun had married Mr. Charlie Soong's second daughter, a kind woman.

Once upon a time, there were three sisters, goes the Chinese saying. *One loved money, one loved power and one loved China.*

The middle daughter, Ching-ling "Rosamund" Soong, was the sister who married Sun Yat-sen. She was known as the one who loved China.

The Soongs were the Kennedy-Rockefellers of China. The eldest sister, Ai-ling, married H. H. Kung, one of the richest men in the world and a direct descendant of K'ung Fu-tzu, Confucius. She loved money.

The youngest daughter, Mei-ling, married Chiang Kai-shek, the lifetime president of the Republic of China. As Madame Chiang Kai-shek, she was one of the most celebrated women in the world and perennially one of the most admired women in America.

The two older sons, T. V. and T. L. Soong, became the prime minister and treasury minister of the Republic of China.

T.A., the youngest son of this mighty clan, always tried to guide his friend Zee Zee. "Father said to me, 'If Zee Zee makes good grades, he can name his ticket.' In other words, you can control your destiny. Because of my father, I have no choice; my destiny is to be a banker. Because of a different fortune, Zee Zee, you are a free person. I envy you."

"Well, my family envies your family," said Zee Zee.

"Everyone wants money. This makes banking very natural."

"Like indebtedness," said Zee Zee.

The Soong mansion sat among southern palm trees in Hongkew, away from the Shanghai Chinese mainline. Mr. Charlie Soong was a short Hainan

Islander with irresistible charisma and matchless drive. Zee Zee had met him when the Soongs visited St. John's three springs ago. He had been surprised when he saw Mrs. "Mammy" Soong's unbound feet. So she had come from a poor family or was a later-born daughter. Zee Zee had been even more surprised by Mr. Soong's personal questions.

"*Hao, hao,* good, good. Fine answers. Lee Zeu-zee, you're good for my youngest son." Mr. Soong spoke in southern-accented Mandarin. "My son is fast in the head, you're fast on your feet. My son worries about new things. You fear nothing. T.A. doesn't like to talk . . . you give speeches to the school! He comes from humble beginnings but understands money. You come from the gentry upper class but know about real life. Tell me, how is your honorable father, the son of the great salt-tax administrator of Yangchow?"

Mr. Soong had inverted tradition, establishing personal connections with an unremarkable boy before asking about the father. He had the curious American habit of shaking hands while still speaking. His hand was muscled and tough, and Zee Zee's calluses rubbed against Mr. Soong's.

"My father is fine, thank you, sir, and he sends his respects." It was what one said. Zee Zee had not spoken to his father for nearly a year.

A week later, T. A. Soong read a letter to Zee Zee. "Father paid a high-peak soothsayer to throw sticks for you and me. *I Ching* says you and I will be friends through many adventures. Our only risk is if we like the same girl."

"We don't even like girls."

"This is true, except for my *tsiatsia,* my older sisters. But someday men have to marry. What if we then like the same girl?"

"No problem," said Zee Zee. "You're older, you win. What if we don't ever get married? What if we are just adventurers?" His eyes were bright.

"That is not logical. We have to have sons and be remembered for great things, like our fathers."

Classmates ignored the rebel who was always in trouble and could run like the wind, and admired the earnest, introspective straight-A scholar who could find "trouble" only if he looked it up in a dictionary. One had a baba who ate opium. The other's father, a great man, had died shortly after his only visit to the school. The mourning period had just ended. For three years, T.A. had worn white sackcloth and sandals and had said little, which was very Chinese. He had stayed in school to honor his father's wishes, which was very American. A good Chinese son would have withdrawn totally from life for three years.

They could now see the place on campus where Mr. Soong and his wife had stood that day. "I can't believe your father is dead," said Zee Zee.

T.A. was his closest pal, but even so, he couldn't say, *People think your dad was poisoned. Two weeks after visiting us, he was dead. Your older brother said it was the cancer god. I don't think so. He was strong when I met him! But he had too much money and power, I bet big cash he had bad enemies. Pan says you dad was a Chingbang elder.* There was no shock there—to be a Chinese revolutionary, you had to be in the underworld. It was the only way to be safe from the imperial secret police.

"I remember what you said to me at his funeral," said T.A.

Zee Zee had said, *Your father must have been dying when he visited St. John's. So the last thing he wanted to do in his life was to see you again.*

"I think Father wanted to make sure that I had a friend for life. Do you think we will be friends for life?"

Zee Zee liked T.A.'s brains, but he also feared them. T.A. always tried to change his mind about things, and he didn't like that. Furthermore, T.A.'s money was trouble. The Lee family didn't have enough, and the Soongs had too much, so their geomantic balance was way off.

Zee Zee stopped; they were alone. "Know why we're out of money?"

T.A. nodded. He knew, but if his friend said it, the words would be an affirmation of their modern friendship, because it would be the boy's acknowledgment of his father's sin. From that, redemption was possible. Redemption was a Christian concept that many Chinese found appealing.

Zee Zee spoke slowly, saying that his father was a *ta-yen* addict, a friend of the smoke, a sucker of pipes, a resident of hard *kang* opium beds. He spent his money on Indian poppy seed and concubines. But it is a father's right to do as he wishes. It is the definition of a patriarch. There. He had said it in the open. He felt like a rebel, and he also felt bad.

"I am sorry, Zee Zee. That must be hard."

"Nah. Hard is leaving your home and running from cops. Because of the Revolution, that's all your family has done, move from city to city, avoiding the Manchus. I've had it easy. Look, I have to bathe and change. See you tomorrow." Zee Zee waved as he ran off towards the gymnasium.

T.A. was still changing when Zee Zee emerged from the showers in a Chinese blue high-collar jacket and blue cotton slacks. Zee Zee's Western blue blazer was rolled into a cloth sack with his books.

"Wait for me, Zee Zee," T.A. called, methodically brushing each article of clothing before donning it. Zee Zee impatiently tapped his feet and paced as his friend put on clean Western clothing.

"You have been up to something," said T.A. "Now I will see what it is."

A wall marked the west end of campus. T.A. had to run to keep up with Zee Zee as they headed towards it. On the other side of the wall was St. Mary's high school for girls. The boys of St. John's had a large, multibuilding wooded campus and a golf course; the girls had a brick structure and the loop of Soochow Creek. Across the creek lay the badlands of Shanghai.

"I thought you did not like girls," huffed T.A.

"I don't! But I'm sort of responsible for someone. Turn around, I'll be right back. Meet you at the Gate."

T.A. gratefully reversed course and began the long walk to the Jessfield entrance. He passed the administration building and the medical school. He passed a few amahs who had entered the Gate and would escort their St. Mary's girls from the dividing wall.

Outside the Jessfield Gate, a broad-shouldered Soong clan rickshaw puller waited to carry T.A. safely to and from school. The Soongs were revolutionaries who for decades had to worry about being arrested by the Manchu secret police. Now, as bankers, they had to fear kidnapping. The puller was a Cantonese expert in Chinese boxing. In his rickshaw were *liang-jiang*, double fighting sticks, several throwing daggers, a hatchet, a short sword, a long fighting knife and a well-oiled revolver. He was thicker and darker than most pullers, and wore no hat so he could see in all directions.

T.A. was approaching the Social Hall when Zee Zee caught up with him.

"What did you do at the wall?" asked T.A.

"Just making sure she was coming," Zee Zee said. Time wore on his emotions like bark rubbing on skin. He would rather run back and forth across campus to see when someone was approaching than wait helplessly while the sun began to set.

"So she is coming, whoever she is?"

"Not yet."

"Who is she?"

"Just a girl."

At the Gate, Zee Zee left his bag with T.A. and sprinted back.

T.A., like his father, was an observer of people and was happy to watch students emerge from the Gate and hail waiting pullers or pass their bulky book bags to waiting amahs. A few were greeted by their true mothers. Some proudly stepped into taxicabs and waiting limos. Older siblings watched over younger ones as the queue of rickshaws rotated forward to pick up their fares. Some students kept their bags and offered an arm to their elderly, slow-moving amahs, who came not to help their young charges but to honor them. Many kids were closer to their maids than to their parents. T.A. wondered if the same was true in the Western world.

The students knew T. A. Soong and the fame of his family. They knew that he was a private person who did not enjoy being a *wen ren* celebrity. His closer friends nodded discreetly at him. Boys studied his short, muscular Kwangtung puller, who clearly was a bodyguard.

First to come out were the St. Johneans who hadn't run the mile; then the St. Maryanns with big feet and the boys who had run and showered. The last were the schoolgirls with tiny golden lilies, walking with small steps, escorted by their amahs. Mixed among the groups were students of both sexes who had changed into Chinese garb. Occasionally, a Chinese or American teacher would emerge in tweeds and herringbone, bound for a special appointment that took them early from school.

Some pullers haggled and bargained, and everyone watched with keen interest as students and rickshaw men displayed the extent of their forensic skills and talents for negotiation. Some St. Johneans wagered on outcomes while St. Maryanns giggled behind their hands.

Zee Zee ran up. "She won't show up until everyone's gone," he said.

"Why?" asked T.A. "Is she very shy?"

"She's washing dishes," Zee Zee said.

"Oh," said T.A. "She is not a student?"

"Some students work to pay off the fees. I think she saves money by walking to her next appointment. After that she takes a rickshaw home."

"Really? Students *work* at school? How extraordinary. You know a lot about her." He didn't ask why Zee Zee would run back and forth rather than wait, or why he was following a dishwasher. It was Zee Zee. It was what made him intriguing. Money was security to the Soongs, for it bought power in an ungoverned land. Money had evaporated from the once-wealthy Lees, and this inspired conflict. The Soongs found political leverage while the Lees slowly edged towards bankruptcy. These differences made Zee Zee the most interesting person in T.A.'s ordered life. T.A. lived according to rules.

"Does the girl *enjoy* washing dishes? I never thought of this. Do people enjoy labor, Zee Zee? How does a student select a job?"

Zee Zee shrugged. "T.A., do you know a *Chingbang* gangster named Tung? Drives around in a car. Has a mole on his face. Ever hear of him?"

T.A. frowned. "How would I know any *Chingbang*?"

"Just asking."

"Do not ask such things. It insults my family. Ask your friend Pan, who *is* Green Gang. I still cannot believe that you associate with a Hongkew gangster who routinely takes money from gambling and sin. And that you learn *gong-fu* from his henchmen, who kill people for money." Whether his father had been a Green Gang elder was not the point. The point was that good Confucian sons did not speak about their fathers.

"I already asked him. See here, now, I have a plan for Mr. Tung. . . ."

In the street, the rickshaw puller waited patiently for Youngest Son, who had never stayed this late. The puller admired the boy's enormous control of his face and emotions. The puller was prone to screeching epic curses and even to trading blows with less respectful rickshaw men of competing guilds, and had even knocked out some suspicious men who tried to approach the Soong boy.

I learn from the boy, he thought. *And why not? His father was a great man, a father of China, and I'm seventh offspring of a nameless turtle.*

The crowd of students thinned. Only four or five amahs remained with a small clutch of waiting rickshaws. The puller stretched his hamstrings as he watched Young Master and the Lee boy wait at the Gate. He'd seen the Lee boy before, had watched him stretching his legs. Another student, always older and bigger, accompanied by friends, would come out of the Gate. The two would fight. The Lee boy knew *gong-fu* yet fought with anger. It would be over with a few blows. The puller thought it was good for Young Master Soong to have one such friend. But no more than one.

The students were gone. Any who came now, he figured, had jobs. The Lee boy watched a pretty girl approach. She wore the foreign blue jacket and skirt, white socks and shiny black shoes, but these were big shoes and she took peasant strides, shoulders and arms swinging with her books. She walked with two other *da-jiao* girls.

The girl said goodbye to her friends and hurried. A portly amah greeted her and took her books. They began walking down Jessfield Road, which meant they must live close by.

The Lee boy began following them with Young Master Soong trying to keep up. Confused and alert for kidnappers, the puller lifted the poles of his rickshaw and followed the Young Master at a respectful distance.

Jessfield Road follows the curve of Soochow Creek to Bubbling Well Road, which takes a hard left to the east toward the Bund. Bubbling Well becomes Burkill, where, five miles away, at numbers 30 and 625, lived the Lee and Tzu families. Beyond them were the Whangpu and the Great Sea, and beyond that the great foreign world and unknown mysteries.

The puller discovered that he was the last entry in a small convoy that was proceeding down Jessfield towards the Episcopalian mission. Young Master was in front of him, taking quick, awkward strides to keep pace with his friend, who darted from side to side in a juvenile's attempt to remain hidden behind the shrubbery and trees that lined the road. At first the puller laughed aloud, but when he saw the intensity in the boy's movements, he watched more carefully.

In front of the Lee boy was a big black Western four-door *chi tz* being driven by a Chinese man in a foreign jacket and cap. He was either drunk or homicidal, because he kept running up on the sidewalk, startling horses and nearly flattening several innocents. In the back of the car sat the vehicle owner. He constantly bobbed his head to look at the pedestrians.

What kind of modern sickness is this? wondered the puller.

In front of the black car were the awkward St. Mary's student and her waddling amah. The amah was doing a great deal of talking and looking about. She was a rural countrywoman who shined an eight-trigrammed *ba-kua* mirror at dark corners and oncoming traffic. She was trying to scare away ghosts and light-sensitive devils while looking up for flying demons, bad-luck signs and flying spirits.

Each time a new group of pedestrians screamed as it was terrorized by the homicidal driver, the country amah turned and flashed the mirror at the driver, which only worsened his behavior. One time, with a great crash, the car struck a camphor tree, gashing it with the fender and making birds squawk as leaves and branches fell.

The Lee boy hid behind a tree. Young Master, caught in the open, froze until Lee grabbed him and pulled him to cover. The rickshaw man had seen enough. He reached behind and slid the dark revolver into his waistband and palmed a throwing dagger. Carefully, in the shadow of trees, he waited. The girl and her amah were now some sixty or more paces away.

He saw the scene with the Lee boy's keen eyes—the man in the car was probably a *Chingbang* or a *Hongbang liumang*—a Green Gang or Red Gang hoodlum, now bent on kidnapping a girl for ransom.

The puller hadn't seen it at first; a girl walking home on big feet could not be a rich man's firstborn daughter, or her feet would be bound. And it was unusual to grab girls. But this one was very pretty and had obvious personality, so her father probably loved her, and maybe there were no sons. Her baba would pay clumsy kidnappers who didn't know better than to grab schoolgirls. Or perhaps this was a family feud of some sort. No matter, because it now involved, by connection, Young Master Soong.

The Lee boy was crouching, ready to spring at the car.

No, don't do it! thought the puller. The kid was quick, but this would be stupid, a boy with fists going up against gangsters with guns. He cursed bad luck. *Dung! What to do? Help him. He's Young Master's friend.*

The big black car disengaged from the bent tree, screeched recklessly in reverse, braked hard, rocked and jerked forward in fits and starts.

The Lee boy dashed from cover, vaulted the hood, pulled open the driver door, delivered a quick punch that drew a cry of pain and tossed the moaning chauffeur into Jessfield Road. The rickshaw puller began sprinting. Young Master Soong was attempting to run, his arms down and his legs scissoring curiously. He was moving towards the girl and her amah, who was screaming to all ancestors.

What under frigging heaven is Young Master doing?

The puller ran hard. Drawing his pistol, he yelled, "I have a gun!" at the hoodlum in the car. He ducked to avoid the Lee boy's quick wild swing. *"Tsou goh wan ba dan!* I work for Soong! I'm helping you, you *pigun!* You *huatou liumang!"* yelled the puller over his shoulder, calling the Lee boy a rowdy and a thug after casting aspersions on all his ancestors who had descended from turtles and running dogs. The puller stopped when he reached Young Master and the females.

T. A. Soong was breathing hard but managed, "Ladies, your honorable landlord's Second Son is saving you from kidnappers. The hoodlum in the bad black *chi tz* has been following you for days and was in danger of running over you. Ah, this is my puller, who will now take you home safely. Please to stop screaming . . . I believe I am out of breath."

Ah Tsui had seen the car hit the tree, the Lee boy jump over the car, the driver being thrown into the street, then the puller running at them with a pistol. She had dropped her mirror, which shattered on the sidewalk, destroying all her good luck and making her wail as she prepared to die, covering her girl's body with her own.

The puller exhaled, stuck the pistol in his waistband and bowed.

"Thank you both," said Da-tsien, looking over T.A.'s shoulder at Lee Zeu-zee, who was still yelling at the obese passenger in the car. Occasionally, the boy turned to curse at the driver, who had found his hat and was hesitantly running away with occasional backward glances.

"We're indebted to you." Da-tsien tugged on her amah, who shut up, dried her tears and bowed with her young charge to the two men.

Straightening, Da-tsien saw a tall, portly man in a fine long blue gown step from the vehicle. He had a pleasant face and seemed amused by the berating from Zee Zee. The older man was not arguing or even protesting, and Zee Zee was slowly losing energy and words, since he had no one to fight. The older man had a mole on his face.

"Aiya?" she tried.

"Yes," said the amah, sighing. "That's your honorable rich husband and caretaker of your future and father of your children and patriarch of your new clan, being threatened by a young gangster who is the son of an opium eater and our landlord."

fifteen

The Wild One

DA-TSIEN READ WHILE imagining a handsome boy-husband on a heroic black Manchu pony. She lurched and gasped as explosions shook the house. Downstairs a pot crashed. Worried backyard chickens ran in circles and angrily bit one another. Crows clattered from rooftops toward the misty harbor.

She had jettisoned her book during the last explosion and waited for Amah to retrieve it. But the booming drove Ah Tsui to quiver beneath a table, her bun shaking as she covered her eyes; she knew that if she couldn't see the Noise Devils, they couldn't see her.

Da-tsien hoped that Fatty Soo had shattered the white tile kitchen floor with the monstrous soup pot. That bad luck might encourage Mr. Tung to cancel her wedding date and free her from the wrong life with an old man! But then she remembered that Tung did not seem to be the sort of man who was deterred by trifles.

The unfortunate misunderstanding between Mr. Tung and Zee Zee had drawn the Shanghai Metropolitan Police, a detective in a blue gown and a Western rain hat, a hundred curious bystanders, a *Shenbao* reporter and the naked wrath of her mother.

Da-tsien had to rely on Mr. Tung's steadfast ardor to calm Mah-mee's rage. Only Tung could quiet the matchmaker's babbling hysteria. Da-tsien could still see the *chih huo's* gold bangles jangling in tune with her hounding voice as hot, angry spittle flew like summer rain.

The idea of marriage saddened her, which was normal for a Chinese girl whose only job in such matters was to show up and say, *Yes, Husband,* fifteen million times until she could safely retire by dying. Da-tsien had been reading Harriet Beecher Stowe's *Uncle Tom's Cabin* and was romantically inclined to try running for her life from her mother—the embodiment of Simon Legree.

The house shook again, but this time something strange and unknown moved her—she wanted to see the monster. She stood, waiting for Amah's challenge, then glided away under the cover of the noise to the grand staircase. Singh, the Sikh guard, was gone. Da-tsien crossed the marble foyer and stopped at the vibrating front door. The noises were louder now and the reality of danger unavoidable.

She had never in her life opened the door; it was the job of a servant. She missed the old Soochow home and its brave stone lions to scare robbers, the tall, dark spirit screen to deflect hungry ghosts, the lush garden that confused burglars, the thick walls to stop tigers and the canal that gave warnings of approaching boats.

Here, on a Euro-Shanghai street, only a door stood between a girl and the evils of the city. Outside lurked evil spirits that made her breath thin and reedy. Defiantly, she showed her fine, pretty teeth, then opened the heavy door and stepped into the brilliant sunlight of a summer Shanghai morning.

The racketing, rebounding thunder came not from a dragon but from an angry machine with two wheels that hurt her ears and put pressure on her chest. On it sat a tall foreign man in a leather jacket, goggles and cap. No— he was Chinese. She giggled—it was Zee Zee. A Chinese boy on such a thing! *Euew!* She wrinkled her nose at the stinky exhaust that blew from the machine's incredibly foul bottom.

Zee Zee looked at the girl. She had materialized tentatively. He thought, A *Big Shot's grandkid*—but he wore the same label. She studied him as if flames were shooting out of his head. He lifted his goggles, and the two youths studied each other in a rare moment without their amahs. She gasped as he revved the big seventy-four-cubic-inch engine, loosening mortar in the brick street and making her jump. He motioned: *Come.* She shook her head so emphatically that he laughed, his eyes glittering brightly in a smile that made her heart both heavy and light.

Later, she would wonder how she managed, in a red cheongsam with a modest slit, to mount the motorcycle's tall backseat, for she had no memory of doing so; and she denied that she had touched "that bad boy," much less actually held on to him, a fact that would have shamed the entire family for a hundred generations.

But this was to be the manner of their relationship—crazy impulses, stunning sensory treats, attacks on their culture and lasting wonder that they had warmly embraced adventure again and again while risking death. She couldn't touch him, so she sat primly out of contact.

Zee Zee gunned the engine, raised the front wheel and spun out, dumping the delicate girl on the bricks and rocketing away like an angry devil towards the Bund. He raced wildly through the crowded streets of the International Settlement to the French Concession to the Whangpu, faster, left, right, racing around turns, scattering pedestrians, cars, honey carts, donkeys and yowling rickshaw pullers, laughing at the world, before he realized that she wasn't behind him.

Ah Tsui found her girl wailing in the street, so she generously offered her opinion of the situation directly into Da-tsien's ear. "What the hell were you thinking, you fool! Insane idiot! Getting on that machine! You! Practically married to Mr. Tung! What do you think your mother will do to you? And then to me? Are you crazy? Are you completely nuts? What will the Taitai do? I'll tell you! She'll beat you! And I'll help her! And look at your dress! It *is* torn, just like I said!" Anger made Ah Tsui seem angular and sharp and her voice ferociously loud, for she knew that in good families, servants were beaten for the mistakes of the children, and if her blood was hot from yelling, the Taitai's blows would hurt all the less later. Besides, the loud voice kept hungry spirits from invading the wounds of her girl; she waited for more bystanders to appear and wail with her.

Luckily, this was not a good family; the Patriarch was soft and the Matriarch was quick with tongue and not fists. Now the clan women arrived on tiny bound feet. They fanned the girl's face, cursed foreign machines, lamented the horrible Lee boys across the street and wrung hands, adjusted jewelry and wailed to befit a planetary catastrophe. They acted out social mishaps with fierce emotion. That this energy was offered for such a small event, complete with gawking crowds and officious interlopers, was foreseeable. These were women who had no voice in life, and many of them were simple country people without access to opera and circuses. Both the poor and the privileged lived more fully in a crisis, for then full emotional expression, including misery, became entertainment. If relating was life in China, then life was good.

At the center of the commotion was miserable, red-faced Da-tsien. Her posterior hurt incredibly. She wondered if she had really sat on the foreign gas machine. Was it something a girl in a book would have done?

Peddlers appeared, offering popcorn. "*Chiao-tze*, dumplings!" "Fresh ginseng, good for nighttime energy!" "Fried giblet!" "A fur hat or a foreign-country soldier shirt! Brand new!" It was a tough city; only the dumplings were hot and succulent. The ginseng was old, the giblets weren't giblets and the apparel had been taken from the dead.

Auntie Gao shook her head, holding a black silk umbrella to keep the sun from Da-tsien's delicate, tear-stained face. Gao scowled at the Lee mansion. You could smell opium from the top windows. The Lee men were handsome but no good. *Poor girl! I'll put a red medicine dot on the right place to let illness and hurt escape her pained body.*

Da-tsien's mother hid in the house to be alone with her humiliation. Slowly, Taitai worked her way to the hall of ancestors to offer apologies, to share her shame, to unburden herself from this worthless girl, so good at bringing disappointment and now public disgrace.

Singh, the black-bearded, red-turbaned Sikh guard, had feared disaster. He had rushed on short legs from the side-garden latrine to the wailing women, his rifle at the ready, a clean round in the chamber, and was relieved to learn that the girl had only fallen. The women regarded him as a dumb steer that passed periodically through the house. He squinted at the warming sky, feeling the tugs of home. He missed India and longed to trek to Amritsar, to touch its holy nectar to his eyes and his forehead for true insight, to cleanse himself of this clogged, angry land of other gods and other tongues.

Only the crying girl had ever cared to know the holy meaning of his name. Interested in his faith, she had listened when he told her that The Elixir of Life, Amrit, was taken from the Five Beloved Ones and the all-powerful God. She appreciated that he protected her father from kidnappers, somehow knowing that he would die for the Tzus. She and she alone treated him as a member of the household.

Singh was glad no one blamed him for the girl's mishap; everyone knew it was Ah Tsui's fault. It was the amah's duty to keep the girl inside, not his. Still, it was bad luck that she had gone out the door when he was busy. There had been a lot of bad luck recently to lower the mood of the Tzu household.

Da-tsien knew the terrible fall had consumed her *chi*; standing could unbalance the intense life-and-death struggle within her organs. She sat, offering passivity to keep the greasy spirits from invading the seven openings in her head. She looked towards the house, but her mother now kept a distance from her, something everyone could see. The engine roared up the street, and she cried louder as others wailed. Singh unslung his rifle, thumb on the safety.

This is so shameful for Mah-mee, thought Da-tsien. And then it hit her: *What if Mr. Tung had seen this?* And she began to think in the manner of a girl doing business instead of a girl weeping in public.

Zee Zee spun his cycle, spitting gravel, and cut the engine. In the sharp silence, he ran like a foreigner, no care for decorum or civility or clan, tearing off his hat and goggles. The guard recognized Lee Zeu-zee, the neighbor, a weak student, a dice player and a colossal pain in the ass who used to jump in the Tzu house through the windows when he was younger.

Boots well apart, hands on hips, Zee Zee towered above the girl, shading Auntie Gao and her umbrella. "Why did you get off?" he shouted. "I drove halfway across the city without you!"

"Careful, young one," growled the Sikh, standing by her.

"Silence, guard!" snapped the boy with a glare.

"Not a word," whispered Auntie Gao to the girl, "just breathe! You need air! Then I'll get you medicine and a red dot for pain. No exertions, Young Missy!"

"Well?" asked Zee Zee, ignoring everyone but her. In the sunlight, in his brown leather jacket, he looked regal. No—imperial.

"Aiy," whispered Ah Tsui, the girl's amah. *"He's so handsome!"*

He's a pig, thought Singh.

Here's trouble in twenty baskets, thought Auntie Gao.

He's like a movie actor, thought Da-tsien. *So passionate! So much t'i-mien, personal force!* She imagined him mounted on a Manchu pony.

"AMITABHA! BUDDHA!" CRIED Taitai, tiny bound feet elevated by dismay, red clan inscriptions on the wall vibrating. "Oh, Dead Father, tell me these words are not of my world!" A bad sign, talking to the dead before noon. She turned to her daughter, soaking in an herbal bath to leach out the dark blue bruise that was darkening her posterior. "Are you crazy, are you completely without brains? We can't refuse marriage to a good man, so you can chase a wild one on a demon machine! You cannot do this! You *cannot* meet men on your own! Particularly males like *him!* Touching him! This is not done! I go crazy from your insane thoughts!"

Unbalanced from the fall, Da-tsien argued. "Mah-mee, we met through family business. You sent me to him to reduce our rent."

"This does not make it legitimate! Seeking a discount does not mean *touching* him! I would scream, but I lack strength. Aiya! It doesn't *matter* without clan introductions. This is so typical of you! Look at the signs. You have fleeting contact with him, you lose judgment and you find yourself upside down on the street in front of the world, wailing like a baby, hurt, disgraced and humiliating the *jia* and me. And now you argue with *me.* . . ."

Da-tsien's mother sat by the window, where she could see brightly colored birds in her garden. The light played on her regal profile. Da-tsien sat in the tub, partially concealed, head down, remorseful but defiant, confused yet delirious.

"Da-tsien, I am the smartest person in this house. You love Baba, but he has the good sense of a leaky teapot. He says, *Marry a modern man who can protect us in bad times.* Ha! It is laughable, so I say again, *ha!* All men need money. Tung is rich. The Lees are almost poor."

"So are we."

"Which makes money *more* important. Daughter, you have to marry *up* for your sons. Not *down.* This man, he has money!" She held up Mr. Tung's gold-framed photo in both hands, nodding to it solemnly as if it were a holy Buddhist icon. "Tung is wise, bighearted, kind."

"He's old and has a mole on his face," Da-tsien said.

"Aiyaaa! What counts—a gentle man with a mole, or a boy with no heart who wants to fly airplanes and kill? That's not honorable!"

Merely thinking about airplanes and their frightening bad-luck sounds made Da-tsien feel ill. She forced herself to respond to her angry mother. "Zee Zee just wants to protect China."

"Ridiculous. He can't even protect *you*."

"Mah-mee, he protected our house by lowering our rent."

"He did not do that. Their domo did." Taitai stopped and raised a finger. "Okay, it's true, Zee Zee helped in some mysterious way, and I'll repay him with gold and warm thanks, but not with my only daughter and our future grandsons. Hey, Tung has good calligraphy, good character. Lee writes like a rooster."

"Mah-mee, Zee Zee is handsome and that man isn't!" Her palms splashed water helplessly.

Taitai's face radiated pain. "You are not in an American movie. This is about your husband and your future sons. Handsomeness means nothing. Character determines fate. Calligraphy reflects rectitude."

"No, Mah-mee! This is my life! Handsome men have handsome sons."

"Where do you get this stupidity about your life and looks? Movies?"

"I got it from you. You said that about Baba."

"Aiy. You kill me with disrespect and destroy *shiao*, filial piety. Well, maybe I did and maybe I didn't, but looks were *nothing* compared to his name. His family name was nothing compared to the debt our wedding fulfilled for our fathers. You are part of a *jia*. We're tied tight, not free-floating ghosts! Ah, your baba exposed you to *Da-Bi*, Big Noses, the Christians. He gave you a tutor when what you needed to learn were life lessons and wisdom."

"The foreigners made me better."

"They made you worse. This man we found for you, Da-tsien, he's honorable. You shame me and the clan by your evil resistance to what is right."

"Zee Zee wants to protect us," Da-tsien said, subdued. "That's honorable."

"Oh, like hell! He can't even protect his new money. Those people have salt in their ears! The only thing dirtier than salt work is the opium trade, and his father smokes that! They got lucky in the Taiping trouble, winning a franchise without scholarship. And it was in *salt*—the poison of brigands, pirates and thieves. Da-tsien, his grandfather was a prisoner of the Taipings *and* the

Manchus. A double thief who knew where the Taiping loot was, winning wealth with a cheap country abacus. Now the grandson talks *airplanes!*"

"Oh, Mah-mee, airplane pilots earn lots of money. And he says if we don't stop the foreigners, they'll take everything."

Taitai couldn't argue with that, so she quickly said, "Who cares if there are no sons of good blood? The Lee boy gives us heart attacks! That is not honorable. He is a so-so student, also not honorable. He has bad friends, which is below mention. Tung pays his debts. *That's* honorable."

"Zee Zee's friends are rich!"

"Then marry his friends." Birds called against the darkening sky in tiny, high summer chirps.

"I don't want to marry anyone! I want to make my own choices!" She had blurted the words without thought.

There was a long and sad silence. "Oh. So. This is it. I see. Now the truth, from a stupid person." Her mah-mee was then so quiet that Da-tsien had to shut her eyes. She was going to take it back, but her mother spoke.

"You cannot talk like this and be my daughter or a daughter of this *jia*." Whispering, she said, "The foreigners have stolen your heart, and you are without value. You argue with me about a boy you do not wish to marry, hiding your secret, your inner desire to be an individual without family. You know, Daughter, I just now tried to imagine Zee Zee as your husband, but all I see are loud, burning airplanes falling from the sky."

"I'm sorry, Mah-mee, to be so weak. For not wanting to marry."

"Then change your mind. Your disturbing thoughts will not give you sons or support you. Or give you a house and cash, a good clan name for your grandchildren and security in old age."

"I don't care about that. That's old-fashioned. These are modern times."

"Then you'll die alone. Life's becoming more dangerous, not more safe." Taitai had a habit of inspecting the backs of her hands for liver spots, as she was doing now. "You don't see Zee Zee for who he is."

Da-tsien closed her eyes. Mah-mee had aged so much. Running her web of relationships had worn her down. Da-tsien's heart broke as she realized, *I made her old.* She felt the disappointment of ancestors.

"Second sons of sick men should honor their elders more than anyone, living Confucius more nobly," said Taitai. "Does he have *guan shi*, links? No, the boy's almost an outcast. He runs with Hongkew gangs and *Chingbang liu-*

mang hoodlums, no *shiao* for his father or peace for his community. He's like his machine—loud, angry and very dangerous."

"You don't see the good in him," said her daughter softly.

"Daughter, what if there's no good to see?"

"Mah-mee, you said I have a good business mind, that I can measure the insides of men. Why can't you trust me like you did with rent? I can see inside this boy. He's good! How can I be so wrong about this?"

"Because you're young, and because rent and marriage are like lakes and desert. I see what you can't. I'm your mother. I know what can hurt you. I have the years and the tears on you." *I forgive you for raising your voice to me, because I have failed you. I failed to instruct my husband, and I couldn't teach you. Ah, so it is. This, this is true misery.*

"*K'e ji fu li,*" Taitai whispered, the great Confucian saying, *Subdue the self and do right,* rolling across her tongue like an ancient benediction. She was lost in her own thoughts and didn't hear Ah Tsui dry and dress her daughter, clucking as she inspected the bruising.

Taitai studied the birds in the sunlight. "Da-zee," she said, forcing kindness to push away the hardness of her last words. "His father smokes opium and collects women, so the son is angry, racing around, looking for his unloved heart and trying to kill people with a Big Nose machine. You're one of his accidents. He means you no harm. But harm is what he offers. He does not submit himself to anything. Such men invite ungodly disasters."

"But I think I could love him. . . ."

"Listen. You're stricken with the *idea* of him. Even if you did love him in time, such love only makes misery. Have you ignored all the stories of antiquity, of so-called *love* destroying hearts and clans? *Family* makes life. The great powerful network of people in the *jia,* dedicated to you, promised to your safety, people who care. People who will die for you—*this* is how we live. We live on good relationships. Zee Zee doesn't have them. It's not his fault that he lives for hot moments that produce all the tragedies of human nature; his father did not guide him, and his background tastes of salt.

"Do we know his sixty geomantic signs and if he is in the Tao water cycle? No. Have they been measured against ours? No. What do the sexagenarian calendar and its permutations of fate say about the portent of his hour, day, month and sign of birth for us? We do not know. Do we even know his eight characters? I do not. Do you? Are you serious, Daughter, that you would flirt with a stranger unknown to us *and* heaven?"

She gathered her final argument. "Da-zee, do you remember Soochow? The household on New Year's, feasting in joy, trading good wishes, toasting with hot wine, forgiving all debts, repairing broken relationships. The music of the *p'i-p'a*, the boats with moon lanterns, the tough canal men singing to us? The sweet laughter of children and old women. The two hundred of us, unified by commitment to each other. Oh, I do! Believe me, I do! I can close my eyes and feel them and see them and hear them, even now with my fading senses. With *that*, we are *so* strong. Daughter, there, you are so safe. Can you see Soochow, and then the dark house across the street? The Lees have none of that. You need to remain Chinese!"

"Mah-mee, I am Chinese. I haven't taken a Western name, like so many of the girls at St. Mary's."

"That means nothing! We Chinese can change our names at any time to change our luck. And you didn't pick one because you couldn't make up your mind! Lily, or Pola, or Greta, or Lillian—all for foreign actresses who have fat bosoms, ghostlike hair and sightless, colorless eyes. Remember, Daughter, you need your clan!"

Da-tsien didn't need clan, because that clan in Soochow was gone, and its days of greatness had passed. Her mind was soaring on modern thoughts of freedom, her spirit intoxicated with the alluring idea that she could carve even a part of her own path. She could take the name Diana, so similar to Da-tsien. Or Diane. Or Dolly . . . She thought, *I need my freedom.*

"We gave twelve hundred dollars to the matchmaker. Wait one month and Tung will withdraw. We have no money for another deal."

Silence.

Her mother smiled. Her face was handsome, but in joy, it was beautiful. "Thank you for not arguing. You know, Da-zee, when I was a girl, I fell in love. Yes, Old Me, your ancient, rickety mother! I know the sharp heartache, the sweet yearning to see him again, how the mind goes back to him again and again.

"Oh, Precious, it'll pass. See, Daughter, deep down, where *ganjin*, emotions, live, I'm proud of your accomplishments. Yes, it's true. You saved us much money. You'll be a good—" She turned.

Da-tsien had said nothing. "Da-zee? Why don't you answer me?" Slowly, Taitai inched forward and pulled back the bath curtain.

Her daughter was gone. Trying to hurry on broken stumps to the stairs, she heard the door open.

"You can't marry him!" she screamed down the staircase. "You'll shame us forever! Aiyaa! Ingrate! Spoiled egg! Fox Spirit Girl! I wash my hands of you! I curse the bastards you want with this rebel, this wild person with filthy foreign ideas that can only pollute you!"

sixteen

You Are My Pleasure

IT WAS JULY in Shanghai, a time when wet heat killed old rickshaw pullers and shops closed before the owners fainted, but still her father fished in the direct sun. "Hook the shrimp," he said, offering the squirming bait and the barb. Baba sat among other men at the Whangpu River's Nantao docks in a wicker chair made in a port town of the Philippine Sea.

Da-tsien and her amah shuddered. When she was small, Da-tsien had set the bait eagerly. As she grew older, the hook became barbarous and the poor shrimp drew all her Taoist sympathies. She had become a young lady.

"Bait tastes better than the fish," whispered Ah Tsui as the humid heat beat down. Baba placed the fish he had caught in a tub of water, hating to kill his catch. He trailed his hand in the water, petting their glistening skin. "Ah," he said, "the pleasure of the tug on the hook! The good luck of so many fish!"

Her father took a wet towel from Singh and draped it over his head, sighing as water coursed down his thick neck. He faced the river with his pole; Singh set his campaign hat, cocked a hip for a long wait and faced the city with a slung rifle, missing his people of the Ganges.

"Your mother is right," Baba said. "I've taken big chances with your feet and your brain, letting both grow big. But marriage, that's her business, not mine. I have to leave her something."

"But Baba, this is my life."

"This is a very strange idea, that your life belongs not to the clan but to you alone," he said gently.

"I've seen foreign movies, Baba. Girls can own their lives. My marriage is my life!"

"Just *part* of your life. Look at me, *mian du mian*." Face-to-face. Singh, understanding more and more Chinese, respectfully moved away. Da-tsien faced her baba, smiling at his kind expression.

"Here I sit. I'm a little on the big side, right? I have an easy heart, no anger, no rushing about. A relaxed person, isn't that right? Bad things happen to me, but I don't take it out on small people." A tug on his line, then nothing. "I grew up with money, but I don't live for it. Everyone knows this about me. I like children." His eyes twinkled. "You are my pleasure."

His daughter beamed, looking into his eyes.

"The matchmaker, she's a funny little lady. She says to me and your mah-mee, 'Tzu *syensheng*, she says, here is Tung. He is a big man, like you. No anger in his heart. Slow and careful. Grew up with money, doesn't live for it. Likes children. Yes, the old *chih huo*, she knew how to set a deal."

Da-tsien stopped breathing.

"Am I so bad that a similar man is unacceptable to you?"

She wanted to throw her arms around him like a little girl, but while the Tzu family had learned many new things, there were still limits.

"I don't need two fathers," she said softly. "Baba, I have you."

"Is Tung so bad? A man who follows his arranged bride around town in a car for weeks can't be too terrible. He obviously has some actual affection for you. He looks forward to being your husband."

"You said I should marry a man who can protect me. Tung is old and fat."

Her father smiled. "Tung is rich. Money means safety, bodyguards, many men like our good man Singh. He can take care of you." Pretending to look at the great smoking, churning harbor, he studied her. "You don't want Tung because you don't want an arranged marriage."

She put her face in her hands, ashamed, trying not to cry.

"Ah, not your fault, Daughter. It's mine. I'm not a good man. If I were, you would take to the rituals. See, I resist our own culture! And so do you. Confucius has become something of a stranger to both of us."

She looked up with wet eyes. "But you are the best man I have ever known! Ever!"

He smiled. "No more words for a while." He needed to think. He needed to see the future. He turned away from the river and faced *hsi*, the west, the past, where he could see tomorrow returning as it always would for the Chinese. His breath was ragged, and he shut his eyes and ears. He heard bronze Tibetan bells, Mongol cymbals and Korean hourglass drums. He saw the words of Men Fu-tzu, Mencius: *Love heaven, and the world is right. If you rule your own nation, who can insult you?* He had done this sort of reflection as a youth. He had never before done it in the presence of his daughter. He heard ship's whistles and returned from his thoughts.

"Da-tsien, does Zee Zee like children?"

"Probably. I'm sure he does." She frowned, trying to remember what made her think this.

"You have a modern relationship. You met like storybook people in a dream world, like butterflies in a flowered field, without caring for the future, without the *chi huo*'s pricey brokering to ensure that the families matched and the auguries promised good fortune. You took your own chances and risked your heart without the counsel of family. Right?"

She nodded. Described that way, she sounded incredibly stupid.

"So now *you* must get the answers that count. Ask him, *mian du mian*, if he likes children. There is no more important question."

"Why, Baba? Why's that so important? Many men don't like children. Only the mother must like them." She paused. "I thought you'd ask about his birth year, geomantic signs, the signs of his father, if he has the high Tao sign, which is so good for the Tzus."

Her father checked his pole, a strong classic Kiangsu bamboo rod with a French spinner and a fine thumb lock, good for pulling a fighting cod or a stubborn crappie from the tidal currents of the Whangpu. He didn't look at the massive gray foreign battle cruisers anchored darkly upriver off the Bund, or at the clouds of black factory smoke that hung as if the city were afire, choking on its modern advantages. He looked into a middle distance. "Bad times are coming." He smiled. "It's the Taipings all over again. Very bad times. If it gets terrible, women will have to run with their small ones. The women who survive will have husbands who like their children. Best for you if your husband loves your daughters and would rather die than drop them on the road like paper money. Blood must survive." The line quivered; he relaxed, ready to set the hook in the mouth of a great river cod.

Teacher Chen the Hanlin had taught her about the Taipings, the foreign-god rebels who cut off their slave queues and tried to wipe out the Ch'ing, the Manchu Dynasty. Taipings took the great southern capital of Nanking by siege and threatened Shanghai until Chinese armies under Lee Hung-chang and Tseng Kuo-fan beat them. It took fourteen years, set China aflame, ruined historic croplands, turned orchards into cemeteries, made Christianity a deep Chinese sin and killed twenty million souls.

Of course, she knew that girl babies had been abandoned by refugees. Da-tsien said a quick prayer for them. She remembered that some clans, like the Lees across the street, had taken advantage of the war to become rich.

The fish nibbled the shrimp. A Japanese longboat sounded its bell as it approached the quay, bobbing her father's taut fishing line, which went slack. Japanese sailors in duck whites modeled after the British navy stepped out, forming flanking lines for an officer. Soon the Japanese empire would take this smoking foreign city and conquer the fabled Dragon Empire of Great China itself. A sailor spat at Singh. The guard bristled, praying for control of himself. The sailors left. Baba wiped his hot face and handed the dry towel to Singh, who took it while handing him a fresh one. Silently, Baba gently patted his bodyguard's shoulder, his comforting hand saying *Thank you.*

Da-tsien did not look at the sailors. Their appearance hurt her eyes and put pressure on her heart. Whenever she wanted to dislike Zee Zee Lee, all she had to do was imagine him in a uniform. It made him ugly.

Her father was speaking. "Little Precious, you're number one at *lun*, relationships. Already elders seek your advice, like Fatty Soo having you mediate her problem with her second brother-in-law, and Auntie Gao asking whether she should break the toes of that Jin clan daughter.

"You have only one bad *lun*, you know. Which one is it?"

"Mah-mee."

"That's right. No, don't feel bad—it's my fault. I don't give her enough respect, and you always take my side, making it two on one. I never thought it mattered, because she always wins anyway. If I were virtuous, I'd respect *all.* I'd work very, very hard; Confucius did and my wife does and you do, but I won't." He laughed. "I like reading and fishing too much. I'm too picky about my employer.

"Little One, you can't be good with everyone else and be a disrespectful daughter. Listen to her. Honor her. *Then* see if you can work your magic on her where the Lee boy is concerned. Don't do it to change her mind, although you very well may. Do it to change your heart's attitude. Be a good daughter first."

"Yes, Baba." She bit her lip. "Baba, do you approve of him?"

"I admire your spirit. But be ready; this Zee Zee might be too much for even your mother's great abilities to adapt. There is no question that she is opposed to him." The sailors had scared away the fish. Gently, Baba poured his tub of fish into the river, patting the last one into stirring before it flopped into its brown, muddy, oil-streaked river home. "We've had enough diversion. Let's go back."

"I told Mah-mee that I think I love him, Baba," she said so softly that he thought it might have been the fish's tail saying goodbye. "But it's not true. I think he's very dashing. I don't want to marry him. I don't want to marry anyone. I'd rather stay here, with you."

He was without words.

Brandishing a fistful of American dollars, Singh immediately started to wave down an old taxi while shaking the water out of the empty fish tub.

She said, "If she thinks I'm headstrong, maybe she'll free me."

"If she *thinks* you're headstrong?" He roared with laughter. "You're as stubborn as a hundred angry Mongolian mules in the middle of a road!"

Da-tsien loved these rides with her father, and she wondered, *If Tung is like Baba, why don't I want to marry him?* Then she remembered the dashing actors of the American movies and the irresistible tug of independence that had become a siren song. She leaned near him, absorbing Shanghai's din as the vehicle sped and slowed around rickshaws carrying hard-faced men in long high-collared gowns, trucks overloaded with green melons, bare-chested men on bicycles, French colonial policemen walking in pairs, armed soldiers of twenty nations, tiny girl prostitutes from throughout central China and laughing male pals from the countryside, holding hands in the habit of peasants. They all passed as in a dream.

Outside the City, China was dying; so refugees packed Shanghai, some bringing money, others poverty, but all nourishing an eager, thin hope. The old habits, made obsolete with the Western economic and military intrusion and the weight of social inequity, would die hard, taking millions more with them.

In Shanghai, everyone competed for single grains of rice. Here, where refugees were stacked upon other refugees and fortune-tellers were doing heavy business to alleviate mass psychological anxiety, the foreigners felt rich and safe. But the Chinese knew the winds of heaven were shifting, and that a catastrophe to exceed all Asian catastrophes was on its way.

Da-tsien had seen the early snow last autumn, had heard rumors of the rise of birth defects in the countryside. A pale red ring circled the sun. Baba had also seen and heard these things and more. He knew horror would come from *tung*, the east, Japan, and he was right. Yet what awaited them was greater than war. China, after eight thousand years of remarkable stability and good government, was going to change everything by killing itself first.

"Help me with Mah-mee?" Da-tsien asked.

He could seldom deny her. He nodded amid the blare of horns, the screech of Sikh police whistles from elevated traffic stands, the roar of the Far East's grandest downtown, the urgent, hot, emotional, sensual aggression of too many needing too much during a deprivation that would dwarf all the histories of need.

"Daughter, I confess that I like Zee Zee. He's reckless, but he's a fighter. Ten years ago, when Dr. Sun Yat-sen pulled off the Revolution and the Manchus fell and we lost our slave braids to the barbers in the street? There were no warlords, and good hope was in the air like Soochow on a summer night.

"Zee Zee would've been wrong for you back then, and I would've stopped you from seeing him. Then stability, good family, good clan morals and rectitude were everything."

The driver swerved wildly, then hit the brakes with a squeal, heads jerking as a line of monks and beggar children passed. Baba held his daughter securely, then quickly released her as if it hadn't happened.

"I don't really want to marry him. I don't want to marry anyone! I just need an excuse to not marry Tung."

"Talk to your mother. Talk to her like you talk to me."

"I don't think I can do that, Baba. She's so angry. All she does is yell."

"Aiya, Da-zee, listen to yourself! You're criticizing her."

"I'm sorry, Baba. I was wrong. Please forgive my worthless self."

LATER THEY STROLLED in their central courtyard garden. Shaded by tall magnolias and *wutung* trees, in a crook created by a curving stone path, a tiny lotus-encrusted pond, sheltering plums and flowering bushes, in a space redolent with the fragrance of Chinese gardenias, Baba sat. This was his favorite stone bench, its center worn with age. Facing it was a small stone shrine of the earth god, flanked by miniaturized *penjing* cypresses that had the scale of full trees. The bench and shrine had belonged to his father, a fine herbalist who used to tell stories from this bench when both sat in a Soochow garden. Now Da-tsien sat at her father's feet.

"Your mother is angry because you don't confide in her. She is your *mu-chin*. She deserves your confidence, your inner thoughts. If you trust her and reveal to her your inner heart, do you know what that means?"

Da-tsien knew. It meant she loved her.

"Isn't this what life is truly about? Isn't it true that life and death are governed by fate, which we can't influence, and that love is our own decision, the only thing we can dictate by ourselves?"

seventeen

The Pledge

ᴢEE ᴢEE SAID, "This dingus controls air. It was totally closed."

The sunlit garage rang with iron hammers and the sweet, undulating music of rich Cantonese oaths. Pan welcomed his pal's diagnosis of his unhappy motorcycle, which seemed to have the chest disease every time he tried to push it up the city's western hills.

"It coughed 'cause it was suffocating?" he shouted. "Hey, air's everywhere! Why not inside that dirty little bastard?"

Zee Zee loved machines, and Pan's new '22 Harley-Davidson motorcycle, gleaming with power, was no exception. In Asia, it came in any color as long as it was black. Zee Zee had a '21 Harley, and the two boys enjoyed terrorizing foreigners, roaring at top speed dangerously close to Big Nose cops and armed Big Nose troops.

In the din, T. A. Soong tried to study economics. He distrusted machines and disliked a shop filled with hot banging steel and sweating profane workmen. Before sitting, he had cleaned the chair several times with his handkerchief. He visited industrial Hongkew only under Zee Zee's charming insistence. Here, God was absent and Confucius was a stranger.

"That is so dirty. I would not put *my* hands in there," said T.A.

"T.A.," said Pan, "you wouldn't put your *servant's* hands in there!"

Laughter. Zee Zee thought of T.A.'s many servants and their pristine fingernails. Pan thought of pretty Hongkew *dongzhi* singsong girls who had taught him embarrassment and pleasure in one lesson.

It was Pan's job to visit the red-pillow honky-tonks of the French Concession brothels, ostensibly to perform quality-control checks. He dragged Zee Zee with him, and wherever Zee Zee went, T. A. Soong followed. Constantly exhausted, Zee Zee would fall asleep the moment he sank into the down cushions of the opulent French sofas. T.A. would sit next to him, reading the Bible with a frown. The carousing always made T.A. focus on the Old Testament, with particular attention to the laws of Leviticus, until Pan finished his unspeakable business and they could leave.

That Pan actually worked in these establishments was verified by the constant presence of two armed thugs named Hwa and Fen, who kept one eye on Pan and his payment bags and another on possible robbers.

Soong's guardian was the Christian god of retribution and a tough bodyguard rickshaw puller from Canton. Zee Zee was alone. The three were joined not so much by sin but by their complementarities, for each had a trait missing in the others.

Zee Zee wanted to smooth the differences between the scholarly T.A. and the streetwise Pan. "This," he said, holding up his blackened hands, "is the price of learning about machines. This is how we get strong against the foreigner."

"Nonsense," said T.A. "This is how you get filthy."

Zee Zee stood. "How'd the foreigners kill thousands of us, huh? With *machines!*" He pointed at the engine. "There's the answer!"

"I shudder to think of the question to which that horrible, smelling thing would be the response," said T.A. "It's better to make money."

"Yes, because money buys gas," said Zee Zee.

"'Those who use their minds govern others,'" said T.A. "'Those who use their hands are governed by others.'"

"Brothers," said Pan, trying on the unusual role of peacemaker, "machines or money, both are okay. But I should be focusing on the Angel!" He extolled her beauty and then spoke of her loveliness.

"You marrying her?" asked Zee Zee, angrily speaking to the engine.

Pan laughed. "Shit, man, not me. You're the one with a girlfriend!"

"I don't have a girlfriend," said Zee Zee.

"Pan, you should marry Angel," said T.A., holding his place in the Bible as he looked up.

Pan ignored him as Zee Zee wiped down the engine. They were in the Hongkew garages of Pan's father, where sweating southern workers camouflaged stolen vehicles by switching bumpers, light fixtures, licenses, handles, hood ornaments, doors and paint. The workers were especially valuable because they didn't speak the Songhai dialect, and were therefore protected from being corrupted by the police. More and more, non-Shanghai men were being hired as cops so the old crime networks couldn't corrupt *them*. In the fall of dynasties and in a growing confusion of dialects and politics, crime and corruption were rampant. In fact, Soong and Lee believed Pan's father was armoring cars for rich clients, and because they had been raised Confucian, they never questioned an elder's story.

Lee was the tallest and the most physically gifted of the three. His face had an inner light that drew others to him, but his antics had always caused him problems. Now, because he had shown poor judgment during the tumult of a revolution, he had admirers.

Soong's face was smooth and untouched by the sun. He was close to being the best student at St. John's, while Zee Zee and Pan struggled with academics. During these long afternoons at the Hongkew garages, T.A. studied while Pan got involved in shady deals and Zee Zee did pull-ups, gymnastics and *wu-shu*, toughening his hands by crumpling industrial paper and hitting bricks. He engaged in high-risk brawls with the underworld thugs who were Pan's friends, rough young men who salivated at a chance to thrash a child of the upper class. Zee Zee's tall Christian mother wept as her son's shoulders, back and arms expanded to the size of some illiterate, sun-baked, *k'u-li* boat puller on the Yangtze Gorges. He was forfeiting the advantages of a moneyed birth and preparing openly for a dangerous life.

The three friends had a pact: T.A. would not try to convert Pan to Christianity; Zee Zee would not try to persuade T.A. to exercise; and Pan would not involve the other two in the criminal underworld.

Pan was an amusing youth who joked when he was in trouble, which was often. He carried multiple passports, lived hard, slept with women and expected little from his natural gifts.

"What if," Pan asked, jingling his keys, "women had ignitions, like Harleys? But no brakes!" He laughed heartily, guffaws echoing in the garage.

His mirth and his infectious, unrestrained laughter at his own jokes always made Zee Zee giggle.

"Pan," asked T.A., "do you think such thoughts please God?"

"Christ, Soong! God's too busy to hear what I think," said Pan.

"God knows all, sees all and has all power," said T.A. "Please do not use His name as an oath or as a method of expression. Even here."

"Yeah, yeah, yeah. Your god's foreign. Look around. This is Shanghai."

"And Shanghai's ruled by foreigners," snapped Zee Zee. "Besides, females are trouble," he added, changing the subject, tired of his friends' frictions.

"Hey, I love their kind of trouble," said Pan. "But what about the Tzu girl, the granddaughter of the Kwangtung viceroy? Damn, she's special!"

"She's an aristocrat. A real one." Zee Zee was of the merchant class. The increasingly poor merchant class. There were three strata in China: scholarly aristocrats at the top; farmers, who supported the world, in the middle; and businesspeople, who tried to take your money and therefore couldn't be trusted, last. It had been that way for five thousand years, until the foreigners invented Shanghai.

"I don't even like her." The words caught on his teeth. Pretending to dislike girls was an old habit from being fourteen, but he had liked her eyes, her face, her wonderfully rapid way of talking without pauses, even her funny way of walking. For some reason, those things endeared her to him. He sometimes thought about her when he exercised and wished she could see him fight.

"It would be a strong match," said Soong. "She is of a scholarly line."

"Yuu!" said Zee Zee. "Ever see her mother? A spitting dragon from a black cave. Eyes of a Yellow Springs devil, a ghost from the dead!" Pan had taught him how to disrespect scary elders, which, if he thought about it, were all of them.

"Yes, but I think the daughter of that dragon loves you," said T.A.

"You're wrong, but it doesn't matter. I treated her badly. First there was that deal with Mr. Tung and his driver and the police. Then I caused her to fall off my bike and got angry at her in public, in front of her family."

"Oh, this is indeed unfortunate," said Soong, frowning ferociously, which for him was a wanton exhibition of emotion.

Zee Zee couldn't erase the memory of that crazy scene in front of her house. He had hurt her and she had been crying in real pain and he couldn't stand it, so he had yelled.

"You keep saying her name," said Pan accusingly.

"Pan, she's betrothed. You see the Angel more than I talk about the Tzu girl."

"I hear the Tzu girl is very headstrong," said T.A. "What if her family asks you to marry her?"

"Won't happen. Couldn't happen. They're Confucian. Crazy talk."

"But what if the Tzu daughter wanted escape from an arranged marriage?" asked T.A. "She's *da-jiao*, and quite independent. We have seen that such girls can act quite surprisingly. After all, she washes dishes and walks home from school. What if she were interested in you, what then?"

Zee Zee laughed. Marrying someone like her was impossible. She had royal blood. He was a second son in a poor clan. The clan had bad habits, passed on by the males. He would never marry.

"Yeah, Zee Zee, what then?" echoed Pan. "Hard to turn down, huh?"

Zee Zee glared at them. "Forget it, her family has standards!"

Pan slapped his thighs as he roared, and Soong quietly chuckled.

Suddenly, the garage had visitors, and the Kwangtung workers were in a hubbub. Women appeared without escorts, one drawing more attention than the other, a condition the men verified with open staring.

"Hello, Pooh. *Hsia An.*" Summer Peace. A lilting voice. Li San-t'ien, the sixteen-year-old Angel of Three Heavens, wore a foreign dress and a feathered white hat under which flowed her long black hair. She was a *wünu* dance-hall girl with a beatific face who dressed like a French model and was fond of Pooh Pan.

Behind the Angel was Lady Du-chin. Angel had a perfectly oval face and bright eyes that made men's vision blur, while Lady Du-chin's face was long and square with a hauntingly deep black gaze. An off-white sheath dress respectfully concealed her form, unlike Angel's tight outfit. Below Du-chin's long dress poked tiny golden lotuses in gray slippers. She was a woman with an unknown past. Her bound feet and cultured voice meant that she had come from money, but now she obviously had no family. Also, Lady Du-chin was cursed with the abilities of geomantic prophecy. Being a seer was a fine gift for a poor, single female who disliked prostitution, but it meant that no nobleman would marry her, for her job was to touch other men's hands, to cast the sticks and to read the future. The future always included death, hardship and the loss of hair. What man wanted a wife who touched such things? Zee Zee thought she was in her late twenties, but no one knew.

"*T'ien-shih*, Angel," said Pan. "Looks like you stepped off a cloud. An expensive cloud!" He laughed happily, and everyone joined him. "What do you need? Cash? A problem with the Shanghai Municipal Police?"

"Can't a girl just miss her guy? Hello, Mr. Soong. Mr. Lee. Summer Peace."

"Hello," said Zee Zee.

T.A. studiously ignored Lady Du-chin standing there in white, the color of death. He had gone to a seer once on a Pearl River sampan, back in the days when his family had to flee the axmen of the Manchu secret police, in pursuit of his revolutionary father. The seer had told T.A. that he would live long, but that his charismatic father, known as Charlie Soong, would not. He remembered his father's funeral, the shock of his strong, undefeatable baba lying in a good red coffin. He had felt unsafe even among family, for he had no close friend to stand near. His older brother and he were the only siblings who attended, and they had always competed for the favor and the fortune of the father.

Lady Du-chin bowed pertly. "Mr. Lee, Mr. Soong. Hello, Mr. Pan. How handsome you young gentlemen are. Your presence makes us safe in changing times." She had a pleasant voice and enjoyed speaking. With her talent, she was much in demand in Shanghai, for from change comes anxiety. Anxiety begets a need to know the future. Knowing the future was her business.

"Still casting fortunes and saving for old age?" asked Pan.

"I am grateful for work," she said humbly.

"Zee Zee, Lady Du-chin still wants to read your palm," Angel said, then turned back to Pan. "Pooh, take me to the picture show, okay? A Chinese film with lots of crying. I feel happy today, so I can give lots of tears. Then you can take care of this." She handed him a citation from the French police for pandering—a standard request for a bribe and as routine as a parking ticket.

"We're working," said Pan.

"Then we'll watch while you do what you do."

Pan shook his head. "You'll mess us up. We're too modern—we can't ignore you and pretend you're not here. Go wait in the corner."

The two walked away with the same slow gait, one on bound feet, the other in heels. Zee Zee found two folding stools, opened them and wiped them off with his machine rag. They thanked him and sat. Pan studied Angel as she crossed her legs and lit a cigarette, looking around the dirty shop and whispering to the *wu*, the witch.

"Want to go to a Chinese film with us, Zee Zee?" Angel called out.

"Nah, go without me." Zee Zee loved cinema; movies were like real life, only better. But he preferred foreign films. Chinese *ch'uan shu* boxers had sworn to their guild not to reveal martial-arts secrets on film, making Shanghai's Mingshing Studio movies incredibly boring. Worse, Chinese women characters in these slow, romantic stories always made mistakes and then had to kill themselves. He did not find this entertaining and hated the sound of women weeping in the audience.

"Please, Zee Zee," said Lady Du-chin.

T.A. said tightly, "We pledged." Many St. Johneans had pledged to marry only Christian girls, or to convert their wives to the cross after marriage. Zee Zee had said the words because Soong had said them. When they had told Pan, he laughed so hard that tears ran down his round cheeks. "The great foreign god!" he had cried. "Holy fat dancing *bonze* monks on hot defiling coals! You know what that means! You can only have *one* wife! For life! And it's a sin to have another! Yuuu! What bullshit! Say you didn't promise! Christ, Amitabha and Tao! You're not even men now!"

"It is okay for you to offend me," T.A. had said, "but it is not acceptable for you to offend God. Zee Zee and I are striving to be—"

"*Frigging monks!*" cried Pan through hysterical laughter.

"Pan," said Zee Zee, "you could piss off a dead Taoist."

"Okay, okay," gasped Pan. "I'll be good. Just don't ask *me* to pledge!"

"It's just a movie," Zee Zee now said to T.A. He didn't want to think about the pledge, much less discuss it in front of a prostitute and a fortune-teller.

"The pledge," said T.A. softly, "affects everything you do with girls."

"I took the pledge," said Zee Zee wearily, "but it has nothing to do with movies. I said *if* I married, I'd marry Christian or convert her. Listen, Jesus used to hang out with girls like Mary Magdalene. Besides, most of us at St. John's aren't real Christians." He suddenly wondered: *Is the Tzu girl a Christian?*

T.A. coughed. "Well, remember that Confucius said that men—"

"Confucius is dead. No time for wives," said Zee Zee, grunting as he tightened the last nut on the engine guard. "We're going to change China, *right?* Going to move fast against many enemies, *right?*" He was done. He stood, stretching, seeing the future. "We're men without backward glances, *right? Able to fix the future, *right?*"

"*Hao, hao!* Empty cup to that!" Pan loved to yell male drinking toasts.

"But we are expected—" said T.A.

"To inspire proverbs! *Kan wu k'o yen*," yelled Pan, even though the garage was now quiet. His words echoed hollowly and caused the staring Kwangtung shop men to grin. Six of them were conscientiously sharing a very expensive American cigarette butt. It was like high theater for them, watching teenage boys talking to a fortune-teller with tiny feet and a woman in curious Western clothes that showed her body.

Angel was amused. She knew that boys made big noises about the future—*China for the Chinese, victory for the good!*—but all they wanted was sex. She liked Pan because he made her laugh. She slept with him because he had saved her life by letting her become a dance-hall prostitute instead of a Whangpu River corpse. She didn't like T. A. Soong in the least, but Zee Zee was a curiosity. She had been watching him, the tough salt-tax kid who liked to run with choirboys and river pirates, but she knew that deep down he was a romantic, and therefore a fool.

Seeing the Future

Lady Du-chin, in a death dress and tiny slippers, had cast the *baodze* for Pooh Pan, remaining silent as the sticks kept rolling against him. They said he would die hard, but the news was no surprise; the boy was trying to use up all his laughter before his years ran out. He even tried to laugh when, under the strict demands of her oath and her guild, she told him the truth.

"You will die while suffering," she said, hating the words. "People will spit on your grave." Most fortune-tellers were not as honest, but most of them didn't have Du's gift for seeing what lay ahead.

She admired Pan's life energy, but like her friend Angel, Du-chin didn't like T. A. Soong, a *huaren* upper-class snob who closed his face to her. Zee Zee was another matter. She wished to know his future.

The male energy in the garage caused Du-chin to tremble. Not just *yang* male power from the mechanics who, by living in Shanghai, had lost their manners and their sense of respect for women; everything was humming, as if the future were already here.

Angel's future was her past. Her gambler father, who owed the Green Gang money and a life, had sold her at the age of ten to the crooked path. She was treated cruelly by pimps until Pan pulled her from the *dingpen* shed where she was being sold to a troop of *k'u-li* laborers for two coppers each. Pan was adept at pilfering stored goods. It was still up to him when he chose to work. In a few years, he might graduate to taking merchandise in transit, which would require teamwork. Then he might become an opium dealer and later move on to the new high-profit commodity—guns. First he and Angel became friends, then Pan discovered sex. Angel hated it. Pan didn't.

Angel of Three Heavens was a beautiful child. Her rescue let the *toutsi* capos recognize that she should never again be condemned to the *dingpen* nail sheds. The proof came when a boss walked the little girl by a nail shed similar to the one in which she had once been placed, and she fainted. No, Angel could be a delicately flowered *changsan*, one of the famed Chinese courtesans upon whom the singing Kyoto geishas of Japan were designed.

A *changsan* was refined, well-trained, deliciously scented and captivatingly beautiful. She dressed in exquisitely swishing Shantung silks, hosted elaborate and complex banquets, moved like the leaves of the spring willow, recited T'ang poetry, beguilingly told gentle, erotic tales, exquisitely caressed favored clients while singing lovely *huagushi* flower drum songs, gave physical pleasure at supposedly storied levels. The problem was that the underworld leaders found Angel too pretty to be left alone. Eventually, they stopped her lessons and made her a dance-hall girl who served the bosses and hooked on the side. Pan had argued for her continued *changsan* instruction until the boss's disciples slashed his baby face and threw him down a staircase. If Angel loved anyone, she loved Pan. Ever since, Pan's father had assigned Fen and Hwa to watch over his son.

While Angel was becoming a dance-hall hooker in Shanghai, Du-chin was downriver in the Yangtze Valley, suffering from recurring nightmares. As a child, she could look at people and sense foreboding; she was less competent at sensing the coming of good. It was said that her mother forbade her use of prophecy except for predicting clan farming and marriage requirements, but the girl was under the control of the spirit of prophecy and uttered forecasts in her sleep. She could not stop helping strangers with a prophetic word. The rumor was that her family fortune had been dashed by a foreign company that bought up all the clan's workers, and so she had been sent into the world by starving parents. Such girls often wound up in Shanghai, the accents of original dialects lost with their hopes. No one knew her home province or what she saw in her own future. It was clear that she had probed the mysteries of I Ching geomancy and the Book of Changes with the steady scholarship that comes from being personally linked to your homework by redundant nightmares.

Du-chin knew Zee Zee's biography before it was explained: indifferent student with dwindling funds and a strange fire in his heart. For some incredible reason, he believed that not studying was patriotic. He spoke the upper-class Yangchow dialect and seemed to have brains, but he wanted to learn Chinese boxing and be part of another world.

Wanting a better future, Pan had to be able to read and write; all the new generation of rising Triad criminals could read ledgers and codes. To move up from being a mean river smuggler, he had hired Zee Zee as his tutor. It was no small accident that he had picked a guide who would rather fight than crack a book.

For payment, Zee Zee was allowed to train in martial arts with Smelly Man Him Yao. Him Yao wasn't a very good *wu-shu* instructor, because he was fat and he drank and smoked, but he remained a steady bodyguard for the Pans and a capable fighter, his muscle mass imprinted with a lifetime of linear and circular killing moves. He was a man of China's past, the part of history that appealed to Zee Zee.

Inside an echoing Hongkew warehouse filled with stolen goods and occasional bloodied prisoners from episodic opium trade wars, Smelly taught the aristocratic Lee boy to take a blow, to fall, to jump, to leap, to kick, to punch, to empty his anger and to defend with *chi sao*, sticky hands, and with the iron hand of the White Crane.

Yao had stopped his rigorous *ch'i kung* disciplines after the Boxer Rebellion of 1900, when half his teachers and comrades had been slain in battle, while the surviving half had been lined up and beheaded by the foreigners. In one summer, he had gone from being a young keeper of the Sacred Fighting Books of Wudong to becoming a juvenile delinquent in the alleys of Hongkew. Of the 365 vital attacking points, he remembered only twelve; of the Pa-kua fighting style's first one hundred linear moves, he taught ten or eleven, depending on his distance from the wine bottle; of the twelve Kao cycles of one-finger attacks, he taught three if his blurred vision permitted him. When teaching Going Three Roads, his legs trembled on the first path. The more he drank, the more he thought he remembered.

Zee Zee once asked him where the Sacred Books were hidden. Yao pointed to his head and belched. Lee was an avid but undisciplined pupil who never seemed at ease in Hongkew. Zee Zee was twelve when he realized that he did not feel at home anywhere. His eyes were always on the next street over, and he would look down alleyways as if searching for someone.

Smelly Man Yao liked Zee Zee because he had a high pain threshold and good luck. Yao avoided Pan because his old magic *gong-fu* skills allowed him to see the death mark on his scarred baby face. Pan's closest pals were his bodyguards: Hwa was heavy and Fen was a stick, and both could kill with their hands. As unalike as the bonded friends of Chinese mythology, Lee and Pan became friends.

Zee Zee liked T.A. and Pan, but his closest companion was Smelly Man Yao, who was quick to anger, yelled at the top of his lungs when he spoke and liked to drink a bottle of *maotai* yellow liquor so he could argue with imaginary dead comrades before falling asleep in the middle of a crowded room.

But if Pooh Pan's father asked Smelly Man Yao to escort him on a business trip, the bottle disappeared and he would pay a local *wünu* dance-hall girl to bathe, shave, massage and dress him. He would lovingly clean his throwing knives and store the scabbards in his outfit, then polish the killing sword he carried as openly as an umbrella. His young associates and students would curtail their thievery and gangsterism to watch him lumber to the limousine to await the Boss, his face young and clean, his long gray formless *ma-gwa* gown bursting with his barrel chest, his black homburg spotless, the huge sword bright on foggy days.

Three years ago, Zee Zee had brought his monkish friend T.A. to the Hongkew factories and teashops. It wasn't until later that all had learned the boy was a scion of the Soong clan.

At his foreign, modern Big Nose school, Zee Zee had seen a crowd form around a lone boy. In the better Chinese schoolyards, there was no single bully who drew occasional blood, but a gang of clan-bound students who tormented, extorted and tortured weak victims for years.

Zee Zee had stood up for the boy against the small mob without knowing the Chinese preliminaries—what were the relative ages and social ranks of the combatants? Whose fathers were the more powerful? Whose clans were the more respected? Was a blood fued involved? What villages would be concerned? What consequences would flow from the actions?

Zee Zee hadn't cared; he liked adventure, had a natural affinity for the underdog and felt like hitting someone big.

The underdog had been Soong Tse-an, the third son of Charlie Yao-ju Soong, the treasurer of Sun Yat-sen's Chinese revolution. Zee Zee was a minor school *pigun*, a rowdy who climbed buildings, and the Soong boy was a true scholar with a wise heart. They were strangers of different classes speaking different dialects from different parts of China. The Soong boy was a southerner, and even though he was tall and pale, the gang had ridiculed his height and dark skin. Tall northern lads knew the *yu* people were almost as short as the dwarfs who lived on the Japanese isles.

On this day, the constant ridiculing by tall northern boys had come to blows. Zee Zee knew his lessons. *Dodging and striking always beats blocking. One good move beats ten so-so ones. Hit eyes and groin, because* chi *can't live there. Confuse the enemy by varying attacks between fast and very fast. Top fist beats flat fist.* Zee Zee dodged some punches and hit the leaders hard enough to end it. In this action, Zee Zee was instantly resented; he had defended a weak, unrelated individual against a gathered clan of thugs. Only the victim admired him. Soong had to ask his rescuer for his name.

"Lee Zeu-zee," T.A. had said after the introduction, "my debt outweighs my manners. My unworthy family is enjoying momentary good fortune." In other words, they were multimillionaires. "Zee Zee, as long as the Soongs have money, the Lees will have no worries."

All Zee Zee's life, doing what came naturally had gotten him in trouble. Now, in the time it took to put his body between a bookworm and a bunch of punks, he had changed the destiny of his *jia*. In an instant, his father's consumptive opium and concubine habits and all their negative moral and financial consequences had been canceled by the allied power of what would prove to be one of the world's richest and most powerful families.

"Zee Zee, will you accept my friendship?"

Zee Zee looked into T.A.'s normally cloaked eyes to see passion and fire, gratitude and sincerity. Zee Zee nodded. He held his right fist in his left palm in the traditional posture and bowed ever so slightly.

"I'm just a, a *pigun*. I don't know what to say."

"Say you accept my offer." T.A. opened his hand. Under the shadow of an

Episcopalian campus chapel in the International Settlement of Shanghai, they shook hands like American kids playing sandlot ball. Neither smiled; T.A. was not given to levity, and to Zee Zee, the offer was too awe-inspiring for his typical, disrespectful grin.

T.A. felt his bond to the Lee boy so sincerely that he tolerated even the company of Pan. T.A. became physically ill when he realized that Pan had broken the First, Second, Third, Fourth, Seventh, Eighth, Ninth and Tenth Commandments. For all Soong knew, Pan had also broken the Sixth. *At least*, thought T.A., *the Fifth is safe; the boy is filial and honors his parents. He follows his father, even if he is a Hongkew syndicate member who walks the crooked way.*

Miss Du-chin knew the mechanics of this friendship before she knew the facts, for clearly, the Lee boy had little culture, and the Soong boy had enough for five men. Someday these three friends would clash. She really wanted to know if one of them would be involved in the Pan boy's difficult death.

She thought that Zee Zee ought to know from his boxing background that these unbalanced relationships would inevitably fall. It was then that she saw Zee Zee's lack of *chuming*, insight. There were things he did not wish to see about himself, so he did not look.

It hadn't taken T.A. Soong long to issue marching orders to his two associates. The three would (1) save China; (2) establish a superior modern banking system; (3) build a complete national railway system—the dietary basis for twentieth-century modernization; and (4) kick out the bad foreigners.

"I like it," Zee Zee had said, tightening his fists.

"What'd you say?" Pan had asked, scratching his head.

Of course Soong would be the national banker, for everyone needed money. He'd have to beat out his two older brothers and his three older sisters, who had unbelievable power and seniority.

"You be the orator, Zee Zee, so we get the money we need. I will learn finance. Tax reform. Land values. Railroads. Dr. Sun Yat-sen says that is essential. Pan learns Western police methods. Pan will be China's police chief."

"Jesus frigging Christ, that's ridiculous, Soong," said Pan. "Me, a cop!"

"No, it is not ridiculous. Shanghai's criminal underground—the Triads, the Green and Red Gangs—exists only because the government is corrupt. With good leaders, the crooks can take good jobs. No more corrupt police and bribes! And please do not swear in front of me."

Pan said, "You're crazier than a rooster humping elephants! We don't work the docks and rivers 'cause we can't get other jobs. We do that because those other jobs suck!"

"You were produced by unfortunate events," said T.A. "I forgive you." Unspoken was the fact that if Pan didn't agree, he'd become an enemy of the Soongs. Lee Zeu-zee was a Soong man, bonded by a pledge of *jias*. Zee Zee didn't do it for the money—he did it for the security it gave his weak father.

Pan cursed his lineage. He had a strong father, but his baba had riverboat blood and could never win a patron like Soong. He could walk near T.A. but never be close.

Lady Du-chin remembered Pan's words: *To inspire proverbs!* Pan wanted fame so much he could spice plain noodles with the thought of it. Soong had so much celebrity it was dangerous, for it inspired jealousy. Most men wanted beauty over life; Lee wanted adventure over beauty. He had bought his Harley with funds borrowed from the local salt-tax office, where his family name still had minor purchase. To pay it off, he'd have to work for the tax police and harass farmers and widows for payment.

Pan stared at Angel, reflecting on heaven. T.A. had gone back to reading; Pan would go to the movies with pagan girls, to no good. Lady Du-chin no longer invested much hope in young men; the life expectancy in Shanghai was twenty-five. Once she had read the hands of a foreigner. He said that China was like Europe's Dark Ages, when plague, war and famine made life nasty, brutish and short.

Du-chin's concerns for the future had been slowed by her knowledge that Shanghai was going to die. But in the meantime, she liked these boys. They trusted one another. Soong liked Zee Zee; Zee Zee needed Soong. Pan liked Zee Zee; Zee Zee needed Pan. Pan and Soong accepted each other, but only as long as the Lee boy was present. Miss Du knew that Soong and Pan would make history, and that was related somehow to the Lee boy. That was why she wanted to read his palms. Professionally, she wanted to know the details of the coming catastrophe.

She felt a momentary uplift from the boys' unspoken connection, their belief that they would remain friends forever, their conviction that nothing under a bright heaven could change their commitment. It was an old Chinese story of friends making pledges in peach orchards, fighting to protect clans and to restore rightness. This, truly, was the best of China.

But all Chinese knew that none of these stories ended well.

nineteen

Talking to Stars

THE STUDENTS LIT matches in the darkened theater, scribbling down unfamiliar English subtitles on notepads. The amahs of rich, high-achieving students held the matches while their charges wrote. The theater seemed magical, alight with fireflies.

Young kids watched openmouthed as Billie Dove, John Gilbert, Alice Terry and Pola Negri did silently on the screen what Confucian youths could not attempt even in their dreams. Boys came to see shockingly happy foreigners who constantly touched each other. (They also came to see the skin.) Girls came to escape tightly constricted lives and to empathize with a foreign girl who could make decisions, show emotions and wear minimal clothing. Elders, fearing foreigners, mostly stayed away.

Da-tsien, a good pupil who feared flame, had practiced writing without looking down so she could record the subtitles in the dark as the magic lights of American film soaked into her bones.

On this day, she stood outside the Golden Dragon Theater in an azure high-collared, pearl-buttoned, straight-lined *chi-pao*, drawing the stares of stylish women, foreign males and street orphans. Shoppers jabbered, and moviegoers exiting the theater blinked in the sunlight. She liked the chattering *le hu*, the entertainers—heavily painted females, expressive males and animated people who were neither one nor the other. The *le hu* were despised, rejected and could not be buried with good dead people, but they fascinated her. Her feet made her interested in people who were different in a hot, sooty city where the world's tribes had collided without apology or explanation.

Round Amah stood by her girl, watching for ghosts and planes, glaring at beggars, scowling at actors, shooing flea-bitten dogs and estimating what was going to happen next.

"We're going to die," she said, pushing away an emaciated street dog.

"Aiya, we're just going to see a movie!" said Da-tsien.

"You say that like we're just going to buy a chicken!"

"Well, it's not much different, but a little better for the chicken."

"Your dress is too pretty, and you'll be kidnapped!"

"The dress is nothing. My big feet discourage criminals."

"You don't know what you're talking about. Get away, dogs! Yuuuuu! They stink of garbage and filth! Get away!"

Da-tsien turned her hips from the dogs and raised her shoulders. Just then Zee Zee hurried around a corner.

Amah narrowed her eyes and shook her head, disbelieving what she saw. "No! My eyes trick me! An accident, yes? Missy—say you didn't arrange this, please!"

"He's a student. He speaks English. He can help me," Da-tsien said. "Do not raise your voice or you will upset my heart and liver."

Her amah could deliver a diatribe at any moment, in any part of the city, with the same staccato rhythm that was like the breaking of dishes.

"What the hell are you doing! You shame Mr. Tung! What will your mother do to you? And then to me? What will Taitai do? I'll tell you! She'll disown you! I'll never be able to work for you or anyone again, and I will die alone! You know you *cannot* see a boy on your own unless it's your husband, and then only *after* the wedding! You shame even me!"

The girl's pained look told her amah to be quiet. The daughter was like the father—giving too much to unhappy women, deaf slaves, chubby amahs and Whangpu fish. Ah Tsui softened her approach. "I thought these boneyard dogs spitting the plague was bad. I was wrong. Here. Here comes the best part of the day! Here comes the gangster."

Da-tsien held an inward smile. Zee Zee always rushed, racing as if his destination had a finish tape and St. John's coaches were after him with guns and stopwatches.

It was a fine day, but Zee Zee was angry. He tried to calm himself by petting the smelly, scruffy mutts that tried to nose his groin. Amah showed all her teeth and resisted fainting as dog dust, hair and jumping fleas floated in a dark living cloud around the boy.

"Where were you?" Zee Zee demanded of Da-tsien. "I was here half an hour ago! I waited! Then I left. I got some noodles. They were pretty good, but I was so angry!"

"Sorry I'm late," she said, recoiling and brushing away dog dander while avoiding his eyes, which blazed like unbanked fires. Still feeling Ah Tsui's hard, loud scolding, she added, "It was Amah's fault."

Amah nodded and recited her usual assumption of responsibility. She had dressed Da-tsien in plenty of time, but all mistakes were her doing.

Zee Zee ignored the servant. He tried to ignore the girl, but he kept glancing at her eyes, still not meeting his. "Why did you ask me here?"

Da-tsien marveled. *Everything he does makes smoke!* "My brother, Da-shing, admires your fast brush. I'm too slow and stupid to write down the new English words, but I want to be a better student in Teacher Roberts's class. I was afraid to go, and . . . and you're quick, and can help my slow and addled—"

"No, no old Confucian expressions with me. If we're going to see a foreign movie, then use up-to-date words. Be Western. Be modern."

Da-tsien took a breath. "Write words for me."

Ah Tsui wanted to spit. *Be modern,* she mouthed. *Be an idiot! Shame your clan! Make it impossible to be seen as a moral female!*

Zee Zee sent the round amah a withering look that made her drop her face.

Da-tsien politely coughed. "Zee Zee, where is your foreign black gas machine engine on two wheels?" She tried to comfort her quivering servant, prodding her to take deep breaths.

"In the shop. I can't leave it here—someone would steal it."

Da-tsien doubted it; no one would want to steal such a thing. Not from a boy who could make the formidable Ah Tsui tremble with a look.

D. W. Griffith's silent classic *The Birth of a Nation* had been released in America five years before and had been playing in Shanghai for three. The theater was jammed, yet younger students automatically gave up seats for the older. Da-tsien, her amah and the young gangster sat in the center. With a loud clack, the lights dimmed as thin stage coolies drew back the curtains. Vendors called out, *fried squid, grasshoppers, shrimp!* After the film, the stage coolies had rights to whatever scraps lay on the dirty floor. The piano player began sourly, and Da-tsien, who was studying Mozart, gritted her teeth.

Then, the noises of a Shanghai movie theater gained momentum. Students began lighting matches, their pens racing on paper, sometimes repeating English words to slower buddies. Occasionally a student cried out as a match burned down to a finger. Kiangsu country folk who had never before seen a movie gasped and cried aloud and pointed at the magic as images rolled past their widened eyes. Some translated at the top of their lungs in Songhai or Mandarin or Kiangsinese for the honorably old and feeble. A girl appeared on-screen, her face the size of a Ming Buddha, her hair as tall as a horse, and field boys who had saved their coppers for a year to buy these movie tickets hit one another and howled in amazement. Peasants felt very sorry for the poor foreigners, who apparently had lost the power of speech.

When lovers kissed, the whole audience fell silent. When sons kissed their mothers, there were cries of disbelief and murmurs of disapproval. *Such forwardness! Touching his mother! Kissing her! Strange foreigners!*

Da-tsien was not scandalized, and accordingly felt awkward and embarrassed. Sons watched over you and kept you safe as your bones grew brittle. *I would love my son to kiss me every day of my life.*

Da-tsien prayed for the people in the story and for a good ending. To her, this was reality. She felt very emotional; the people on the screen were interacting with her, sharing deep feelings and terrible crises. She cried as they did. She was not surprised that foreign people's emotions were much like the feelings of real people. Amid this cresting and falling of emotion, she found herself looking at Zee Zee without knowing the why of it. His face drew her to him. He wasn't the handsomest boy, or the smartest, and he came from a decadent clan; but something secret and unknown was making her yearn for him while the off-key piano played and the larger-than-life men and women showed their hearts.

Teacher Roberts from America had told her that God had a plan for her. She had a personal destiny that was related to her gifts. This was stronger than *yeh*, karma, which was related to her faults. Roberts, an Episcopalian, said that the Methodists were right: God was "prevenient"; He went before you, preparing the way and setting up help before your need was even known. China's future lay in her past, but God lay ahead.

When she was sitting watching a movie, Da-tsien knew with even greater clarity that she needed to escape her arranged marriage. She did not want to be chattel, and she did not want her own daughters to be chattel. Each time she went to the foreign movies, she found her resolve strengthening. Surreptitiously, she kept looking at the boy next to her to see if his rebellious ways were a part of her future. She looked at him and shivered with the memory of the missionary's words. Could she be connected to him by *chi tz* gas machines, road accidents and English? By sitting next to each other, they were defying her mother and the ancient habits of Confucius.

She liked his voice, which she knew some might find rough and streetwise. He had a good face, but his manners were atrocious, for a good Chinese man can show only kindness to subordinates. It was the way of her father and the way of his father and his father before him.

She shut her eyes during battle scenes—actors were being killed for this terrible and amazing movie! Waving her arms, covering her eyes, she actively advised the women in the story while fighting off Amah's strong-armed attempts to pull her outside. She could no more leave than pluck out her own eyeballs. She loved Elsie the heroine, who wisely followed all of Da-tsien's good advice, doing exactly what she, from her theater seat, directed.

The air stank of phosphorous, sesame balls, fried foods and nuts. The pianist took random breaks to highlight the sounds of eating, talking, pranks and the yelps from match burns. Quickly, the score mismatched events on the screen. No one cared. It was a foreign American film that showed a strange and different world to an audience that had lived in the singleness of the Chinese universe; yet they felt the tumult and madness in the story, and the disjointed piano made perfect sense.

Zee Zee identified with the mounted heroes wearing white robes. He knew he'd be a soldier—an occupation so despicable in Chinese culture that every member of his family viewed public hanging as a better choice. Amah, meanwhile, studied the geography of the floor and elbowed her Young Missy, while the evil spirits of the theater leaked from the screen and inspired the girl to talk aloud to the giant foreign images.

Emerging at the film's end, three hours later, Da-tsien blinked and bumped into the crowd, unable to find her feet. She wanted to recover a sense of her body, her mind, all of which she had left behind in the theater. Drained, she tried to understand what had just happened. She wanted to talk with Baba and ask questions, but there was only Zee Zee.

"Great film, huh?" he asked. "Hmm! I'm hungry!"

"I have just felt war and loss," she whispered. *God, Fo, and Amitabha, please, never let me see such things in person.*

twenty

A String of Girls

"SO VERY DUMB to sit in the dark with a boy," hissed Amah to Da-tsien, "but talking to him alone now is immoral. To do this right, you'd need the matchmaker's blessing—no way you'd get that. And Taitai's approval—impossible. Or fifty family members with us, and even a *mo li* magician couldn't do that! You are a bad girl! Come home now."

"The teahouse is this way," said Zee Zee cheerfully, starting off without looking back.

Da-tsien was afraid to move. She feared breaking convention and hated Amah's badgering. Awkwardly, she followed Zee Zee, hissing and shaking off Ah Tsui as the servant tried to tug the girl away.

Cinema was a new enterprise, and older industries, such as manufacturing, shipping and drug trafficking, had already taken the best real estate. Most theaters ended up in questionable outer districts like loud Hongkew and low-rent Chapei, where the neighbors were factories with smokestacks and a variety of foreign people and their failing shops.

The Hongkew Cinema Company owned twelve theaters that showed U.S., German and Chinese black-and-white silent pictures. Because of Pan, Zee Zee knew about Hongkew's alleys; he led the two females through pickets of begging children, hawkers and cigarette-smoking arms dealers to a robust, smoke-filled *chijiancha* crime-den teahouse called Twelve Goddesses, which in Hongkew street jargon meant "A Dozen Prostitutes."

Da-tsien stopped. Two coolies with sticks herded a gaggle of girls down the crowded street. The girls threaded through shoppers; ladies in elegant, gold-dangling imperial headdresses; cloaked Chinese Muslims and bawling merchants. Some of the girls were tiny, no more than seven years old; all were emaciated, dumb with fatigue and filthy. Each dragged a scrap of metal for the foundry, making a painful sound to compete with the gongs of monks and the cries of competing peddlers. The little panting girls were tied by their necks to a heavy, abrading rope, like animals on a death march. A few who were not much younger than Da-tsien helped the smallest with their loads.

Da-tsien stopped one of the men. "Please, sir, who are these girls?"

The man bowed. "Factory girls. But Missy no can buy. Belong to the *Toutzi*, the Big Boss. No good for your house. No fingers!" He pointed. "Hands live all day in boiling water, shake threads from silkworm cocoons. No skin left." He smiled toothlessly at her outfit. "Make pretty silk dress." A girl fainted, and the rope tugged as the little girls were jerked to a halt. Da-tsien saw their tiny fingers trembling to hold on to the jagged metal scraps they were carrying.

"Sir, they need sleep and food and care!" said Da-tsien.

"Sleep? Hey, Silk Dress Lady, little-girl animals don't need sleep!" He laughed bitterly and bowed and picked up the collapsed girl by the neck like a sack of flour. He kicked the lead girl, and they moved.

"No, no! Don't look!" hissed Ah Tsui. "Not for your eyes!"

Da-tsien couldn't shut her eyes: One girl was looking at her, seeing the rich Young Missy cry for her. The little train of roped girls disappeared into the mass of the crowd. Da-tsien was paralyzed, not breathing, tears running down her cheeks. Ah Tsui pushed her into the teashop and to a chair, fanning the air and pinching her to breathe. Da-tsien sat, panting like the girls outside. She had enormous empathy, her emotions close to her skin.

"Zee Zee, did you see those girls, did you see how they were tied by their little necks, dragging those things?" She had to say it twice; the first time no sounds came from her mouth, which was as dry as an old man's face.

He nodded.

"Zee Zee, what can we do, this is so wrong! Do something, please."

"What can we do? Join the Revolution." His eyes narrowed. "Fight the foreigner and the evil men who make children into slaves, who buy slaves from starving families." He was angry again.

"Tsa!" hissed Ah Tsui. "Say not a word, Young Missy! If someone hears you even playing at politics, you endanger your whole clan."

"Amah," snapped Zee Zee, "this is a Hongkew *chijiancha* crime den. Everyone's a Triad, a Boxer descendant, a guildsman or a Green Association man. All they talk is revolution."

Ah Tsui hunched her shoulders and said, "They do kidnapping! We should not be here."

Da-tsien shivered with the thought, but Zee Zee's intensity drew her. "I don't get it," she said. She hadn't been taught history in great shouts by Smelly Man Yao. "What do Boxers have to do with those poor little girls?"

"What happened when the Manchus crossed the Great Wall and beat the Chinese Ming Dynasty three hundred years ago?"

"They made our men wear slave pigtails and defiled our women. Clans lost land, jobs, horses, ships. Everyone knows this. Why?"

"And so who fought the Manchu from the start? Not Sun Yat-sen in 1912, or the Taipings in 1850. Who fought them three hundred years ago?"

Da-tsien shook her head. She thought: *No one. We were slaves.*

Zee Zee gestured at the room. "These guys did." He lowered his voice. "Triads. Boxers. Guilds. The underworld. Guys who pull barges, haul honey carts, sell human manure. Dirt merchants. For centuries, the secret-society men killed evil Manchu magistrates and sprang Boxers, Shao-lin priests and rebels from prison. From torture." He paused. "The societies helped any man who said *Down with the Ch'ing, up with the Ming.* In this century, they helped Sun Yat-sen. Our clans spit on them. I call them *patriots.*"

This went against everything she had learned. Teacher Chen had never mentioned Triads, whom she knew as robbers, tramps and thieves. "They kidnap people like our fathers," she whispered, her eyes large.

"Yeah, they kidnap rich men. Very rich men. How do men get rich in China? Not the old way—buy cheap, sell expensive. Now they do it by using children and laborers, *k'u-li* men from Chekiang and up-country Kiangsu, as slaves until they kill them. They steal these people at night! They sell opium and guns to other Chinese so we can kill each other. So we can make foreign people rich. People here, they owe the rich *nothing.*"

She trembled. He was talking about her baba. Ah Tsui covered her ears and sang a Taoist chant to drown out the rebellious boy's bad words.

"But you go to St. John's, a *huaren* school, and your best friend is a Soong, and you live in the Concession, with the rich." *You're our landlord.*

"I go to St. John's to learn English. Machine instructions come in English. Books on how to fly are in English. And I go because my father wants it. Soong's my friend because he helps my father. Remember, Soong's father was a revolutionary, and I'll owe him forever."

Zee Zee snapped his fingers, and steaming green tea, *kuo-tieh* dumplings and hot napkins appeared. The waitress inspected the red-cheeked *huaren* upper-class girl in her blue silk *chi-pao*, holding her school notebook against her chest and attended by a worried amah, then curled a lip and smiled as she deliberately mussed Zee Zee's hair until he told her to stop.

Da-tsien gulped hot tea to cleanse herself of many bad feelings, one of which was directed at the waitress. She wanted to ask how Zee Zee could recover his honor after a girl had touched him so privately in a public place, but instead she said weakly, "What if some of these men kidnap your father?"

"They wouldn't. He's kind of out of cash right now."

"Say they made a mistake and took him anyway, then what?"

He laughed. "You ask questions like T. A. Soong. If they took my father and I couldn't reason with them, I'd find cash and pay."

"And never have anything to do again with these Hongkew people, because of how terrible and dangerous and scary they are to us?"

"Hey, some of these people are my friends. Look, Miss Tzu, almost everyone in China's poor. Only about five people in a hundred live like us, but our class owns ninety percent of the land and has access to most of the cash. The peasant, the *k'u-li*, the factory worker, they work bitter hard, then they die. We rich have to pay our debts, too, in money. We pay in taxes, bribes, ransoms."

She sat back. "You're a Western radical. You agree with gangsters. You think kidnapping to get money is just another job!"

"No, it's wrong, but I understand why it happens."

"I want to go home," she said. Her amah quickly stood.

"Sit down, Amah," said Zee Zee. She sat.

Her eyes down, her lower lip trembling, Da-tsien said, "You cannot speak to my amah that way," *Too much is happening at once. It's always this way with him!* "I just wanted to talk about the movie. . . ."

He poured her tea, and then he was gone. The girl looked at her servant, both shrinking from the gangster patrons in the teahouse. They weren't sure about being with the boy; now they feared his absence.

Suddenly Zee Zee reappeared, bowing, clasping his right fist. "Young Miss Tzu, I am deeply honored. Your presence lends learning to a low setting. Thank you for allowing an unworthy such as myself to greet you. Might this unworthy one join you, but only to improve my thinking? Thank you," he said immediately, sitting tall and erect like a good student. "Miss Tzu, how many words did you write during the movie? You're smart and I'm not. I meant to write, but the movie took my mind. Did you like the war scenes? Weren't they great?"

Da-tsien was shivering from too many sights and sounds, too many new ideas and feelings. Her eyes were still wet from crying over the girls, and she had felt fear in the heartstopping moment when Zee Zee had left them. She nodded at him and then burst into tears. "They killed innocent people for entertainment! I can never see another movie."

Zee Zee, upon his return to the table, was trying hard to act like a Confucian, but the girl's naïveté ended that. "Hey! It was a *movie*! They don't kill anyone. It's all playacting."

"I saw blood! The tears were real! Explosions . . . oh, they were terrible!"

"They were fake. Make-believe. Stop crying. You embarrass me."

"No, it was real!" she cried, stamping her feet. "I'm *so* sorry for them and for their families. Oh, Zee Zee, please tell me that foreign film companies pay for the dead, and buy good red wood caskets."

Hard-looking men were frowning at her. Zee Zee shook his head. *And they say* I'm *crazy*. He looked around and found a hot-chili seasonings dish. He made a sound like a gunshot in the back of his throat, like boys do around the world, and jerked the dish so hard that his hair flew. Da-tsien cried out, Amah sagged, bodyguards covered their masters and drew an international assortment of handguns—British Weatherbys, American Colts, Smith & Wessons and Japanese Nambus—eyes scanning wildly for the shooter.

In the center of Zee Zee's Sun Yat-sen jacket was a bright red splotch. A bullet wound. Zee Zee grabbed his chest. He leaned slowly backward in his chair until he flipped over with a loud crash.

Da-tsien screamed, "*Amitabha! Oh my God!*" Other women cried. Bodyguards locked the front doors as others checked the kitchen.

Zee Zee stood, picked up his chair, straightened his hair, bowed with a bright smile. "See? Make-believe! Just like in the movies."

Excited murmuring became laughter and loud applause—just a joke, no one was dead and the boy was a *le hu* acrobat! Others cursed colorfully and put their guns away before throwing a variety of cooked vegetables at the boy as he grinned and dipped a handkerchief in his teacup to wash out the red sauce.

Amah, panting and crying with murder in her eye, struggled to adjust. Da-tsien's shock was overborne by the fact that he wasn't dead. *He's impossible! Incredible!* She wanted to cry and to laugh and to breathe deeply. She was clapping for his magic as her amah tried to stop her. Da-tsien had never known anyone so crazy. She saw him on a black pony, freeing little girls, then burning down his house with his foreign gas machine. She imagined him fixing all of China. "Oh, Zee Zee, that was terrific! How did you know? How do you know so much about everything? Oh, tell me!"

"I don't spend all my time at St. John's."

"Maybe you should spend more," said Amah.

With a quick look, the girl sent Ah Tsui to a different table.

"You are a very interesting person, but you haven't helped me with English. Now a request, please, no more rudeness to Amah. You've been mean to her, almost like those bad men outside, whipping the little girls. You know? Things like that make me feel sick inside. Amah was rude, but you're her superior. Men of learning must be kind and gentle, regardless of circumstances, regardless of emotions."

"Hey, no fair! You just gave her a mean look yourself."

"It was a *corrective* look, which is very different. I had no rage, only a wish to do the right thing. When you don't get your way, you show big anger and your nostrils flare and you frown and I feel sick. You must understand that she's my amah, and her job is to protect me. As a man, you must be courtly and show rectitude while she performs her duty."

Zee Zee drummed his fingers. He could get this treatment at home. This was like being with his mother or Tall Amah—his mother was constantly harping about his soul and his prayer life when it was his mind and his heart and his liver and his stomach that spoke with greater energy. And Tall Amah was his mother's agent. Females!

"Well, what do you say, am I right, do you see my point?" asked the girl, wishing all her missionaries were here with her.

"I don't have to answer to you," he said.

"No, you don't." She prepared to stand. "Thank you for the honor—"

"Don't use that old-fashioned talk—"

"You did, and I don't have to answer to you, do I?" She stood with a faint smile. Round Amah appeared at her side as if she had popped out of the girl's pocket.

"Okay, look, I'm sorry!" The words were uttered before Zee Zee understood them. He started to retract his apology.

"I am moved, Mr. Lee," said the girl, "by your graciousness. My own shortcomings are a burden to all who know me, and your generosity—"

"Don't talk like that!"

"—sets an example for all to behold and emulate, and your patience would do credit to the Son of Heaven himself."

"Farting mice! Talking to you is like being beaten up by Master K'ung and all his ranting disciples and my own mother!" He lowered his voice. "The emperor's deposed. I wouldn't mention him here in Triad country." The secret societies hated big government.

"How kindly you compliment my learning, how gloriously you grow my mind! And please, may I ask that you never speak like that again? Do not appear confused, you know what I mean. The thing about the mice."

He tried to argue, but Da-tsien sat. Amah returned reluctantly to her table, scowling ferociously and then violently turning her back.

"What," said Da-tsien, "did you think of American family members fighting each other because of their beliefs?"

Zee Zee took a deep breath. *What a crazy girl!* She was confusing him, but she had asked a good question. He resented his imperious older brother, and that was normal, but the movie had been unbelievable. Brothers killing brothers, blood against blood. "Unbelievable," he said.

"So you would never fight your family over your independent beliefs? You are more Confucian than you appear?"

"I couldn't fight my family!" he said, sitting up straighter. "Would you?"

"I'm doing it right now, by being here, in a Hongkew teashop with cutthroats and pirates and kidnappers, with you, while you pretend to be shot and make all the gentlemen here pull out their guns." She smiled, almost like a foreign actress without emotional brakes.

Zee Zee opened his well-trained oratorical mouth, but no sounds came out.

"Nothing? Do you want another question? This is so much fun! Does your honorable father like you knowing Hongkew ways and riding a very loud black foreign gas machine? A machine that makes babies cry for hours and makes our house guard want to shoot you from our porch, yes?"

Zee Zee shrugged, happy with the recognition of his skills.

"What does your honorable mother think of such habits? I mean, your actions must give her headaches or stomach problems and sleepless nights, yes, and encourage her to see soothsayers and geomancers?"

"Well, what about you? Does your mother know that you're in Hongkew with me?"

"She knows I'm with fellow students." Da-tsien cleared her throat and said a quick silent prayer. "But my answers aren't nearly as much fun as my questions. What did you think of Miss Elsie Stoneman?"

Zee Zee had to think who she was. "She just sat around, right?"

"Oh, but she had a great spiritual center. She followed all my advice, so she lived to make more movies! And she was very strong."

"Too strong, I think," he said.

Da-tsien's eloquent face couldn't hide her disappointment.

"But I admired her," he tried. "She held everyone together, didn't she?"

"Good! Do you want to see another movie and study English?"

"So we can argue and you can drive me crazy?"

She covered her mouth to laugh. "So we can learn English. Zee Zee, I *have* to learn English. I have to be the best. My teacher . . . has given me gifts of the spirit. I *have* to be the best for her in academics, or I shame her generosity, don't you think?" She did not mention her mother's expectations.

She had told him a great deal. Guys talked all the time, but they never transferred this much information. Her words buzzed inside his brain. Her rapid-fire speech was dizzying. "Miss Tzu, you're betrothed, and we're both taking chances. Someone could see you at the movies with me. And your betrothed could still be following you."

She tried to be offended but giggled instead. "Are you afraid of the honorable Mr. Tung?"

He shook his head. "I'm afraid of your mother."

Da-tsien laughed so abruptly that her amah leaned over from a neighboring table and hit her. She blushed and lowered her head. "Please forgive me. I shame all I know. But *you*, the gangster, afraid of Mah-mee!"

"Gangster?" he asked.

"Zee Zee, you hang out with Pooh Pan. He's a *Chingbang*. You know the saying. How can one gauge a person if not by his friends?"

"How about judging him by his motorcycle?"

"That wouldn't help you." She couldn't stop smiling. She was talking with him as if he were a classmate, a girlfriend; but he was a boy, a crazy, rebellious boy who was so unconventional that he scared her, and they were practically alone with each other, talking and feeling emotions together like married people, and these facts, representing so much *jing ji*, taboo, made her stomach jump.

"Don't think of me that way," he said softly. "I hang out with Pan. His *jia* has been incredibly generous to me, for very little in return. But I'm not a gangster. I would never do business in that field."

"Why not? You do outrageous things at school."

She had said it so nicely he had to smile. "Like what?"

"Like gluing political posters on walls for the *Tung Men Hui*." Sun Yatsen's new Alliance Party, a provocative blend of bearded intellectuals, *di-ren* peasants, energetic students and angry radicals who were fighting for a new, democratic China. "I saw you do it, running away afterwards like the wind! Did you do it on a wager, or did you do it to get in trouble, or did you do it because you're part of the *Tung Men Hui?*"

He laughed. "Do you think I was wrong?"

The question surprised her. "Oh, that'd be something," she said, "if a female could judge the acts of a male! I'll take your question as a compliment. I want to know why you did it."

"To stop opium trafficking. To free children from factories. To kick out the foreigner. To give China back to us. The posters say brave things!"

She looked up, smiling to herself. "You know, Zee Zee, I think Hongkew would be a better place to hang posters. If I could, I'd put them on factory walls, using *pai-hwa* common words, not classical characters, and I'd hang them for the workers, who need inspiration from intellectuals. Not for students, not for the St. Johneans, who get lots of political training. It's the girls at St. Mary's who don't know that much, so I'd definitely hang posters there. And I wouldn't get angry that they take them down, because Christian schools have to do that. So why wouldn't you do some sort of secret business with Pan?"

Now she was talking like a guy, and he relaxed. What she said about the posters made sense. And she had asked a big question. She talked with her eyes and her hands as much as with her mouth, telling him things from inside herself. He wanted to keep talking to her. Doing so, however, put her at risk. It didn't matter how modern he tried to be; what they were doing was wrong. He didn't mind for himself; he minded for her.

"Miss Tzu, my Master Lee was the Yangchow salt-tax administrator. Before that he ran some Kiangsi pawnshops. We have salt in our skin. No scholars." No honor, no royal line. "Trading salt, you deal down. It's bribes, smuggling, salt merchants who double as bandits. It's back-door business, all *ho-men*. Father told me to deal up, look for the front door, the main floor. So I try to not think about what Pan actually does."

Da-tsien nodded at the truth of it, loving his honesty. China's salt enterprises were the great mothers of corruption. "You want to do good for China, don't you," she said. "I mean, from something deep inside yourself."

He nodded, hands forming hard, gnarled fists.

"Zee Zee, what happened to your hands? If it's not too rude of me to ask." She blushed. "I'm always asking questions. My mother hates it, but my foreign teachers seem to appreciate it. Anyway, please tell me, if you can."

He looked at his hands palms up, opposite of the way her mah-mee inspected hers. He didn't say, *I hit really hard things. Like people's heads.* So he asked, "What do you want in life? You know. If you had a choice?" It was a question to the heart and liver, since Chinese girls, in the face of their families' marital requirements, could hold only secret wants that could never be heard except by the gods. "And don't say, *Marry rich and have ten sons.* Or the Four Virtues and the Three Followings and all that junk."

"I would never say that! Not that I disagree with the commandments, but it's just that I want to marry a handsome man and have one perfect son, ten in mind, ten in heart, ten in handsomeness."

"Why only one son?"

"So he won't have a Younger Brother to lord over, a Younger Brother who'll hate him all his life; so we could have a household without bickering."

"Yuu! That goes against logic! What's a little bickering if he dies, and you have no sons at all and no one to care for you when you're old?"

"Then part of me dies with him, and I won't care about old age. But it won't happen. Oh, Zee Zee, I want my son to be happy, at peace with himself because his mother loves him and approves of him."

"Mothers love their sons," said Zee Zee, realizing it for the first time.

"But I don't want to have lots of sons just to fight the odds of survival. I want one special boy to focus on, to develop, to teach to read, to write, perfectly. To be an ideal person of scholarship and virtue, yes?"

He glanced at her and looked away from her intensity. "Mr. Tung can give you one son," he said.

"I don't love Mr. Tung."

"Of course not. You don't love a husband until *after* you're married."

"Miss Elsie Stoneman loved before she married. It's the Western way. The modern way. If you're going to talk modern, you should *live* modern."

"You're unbelievable," he said. "You're probably more radical than I am. I bet you're in more trouble, too."

"I don't ride stinky motorcycles."

"You should! They're incredible fun. Exciting!"

She turned away. "Never! How did we get onto motorcycles again?"

"Would you ride one for the man you loved?"

"The man I loved wouldn't ask me to, knowing how much I fear machines and their noise, so he wouldn't ask, he'd never, ever ask."

"But you got on the motorcycle."

She covered her face. "I know. That's because I was asked by someone who obviously didn't care about me or my future! I think from now on, we should say that I didn't get on the machine. It will extend Amah's longevity."

"Why'd you ask me to watch the movie with you? And no polite answers. No indirect answers. Give me the real reason."

"I told you. You're quick and smart. I'm slow and—"

"Tell me the real reason."

"Now I think you ask too much. Agreed?"

"No." He thought. "I've known you for years, since we were little. I'm friends with your brother. We go to side-by-side schools. We're in the same *bao-jia*, collective responsibility unit. If your baba gets arrested for killing too many fish, they could take my head, too. If the foreigners decide to kill Chinese students, we could die together."

His words made her shudder. More accurately, if Zee Zee killed someone with his gas machine, everyone in the neighborhood was subject to punishment. In China, this ran the wide spectrum from private strangulations to public beheadings.

"I can handle the truth," he said. "I like truth."

"I can't tell you the truth," she said. "So let's just say that you're very interesting, and you make me laugh when you're not frightening me and making my amah lose her ability to think. As I learn more about the Western world and the Christian god, I should know more about the world of men. And how they think. Or don't think."

"I'm okay as a thinker, but not the best. You should've asked T. A. Soong. He's a thinker like Hanlin is a reader."

"I don't know Soong, and to be honest, I'm not sure I'd want to be around such a powerful family when the political situation is so shaky."

Zee Zee was sixteen and skilled at many things. He had once pried secrets out of household staff by tickling them. "Are you ticklish?" he asked.

She backed up, grabbing and startling her amah. "You are an incredibly evil person! I would die right here, and you'd be a murderer!"

"But I would know what's in your mind. I'd get your last, dying thought."
He saw that her amah was glaring at him. Now he couldn't quell her with his
hard glance.

Ah Tsui was speaking with great authority. "Come on, Young Missy, time
to go. Stop using this boy to mess up your betrothal to Mr. Tung."

twenty-one

Dancing

SPRING CAME EARLY in 1922. It made May as torrid as July, and July in
Shanghai was like being boiled in hot-and-sour soup. The heat was so punishing that it justified inequilibrium, delirium, some homicides and the spon-
taneous removal of clothing in public. Into this searing world emerged
Da-tsien and Zee Zee from a suffocating theater in which the piano player had
expired after a few moments. Wilted by humidity, drained of emotion and
hounded by Ah Tsui, they stepped out to be stunned by the coiled heat.

In the direct sunlight, Da-tsien briefly considered suicide, but that would
require effort. She wanted to go home, take powdery doses of medicinal herbs
and allow Ah Tsui to fan her and rub her feet until sundown. Night would be
too hot to sleep, but she'd rather toss in bed than be punished so cruelly for
being outside. Every summer she desperately missed moderate Soochow, and
now she was doing it in the spring.

"Let me show you something," said Zee Zee, and Da-tsien tried to decline,
but she simply couldn't react. Ah Tsui filled the silence with a suggestion: "NO!"

Zee Zee had already shown her something. Two weeks ago he had pulled
her out of the St. Mary's music recital. Without lauding her performance,
which would prove to be the third best of the evening, he handed her a garment bag and suggested she change in the girls' room.

"We're going dancing," he said.

"I don't think so," she said. It had been cooler then, and she could speak.

"*Ching ni,*" he said. Please. And he smiled.

In the girls' room, she looked in the mirror. Her hair was dark and full in a loose net. Her blue uniform jacket, white shirt and skirt, white socks and oxfords were clean. *Why change?* In the bag she found a long black scoop-necked, bead-bordered dress with see-through sleeves, nylons like Clara Bow's in *Mantrap,* three pairs of fancy shoes, each a different size, and a white flapper hat. The clothing was clean but not new. It obviously belonged to someone else; she wondered who.

Ah Tsui observed that this was a perfect outfit for prostitutes and that Da-tsien would be better off diving *huahui* into the Whampu River. Then Zee Zee barged into the girls' room and yelled at them to hurry—he had a wide-bench pedicab with a good driver waiting, and they'd get ice cream first, and yes, of course he understood that Ah Tsui was coming.

Shanghai evenings were cooler on the river and hotter to the west. The best spots were near the Bund. Naturally, top nightclubs such as Farren's, Paramount, Del Monte's, the Roxy, the British country club's sixty-five acres, the Shanghai Club's hundred-foot Long Bar, the Majestic's grand ballroom, the Cathay's restaurants and the French Club's roof garden on Rue Cardinal Mercier all discouraged the presence of Chinese people except as serving staff. These were exactly the places that Zee Zee intended to crash, but not tonight, not with that scolding amah in tow.

The sweating pedicab driver, competing with eighty thousand rickshaw pullers and a thousand taxis, bowed at the girl in the Western dress who smiled at him as she boarded. He peddled industriously out of the hot western Out-roads to slide into river-bound evening traffic. It was warm and he worked hard, knowing that the breeze would save him. They made a stop at the Chocolate Shop for the *huaren* boy, and then the driver turned south on Tibet Road and headed for the British racecourse. When the heavy amah complained, the boy gave her French chocolate truffles, and the driver smiled as the woman loudly devoured the sweets, storing some in her pockets.

Da-tsien saw looming ahead a garish white illuminated, multileveled tower with a spired facade. This startling pagoda allowed her to feel terror at several levels—of sin, of being seen, of not seeing the unimaginable. "Zee Zee, we're not going to the Great World, are we?"

The *Da Shijie* amusement center was like Coney Island without cops. It was six levels of unrestricted mayhem with gambling, food, acrobats and lewdness. No one of Da-tsien's class could be seen there without repercussions to family reputation. Yet the place crawled with people of all classes, each taking risks in some way.

"Young Missy must go home now," said a goggle-eyed Ah Tsui to Zee Zee. "I'm tired, and I can't do my job for Da-tsien this late at night."

He quickly gave her another chocolate. "They have great food. Can you get us closer to Avenue Edward VII?" he asked of the peddler.

The pedicab weaved through brigades of street kids as they streamed around the saddest beggar guild—women who had disfigured their small children's faces for sympathy, and limbless, sightless elders who advertised facial sores for viewing. Then came beady-eyed pickpockets, small hoods and single-bamboo-pole salesmen offering old bean curd, used clothing and questionable soups.

Da-tsien was looking over her shoulder at the beggar women's children when the pedicab stopped. The driver thanked Zee Zee, who tipped generously to cover his poverty, then bowed to Da-tsien, taking her smile as if it were a hug from a god. Da-tsien remembered hiding her face from Shanghai when she had ridden out of the International Settlement in search of her mysterious landlord. The jolting ride was over. Her amah put her bulk to one side of Young Missy, and Zee Zee took the other.

The Great World was a stack of naked commerce. Da-tsien would now see things that were normally reserved for the survivors of life's ills. She tried to hold her head high, but her eardrums had never been tested by so much continuous noise in a closed space. Slot machines rang, magicians screamed and huffed flaming fireballs, food-stall men hollered, storytellers shouted over microphoned singsong girls in short dresses while firecrackers exploded overhead. Drunk, unwashed countermen gave young urchins free beer while pimps showed off their stables of sad, poorly dressed street girls, offering an easy path to a terminal disease in the dungeon of the Flower World. Amah kept trying to cover her Young Missy's eyes, but Zee Zee easily moved through the crowd, and Da-tsien kept pace with him. He showed her a display of little jumping Mexican beans, and she tried to laugh.

Zee Zee wanted to go dancing, Da-tsien wanted to see opera and Ah Tsui felt like fainting. Da-tsien, an avid storyteller in her heart, saw an intriguing *Shaoshing*, country opera, about true lovers and stopped to watch, her lips parted. Zee Zee got the amah tea in a paper cup, which she spilled because it was so hot.

The opera ended, and they climbed stairs until Ah Tsui had to stop on the third floor to have ice cream, too exhausted and hot to remember her duties.

The two youths continued without her to the roof. The girl walked unsteadily, unaccustomed to stairs and exercise, and he slowed. Occasionally, she bumped into him.

She arrived panting and heard the band playing sweet foreign music before she stared at red-uniformed rooftop acrobats walking on incredibly high wires while twirling plates on long poles.

"Don't look at them," said Zee Zee. "Look at the city."

The view made her put a hand to her throat to find air. He stood by her until she could breathe and take in the surrounding vista. The dark river snaked to the east, dotted by brightly lit ships that looked like toys, reminding her of the Soochow night fisherman who sang to the Tzus on the night of the new year. Darkened Offroads and St. Mary's and St. John's lay to the west, the huge racecourse and Chapei to the north, the somber shadow of the Chinese City to the south, their Hongkew movie theaters and *le hu* communities to the northeast. Above, fireworks burst in bright good-luck reds, the explosions making her jump. She had always loved Soochow, but for a moment, she was enchanted by Shanghai. This was her new city, and she could see so much of it.

"Thank you, Zee Zee, for bringing me here."

"Want to dance?"

Gay foreign music seemed to cleanse her mind. "Why do you want to dance?"

"I thought you'd like it."

"You don't like to dance for your own pleasure?"

"Not by myself."

A breeze cooled her. "I'm sort of awkward. I walk like a duck. And I don't know how to dance."

He laughed. "You look like a princess. I'll show you."

She was happy and nervous. "Do we have to dance with everybody over there? Can't we do it here, where no one can see?"

"Doesn't count unless you do it where people are looking. And I'll get some credit for being seen with you."

"From whom? Who do you know here? Not from school?" Suddenly she was scared.

"Just acquaintances. Come." He took her trembling hand and walked to the dance floor, a section bordered by the relatively staid table activities of mahjong, money changing, and palm reading.

Holding her at a distance, he guided her, moving her around the floor to a song with an enduring melody, grinning while she frowned as if struggling with a troublesome new English word. He reassured her when she stepped on his toes, and looked at the fireworks overhead when her face turned red. She was panting from exhilaration and fear—it was so wrong to be this close to a man, any man, even her father.

"Breathe gently, from your belly," he whispered.

She followed his instruction, gaining air. He pretended not to see Ah Tsui as she appeared, wheezing and out of breath, ice cream on her lips.

He looked at the girl, and she seemed to look into him. At that moment, he sank into her as if she were a Hainan sponge and he were a drop of rain. His body became mist like a mystical Shao-lin boxer, and he lost his way as surely as a man looking for a path on a moonless night. He felt an unanchored affection that ran the length of him, a magnetism that warmed his soul. It was as if he were a part of her.

She sighed, and he knew he needed her and wanted her and could not live without her. Her personality, her magic, carried him, and he felt wonder and tried to understand how he could save China while never leaving her side. He was delirious, as if Smelly Man Yao had hit him with a deadly right top fist.

Da-tsien saw him clearly that night: his love of risk, his kindness, his tender heart. She didn't know the whys of his feelings, unaware of the tugs between his desire to be a soldier of fortune and to never leave the scent of her, but he was so wonderfully close, interacting with her, enabling her to assess him as simply and directly as reading the first primer of the Chinese language.

Zee Zee didn't remember descending the stairs, but he did recall standing beside her and the amah as they watched a country opera about love. He was in a daze, a condition he found particularly unappealing.

Later, he'd remember that the rooftop band was from Luzon and wore white coats and that the violinist was a woman. Although he had a tremendous memory, he would slap his forehead in old age, unable to bring back the tune to which he and Da-tsien had danced.

She knew it. Again and again, he would ask her for its name, and she would smile and shake her head. He would hum it for musicians, but his tin ear made the rendition useless. On warm nights throughout their marriage, Zee Zee could hear her humming that haunting melody from a lovely throat.

A thin kid appeared and guided them through thick crowds to a reserved side café table near a fortune-teller. At the table, holding it for them, sat a round boy in worker's clothes. Fen and Hwa were Pan's bodyguards. Their unhealthy complexions identified them as opium addicts. The sagging weight of metal in their pockets identified them as killers. They left, nodding almost imperceptibly at Zee Zee. Da-tsien sat, Ah Tsui almost collapsed and Zee Zee ordered steaming pot stickers, spicy aromatic soup, translucent rice noodles with fat prawns and minced pork, hot jasmine tea. A small feast. They ate with loud slurps that were lost in the roar of the *Da Shijie*.

"Oh, this is wonderful!" said Da-tsien. "The food is delicious, and this is such an incredible place! Zee Zee, I feel so strange . . . elated and sad, stupid and smart, excited and melancholy. All at once! Why do you think that is? Do you feel the same? Am I the only one who does?"

Zee Zee grinned. "Upstairs is Shen the chess master. He just came back from America. He plays twenty chess games at the same time and wins them all. Most people have one feeling at a time, but you play all your emotions at once."

A group of men approached, led by a shorthaired man Da-tsien had seen upstairs. One of the lead actresses from the Shanghai film industry walked behind him, waving at admirers, their path parted by a group of serious-looking men. One of them nodded at Zee Zee, who nodded in return. Da-tsien asked, "Zee Zee, who are they?"

"That's Tu Yue-sheng, Big-Ears Tu, known as Yue-sun in Songhai," said Zee Zee under his breath. "The younger ones are bodyguards like Guard Man Singh. I know one of them from Hongkew. His name is also Lee."

Da-tsien covered her lips, while her amah sat straighter, alerted like a guard dog. Big-Eared Tu was the leading gangster of Shanghai and all of China and all of the Far East. He was the master of opium street dealers, of murderers, of kidnappers; the enemy of her baba. Everyone knew he cut off the ears of hostages if their families hesitated to pay the ransom, and that he sold thousands of little girls into unthinkable horrors. He was the kind of person who protected big factory bosses, men who led strings of little bound girls from factory to factory, working them to death.

Sleep? Little-girl animals don't need sleep!

Trembling with fear, she saw that the young braves had hard faces and bore not the slightest resemblance to dear Singh, who was a faithful man of his god. With a start, she realized that they resembled Zee Zee.

"I want to go home. Please. Now."

Even after they found another pedicab and began the return to Burkill Road, she found that she could not stop crying.

THE HEAT OUTSIDE the theater was stifling. "Young Missy must go home," said Ah Tsui. "I'm hot and can't do my job and protect her in this heat." Blaming heat exhaustion on an aristocratic girl who was ready to faint would be impolite. Only servants perspired and experienced fatigue. "It's my fault. And no more showing her anything! No more Grand Worlds."

It was a veiled warning, not from Ah Tsui, but from Mr. Tzu.

After the visit to the Grand World, Baba, Da-tsien's slow-moving father, had gone to the Lee mansion to meet Zee Zee for himself. The boy's mother, Lee Taitai, was at the foreign-god church with her firstborn son, Gee, so Zee Zee would be at home, using his hands to work on his horrible two-wheeled machine. Sundays for Baba were otherwise idle; the foreign church bells rang all morning and scared the hell out of the fish.

"Young man," said Baba, "I bid you good morning." He had studied the boy for some moments before speaking. He saw a handsome, well-muscled youth covered in black grease, and he marveled at the teen's enjoyment of dirt.

Zee Zee looked up in the sunlight to see Da-tsien's father. He stood, bowing courteously, spilling flowery conventions about unworthy sons performing unworthy tasks in the presence of the truly worthy. Baba returned the favor by admitting his abandonment of protocol.

"A scholar attacks issues with study. I'm not that smart. This is my bodyguard's holiday. I want to fish but promised I wouldn't go alone. I don't think I'd get kidnapped if you were along. It's a nice day, don't you think, except for the weather? Why don't you come with me and guard an old man from Hongkew and French Concession gangsters?" Baba smiled shyly, knowing he had speared the boy with his underworld connections.

At the Whangpu, Zee Zee watched the bearlike man bait his hooks and pull fish from the river. Opposite them, coolies loaded opium at the Laobatu Ferry. Behind them, on Maloo Road, coolies off-loaded the opium for shipment to the French police station. Rail-thin, sunburned fishermen traded bait news with Baba.

"You wonder why I fish here," said Baba. It was crowded. There was no shade. "Here I can't see the Native Customs House. I can't see my countrymen kowtowing to foreigners."

"This is a better view," said Zee Zee to the sound of ringing bells. He studied the foreign battleships. *Power and steel, and we have none.*

"It's good to agree with the politics of your elders. Not so good when elders don't like what you do with their daughters."

Zee Zee froze. He had a Confucian center and felt burning guilt. He had loved dancing with this man's daughter—too much.

"Sitting here, knowing history, I feel changes coming." An airplane flew lazily overhead, and Baba waited, observing the boy's totally rapt focus on the machine, so high above them that it seemed unreal.

"You see my daughter against her mother's wishes and in violation of the contract with Mr. Tung and a costly matchmaker. Da-tsien is headstrong, but she's no dummy. She sees something in you worth pain and censure. I had to see who you are. I've watched and heard you. All our ancestors going back a thousand generations have heard your machine.

"Young man, sons must honor fathers. Your honorable clan has modern problems, as does mine. I ask that you not let any trouble splash on my daughter. Your relationship with her hangs by not even a thread. You must act with her as if K'ung Fu-tzu himself were with you every moment. I think young people now do modern things of which the Sage, and all reasoning fathers, would not and could not approve."

"I hear you, Master," said Zee Zee.

"And will comply?"

"And will try to comply, Master," he said.

"Lee, please understand that if you do not, I will not bless you. You will find the House of Tzu opposed to your interests. Hey now, young man, thank you for fishing with me today! You give an old man pleasure."

twenty-two

The Kiss

Y ou," CRIED THE round amah, "have been alone together enough for fifty married couples! So wrong! I hate it that you drag me to these movies. You humiliate me. Missy, come with me! Must go home now!"

Zee Zee nodded in agreement, then led Da-tsien away with long strides. The amah squeaked. *Aiyaaa, physical contact in public!* She tried to shout, but it was too hot and they were walking so fast and she had to rest, panting in a narrow band of shade. She frantically dug her new eight-trigrammed, red-framed geomantic mirror from her purse, pointing it in all directions as flea-bitten dogs nuzzled her and the crowds passed by and the sun took vengeance.

Oh, no! It's the huge foreign farting machine! Had there been a table, Ah Tsui would've been under it, but now the machine seemed to be after her, roaring, hungry and mean. It lurched at her from the corner, and she held the mirror like a shield, reflecting away the evil spirits as Young Missy, mounted on its back, held the boy and they roared off.

Ah Tsui screamed and jumped with unusual alacrity into a rickshaw, bellowing orders. The puller, hating a chase, demanded extra coins before running in pursuit with the screaming amah. It was not a fair race. The Harley could do an incredible forty-three miles an hour, and a well-conditioned runner, dragging a cab and a rotund, jumping passenger, could maintain little more than five miles an hour. But the streets of Hongkew were built for foot traffic, so the motorcycle had to stop constantly and then was halted by an Indian street cop at the Woosung Road bridge. Ah Tsui, praying to all gods, perspiring wildly, yelling contrary directions, fingering her Buddhist worry beads, shining her mirror at bystanders and drivers, saw the machine make a right and several lefts to end up on Wayside Road, a dangerous, foreigners-only storage area. She couldn't read the sign, which said WATSON'S MINERAL WATER CO. FACTORY, MANUFACTURERS OF AERATED WATER.

Outside the factory was Zee Zee's horrible machine. From within the gray building came the sounds of dragons dying. The clanging, banging and huff-

168   GUS LEE

ing was a thousand times deeper than the gongs of hell, which she had heard on those occasions when the Taitai was really mad. The terrible noises paralyzed Ah Tsui and even stilled her tongue.

"*Shemma?*" the sweat-drenched rickshaw man kept asking, his bursting lungs keeping pace with the racketing machinery within. He didn't like it here; it felt all wrong and bad, a place where you could break a leg.

"I can't leave her here," she said, paying him three times the normal charge without a word of barter. "We wait."

The puller wanted to argue but instead found a tiny bit of shade and sat against the hot wall, his rib cage heaving, his body gleaned of liquid.

DA-TSIEN AND ZEE Zee giggled, then laughed so hard they bent over, their sounds lost in the crash of machinery. She had fled her amah. She had held on to "that boy." She had ridden on his roaring motorcycle, her heart still pounding from each acceleration as they outran every devil in China. Now they were hiding from Ah Tsui and a fast rickshaw puller. They were hiding from her mother, her father, from Confucius himself, and it was as delicious as being on Tungting Lake after the last day of school. After noticing his resemblance to his gangster friends, she had meant to have nothing to do with him ever again—until he asked her to the movies.

They recounted the trip, babbling, reliving common experiences; they had faced the devil, escaped death and had yet to pay their ancestors for their many weaknesses.

Behind them, at stops, she had seen Ah Tsui mouthing curses and flashing her magic mirror. Then they were racing, going faster than ever, and then there was no amah, no mah-mee, no past life, and Da-tsien could feel the muscles in Zee Zee's torso and had no choice but to hold them to her with fear and wonder. Such thrills, such violations, would cost dearly, and she knew with the certainty of scholarship and the promise of faith that she was going to die a horrible death for violating so dramatically and openly all that her mother had wished her to be. She held on to Zee Zee with all her might so she wouldn't die alone.

Each time she survived a collision or fall, she experienced a small internal Chinese baptism, a soft spring bath where the gods were blessing and saving her, where Jesus smiled on Buddha as they lit Taoist candles and placed a halo over her head. She had been transported outside of her body, and she had done it with the son of her landlord, the grandson of a salt man, a boy her mah-mee feared and her amah called the Gangster.

"Hot?" he asked her.

"On fire." She smiled, never before so happy to be uncomfortable.

"Thirsty?"

"Parched."

"Believe in *mo-li*, magic?"

She fell serious. "I believe in God," she said.

"Come." He took her hand and she trembled, keeping her fingers inert. His grip was tight, almost uncomfortable, as if he could squeeze Christ from her blood. Touching him was an adventure, scary and strange.

She followed him into the bowels of the factory. She had never been in such a place. She felt faint. He slowed down and let her breathe a little. He was going to tell her to close her eyes, but they were already tightly shut.

Blindly, she followed him around twists and turns. The air blew on her, loosening her long hair. Her heart stopped—foreign workers were yelling from far away. Of them, she had a deep and powerful fear, more than of kidnappers, pirates and Confucius. She heard Zee Zee open and shut a small door with a latch.

"Keep your eyes closed. Remember, you're thirsty. Now drink."

He put a towel in her hand. Inside the towel was a bottle. He guided the bottle to her lips, a strange contour for a girl used to teacups. She expected heat, but there was no radiating steam. Chinese people understood cooling, and Shanghai people knew it better than anyone. If hot, drink tea that is hotter than the air, and the body cools.

"Just a sip," he was saying. "Be ready for a surprise."

She sipped, waiting for heat. The drink was cold. It was cold, and it tingled and bubbled on her tongue and her teeth. It was frigid, strangely alive, sweet and delicious, and it flooded her innards and made her swallow and then stamp her feet in confusion and delight. He laughed a good, admirable laugh, and she opened her eyes and saw his good face filled with pleasure for her, and she wanted to thank him but instead drank again and again while he laughed. He took the bottle and removed the towel. The bottle said Coca-Cola.

"Want more?" he asked. She shook her head; so he drank the rest.

"Ready?"

She might have nodded. He said, "Close your eyes."

She did. She felt coolness on her brow. Then he was gently caressing her forehead with the cold bottle, making her shiver and shudder, and then he was caressing her cheeks and her chin, and then her neck, and she peeked through her eyelids and saw a boy adoring her. She shut her eyes and let the bottle share its coolness with her face.

"Feel better?" he asked.

She couldn't speak.

"Ready?" he asked again.

"I don't think so, Zee Zee." She laughed. "I think we should go back. But this time not so fast. And please, don't touch me again, okay?"

"We're not done yet," he whispered, taking her hand. She closed her eyes tighter, out of anxiety and delight.

They walked in zigs and zags as if confounding linear-walking ghosts. The drink's coolness had worn off; Da-tsien was hot again, and now, with her eyes closed inside a foreign-machine factory, her blindness and perspiration made her feel almost naked and shameful.

A door opened and it was winter, and they were inside and the door shut. She opened her eyes and the walls were made of a clear white magic substance. She touched it, and it was smooth and cold.

"Ice," he said in English. "Frozen water."

The cold air was like a tonic to her skin, freeing her, pleasing her.

"Zee Zee! It's—it's heaven! Oh, it's so deliciously cold!" She trembled and shivered in joy, the hateful heat, the painful perspiration, dissipating, the oppression of July left only inches outside on the other side of the door. She was in another world, and all she could do was smile.

"Compressors make the ice by changing the pressure between . . ."

She stopped listening. She was focusing on his mouth, which was tilted upward into a smile. No sternness, no anger. Only harmony and pleasure. A *handsome boy who really, really likes me.*

They came out of the ice storage facility to face a dripping rickshaw man in soaked cotton trousers and no shirt, sunburned to the bone.

"Forgive a beggar, but the young missy's amah waits and is suffering in the sun."

Zee Zee was studying the man, who bowed lower in fear of the factory. Dragons would eat you inside such a place and laugh as they chewed.

"Here," said the boy, using a tool to open a bottle, "you look thirsty and hot. Drink this. It's cold, like winter stream water, but it bubbles."

The man took it and drank, crying out in delight, the drink fizzing over his lips and chest, and he danced in pleasure and drank it all.

SHE CLOSED HER eyes, remembering his kiss. She would never think of winter again without pleasure. It had been a movie kiss, an American-movie kiss, and she had been like a girl in a storybook, doing the impossible in an unimaginable place.

Chinese movies were about punishment and pain. German movies were about love and pain. American movies were about laughter and happy endings. Da-tsien loved American movies. Out of respect for the actresses, she had initially avoided looking when they kissed. Later, she had never breathed when they kissed. When Zee Zee kissed her inside the ice factory, she closed her eyes and forgot to breathe.

Now she thought of it as a kiss worthy of antiquity. A thousand years from now, Chinese girls would secretly tell one another that they had enjoyed a first kiss just like Tzu Da-tsien, the granddaughter of the viceroy of Kwangtung and Kwangsi, who had then married the future savior of China, Lee Zeu-zee, the grandson of a tax administrator.

She closed her eyes to the city of Shanghai as they approached Burkill Road and quickly reviewed everything that had happened, then pressed each detail into her deep Chinese memory.

Ah Tsui had been so angry that her ranting had sobered Zee Zee and left him with a range of self-assessments stretching from Stupid to Very Stupid. He then offered her a Coca-Cola. It distracted Amah so much that she didn't notice that Da-tsien had changed.

ZEE ZEE WENT to the Outroads, the western edge of Shanghai, bandit country, hoping for trouble. *Try to steal my Harley.* He tried not to think of the kiss. He had been given a choice by the girl's father: Respect my daughter and have a thin chance; disrespect her and make an enemy of the Tzus.

He didn't go back to Hongkew, because Pan would see his sadness and make fun of his infatuation. He didn't go to the French Concession and the new Soong mansion, because T.A. wanted him to get married and he didn't want to marry anyone, especially not Da-tsien, who was way beyond the reach of his clan.

"Christ," said Zee Zee, looking to the west in the ungodly heat. *How do I get out of this? I want to fly and leave this place, right? I don't want to stick around and get stuck on a girl. Yuuuu! A girl who's going to reject me anyway, the moment she thinks about the Lee family. That is, if her father doesn't have me strangled outside the Confucious Temple first.*

His father never said *Study*, but that's what all fathers demand. Smelly Man Yao said that to study in a Western school was to piss on the Boxers, who had been beheaded by the foreigners. Zee Zee had promised T.A. that he'd help change China, and he wanted to fly airplanes and kill the bad people, but white people were the ones who trained you to fly.

He felt her lips on his and had to close his eyes. She was magic and she was beautiful and she had tasted like peaches and jasmine, and he even remembered the scent of the girl's powders and creams and her skin, and she was a wonder and a threat to all that he was. Being close to her at the Great World had uplifted him. He could not live without that feeling.

twenty-three

A Man of Excellent Fortune

HIS OLDER SISTER, the formidable Madame H. H. Kung, had asked T. A. Soong to visit her estate on the Route de Herve de Seiyes. "Bring as many friends as you can," she had ordered.

T.A. could refuse vices and frivolities, but he couldn't refuse her. She was Firstborn, and their father had invested in her his heavy dreams and inflexible will. There was a purpose to this meeting, and T.A. did not like it.

His entourage met at Jessfield Gate—his part-time tutor, the dignified, pencil-mustached chess master S. Y. Shen, an honors graduate of Princeton University. Shen showed his earlier Peking schooling in a fastidiously clean blue gown and a scholar's black hat with the red top button of distinction. Fully trained in totally antagonistic academic orthodoxies, he moved slowly but nervously. Able to defeat anyone at chess, he made all other moves hesitantly, as if the next one could prove galactically fatal.

There was the tough, sunburned Cantonese bodyguard/puller with a revolver and a medieval arsenal. The puller disliked Shen, who was stingy, but liked the Lee boy, who was good in a fight. There were six or seven other students from various grades, excited to visit the house that now belonged to the descendants of Confucius.

Zee Zee was trying to hide behind the puller while glancing at the gate, where Ah Tsui waited. The spring rain had passed, but she held the umbrella open, ready to cover Da-tsien from the sun. The amah had seen the Lee boy and viciously ignored him.

"C'mon! Hurry!" said Zee Zee. It had been only days since the debacle at the ice factory, but he had avoided all contact with the Tzu girl and her critical, adhesive amah. He felt like a fugitive.

T.A. boarded his rickshaw, and the puller scanned the street and began jogging. Shen and Zee Zee shared another. Looking over his shoulder, Zee Zee got a glimpse of Da-tsien as she came through the gate, and the sight of her made his heart sad.

The passengers studied Russian immigrants who filled Little Moscow in southeastern Shanghai. These were White Russians who had fled the 1917 Red Bolshevik Revolution, abandoning their homeland, their goods and their many dead. They had come to Shanghai haunted by the past, worried about the present and frightened by the future.

Russian Cossacks were the vogue in personal bodyguards for the Chinese wealthy, while Russian Jews competed in antiques and banking. Russian blondes monopolized the American prostitution market.

Two more right turns, and they were at the Kung mansion.

Slowly, S. Y. Shen exited, paying the fare with maddening exactitude while his puller frowned. "What is the purpose of our visit?" he asked.

"My honorable older sister wants our company," said T.A.

"T.A., tell the truth!" said Zee Zee, who thought he had figured out the reason. "We're supposed to look like bodyguards. Like them." He pointed at the gun-bulging security detail on the portico. "Madame Kung must be having a meeting with Big Shots and wants more security."

"Me? Look like a bodyguard?" S. Y. Shen was small, bookish and physically modest. His glasses were tiny, round and impeccably clean. He looked at himself and said, "I know it is hot, but you cannot be serious."

"Not true," said T.A. Zee Zee took disagreement badly. He had been tired and cranky since the kiss. The great Kung mansion stood in sharp contrast to the Lees' relative poverty, and he wanted to fight. Insolently, he sauntered up the steps, raised his arms to be frisked by the guards and entered looking for a place to take a nap rather than stand in the heat with the security crew.

Inside, men argued so loudly that T.A., who liked to study, couldn't, while Zee Zee, who liked to sleep, kept awakening. S.Y. loathed politics. He found a cool room in the back of the mansion and sat in a hard chair, silently reciting the *Lun-yu* to cultivate his moral rectitude.

T.A.'s oldest sister, Ai-ling "Nancy" Soong, was Madame Kung. She was an ardent Christian who ran an upside-down Chinese household with willpower and intelligence. No one ordered her to leave, serve or be silent. She was strong, insightful and courageous on a field littered with confused men. This was her house, and she was backed by the majesty of the Kung clan and the wealth of her banker husband, H. H. Kung.

This was not all known by Zee Zee, who merely thought of her as T.A.'s rich older sister. The fourth or fifth time he was awakened by an imperious female voice, by the high, sibilant tones of a Chekiang accent and by a deep-chested foreigner, he stood with a snort and marched to the sitting room. A bodyguard stopped him cold. Angry, Zee Zee entered through a side door. Inside were T.A. and the other St. Johnean students, who jumped as he opened the door; they had been eavesdropping.

"They're arguing about taking over the new republic," whispered one.

"Who cares?" said Zee Zee too loudly, making his schoolmates say, "Shhhhhhh!" Troubled by his feelings for Da-tsien and now unable to sleep, he concluded that he had nothing to lose.

Suddenly they heard from the next room, "You want me to go to Hong Kong and create miracles from mud. So I can be a hostage, too? You drown me in bad ideas." It was the man with the Chekiang accent.

"He is my sister's husband," said the woman carefully, her words like blows. "As Father of China, Sun Yat-sen should not be a hostage, and certainly not to your old boss, a *jun-fa* warlord shrimp like Ch'en Chiung-ming!"

The boys looked at each other. *Sun Yat-sen, a hostage in Hong Kong!* Then they looked at T.A., who was Sun's nephew by marriage.

"Hey, let's go rescue Sun Yat-sen!" boomed Zee Zee.

Conversation stopped in the next room, and the double doors opened. A bodyguard frowned ferociously at them, his hand inside his Western coat.

The boys jerked upright, but Zee Zee strutted into the room; while his look could make servants quail, the glare from Madame Kung thinned his blood. He suddenly had no desire to fight anyone. He had stumbled into the chamber of the emperor, and court was in session.

There were four men with Madame Kung. Next to her was a small hunchbacked man wearing bright gold glasses and a gleaming gold silk gown. He evaluated the teens over an elegant cigarette holder before ignoring them.

Another man had a boulderlike head with flyaway ears, a hooded eye and fists scarred by street combat: Tu Yueh-sheng, Big Ears Tu, the gangster boss of Asia who had danced alongside Zee Zee and Da-tsien at the Grand World just a few nights ago.

In the corner was a scar-faced foreigner with a thick mustache and a bored look.

The last man had a perfectly erect military posture, narrow shoulders, a thin mustache and a uniform that seemed to provide him with size. He studied Zee Zee and said, in a Chekiang accent, "This one has balls."

Suddenly Zee Zee remembered the voice of his *na-ma*, his wet nurse. She had been a Chekiang country girl with the same accent. To the room he said, "I am the unworthy Lee Zeu-zee."

The bald soldier stood and faced Zee Zee. He moved fast like a tight spring, an engine ready for the spark.

"Boy, my friends want me to go to Hong Kong to rescue Dr. Sun from his own renegade warlord army." He lowered his high-pitched voice. His eyes twinkled. "It's like asking me to go catch fish in a tree. It's *yu yung wu mou.* Brave but no plan. Something a kid would think up, right?"

Zee Zee said nothing. The soldier beckoned, and T.A. and the other male students stepped tentatively into the room.

The soldier said, "Look at the schoolboys Madame Kung brings us as recruits. Can they kill hard men? No! We need *training!* We need to create discipline! Toughness!"

There were quick arguments from the hunchback in gold and the foreigner, who spoke Russian-accented Mandarin Chinese.

"Yes," said the soldier. "But when the Kaiser surrendered at Versailles, unlike the Cossacks in Russia, the German soldier still felt he could win. He had won many battles. The German army was intact."

He spoke to Zee Zee. "The Versailles Treaty restricts the German army to a hundred thousand men total. Each has to serve ten years. So now there are a million good unemployed German officers.

"What my friends don't know is that I hired some of these out-of-work Germans to train a new, disciplined Chinese field army. They're in the Gobi Desert now, preparing a training program that exceeds anything in Europe."

The soldier turned to the St. Johneans. "Are any of you patriots? Ah! Here's our hostess's baby brother, T. A. Soong! Greetings, Little Brother. One sister married Sun Yat-sen, and another married the descendant of Confucius! I know *you're* a patriot to New China! But to go to Hong Kong alone is silly. To develop the new army in the Gobi requires true patriotism.

"Students," said the soldier, "are you brave enough to take German training? For only one year! Do so and I promise you excellent fortune. I would find a place of honor for you." His eyes glowed, and Zee Zee couldn't turn away, couldn't swallow, couldn't breathe. He was now a quiet lad, drawn into a Chekiang stillness. German troops in the Gobi. His Chekiang wet nurse had to be somewhere in the world. *Na-ma, my na-ma.* He bit his jaw.

"Those who return from the Gobi as trained officers will be men without fear who cannot be stopped by derision, misjudgment or evil in others. Who will do this? Who will join me?" The soldier smiled with irresistibly bright and promising eyes.

twenty-four

Gobi

Y OU CANNOT DO this," said T.A.

"To do it would be exceptionally foolish," added S. Y. Shen. "You would fall behind at St. John's, and your father would be disgraced. I fear the desert sun will cook your already limited brains like a pot sticker."

"That soldier is a patriot and a good man," said Zee Zee.

"There is no such thing as a good soldier," said Shen. "I have heard of him. He is incredibly dangerous. T.A., you must advise your friend!!"

"The general could be important in the future," said T.A. carefully. "He believes in loyalty. I have heard this many times."

"Does he keep his word?" asked Zee Zee. "He promised me an airplane if I finish."

"An airplane?" asked Shen. "Why would he promise such a thing? What would one do with an airplane? Does this not prove my point?"

A Soong banker and kinsman by service, S. Y. Shen knew secrets inside secrets. But he closed his face, and Zee Zee saw it.

"Instruct us, Uncle," said the Lee boy. "Your wisdom will improve life for many." When Zee Zee was polite, few could refuse him.

"Okay, okay. He is a soldier from Chekiang," said Shen. "The far side of Wuling Mountain, the son of a low salt merchant and a concubine. As a boy, he saw injustice and became a revolutionary. Which means he had to walk the crooked way." To fight for political ideals, he had to become a criminal in the underworld.

"He rose in the Green Gang in this city, which actively supported Sun Yat-sen's independence party. That is how an underfed, lower-class Chekiang-nese with a dead father got into a top Japanese military academy. Inside patronage." The Japanese had modernized while China had not. Their military training system was the best in the Far East. Shen shuddered at the thought.

"The soldier in the other room was a *Chingbang* like Pan. He was a blood brother to Big Ears Tu."

"Uncle, what's that general's name? He's suddenly my patron. I guess I'm a *mentu* now." A disciple.

Shen said nothing. He studied his thumbnail.

T.A. said, "His honorable name is Chiang Kai-shek."

"A Cantonese name," said S. Y. Shen. "He knows Big Ears Tu of the Green Gang, and Curio Chang, the banker with the curved back and untold millions in gold. He has other friends. The Russian, Borodin, agent of the Soviet Union, is in the other room to start world disorder. Chiang Kai-shek will take his money and guns, and then, I think, it will be very unhealthy for Mr. Borodin and his friends to stay here. Chiang hates the Reds. He doesn't think they have Chinese values. Aiy. There is much risk in every direction. It is like *San Guo*, the Warring Kingdoms, full of tragic endings. Much danger! Do you see? Can you heed warnings, Young Lee?"

"You know a lot for someone who doesn't like politics," said Zee Zee.

"This is not politics, Mr. Lee. It is family banking in hard times."

"If Chiang Kai-shek," said T.A., "agrees with my sister and rescues Sun Yat-sen, he would be the number two man in China. But—"

"Then he should go," said Zee Zee.

"He could be killed," said T.A. "Sun Yat-sen no longer has an army. He has only Chiang and my sister and the few friends who were in that room. If the warlord troops should capture Chiang Kai-shek in Hong Kong, it's all over. This is too risky."

"I agree," said Shen. "That warlord Chen is setting a goat to catch the tiger."

"Chiang should go to Hong Kong and save Dr. Sun," said Zee Zee. "As for me, I'm going to the Gobi! I'll take my school exams early, ride the northern Peking train, find one of those outbound camel caravans and follow the map to the Germans." He patted his pockets and made a face at their disapproving expressions. "Yuuu! Don't you see? This is *adventure*!"

"MAH-MEE, IT'S NOT an adventure," said Zee Zee. "It's education." He had little practice talking with her. He was often gone, and she was usually at the foreign-god church, lighting Buddhist candles, giving money to compensate for her husband's vices and inviting Jesu's return. Jesu would come back to scold her husband and set China right.

His tall mother was bathing. She had beautiful skin and wanted members of her family to admire it while it glistened under soap and water. Her eccentricities had increased in direct proportion to the number of opium pipes her husband purchased. Male servants would bare their teeth in false smiles, uncomfortable looking at something that would normally lead to their executions. Her son studied the window, hoping to see an airplane fly past.

"Chiang Kai-shek is a gangster! I heard the British arrested him once and they have warrants out for him for murder and armed robbery." She reached for a thick sponge. "No, do not tell me that these are crazy times. God will hear your despair. How do we tell your father that you're going away?"

"We don't, Mah-mee. He won't even know that I'm gone."

"You have such a mouth," she said, splashing him with water, while making sure that some of it hit her face to cover the tears on her cheeks.

"I'll be back in a year, ready for classes. I'll take English books with me and study at night." She had never emphasized his study of English, but it was the correct thing for a Shanghai youth to say.

"You'll take your Bible," she said solemnly, and he groaned as she began praying loudly to Jesu and the Holy Ghost for the soul of her son. Her voice cracked, and he knew he had made her cry again.

"Promise me you'll come back a true Christian," she whispered.

He said nothing, but he was thinking, *The Christians are foreigners, and they preach love while they look down on us from their battleships and kill our businesses. They take children at night. They rape China in the name of God.*

"Take my Bible. Promise me you'll carry it." She always had it within reach. She passed it to him, her hands and arms dripping. He reluctantly took it.

"Look at my skin," she said. "Smooth, heh?"

He nodded. "Very smooth, Mama."

She thought for a moment. "What will you eat in the Gobi?"

He shrugged. "German soldier food?"

"You could say nothing worse to me." She shook her head. "Now, for the first time, Zee Zee, I'm glad you're thick and muscular like a peasant or a Manchu soldier. You'll need all your fat up there." She began crying, and Zee Zee shut his eyes and imagined the roar of a motorcycle engine.

"Are we never to have grandsons?" she wailed, clasping her dripping hands as she looked at the ceiling. "Oh, dear Christian God, will my son *never* let himself be interviewed by a matchmaker? His older brother allowed me to do this for him, and we will find him a fine wife with many male children! Why is my Second Son so stubborn? Why do I love him so deeply in my broken heart, when all he does is cause me pain and grief, and now he leaves me?"

Zee Zee lowered his head, his cheeks hot with Chinese shame. He had been a terrible son. He had angered the principal, antagonized teachers, earned low grades, never obeyed his older brother, rode a ferocious motorcycle, refused the kindly *chih huo* who wanted only to find him a kind and loving wife, ran in the sun until he sweated, consorted with gangsters in Hongkew and did not love Confucius. He had kissed a girl when he had no right. What had he done that was good and noble, besides hating Christianity?

He had won the kinship of T. A. Soong. If the Lees needed to borrow money, it would be there, at no interest, with a kind nod. But no one in his family knew this, for mentioning such a thing before the need arose would be *ji hui*, inauspicious talk, the inviting of bad luck and poor crops of weak-hulled rice for twenty years.

She asked, "Remember the poem I recited the first day you went to St. John's?"

He nodded.

"When you leave my heart goes with you, taking spring
Every night I'll hear the wind in the willows
And light my lantern for you across white snow
Praying that my son is coming home with my heart intact.

"I won't cry for you now," she said. "I'll save my sadness, and give you happy tears when you come home, so I can breathe and sleep and eat."

Chinese mothers could not embrace their sons, so they used words to stitch their boys to their souls, using tears to bind instead of arms.

DA-TSIEN SAT, ENJOYING snow-white gardenias and red show-off magnolias. A hot breeze rustled branches and freed shimmering petals to sail downward. She sat on Baba's favorite stone bench, while he slept in his study with his books. How close her heart was to his! But it was true—she wanted a man who ran with the wind. She closed her eyes to see Zee Zee—his glowing eyes, his intensity and passion for her. She caressed these memories of him the way she held a dream before awakening, beguiling it to stay in her warm bed, holding it in a secret place in her memory where it could remain hers alone, unscathed by the real world, untouched by the many prying eyes of a multi-generational household, completely beyond the reach of her mother.

In the garden, shaded by arching trees and rustling branches and sere-naded by small birds, she saw with young eyes and felt in small soft bones that Lee Zeu-zee, whose name meant Plum Tree, Longevity and Mercy, would save her from kindly, fat Mr. Tung. She began to demonize the older man while deifying the younger. She imagined Zee Zee was with her, here in the courtyard. She remembered when he would jump through the dining room window. She imagined him vaulting all the way into her magical courtyard, and she giggled.

"Yes, fly away," she said to a small, bright finch that had been on a nearby branch. "And bring my heart's love to me, in this garden. I know he'll come . . . I'll wait right here!"

"Yuuu! The Gobi?" asked Smelly Man Yao, rubbing his iron-hard feet.

"Just for a year," said Zee Zee. "I'll be back when it's cool and bricks break easily, and you'll be sucking hot yellow rice wine."

"You do all my crap jobs. Who does the dirty work when you're gone?"

Zee Zee laughed. "I'll do them when I get back."

"Defile limping dogs! You'll forget what I taught you. Who's your teacher going to be?"

"A German with a name no one can pronounce."

Yao spat at the word. *Germans!* They were as bad as the Japanese after the Boxer Rebellion. They enjoyed beheading prisoners—the proud, bloodied men who had been Yao's teachers, the greatest martial artists in the world. "You're upside-down crazy," said Yao. "Go. Your words age me."

"Wish me luck, Teacher," said Zee Zee, not budging. "I'm following a sol-dier who has iron will, just like you." He could not say, *I'm running toward adventure. I'm running from a girl. Please say it's the right thing.*

"You'll spawn turtles and running dogs!" Yao growled, walking away. "Defile you! Get off my frigging road, then, drop dead!"

"Thank you, Master Yao. I'll be back. Hey, Teacher, don't forget me! I'll see you later, okay?" Zee Zee took a few steps, then stopped and let his angry *lao-shr* leave, wondering why he felt so sad when his life was about to begin.

HE LOOKED AT the Tzu home across the street. She would be inside, reading or embroidering or doing what girls do. Hot, he entered his own home's interior courtyard. It was not a miniature forest like the Tzus'. They were people of learning, admirers of poets and scholars. The Lee courtyard was a merchant's costly but inartistic space created by abacuses and shovels. Here there were no wooded creek or wind-swept cypresses climbing misty mountains. In the Tzu courtyard, the air was cooled by high *feng shui*; here the sun beat down. *I ought to say goodbye. No, that's just an excuse to see her.*

He stood by the grapevine walkway. Had he looked up, he could have seen his father's apartment, but he didn't look up.

He went upstairs and worked out until he felt no pain. He bathed but fasted, avoiding the table with his brother, mother and tutor. He waited until the cooks ate and cleaned the kitchen and the servants fanned the rooms while his mother played mahjong with sleek and painted ladies he didn't know. His brother returned to the dorms at St. John's. Finally, the laughter and the jokes stopped, and sleep came. His father was upstairs with his concubine. Mah-mee was with God. It was not a good house. He didn't care about anyone in it; they were part of his past.

In the dark, he walked down the stairs and stood in the kitchen. He lit candles; electricity would bring attention and cost money. He emptied his pockets: a desert map. Cash from T.A. Chiang Kai-shek's letter of introduction to the German cadre. A green Peking railroad pass for hard seats, coach. A travel permit signed by Sun Yat-sen, useless in the north. His favorite knife. The pin with which Zee Zee had pricked his thumb to press a blood seal, which Chiang had given to an aide; the general had thousands of blood promises from men who had pledged to die for him.

The Bravest Wife looked outward, her cool tablet unperturbed by Reds, warlords and pretty girls across the street. Zee Zee bowed, praying. If he asked for bravery, it was reflex. Checking his bones, he found no fear of the Germans. They intrigued him. *The Gobi!* He would walk in a young man and emerge a professional soldier, able to do anything, ready to fly. He was leaving in the morning. He would never look over his shoulder again. He could not describe the wonderful feeling that idea brought.

When he came back, Da-tsien would be Mrs. Tung, and he'd be free to beat the hell out of the enemies of China. He looked in the mirror, disliking the pleasant, handsome, affable face of a schoolboy. He wanted to look older, harder, crueler. He made a face like an American or a German actor, smoking a cigarette, narrowing his eyes to block out all that was weak.

He didn't know that the trench-war veterans of the Kaiser's Imperial German Army would teach him *operativ*, the blend of strategy, tactics and immediate action, and the principles of war: initiative, mass and surprise, placing the greatest emphasis on surprise.

Had he known that the German cadre would scorn their Chinese pupils, killing them in great numbers with hunger and careless friendly fire, he still would have gone. He had made a blood-seal promise, and he was to be a soldier of excellent fortune. Such men cannot be stopped by the derision, the misjudgment or the evil of others.

The Emperor of China

THE LEATHER FACTORY was dark, loud and rancid. Da-tsien lowered her face in the amber light, breathing shallowly. Ah Tsui trembled as the tiny demons that festered in the factory began to work their way into her skin.

Gently, Da-tsien declared herself to be a disobedient daughter, weak in tradition, ungifted in speech. She said that she was an offense to all that was good. She apologized for her many weaknesses and asked his forgiveness. Below, vats bubbled, and she hoped she wouldn't become sick.

"I hear your true words," said Mr. Tung. "I am astonished to see you, but everything about you is extraordinary." He wished she would lift her face and that her amah could relax and stop praying in a low hiss. He didn't know that Ah Tsui was his ally, praying that spirits would change her stupid girl's mind and make her accept this rich, kind man. Ah Tsui rejected the rumor that a fifty-five-year-old man who had always lived with his mother and female servants had lost his *yang* power to make sons.

"Miss Tzu. I will always remember this visit. I will, of course, withdraw my marriage suit so the *chih huo* can find someone who is more suitable." He paused. "I have a request that may dishonor you. Might I ask, Young Miss, if I may keep your photograph, sent to me by the *chih huo*?"

Chinese youth must hide their emotions, but Da-tsien had never been good at it. In the year since Zee Zee had left for the northern desert, her schoolwork had slipped as her emotional sensitivities had strengthened. If a troubled kinswoman consulted with her, she could see the truth and offer wise counsel. Swept away by the emotions on movie screens, she wept openly in theaters.

Now she cried for Mr. Tung's kindness. Blubbering, she thanked him, bowed gracefully and stepped into the sun, crying for the pain she had caused for so many people, crying for her mother, who would be blind with anger, and crying for Zee Zee, whom she feared was dead. She wanted to see him again and feel his confidence, to let his boundless energy pull her from sadness and loneliness, and she wanted all soldiers to disappear from the earth. Ah Tsui followed her, shaking her head at a girl who refused money and kindness, even as she looked overhead for devilish airplanes.

IN THE SUMMER of 1924, when Da-tsien was eighteen and depressed and unacceptably unmarried, and Shanghai was a hotbed for the now chronic Chinese Revolution, she left her amah to attend a meeting on her own. She had been invited by one of her former teachers, who said the Kuomintang, Sun Yat-sen's new Nationalist Party, would bring China into freedom and the new age. Her teacher said that she would like the high energy of revolutionary politics, and many students were now confusing their parents and scandalizing their amahs by openly imitating the actors they watched on the movie screen; they were going about the city without servants.

She went because Zee Zee's friend T. A. Soong was related by marriage to Dr. Sun, and so she thought that T.A. might be at the meeting. All last year she had written sentimental letters to Zee Zee and given them to the Lee majordomo for delivery. But she hadn't received a single letter or message in response. Nor had the Lee domo heard from the boy. She had sent letters to T. A., asking for news, but he had not answered her, either. She would look for the Soong boy on campus after her kitchen duties, but without Zee Zee for company, he apparently left with his bodyguard directly after class.

She shrank from the roar in the auditorium as factions shouted at each other. She instantly regretted her reckless decision to come to this place of screaming men.

The political caucus of the Nationalist Party was held in the wide-open French Concession of Shanghai, where activists, students, prostitutes and criminals could gather without risking arrest. Those with political views could rant in an escape from the usual heavy rules of society, acting as if Confucius had never been born.

Da-tsien added mournfulness to regret when she learned that Dr. Sun was not at the meeting. She wanted to see the father of the Chinese Republic, whose presence might increase her chance of seeing T.A.

Sun's deputy, the charming Wang Ching-wei, an intellectual with a kind face, curly hair and thoughtful eyes, conducted the divisive meeting. While Rightists screamed and stomped in fury, he tried to welcome the Communists as full members of the party, drawing cheers and hisses.

A lean, uniformed Chiang Kai-shek supported the protest. Da-tsien studied him carefully—this was the man who had inspired Zee Zee to leave his home. Da-tsien recognized Chiang and Wang as rivals for the favor of the absent Dr. Sun. Chiang said that he had founded a military academy for Chinese cadets at Whampoa, near Canton. Whampoa, he declared in a high Chekiang accent, would provide the leaders for the revolution.

Wang pointed out that the Russians were funding the revolution and that Dr. Sun was ordering all patriots to welcome their Red brothers.

Later, a bright, articulate man spoke. The roar subsided as most of the delegates and onlookers paused to listen. His name was Chou En-lai. People whispered that he had just returned from overseas. He was urbane and persuasive, and a Communist.

Chou En-lai said Nationalists must do four things: one, beat the *jun-fa* warlords; two, help the workers launch a socialist revolution to free them and end peasant slavery—with this, Da-tsien sat taller—three, end the poverty of China's people; four, eradicate foreign imperialism by chasing all foreign armies, warships and missionaries from China.

Da-tsien agreed with everything except the very last thought. The missionaries had taught her English and let her add the most powerful God of all to her growing panoply of deities. She knew that with her big feet, angry mother and awkward ways, she would need every one of them to find happiness.

She wondered why the meeting adjourned with little decided. She remembered Soochow business negotiations that lasted for days. Women, who enjoyed interaction, would have kept at it until resolution.

Tea was served. The Communist delegates treated the few female students in attendance with enormous accord. Da-tsien held court, enjoying for the first time in her life the ability to entertain several men. They were smart and quick, and it was all tremendous fun, listening to them speak their minds and reading their motives. The men were intrigued by the pretty girl, pummeling her with political questions to show off their knowledge while trying to lure her into their caucus of political thinking. Not one seemed to notice that she had big feet.

In the hall, conservatives and liberals argued, then pushed and cursed while the charming Wang Ching-wei, the rigid, eagle-eyed Chiang Kai-shek and the debonair Chou En-lai recruited disciples. It was a job fair for revolutionaries.

In the uproar, Da-tsien suddenly noticed T. A. Soong. She begged pardon from her admirers and chased after him, bumping into miles of shoulders, crying in the din. "Mr. Soong! Please, Mr. Soong! Mr. Soong!"

When she caught up with him, he was assailed by breathless questions. T.A. was flustered by her urgency, blushing from her proximity, nodding, speaking erratically, undone by the press of the crowd and the girl's intensity.

"Oh, certainly, Young Missy, I remember you from the unfortunate incident on the road with Mr. Tung. Oh. Zee Zee hasn't contacted you? That is most strange . . . when will he return? Oh, you see, Young Miss, he has returned already. Yes, it is most surprising, yes, yes, very, very. Where is he? Ah, a truly excellent question. I believe he is, he is still in the hospital. Well, he was there, very much there, this morning. . . . No, not terribly sick, not at all . . . the doctors say he should be able to talk, perhaps in a few weeks."

Zee Zee's high fever no longer puzzled the hospital staff; they were now convinced it would kill him. A sun-blackened Mongol medic in the Nei Govi, as he called his home, had said the fever had come from an animist Silk Road spirit that the boy had accidentally angered during an artillery barrage. The German army doctor said the fever was caused by a spectacular form of terminal desert dysentery. Zee Zee wanted to be modern, but in this case, he preferred the Chinese explanation.

The fever would have had less effect had he not lost twenty pounds during training. More trainees died from friendly fire than from disease and malnutrition; too many peasants ran from German machine guns, as if from summer lightning, when they should have dropped for cover.

Zee Zee had shivered during graduation, which consisted of receiving an unintelligible speech from a badly sunburned German colonel, a tan uniform with Prussian collar pips, a clean 1898 Mauser rifle, and an impersonal hand-shake. Before Zee Zee could pack, he succumbed to the fever that had plagued him for weeks. He was placed in the dispensary, critically ill. Because he was literate and had been a fine, arrogant, upper-class, *junker*-like trainee, the Germans tied him on a raggedy camel, took back their rifle so it wouldn't be pilfered, and paid for his passage to Peking.

The half-bald Sergeant Dieter, a friend of Zee Zee's, was negotiating with the tough little creep who was assembling the next caravan. Dieter was relying on thin language skills and a one-legged Tartar who claimed he could trans-late using fifty unrelated Portuguese, English, Japanese and German words. A one-legged man can ride neither horse nor camel and therefore must do some-thing new. Sergeant Dieter spoke, emphasizing his points with huge pan-tomimes as the one-legged purported translator watched, his mouth no less agape than that of the caravan master.

Dieter pointed out that he wanted Zee Zee on a healthy young red Tushe-gun camel with good, unblooded footpads; a tall, wet, haughty nose; fair cud and a soft cargo with a gap, so the boy could sleep tied down. *No boxes! No metal! No opium chests! Tea bricks, okay!*

The Tartar pretended a translation. The Head of Caravans played for higher fees, pretending incomprehension and of course saying nothing.

The sergeant then insisted on a good camel puller with a family name, a man who would not get drunk, steal water or kill the boy to lighten the load. He wanted the puller to be in a good *pa*, a string of unabused and peaceful camels of fine lineage, in the middle of the caravan, protected from bandits, internal larceny, abandonment, sandstorms, with a chance of discovery if the boy fell off.

The translator reminded Dieter that all the camel strings were bad because this was the return trip to Peking, the inward trek. All the beasts were almost dead in these hard times because the Silk Road wells were running dry and feed had dropped in quality.

"Ya, ya, I want the best of whatever this cretinous bastard has."

The translator turned to the Head of Caravans. "He wants your best *pa*. Don't know how, but he also knows your parentage and schooling."

"I listen despite this foreign pink man's origins. I assume that, like all foreigners, he doesn't have a male organ," said the Head, "but the price for this unbelievable piece of goat turd has become astronomical because of Pink Man's lack of bones, his rudeness and his lack of an organ."

Sergeant Dieter had been in the Nei Govi for five winters and knew more about camels than he did about sex. In the spring of 1920, a big bull had spit a massive goober on him, and Dieter had disciplined it with a rocking blow to the jaw. He was grinning at his comrades and checking his barked knuckles when the camel ripped off part of his scalp. Dieter hit the camel in the throat until it choked, and then it bit him on the arm and now it was a real fight that knocked over three strings of complaining beasts, inspired heavy betting and finally left the camel heaving on the ground. Dieter racked a round in his Mauser and fired it into the sand an inch from the camel's head, rousing it so he could knock it out with a clean butt stroke to the head. The Mongolian camel pullers cheered him, for the load-bearing beast had been mean. The pullers with bitten, uneven scalps who had bet on the foreign devil had cheered the loudest. Everyone admired Dieter the Camel Boxer.

By then, Dieter had also learned that the men who pulled camels across the wastes of the Gobi and the Ordos were casual killers, dwellers in a mind-numbing wasteland at the top of the world. Here death was a relief and life was a curse, and cities disappeared into dots as you went into a golden desert. Dieter was a long-boned training sergeant and an enormously tough son of a bitch who hadn't lost a fight to a man, a horse, a camel or a good-time house madam since he was sixteen. Yet he hadn't figured out that relationships were everything; he should have negotiated with other caravan drivers who'd done fair business in the past. Or he could have removed his hat and been recognized as the Camel Boxer, which was worth a free trip for his sick Chinese cadet. But he had a railroad mentality—one locomotive was no different than the next.

The Head of Caravans, lean, patient and brown, kept upping the price with each European demand until he reached an exorbitant eleven *yuan*— three dollars U.S.—for the boy's soft seat to faraway China.

Then the Head of Caravans saw the passenger, a sickly kid on a stretcher carried by two Chinese soldiers. The Head screamed hoarsely at the German. He was hoarse because his commands had to cover the length of fifty camels over the howling winds of the Gobi. He yelled because otherwise, how could a stupid foreigner understand him?

"I assume, like all foreigners, you are irretrievably stupid, yes? You waste your money, yes? That boy of skin and bones will croak before we even see the basins of the Bayan Obo! He'll waste our water and you'll blame my clan. That's no passenger—that's a corpse looking for a hole!"

"I think he's afraid the boy may become more ill on the journey," suggested the translator to the German sergeant from Bavaria.

With a muscial *zing*, the sergeant drew his bayonet and said with broken words and threatening gestures that the boy was his soldier, and if the defiling boy didn't reach Peking alive with his defiling uniforms, his gear and his three excellent, unpatched defiling water skins, the Head of Caravans would end up eating a defiling oversharpened Prussian long knife from the south end of his wretched defiling stinking body. "Full defiling passage!" he bellowed. "You treat that boy like he was the fucking emperor of China!"

"The sick Chinese boy is a relative of the German general, and good treatment is recommended," offered the translator.

But the Head could interpret profanity in any language. "Defile you, pig!" he screamed. "I'll deliver full passage! I'll give his dead body to those army bastards in Peking! I am master of life and death on the Silk Road between China and the Always Snows. You filthy befouled forgotten son of defiled dogs and maggots, no one threatens me! That'll cost you *twelve yuan!*"

The sergeant paid, the puller nagged the camel down and Zee Zee was lifted onto it. He had smelled it before he saw it.

Had it been a year since he had ridden a personable female camel from Peking to the tent camps at Ulaanbandra? Snake Head had thrown him so many times into the rocks before they reached the wells at Hohhot that Zee Zee had become famous, and never had to fight for good yak meat or a warm seat at the grease-spitting fire.

Dieter strapped Zee Zee to the camel's rig and soft load with a good alpine rappelling rope, the kind a rock-soldier never stands on lest it be degraded by one granule of sand. By rote, Zee Zee completed the Swiss seat cross-hatch and tied himself onto his camel, half-hitching the center knot to secure it against slippage. He could fall asleep and still end up in Peking instead of flopping alone on the desert floor.

Dieter gave a handful of random cash and coins to the puller, who thanked him for the rest of his days.

"*Tsai jen,*" said the Chinese stretcher bearers, two young Kiangsi peasant boys who were in the new training class. They had never seen a boy cared for by a foreign middle soldier, the term for a sergeant. Zee Zee wished them luck, and his puller spoke to his camels. Mongol shouts led to great honking complaints and camel nattering as the beasts rose with partial loads for the long journey.

Dieter stayed at the watering hole to ensure that Zee Zee's string was centered in the line of march. The sergeant removed his forage cap, revealing his half-evacuated scalp, to shake Zee Zee's hand. He smiled as if the boy weighed his normal 150 pounds and could eat goat meat and defecate like a human. Zee Zee smiled faintly, using muscles that had atrophied along with all the others.

Dieter put on his cap. *"Auf Wiedersehen, faehnrich,"* he said, coming to attention and saluting, sunlight on the golden hairs of his hands. Strapped in like a mental patient, Zee Zee returned the salute. The camel picked its way into the rocks, and the boy looked over his shoulder. Dieter and the two Chinese troops become tiny dots, and then one dot, and then nothing.

During the trek with pullers, cooks, bandits, black-marketeers, thieves, soldiers of fortune, deserters, merchants, monks and the severed heads of wanted criminals that were prominently displayed to discourage marauders, Zee Zee became sun-scorched from the invasive glare and nauseated by the rocking. He kept hearing a musical woman's voice chanting, "for we are one . . . for we are one . . ." In acute stomach pain, he refused to submit to the hallucinogenic babble that the deep desert invites. He welcomed subzero evenings, when his comical shivering seemed logical, and celebrated desert sunrises by making teeth and laughing. In time, even the deserters, who were the most arrogant, stopped making fun of him.

His camel puller was Moslem. Zee Zee thought all Moslems were named Ma, for horse, but this man was a Yeh, which means fate. He was devout, he was a friend, and he protected Zee Zee from theft, death and bad camels, offering fine rations of brown well water. Yet Zee Zee shed another twenty pounds and most of his muscle. It was unfair that years of exercise had been undone in only weeks. He couldn't hold food. In that void, the body consumes water-rich muscle before fat. His features had turned sallow, his eyes pink, his nail beds black, but he was lucky. Most who got the stomach illness had expired begging for death.

He sustained himself by remembering, in excruciating detail, the location and splashy, wasteful exuberence of every fountain in Yangchow, from the gardens to the gates. Zee Zee promised to never again take water for granted.

Often he recalled a Shanghai ice factory in which he had cast his fate by kissing a girl who was above his blood.

"Yes, talk to me, talk to me in your fast voice," said Zee Zee.

"You'll live, you'll live," said Yeh, patting his own empty stomach, thinking of the noodle and lamb shops outside the Forbidden City.

Zee Zee knew he would live. Chiang Kai-shek owed him an airplane.

A KUOMINTANG AGENT had informed Madame Lee that her second son had been returned on the Peking train and was in the Shanghai Chinese City Hospital Number One, courtesy of the Chinese Nationalist army.

His mother and Tall Amah now sat with him, day and night, crying over his once handsome face until they were sick. Household servants came to serve meals that were ignored, praying to the household gods and ancestors while the two women tried to quench the boy's fever with cold cloths, medicinal candles, prayers and an acupuncturist who could find each of the boy's key *chi* points with ease, for his patient had neither fat nor muscle.

The two women looked at Da-tsien standing in the doorway and saw a stranger. Da-tsien had known Zee Zee for nearly half her life, but she should not have even glanced at him without first establishing a relationship with his mother. She was surprised by the height and robustness of Zee Zee's mother. Even in bad light, she saw that the woman had wonderful skin. Lee Taitai wore a gold cross, so she was a Christian. As with other systems of faith and ethics, this could mean much, or it could mean nothing. Appropriate to teens, Da-tsien knew almost nothing about her own parents and even less about anyone else's. Chinese elders actively supported this ignorance because it covered up their past mistakes and made them hauntingly mysterious and even more powerful.

The girl spoke, trembling. "I am Tzu Da-tsien, the worthless daughter of your grateful tenants on Six Two Five Burkill. I am honored to call myself a school friend of Second Son. Please forgive my rudeness in this moment of privacy. I only ask—"

"He has a fever, and it won't leave his body," said Zee Zee's mother, wringing her hands, her eyes puffy and scratchy and dry of tears.

"So where did Lee Zeu-zee meet a Soochow female who walks into private rooms?" asked Tall Amah, not too tired to be mad.

"Disregard her," said Madame Lee. "She's from Shantung," which explained everything. "Tall Amah, explain everything to Zee Zee's friend. I'm too tired."

"Yes," said the amah. "Doctors tried everything. Even used foreign potions. Dr. Wang used best herbs and needles. Nothing worked. Taitai asked the missionary doctor to come, but he's not like the Old Ones. He fears the Chinese City. Taitai also asked Western doctor from Lester Hospital to help, but no one has come." Tall Amah's reddened eyes were vacant.

The darkened yellow room was shrouded from evil spirits, capricious ghosts and bright sunlight. The air was heavy, humid. Amah had feared that Shanghai would eat her boy; she never thought about the Mongolian sand devils of the Gobi and free-floating girls who showed up in private rooms without their amahs.

"Who is Dieter?" asked Tall Amah. "In his fevers, he says this name. Is this a person you know?"

"No," said Da-tsien, hoping that Dieter wasn't a girl.

If Zee Zee suffered from gut pain while pinned to a wet bed, he felt infinitely worse when he realized that Da-tsien was in the room. He groaned, using all his willpower to turn away, trembling, drenched, miserable. He could not be seen like this! He was ashamed of his painful skinniness, his weakness, his vulnerability, his badly sunburned lips and face. He had worked hard to not look like an underfed *k'u-li* at the edge of death. Now he was one. Slowly, he recognized the depth of his vanity. Thinking and insight were too much work, and he passed out.

"I will pray for him in every temple," said Da-tsien, holding her tears. She bowed and left without ever setting eyes on Zee Zee.

THAT FALL, ST. John's University, upon the urging of the illustrious Soongs, accepted the scholastically deficient Zee Zee as a freshman, even though he hadn't graduated from high school, was unprepared for college and looked as skinny as a dead beggar in a famine year. But he was once again T. A. Soong's classmate, and now owed his friend more than ever.

Da-tsien was happy for his survival but angry with him; he wouldn't talk to her. He spoke to Pooh Pan and T.A. about mundane matters, while answering her wonderfully insightful questions with a camel puller's head nod or a Teutonic grunt. He had a habit of standing by the Whangpu and staring at the river for long periods of time. Once he removed his shoes, which no gentleman would do, to stick his feet into the fountains on Rue Cardinal Mercier, his eyes lost in a distant place.

She prayed for the return of his bold spirit, to no avail.

The great adventure in Shanghai was politics—the work of deciding China's future. To inspire the orator in Zee Zee, she asked T.A. to take him to a Kuomintang political meeting in the French Concession. T.A. said that she should ask Zee Zee's uncle Chu, who had connections.

Uncle Chu Lin-da had been a guest in the Lee family house the night that Zee Zee's Chekiang wet nurse had disappeared into Master Lee's apartment. Now he was a textiles engineer in Chapei.

Da-tsien asked Auntie Gao to accompany her. Gao was feeling robust despite the absence of any more baby feet to break. The two females rode a pedicab to Chapei, the north side of the Whangpu, on a nice day when the grayness of Shanghai had been cleared by a sea wind that lifted spirits. Auntie Gao was gay and pretty, her widowhood improving her appetite and giving her a quiet radiance. Da-tsien had little judgment, and smiled at everyone and conversed with the uneducated.

Auntie Gao knew better, saving her best glances for those whose eyes had been trained to read and discern. Everyone knew that if you gave your eyes to the unlearned, they could enlarge the hole in your eye through which you see wisdom. She didn't think of herself as arrogant; she was merely conserving her brains.

After a terrible ascent up a very steep metal staircase, they had to rest. Da-tsien and Auntie Gao allowed half an hour to pass so that they were no longer in danger of fainting, then they permitted themselves to be introduced to Uncle Chu. He sat behind a desk in an office above the racket of the factory floor. He was young, in a Western suit, drinking tea from a fine porcelain cup with a small lid, signing papers and acting like he was perpetually late. He looked up, jerked and greeted them pleasantly.

"Yes," he said, "I know Zee Zee is ill. How kind of you to care about him so much that you came out here alone. When you return across the river, you must use my personal driver. No, no argument, please.

"But I don't see how getting Zee Zee involved in politics will make him well. Chinese politics are very upsetting right now, especially to the sensitive stomach. I think politics are headed for very hard times. That is why I got out to make business. May I offer you some poor tea?"

"But Zee Zee was such an impassioned orator," said Da-tsien. "He used to give political speeches at St. John's. He cares about China's future. This could be what he needs to become what he was before."

Uncle Chu was trying to find a decent way to say no. He could feel his Western watch on his Chinese wrist in his Japanese factory and knew he had little time for females or politics and none for both.

"Won't you help us?" asked Auntie Gao. "And we would love tea to help us settle our poor stomachs, so disturbed by politics. What an impressive office. You know, we're all very proud of countrymen who have the courage to travel overseas to study." She smiled warmly.

Uncle Chu pulled a servant's cord to keep from studying Auntie Gao. He saw Da-tsien assessing him with a tiny hidden smile, and he jerked himself out of a spiral of careless wandering.

"Tea is coming, I'm certain it is. Hot tea. Won't you have some? Ah, I already asked, didn't I? Good to have tea, yes?" He scratched his eyebrow. "Even on hot days. Is today hot?"

"Wonderful," said Da-tsien, because Auntie Gao was blushing. "We understand, Chu *syensheng*, that our request was most unreasonable. How wrong of us to inconvenience you, with so much work before you."

"No, no, of course I'll invite Zee Zee to the Kuomintang meeting. It will be very good for him!" Uncle Chu caressed his chin with the delicate fingers of a scholar. He had heavy eyebrows that made him look older than his twenty-five years. He couldn't help glancing at Auntie Gao, who, blushing, had found something interesting on one of her perfect cuticles. Heavy mechanical looms clacked below like the fangs of giants.

twenty-six

Sun, Chiang, Mao, Chou and Teng

THE MEETING WAS yet another to establish cooperation between the two wings of the party—Dr. Sun Yat-sen's Kuomintang Nationalists and Dr. Ch'en Tu-hsiu's Gungtsetang Communists. Sun was a former physician; Chen was a former dean of Peking University.

The lack of leadership, money and industry had finished off the Chinese Empire and now crippled the revolution that sought to establish a new republic. It was obvious that national change could not occur without the financial backing of another country. Dr. Sun had hoped America would help, but it was in an inwardly directed boom economy and was not interested.

The Soviet Union, on the other hand, was critically interested. The Russians recognized Sun and the Nationalists as the power in China. They backed him, telling their own Chinese Communist members—who rightfully feared the Nationalists—to follow his lead.

Nationalist soldiers admitted no onlookers, but they smiled at Uncle Chu in his Western suit and at Zee Zee in his Kuomintang army uniform and Da-tsien in her blue cheongsam. T. A. Soong was already inside, standing near Sun Yat-sen. They worked their way towards the great revolutionary, who nodded at Uncle Chu. Sun then sat, making him barely visible to the throng on the floor. Yet his quiet self-control permeated the noisy, smoke-filled cafeteria, making this meeting more orderly than the one he had missed the previous winter.

In the press of the crowd, Da-tsien felt some anxiety, while Zee Zee was nonchalant. T.A. introduced them to Wang Ching-wei, Sun's deputy. Up close, he was handsome, his large eyes compelling. They felt his warm handshake, thinking, *This could be the next president of China!*

Spirits were high as friends shouted to one another and intellectuals gave their passionate hopes free expression. No more Manchu secret police! Jostling forced the milder delegates to the margins of the room. Da-tsien wanted to escape the mob, but Uncle Chu, with two men in tow—one compellingly handsome; the other incredibly short—was waving to Zee Zee.

"Nephew! Nephew Lee! This is my brilliant friend from Paris I told you about. Lee Zeu-zee, this is Chou En-lai, who speaks French better than Foch." Uncle Chu lowered his voice. "He charmed ladies from Versailles to the Rive Gauche! Chou, this is my nephew, the one who just came back from having the Germans almost kill him in the Gobi. He was a track star at St. John's."

Zee Zee shook hands with the future premier of the People's Republic of China, the rationalist who would succeed Mao Tse-tung and meet with Richard Nixon. Chou's death would break China's heart.

"And here," said Uncle Chu, "is our own Panda Bear—he's just a kid. Zee Zee, this is Teng Hsiao-peng. I think he's only two years your senior, and he's already spent three years in France."

Zee Zee shook hands with the man who would orchestrate China's modernization. Zee instantly liked him, a little shrimp under five feet tall, who kept puffing on a French cigarette even as he spoke.

"You're pretty skinny," said Teng. "German food disagree with you?"

"I used to be seven feet tall and fat as a foreigner," said Zee Zee, "but I smoked."

Teng was taken aback, but Chou En-lai quickly laughed and slapped his shoulder. Then Teng laughed, delighted, and everyone joined in.

"Chou says I should quit," said Teng. "It's my only weakness. I'm going to the Soviet Union next. Their cigarettes are just awful. I'll quit then."

"Why not go to America?" asked Da-tsien. "I understand they make the best cigarettes in the entire world."

Teng smiled and was about to speak, but his friend interrupted. "I am Chou En-lai, of a Kiangsu family without distinction," he said with happy eyes to the girl. In other words, he was of a distinguished, well-educated Mandarin line, and he found her dazzling.

"Tzu Da-tsien, a mere daughter, once of Soochow." She offered her hand, consistent with the etiquette instruction of St. Mary's. Chou took it. Bowing, he kissed her fingers, and her face reddened in the same instant that she curtsied. Without looking, she sensed Zee Zee's discomfort, and she surprised herself by smiling.

"America doesn't want me or I'd go," said Teng. "Brother Chou here tried to get into American schools, but America's presidents, Harding—who had all his cabinet prosecuted for fraud—and Coolidge, who's encouraging Americans to gamble wildly in the New York stock market—don't care if we're democratic or imperialistic. I don't think they know where or what China is, except a place to send missionaries." He lit another cigarette. "Only Moscow cares. I tell you, if I quit smoking, that'd be something, wouldn't it?"

"It would be," said Da-tsien. "May you have good luck and quit!"

Teng was going to say something clever, but Chou interrupted him. "Enough politics, Teng. Show some mercy! Missy, can I interest you in joining the Communist Party? We're the most progressive of all, and we have the most modern attitudes towards women."

"No way," said Zee Zee.

"Oh, Zee Zee! Tell me more, sir," said Da-tsien. "I've never understood the difference between Engels, Marx and Lenin—"

She fell silent as tramping jackboots filled the hall. Fear replaced the roar of hundreds of conversations. A hard, menacing phalanx of armed KMT, Kuomintang, troops marched into the center, forcing back the crowd as it formed a cordon. Chiang Kai-shek, wearing white gloves and a bright look, entered, passing his troops, seeming to enjoy the new sense of order. Dr. Sun looked up at him from his chair, but there was a mournful quality to his gaze. The two conferred while the assembly, and Wang Ching-wei in particular, respectfully watched. Da-tsien, who would not have given a kernel of barley for a lesson about the dynasties, had an irresistible sense that history was unfolding before them, that somehow Sun could not resist the power of Chiang Kai-shek. Neither man showed any emotion, but Da-tsien saw that they were struggling to find a basis to agree.

The general ended it. He looked around the hall, accepting the greetings of some, then marched out without noticing T. A. Soong. Yet he nodded curtly at Zee Zee. No doubt the general was acknowledging the KMT uniform, for few people who had known Zee Zee last year could now recognize the transformed youth. Chiang left, and Zee Zee was disappointed that he hadn't been able to ask for his airplane.

The thick roar of dialogue resumed. The delegates were impassioned students, tough labor organizers, soldiers, teachers and actors. The teachers sat close to the actors, who had the lowest status of anyone, since they were in entertainment. Da-tsien waved at a few she recognized from the Hongkew *le-*

hu troupes, but Zee Zee did not notice either group. Had he been his former social self, and approached that caucus to joke about Pan and gangsters and double-jointed acrobats, he would have met a dreamy, longhaired forty-year-old married man in a plain blue cotton jacket. He was a teacher and a Peking University librarian from Hunan Province, and in three years, Zee Zee would risk everything he had to kill him. The man's name was Mao Tse-tung.

The room was electric with revolutionary energy, the voltage of change, the sizzling promise of overthrow and violent renewal.

Sun Yat-sen asked to speak, and the hall fell silent. This was the father of China, a man who had dedicated his life since birth in the little town of Tsongshan, near Macao, to the welfare of China. He explained the need for Chinese unity before national change. All Party members must be aligned with the Three Principles of the People—nationalism, democracy and social-ism—before the true revolution could succeed. It was a short speech. Thundering applause and approving whistles and shouts followed. He was adored.

"Isn't Dr. Sun *wonderful?*" asked Da-tsien. "He makes it so clear with just words. Oh, he's a hero! His words still hold my heart. Zee Zee, this is magic, being here, feeling China being reborn with hope and goodness. Isn't it just terrific to be here, to see this, to hear a great man?"

"He's a tired old dreamer," said Zee Zee, who knew about fatigue; he had trouble putting on his pants every day. He was a boy of seventeen with the energy of an ancient and the worldview of a German rifleman. "Sun can make clear all he wants. It doesn't matter if he doesn't have guns."

"Guns didn't save you," she said softly, looking into his eyes. "It was prayer to all the gods and to the Jesus God. It was many good wishes."

He didn't know what to say to that. Once he had been an orator. He felt her emotions but was too tired to know what to do. Now others were talking. Wang Ching-wei was droning on about Dr. Sun's posters.

Da-tsien wanted the old Zee Zee back. But most of all, she needed a husband and was now beginning to think that it would not be this skinny boy. Others in the room had political dreams of a China without warlords or girls tied together by their necks. She could imagine a healthy China, but her dream was about a good husband who would take her from her parental home and care for her and love her and never let her be alone until she had her son.

The Christians had gotten inside her heart. Teacher Roberts and others at St. Mary's extolled Christian weddings in which God, the Holy Ghost and

Jesus Christ were all invited to bless the marriage and to guarantee later entry into Heaven. Even better, the missionaries described the Christian marriage that would follow the wedding.

"A Christian husband promises to love you and none other," the American lady missionaries had said. "Forever. For his entire life."

"Forever?" Da-tsien had asked.

Forever, they repeated. "That's right, Da-tsien. No concubines or second, third or fourth wives. No competing for attention or love."

Oh, the Christian God was brilliant! Except for one detail.

"Why would Christian men give up other ladies?" asked Da-tsien. "Many Chinese gentlemen are refined but keep secondary wives."

"Because they love God more."

Da-tsien frowned. "What if the husband doesn't really love God?"

"Then the man makes the promise just to win his bride."

"Ah, of course. *To win the bride.* Do all foreign-country Christian men keep their promises to their wives, to love and honor only them?"

"All *true* Christian men do, from whatever country they may be. Did you know that many St. Johnean boys took pledges to marry only Christian girls, and to remain totally faithful to their one wife, forever?"

IN THIS POLITICAL meeting full of conflict in which China's future was being shaped, Zee Zee was still angry with Chinese City Hospital Number One and frustrated by his motorcycle. The hospital had uneducated country girls administering Western medicines, and he knew they were untrained, fearful of the West and deeply superstitious about anything new. To the end of his days, he believed that he had lost his true longevity, his musculature and much of his male vitality not in the Gobi but under Chinese health care in the city of Shanghai. This kind of bad treatment never happened in the West, in Germany or in America, he would say. He knew this because none of the American or German men in the movies ever got sick.

Zee Zee imagined becoming more Western. He would get his airplane, and then he would chase all the foreigners out of China. Meanwhile, he felt sick because he was too weak to operate his Harley, which Pan had kept for him, albeit poorly. Pan had changed in the last year; he now looked younger. He had always emanated an undefined look, militated perhaps by his desire to avoid arrest by any number of police agencies. Now, as his facial scar faded, he looked even more baby-faced. "I look like a kid," he groaned. He imagined holding up a diamond courier and having the courier offer him candy.

Zee Zee's problem wasn't youth; it was the Germans. He had received their remarkable cruelty and their prodigious military skills. The sergeant-veterans of the western front were still pissed by the Kaiser's 1918 order to surrender to the Allies in the trenches, and they were even more pissed to be in a Chink desert without beer, blondes or sausages. They had relieved their anger by torturing their young Chinese peasant trainees. But they had also taught Zee Zee to strike the center of a man-sized target at four hundred meters with an elevated rear-sight Mauser, fire a trench mortar, direct artillery fire, fight with a bayonet, coordinate an envelopment, and use Maxim guns to defilade attacking infantry and horsemen. At the end, the Germans had called him *faehnrich*, officer cadet, and *jaeger*, rifleman.

In the desert, Zee Zee had also learned that foreign-country people could love a faraway woman with blond hair almost as much as some Chinese men loved distant women with black hair. It was a revelation. *In so many ways, they're just like us. Do we kick out the Germans, too? Or let them stay, because I owe them for teaching me so much?*

twenty-seven

Da-tsien's Prayers

DA-TSIEN HAD ASKED the smartest women of many clans the key question—how do you get a man to marry you—and received the same answer: *Are you crazy?* Proper girls didn't ask such questions. Proper girls had matchmakers, as they couldn't decide such things for themselves. Proper girls had bound feet and much better judgment.

Zee Zee's withdrawal confused Da-tsien. Steeling herself, she rode a rickshaw to the places where earlier she had purchased Zee Zee's health.

She began with the imposing Confucius Temple off Chung Hwa Road, where she prayed to ancestors and said the Three Followings (*Follow Father as* a child; follow Husband as a wife; follow Son as a widow) and the Four Virtues (obedience, appropriateness, seemliness and domesticity). She asked K'ung Fu-tzu to open Zee Zee's eyes so he could truly see her, and to help her mother be less angry, her father more spirited, her brother less forgetful, the leaders of the KMT more generous.

At the cavernous, candlelit Buddhist Temple of Assured Peace on Nanking Road, she burned incense, clapped her hands to the bodhisattvas to awaken them from their slumber, and prayed over worry beads to Guan Yin for strength. It was a good sign that the seng monks smiled at her as she begged the god to give chuming, insight, to Zee Zee so he could see how valuable a wife she would be for him. Please, she prayed, give him a soft heart, and make him open to long conversations.

At the congested Chengmiao Temple of the City God, she left paper money for good luck so Zee Zee could be rich. Cash would make their marriage safe and give education to her precious son, while everyone knew that soldiering was a very stupid way to earn a living. Please give him a job in banking!

At the Taoist temple on Wenmiao Road and the peaceful Ching An Ssu Temple of Tranquil Repose on Bubbling Well, she prayed to Ho Hsien-ku, goddess of single girls. Please bring love to barren hearts. She wrote wishes on paper lanterns so the wind would carry her messages to the spirits. Sky and rain, wind and water, the feng shui, would then whisper to Zee Zee: Marry the Tzu girl and have happiness always.

At St. Mary's and the American Presbyterian Mission on Yuen Ming Yuen, and the China Inland Mission on Sinza, she prayed on her knees to the Christian God, the Holy Ghost and Jesus, repeating the prayer from the Book of Matthew, Thy kingdom come, Thy will be done. She left real money. She asked Jesus to inspire Zee Zee to marry in a Christian ceremony, forswearing all other women for the rest of his life, asking Him if she should be his wife. All I want, Lord, is happiness and a son.

Behind her came Round Amah, who was being worn out by all the travel. She displayed her ba-kua mirror against the devil hordes of Shanghai and prayed very intently, frowning with concentration, sending directly opposing wishes to the gods to cancel the unholy requests of her gangster-chasing girl, including her silly request for only one son. Everyone knew trouble was coming, and trouble required many, many sons.

Da-tsien had graduated from St. Mary's high school and was ready to try college, a bold idea for a musical girl with uneven grades. But college would be costlier than high school, and there was no money for such things if the student was a female. Further, a British cartel had squeezed the cash from her uncle's once prosperous real estate business. The gentle, walleyed man could make no more loans.

So now Da-tsien spent many hours reading with her father, discussing French authors whom he knew, German philosophers whom he admired, American films that he had never seen. Neither was happy because Taitai was miserable, ruining meals and moods. For fifteen years, Da-tsien's big feet had cast a pall on the house. Now the refusal to marry Mr. Tung and produce dowry and grandsons had made earlier depressions seem lively. Da-tsien needed escape. There was only one righteous way.

twenty-eight
The Fortune-teller

THE SQUARE-FACED WU Du-chin was trying to look at Zee Zee's hands to better understand the direction of Chinese history, while Angel Li Santien, the dance-hall prostitute with the face of a cherub, was trying to get Pan to spend money on her wardrobe so other girls would be jealous.

T.A., an ardent student at St. John's University, never came to the outer Shanghai districts unless there was a political purpose. Today's purpose was the hanging of KMT Nationalist Party posters on factory walls. He was waiting impatiently for Zee Zee and Pan to stop playing cards with the girls so they could start. Zee Zee had brought the posters while T.A. pretended not to know him; the SMP, the Shanghai Metro Police, were now arresting students with political signs. Shanghai was a microcosm of China.

SMP cops were Chinese, but they were hired and paid by the foreign powers, which were in the business of the radical exploitation of Chinese workers. The posters directly blasted the foreign powers, and as a result, Chinese students carrying political materials were liable to be arrested, tortured and then shot by their countrymen.

In moments like these, Soong wondered if Zee Zee would ever show the steady discipline required to participate in the creation of a new Chinese nation. The Lee boy seldom studied but always played American football, a truly vicious game in which players were rewarded for being cruel. Zee Zee played sports as if he were still a sixteen-year-old wunderkind. But ever since his year with the Germans, he had been skinny and weak. His efforts to recover weight and muscle had failed. T.A. refused to watch him play football; it was like watching his friend get punished. *Americans*, he thought. *A very dangerous people.*

"I want to hang posters," said T.A. softly. More precisely, he wanted Zee Zee and Pan to hang them; he would show them where. He had told Zee Zee that Dr. Sun Yat-sen had personally approved the posters, and that the Soongs were expected to hang them. T.A.'s bodyguard had offered to do it, but T.A. knew this would be wrong. He had to do it himself.

"Can you help me, Zee Zee?"

"Of course," he said. "I can refuse you nothing." Zee Zee got Pan to help. Pan brought his pals, wiry Fen and chubby Hwa. T.A. had not missed seeing these people during the year that Zee Zee had been away. For strangers to the crooked way, the underworld seemed intriguing. To T.A., there was no romance about larceny and no great warmth or camaraderie between thieves. They were simply people without the benefits of education or redemption.

Finally, the card game ended and Zee Zee picked up the long, heavy posters while Pan picked up the glue buckets and brushes. Angel and Lady Du the sorceress couldn't hide worry wrinkles on their foreheads.

"Have small heart," said Angel. It was a Chinese way of saying *Take no chances*. Particularly if you couldn't make money from the risk.

"You should let me read your fortune first, Zee Zee," said the *wu*. "I have a sense of foreboding about—"

But Zee Zee saw Smelly Man Yao standing in the sun, and despite his weakened appearance he was out the door.

"Hu-hu! It's true," said the big man. "You're skinnier'n a bug dick."

"Hello, Teacher," said Zee Zee, bowing. "How are you?"

"I am very angry with you! When are you coming back to train with me?"

"Teacher, I'm not. I've lost my strength. I even lost my speed."

"Oh, no kidding. You're as smart as a maggot. That's what happens with no training—no speed, no power! Train and get 'em back."

Zee Zee shook his head. "I'm sorry. I've lost my way with the fist."

"Crap! You mean you lost heart. Chasing girls now? Becoming a painter? Training with men too hard? No guts? Son of a dropped egg!"

Zee Zee walked around his old teacher. The teacher offered to show the boy his secret books and new moves, but Zee Zee didn't look back.

They were on Boundary Road at the North Shanghai railway station in Hongkew. Looming above was the BMEA, the British Manufacturers Export Association factory warehouse. It burst with racketing noise and acrid red fuming smokestacks. Inside worked textilers, sewers, binders, carters, stackers, machine laborers, stokers, fuelers, men, women, children and families, blackened with coal soot, making exports for Europe.

"That wall," said T.A., "hurry!"

Zee Zee, Pan, Hwa and Fen hung the posters, moving fast and not sparing glue, racing against discovery. Hwa and Fen, having no brushes, used their hands to quickly spread the slick, pungent adhesive.

The posters extolled the Kuomintang, Dr. Sun and the necessity of labor organization. They revealed the evils of foreign exploitation and their military forces, and advertised the benefits of Nationalist army recruitment.

Zee Zee was the first to see the guards. He snapped orders; the boys hid behind loading pallets and sea crates, laughing until they heard the gunshots and the whine of bullets ricocheting from chipped concrete. Pan and Hwa ran. Zee Zee pulled Fen and T.A. in another direction.

"I'll never do that again," announced T.A. when they were safe.

"Next time we kill them," said Fen.

"Next time we go at night," said Zee Zee.

"Every time workers enter that factory," said Pan, "they'll think of me! Why? Because I signed every one of them, Zee Zee, like you taught me!"

That night Zee Zee returned to Hongkew. Using a calligraphy brush and heavy ink, he blackened C. C. Pan's autographs, saving him from another arrest and bribery requirement.

Days later, the boys visited the BMEA factory to discover that their posters had been painted over in green. All that was left of their work was a hint of the black ink Zee Zee had used to conceal Pan's name. The moment of common political activism for the three friends had come to an end.

ZEE ZEE WOBBLED from the football practice field, bruised, tired and thirsty. He took a long turn at the hot-water kettle, where he drank cup after cup of the warm fluid while other players harassed him.

"Run-Run Lee thinks he's still in the desert! He drinks like a camel!" "No wonder he's skinny! The guy only drinks water!"

Lady Du-chin, the serious, unsmiling *ba-kua* seer, was waiting for him. The curious sight of the Lee boy's emaciated form lurking inside a bulky American football uniform amused her. It was so funny of boys to put pads inside their clothing to look bigger. Didn't they know that it didn't look like real muscle? She kept wondering why she had so much hope for this person, when it was clear that the Chinese people were about to enter a time of unprecedented pain and suffering.

But her ability to read bad moons was the best in the province. This boy had luck, and she wanted to reach his good secrets. Great military success? Great financial prosperity? Big luck in love?

Knowing of two ways to reach the male heart, she carried a small metal pot. She preferred one road to the other.

He grinned at her. "I apologize for my unpresentable appearance."

"Zee Zee, I think you look fine. Doesn't this smell good?"

"Yeah, sort of." As hungry as he was after exercise, he was unable to hold food down. Surrounded by scores of students as they changed classes, the two had never been this alone before.

"You returned from the Nei Govi without appetite. I wonder if you've eaten bland, unseasoned foods since you've been back?"

He frowned. There was no such thing as bland Shanghainese food. If the Hu family cooks still served the House of Lee, Zee Zee would have enjoyed this simple remedy. But the Hus had left, taking with them the best pots and the medicinal benefits of their cuisine. Sesame Face Wong and his nausea-prone assistant had replaced them. Knowing they were weak in the culinary arts, they simply overseasoned everything.

Du-chin cleared leaves from a bench and sat. "Try it." She offered the pot and a pair of ivory chopsticks covered with helpful red geomantic symbols.

He lifted the lid to find unspiced *dofu*, bean curd, in a very light oyster sauce without scallions, chili or ginger. Carefully, he tasted the dofu, then tried another small bite. He waited. He eyed her tea thermos, but she didn't offer it, watching him.

"I believe in eating completely, then drinking completely," she said. "Much better for your internal system. Otherwise, too much shock."

"Okay." He had counted paces for distance, different on rocks than on sand or hills; seconds for fuses; heads for patrolling; coppers for water; kilometers for running. In four minutes, his traumatized guts would reject food of any sort. Six minutes later, nothing happened, so he tried more dofu. Again he waited. In time, he ate it all. They talked, but of what, he had no memory; the wonder of eating quashed the other senses.

The *wu* then offered him cooled southern black tea, which he drank.

"See? You eat all, then drink all. The stomach is then most happy!"

It was true. He rubbed his tummy, which had stretched more than it had in months. With the warm fluid at the top, digestion was optimized. "Hu hu! I'm pleased! You're a wizard, knowing everything."

"But I don't know your future," she said.

"Oh, that's why you're here. Fair enough. But only on one condition."

"I don't read palms on conditions," she said slowly, her pupils large.

"Okay, but you have to tell me the truth. Absolutely. I can't stand lies. I'd never forgive you if you lied. Never."

"I never lie, Zee Zee. I do *ba-kua*. I follow Lao-tzu. I don't work in the street. I have steady customers." His penetrating look made her inch away. Of course she'd tell the truth! She sensed his positive future, full of strong sons and long vibrant years, his ability to pull at history itself. He was a friend of two men who would change China, but Zee Zee's personality was the most interesting of the three. Pan's geomantic future was vested in bloody conflict, and she didn't have to see Soong's hands to know that he was a brilliant member of China's greatest clan.

She placed the green octagonal *I Ching* stick container next to him so his aura would warm and prepare and personalize the throw. She began asking him questions, making notations, nodding, saying, "Hm hmmm, hm hmmmm." She shook the container, then held and threw the sticks, saying nothing. She asked for his hand.

Licking her lips, Lady Du compressed, stretched, pressed on the flesh of his palm, her eyes so close that she tickled his hand with her warm breath. He had seen her study the hands of her clients, but never by using her eyelashes; it was as if she were reading difficult passages.

"There can't be that much there. Hey, Du, come up for air!"

She kept her face down. "I can't read this," she said, scraping as if to clear away dust. "So many abrasions . . . probably the rocks of the Gobi." The Gobi Desert was more rock than sand, something that pleased men but not camels. She acted disgusted, throwing away his hand as if it were filled with scurrilous graffiti, unfit for her discerning eyes.

"Remember," she said, "to eat unspiced dofu and drink only after eating." She recovered her notes and sticks. "In all my years, up and down the Long River, I've never seen such a worthless hand!" She bowed to him and left before he could speak.

Zee Zee shrugged. He never would have remembered this incident but for the realization that she had forgotten her small metal food pot. He ran after her with it, puzzled, and found Lady Du outside the gymnasium building, weeping into her hands.

twenty-nine

Crazy for You

DA-TSIEN, UNDER GOLDEN chandeliers, appropriately asked Zee Zee about his honorable mother, father and older brother. She wanted to appear Confucian, because she wasn't.

With equal hypocrisy, Zee Zee gave a fine Confucian report. "My father makes our days richer with his company." In other words, *We haven't seen him for months and he's killing us with debt and we suspect Mei-yi, his latest concubine, of pawning our goods for his opium.*

"My mother's judgment is an example to all who know her." That is, unless you see how much cash she gives to the foreign-god religion and are called to witness the quality of her skin as she bathes.

"Older Brother Gee's marriage is an example of virtue. My new *sao-sao,* sister-in-law, outdoes the legendary Chiang Kei in filial propriety." Chiang Kei was the icon of proper family behavior, a complete sucker for the old ways. Gee was cruel, and his pretty new bride was a sad victim.

Zee Zee forced himself to ask about Da-tsien's fearsome father and even more frightening mother. He already knew about Da-shing, who was a schoolmate, famous for his good looks, quick mind and forgetful ways. Da-shing wanted to be a businessman, to rescue the Tzus from their debts, and few doubted that he could do it.

"Baba is quite wonderful, although I worry about him. He eats less now, fishes not so frequently. I'll tell you the truth—I think my mother's criticism of him is making his hair fall out and his ears go deaf."

Zee Zee recoiled from her frankness. "Yuuu!" he tried.

"Zee Zee, I'm eighteen," said Da-tsien. "I'm an unmarried *da-jiao*. I don't know what to do with my life. My parents want different things for me. You're a boy, like Da-shing. You can make plans for yourself."

"You're smart and beautiful and you're the granddaughter of a great man," said Zee Zee, who had finished eating long before. "Having big feet now is a sign of being modern. You have no problems."

"No problems! I can't afford college. I have no prospects."

"You should be betrothed!" said Ah Tsui, still coveting Zee Zee's hearty leftovers.

"What about your famous Mr. Tung?" Zee Zee asked.

"Oh, no, not him! I told him that was not possible."

A shrug. "Doesn't stop him from making money."

"His factory stinks terribly, you can't believe how bad."

"Of profit."

"Of very sad dead animals and bad luck. It's incredibly unclean. I have a feeling about his *yeh*, his karma. He has money, but he's not safe."

"I can't believe he would ever hurt you."

"I don't mean that. I think, in hard times, he couldn't protect me."

Ah Tsui made a face. Money was the best protection.

"Some girls go to college," Zee Zee said, thinking. "But most get married. Which do you want?" Certainly she'd want college. College was fun. You could sleep late and miss morning classes. You could debate politics and feel the warmth that came from an audience's passionate applause as you explain the world to them.

Two of Da-tsien's high school classmates, known to the Americans as Elaine Yu and Grace Sun, were from prosperous mercantile families and had gone on to college. Elaine was enrolled at Chiao Tung University in the International Settlement, and Grace, who was adept at languages, was at the

Marists' College Ste Jeanne d'Arc on Route Doumer. Both said that they could never disappoint their parents' expectations for arranged marriages, and both said they dreamed every night of picking their own husbands.

Because their parents were Christian converts, Elaine and Grace were *da-jiao*, big-footed maidens. The three girls had avoided one another for years, too embarrassed to greet openly, since associating would emphasize that which made them ugly and undesirable. When Da-tsien began washing dishes at St. Mary's, the other two had decided to wait until she was finished and the crowds were gone. On those afternoons, they talked happily and gaily. After they graduated, they became deep friends.

"I hope we're friends for life," said Grace. "I've always wanted to be your friend. You're so kind and so wise, and everyone talks about how you give such good advice. Could we be such good friends?"

"Oh yes, Da-tsien, give us all your advice, all the time!" said Elaine.

"Oh, Grace, please!" said Da-tsien, squeezing her hand in happiness. "I've always loved your strength, your intelligence, your academic work, the way the teachers admire you! I'm honored to be your friend. Just being with you will make me smarter!"

"Isn't this wonderful?" asked Elaine. "We'll never be alone again!"

This week, Da-tsien had surprised them by asking *their* advice.

"He asked me to have dinner with him," she said. "My father's going to let me do it!"

Her friends squealed, but stopped when they saw her face.

"Now," said Da-tsien, "we know the ten-ten result, right?"

"His love," said Grace, "matches yours, and his Christian pledge equals yours also, making everything quite perfect."

"And zero-ten?"

"You love him," said Elaine, "and he loves his motorcycle."

"Zero-zero," said Grace, "is he loves his motorcycle and hates you."

They laughed, somewhat painfully. "Oh, dear friends, here's the hard one. What's a five-five?"

"He doesn't like you *or* his motorcycle?" asked Elaine.

Da-tsien shook her head. "Halfway means he doesn't love me. But he's willing to marry me to help me escape an arranged marriage."

This caused an airless silence.

"That would be wrong, wouldn't it?" asked Elaine. "It'd be lying."

It was the Festival of the Eleventh Moon for the *Da Hsueh* Big Snows of December. For foreigners, it was Christmas Eve, 1924. The cursed football season was over, and St. John's, with its heavy assortment of American coaches, had beaten the other Bible-inspired colleges in the Shanghai area. Zee Zee had been a reserve running back and had escaped major injury. Each of the women in his life—his mother, Tall Amah and Da-tsien—privately claimed full credit for the work of their own individual prayers.

Green and red lights had been strung in the concessions to celebrate the epic alcohol consumption and bad behavior that would occur in the private rooms of the Astor, Cathay, Metropole and Park Hotels. Green was the Chinese color of hope, red the Chinese color for good luck, and Shanghainese believed that the foreigners shared the same preferences.

"Happy Christmas," said Zee Zee to one of his American teachers. "Good hope and good luck!"

"Yes, good hope and good luck to you, Zee Zee."

As was her custom, Da-tsien had attended Christmas Eve services at St. Mary's, praying zealously for her future husband, whomever he was. Zee Zee had scrupulously avoided the services at St. John's. A light snow had fallen, and temperatures were in the low forties. Foreign naval vessels were on minimum watch, and the city was awash with sailors, soldiers, foreigners and lost Chinese youth in a long night of breathless merrymaking.

Da-tsien, her amah and Zee Zee were in the dining room of the Paramount Ballroom and Hotel at the corner of Yu Yuen and Jessfield. He had wanted to take her to the Cathy Mansions on Rue Cardinal Mercier in the French Concession, but Da-tsien had asked to hear the Paramount's famous orchestra. The international band played as Chinese waiters and French bartenders served the global assemblage of diners. Zee Zee couldn't tell if the music was outstanding or deplorable. Laughter, warm toasts and the tinkling of champagne flutes floated above them. Two other Shanghainese groups were in the establishment, and these unknown Chinese had waved at Da-tsien and Zee Zee, happy to see that ten out of five hundred people were natives.

Da-tsien loved the Mansions because it reminded her of Hollywood, a brighter world where emotions were honored and endings were glorious.

Tonight she discovered that if a Chinese man wore a tuxedo with a white bow tie, and a Chinese woman wore an elegant Soochow silk high-collared *chi-pol*, and they were willing to pay outlandish prices, they could eat to the sounds of excellent music with rowdy Europeans. It didn't matter what Ah Tsui wore; she was a servant.

"I want you to dress up pretty on Christmas Eve," Zee Zee had said.

"Why? What are we going to do? And where? Will Baba be angry?"

"Why do you think I want you to dress up? To teach you engine mechanics? I'm taking you to dinner and dancing. You know, to celebrate your Christian holiday." He suppressed thoughts of her baba.

"Zee Zee, I'll go, but you have to talk to me. *Really* talk to me. Like you used to. You have to answer my questions, okay? If you don't do this, we can't be friends anymore. How fancy should I dress? Will it be foreign food, and do you think it will be better than the high school cafeteria?"

Zee Zee had borrowed money from T.A., which was his Friday habit. He rented a tux from Baroukh's, serving gentlemen of leisure and ladies of taste. He struggled for an hour with the bow tie, then crossed Burkill and called on Da-tsien and her amah. He was ten minutes early, which for him was twenty minutes late. The Germans had been very clear about punctuality.

The tux concealed his painfully thin frame, which was good, but he did not look forward to the meal, which would be as easy to digest as rocks.

Gaudy crystal chandeliers, wall sconces and table candelabra illuminated the gold-hued, mirrored dining room. Da-tsien softly hummed to the music, imagining her fingers on the piano keyboard. Zee Zee drummed his fingers, waiting for the answer, then stopped.

"Well?" asked Zee Zee.

"Well, what?" she replied.

"I asked what you wanted to do—college, or get married."

"Such a question! You think you can sit there and ask like that?"

He frowned. "I think I just did. Didn't you say we had to talk, or else?" He made a fatal slicing motion across his neck.

"Yes, but that means you telling me about yourself."

"Oh. For me, I want to know what you do. What you *want* to do."

"She needs to marry money, quickly," said the round amah.

"The matchmaker would find only rich men," said Zee Zee.

"Oh yes, good idea," said Ah Tsui.

"Amah," said Da-tsien, "please check on my coat."

Ah Tsui shook her head against the dismissal. "You should eat your food," she admonished Zee Zee. "Don't gangsters eat like regular people?"

"Amah!" hissed Da-tsien.

"It's okay," said Zee Zee. "No, we usually eat children. Here." He handed Ah Tsui his plate. She took it in an instant and left.

"Zee Zee, what happened in the desert with the German people? You were once so full of life! Now you're quiet. Reserved."

He thought. "I'm the same. I just don't eat the same."

"No, you're different."

He liked that. "Yes, I am. I'm a soldier now. I know how to do things."

"You used to run everywhere. High energy. Lots of talking. Teasing. Laughing. Do you remember? Do you know what I'm talking about?"

"I'm older." He had seen boys die. Sergeants remained stoic about sudden death but got angry over the continuous absence of beer. He remembered tall, lean Sergeant Dieter kicking and cursing the absentminded German machine gunner who'd accidentally killed an entire rifle squad of Chinese trainees. Zee Zee had tried to record the German swear words in Chinese and English phonetics, but he couldn't manage it.

Da-tsien wondered where Zee Zee's mind was drifting. Probably to the desert. She had chased better answers out of tougher men during the negotiations that led to her father's position with Jardine Matheson.

"Zee Zee, what do you think of me? Am I important to you?"

He leaned back. "You talk like an American movie star."

She smiled. "And you talk like an old man."

He nodded, trying to be modest. "Well, I am an orator."

"Oh, Zee Zee, orate then on this: *Am I important to you?*"

He cleared his throat. "Of course. God, what a question!"

"Give me the details. Give me *all* the details. Every one. Every detail you have. Nothing held back!"

He rubbed his nose. Big noses had been considered good facial features until the foreigners arrived; the noses of the *Da-bi* were *too* big. "You're a good friend," he said. "A very good friend. We're both part of the same—"

"No, no, tell me how you *feel* about me," she said, knowing that there were wives of half a century who had never asked such things of their husbands. "Zee Zee, we're modern young people. I want to know your *feelings*."

"Why?" asked Zee Zee. He leaned forward. "I'm not in trouble, am I?"

"I want to know because this will decide my whole life, forever, right now, and Amah's going to come back and ruin it all before we can decide anything! Are you sure you can't eat? Do you want some of my food?"

Zee Zee had been trying to be calm. Now he was worried. He wiped his hands on his trousers as he had in the desert before setting the sights for a long shot in a hot desert crosswind.

"What do we have to decide?" he asked.

"Whether I'm going to be happy or not. Whether *you're* going to be happy or not." Her eyes glittered, large and compelling. She was Shih Shi, the most beautiful woman of Chinese antiquity. Her hair was piled atop her head, her heart-shaped oval face illuminated by candlelight and the moon. It was a perfect face, and he shook himself from the thought. She was focusing all her attention on him, smiling, so he shifted in his chair, unable to displace her energy.

"Zee Zee, what do you feel for me?"

"I think you're a very nice girl."

"No, tell me what's inside you, inside your heart."

"I want the foreigners out of China?"

"No, Zee Zee! No politics! What's deep inside you? How do you feel about *me?*"

He didn't want to think about it. He had become good at not thinking about it. He pulled on the constricting bow tie.

Da-tsien knew Zee Zee had to be guided and not rushed, but she was running out of time. Amah could not hover indefinitely at the coat closet, gobbling European food, without the staff chasing her into the dangerous streets or—worse—back into the dining room.

The music was soft and beguiling. Her heart was full of affection sliding towards infatuation, but there was also sharp anxiety edging towards fear. She felt cosmic forces as she closed her eyes in instant prayers to all her gods and the Tao and the Holy Ghost and the high-water-sign god of Soochow and her dead ancestors, including her grandfather the viceroy.

"Am I pretty to you, Zee Zee?"

"Aw, come on, Da-tsien, you're beautiful!"

She smiled. "I'm not, but what a wonderful thing to say to me. Oh, Zee Zee, being here is like a dream! Do you like me?"

He nodded carefully.

"Do you like me very much?"

"Da-tsien, we're great friends, great, great friends."

She closed her eyes to let the words sink all the way into her heart so she could taste them. It felt almost like love. But it didn't sound like love. It sounded like *You're beautiful, but I love my motorcycle.*

"What does that mean, exactly, Zee Zee?"

She saw that this question was a mistake, because he backed up. "It means we're great friends."

"Do you know how I feel about you?"

He shook his head. He kept tugging on his collar.

"Zee Zee, do you know the story about the butterfly lovers? No? It's a wonderful old Soochow story. Can I tell it to you?"

He exhaled. "Yes. Please." He resumed breathing. "Take your time."

"Zee Zee, *kai t'ien pi di,* when the heavens separated from the earth long ago, there was a girl and a boy. The moment they met, each knew that theirs was to be the most fabled love in all the histories of happy couples in the world. There was a light in the sky. She was beautiful and wise, and he was handsome and brilliant, and they knew in that instant that paradise was for them. But it turned out that their clans had been opposed to each other in a blood feud that was centuries old, and so their matrimony was impossible. They were forcibly separated. Each then refused to marry anyone else and both died of broken hearts, young and very sad. You've not heard this before?"

He shook his head. "Wooo! That's a pretty lousy story."

"But heaven, Zee Zee, heaven looked down on the two lovers and turned them into butterflies. Now, every spring in every year, they meet again in flowered fields, so happy to see each other!" She clasped her hands together, blinking to stay the tears. "They flit together with unrestrained joy, having love without any sense of time, or any duties, other than to enjoy each other's company and to love the world. And when summer passes to winter, they know that spring will come again for them."

Zee Zee wrestled with the meaning of the story. This was like being in school, which wasn't encouraging. Was one of Da-tsien's girlfriends going to die? Was this about spring? Angry families? What was that thing about no duties? Maybe she was saying that the two of them could be butterfly lovers and not have to do anything on earth?

"Zee Zee, what if the lovers were from families that weren't opposed? Think of how happy they'd be! They'd have the world all to themselves. Don't you see? If young people today had such a chance, they should take it! Doesn't this make perfect, perfect sense, ten out of ten? Tell me you agree!"

The music picked up. They watched couples glide towards the dance floor. The waiters returned to offer champagne. Zee Zee vehemently shook his head.

"You don't agree, do you," said Da-tsien.

He wanted to rub his nose again. "I don't know what to say."

"Would you miss me if we didn't see each other anymore?"

He tried to say nothing, but words came out, each one a surprise to him as it became audible. "I can't imagine not seeing you. I'm, I'm very used to seeing you. I'm, you know, I'm used to it now." He made it sound like a bad thing.

She had tried too hard and broken too many rules. It was her big feet giving her big ideas and big words for a boy with a small heart. She had waited for him in the garden to say goodbye before he left for the Gobi, but he had never appeared nor written a single letter. She had expected the desert would mature him the way storybook adventures made boys into tall heroes, but he had returned stunted, younger, less sure of himself. She wanted him to be strong, and she wanted to not cry, and now she prayed for strength and dry eyes, and the gods heard her and gave her composure and gave Zee Zee some of his old decisiveness.

Zee Zee couldn't sit still any longer. Suddenly he wanted to run and climb trees and shoot at distant targets. He wanted to fly an airplane, to be his old self. He didn't know how to dance fast, but he watched the foreign couples on the floor, the women wearing short, tight, fringed dresses and heels, the men in studs and tails, and he knew he could do it. He stood and took her hand, leading her to the music. She went sadly, almost resisting, hardening herself, her mouth turned down, fearful now of further failure.

They had danced before, but that had been slower, without any connection to the type of dance-floor activity inspired by the flappers. Clumsily, she moved as Zee Zee directed. He guided her, and she closed her eyes in embarrassment. Looking, she found him smiling at her, liking her. She danced more fluidly, letting the music reach her big feet, and they were a couple, touching hands in the joy of this new connection as they spun and swayed and the music crested and stopped with a flourish, *tum tum tum!* Couples applauded and those at tables applauded, and they looked into each other's eyes.

The orchestra began a slower number, and now, for the second time, he held her. She trembled at his closeness. He was thin, and she remembered dancing with him at the Great World, holding him tightly as they prepared to ride his terrifying motorcycle. She remembered his strength and his muscles, feeling now his painful self-consciousness. Something moved her to nestle closer.

Calmly, he held her in his arms, and years of her Confucian rigidity flowed into an anticultural intimacy that was more powerful to her than a long-ago kiss in an ice factory, his strict Confucian training falling off of him as easily as muscle in a stomach fever. She knew she was breathing with him, both of them using the same tempo, and the golden light was something of her eyes and not of the room. The music was now hers, beating time to the rushing of her blood. She prayed that the music would never end, that the moon would remain suspended in the night sky, that the magic would continue.

Zee Zee had always looked upward. For a moment he was back in the desert, seeing stars so bright that they threw shadows on the tents of stacked rifles that dotted the rocks and sand like tiny Mongolian yurts. He was surrounded by tough peasant boys from Baotou, Ningshia, Kansu and Meiyuko who didn't speak *Han yu* Mandarin or Songhai or Yangchow, and none of them spoke German. He missed the sounds of Shanghai and Yangchow, and he remembered Da-tsien's beautiful, breathy Soochow voice. He thought of her as he studied the black, glittering night, wondering what she was doing and what she was eating and if she really liked doing homework or if she did it the way he did—by gritting his teeth. As the training hardened, and boys were killed by disease and thoughtlessness and horrible accidents, he came to regard his thoughts of her as signs of his old weak self, of a second son without chances or resolve or plans, and he shut her from his mind. Later, when bone-deep exhaustion from hundred-mile forced marches stole his mental discipline, her face came to him unbidden, and he began to think of her in deeply subconscious ways for countless moments, and then countless days. On the camel trek back to Peking, stripped of resistance by the fever, he had thought of her and believed she was with him.

He knew the Confucian way of love, founded in unyielding *tze ren*, duty, and he admired it without much affection. In China, a man's closest relationship was with his father, the only human who could grant genuine approval. A woman's most intimate connection was with her mother-in-law, who would rule her hard daily work for most of her life. In Hollywood, great love was between a man and a woman. What a crazy, wonderful idea, he thought. In a scorching desert, he had thought about the Eastern and Western ways of love.

Now her feelings were flowing from her. "What do you feel for me now?" she asked.

He said "*digga, digga, digga,*" the busy, meaningless equivalent of *uh.* His voice choked, and then he surprised himself again as he told her that he was crazy for her.

Da-tsien's hands squeezed his. There was a long moment of silence. Somewhere on the dance floor, surrounded by foreigners and bathed in foreign music, Da-tsien told Zee Zee that she loved him, and had since the day that he had taken her to a crime-den teahouse in Hongkew, falling over backwards in a chair, making the *liumang* pull their guns, an act that she had thought was even better than the movies.

She wanted to cry, but she wasn't done, telling him in a great rush that if he wanted to ask her father for permission to marry, she could marry only in a Christian wedding.

"You know what that means?" she said in his ear, her heart thumping so hard that she thought she would faint.

"I know. No need to say," he said. He had taken the St. Johnean pledge.

"THAT'S A LOT of bullshit!" said Pan. "Pure *ma-fen!*" Horse manure. A typical expression in a Hongkew den.

"Yeah, okay, but Christians do this. Look, I have to pick a best man, and T.A. helped my fa—"

"I'm not talking about that! I'm talking about *you getting married!* What about all the plans we made together?"

"I'll still do them."

"See here, Pan, being Christian," said T.A., "is crucial to—"

"Shut up! I'm not yelling at you!" shouted Pan. "I'm yelling at him!"

"Goddammit, there's no need to yell!" shouted Zee Zee. "*I'm* the guy getting married! *I'm* the one who made the promise! Why are *you* upset?"

Pan kicked over a table of teapots and cups, bringing a crowd. "It's white bears and red cranes, and you're fucking up everything under heaven! You're the asshole who left last year, just when I needed you. I had the perfect frigging opium exchange going, but I needed your damn family name and the salt background to make it happen. Where were you? Humping scorpions in the desert! You're the greasy brainless duck who said *No wives, move fast, nothing holding us back!* You're breaking the promise to me, to us, to our future!"

"Hey, I didn't promise I wouldn't marry. I just thought I wouldn't."

"Listen, man," said Pan, "we got big chances in this city. Know how many *taels* we can make shipping guns and opium? *Millions!* Then you pay off your baba's debts and buy a thousand Tzu girls to diddle!"

Zee Zee was frowning; Pan had gone too far. "Defile you, Pan," he said.

"Defile *you!* Dog molester! Rat bugger! Turtle lover! Man of no bones! Maggot crap!"

"No, no such words, please," said T.A., as Zee Zee took a fighting stance. Zee Zee stopped at Soong's urging, and Pan whacked him in the jaw, staggering him. It took Smelly Man Yao and three other men to pull the boys apart.

"Bastard! You're not invited to the wedding anymore!" screamed Zee Zee, his mouth red with blood, trying to break Yao's iron grip on his neck and his trousers so he could kill Pooh Pan.

"Idiot! *Kuei* devil! I'm not coming anyway, frigging one-eyed stupid back end of a north-facing whore!" shouted Pan, one eye closed and bleeding, making obscene finger gestures at his best friend as Hwa and Fen and a third man struggled to pull him out of the room.

"This must mean," said T.A., "Pan does not mind that I am best man. Zee Zee, how much money will you need for the wedding? And be very clear— you cannot speak like this during the Christian or the Confucian ceremonies."

thirty

The Dress

DA-TSIEN," SAID MISS Roberts, "it's beautiful!" The single female missionaries agreed loudly, clapping with misty looks. The shop was filled with women's English-language exclamations, which made most of the Chinese staff cover their superstitious, noise-sensitive ears.

"Say your minds," Da-tsien said in Songhai to her family and friends.

Little Auntie Gao, round with good luck and meat, embraced her niece so hard she almost scared away her air. Cousin Miao-miao kept rubbing

Da-tsien's arms, glowing, stopping her tears on the sleeves of her long dress, trying to say between sobs, "You're gorgeous! Beautiful! Incredibly terrific! More beautiful than Shi Shih! My God, look at your cheekbones!"

Elaine Yu and Grace Sun said that they had never seen a more beautiful bride. They didn't care that Da-tsien's groom was a young man with prospects as lowly as a peasant's toes. Picking your own husband, even if he came from a condemned clan and the smallest village with a history of pox, was a heavenly dream, and Da-tsien, a Christian girl who refused to take a Christian name and was in so many ways loyal to the past, had actually pulled it off against Confucian parents. They marveled at her. The girls were true modern friends, their fates tied together by their big feet and big hopes.

Because of what Da-tsien had done, and because of their bonded closeness, Elaine and Grace believed that they also were destined to pick their own husbands. Close Chinese friends always share a common fate.

Da-tsien was surrounded by many who loved her. She was even happier than in that moment on the Paramount dance floor. Maison Lucile Modes de Paris on Avenue Joffre was perfect for her because it was Western and modern and took credit. The white wedding gown was made of satin and silk and was now being tailored to fit Da-tsien's slender form. Taitai, her angry eye closed to a single line, had been required to pawn a highly prized Ming red sandalwood lace fan and some cheaper Ch'ingware pottery to cover the down payment. Loudly, she had counted out each *yuan* that would go to commemorate her only daughter's marriage to a house of corruption and low values. Through clenched teeth, she had made Da-tsien promise on the ancestral spirit tablets that all her coming worthless granddaughters—the matchmaker had seen that this girl would produce no sons—would use the same dress again and again, in their own time. There were no more vases, fans or artwork that could be spared. The dress had to last a millennium. Da-tsien had promised her mother that the dress would last a thousand generations.

"It better!" hissed her mother. "It should last even *longer!*"

"We love it, we just love it!" came the chorus.

"Oh, Miss Roberts, it *is* glorious!" said Da-tsien as she paraded in front of the floor-length mirror.

Miss Roberts's approval was essential because Miss Roberts said the words Da-tsien yearned to hear from her mother. The tall American lady never criticized, never gossiped, and never uttered words with sharp corners that hurt the ears as they went in. She was like a *ni ku* nun, except that she lived fully in the world. May Yang thought Miss Roberts was boring; Da-tsien thought she was a saint.

Later, when asked to describe his wife's wedding dress, Zee Zee would say that it was white and had an itchy veil.

Earlier, he had tried to follow convention by having his house domo convey a message to the Tzu domo. In ten seconds, both old Empire houses, 30 and 625 Burkill Road, were electrified by the news that Da-tsien and Zee Zee were in a scandal, bypassing the traditions of ten thousand years and offending all known elders by seeking their own private marriage without the blessings of the dead, the living or the fates. It was as if the two youths had sprung from rocks and moss instead of from two honorable, well-named tradition-bound clans.

"What will Nu Kua, Goddess of Matchmakers, say to *this*?" screamed Taitai. "What will our banker say when there is no dowry to give *or* receive? You must have given lots of our clan money to Ho Hsien-ku, the Goddess of Unmarried Girls, to win this great prize of a gangster, heh?"

Da-tsien received these responses, and others, from a kowtow position. Half of her wept, but the other half was too happy to care.

The next day, Ah Tsui arranged a meeting with Tai Yueh and Kwok Lu, two of the funniest girls who had ever attended St. Mary's. The three girls met in the Tzu courtyard, and Tai and Lu carried small bags.

The three girls held hands with warm smiles.

"Ah, you're a house of robes and caps!" said Tai Yueh happily.

"And we're a house of buckets and scraps!" said Lu, laughing so hard that everyone had to join in, even the round amah.

"You always make fun of yourself," said Da-tsien, "but I can't stop laughing anyway. You know, Zee Zee has a friend just like you. His name is Pan, and no one can remember if his jokes are any good, because everyone's laughing so hard!"

"You know, Da-zee," said Tai Yueh, "we understand. Your guest list can't be big enough for us, so we brought your presents today."

"But you have to give us tea, Ah Tsui, for good luck," added Lu. "Hey, did you hear? I took a Western name. I'm now *Lucy*."

"It's a lovely name! Now the two of you really go together as friends." Tai Yueh's name meant a beautiful blue-black moon, and has a grace in Chinese that evades translation. "But you're completely wrong. Here are your invitations! Please take your perfect presents back, and bring yourselves on my wedding day."

"Oh, Da-zee!" cried the two girls. They honored her and her kindness by lowering their heads and crying, and Da-tsien held their hands.

"MOTHER," SAID ZEE Zee, "I have news." He sat by her tub, which had been moved into the center of the entry hall to maximize viewing opportunities of her wondrously sleek skin. Various people had tripped on the stairs because they were either looking at her or trying not to.

"See, Zee Zee? Your skin doesn't look this good! Mine is incredible, right? You come to break my heart again, yes? Going to tell me that you now go to Hong Kong to find your old wet nurse, right?"

It was a startling idea. "No—"

"Oh. So you go to the Ordos Desert to finish the job of killing yourself that you began so brilliantly in the Gobi, right? Look how my skin shines in this light!"

"Ma, I'm getting married. To the Tzu girl, across the street."

"Whaat? *Shemmma?* What's this you say? Zee Zee, you *serious?*" She stopped inspecting her leg, dropping it with a great splash.

Zee Zee wiped the water from his eyes. "I asked. She said yes."

"She said yes? What in monkey kingdoms does *that* mean? What does her father say? Her mother? Have you cast the calendars? What does the Tzu *chih huo* matchmaker say? Have you—"

"I'm going to ask the father for permission tomorrow. You know the girl, right, Mother? Do you like her?"

It was not a small question. If she did, Da-tsien could have a very good life; if she didn't, Da-tsien would live in hell. That is, if his mother didn't rise out of the tub and cross the street stark naked to confront her future daughter-in-law, which would probably sink the deal.

"How can I like or not like her? You picking her out without a *chih huo*, who cares what I think? Does your opium-sucking father ever ask my opinion about *anything?* How many ways will the males in this house break my old heart? How cruel of you, asking me when you have already made up your mind. Oh, to take this from my favorite son! I'll show that little Soochow brat. Oh, oh, I tell you this, Zee Zee: I have better skin than hers!"

THROUGH THE DOMOS, Zee Zee requested a formal audience with Mr. Tzu. He was told that the master was doing big financial business; he hoped to be available by the third moon, three months hence.

Perplexed, Zee Zee asked T.A. for help.

His friend sucked air through his teeth, never a good sign. "Zee Zee, it is a wonder that you have lived this many years. First, before drawing a breath, you must go to the matchmaker and ask her permission to disturb the contract. Otherwise, she loses face and will speak badly of the good House Tzu until the end of her years—and these *chih huo* outlive everyone.

"Second, never have house staff convey messages of clans." T.A. forced himself to be calm. Poor Zee Zee. Even before he went to the desert, he was such a lackluster student that he was hardly Chinese anymore; now he was German, with an old winter melon for a brain. There were little palace lion dogs that sniffed things that should never be sniffed but understood family protocols better than Lee Zee Zee. "Servants talk and your secrets are no more, and elders learn the news through a cook with a runny nose. Very bad." T.A. coughed. "Third, pray to your ancestors and ask for guidance before you approach your parents for counsel. Fourth, never announce to your honorable parents what you are going to do; instead, ask them for wise direction."

"But you're Christian!" said Zee Zee. "What's all this praying to the old ones?"

"Interesting observation, Zee Zee, from someone who probably last prayed when God created snakes without feet. Yes, I am Christian. Am I not also an honoring son of Han? So I pray to God and to my Before Borns at the same time. God made all ancestors. It is very consistent.

"Fifth, be a good student! Good grades can change the future. You are to be an orator. Learn English very, very well. Learn the classics of our language and of the foreign tongue. As a better student, you will follow my advice with greater skill. You like history, right? Not so good at math, right? So at least study history and reading.

"Now, this is my final point. Please heed it. Zee Zee, do *not* speak to Mr. Tzu. Ssss! Nothing could be more disgraceful, an unbidden suitor speaking to a gentleman's face about his unmarried daughter."

"But T.A., Mr. Tzu spoke to *me* alone! He came to see *me!*"

"Yes, yes, I know, I know. That was to castigate you. He is the elder and has the right to address you at noon in front of the Gate of Heavenly Peace while picking his teeth; you are the subordinate and cannot make the sound of a thrush, your face buried in the dirt. Lee, tell me you understand. I do not intend to allow you to repeat these grievous errors."

"YOUNG MAN LEE," said Da-tsien's father, putting down his book, "before drawing breath, tell me if you in fact have feeling for my daughter."

"I do, sir, deeply."

"Now tell me how you'll support her and your sons."

"Sir, I'll fly airplanes—"

"Excuse me. My wife put up with losing our Soochow house and our staff and the clan wealth. However, you can't expect her to tolerate her son-in-law flying airplanes. Best to try an alternative answer."

Zee Zee felt like banging his head on the ground while lighting his hair on fire. He took a deep breath. "My honorable grandfather once ran the Salt and Tea Tax Administration from Yangchow." Snarling, he went on, "I can work for them again."

"Lee, are you a Christian man? I'm curious only. I myself am not."

Zee Zee shook his head.

"Are you a Confucian?"

"I have studied the Sage." Then another shake of the head. Zee Zee was a modern young man.

Baba leaned forward in his great French chair. The boy stood before him, taking half the width he had occupied just a year before.

"What are your beliefs? What will be the values of my grandsons?"

"I believe in a China free of foreigners."

"Good. So do I. This is a belief in a negative. Any positives?"

"I believe that only Chinese soldiers can free the country."

The Tzu patriarch sighed. "Another negative. But what happens after the soldiers kill many, including innocents? What will all these deadly soldiers do then?"

"They'll guard the country. There are always enemies."

"Well, I hear your words. My daughter is a dreamer. So are you. I give you one more chance, yes? What are your beliefs, your values?"

This was like being back in school. Zee Zee shrugged.

"Ah, I see. Well, I wonder where the money will come from. And I hope it won't be the Soongs. They're good people of good education, but they'll be part of a coming tragedy. This is like the end of the Han, do you see it? There is no way for them to escape it. If you stay connected to the Soong boy like marrow to bone, you will take my daughter towards catastrophe. I say this not to warn you but to ask that you consider alternatives to disaster. Tell me if you agree with this last thought."

"I think war is coming," said Zee Zee. "Knowing how to fight, I can protect your daughter better than a man who can only cry at a fire."

METHODIST EPISCOPAL CHURCH South was a classically grand Western structure filled with painted glass and foreign spirits. It inspired the faithful and scared the rest. Da-tsien had picked it because it resembled the edifices of American movies in which starry-eyed brides married well-mannered men. Her passionate desire for the perfect wedding and her perfect gown would defeat all bad thoughts.

"Isn't it beautiful, Mah-mee?" she had asked, displaying it and tripping only once on its long hem.

Taitai caught her daughter, biting her lip. Da-zee should have a beautiful red good-luck, gold-embroidered wedding gown with the lucky gold-bejeweled four-cornered veiled hat that would cover her face and, in combination with good posture and good teeth, would say everything positive about a once proud house. Instead, her daughter would wear an unlucky white wedding gown in the color of death and mourning that showed her arms.

Taitai would have gladly given away her best heirlooms to purchase a correct gown and an appropriate wedding in their own living room with their own food. The subsequent public ceremony could be held at the grand Confucian Temple on Chung Hwa Road. There the souls of the great House of Tzu could gather to honor a miserable joining between her stupid big-footed daughter and an unemployed thug, a union that would produce only daughters. The power of dead ancestors could reverse the worst of curses, but now they wouldn't even come to the wedding, since the dead were far too smart to glide into a foreign-god temple.

Taitai summoned her fortune-teller, who threw the sticks and read the tea leaves. "Yes, no problem," she said, "you can have two weddings! One for the evil foreign god and a second for Confucius, which would cancel the bad of the first."

Baba had no view on the matter. He was sleeping more in the past months, and his waking response to his wife's harping was a light lifting of his shoulders, which had grown narrower during the slow and tentative passing of this last winter.

Madame Lee, Zee Zee's mother, had insisted loudly to all who would listen that the wedding had to take place at Moore's Memorial Church on Tibet Road, where she worshiped with an all-Chinese congregation. Moore's would result in more guests who could see her skin and her complexion and, naturally, compliment her.

Her firstborn son, Gee, and her lovely new daughter-in-law, Fong Ying-oh, agreed with her; but she had no other allies in this, and her voice failed when she saw the fire in her prospective daughter-in-law's eyes at the suggestion of the Episcopal church. That was okay; she knew how to dampen the will of a young, prideful *Jiang-nan* Soochow girl who came from below the Yangtze and thought her little nose was so special.

thirty-one

Promise Me

MADAME LEE WAS in her sitting room, gossiping with church ladies, when the domo whispered in her ear. "What?" she said. Again, he whispered.

"Sisters, excuse me," she said. "My husband requires me." The ladies hid their shock as the domo escorted them to the door. They couldn't remember when Lee Taitai's reclusive husband had asked anything of her.

She sat and composed herself, sitting even taller than was her wont. Silently, a willowy woman of small feet, small features and short thoughts appeared and gave a low bow, holding it for a tall moment.

"Permission to speak, Taitai," she said. It was Mei-yi, Master Lee's latest, virtually invisible concubine. Not that long ago, she had been Taitai's second maid in the grand Yangchow mansion. But the Master had noticed the girl's soft, lovely Soochow accent. The silken voices from the city of canals were to the men of central China as Marilyn Monroe's breathy voice was to American men of the Fifties. The tones suggested the possible and caused ears to perk and money to change hands in a fair rush. It was said that the world's best concubines came from Soochow and Wushi, and Soochow was closer. Mei-yi was pretty, delicate, pleasant and uneducated, but she had somehow gotten her feet bound, which added to the effect of her voice.

Madame Lee hated the sound of Mei-yi's carnal voice and hated the hints of Soochow in her home. While Yangchow, their home city, had been a notorious community of drunken poets and renowned literati, Soochow was a palace of evil, adulterating women. Very, very unchristian. The bowing concubine heard Madame Lee snort at her.

"A thousand pardons, madam. Master wants to see Second Son."

"*Shemma?* Second Son? Why?"

"I don't know, Madam."

ZEE ZEE HAD not seen his father's quarters since he had illegally crawled in the window, an age ago, looking for his wet nurse.

He stood almost frozen at the door. He was struck by the wealth of artwork on his father's walls. He saw beautiful K'ien Jung paintings that made men look like ants on the mountainous landscape of earth. There were expensive paintings by the Jesuit painter Castiglione, who had visited the Ch'ing court and stayed, hoping for converts; these depicted mounted warriors and noble black steeds. Zee Zee was spellbound by sepia paintings of tall peaks and fair clouds, recognizing the square red ink chops in the lower corners—painted by his father before he had given his gift to Indian opium. Zee Zee didn't know that his father could paint so brilliantly. It was a collector's fortune in art, and a son's revelatory archive of his unknown father.

Master Lee reclined on the *kang*, his contoured red teak bed where he smoked and dreamed and lived. He lay in dungeonlike light thrown by one of his own father's old beautiful stork-necked Yangchow lanterns. The room was an opium den, reeking from the accrued chemical imprint created by twenty thousand sequentially burned opium pipes. Zee Zee winced at the bitter smell.

His father spoke so softly that Zee Zee missed much of what he said. Master Lee was rambling about his own father, Shui-feng. Zee Zee leaned forward, holding his breath, wanting every word. He knew nothing about his paternal grandfather, except that he had been a commoner who got incredibly lucky by becoming a salt-tax lord.

"My father," said the Master in a voice roughened by the hot river of opium gases, "came from Snail Creek village in Kiangsi Province. He was a rice farmer who rose up on good calligraphy." Then he was quiet, and Zee Zee realized that he had fallen asleep. When he awoke, he gestured impatiently at his son. It took several tries, and then the Master pointed and, frustrated, gave sharp instructions.

Zee Zee fired the gum burners and reached into the dark chest to remove a slug of black opium. He dropped it in the burner cup, watching as it softened and sagged. He had to guess when to remove it, his roughened hands taking the heat too well as he rolled the hot opium into a ball. He pressed the ball into the pipe, but it wouldn't fit—the mass was too big, and now it was cooling and hardening. Angrily, Zee Zee pulled out his folding knife, dug out the softened slug and viciously cut it in half, sweeping one half into a corner and dropping the other in the burner. Again his father slept, and Zee Zee imagined hurling the opium chest through the window and machine-gunning it and hacking at it with a long Prussian bayonet.

This was not what he had expected. Zee Zee had imagined his father giving him marital advice, telling him how proud he was that his son had trained with the Germans and was now playing football, how happy that he would marry a pretty girl with royal blood who would produce sons to support him. Instead, he was helping kill his baba with opium.

Zee Zee violated propriety by studying his dozing father, truly seeing his face for the first time since he was very little. His father looked tragically old, breathing poorly, his once good lungs forever wasted. Zee Zee was actually too Confucian to curse the fate of having an opium-addicted baba. He thought, *Heaven decides all matters, not men.*

He wondered instead about how great men seemed to produce lesser sons, how the great tax administrator could have raised an opium addict who had trouble speaking. Each man can do one thing well. His father smoked *ta-yen*. What could Zee Zee do? The idea of flying pulled at him and seduced him. The opium was soft; he pressed the hot ball into the bowl, and it fit. Baba knew and awoke, gesturing for his son to light it.

It was a test, as everything in China seemed to be.

Zee Zee lit a long, splintery good-luck Hunan-forest wood match. Grimacing, he put the yellowed, gnawed pipe stem to his lips, sank the flame into the bowl and drew inward to light the bitter opium paste, puffing until the ball was in heat. He spit out the hot smoke. Feeling as if he were committing murder, he passed the smoking pipe to his father.

On his father's orderly, unused desk, Zee Zee found an old salted plum, a woman's snack. He quickly bit into its stale hardness, hurting teeth that had been loosened by malnutrition and hand-to-hand fighting and years of *gong-fu*, letting the bad taste seep in to attack the bitter burn of opium, wishing for hot tea.

His father smoked, dozed, relit his pipe, fading, drifting, riding the gray cloud as it took him to a better place. There was no sense of time. He awoke, surprised to find Second Son standing attentively but invasively in his own private room. He got angry, then remembered that he no longer gave himself to the Fury God, that he had taken the Big Smoke to quell the fires inside his heart. *I am Lee Kung-doo, son of the great administrator and lord Lee Shui-feng, and I no longer strike my unworthy wife or push the faces of my worthless sons into buckets of Yangtze water to silence them when they cry out for their wet nurses. No, I am an honorable man and I produce excellent calligraphy, and I am a painter of antiquity, and my concubines honor me and know me as the rising sun, the rampant dragon, a man of thunder and great clouds.*

"What are you doing here! Oh yes, you lit my pipe. Yes, okay, good. Now, listen to my words. . . ." He told the story of Zee Zee's grandfather, telling of his sacred name, Lee Shui-feng, which could be spoken only by a son from another world. His father kept dozing, starting again each time from the beginning. The story took most of the day. Zee Zee was supposed to be arranging his wedding, because Mrs. Tzu, his small, evil-eyed future mother-in-law, was not inspired to do the work. She was spending her time commiserating and cursing bad luck with the *chih huo*, the short, unhappy matchmaker who had failed Mr. Tung.

His father was saying, "Be a modern person. Learn all you can from the West. Yes. Do this. Become an engineer . . . ahhh, light another pipe, this one's gone dead on me, just like this stupid house. . . . Promise me this, Gee, promise me. You're a good son."

Master Lee had been confused by fatherhood. *Digga, digga, digga . . .* "Listen, Gee, I was so angry back then. You're not a bastard. I am! Ah, I think I'm dying. . . . Gee, you're Firstborn and have to know . . . you're cruel but sensible, not like your idiot younger brother. Where was I . . . what are we doing? Why—why are you here?"

"You were talking about having to know something."

"No, I was talking about what you needed to know. Is it dark in here? I have so much trouble seeing. This makes me so angry! I can't even do my calligraphy . . . no light . . . the light hurts my eyes. Gee—you should know, but don't tell my grandchildren. Your grandmother was a Small Wife . . . yes, my mother was a concubine, not the Taitai.

"See, the day I called you a bastard, I remembered that I got the big Yangchow house with Father's garden, but not enough money to keep it. Father wanted me to work! *Me!* Everyone knew I was an artist, not a *worker!* He said if I worked, I could keep the house. But he gave me awful jobs in the salt business. I had to do so many things. I hated it!" He gathered his breath, seeing everything, but nothing in the room.

"Gee, be an engineer. Engineers will have the cash . . . but you have to keep your brother away from me. I do not like Second Son's face—it reminds me of my Older Brother, the son of the Taitai, who got everything. Oh, he mistreated me, disrespected me, the dirty bastard!"

His father wept, and Zee Zee was surprised by the emptiness of his own heart.

He jumped. His father had grabbed his hand and was pressing it against his head, weeping pitifully on it, smearing him with hot tears.

"Oh, oh, son, oh, I'm so lost! So alone. Don't leave me! Promise me you'll stay by me. Times are so dangerous! It's going to be like the Taipings all over again. They're going to come after me with drums and spears to kill me in my bed. Promise me, Gee! You hear my words?"

"Yes, Father," said Zee Zee.

"Promise me!"

"I promise, Father," said Zee Zee. "I promise."

thirty-two

Phyllis Thaxter Eyes

AD HAD SAID things about his father that were beyond forgiveness. He was tired, a prisoner of war who had given answers to the enemy. Dad loved history but hated to look back at pain. He liked to look out his window at snow-capped Pikes Peak. He said it reminded him of Tibet, and of flying in military transports over the windswept Himalayas. I waited, feeling Chinese guilt and American hope.

"Then I married your mother," he said.

"Was it a happy day, Dad?"

"You remember the movie *Thirty Seconds over Tokyo?*" I said that I did. "Who starred in it?" he asked.

I named the cast: Van Johnson, Spencer Tracy, Phyllis Thaxter.

He laughed. "I knew Spencer Tracy. Learned so much about him in just one day. Two days," he amended. "Second day a bad day. Surprised?"

"Yes, but not that surprised. You knew everyone."

"But this not about him. Later, more about him. More than I want to say. This is about Phyllis Thaxter."

"You know, she had eyes that seemed to melt."

"Oh, good, very good. See, that's how your mah-mee looked. Her eyes, just like that, in that movie."

"ARE YOU READY?" asked T.A.

"Hell, no," said Zee Zee. "Dammit, don't make me do this!"

"Zee Zee, she has been waiting all night for you! You must!" T.A. was adamant. He opened the door, admitting the excited chatter of the crowd pressing into a packed church. "You are beautiful and wise as always," he said, bowing. "Please honor us with your company."

She entered. Miss Wu was the smallest and oldest adult Zee Zee had ever seen. He had met her earlier and had long feared the idea of having to deal with her. She hobbled in as if partially paralyzed and attempting to negotiate a slickly frozen lake. One arm was unsteadily extended; from it a tiny, sawed-off cane oscillated like an activated divining rod. Thin, white, wispy hair seemed to stream behind her as she approached, as if she were flying in mountain winds instead of moving at the speed of glaciers. She had a thin jaw that jutted outward like a pike, a weathered face and the blazing eyes of Chong Kui, the scary ghost catcher with devilishly upturned, U-shaped eyebrows. In her other hand she carried an extremely worn Chinese Bible.

Zee Zee groaned, stood and bowed.

Miss Wu passed him, bowed to the portrait of Jesus—depicted as a solemn Chinese man with a thin mustache—and sat with surprising nimbleness in the groom's special red satin–pillowed chair. She sighed, her bound slippered feet a foot from the floor. Her smile made her a different person. Her forbidding eyes were now soft and beguiling, the black-gummed, toothless grin warm and kind.

"Ah, Young Lord Lee, your face brightens tired eyes. How fine and handsome you are! So clearly are you a man of fine taste and good manners. You could marry any number of girls by just standing there, flashing your teeth. Clans will applaud, and many sons will be produced! No, no, no formalities. I was speaking from the heart, and you are a young man who has no interest in ancient persons like myself and will only offer fake flattery that I don't want to hear. Did my godson T.A. tell you of what I will give you today?"

Miss Wu had been a friend of T.A.'s revolutionary father, "Charlie" Yao-ju Soong. She had lived in the Soong home, but no one could remember how or when she first appeared. Charlie had truly and sincerely eaten the Christian faith, but Miss Wu was, in that regard, his superior. She was a fundamentalist of the first water and had inculcated Christianity into Mr. Soong's children, with varying degrees of success, a thing that could be said of many rich American Christian families.

"Ah, so no one has told you anything. No problem!" She rubbed her palms as if to lift a hoe. She handed him her Bible. "Open it, yes, open to any page."

He deliberately opened it in the back, to the New Testament, thinking that it was in many ways easier than the Old.

T.A. offered his godmother a cup of tea, which she courteously refused. Without looking down, she pointed randomly at the page Zee Zee had selected and began to recite. It was something about being weak to win the weak.

"See?" said Miss Wu. "God tells you to be strong and hold the pledge of only one wife! Pick another!" Zee Zee flipped to a new page. Blindly, she pointed. The passage described Herod and the star of Bethlehem.

"Ah yes! The one single star in the sky, among millions of alluring stars, means fidelity to only one wife!"

This went on for some time. It didn't matter what the passage said; she interpreted it to mean that he was becoming a man of one wife.

Zee Zee knew that part already. He quietly detested his father's love of concubines and was resolved against opium and adultery. He fought to stay awake.

"Pay attention," said T.A. "Miss Wu is a Bible scholar."

"Take my wisdom, Young Lord. Let me pour my years into your ear. I knew your father and saw your grandfather, the Yangchow salt-tax administrator. Yes, very true. I saw his mistakes from far away, but I saw your father's errors from very close. Young Lord, if you do not take this good Book inside your heart, you will become him and your son will become you and his son will become your father."

Zee Zee laughed. "You make that sound like a curse."

"Aiy! Don't make light, it's a warning! A warning for a smart young man. I see the ugly fires inside you. The devil's anger. And pride, so much pride, so much arrogance. Will you take my warning or spit on it?"

"Miss Wu, I take it as a wedding gift. From you. Your generosity can never be matched by my inadequate skills."

She turned to T.A. "He talks like a beggar in a whorehouse. Trying to get trouble for nothing. Using flattery when he should bow to truth."

T.A. coughed. "Mother, he tries to honor you."

"Lee," she said to Zee Zee, "you want to honor me, then pray with me. Pray with me now! When's the last time you prayed, boy?"

Zee Zee tried to remember. He hadn't prayed in the Gobi. Man was invisible and there the gods had come into the open. "Last year, Mother," he said, using the honorific. "I prayed to ancestors in the clan hall. I prayed to a female. Called her the Bravest—"

"Pray with me now, Lee. With your heart. Boy, pretend I'm still a beautiful young girl and you look just one look, and you see me at night when I'm a thousand *li* away. Will you pray with this beautiful girl?"

PAN WORE AN ill-fitting Western suit with a black panama hat. He chain-smoked, was half drunk and, snapping his fingers, refused to enter the sanctuary.

Barrel Man Yao's thick chest burst out of a formal celestial-blue gown that last fit him when the empress dowager ruled in Peking. His eyes narrowed as he looked upward at the tall, death-white bad-luck cross that pointed rudely at heaven like a spear, disturbing harmony by suggesting that men could jab at gods. But this was not his day; it belonged to Lee, and today he would become a man. Pan was leaving.

Smelly Man Yao, wonderfully redolent with fresh Ningpo sandlewood soap, stopped Pan with a hamlike hand, whispering, "This is your best friend and the only *gaodeng huaren* you know. He's your teacher. He taught you good calligraphy. Don't fart it up!"

"He broke his promise to me, Yao. So defile you!" Pan spat hard on the church steps, pulling away to the church doors, letting the thinning crowd move past. Next to him were Hwa and Fen in gowns, wearing their smallest pistols to avoid breaking the lines of their garments.

The Pan family rickshaw puller was an old, bearded man who was seldom used since the Pans had acquired Chryslers and Harley-Davidsons. He quickly lifted all the wedding presents and carried them to the church doors. This way he could guard the gifts while being able to see what devils did to Chinese people inside their dark, frightening temple. He had swallowed the foreign-god religion during an Anhwei famine just before the turn of the century, because the missionaries gave food with their lessons. With a full tummy and a fear of ending up on a cross, he quit the mission and went back to honoring his ancestors and the unimpressive and extremely unresponsive god of rickshaw pullers.

He saw Pan reach into his jacket and pull out an enormous automatic pistol. He did something to it, then slipped it inside his waistband and went in. Behind him trailed the two gunmen and Him Man Yao, wearing his black homburg.

ZEE ZEE WAS so angry that he could hardly think. He hated Miss Wu and her proselytizing. He had already been anxious, and then *her*! And he couldn't do anything about it because she was T.A.'s godmother, responsible for his faith.

He felt like punching the minister, one of those American-tainted Chinese who were trained by foreigners in a foreign school to make him a real foreign devil. Because prejudice was easier to deal with than fear, he let the bigotry wash over him, his anger giving him comfort. He wanted to keep the pastor from speaking. He wanted to hit someone. He wished someone would start a melee.

Da-tsien knelt on satin pillows, praying to all gods. It took a while. Auntie Gao lit incense and rearranged the offerings at a makeshift Taoist shrine. Miao-miao was an atheist, so she spent the time thinking about food. Grace and Elaine, Da-tsien's school friends, prayed to Jesus. May Yang looked at herself in the mirror, head at an angle, adjusting her pretty hair.

"He's so handsome!" hissed Miao-miao, who was peeking through the curtains. "You're so lucky!" She hushed with a gasp as Taitai entered. Da-tsien's mother wore a bright red silk cheongsam that made her look like a young bridesmaid. In her hair she wore a small white gardenia.

"What's the delay?" she snapped. "You're supposed to wait for others, not make others wait for you. God, I hate foreigners!"

Da-tsien jerked, almost falling, and apologized as Auntie Gao and the Christian girls prayed louder and May checked the fit of her dress.

Taitai stepped out from the curtains and fixed her evil eye on the organist, who jumped and immediately began the wedding march.

Zee Zee saw the bridesmaids running down the aisle to take their places beside him on the chancel steps. He was angry at the world and at the horrible organ, and he took pleasure from the girls' lateness. Sergeant Dieter had said that the Germans had a word for it: *schadenfreude*—a malicious satisfaction drawn from the misery of others. Zee Zee had a large serving and smiled, relishing how badly the wedding was going. Because he was afraid, he even hoped something would stop it, but armed gangsters were in the pews and Sikh guards, including the Tzus', lined the back of the church at parade rest.

Then Pan walked in, followed by Hwa, Fen and Barrel Man Yao. Pan sauntered towards Zee Zee, waving at fellow gang members in the sanctuary. Smelling of whiskey, he ignored Zee Zee and casually stood with the other groomsmen—T. A. Soong; F. C. Fong, a classmate from St. John's; and Zee Zee's brother, Gee. Of Zee Zee's four men, one was good, one was patient and two hated his guts. It amused him greatly. Some wedding!

There she was. Da-tsien was walking down the aisle to him, keeping pace with the music, which he understood for the first time. She was accompanied by her father, who today looked strong and robust. Zee Zee looked again at his betrothed, the sight of her making his mind vanish. Her baba wore a blue Chinese gown; she wore a Western white wedding gown with a veil and train. He had trouble breathing. Two pretty little girls in pink dresses carried tiny pillows with rings.

She was beautiful, exquisite, intoxicating, her face shining under a galaxy of desert stars. He looked at her as if he had never seen her before and she had stepped from the screen of the most powerful American movie anyone had ever seen. She stopped next to him, and he wondered where her father had gone. The pastor was speaking, and she looked up at him with melting eyes. Her love was so pure, so unconditional and so generously given that his heart softened, shedding anger, fear and *schadenfreude*.

When the words were said and the rings exchanged, he held her hands and kissed them as Chou En-lai had done with her fingers at the KMT caucus. He had seen Chou in the audience.

He held the kiss. When he looked up, she was crying with joy.

thirty-three

Bow to Ancestors

SHE SAT IN Zee Zee's room with her dearest friends. A thousand feelings ran through her heart and liver. As far as Jesus was concerned, she was a married lady. As far as her stomach was concerned, she was ill. Zee Zee had said the words in front of the Holy Ghost and the pastor, but he hadn't said them the right way, and so everything was wrong. And what was coming—the Confucian ceremonies—would be even worse.

Auntie Gao, Miao-miao, Grace, Elaine and Ah Tsui were helping Da-tsien change while pretending not to see the native disorder of the room. Servants had cleaned it for them, but the walls were covered with movie stills, photos of the St. John's football and track teams and soldiers with ugly camels. Above them dangled two rings from the ceiling, and they uniformly hoped that these had nothing to do with sex. The windows were open, and a cool breeze blew the old lace curtains while each woman discreetly tested the bed for strength and stability.

Da-tsien was surrendering her Western wedding gown, which made her feel like an actress, for the heavy red high-collared, gold-embroidered, front-paneled Chinese dress, which made her feel like a slave.

Awaiting her was the heavy wedding cap and its square red opaque veil. The only important thing now was not to tear the dress, which would be a bad omen. Tearing wedding fabric meant death.

Ah Tsui kept perfecting Da-tsien's elegantly coiffed hair while complaining that her girl should have had the red palanquin journey from her house, across the street, to the groom's house, as custom required.

"It's okay, Amah," said Da-tsien soothingly, "this dress is a spooky reminder that Mah-mee wanted me to marry Mr. Tung, so the less we do the traditional way, the better, don't you think?"

"Don't ask questions! I can't argue when you ask questions! Oh, poor Mr. Tung!" And then she screamed, "*Aiyyyyyyy!*," making Auntie Gao and Miao-miao shriek as Da-tsien lurched awkwardly from her chair, ripping the hem of her red wedding gown. Everyone froze.

Da-tsien counted fifteen seconds. Singh the guard opened the door. Taitai burst into the room, her evil eye shut. *"Now what?"*

"A devil tried to find my secret coins! I felt it!" cried Ah Tsui.

"Aiyaaa! Poxes take your secret coins and secret devils! There isn't a spirit in the province that'd mess with your fat to find the greenest jade in China. Hush! You scream again, and the Lee women will come! This is their house! You want a six-foot Amazon here? *That's Lee Taitai!* You want the dwarf with the Bible to take your souls? *That's Miss Wu!* Or Miss Wong, the strict witch tutor who taught the Lee boys nothing? *You want her in this room?"*

Ah Tsui slowly got to her knees, bowing and chanting, No, no, no.

"Tell me I did not hear fabric ripping," said Taitai. *"Did I?"*

"It was nothing, Sister," said Auntie Gao, her needle ready to work.

"It was the slip," said Miao-miao, then realizing that this would be equally unlucky, for it meant the foundation of the marriage was torn.

"We can't lie," said Grace, who was Christian. "It was my dress."

"Hey, know what?" asked Taitai. "You are all as stupid as headless chickens running for the pot! Now, not one word of this to the Lees or you disgrace us even more! Some wedding!"

Zee Zee couldn't discern Mozart from a train wreck, but his tin ear heard the screams of women even amid the roar of two clans compressed into the Tzu sitting room. Everyone either family had ever known seemed to be present: herbal pharmacists, Soongs, Christians, salt-tax luminaries, Kuomintang military and political types, St. John's faculty, dishwashers, Bible salesmen, foreign missionaries, students, gangsters, labor activists, Communists and a small lean Gobi Moslem camel puller named Yeh.

Zee Zee heard the commotion upstairs in his bedroom. *My wife is in my room! Holy Christ, what'd she think of the Roman rings bolted into my ceiling? Were my boxer shorts on the floor? God, I'm married.* He was convinced that everyone could see that he had changed. The wedding band on his left hand weighed more than a mortar. Yet he liked the attention and uproar, well-wishers slipping cash in his pockets and stacking presents, sipping wine and tea and eating southern Chinese dim sum treats.

"A toast to the lucky groom! Say goodbye to sleep, Zee Zee!"

Tall Amah pulled him aside as if he were a small boy. She wet her fingers and plastered down his cowlick, a sprout that she always thought had come to him from the spiritual courage of the Bravest Wife. Amah looked directly into his eyes for the first time since he was little.

"Zee Zee, you remember Na-ma, your wet nurse?"

He couldn't speak at first. Then, he whispered, "God, yes."

"Her name was never spoken in the house, but I knew it."

"Hey, congratulations, Zee Zee!" cried a St. John's classmate. Zee Zee tried to smile at his friend but could only look at his amah.

"Tell me," he said hoarsely.

"Her name was Fu, meaning good luck. Her given name was Sweet Plum, plum just like our family name, Lee.

"You know what, Zee Zee? Sweet Plum was like your Da-tsien. She talked fast and had a very pretty voice. She loved everyone in a way I never could. She talked to all persons. Horse people, honey carters, slaves. That's why you can get along with so many people, because of her. That's why you talk many dialects without thinking—that was *her* habit. You've been talking to Soongs in Cantonese without even knowing."

"Was she really good and kind?"

"Oh, yes. She loved you, I think, even more than me."

He nodded, smiling sadly at her. "Was she beautiful, Amah?"

Tall Amah reached up to pinch his cheek. "Men! Zee Zee, she wasn't really beautiful on the outside. God, she was very strong! Good legs, walk forever! But she was beautiful inside. Very beautiful inside. Like your Da-tsien. Oh, Da-tsien's plenty pretty, but inside she's like your na-ma. Zee Zee, this is a good thing. Na-ma was a country girl, but she had heart. Da-tsien is a gentry girl, also with heart. Look, I know you're worried. But a wife is no worry. This girl, she loves you. You be good to her, you hear?"

The big-bellied Lee majordomo and the Indian guards, called up for special duty from the Tax Office, began pushing everyone outside. Only family and inner friends were allowed to stay for the ceremony. The outsiders pushed to look in through the windows, and Zee Zee was surprised to see so many noses flattened against the French panes. His groomsmen remained. He didn't see Pooh Pan.

Taitai nodded at Madame Lee, Tzu Taitai acknowledging Lee Taitai, the two mothers taking command of clans.

Deaf Man Fu struck a Buddhist bell with just the right tenor to invite the families to reflect. Quietly, servants laid Confucian rice bags on the staircase and the hallway leading into the sitting room. East Asian *p'i-p'as*, flutes, drums and gongs and a wonderful, traditional seven-stringed *ch'in* launched into a solemn march that proclaimed the survival of the clans and that the young couple was but an instrument of a greater plan. Healthy children can be made only by a good man and a good woman who have given each other the lifelong promise. Thousands of Lee and Tzu ancestors and the two living clans had joined today to ensure that Zee Zee and Da-tsien remained loyal to the needs of the greater community and to raising healthy sons.

The music stopped. No one breathed. Ghosts were coming down the stairs. Footfalls on a carpet of rice paper creates an ephemeral effect of angels tiptoeing through the house; the sounds were intended to remind all that the ancestors had been summoned and were there, eerily walking among them, watching and judging everything.

Zee Zee wanted to clear his throat, but it was too dry. T.A. was looking at him with smiling reassurance, patting his jacket, hinting at the gift within, as if money would help.

Grace Sun and Elaine Yu led the procession. Each carried an enormous red candle, twenty inches tall and four inches in diameter. One symbolized the *long*, the dragon, and the other the *feng-huang*, the phoenix. Together they represented male spirits, female spirits, justice on earth, harmonious union and hints of good intercourse. The candles flickered as they walked, as if the ancestors were huffing on them.

Behind them came Cousin Miao-miao and Gee's new wife, Ying-oh, a beautiful girl with long ebony hair.

Da-tsien was next, approaching her ancestors, her new mother-in-law, her husband and her parents. She was guided by Auntie Gao with her brave limp; Da-tsien's square red veil draped over her head and blocked all but a hint of light. She couldn't see the good-luck red banners stretched across the helmeted doorways of her home, but she could feel the separated red hanging banners as they brushed her body in passing. She could hear round Ah Tsui sniffling, and behind and alongside, she felt the spirits of the dead, wishing her well, their hands ensuring that her veil didn't fall from her face.

Often a prosperous matchmaker would open the ceremony and pass the formalities to a Confucian or Buddhist priest. But this was Shanghai, and Zee Zee's mother had majored in faith and minored in exhibitionism.

"Now we begin," she said in a small voice that didn't match her height. The ensemble knew four tunes—for ancestors, for weddings, for funerals and for moon festivals. They had finished the first and now played the second, which was upbeat and positive.

Auntie Gao led Da-tsien to stand next to Zee Zee. Da-tsien could sense her husband next to her. *What is he thinking? Does he hate me?*

Good God, thought Zee Zee. *My shoes are killing me.*

"Bow to heaven, and bow to earth," cried Madame Lee in an operatic voice. The couple bowed twice, straight ahead. Everyone saw how they moved as one. Only Amah knew that they had practiced by dancing together in public, in front of foreigners, to ungodly devil music that polluted their hearing.

"Bow to ancestors. Bow low to the Bravest Wife!" They turned and bowed to the wall on which the ancestral portraits hung. They'd been moved from the upstairs Hall of Ancestors into the sitting room. The ancestor portraits showed very formal, judgmental people. Next to them was the marble spirit tablet of Shui-feng's first wife.

Da-tsien thought, *How wonderful to honor a female ancestor!*

"Bow to your parents and thank heaven." They turned toward Madame Lee and bowed to her, to Baba and to Taitai. Master Lee was upstairs with his pipes. Mei-yi, his ghostlike concubine, had appeared for him. Madame Lee had banished her with a single frown to a distant corner, where she still huddled, sad and alone. Zee Zee's mother knew that she was acting shamefully in both Confucian and Christian terms, but she didn't care. This was her Second Son's wedding, and she hated that woman.

"*Men and women are meant to love each other and complement each other,*" said Madame Lee. "Thus Lao-tzu said in the *Tao Te Ching.*"

Zee Zee saw Tall Amah and his tutor, Miss Wong, looking at him so proudly, tears in their eyes. His unhappy brother. Sesame Face Wong. Servants with whom he had carried coal, chickens and fish when he was a boy. The old Yangchow horse master who had caught him when he jumped from trees, now older and frail. Zee Zee thought of his father. He looked down to contain his feelings, his fear of change. His mother was speaking.

"*What you do not want done to yourself, do not do to others.* Thus K'ung Fu-tzu instructed us in the *Lun-yu. To do five things everywhere under heaven is perfect virtue.*" She smiled as Zee Zee soundlessly recited, with her, *Courtesy, generosity, sincerity, earnestness and kindness.*

"We, the House of Lee, welcome the honorable House of Tzu, and we together, as strong *jias*, petition the good wishes of our ancestors. Together we wish much fortune, long life and many sons!" With that, Madame Lee began crying, for she was gaining a fine new servant in Da-tsien. She was comforted by Ying-oh, her first daughter-in-law, who would outrank this newcomer, this Soochow wife of a second son.

The ensemble broke into a more energetic rendition of the wedding song as family inside, and friends outside, burst into applause.

Auntie Gao, Miao-miao, Grace Sun and Elaine Yu slowly escorted a blind Da-tsien back across the crinkling rice paper, with the invisible ancestors in tow, and up the stairs to her new room, which was Zee Zee's.

Someone opened the front door and the mob entered, rushing upstairs to beat the bride into the bedroom. Children, students and grown women snatched items of clothing, shaving gear, toiletries and mementos from Zee Zee's room and flooded down the stairs, giggling and whooping.

Da-tsien laughed at the tradition that now applied to her and her husband; the friends would barter these snatched items for candy, a good-luck trade if they came from a happy couple.

She sat on his bed in the ransacked room. Her friends tried to straighten the mess. She would sit here alone, without him, *fong chun*, until he chose to join her, and then she would stand. She trembled, feeling very young. Auntie Gao and Miao-miao had warned her about sex, and she alternated between panic and terror. Grace and Elaine felt her anxiety and wept with her, and soon all the women were crying.

Downstairs, the hungriest of the guests were filling their faces. Some smiled as Zee Zee stuffed his mouth with dark, cured, soy-saturated, good-luck Thousand-Year Eggs, thinking that he was loading up to make sons, not knowing that Zee Zee mostly ate for the harmony of his digestion.

Baba, with Taitai uncharacteristically next to him, accepted Zee Zee's low bows and statements of humility and respect.

"Good," said Baba, "that she's only moved across the street."

"She'll need to learn how to cook," said Taitai. "And sew. It's all my fault, Son-in-Law; I taught her nothing. Your mother will teach her."

"Honored Mother, you taught her to be strong, and to be good."

"We'll see," said Taitai. "Brother, this is your new nephew, Lee Zeu-zee. Zeu-zee, my brother, Wong *syensheng*, the distinguished scholar."

Zee Zee bowed to the small, shy, walleyed man in a simple blue Chinese housecoat. Taitai's brother gave Zee Zee a fat envelope.

"Thank you, Uncle," said Zee Zee. "I am not worth—"

"We go," announced Taitai.

"Allow me to escort you to your door," said Zee Zee. Graciously, he walked his new parents-in-law and uncle through the throng across the street. Neighbors were on their verandas, watching the wedding, enjoying the fashion show of well-dressed ladies and the bustling of two households of servants from two clans that were running out of money. "It took four thousand *mou* of silkworms to dress those women," said one.

Zee Zee looked for Mr. Tung's black car but didn't see it. He left his new relatives at their door, standing alone for several seconds out of respect, in case they came back to ask for a favor. They didn't.

He then escorted the tiny Miss Wu, her Bible and diminutive cane to her pedicab. "You're a good boy," she said. "Be sure to stay that way."

Inside, Gee, T.A. and F. C. Fong began to encourage the guests to leave. The Communists, the gangsters and the women were the first to show consideration; the political types, the salt-tax people and Yeh the camel puller were among the last.

Yeh congratulated Zee Zee, who tried to give him some of his good-luck wedding money, but the puller refused. "This is your day, Young Master. You come to my wedding and then give me riches, okay? Oh, I pray for a wife as wonderful as yours!"

Angel kissed Zee Zee on the cheek, a very Western thing to do. "Lady Du the fortune-teller is sick and couldn't come. That's from her."

"Congratulations," said a slurred voice.

Zee Zee turned to face Poo Pan. "You mean that?"

"You bet. Here's your wedding present." He reached into his coat and extracted a U.S. Colt .45 1911 automatic, a huge black-market item, pointed it at Zee Zee's heart, then flipped it and offered it, handle first.

"That's your favorite sidearm," said Zee Zee.

"Not anymore. It's yours. Protect your wife against other men." Pan pulled extra clips from his pockets and gave them as well.

"I'm sorry I hit you, Pan," said Zee Zee, his hands full of ammo.

"It's okay. You know, I didn't mean that about your girl. Your wife." He grinned, slapped Zee Zee on the back as hard as he could, popped a dim sum in his mouth, snapped his fingers and left. Hwa and Fen followed him. Hwa's chubby hands were filled in case Shanghai ran out of food the next day.

"Hey, this is your time," said Barrel Man Yao. He faced his former pupil and smacked his huge right fist into his open left palm, nodding.

"Thank you, Teacher," said Zee Zee. "You honor me."

"Not really. Gain some sogging weight."

"You have curious friends," said F. C. Fong. "Gangsters."

"Friends, F.C. You must learn to be diplomatic."

"Diplomatically, here are my congratulations, my wishes for prosperity, longevity and many strong sons." F.C. passed him an envelope.

"Thank you, F.C. Thanks for standing up for me today."

"Did you say hello to Uncle Chu, Chou En-lai and Teng Hsiao-peng?" asked T.A. "They were trying to reach you through the crowd, and then your brother told them to leave. I don't think Gee likes the Reds."

"Like you do?" asked Zee Zee.

"They are terrifically smart," said T.A. "And Brother Sun Yat-sen asks us to welcome them openly. He made that exceptionally clear."

"I don't trust them," said F.C. "Stalin tells them what to do, and the Russian Bear is always hungry for Chinese chops. Dr. Sun's making a mistake. If Chiang Kai-shek takes over, he'll wipe out the Reds."

"That will cause problems," said T.A. "What do you think, Zee Zee?"

"I think Da-tsien loves Chou En-lai and my uncle Chu and that little Teng

Hsiao-peng so much that Chiang will have to welcome the Reds." Zee Zee was happy. It was the only time he ever made a political joke about the Communists.

"There'll be a bloodbath," said F.C. "the moment Dr. Sun dies."

"Here, Zee Zee," said T.A., changing the unpleasant subject; it was known that his brother-in-law Sun Yat-sen was ill in Peking. "Zee Zee, I am happy for you. Your wife is remarkable, worth all futures. Do not forget the music. See where I placed it?" He passed an envelope. "Let us shake hands and remember this day."

They shook hands, and Zee Zee watched his friend and patron leave with S. Y. Shen and F. C. Fong. Among a forest of poles, the tough Cantonese rickshaw puller waited for them in the street.

Sesame Face Wong, his assistant and the servants began picking up the rice paper and the dishes. The lovely Tzu women came swishing down the stairs in their silk cheongsams, keeping their eyes from the men and exiting with short bows to Zee Zee. Last down the stairs was little Auntie Gao, who smiled. Waiting for her was Uncle Chu.

Such pretty women over there, thought Zee Zee. *Now there are two here— Da-tsien and Ying-oh, Gee's wife.*

Singh the guard was the last. He stood at the foot of the stairs, looking up at the girl's new room. He disliked Zee Zee but was a man of faith; he bowed and wished him well, giving a small monetary gift.

"Thank you, Singh," said Zee Zee. "You know, you were right. I was a pain in the ass. I hope you can forgive me."

"Nothing to forgive, Young Master. Bless your kindnesses."

DA-TSIEN HAD DRIED her tears, reapplied her makeup and prayed to the gods for an escape from the pain of sex. When she was three and in Soochow, her baba had saved her feet from being broken. She knew that God would now save her from agony this day.

Da-tsien smiled when she heard the music float up the stairs. T. A. Soong must have brought a victrola and his Mozart collection. "Jupiter" wafted up the stairwell, and her heart melted for her romantic husband. She couldn't wait to hear his footfalls—there! There he was! She stood, her red veil vibrating slightly. The door opened. Footsteps. Silence.

"You're beautiful," he said.

She closed her eyes and absorbed the moment.

Items were being placed on the dresser.

"No, stop, please!" she cried. "Keep everything in your pockets, just the way it was. We have to do this right." She smiled as she heard him scoop up his stuff and return it.

"Stand by me. Yes, that's right. Now we have to think the best thoughts we've ever, ever thought, with whatever it is that represents our normal life, such as what's in our pockets, and then we send our thoughts, together, at the same time, to Guan Yin and heaven!"

"But Guan Yin is a female god—"

"Shush shush! Who's going to give us boys, Zee Zee? Guan Yin will! Are you ready? Now think, think very, very hard! This is important!"

He frowned, trying to comply. Soon his mind began to wander.

"Good!" And then she thought of another god, and more wishes, and another after that, until she came to the Christian God, and Zee Zee had regrettable images of Miss Wu badgering him with her worn Bible. His young wife prayed to Jesus, thanking him for her husband.

"Oh, Zee Zee, this is as I imagined it! Oh, listen to the lovely music! It's a dream! Aren't you just incredibly, incredibly happy? Oh, no, don't move! Not a *yingtswun!* We *have* to sit down at the same time, don't you remember the old custom? Then no one's in control over the other! We're both equal, for all time! Oh, Zee Zee, hold my hand, and let's sit at the same time, and then you can take off my veil, and the day will be ours! Oh, Zee Zee, do you promise to love me, forever and ever?"

AT DUSK, THEY were on the roof of the Lee home. Shanghai was stirring into its old sins, the great lights of the city burning brighter.

"Have you ever been happier?" Da-tsien asked.

He smiled. "You know, I think not."

"Oh, My Heart, it's like we're in an American movie and you're the hero and I'm the lucky girl who gets two weddings at the end!"

They were holding hands when the church bell at Moore's Memorial Church, the Chinese church of Zee Zee's mother, began to ring. Then the Methodist Episcopal, where they had married, also rang its high bell. They looked at each other, and then the Church of England's Holy Trinity Cathedral, with the grandest bells in Shanghai, began pealing loudly. Crows took flight, and then swallows, and the dark sky filled with birds.

"What are the Christians celebrating now?" asked Zee Zee.

Da-tsien raised her shoulders. "They only play on Sundays, and this is Thursday. Listen, Zee Zee, to how slowly the bells play. It's not happy, not like us! Oh, sweet honey, is something wrong?"

They went into the street to find neighbors they hardly knew milling in small groups under the din of the bells, louder in the street.

The Tzu majordomo found them and had to yell. "Young Missy, I mean, Lee Taitai, have you heard? Dr. Sun Yat-sen has died! Oh, so sad, yes? So strange! He died the same day you were married! Aiy, the Reds are in trouble now, don't you think?"

thirty-four

Soochow

OH, ZEE ZEE, I have to look!"

"No, not allowed. Remember, you promised."

"I'll go out of my mind! I can't stand not seeing! Are there other people staring at me?"

"Relax. Take deep breaths from your tummy. We'll be to the new church I'm going to show you, and you can pray there. I promised your parents not to scare you, and the sight of all these dead people from the plague would destroy your *chi*, so please listen to me, and honor me, and go to sleep! Right now!"

The train clacked steadily west, passing through an idyllic countryside undisturbed except for a black plume of locomotive smoke. Their traveling companions in the first-class soft-seats compartment looked quizzically at the young man with his lovely bride, for they saw no dead people anywhere and couldn't understand why the girl was blindfolded. Behind them, in the lower-class and baggage cars, were country merchants, families, soldiers and peasants with pigs and chickens.

By the time they reached the twelfth stop, the girl was asleep. Zee Zee paid porters to carry their luggage, and he carried Da-tsien to a taxi. He was recovering his strength but was relieved that she was so light.

She awoke in her traveling clothes in a feather bed in a strange room. Her blindfold was off. She smelled jasmine tea and water lilies. She was going to call for Ah Tsui to get her slippers, then remembered that she was alone with Zee Zee.

She covered her mouth in surprise and pleasure. Her husband, Zee Zee! Oh, dear Lord.

"Honey?" she called. No answer. Where was he? Where was *she*? It was a lovely room, perfect in size and comfort and decor, with the same flourish of flowers that Lee Taitai had arranged for their church wedding.

She stood and padded to a curtained door. She opened it slowly and stepped onto a fine balcony and the call of cicadas and frogs. Zee Zee dozed in a chair, his bare feet on the railing, his jasmine teacup cooling on a small black table. She studied his feet for a while, marveling at their perfection. Beyond his toes were the canals of Soochow.

She cried out, and Zee Zee bolted out of his chair, ready to fight. "What, Dieter?" he said.

"Honey, it's me! Oh, we're in Soochow! You brought me home!" And she wept and wept in his arms, hitting him and hugging him and crying as she gave herself to so many emotions all at the same time.

"Surprised?" he asked.

"Oh, darling, yes! So surprised!"

THE FIGHTS BEGAN in the morning.

"You asked about what I saw in the Gobi Desert. I'll tell you." He smiled wonderfully, and she rested her chin on his leg.

"One day, not long after dawn, after a long night march by the stars, we heard a noise. The peasant boys thought it was dragons. I tell you, out there, for a moment, I thought the same thing!"

Her eyes glittered.

"Then there, out of the south, came this incredible airplane. It zoomed over us and then banked like a hawk!" He demonstrated with his hands, a thing he'd noticed Da-tsien did frequently when she got excited. This was something ladies did not do. Gentlemen, either. She was unaware of her own extravagant gestures.

"Oh, Da-tsien! I imagined flying up there, being out of the sand!"

She shook him. "Now you're out of the sand! Oh, look at all this wedding money! So much! Zee Zee, we can pay back your father's debts and buy baby things!"

"No!" he yelled, making her lurch, his gestures violent and extravagant. "It should go for food and for flying lessons! Guns and equipment! T.A. didn't give me ten thousand dollars to pay for *ya-pien* opium and concubines! There's a war coming! A big war!"

"But he's your *father!*"

"He's not like your baba. It's different."

"No such thing! All fathers are fathers!" She was getting angry, so she stifled herself, pursing lips and frowning.

"Well?" he asked.

She shook her head.

"Okay, it's settled. There are American and German instructor pilots at Hongchiao Airport and—What's that look on your face?"

"Nothing," she snapped.

"Da-tsien, you're turning red. Hey, you have to breathe. Look, it's okay to argue! My household does it all the time. Go ahead and fight me. It's good for circulation, and it's better than reading the Bible."

"I can't stand how you treat me! It's so unfair! You just give orders!"

He looked perplexed. "Yeah, so?"

"We sat down on the bed at exactly the same time! We're *equal!*"

"I don't think so. I'm stronger. I'm bigger. I'm the man. I have the you-know-what. Hey, you're turning red again! Breathe!"

"No! I'll just die right here, right now, in Soochow!" She began to cry.

"Aiy, you drive me crazy! I suppose you also want to give away the silks, the clothes, because they're too much for us, right?"

She brightened. "Oh, yes, darling! We can give it to the Christian missions and—"

"No way! Impossible! Why give such good things to the poor?"

"Because they need it, and we couldn't use all these clothes if we wore them three at a time!"

"I'm getting flying lessons. No, don't turn red!"

"You want me to argue? Okay, I'll argue. Flying lessons? We don't need flying lessons! We already fly the way God intended. You can't talk about flying lessons anymore. Not to me. Not if you expect *chun ching* anymore!" *Chun ching* meant spring feelings, and it meant sex.

That caused a silence.

"Fine!" he shouted. "Who needs it?"

"Good!" she cried. "I don't!"

"I don't like it anyway!" he yelled.

"I don't, either! It's too messy!"

He was going to yell, but he surprised himself by laughing. "The *chun-hua* never told us about that." These were the pillow picture books that showed virgins how intercourse occurred.

"I never looked at them," she said, blushing. "They're not Christian."

"I didn't, either, but Pan looked at them all the time."

"I don't believe you. You must've studied them for years!" She was so angry, and then so happy, her laughter turning to tears as he slapped his thighs and laughed. He was holding her, and she giggled through wet eyes, and then she blew out the candle.

THEY SAILED ON the canals, sliding under each of the fabled water gates of the city.

She smiled and rubbed Zee Zee's hand all over her lovely, smiling face. She kissed each knuckle, uncaring that people in their gardens and on their flowered rooftops could see such shamelessness. But this was Soochow, a city of love and beautiful women, and she was in love and she felt totally beautiful inside.

"Zee Zee," she said dreamily as the waters gently slapped the canal boat, "isn't this like Peach Blossom Spring, where Mr. Five Willow Tree recites *shi* poetry, just for us, under a perfectly round moon? Is life not wonderful?"

The spring was the legendary place of Hunanese dreams, where all the cares of the world drifted into another space governed by Tang poetry, well beyond human reach. Hunan was a province of big dreams and big trouble.

Yes, Zee Zee breathed, like a poet, softly, in rhythm with the wind. He caressed her beautiful long hair as she cried on his hand.

Zee Zee was enjoying himself. The water was stupendous and fed his soul.

He vowed to always live near the sea, and not near rocks or mountains. In all of Lady Du's geomantic gibberish, he had heard her refer to his heart line, life line, fate line, mind line, so much rubbish! But she had said that he was of the high-water sign. This he believed.

He smiled at Da-tsien as she prayed before every pagoda, temple and god's station they passed. She even prayed to small door gods and gods of gardens and watery backyards. He marveled at her beauty, her sweet voice, and he loved her, knowing that their memories of Soochow and its waters would provide comfort in the trouble that was coming.

Once, long ago during the Taiping rebellion, Soochow was destroyed, ruined, its architecture set back two centuries. His wife slept. *His wife.* He stroked her scalp, her hair, in what would become his signature caress. She stirred with a sigh, then fell back into sleep.

It was dusk. The boatman, using the fishtail Chinese oar that allowed one person to row for days and to negotiate narrow channels, had become a steady machine.

"More canals, Master?" he asked.

"Yes," said Zee Zee. "Now we go to *Shi shr er*, Lucky 72 Way." They entered a wider passage framed by great trees, weeping willows and greater houses illuminated by soft electric lights and paper lanterns of many colors. There it was, and he told the boatman to slow. He was about to awaken her, to show her the great Tzu mansion where she had been saved from foot binding and had learned to read and write, and ladies in silk dresses on a flowered balcony had once bought fresh vegetables from rib-thin farmers on bony rafts. To the north, there was lightning flashing across a fifth of the horizon. He sat up. It was artillery, and his heart sang. French 75mm howitzers, firing by batteries.

He knew their sound better than their light splashes. Fifty-plus kilometers away, but factoring in this city light, maybe less. He timed the barrages and recognized the old rhythm of German-trained gun crews ejecting hot smoking shells, seating the fresh round and pulling lanyards to kill a distant enemy. *Ein, zwei, drei, vier, vorgehen, dickköpfig! Beste, beste!*

Chiang Kai-shek was beginning his campaign against the *jun fa*, the warlords, the scourge of China. Chiang would need his cadets. They would see the flash of his cannons and would come to honor the blood chits they had signed as boys.

With a start, he realized they were no longer on Lucky 72, the numbers that described the years of Emperor Yao's rule; and that he was married. Zee Zee wondered how his wife would accept his leaving her for long periods of time.

thirty-five

Marriage

LEE ZEE TRIED to make his ears stop ringing by covering them.

"If you go now, I'll just die!" cried Da-tsien. They were in bed, the now familiar site of their best communication and their worst fights.

"Come on! You already said that. Say something different!"

"Well, I *will* die! You can't be saying this to me. You promised!"

"I promised not to run around with women! I promised to support you through bad times and worse times! How am I going to earn money to do that if I don't join the army?"

"Oh, you make me crazy! What about working the Salt Tax? No one earns money fighting and killing people! They only die!"

"I'm trained so I won't die! Chiang spent a lot of money on me—"

"Yes! In medical expenses! Why can't you get a *real* job?"

"Like Mr. Tung?"

"Mr. Tung? Aiy, no wonder you were no good in school! That doesn't make sense! *I turned Mr. Tung down!* Want me to ask *you* about those *wünu* dance-hall girls or that slinky fortune-teller who follows you around? Well, I don't ask, so don't ever mention Tung to me again!"

"Dammit, this hurts my head. Christ, is this what marriage is?"

"Only when you're stupid and you say you're going to leave me!"

"What's so wrong about going?" He thought of his father, who never left, when, no question, he should have.

She buried her face in the pillows. "And you shouldn't swear."

"Don't hide. What's so wrong about my going to work?" He looked at his orders from the Kuomintang army, written in Nanking, by a good clerk with a good brush. It named him a lieutenant of scouts for the Nineteenth Route Army. It was a good job, being in advance of the main army. Chiang Kai-shek was going to use his German-trained officers to defeat the *jun-fa* warlords and reunite China.

Zee Zee could hardly hear her as she spoke into duck feathers. "You're leaving for a long time, maybe forever. And that breaks the promise. And you can't leave me here with your mother and your sister-in-law."

He lifted her face from the pillows. "What about my mother?"

"Oh, Zee Zee, they torture me every hour you're gone. Your mother hates me! She makes fun of my Soochow accent and gives me all the chicken-poop assignments and give Ying-oh the indoor, sit-down jobs. She's making me into a kitchen girl to help Sesame Face Wong. And the worst is, Ying-oh isn't friendly to me, just because she has lovely little bound feet and I have huge clodhoppers. She's always making fun of my feet!" Da-tsien wept into her hands, her shoulders shaking.

"No, no, don't do this!" he urged. "I can't handle it!"

"But you have to help me!"

"It's woman problems, right? And I'm a man, right?" He grabbed his clothes and fled, dressing as he pounded down the stairs. At the door, he zipped his pants, stepped into his shoes and ran to his Harley, uncaringly risking death by driving a machine with dangling laces. The ride to Hongkew took half an hour on bad days. This was a bad day.

"I HAVE WOMAN problems," said Zee Zee. "Help me."

Lady Du-chin laughed. "You mean you have communication problems. Ask your wife! She's a girl, but she has a reputation for knowing these things. Hey, you know, I can't wait to read *her* future! She's a very interesting person. Very smart!"

"If she's so smart, why doesn't she solve these problems?"

"Advisers specialize in other people's problems. Not their own."

"That include you?" he asked.

"Why, Zee Zee, that's a *chuming* question, a question of insight. How exciting! I think your marriage is doing good things for you."

"I love her, but she drives me out of my mind."

"Naturally. This is your first month together, and you're young and probably quite stupid. It's cats and dogs."

"Just me, stupid, and not her?"

"I don't know. That's usually the story, though."

He looked at his hands, and then at her. "Du, I have a mother-in-law. She's big in *ba-kua*, has her own fortune-teller and everything. So my *yueh mu* has her *ba-kua* lady read my hands. I told her, 'You can't read them—they're sand-damaged.' The *wu* said, 'Nonsense.' But her face fell when she read the lines, and she wouldn't say anything. Just like you, except she covered her face like she was ashamed. Du, tell me what you really read in my palms. Don't lie! Tell me the truth."

Du hid her own face in her hands. "I can't," she said.

"Hey, did I turn suddenly ugly? Why does everyone hide their faces when they're talking to me? Here, here." Zee Zee pulled down her hands. "Look at me, *mian du mian*. I've seen hard things. I can handle it."

She shut her eyes. "Oh, I was so wrong about you. I was sure all the auguries would be great. I thought they'd tell me about our future, the future of our country." She dried her eyes. Zee Zee was glad she wore no eye makeup; there was no smudging, as with Da-tsien.

"Zee Zee, fortune-tellers give more than just answers. Good ones give advice, yes? My advice, after I say what I say, is for you to do what your wife wants, not what you want. Do you hear my words?"

"Sure," he said. He felt calm. He was surprised that he felt no anger; he would have guessed that he'd be furious.

"Okay," she said, wiping her nose. "Your life line is very deep and very strong, but it's short, so short, I expect you to die any day now, in a most violent and rapid way, but strangely, without pain."

ZEE ZEE TOUCHED his KMT khaki uniform with the officer's bars on the high collar, then angrily put on the Western pin-striped suit. He fought the Windsor knot, cursing darkly as Da-tsien watched him with wet eyes. He didn't care. He was a college student learning to be a banker, and T. A. Soong was in ecstasy that his pal Zee Zee was going to be a rich man while Chiang went to war without him. Zee Zee had explained to the military adjutant that his wife needed him, his face beet red. The adjutant accepted the explanation because Lieutenant Lee was connected; he was a kinsman of the Soong *jia*.

Like a good wife, Da-tsien followed Zee Zee down the steps and stood on the porch, respectfully watching him roar off to St. John's on his bellowing motorcycle. She looked at her list of things to do: Attend a student rally at St. John's; work in the Methodist Episcopal's soup kitchen; teach the literacy class to the *dingpen* nail-shed street prostitutes; bathe the orphans.

She didn't want to do any of it. It was all back labor, hand work, peasant duties. It was all because she had learned English to gain the favor of her mother. Instead, Miss Roberts had introduced Da-tsien to every foreign mission and ministry leader in the city.

Da-tsien almost stamped her foot in anger, but the last time she had done that, during an argument with Zee Zee, she had fallen. Now she argued with him only in bed.

She jumped at the crack of Madame Lee's voice as it replaced the roar of the motorcycle.

"Stop daydreaming! Are you against work? Do you oppose our house? Time for market, time to carry fish, time to clean floors, time to watch the servants hang laundry! Not time to stand on the street!"

When she was in the middle of these chores, Da-tsien decided to stop. They could starve, they could live in filth and wear dirty clothes—she didn't care. And then her nemesis, the wife of the Firstborn Son, Ying-oh, padded into Da-tsien's world on her tiny slippers.

"P'o-p'o wants to see you." *P'o-p'o* means the wife's mother-in-law. *Yueh mu* means the husband's mother-in-law. In a class-conscious society, titles of distinction were everything. "Wife" actually meant servant to the husband's house and lackey to the mother-in-law. P'o-p'o could be an overseer. In the House of Lee, there was an added distinction to being a female in-law, or outside, descendant.

"Sit!" said Madame Lee, Da-tsien's p'o-p'o. Da-tsien sat on a stool.

"Ying-oh, you sit over there, on the soft chair." The pretty young woman stepped daintily and sat.

"Da-tsien! You see the picture above my head, above all of us?"

"Yes, Mother," said Da-tsien.

"Who is that?"

"It is *tsu fu mu*, Honorable Grandmother."

"No! You couldn't be more wrong! This is the House of Lee, and she is *Ch'i tzu yung kan te*! Has my worthless Second Son told you *nothing*? Do you know nothing about your Before Borns or your new *jia*?"

"I know, Mother," Da-tsien said softly, "that word of your faith and your kindness to others has spread farther than across the street."

"Respect P'o-p'o!" hissed Ying-oh. "This is for your own heart!"

"Yes, thank you, Daughter," said Madame Lee, touching her throat, inviting both girls to see the beauty of her skin. "I see that manners have not completely died in this strange city, so polluted by Soochow ways. Ying-oh, what would I do without you?

"This woman," she whispered violently, "is the *Bravest Wife*! She was polite and respectful. Of course, this is said of all the Before Borns, but this woman truly was. Honor her!"

Da-tsien stood, then knelt, her forehead to the cold floor.

"Yes, bow to her! Kowtow! Yes, nine times! Ask her for strength to fill your weaknesses! Listen to my words.

"The Bravest Wife, she had golden lily feet, but she marched thousands and thousands of miles on them because her clan required it. She was a delicate girl of manners, but she used a huge broadsword to kill hundreds of bandits and thieves, to protect her husband, Second Son's honorable grandfather, a fine scholar. Yes, she killed to save!

"The Taipings were coming to kill them, again and again." Madame Lee gestured as if she were the Bravest Wife, flashing an imaginary sword. "Again and again, she fought them off, her sword drinking their blood. Oh, so many fell! She could fight, but she couldn't run. So to save her husband's life, she threw herself down a well, laughing all the way down because of the pleasure she experienced serving her *jia*.

"She always told her husband, who was your husband's grandfather, to hide that which was obvious. So her husband followed her advice and became a lord of salt and tea, and gave us all our money, which is being smoked up to heaven by my worthless husband, even as we stand here and chat. Bow again! Look at her! Look up now.

"See here! No spirit tablet, no ancestor portrait, can do her justice because she was the most beautiful girl in Kiangsi and in the double provinces, and she had lovely, lovely skin, almost as good as mine!"

"Oh, wonderful, wonderful!" cried Ying-oh, wiping a tear. "We can never match her courage, but we have her standard to measure ourselves against."

"Yes, well said, Daughter. Understand, Da-tsien? I give you small tasks, nothing bitter, but you complain and work slowly, offending not only Confucius and the ancestors of the House of Lee and my House of Han but also Jesus

Christ and the Bravest Wife! Do you see how little you are, compared to the weight of tradition and the past?"

"Yes, P'o-p'o."

"Do you swear to me that you'll strive to be remembered as a woman who tried to be as noble as the Bravest Wife?"

Da-tsien hesitated. *I don't want to be remembered as someone who threw herself down a well.*

Madame Lee gestured. Ying-oh immediately stood and offered her Bible to Da-tsien.

"Are you truly ashamed of your shoddy work, Da-tsien, or are you silent to avoid trouble? Here, swear on this in your little Soochow accent!"

None of the missionaries had ever asked her to do such a thing. Her word had always been believed. Da-tsien's cheeks turned red. She wanted to run away on her big, ugly feet, but she calmed herself and placed a hand on the Bible. She had always admired it; now it felt like a hostile surface. *How the Bible is used defines its worth*, she thought.

"I swear to you that I am sorry for not working harder."

"Uh-huh, yes, and what else that you're not saying?"

Imperceptibly, Da-tsien lifted her fingers from the book. "Nothing else, Mother." And now her feelings and thoughts ran through her.

I would serve you gladly if you were kind. Your ho, your harmony, would fill my heart and I would work like a dirt farmer to please you. But your unfairness, your anger, have stopped my heart, and I feel myself closing up against you more and more every day.

And I don't care about the Bravest Wife! That was during the Taiping wars. Nothing like that could happen to us. And the whole thing was probably made up, anyway. Who'd walk thousands of miles for her husband, and what kind of husband would put her through such a test?

Part Two

FIRE

DA-TSIEN, YING, MARY and ELINOR, Chungking, 1944 [left to right], not long after the Run.

LON-LON, JANE QIN, LU-LU, ELINOR, YING, Shanghai, c. 1936. The house's three marriages and its opium-and-concubine-plagued finances are dying "like a centipede" inch by inch, but the cousins remain loyal to one another.

JAMES WONG HOWE, CHINESE COUNSEL, JAMES CAGNEY, T.C., Hollywood, 1941. Zee Zee met many celebrities, but would not meet the great Katharine Hepburn until his second trip to Hollywood.

T.C., Cairo, 1943, awaiting Chiang Kai-shek's arrival for the meeting with Roosevelt and Churchill.

ZEE ZEE WITH HIS O2U-1 CORSAIR, Changsha, Hunan, China, 1927. From this airbase, Zee Zee tried to kill Mao Tse-tung, warred against his commanding officer and got grounded.

thirty-six

A Heart for People

I'M FIRST OF all an honoring daughter," Da-tsien would later say, thinking of her father. "And of course I'm wife to my husband, whom I love more than respect. And I'm a Christian lady and a mother to my unborn son."

Asked if she were a Nationalist or a Communist, she'd say, "I don't get the difference between right-wing Nationalists and left-wing Reds. They both talk about the same ideas, don't they?"

But she saw other differences. Both sides had people of privilege, but the Nationalists had the wealthy bankers and business owners and the Reds had laborers and peasants. Not liking commerce because of her father's views on foreign trade, and identifying with the downtrodden because of her mother's lack of affection, she preferred the Reds. They were more passionate. As she matured and approached her twenty-first birthday, passion had begun to underline everything she did.

"We have to organize the workers so they can help!" she exclaimed to her friends, waving her hands like a person of no education.

"Radical talk," said Elaine Yu. "Girls can't do that!"

"I don't think we should even talk about it," said May Yang, fixing her hair and wetting her eyebrows.

"But Da-tsien's right," said Grace Sun. "If Chiang Kai-shek starts the Northern Campaign from South China, and beats all the *jun-fa* warlords from here to Manchuria, he'll *have* to come to Shanghai. This is where the money is to feed his army. We have to organize the Shanghai workforce, or else the foreign armies will kill our army brothers when they get here. We have to shut down the city to make it safe for them!"

"My God, Grace, you're a Communist!" said May.

Grace pulled her head back. "I'm not, but I've attended their meetings. They're so smart, and so, so—"

"Passionate!" said Da-tsien.

"*You* go, too? That's no place for a Christian girl like you!" said May.

"They're nice to us," said Da-tsien. "We even meet in a girls' school."

"Don't say that!" said Elaine. "They're Communists!"

"They let us talk very freely and openly," said Da-tsien.

"Yes!" said Grace. "Da-tsien asked if they wouldn't do better to ask questions when they were angry, instead of yelling. They agreed."

"So, you're a Big Cap, a big thinker, who can walk into a Hongkew factory and tell the workers to organize, and they will?" asked Elaine.

"The Party," said Grace, "establishes relationships first—"

May almost threw down her hand mirror. "I think that's really stupid and that you're both going to get killed!"

"Oh, May," said Da-tsien, "can't we even talk without pain?"

"No, we can't!" cried May, "and when the KMT gestapo investigate, I'm going to say I don't even know you!" Looking about as if the *Dong Tang* Blue Gown secret police were already coming, she retrieved her cosmetics and fled. When she got home, she would burn the photos of Da-tsien's Christian wedding, in which she appeared incriminatingly as a bridesmaid.

THE NEWS FROM the war front was driving Zee Zee into two moods—depression and anger. Chiang Kai-shek's Kuomintang army was pushing outward from Canton on the Northern Expedition. Chiang fought the warlords, beating them and taking their arms as he crossed the passes out of the Kiangsi River systems into the Yangtze watershed.

Zee Zee picked up intelligence reports from the KMT army liaison office and marked the progress of the army with map pins. He knew Chiang would turn up the Hsiang and Kan Rivers to the great lakes and the Yangtze, the Long River itself, which would lead to Shanghai. Chiang was following the old Taiping line of march.

Sitting in class, Zee Zee imagined the rumble of artillery, the mutter of machine guns, the shrill whistles and waving of battle flags to direct the maneuver of rifle companies. He could feel the whumps of mortars and see the cruel, rapacious, peasant-scourging armies of evil warlords fleeing from a disciplined and modern Chinese army. He could feel the sweet kick of a Mauser on his shoulder, the smell of fine cordite.

He heard the powerful diving whines of artillery scout aircraft, piloted by goggled men who had already graduated from college and completed flight school. He angrily snapped his pencil, his knee rocking like pistons in an aircraft's radial engine. He ignored a frowning T.A. who was trying to encourage him to focus on differential equations. Zee Zee remembered that he was supposed to ask his father-in-law, Da-tsien's baba, if the two of them could move into the House of Tzu.

Only a concubine could live with his father. Now Da-tsien couldn't live with his mother. In bed, she had begged him to move into her own home across the street. Tzu Taitai was a critical harridan, and Da-tsien's willingness to move back was clear evidence that her life under his own mother was hell. *But this is unheard of—newlyweds living with the* wife's *family! Christ!* The anxiety of that made him involuntarily snap his fingers, drawing the criticism of Professor Far.

To Far, inattention was the act of a defiant apostate with Communist leanings, and he had observed young Lee's indifferences. Such students, he thought, ought to be flunked out.

T.A. invited Zee Zee to his home in the French Concession in an effort to induce him to study math and read the Bible. His kitchen was better than the Lees', and after Chef Chen had softened up Zee Zee's tummy, T.A. would hit him with the books. Zee Zee disliked math and loathed the Bible, which he associated with his mother's baths. He also was afraid of Miss Wu, the tiny fundamentalist who always abused him with Scripture when T.A. began his tutoring.

He never saw T.A.'s oldest sister, the stunning Ching-ling, widow of Sun Yat-sen and the most distinguished woman in Asia. She had fled the dangers of Chinese politics and moved to Japan. Also absent was sister Ai-ling, who had called the meeting at which Zee Zee met Chiang Kai-shek.

Zee Zee liked the youngest sister, Mei-ling Soong, who was very pretty and bright. She was a terrific painter, drawn, like all Chinese artists, to studies of bamboo, the symbol of solitude, of strength, of timelessness.

"Nice job," said Zee Zee, looking at her work.

The appropriate response would have been a modest objection. "It *is* good," she said. "I practice, so it ought to be! Tell me, Lee Zeu-zee, will Chiang Kai-shek give you a plane when his army arrives from the south?"

"Your small words crush my heart," he said with a laugh. "Everyone in this house makes fun of my deepest desire. You know, he promised. He just never said when. So, what do you think of the General?"

She smiled and put down her brush. She had a square and open face that had no fear, a little like his wife when she had an idea.

"T.A. tells you too much, too many family secrets. Have you heard that General Chiang proposed to my sister Ai-ling in Japan? How could my thoughts about such a man bear any relevance to anything?"

"That's not true," said Zee Zee. "And if it is, you know it's just political. Ever since Sun died, every politician claims now to be his son."

Mei-ling didn't react. She looked at him as if he were something she might try to paint from memory. "Zee Zee, I hear you're pretty good. Here's a fresh canvas. You try painting a bamboo trunk."

He was going to die soon. No time for painting, not with a woman like this. She was too attractive, her ambitions too strong.

"*Tsai jen*," he said. See you later.

EVEN DA-TSIEN, ON the other side of the Settlement, sensed the approach of Chiang's army. Her friends and fellow volunteers and workers at the local churches and orphanages spoke of little else.

"The Party wants us to feed Chiang's soldiers when they get here," said Grace Sun. "They'll be hungry and thirsty and will be carrying their wounded. Do you want to do noodles or hot water for drinking?" All water in China was boiled. "Or help the wounded. I hear there'll be a lot."

"Noodles," said Da-tsien, who feared making hot water and couldn't imagine working with the injured.

"You're such a worker, Da-tsien!" said Grace. "Everyone wishes they were you! Everyone asking you advice, wanting to share their problems and cry with you."

"Oh, Grace, I'll tell you the truth." Da-tsien pulled a few stray hairs into obedience and exhaled, dropping her narrow shoulders. "I came here to escape P'o-p'o. Grace, she's a tyrant! She calls herself Christian, but she's more like the pharaohs. I couldn't stand mission work, either. The sadness. All I did was cry. Beggars with open sores, women raped by hoodlums and robbed by thieves, babies dying of so many diseases—it was all too horrible. You didn't know, but I was constantly ill.

"But you know? None of these sad people cursed me. They appreciated everything. A girl with one hand tried to comfort *me!*"

"Oh, my dear friend," said Grace, "you have a heart for people. You're like a nurse."

A tiny, emaciated beggar woman whom Da-tsien had earlier given a set of clean clothes approached them.

"Ah, Mother," said Da-tsien. "How good you look! The gown fits you as if tailored! How can I help you?"

"I love your lies! I'm old river spit!" The old woman took several steps, rested, then took more. She motioned for Da-tsien to follow. Stopping and looking in all directions, she whispered, "Listen. The Beggar King"—head of the beggar guild—"says *Chingbang liumang*, Green Gang hoodlums, will pay us to mark Red students. Young Lady, I hope you're not a Red. You aren't, are you?"

"No, Mother, I'm not. I don't understand. What does *mark* mean?"

"We wear a strip of white cloth on our heads. We follow Red students. Find where they sleep. Wait outside. For this, good cash."

"But why, Mother?"

The woman shook her head. "Well! Not for good reason, right? Red students say *strike* because bad work conditions. Green Gang lose money if factories close—they make factory owners pay or they break the machines. Maybe they beat up the Red students. Maybe much worse. *Liumang* very bad! Young Lady, please, you stay away from all Red meetings!"

Up and down the Yangtze—which the people called the Jiang Chiang, Long River—the oncoming war packed the small, dark shops of fortune-tellers. Customers of prophecy had long memories. A new war was part of the old.

Da-tsien always had trouble remembering the sequence of events that year. She would often confuse whether the executioners preceeded the firing squads or followed them. Mostly what she remembered was that Shanghai went crazy and that her friends died.

The craziness began when St. John's students debated the pros and cons of Communism. The Nationalists demanded an open symposium that would include the business leaders from the foreign community; many of them were counting on good jobs after graduation. They threatened to beat up anyone who disagreed. The Reds urged a campus sympathy strike with factory and dockworkers. They also demanded that a few workers' sons be allowed into their school to study with the scions of the upper class.

Zee Zee didn't want a symposium, and he disliked strikes. Strikes were mob actions that could burn the home of his father. On the other hand, if the campus struck, there'd be no calculus class.

"What do you say, Zee Zee?" asked C. K. Chen.

Zee Zee took the stage. "Admit the sons of workers! Are they not people, too?" he cried in the mike, his deep voice sounding like Guan Yu, god of war and business, shouting at the devil at the Three Gorges. "Strike—and hold symposia in the streets!" The cheering was thunderous. How he loved stirring a crowd!

"STRIKE! STRIKE! STRIKE! STRIKE!" The students swept outward.

Professor Far was outside the auditorium. He knew Zee Zee's distinctive voice, and he didn't like it.

IN THE FRENCH Concession, prestrike fever was consumptive. But in the empty Boai Girls' School on Joyful Undertaking Street, the small Chinese Communist Party, composed of freethinkers, radicals, intellectuals and labor organizers, argued about Josef Stalin. The meeting was attended by hundreds of student and labor organizers and a sprinkling of peasants.

"Stalin orders us to support Chiang's Northern Expedition," said Li Ta-chao, a stout, square-jawed, bullet-headed Peking librarian with a dark mustache and small round apothecary spectacles. He spoke in a fine, deep-jowled Mandarin accent. Recently, he had hired a new assistant librarian, a Hunan schoolteacher named Mao Tse-tung.

"But it just seems wrong," said Phyllis, his teenage daughter. "Stalin doesn't know how much Chiang Kai-shek hates Communism."

"Stalin knows," said Chou En-lai. "His agent Borodin told him. And everyone here knows that Chiang imprisoned members of our party—members who actually helped him launch the Northern Campaign.

"But we have no choice. The strike is ordered. We'll have a million workers on the street. We have to shut down the warlord's army and avoid the foreign armies. But if foreign troops shoot at Chiang's army, we must fight and protect them as brothers."

"With a hundred and fifty old rifles," said a student. "Against thousands of foreign troops in Shanghai, which the Americans, Japanese and English have reinforced with another thirty thousand troops to protect their big businesses."

"We fight with what we have. Our numbers should help. But what do you think? Should we disperse our leadership, protect the head?"

"Yes," said Da-tsien, unsure if anyone listened.

"Tell them!" urged Grace Sun.

Da-tsien shook her head.

"Pardon a mere girl," said Grace.

"No, Sister, don't say that here," said Li Ta-chao. "All are equal."

"Thank you," she said. "The Green Gang is paying the Beggar King to have his people track us when we leave here. His beggars will follow us and sleep outside our dorms. Then they're to point us out."

A long silence followed. Someone thanked her.

Chou spoke. "We should increase our escape routes and confuse them. Li Ta-chao, get Phyllis back to Peking. I know the big strike's here, but we need you at Peking University. Teng," he said to Teng Hsiao-peng, "you go, too." He named others. Many argued that leaving now was impossible; the strike was too important. Li Li-san, another leader, refused to leave.

"Nothing's more important than you," said Chou. "Than our people."

There were arguments. Someone said, "This strike, before Chiang's army even gets here, is suicide. Screw Stalin! I don't know why, but he's trying to get us all killed. I say we delay the strike until Chiang is at the gates. Although I tell you, I fear Chiang, too."

"We knew," said Chou, "that we couldn't have a successful revolution without foreign help. We asked the democracies to help us. Only Communist Moscow offered assistance. We take their money and books, so now we take their orders."

"Stalin gives us *books*! And he gives machine guns and airplanes to a warlord who hates us—*Chiang Kai-shek*!" said Li Ta-chao. "Guess which counts more!"

"Yes," said Chou, "but the Russians, our old enemies, are now our only friends in the world. We must disperse. When we leave, don't walk. Get rickshaws, ride fast and pay well. Most pullers are on our side. I'm disappointed about the beggars. The news makes me very sad. They lose most if the Green Gang wins.

"Teens and young women who aren't Party members should stay home until the strike ends," said Chou. "It's not safe. If anything happened, I'd have no words of adequate explanation for your parents or teachers."

Da-tsien knew many of those in attendance and saw enormous resolve in their faces. She knew she had to be brave, but she couldn't. Beggars following students! Students in China held a lofty social station. How could this be? She left the meeting to weep in the bathroom. When she emerged, the meeting room was empty. She walked the hallways—the school was as quiet as a cave.

"Phyllis?" she called quietly. "Grace? Mr. Chou? Mr. Li Ta-chao?" She thought she heard something and froze, her heart trying to leap from her chest. Screwing up all her courage, she looked outside. In the street were some vendors and beggars in white headbands. She began crying.

Huddling in a corner, she tried not to cry again, then gave up and allowed the tears to flow. She hated fear. She was too petrified to leave and too terrified to stay alone in a dark place, but too paralyzed to turn on a light. The temperature dropped. It was dark by the time she thought the streets were free of beggars. Running from the building, she caught a rickshaw home. She never again returned to the school.

"I CAN'T BELIEVE you stayed, Da-tsien!" said Grace. "I'm so sorry! A person like you, all alone in that building."

"Did Phyllis and her father get out safely?" asked Da-tsien. "Oh, Zee Zee, I wish you could meet Phyllis Li and Li Ta-chao. Phyllis is seventeen, and she's so smart! Her father, Mr. Li, is hiring librarians. Wouldn't you like a job like that?"

"I'd rather dig graves," said Zee Zee.

"I'm glad they left," Grace said. "Sun Ch'uan-fang," the Shanghai *jun-fa* warlord, "tortures girls. Oh, Da-tsien, he's so evil! Phyllis fears that Warlord Sun will cut her open and wrap her insides around her body, like he did to the teenage girls who tried to escape his prostitution rings. They say Warlord Sun sides with foreigners because they split the opium profits with him. That money protects the foreigners by keeping him from invading and controlling the whole city. Is that true?"

"I don't know," said Da-tsien. "Zee Zee, is Grace right? Is this true?"

"Sure it's true," he said. He was reading a Russian flight-instruction manual, though he couldn't understand Russian. It was a cool winter morning in the Tzu courtyard, where they sat among graceful, proportionately stunted *penjing* trees.

He felt physically ill. The greatest campaign to unify China since the days of the Yellow Emperor and Wall Builder, Chin Shih Huang-ti, had launched, and all he could do was suggest that students skip math class. He was disgusted and disappointed in his fate. It was all because he was married, yet he loved his pretty wife. He didn't mind dying early, but he didn't want to be in the paddies when the war was in the hills.

Grace no longer felt safe talking politics indoors, so it was she who had talked the young Lees into joining her outside. Da-tsien didn't feel safe anywhere near her mother-in-law, so they crossed the street to her parents' esthetic garden. Zee Zee had to admit that he enjoyed the Tzu house more than his.

Da-tsien was delighted to have her husband with her. She knew that he hated to be away from the army, but the idea of being separated from him was so unendurable that she didn't care.

"Chiang Kai-shek has a general named Niu," said Grace, her breath condensing. "He promises that the Northern Expedition will defeat Warlord Sun and free us from him *and* the Green Gangsters. They'll even end the opium trade once and for all. Isn't that wonderful!"

"Oh, Grace, really?" cried Da-tsien. "Zee Zee, no more opium! If the Nationalists shut down opium in Shanghai, that'll shut it down for the whole country! Oh, that's terrific! I was so worried, fearing every poor beggar with a white headband. I can't wait to not have to worry about that anymore. Aren't you cold? Please come inside and have some hot tea."

"No, forget beggars," Grace said. "They're everywhere! But here's the big news. We're holding a prestrike before the main one. Moscow ordered the Communists to do it. On February nineteenth. In Nantao."

Zee Zee closed his book. "Chiang won't be here until March."

Grace nodded. "I know. It'll show our solidarity with Chiang."

"That's crazy," said Zee Zee. "Chiang *knows* you're helping him. General Niu coordinates with you! But if you strike without Chiang's troops, Warlord Sun's soldiers and foreign troops will enter the city."

"Would they hurt the student leaders?" asked Da-tsien.

"Oh, no, they'll kill them." He sat up. "Don't do it, Grace." He didn't have to warn his wife; she had been terrified since the night she'd been trapped in the Red meeting. Ah Tsui had scolded her for an hour, and Da-tsien, knowing she had been stupid, had welcomed it. She was not an adventurer.

"We can't stop now," said Grace, wishing Da-tsien could join her.

"I don't mean all of you," said Zee Zee. "I mean you individually."

"Thanks, Zee Zee. But I can't stop now."

"Chiang Kai-shek's General Niu, what else did he say?"

"He mostly wanted to know the names and addresses of our labor and student leaders. I think he said that General Chiang wanted to give certificates or medals to them. I think that's a wonderful idea, don't you?"

Zee Zee did not. Only generals and foreign advisers got KMT medals. Students? Never. *Red* students? They'd get a bayonet. He left, put on his leather jacket, fired up his Harley and drove to Hongkew. He went to Pan's garages and the red-pillow parlors, but he couldn't find any of them: Pan, round Hwa, pencil-necked Fen, Barrel Man Him Yao or the slow Pan family rickshaw puller. Most of the underworld workers were gone.

He drove to the French Concession. T.A. was studying in his parlor, which was as notable as finding dirt in the fields.

"I am glad to see you," said T.A. "Please step outside with me."

Zee Zee said okay; T.A. never wanted to go outdoors.

In the beautiful Soong courtyard, complete with ancient spirit screens and great, deep-chested temple lions, T.A. said, "I have news, very confidential. The Shanghai business community is going to fund Chiang Kai-shek's army."

"Now he can afford to give me a plane," said Zee Zee with a laugh.

"This is no laughing matter. I am not talking about bankers. Curio Chang and Big Ears Du Yueh-sheng and the *Chingbang* Green Gang are behind it. The money will give the criminal underworld even more license with the foreign police chiefs. Shanghai will become even more villainous and even less Christian, if such a thing is possible. The foreigners fear Chiang because they fear he is a Red. If this were not all so terrifying, it would be funny. Chiang hates the Reds more than even the foreign businessmen. You know why I tell you this."

"To make me a banker," said Zee Zee.

"No. I tell you because Da-tsien has been seen by the police, meeting with the Reds. It seems she has no political outlook, but the appearance is most dangerous. Now I give excellent advice. On February nineteenth, wear your KMT uniform. Sleep in it. Lock all doors. Keep Da-tsien from doing her mission work. Under no circumstances can she leave the house or even see a Communist. Avoid the Chinese City."

"What are you saying?"

"The Green Gang has the names of the Communists, the labor organizers, the labor leaders. All of them."

"They can't have that list," said Zee Zee. "General Niu works for Chiang, not the gangs—"

"Zee Zee, Chiang Kai-shek, the Green Gang and Warlord Sun are all together in this. The Green Gang and Warlord Sun will fund Chiang's army. Chiang will allow the foreigners to run their businesses in Shanghai, from which the gangs make their money. The workers will get nothing. The students, the Reds, the labor people, are expendable."

That was when Zee Zee remembered that Chiang Kai-shek had once been a member of the *Chingbang* underworld. It was the way you practiced revolution. He saw what was about to unfold.

"Christ, T.A.! This has to be stopped! Will you stop it?"

"I know it is awful," said T.A., covering his face. "*Mayo ban fa?* What can we do? I am an insect in a world of giants. All I can do is warn you so you can protect your family, mostly your wife. But please, if you spread the alarm any further, I will be imprisoned. Chiang's secret police watch all of us. The Blue Gowns are everywhere."

"T.A., this isn't the way it was supposed to be!"

"I agree. There are now circles inside invisible circles. First, warn your wife. Second, we will have to be very, very smart. Can you do that? Will you do that, Zee Zee, and not be impetuous or stupid?"

Zee Zee found Grace Sun still at the Tzus', inside. He kept on his leather jacket and pulled her outside, knowing that it was now too cold for delicate Da-tsien to follow.

"What is it, Zee Zee?" asked Grace. "You look so angry—"

"Promise me that you'll stay in your home on the day of the first strike. If you don't promise, you may never see my wife again. Look at me, *mian du mian*. Do you trust me and believe me?"

"You're holding me too tight!"

"Will you do what I say?"

"Zee Zee, Da-tsien is my dearest friend. You can't blackmail—"

"Am I her husband? Yes. Do I give orders? Yes! Will you stay home?"

"You know something. What—"

"Say yes. Or leave our family and never return."

She lowered her face, angry and confused. "Yes," she said.

"What is it?" asked Da-tsien from a barely cracked door.

"It's a surprise for you," said Zee Zee quickly. "Secret."

thirty-seven

White Terror

CHOU EN-LAI, THE twenty-eight-year-old Paris intellectual, had carried out Josef Stalin's orders carefully. On February 19, hundreds of thousands of Shanghai workers failed to show up at the factories and docks. Hundreds of thousands of rickshaws were idle, poles up like a forest of spears. On the piers, birds gathered where usually fifteen thousand chanting, bare-chested *k'u-lis* hauled tons of heavy cargo. Even the fishermen were absent from the Nantao docks. The thousands of Whangpu sampans were absent. Up and down the wharf, great foreign freighters appeared to be sleeping. The city had come to a standstill.

Da-tsien thought her husband was like a blinded songbird, all feathers and no brains. For two nights, he had risen at midnight to put on his uniform, leggings and boots. Next to the bed rested that terrible dark gun that Pan had given him on their wedding day. Zee Zee had lain on the bed, looking at the ceiling. She awakened later to find him standing at the window, smoking a cigarette in a cupped hand to keep the glowing ash from showing. He had never smoked.

"Zee Zee, what's wrong?"

"Nothing. Go to sleep."

"I can't. Come here and hold me." He refused. When she begged, he put out the cigarette and held her. Through his uniform and the scent of tobacco, she felt his distance; below that, his anger. She had been close to him, closer than to any person. She knew him and could read his deep rivers of feeling. He was angry at China, at politics, at their marriage.

The next night she didn't sleep. She was crying too hard.

WITH THE STREETS of the city empty, the warlord Sun Ch'uan-fang sent his troops into Shanghai. The foreign police, the U.S. Marines, the British and French infantry let them enter the city because they bore passes from the

French Concession police department, with whom Warlord Sun and the Green Gang shared the city's opium revenues and operated hundreds of prostitution and smuggling rings.

Warlord Sun's biggest and tallest men had been appointed the executioners. They carried huge two-handed swords, stuck out their chests and strode down the streets of Nantao district in the Old Chinese city, laughing. Before them ran mobs of terrified, screaming people.

In Nantao, student organizers carrying placards and signs had gathered to monitor the strikes on the Bund and the docks.

Backed by platoons of riflemen and preceeded by Green Gang hoodlums, the executioners hefted swords and beheaded the students thrown to them by the gangs. The death squads executed anyone who looked like a radical, a Red or a labor leader, or who seemed to have such people as friends. Captives were caught, beaten, bound and hauled to the Big Swords in a redundant, mechanical process.

Grace Sun fulfilled her promise to Zee Zee and stayed home on the nineteenth. But thousands of students had gone to support the strikes. Many of them were executed, their heads placed on poles by the warlord army as trophies of good swordsmanship. Some heads were placed inside birdcages and hung from roofs as a warning to all.

"You want change?" called the executioners. "Here's change!"

When Li Ta-chao and his teenage daughter Phyllis learned in Peking of what had happened in Shanghai, they were stricken with guilt. They didn't feel they had deserved a special salvation. Many survivors vowed to never say the names of the dead again, for this was like repeating the executions and giving evil men more pleasure.

Da-tsien no longer felt like a girl in love. She kept trying to understand what had happened but couldn't. She felt frail and powerless.

"How could Chiang Kai-shek do this?" she cried.

Zee Zee took comfort in having saved Da-tsien and Grace Sun, but he said less and less. Ashamed, he removed his Kuomintang uniform and kept it in a chest in a distant room. He kept the gun by the bed. He left messages for Pan, asking his underground pal for a rifle with five hundred rounds. He stayed away from St. John's, pacing and paging silently through his Russian flight manual. "Da-tsien, I don't know what to say," Zee Zee would tell her when she begged him to talk to her.

"Honey, just tell me how you feel."

He loved how she called him sweet names, and he nodded. "How do I feel? I feel old. You know, I used to remember all those golds and reds and purples of the desert. I could see the scene any time I wanted." He rubbed his face. "It's strange. I still see the rock towers, endless sands. But it's all in black and white. Like an American movie."

"You loved the desert, didn't you?"

"I loved the colors. I loved the army."

TWO MONTHS LATER, Stalin ordered the CCP, the Chinese Communist Party, to strike Shanghai again. This was to allow Chiang's army to safely enter the city. Many Communists wanted to ignore the order. After all, the February 19 incident had led to a massacre of their student supporters. Only recently had the birdcages been removed from the roofs.

But Chou En-lai reminded the Party that they had given their word. So he launched his well-trained strike teams to take control of the telephone building and radio stations in the Chinese city. Small teams of armed workers and students surprised Warlord Sun's sleeping troops and disarmed them. Some of Sun's soldiers resisted, and gunfire erupted in short, brutal urban firefights. The students fought bravely and well.

In a few hours, the Reds and laborers had taken control of the city. Following Moscow's orders, they had left the foreign concessions and their troops alone. Even with the gunbattles, there had been little bloodshed. Shanghai was theirs. It was a tremendous coup.

Meanwhile, in a replay of February 19, nearly a million workers simply didn't show up for work. Shanghai's heavy industries ground to a total halt. Smokestacks became dormant and cooled for the first time in decades. An eerie silence and clean skies befell the normally deafening metropolis. The entire city sounded like it was on holiday. Workers had stayed home and were playing with their children.

Zee Zee had once again unearthed his KMT uniform. He wore it as a shield against the killers. He drove around the city on his Harley. The residential areas were packed, but the vast industrial districts of Hongkew, Pudong and Woosung were ghost towns. Again he couldn't find Pan. The old, slow family rickshaw puller hid his face, afraid to talk to anyone, including Zee Zee.

Zee Zee gunned the engine and rode fast to the outlands, expecting to run into motor scouts or advanced cavalry of Chiang's army. The morning strike had been timed exactly with the Northern Expedition's arrival, so it would occur as the troops marched triumphantly into the Hanyang western district. He could see no scout aircraft. There was not a single KMT gunboat patrol up the Whangpu River. It was March 20, the day of arrival for Chiang Kai-shek's army. Something was wrong. The next hours passed with enormous tension.

Two days later, the advance elements of Chiang's Northern Expedition finally entered Shanghai. It was the First Regiment of the Chinese Fifth Army. The regiment was made of many Shanghainese, who happily nodded to celebrating relatives and friends. In good order, they marched down Markham Road to be cheered by students, workers and labor leaders as thousands of women offered them bowls of noodles and hot water. These men were heroes; they had defeated the *jun-fa* warlords. The warlords had chopped China into small, bloody pieces of meat. Now Chiang Kai-shek had beaten them! This army represented a new and better China, and even those who hated militarists and armies cheered at the top of their lungs, waving the new red national flag. It resembled the American flag, with a white twelve-pointed sun in the blue corner.

"I can't stand this!" cried Da-tsien to Ah Tsui. "If Zee Zee were here, I'd, I'd hit his arm, I'm so angry! I should be feeding those poor men! I promised to help. There's nothing dangerous. The warlords are beaten!" They stood on the roof of the Lee house where, only two years earlier, they had heard the bells that marked Sun Yat-sen's death.

"Hush!" said Ah Tsui. "It's the only advice he's given that I like. It's too early to know if it's safe to walk on the streets. Keep your voice down!"

"Who can hear us up here besides God?" Da-tsien asked.

"Spirits! I feel them in my clothes—"

"Okay, Amah, okay, I'll be quiet."

Zee Zee rode his Harley up and down the First Regiment column, stopping when he finally found a Gobi Desert classmate.

"What held you up, Koo?" asked Zee Zee. "You're late!"

"Look at you! So clean! How do I get a motorcycle and a hot bath? My feet are bloody camel pads! Hey, I just hiked through central China!"

The lieutenant was route-marching with his men. Zee Zee was incredibly jealous, looking over the troops, imagining the corrections he'd make, the encouragements he'd offer. Koo was starving for noodles and hot broth on a cool day. But he was an officer, so he passed each bowl he received from a smiling, bowing girl to one of his soldiers.

"Visit the house," said Zee Zee. "You'll get both. Why are you late?"

"It's funny. We were ordered to stop seventy-five *li* outside the city. Something about the labor leaders not being ready for us."

"That's bull. They were ready a long time ago. They took a big chance, striking with you guys halted a day's march away. You hear what happened in February?" Koo hadn't. Zee Zee told him.

Koo stopped. Automatically, his troops also stopped. He waved them on so he could ask Lieutenant Lee if there was treachery ahead.

"You saying snakes and scorpions, Brother Lee?" he asked.

"Not sure," said Zee Zee. "But you remember Dieter's old saying. *If you step on snake droppings, sleep on high rocks.*"

"I hear your words. No sweat, Brother. This regiment will protect the workers and the students and all the little grandmas from Warlord Sun's cheap little snakes. We'll shoot the executioners!"

Zee Zee was encouraged. Three days later, Koo visited for noodles and pork.

"They're pulling us out," he said. *Us* was the Chinese Fifth Army, heavy with local Shanghai and Kiangsu troops.

"Who's taking your place?" asked Zee Zee.

"Chinese Eighth Army." Koo spat, a habit that German training couldn't stop, since Sergeant Dieter spat more than ten Chinese on a bad boat. The Eighth was made up of troops from the south and the Pearl River interior. They didn't speak Songhai. The regiments of the Eighth viewed Shanghainese as being from a different part of the world. They had heard that Shanghainese looked down on southerners.

"Big heart, Lee," said Koo. "No dust in your bore."

"Big heart, Koo. The sun at your back."

Zee Zee had given Da-tsien permission to feed the troops. He was about to tell her to stop when she reported that the new soldiers were rude. Some girls serving noodles and water had been manhandled.

Zee Zee almost exploded.

"Okay, okay, don't say a word!" Da-tsien said. "I won't go back there! But not because of your saying so. I'm not going back because those men scared me."

A strange foreboding settled on Shanghai. It felt to Zee Zee like the accumulation of an emotional avalanche. He went to KMT headquarters and found the Eighth Army adjutants, who had nothing to say to him. He wished Da-tsien were with him; she could always read motives, while he tended to take everything at face value.

Meanwhile, the Communist organizers, under the army's request, told the strikers to return to the factories.

"Zee Zee, everything's okay," said Da-tsien. "Don't sleep in your uniform anymore, okay? The buttons hurt my skin."

"The uniform keeps us safe."

"It makes me black and blue."

"You look good in any color."

She smiled gloriously. In these moments, he forgot that he hated being away from the army.

IN THE PREDAWN hours of April 12, waves of Green Gang members, backed up by Chiang Kai-shek's army, attacked the labor organizing headquarters and dormitories of Communist students and labor activists. The victims were the people who had delivered Shanghai, the greatest city in Asia, to Chiang Kai-shek and his army.

Chingbang gunmen dragged many Reds into the street and shot them in the head. Those were the lucky ones. Others were beaten to death. Some were executed in groups or beheaded, shot multiple times in their beds or burned in their apartments. Tired of wasting ammunition, some gangsters tied leftist students together, bound their feet and dumped them from boats into the Whangpu River to drown. Other organizers were strapped onto bumpers of cars and dragged through the streets of Nantao. The students cried out to Chiang's army for salvation from the gangsters, but the Eighth Army had been instructed to support the Green Gang, and herded refugees towards the guns of the criminal underworld.

Chou En-lai and others were trapped in the headquarters building; he and a precious few managed to escape.

The sound of gunfire caused Zee Zee to jump fully dressed from bed. He grabbed the new Lee Enfield rifle Pan had delivered to him after the February executions. It was a sign of the times that Zee Zee hadn't asked how it came to be Pan's.

He loaded and safetied the Colt .45. Putting on his cartridge belt, holstering the sidearm and grabbing two packed ammo bandoleers, he awakened Da-tsien, who had been in deep sleep.

"Stay in bed. Stay away from windows. Keep the curtains pulled all day. I'll be back."

"Zee Zee, what is it? What's wrong?"

"I don't know yet. But those aren't firecrackers."

"What's going on? Tell me what's happening, Zee Zee!"

He couldn't. He didn't think his gentle, fragile wife could handle the information.

Zee Zee found his majordomo looking out the opened front door.

"Lock the door after me," said Zee Zee. "Draw all curtains. Put storm plywood on the insides of the front windows. No one leaves the house, not even for market. Get my father to the lower level. No one stays on the upper floor." He ran across the street, roused the mustached Tzu majordomo and Singh the Sikh guard and repeated his instructions.

"You guard the Tzu house, Singh," said Zee Zee. "I'll guard mine. Lights out. Elders and children in the storm cellar. No one upstairs. The Communists aren't trained and will shoot wildly." He assumed that the Communist strikers were storming the houses of the rich. Mob shooting sailed high, breaking upper-story windows; so would Red gunfire.

None of the fifteen or twenty personal house guards who lived in the homes on Burkill came into the street. Zee Zee was alone. He took up a position along the sycamores that offered some cover, fair concealment and clear firing lanes. He adjusted the sights for a two-hundred-meter shot, a distance he guessed would discourage a mob's advance. He laid out the bandoleers and unsnapped the individual ammo pouches, wishing that he had been able to battle-sight the rifle. At least he had cleaned it of its Cosmoline packing grease. Most Enfields fired high and to the right, so he clicked two low and one left. He grounded the .45 by his right knee, grateful for the full moon. It made night fire an easy exercise. To protect his night vision, he ignored the streetlights.

Can I kill them, workers from Hongkew factories? Where I hung posters urging them to organize? He had to protect his frightened father. So he'd shoot the advancing mob in the legs. No head shots.

He heard a car. Several cars, honking, celebrating, driving fast and erratically. They screeched around a corner. He aimed at the driver's window and saw the Kuomintang national flags fluttering from the radio antenna. He quickly pulled up the muzzle and stood as the cars passed him, honking, slowing down, passengers waving with white armbands. Some were Hongkew people he recognized from the teashops. The cars were dragging something. Dead bodies. No, some bodies were struggling. His instinct was to raise the muzzle and shoot the drivers.

Shaken, Zee Zee returned to his firing position. He listened to gunfire in the Chinese city. It wasn't disciplined military fire. At first it reminded him of Pan's opium gang-war firefights—different ordnances and calibers firing randomly. But there was no rhythm of gunfire, of combat, and he knew that the gangs were executing people. Not in the rich districts, but in Nantao, the heart of the Chinese City of Shanghai.

Now he also knew the origin of the cars that had passed, and why he hadn't been able to find Pan and his cronies—they had been lying in wait in Nantao. The cars were armored vehicles from Pan's garages. The drivers were *Chingbang* gunmen. Chiang's Shanghainese Fifth Army had been withdrawn and replaced by units that had no love for the city. T.A. had said that the gangsters were funding Chiang's Northern Expedition. The King of Beggars had been paid by the same gangsters to finger Communist students as they left their meetings. The beggars wore white headbands; the *Chingbang* wore blue jackets and white armbands. It was a white terror against the Reds and the friends of Reds.

"*Scheiße*," Zee Zee said, the German word carrying greater weight than a Chinese curse. He safetied his rifle, holstered the automatic, buttoned up his bandoleers, threw them over his shoulder and stood. He felt ill. He found a pack of cigarettes. He lit one, showing his position, illuminating himself. He didn't care. He drew the smoke deep into his lungs, welcoming the acrid smoke, thinking about his father's stained opium pipe in the dark, silent house.

Like most of the house servants, Da-tsien peeked behind the curtains to see Zee Zee smoking on the street. She had heard the cars and the yelling and had hidden, her heart flying in anxiety. She imagined her husband being shot and killed in front of her, in front of his own parents. Tapping on the window, she tried to get his attention and to make him come inside. She tried to open the window but didn't know how to do it. Futilely tapping on the glass, she wondered how she could become pregnant and deliver a healthy son under such conditions.

Later, Zee Zee lay down next to her, fully dressed, conflicted, exhausted.

Da-tsien asked a thousand questions without pause. The questions made him angry. It was her fault that she had Red friends who were probably now dead. This would ruin her mood and cause trouble.

After sunrise, the *Chingbang* caravans happily honked their way through the International Settlement, flying the national flag and passing the foreign troops and police, who were their new allies against the workers, the students and the Reds. Bloodstained, armbanded assassins waved at the young KMT lieutenant and an Indian Sikh guard who stood on Burkill Road, not knowing that these two riflemen were disciplining themselves from shooting them.

The news came through the servants. Skinny Wu, the gap-toothed, stone-faced seamstress with dead sons and no daughters, had disappeared from the Lee household not long after Zee Zee had gone to the Gobi. Some presumed she had been run over by one of those horrible *chi tz* gas machines. Uniden-tified bodies were collected every morning by Buddhist death monks and buried in mass graves west of the city.

Others thought that Skinny Wu had wandered north to find Zee Zee, the way a lost cat will persist in finding its way home. Zee Zee was the only one who could make her laugh.

"I have terrible, terrible news," said Skinny Wu, who now suddenly appeared at the door, thin as ever. She ignored the cries of welcome, the warm patting of her arms to verify that she wasn't a ghost, the shouts that both Lee boys were married but no sons yet, that Zee Zee had been on the street all night with a gun, that there was hot-and-sour soup in the kitchen, the way she liked it, with thick scallions.

Wu was shaking. "Gangsters and Chiang Kai-shek's army have killed thou-sands of students and workers! Thousands! Their blood is everywhere. Worse, they're kidnapping the daughters and wives and sisters of the workers and stu-dents, raping them and throwing them into brothels and factories." She wrung her hands as if they were wet. "It's like February all over again, and the Boxer trouble, with heads on poles, but so much worse! These were young people! I recognized some of the heads . . ." She wept so hard that she fell. Sesame Face Wong caught her and carried her to a sofa. Da-tsien cared for her until Ying-oh, her ranking sister-in-law, rebuked her and took over.

Da-tsien ran to her room, frustrated and terrified and confused by the news. She tried to hit her pillows but had no strength.

The next night, when he was certain that no mob would come after his father or his family, Zee Zee drove to St. John's.

He found T.A. in the library, on the edge of tears.

"Oh, Zee Zee, it is terrible, terrible."

"I *saw* it. Parts of it. I saw the *Chingbang* caravans, dragging bodies of students. What do I do about Pan? He was part of it."

"Yes. Well, Pan has been admitted as a student at St. John's."

"No kidding. Well, that's funny after last night, yes?"

"Zee Zee, listen. This is not about Pan. Please prepare yourself for bitter news. It is about you. Zee Zee, Professor Far convinced the dean to fail you academically."

"What?"

"Zee Zee, you have flunked out. I spoke to the dean. I could be of no help." T.A. carried a look of total despair—a Soong had been unable to help a kinsman. He was so sad that Zee Zee felt sorry for him.

"Professor Far wanted to expel you. He succeeded. Your grades were weak. He used your absence during this trouble, your aggressiveness during school assemblies, to fail you. I think he accused you of being a Communist. I hope you do not blame your wife for this. Lee, I am so sorry. I feel so guilty. I should have been able to avert this. As heaven and earth are my witness, my heart is heavy with sadness and shame."

Zee Zee walked across the campus of St. John's. He stood in the quiet interior courtyard. The full moon that had allowed him to watch the horror of April 12 radiated a cold light that mirrored his paralyzed senses. T.A. had come up to stand behind him. Zee Zee felt incredibly stupid, for he had failed to fully recognize his academic indifference or Professor Far's animosity. He was unaware that he was profoundly depressed, for he presumed that as a young soldier he was immune to feelings of weakness. Yet he was leaving a fellowship that he had never appreciated until it was one moment too late.

"Be a banker with me, Zee Zee," said T.A.

Zee Zee shook his head and walked away.

It was hard to feel self-pity when he could imagine the wailings of many thousands for the dead. He was confused, because most of those killed were Reds, the enemies of his social class. He began to consider sympathy a weakness.

He was walking alone, succumbing to the deep, abiding shame that belongs to the imperfect sons of Chinese families when the mustached majordomo of the House of Tzu called out to him.

"Young Master Lee, oh, I found you! Young Master, you *must* come home!

Da-tsien's crazy with sadness! Classmates are with her, but, but—this is so hard to say—Young Master, her friend Grace Sun was killed. It is true—evil spirits are in control. And her friend Phyllis Li, in Peking? She was tortured to death. Amitabha forgive me for saying—they strangled the poor girl for three days. So all of this was carefully planned.

"This after they made Phyllis watch her father, Li Ta-chao the librarian, being strangled first. I tell you, Master, the world has gone crazy. I am so sad for you young people. Ah, at least they didn't pull her insides out. That was her great fear, I heard her say that many times. You know, I hope she was glad about that. There are so many students who were killed—you remember Auntie Gao's nephew—"

DA-TSIEN WAS WEEPING in the dimly lit *ting* sitting room, which was full of crying women. She saw him and cried, "Oh, Zee Zee!"

He didn't belong in a room with so much *yin*, so he went upstairs.

Da-tsien followed him. She found him cleaning his rifle.

"Is *that* what you do after all this blood? Oh, God in heaven! I hate your uniform! I hate your guns! I hate your army! You're all murderers!"

"You hung out with Communists! They threaten your father and my father and all fathers. They shouldn't have tried to mess in politics!"

"I can't believe you! You're blaming the victims?" she cried. "You're on the side of the killers, the murderers, the stranglers!"

"I'm on the side of the modern world, the future!"

"Is killing girls the future? I pray not!"

"You pray all you want. What's pretty clear now is that siding with power is the only safe way."

"What's really clear is that your general, Chiang Kai-shek, is the worst *jun-fa* warlord of all. He makes Warlord Sun look like an angel! At least *jun fas* are honest about their badness. Chiang hides behind the national flag to kill innocent students and girls and workers!"

"This is a class war, Da-tsien," Zee Zee said through his teeth. "We have to side with our fathers."

"My father weeps for the dead! Does yours?"

"*Don't talk to me about my father! You can't do that!*"

His anger, coming from so close to her heart, struck her like a club. She fainted and fell to the floor. Gritting his teeth, he picked her up and laid her on the bed. Downstairs, the servants looked up in fear. Zee Zee lit a cigarette and paced between the window and the door, trapped and uncertain which way to proceed. He opened the window and fanned his wife. Then he looked out, the curtains gently billowing, and studied the moon. As a boy, he had tried to touch it, jumping as high as he could, reaching, straining.

thirty-eight

Chingkanshan

CAPTAIN JOGHINDER SINGH, Zee Zee's commander, pointed earthward. Tall on earth, he was regal in the sky, his bright white scarf waving bravely in the slipstream.

It was 1928 and this being Zee Zee's twentieth combat mission, he didn't dip the nose as he looked down. Below, Kuomintang troops had displayed yellow panels aimed at targets they wanted bombed. Five flags meant five Communist enemy rifle companies.

"Probably five water buffalo," snorted Zee Zee.

They were at two thousand feet on a gray day. They had flown over Tungting Lake's broad, sparkling salt beds to bank below the cloud cover and attack the nonexistent Communist ground troops.

Few loved to fly more than Zee Zee. Perhaps Lieutenant Pong had greater passion. But Zee Zee crowed and whooped each time he took off, laughing at the sky that he could now embrace.

Singh made a fist, banking left. When his wings were vertical, Zee Zee followed. There were to have been eight aircraft on the mission, but mechanical problems had cut them to five. The all-metal open-cockpit O2U-1D Corsair biplanes arrowed downward at nearly 180 miles an hour in a tight formation to maximize the bomb impacts. The wind screaming through the struts pressed Zee Zee's goggles hard into his face and vibrated his cheeks. He loved the drop in his stomach as the world blew upward to meet him.

Singh couldn't see any targets. He waggled his wings and pulled out, the flight following him. Only one man dropped a single bomb onto the brown scraggly brush broken by a meandering creek. The bomb burst dully, throwing debris in a flowering arc. There was no antiaircraft fire. Birds silently took flight.

Engines roaring, Singh pulled the flight to twenty-five hundred feet and signaled for them to racetrack. The two-ton, thirty-four-foot-wingspan Corsair was the U.S. Navy's top scout aircraft. Designed for sea-level operations, it was a temperamental bomber in the high mountain plateaus of China. Singh dove and leveled out at four hundred feet. Now men on the ground would look like men instead of haystacks. He altered his airspeed to stymie enemy guns, looking to either side for signs of the enemy, hoping to draw fire. Nothing. He tried again, then pulled up, regained formation and pointed towards the mountain to the west.

To the Chingkanshan. Zee Zee whooped. *Yes! No more bomb runs on mud and birds. The Chingkanshan.* Even the name sounded romantic. Mount Chingkan, named for five wells, was as hard as the ridges of the moon and had been the ideal hideaway for bandits and thieves for a thousand years. Now it was the home for the First Workers and Peasants Revolutionary Army of Hunan. This ragtag band in a land of thieves and smugglers was led by the former schoolteacher and librarian Mao Tse-tung, and by a leather-tough soldier and master tactician in tennis shoes named Chu Teh.

"Kill a snake by chopping off its head, not by throwing pebbles at its tail!" Zee Zee urged Joghinder Singh.

"We follow orders," said Joghinder.

"That's old British colonial talk. Orders for rajas and lords."

"The British trained me to fly," said Joghinder. He was tall and refined, a lovely man with the voice of an English country gentleman.

"So you owe them. What the hell does that have to do with following the orders of a stupid Chinese general?"

Joghinder paused. "Zee Zee, I am a Sikh, a fighting man from India. I have received a lead position in the Chinese air force. I must be respectful of that opportunity. I presume the general is not stupid and, in fact, knows more than even my newest pilot, a brilliant lieutenant."

"Crap! You're a fighting man. Fighting men don't drop bombs on bushes! Fighters fly up the damn Chingkanshan and bomb the head of the snake. They kill Mao Tse-tung and Chu Teh and their troops!" Zee Zee pronounced the general's name *Jew Da.*

"Would it be possible, Lieutenant, for you to call me *sir*, at least once a day? It would reflect good morale."

"Oh, piss on that! I—"

"Pilots must not curse. It sets a bad example for the enlisted men."

"The enlisted men," said Zee Zee, "are curs and dogs and roosters of unknown origins. They eat roots and raw barley and would kill for half a ball of cheap *tye* opium residue. I don't think elegant speech'll make them into scholars any more than a curse word'll make them worse."

"Sir," said Joghinder.

"Sir," said Zee Zee.

Captain Singh agreed with Zee Zee. So he secured Squadron Leader Loo's permission to request authorization from the ground commander to raid the Chingkanshan instead of bombing the scrublands. But the Nationalist commander for Hunan, a large-stomached general, insisted that the Fourth Squadron bomb only the area to his immediate front.

Earlier, a Communist sniper had shot the general's aide-de-camp—his third son, and the regimental chef—who unfortunately had been clowning with the general's cap. The general missed his son, and the regiment missed its cook, and so the Fourth Squadron bombed the bushes.

"You tell the squadron leader that he's an idi—"

"The Germans who trained you might have used military protocol. You must respect Major Loo. Understand?" Singh didn't add, *Even though he's an idiot and loves to provoke people by calling them stupid, and by questioning their manhood and insulting their clans.* Lee was crazy enough to lose his temper, for which Loo would have him shot. Finding Chinese men who wanted to fly was not that easy in the early twentieth century.

"I will ask the squadron leader. If we do not find snipers tomorrow, we will see if he allows us to sortie the mountain," said Singh, "on the condition that you not speak to him face-to-face. Agreed?"

Zee Zee beamed. "All right! Sir!"

Now they were going. There were three good passes to the Chingkanshan and four thousand bad ones, and all were hidden in ground fogs as persistent as turberculosis. The mountain wasn't a simple geophysical form—it was a miasmic tangle of foggy ridgelines, tunnels and outcroppings to catch careless pilots. Lacking a single promontory, it was a lunar rock sixty by twenty miles with five villages and a stone barricade that was as easy to bomb as the door to an anthill.

Zee Zee's eyes opened wide. Ancient sod villages clustered in the foothills. Tiny people stopped their hard labors to look upward. Some ran and hid in total fear, and others covered their ears. The aircraft began bouncing as they approached the wind contours of the mountain.

It loomed before them, massive and ancient in clouds of mist, more myth than reality, more red than brown, more sulfur than loam. Small military cooking fires dotted the sparse, dripping pine forests. Here a modern man could believe in dragons and phoenixes, and in schoolteachers and peasants who were shaking their fists at the landlords of the earth. Zee Zee reminded himself that the Reds were after the scholars and fathers of China, and that he was an educated Chinese son.

Focus. Fly. You've been daydreaming for—a minute? Two? Christ, you could be dead from inattention! Watch out! Flying is like a drug.

His instructor had said, "Taking off is Big Fear. Landing is even Bigger Fear. Taking off is optional. But landing is mandatory.

"In between, you're a bird, and your emotions become strong and you stop paying attention. Flying is like a drug. So you crash."

The instructor's name was Anderson, and he had gone to a school called West Point. It was a Chinese name, like Snail Creek, South Lake, North Isle.

"It's a goddamn military academy," he had said. "Which means they empty out your brains and pour in training manuals."

"Did you like it?" asked Zee Zee, who wished that Chiang Kai-shek had sent him to Whampoa Military Academy, where Chou En-lai had been a teacher until the White Terror. Whampoa wouldn't have stripped off his muscle like the Nei Govi, and he'd have a certificate, which St. John's had failed to give him.

Zee Zee was paying Anderson three hundred dollars Shanghai to learn to fly. The top schools at Hangchiao Airport cost nearly a thousand, but Da-tsien had spent the balance of T. A. Soong's honeymoon money paying back ancient Lee-clan debts for rent, opium and concubinage fees. Zee had engaged Da-tsien in an incredible argument that spanned five days. Finally, exhausted by the fight, she insincerely admitted she was sorry and pulled him to bed.

Anderson laughed. "You're not supposed to *like* West Point. Not all four years. Me, I only hated it for three."

"You enjoyed the final year. That's good."

"Horseshit. I quit before the final year."

Zee Zee looked at him with great compassion. Anderson was much older, almost thirty. He was tall and gangly and had a classic huge Western nose. Zee Zee and his teacher were strong men with living fathers. They had gone to good schools but had failed to finish. He presumed that this American was accordingly filled with bitterness.

"Bitter? Oh, hell no. Every day I'm free of that fucking place, I feel better. Now, remember. When you get drugged up there, and your mind drifts off, check instruments and position constantly, front, left, right, rear, then vary it. Front, right, left, front, rear. Embrace the sky, Lieutenant. No one ever crashed by running into air."

He said all of this in superb Mandarin. He had been the son of missionaries and had learned the musical tones of Chinese as he learned the Germanic inconsistencies of English. T.A. thought Anderson's Chinese was better than his English, but of course, that was impossible.

"You miss America, Anderson?"

"Like a hot bamboo plank shoved up my butt. Remember, the greater the angle of incidence to the ground on landing, the greater the chance of never flying again."

Zee Zee had nodded. He understood. Many of his compatriots didn't. There was an invisible cultural wall between feudal China of the twentieth century and Western technology of the 1920s. Most Chinese pilot trainees struggled on that border. Zee Zee hadn't even noticed it. The final flight test was a solo through the Yangtze Gorges while being followed in a chase aircraft by the instructor. The shabby biplane trainers couldn't rise above nine thousand feet, and the height of the river and its gorges required pilots to fly between the cliffs. Zee Zee had loved it; it was like riding a Harley.

"You are unusual, Lieutenant Lee," said Anderson. "Most good students here are farmers with good vision and strong legs and arms. I see about one of those guys a year. The literate ones are pansies who hate dirt and noise and want to fly without having to understand aviation. Were you a farmer before you got to college?"

Zee Zee shook his head. "I rode a motorcycle. I became a soldier at sixteen. Before that, I did *gong-fu.*"

"Yeah, that'd do it. You gotta teach me some of that."

"I don't do it anymore."

"Why's that?"

"It requires all of your life. All of your health."

"Sounds like flying."

"You make flying sound dangerous," said Zee Zee.

"Flying is not dangerous. Crashing is dangerous."

SINGH CLIMBED SO that Pong, the squat, muscular man in the trail aircraft, wouldn't scrape rocks. Pong was Singh's best pilot because he wasn't interested in killing anyone. He loved flying as much as Zee Zee, and never complained about overscheduled sorties, even though he violently opposed war. He flew tail position to make sure none of the other pilots fell asleep, drifted off or collided. He always aimed his bombs away from people. He liked bombing mud and scaring birds.

Singh waggled twice to each side—*spread out.*

The winds hit, swirling and shearing into valleys and saddlebacks. The formation broke as pilots fought to avoid stalls and outcrops. Singh was leading the right way, but the right way was very hard.

The captain had briefed them before takeoff. "Stay together. Drop your bombs when I drop mine. No individual targets. Do not pray or use worry beads while flying your airplane. We will all pray after we land.

"Today, if there are no targets, to please crazy-man Zee Zee, we will seek secondary targets on the mountain. I will signal to open the formation on approach. Remember the winds. Drop bombs where I drop, get off the summit, skirt wide to the east and form up. Pong has the tail."

The summit! In earlier raids, they had first hit the base camps, alerting the gunners at the peak and losing many planes as they climbed. This time they were going straight for the top. Zee Zee snapped his fingers. Pong grimaced. Zee Zee had gotten an extra bomb for the cockpit.

Brilliant white streamers rained down on them—enemy gunners had heard their engines. A pilot jinked too hard and stalled, falling out. Zee Zee bared his teeth and fired long, tight bursts from his single Browning .30-caliber that was mounted above the right wing. It was a trick to press the trigger without changing course, and he had four hundred rounds to spend. The heavy *pukka-pukka-pukka* of the gun reassured him as he gently hit his rudder to swath his arcing tracers into the rows of gunners, the impact spouts of his machine gun silencing them. He juked right, left, and was free, and it was seconds to the top—airspeed indicator at a full 115 miles an hour as the old and overworked Pratt & Whitney R-1340C radial Wasp 450-horsepower engine strained at thinner air. The oil-pump gaskets flattened as he upped manifold pressure, oil bleating out of the heads to splatter on the windshield and stream from the exhaust ports. The air was arctic, but Zee Zee didn't notice; he was cursing gunners that were putting hot pinging lead into his ship, ripping away a panel and a part of his lower left wing while luckily missing the struts and controls. Singh was over the top. Zee Zee followed. There were more guns than he had ever seen, endless ranks of infantrymen shooting at him, machine guns splurging unbroken chains of hot incandescent ordnance on his flight as buildings flashed below with more ahead. He jinked as tracers ripped through his plane; Singh was dropping bombs that fell darkly. Zee Zee pulled his mechanical bomb releases, then reached down to lift the fourteen-pound high-explosive Krupp bomb from the cockpit and throw it below his craft towards a wave of small riflemen. He hauled on the stick and pushed maximum airspeed to break opposite to Singh's left-hand pullout, gravity tugging on him. Bright red ground explosions rocked the plane as it climbed hard, streaming oil and threatening to cough and sputter as the oil pressure dropped. He needed separation and lower rpm's, but he couldn't get one without giving up the other. Tracers whacked the fuselage, but there was no pain and he still had aileron and rudder as the white streamers arched lower; he pointed the nose down and dropped speed, the engine gulping and thanking him as one, then two, flaming aircraft pancaked into the mountain, erupting in painful fireballs. He skirted the peak to the east. Brilliant flames flashed—ammo blowing up—and hot smoke billowed from the summit. Zee Zee whooped, lifting his chin to crow as he pulled out his Colt automatic and dove, firing at the riflemen shooting at him.

~~Hey, Da-tsien, Dear Da-tsien, Dearest Da-tsien,~~ My darling Da-tsien,

Life is wonderful in Hunan. The food is spicy. We use chopsticks like the ones Sesame Face uses for cooking. Seriously, they're as long as my forearm. The people here put hot pepper and chili in everything and then they put in more, and they hang chili peppers from doorways and sing to the god of chilis.

I know why rebels come from Hunan. They fight in taverns and they're as hot-tempered as their food, brawling in streets and markets. Some know good country gong-fu. Others fight like chickens.

I miss your cooking. Just kidding! We have a funny cook who's like the one-legged translator in the Gobi. Maybe I never told you. I don't remember.

Everyone is so poor that there are no restaurants; not like Shanghai. People cook and eat at home. No servants to do it. Children chop and wives cook. Cooking takes up the whole day! So primitive!

For the squadron to get a cook wasn't easy. Soo collects things from the wilds with mountain lions and bears. If tigers show up in our soup, to go with vegetables that defy description, no one'll be shocked. Soo has only one arm; he lost the other in a leopard attack on his village when he was a boy.

My boss is a Sikh Indian, same name as your house guard—Singh! No relation—I asked. His first name: Joghinder. He says most Sikhs are Singhs, like most of us own the Hundred Honorable Names. I never knew that.

He's distinguished and refined. Never swears. Talks like T.A.—no joined words. When I got here, I asked him how the food was. He grabbed his throat, staggering around, making gagging sounds for five minutes. Despite all this, my stomach is very regular.

I'm trying to kill a man named Mao Tse-tung. He was a Hunan school-teacher who worked in the Peking University library.

Mao incites Hunanese to kill the grain-owning landlords, who up the rent in hard times. The peasants complain. There is no harmony in this. Of course, the poor people have a point—their children are starving. But it's not good that Mao upsets these people. It disturbs heaven and is bad for order.

The army fights stupidly and we pilots don't fight much better. We go out and bomb bushes. This is not how the Germans do it.

I exercise because I'm not sleeping with you. More energy now. I'm almost twenty-one! I'm a pilot! I love life. I'm sleeping well. You okay? I may come back in half a year or so. Pray that I kill this man Mao.

Zee Zee

~~*My Dearest Honey Darling, My Darling,*~~ *Honey,*

Thank you for your letter! I miss you so much. Without you, the house was incredibly empty, so I moved back with my family and I think every-one's much happier, don't you? P'o-p'o, your mother, will be saved from my many failures in the kitchen and in the market and in the yard and in life itself. Ying-oh is quite happy with me gone, and I am deliriously happy to be with my father again. I know you don't like this subject, so I'll do the talking and all you have to do is read it.

Baba is frailer, which is incredibly sad to see. Mother constantly criticizes him, and so I pray that she'll accept that he's old now and seldom fishes or reads and it's unreasonable to expect him to work at this age. It's wonderful to be with him, to rub his back when his muscles hurt, but my mother just frowns and I can feel his nerves tense and his chi diminish. This is very sad, just like the separation of a young couple, and just like the absence of a newborn son, yes?

You have to visit much sooner than six months or I'll just die! If I were an adventurer, I'd take trains and boats to reach Hunan, and I could try to cook for you while you think about making sons. My friend Tai Yueh showed me a map, and I think the distance from here to you is about twenty-five million miles, maybe more.

Zee Zee, I am sorry you are trying to kill anyone, especially Mao Tse-tung, who is such an incredibly interesting person and also exceptionally polite, especially to women. He was good friends with Chou En-lai. You remember Chou. He kissed my hand when we met. A most elegant person, don't you think!

Mao cares about the common person and wants to free the peasant from greedy landlords. I don't think that's true about General Chiang. Chiang Kai-shek's people killed Grace and tortured Phyllis and her father and shot those poor people last year just because they were trying to help him. Actually, I don't understand at all why he did that, and I don't want to hear your explanation. Chiang's people torture girls and cut them into little pieces and do even worse things than that. Not Mao's people, who are much more respectful and kind. Li Ta-chao actually hired Mao Tse-tung to work in his library. I know this makes you angry, but now I don't care because you're wrong on this one.

Are you really okay? You didn't mention us. Do you miss me? I miss you. You're supposed to be telling me these things. When we were together, I'd make you tell me, and now, with you so far away, I can't.

I pray to Guan Yin for our son. Ying-oh had a son. His thirty-day Red Egg Ginger party to celebrate survival of mother and son was good— P'o-p'o's soup was positively heavenly—except your mother and brother argued. Gee has been much worse in your absence. The baby is very lovely, and Ying-oh let me hold him for one second. His wet nurse has a sweet voice, which is good for the milk.

I can't tell you of the pressure on me to have a son. You can't even imagine. I would tell you, but it would take a hundred hundred hundred pieces of rice paper and they're now quite expensive. I cry all the time now, except when I'm praying. You know goddess Guan Yin's mah-mee was Hsi Wang Mu, Queen Mother of the Western Skies! You're in the west, so if you pray to her, she'll surely give us a son, don't you think?

Your father sent his scary little concubine downstairs to give your brother's son the name Lee Huo-sun, Hunter-Harvest Grandson, with generation name, for the Ancestors' Tablet, of *yen*, long life.

He named our son at the same time, too—Lee Chien-sun, Healthy-Strong Grandson. A fine name, but unimaginative, not scholarly, reflective, inspiring, promising, spiritual or strong in values. When you're home, talk to your father and get a name with Brilliance or Wisdom or something world-shaking in it.

> I shut the door, hoping to drive away a permanent sorrow,
> Let a spring breeze approach, and I could beg sorrow to linger
> And sorrow would never stay!

Remember that Sung poem I recited to you under the sheets? I pull my coverlet over my face at night, sad to be alone. But I remember you and I love you. In your next letter, don't worry about reporting on food or your stomach. Tell me about your heart and your liver and tell me about how much you love me and miss me and how you will soon give me a son, very, very soon.

Da-tsien

thirty-nine

Killing Mao

THE PLOT TO assassinate Mao Tse-tung evolved when Cook Soo was feeding his strange, lopsided, spike-haired mutt. The pilots always suspected
that Cook Soo gave the best portions to the dog, who had been beaten so hard
as a pup that his spine waved like a dragon's.

"The Yuan and the Wang on the Chingkanshan eat better than you, I
think," said Cook Soo.

"Who are they?" asked Zee Zee. He was one of two pilots who spoke to the
shunned cook. The others believed that talking to a handicapped person was
a risk; the gods obviously disfavored such people. Pilots knew they were better
than all other people—flying proved it.

"Two outlaw gangs," said Soo. "They fight each other, kill everyone. The
lai ko, the Visitors, buy them off, so the outlaws help them now."

The Visitors were Mao and Chu and the Communists.

"Soo," said Pong, "that's the ugliest dog since the emperor scolded Admi-
ral Cheng Ho. Where'd he come from, the egg of a dead vulture?"

Soo frowned. "He a fine dog, Master. He feed very good!"

Zee Zee petted the wet mongrel as he ate, making him growl menacingly,
which made Soo laugh. He liked this young man, whom he called Handsome
One. Handsome One cursed, which proved he was human; and talked to him,
which he considered normal. It was what people did. There were no social
classes on the Hunan-Kiangsi border. There were only various groups of the
poor.

"How do you know what the people on the mountain eat?" asked Handsome One.

"Sir, the big cat that took my arm, also grab my cousin, same time. He lost
fingers, a foot. He not a full man, either, so he also a cook. But he cook on the
mountain."

"He cook as bad as you?" asked Pong.

"Worse!" said Soo, slapping his thighs and laughing with broken teeth. He had slept on dirt all his life. His feet were wrapped in grass sandals, and red soil had tinted his pores since he could walk. He endured enormous temperature differentials, worked twenty hours a day and suffered sharp physical pain without comment.

"Then we don't have to bomb them!" Pong laughed. "His cousin'll kill them!"

It was an idea, even if Soo understood none of it. He thought the American biplanes were large animals that drank black blood, and he hid under bear pelts when the sated beasts roared and climbed into the sky.

Zee Zee sat at the table, remembering Chiang Kai-shek.

Not long after the Shanghai massacres of students and workers, T.A. had insisted that Zee Zee accompany him to his sister's wedding. "Mei-ling is getting married," he had said somberly. "Arranged by Ai-ling," the firstborn sister.

Zee Zee remembered Mei-ling and her bamboo paintings.

"She's marrying Chiang Kai-shek."

"You're kidding," said Zee Zee. "I thought he already had two or three wives in Canton."

"He does, but he is divorcing them."

The wedding was performed in the Soong home on Seymour Road, and the public ceremony held at the Majestic Hotel. It was a wedding of state, combining the country's preeminent military leader with the preeminent political and financial clan.

Zee Zee couldn't manage to congratulate his commander in chief. He expressed his wishes for double happiness to Mei-ling, who was now, and forever after, Madame Chiang Kai-shek.

"You're very kind, Zee Zee. I hope we'll still be friends?"

"I didn't know you knew her," whispered Da-tsien later.

"Barely," said Zee Zee. "She's just T.A.'s sister."

LATER, ZEE ZEE talked to Soo alone.

"Your cousin cooks for the villages at the mountain base?" The villages were Stone Age communities of small people and rotting wood.

"Oh, no! Cousin cook at summit! For Big Pants!"

"Your cousin knows Mao Tse-tung?"

"Oh, yes! He know everyone up there! Who Mao Tse-tung?"

"He's their leader on the mountain."

"Oh, yes! He really not so bad cook as me. Must know the leader."

"Soo, is your cousin a Red?"

Soo scratched his head. "No, sir. He Han man. He have black hair." "Han man" meant the ethnic majority, the people called the Chinese.

"Is he Communist, a *gungtsetang*, Share Wealth Party man?"

"Don't know, Master."

"Do you know what it means to be a *gungtsetang*?"

"Oh, yes, sir! I not selfish! I share all my vegetable with you!"

"Yes, Soo, you do. Thank you." Now he was talking and smiling like Da-tsien. The thought of her stopped him for some moments; Soo waited patiently, blinking. There was no rush in the hills. Winter always came.

"Soo, have you ever climbed the Chingkanshan?"

"Oh, Master, I born in first mountain pass, at Dajing, Big Well, opposite big cliff. I live there until no food! Hey, going up, now—that a long, hard walk for old man with one arm."

"A man who reached the top and came back could be rich."

Soo scratched his head again. "Don't think so, Master?"

"I'd give him a lot of money. To buy shoes, clothes, food."

"Oh. So you want me to bring my cousin back to cook for you?"

"No. I want you to find out where Mao Tse-tung, the leader on the mountain, sleeps. He and his friend Chu Teh change where they sleep."

"Like hunters, Master?"

"Yes! Like hunters. Cook Soo, I want to know where Mao sleeps on Monday. You know the days of the week? Good. I want to know also where Mao sleeps on Tuesday, Wednesday, every day of the week. I want to know what time he gets out of bed and what time he goes to sleep."

"I can do all that? Me? So much to remember!"

"Yes, you can. We'll practice first." Zee Zee knelt and smoothed wet ground. On it he created a pattern of rocks. Soo knelt with him, staring.

"Soo, see this? This is the airfield. This big rock is Hanger Number One. See? This is Hanger Number Two. See this? That's the HQ building. Here's your mess hall. Now, what's this?"

"That a pebble, Master."

"What does it represent? What building? See, next to the Mess?"

Soo thought and thought. "Not pebble? Oh, oh, that my little house! Oh, I see, I see! You make magic! Small world!" He laughed delightedly.

"It's called a *map*. When you get to the top of Chingkanshan, I want you to look around with both eyes. Look at all the buildings! Then make a map of the buildings up there on the summit. Use rocks, just like this. Do it again and again until it's like chopping meat.

"Then figure out where Mao sleeps. Inside which building.

"Then come back to me. Make the map again. Show me where the buildings are, using rocks like this. Up there, I think it looks like this. . . ." Zee Zee moved the rocks to resemble the buildings he had seen. "There's a big one here. Three small ones here. . . . Then show me which rock Mao sleeps in."

Soo nodded, then slapped his forehead in alarm. "Aiyaa! I not kill him for you! I no killer, Master!"

"Of course not. I just want information. The map. And when Mao gets out of bed: before the rooster or after? When does he go to bed: second watch or third watch? Nothing more."

"Nothing more? Go up mountain? Remember? Come back?"

"That's all. Make rock map up there. Come back. Show me where Mao Tse-tung sleeps, every night of the week. Can do? *Gung ho?*"

Soo thought and frowned. He nodded. "Can do, Master. *Gung ho.*"

"Soo, don't tell anyone up there, even your cousin, that you work with us pilots. They'll be so jealous of you, they may hurt you."

"Really," Soo said, stroking his chin. "You think?"

"And ask questions carefully. Also, take apart map when done. Here." Zee Zee filled Soo's hands with *yuan.* "Much more for you when you come back. Hide the money. Don't show off with it, or the gods will take it from you and hurt you. Can you go in the morning?"

"Yes, but who cook?"

"The dog."

"My dog not cook, Master." Then he got it. He laughed, then fell deadly serious. "You feed my dog, sir?"

"I feed your dog."

"Then I go."

"Sir, I need to talk to the squadron leader," said Zee Zee.

Joghinder Singh reclined on his cot in the mud and smoke-filled hut that had a crude fireplace which sputtered with wood that never dried. Heat was more important than air.

"I disagree," said Singh. "I think that is the last thing on earth you need. The two of you talking would be a disaster, like a Hwang Ho flood."

"That's because I don't believe in bombing shrubbery."

"It is because you are unaware that China is a class-driven society, much like India, and that in a class society, manners are everything."

"I need to talk to him."

"Perhaps I can convey your message."

"Okay. Tell him that after sweating through the summer and shivering through the fall and now freezing our asses off in the winter, we can, in one sortie, make this entire sorry campaign pay off."

"How?"

"By killing Mao Tse-tung. In two weeks, maybe three, I'll know where he sleeps at night. The exact building and the exact time. A dawn raid before the rooster, is my guess, and he's dead."

Joghinder sat up. "Does that seem entirely fair to you?" he asked.

"Totally," said Zee Zee. He thought of the incredible brutality imposed on the Reds in Shanghai. He knew that the Reds, given a chance, would return the favor. He had to get them now, before all the peasants in Hunan and Kiangsi and then in Shanghai revolted and killed everyone he loved in the world.

"It is a provocative idea. I will talk to the commander."

"Good. I have work to do. Sir."

THE GROUND CHIEF was a midwesterner who had been hired to clang on unrepairable American engines in remote central China. Chiang's air chief, General Li, had paid Henry Smithson, Jr., of St. Louis, Missouri, the same fee that Chiang paid the German army colonels—ten thousand *yuan* every lunar month. Smithson shuttled between five aero squadrons, cursing blue streaks, banging on old steel and collecting good pay. He had done the same thing behind the Somme for far less compensation and spoke as much Chinese as French.

Smithson was a typical engine mechanic of that era. He was short enough to crawl into tight, hot metal spaces; had strong, sensitive fingers with at least one tip missing from a painful mishap; and liked grease, which cut friction and gave warnings about problems growing worse. He listened to Zee Zee while the young lieutenant spoke, staring at the ugly stump of a wet Cuban cigar that was clamped between the American's stained lips.

"Won't work," he said. "I know what you want, but it won't work. You can't supercharge these old Pratts. Can't make up for altitude with more fuel, 'cause plugs are gapped to prevent fire, which is the big risk with these heavy leaking overheated bastards. Try to supercharge, hell, you put out your own lights and you end up smashing up one more perfectly lousy ruptured OV-1. This ain't even to mention that the damn petrol that makes it to the end of the supply line in fucking Hunan almost won't light if you soak it in kerosene and hit it with a blowtorch. Supposed to be Standard Oil Av Gas Two, but I bet it's Horse Piss Fifty."

"You Americans are supposed to have answers," said Zee Zee, marveling at a people who could make gasoline out of equine urine.

"Yeah, ain't it a bitch? I gave you the answer, Lieutenant. It just ain't the answer you want."

"I need to be on top of the mountain, Henry. I need to pull out without a crash."

"You think you could call me 'Chief' just one fucking time?"

"Mountaintop, no crash, Chief." Zee Zee knew American movies. Americans were the most informal people in the world. He loved it.

"Then go *real* slow."

"Then I'll get shot down and lose the plane."

"Don't go on the mountain."

"I must. Should I try to use more fuel, less fuel?"

"You ain't got legs to cut tanks to the Chingkanshan and make it back. Lissen. Only fuckin' time you got too much fuel is if you're on fire."

"You have to help, Henry. You have to think. Figure out the answer!"

"*Chu ni ma di!* I told you, there ain't *no* goddamn answer."

The expression meant to do something horrible to your mother, something Zee Zee would never say. "You are American. You know all the answers. Make a change. Plug. Fuel. Air. Hose. Pressure. Pump. Gasket. Rotor. Angle. Dingus."

Smithson laughed. "Okay, okay. I'll think on it. 'Specially that dingus."

Cook Soo DIDN'T return for a month. He came back huffing, shocked that the Fourth Squadron actually welcomed him, whacking him on the back and rubbing his dusty hair. Zee Zee, as the junior pilot, and Henry Smithson, Jr., as the only foreigner, had been commandeered into the kitchen with lamentable results. Everything tasted like pork, which was Shanghainese, and grease, which was American.

"Where've you been?" asked Zee Zee.

"Oh, had to see sick brother in Wuhu. Sorry, Master."

"Wuhu! In *Anhwei*? That's almost to Nanjing! What's that—five hundred miles? How'd you get there and back?"

Soo scratched his nose. "Walking? I remember nothing else."

He was like Lee Shui-feng, Zee Zee's grandfather, who had walked from Lo Chuen to Ji 'an and paddled his way to Nanking.

Zee Zee told the pilots and ground crew to wait—Soo would make it to the kitchen right after he answered some questions.

"Oh, Master, look." Soo knelt to smooth the ground. Talking to himself, he made his map. He smiled. It made perfect sense. "I met Mr. Hairy."

"Mr. Hairy?"

"Mao! His name Mao, *hair*. We call him Mr. Hairy! He nice man, Master. Have pretty wife, name Kai-hui. Work hard all time. Write book! Scholar, Big Cap!"

"He works so hard, Soo, does he get enough sleep?"

"Ho, ho, much sleep! Pretty wife! Monday," said Soo, showing where Mao and Kai-hui slept. "Tuesday, Wednesday, same same," pointing. He ran through the week. Zee Zee took notes and sketched the map, orienting to magnetic north. Every building where Mao and his wife slept was easy to remember. There were four buildings. Three had heavy tree cover. One didn't, probably because the weight of last year's snows had broken it. You'd have to approach from the west, which would take more fuel. So you crawled to the mountain and then dashed up the sheer cliffs and dropped everything on Mao's head, hoping his wife was out.

Zee Zee thanked Soo and gave him all the cash he had.

"Too much, Master, too much. No can take. Too much."

"You must," said Zee Zee. "Today you're a hero." He saluted, and Soo bowed and covered his face in embarrassment and pleasure.

Henry yelled for Zee Zee, who left the morning calisthenics to run to Hangar Number Two. The maintenance shop was there, appropriately housed between the wrecks of earlier crashes, which were numerous.

"I got your friggin' answer," Henry said.

"Like I say! Americans always know. Oh, Henry, you're so good!"

"Call me Chief. All my friends do. So you fly over to Nanking in Number 627. Bring back Number 54."

"But 54 is much older than 627, Henry."

"Chief."

"Why the older airplane? Chief."

"It ain't older. It's *newer*. It's a frickin' O2U-2! Has a four-sixty-horsepower Wasp with a goddamn supercharger! You can go up that frickin' mountain and pull two loops with Cooper bombs on every rack!"

Zee Zee beamed. "How do I get it, Henry?"

"They need a shuttle pilot. That's you. Orders at the flight shack. Fill in your name. Six-two-seven's fueled, although she's still as dangerous as a stick a dynamite in a coal fire. Go now."

Zee Zee ran.

"USE THE CHAIN of command," said Major Loo, the evening that Zee Zee returned to Changsha in a shiny new O2U-2 with a new tail number.

"I am! I could see Chiang Kai-shek, who sent me here, or Madame Chiang Kai-shek, who painted bamboo pictures with me. Or T. A. Soong, my old roommate. Here I am, in front of you. Sir."

"You're military-dumb, aren't you? You chase the wrong guy. The threat on the mountain is General Chu Teh. Not a schoolteacher. Mao's a dreamy-eyed poet. Unathletic. A high, mousy voice. A librarian!"

"Chu Teh's as tough as an Anyuan coal miner. He's Chuko Liang, a military genius. He outruns, outflanks and surprises us. Chu Teh's worth a hundred Maos. In war, kill the general, not the scribe!"

"Then let's kill them both. Sir."

"We have one good plane. One chance. See, or are you stupid?"

"Mao," said Zee Zee through clenched teeth, "is the one who creates the armies that Chu Teh leads. Mao's the damn head of the snake! The body is his peasants, who can run all day and all night. People like Cook Soo, who just walked back from Anhwei! Chu is the lungs or the heart, but *Mao is the head*! No Mao, no peasants, no army! Sir."

"You are an idiot. Those aren't *peasants* up there. You think peasants can outfight us, us *professionals*? That's Communist talk! Damn, you talk like a Red! Those troops are probably actually foreigners, Germans and Russians.

Those are pros facing us, not farmers and dumb idiot serfs. Dammit, Lee, how stupid are you?"

Zee Zee's eyes narrowed, neck muscles tensing. "Don't."

"*Don't?* Don't call you names? *Sir,* right? Oh, getting angry? Going to lose your temper? Can't make sense, so you'll throw a tantrum? I know you, crazy-man Lee! Salt in your blood—*ho-men*—back-door man! Are you *Lee* as in tree, or *Lee* as in one-thousandth of a man? Oh, crazy-man Lee, getting mad at your commanding officer? Perhaps you don't know who my father is. Is this true, Manure Brains?"

"*Chu ni ma di!*" snarled Zee Zee, advancing on his commander.

forty

Elinor Ah-wu

DA-TSIEN DIDN'T ENJOY being pregnant—she felt as if the baby had taken over her body—but she enjoyed the mandatory rest from house duties. She was talking to her tummy.

"Lee Chien-sun, be a good boy and listen to your mah-mee." She rubbed the small bulge. "Lee Chien-sun, help me decide. Should you be a wonderful writer or a wonderful composer? I think you should be a Mozart, and then we can have music in the house all the days of my life!"

"How many times I tell you?" asked Ah Tsui. "The matchmaker read your hands and saw daughters. Lots of daughters! Don't set yourself up for disappointment. Accept your fate. Now, think of girls' names."

"I've prayed to Guan Yin and Guan Yin's mother, Hsi Wang Mu, the Great Royal Mother of the Western Skies. Don't interfere with the gods!"

"Hoy! You talk to *me* of gods! What does your Jesu say about this?"

"He's a man. Obviously, no control over babies."

"Okay, first thing you say that makes sense." Ah Tsui stood as Taitai walked carefully into the sitting room on tiny slippers.

"Don't get up," she told her daughter. She sat as if a thousand demons were sticking needles into her bottom. Ah Tsui bowed and left.

"How many women see you every day, every week, for advice?"

Da-tsien tried to count. Math had always been stressful. She responded to arithmetic with big thoughts. "A thousand?" she tried.

Taitai shook her head. "My brother says the Chinese are the best in the world in mathematics. Maybe you're not Chinese! I think you see five or six women a day. So, then how many do you see every week?"

Da-tsien stamped her feet and made a face, then quickly removed it before the bad emotion reached her son. "Five thousand?" she asked.

"Hoy. Thirty-five to forty-two women a week. Now an easier question. How much do I spend on tea and crumpets for them each week? I'll tell you—thirty dollars Shanghai. How much would these women pay a *wu ba-kua* eight-trigram fortune-teller to get the answers you give for free? I'd say four dollars a visit. That's a minimum of—"

"Three thousand?"

"—a hundred forty a week. Start charging."

"Mah-mee, I couldn't!"

"I predicted this extremely constructive answer. And why not?"

"These are church ladies. Many are poor. Some are widows."

"Then charge less. One dollar. You know why I say this. Tell me."

"I know, I know. You say it because—because Baba won't work."

"Yes, you said it! *He won't work!* Once you made big noises about being a comprador. So charge for your services! Da-zee, do you think I, the smartest person in this house, am stupid? For ten thousand years, maybe longer, wives have gone to live in the houses of their husbands. Where do you live? In the house of your parents! Completely crazy! We pay for raising you *and* support-ing you to old age! Never have I heard such nonsense! And you bring your worthless husband with you—he who also earns nothing! Oh, yes, he earned a few dragon coins from Chiang Kai-shek's army of murderers, cutthroats, gunrunners, opium dealers and prostitutes—for trying to kill some simple peo-ple on a faraway mountain who meant him no harm. And he spends it on new clothes for you, to make you stop yelling at him!" She wrung her hands. "And! You fight so much you drive us old people crazy! Where'd you learn to fight so much? To raise your voices so high, trying to puncture heaven! Your fights will end up killing your father. So much yelling! So you charge women who seek your answers and drink my tea. And get Zee Zee a job! I failed with your father. You succeed with your husband!"

ZEE ZEE HAD briefly returned from Hunan in the late winter of 1927 to sleep with his wife, smoke cigarettes and say very little to anyone. When he was totally convinced that he had nothing of value to do in Shanghai, he returned to Hongchiao Airport and rode a Nationalist Fokker Trimotor transport back to Changsha Airfield, Hunan. The army was still trying to catch the Red peasant army on the mountain.

Zee Zee had returned to Changsha to face a possible court-martial for calling his squadron leader obscene names, for throwing his furniture out a closed window and for hurling a chair at a superior officer.

His court-martial was dismissed, but his promotion to captain was canceled. He was limited to unarmed shuttle and engine-test flights. This wasn't to protect Mao Tse-tung but to allay the fears of Squadron Leader Loo, who lay awake terrified that crazy-man Lee would kill him.

Zee Zee was allowed to fly only in the rear gunner seat on days that Major Loo was not on base. Zee Zee acquired competence with the Lewis gun, an American .303 machine gun with a ninety-seven-round drum magazine manufactured in Canada and shipped to China through India. But there was no *ho chi*, harmony, and no sense of being in control in the backseat.

Joghinder Singh taught Zee Zee how to play cards instead of strangling Major Loo. He tried to teach him patience. He also reminded the lieutenant to send his meager paychecks to his wife.

The coming of summer cheered everyone as hundreds of tunics and trousers were laid in the sun to kill the stink of mildew. The longer days cheered Zee Zee, who, in the blossoming sunlight, was convinced that now someone would kill Mao.

Cook Soo had trekked back up the mountain and returned with fresh information describing where Hunan Party Secretary Mao slept. Mao loved red chili-bean paste, and Soo's cousin knew how to make it and where to deliver it. Zee Zee had personally delivered a summary of his proposed air action against Mao Tse-tung to KMT Air Force HQ in Nanking. He had returned to Changsha without resolution. He was awaiting an answer when a different letter arrived.

Dearest Zee Zee,

You should come home now to help me name our new baby daughter. I think she should be Ah-wu, because she's like a flower, born at noon, and she should have an actress's name, because while we disagree on politics, we agree on movies. Ah-wu is not unlike Da-tsien, the meaning of which is logically hidden in poetic double meanings. I like Elinor Fair, the English actress who is so beautiful and dainty, so don't you think our daughter should be Elinor Ah-wu? Yes, me too! I also think "Fair" is a very nice name. What do you think "Elinor" means?

She's very beautiful and very brilliant, ten out of ten perfect. I'm only bleeding a little, but the Western doctor thinks you should come back. Childbirth hurt quite terribly.

Da-tsien

Lee Ah-wu was a beautiful girl. Ah Tsui loved holding her so much that Da-tsien had to chide her. The baby never seemed to cry. Even Taitai enjoyed propping herself on round pillows and opening her arms to her little grand-daughter. Ah-wu's beautiful eyes were huge and seemed to absorb everything in wonder. Da-tsien watched her mah-mee loving little Ah-wu and wondered if Taitai had ever loved her that much when she was an infant.

Da-tsien thanked her baby, born in the trying heat of July, for not arriving in the oppression of August. The doctors said that would have made delivery even more difficult.

"Madam, please try to have babies anytime but in summer. You are very lovely and delicate. Summer deliveries are too hard for you."

Da-tsien was twenty-one years old and more or less had a husband, but she definitely had a baby, and she didn't care that it wasn't a son or that the child had come in summer, or that delivery had been so painful that she had tried to reject Amah's version of salted chicken-broth mother's soup, so good for making milk, because it would mean she'd have to pee later.

She gazed at her beautiful daughter and spoke to her with the same ani-mation she would have directed at a boy.

"Ah-wu, Ah-wu, you're so perfect! You are a magical baby! You're so bright, with so much intelligence behind those very wise eyes! You'll be the great composer, the brilliant mathematician, and you'll fill the world with music that will bring tears of happiness and add up mountains of numbers that will make wonderful sense!"

ZEE ZEE RELUCTANTLY came home without having received the orders to kill Mao. The KMT army sedan had dropped him a block from his house so he could avoid being seen by his family. He thought of his father in his upper room with his short concubine.

I am sorry, Father, he said silently. *I didn't get the man who'll probably set the country on fire. If you're lucky, you'll die quietly in your bed first.*

For a moment, he missed his mother, and the house servants, and then he remembered his opium-sucking father, his mother's exhibitionism, his wrathful brother and jealous sister-in-law and the deteriorating cuisine.

He thought of the House of Tzu, where people were simply odd. He came to the veranda, where Deaf Man Fu was snoring. The man didn't look a day older. All he did was eat and sleep.

Zee Zee sat on the porch. He was twenty-one and employed by the most powerful military organization in China. He was paid very little, and he had married a girl who had been raised as a princess. And now he might be fired, just because he had lost his temper for one lousy moment. Maybe two moments. *Be grateful you didn't kill that son of a bitch,* he told himself.

Zee Zee would make sure Da-tsien was okay, then report to Air Force HQ at Nanking and make sure that they killed Mao Tse-tung, with Chu Teh thrown in as a bonus. Mao must never be allowed to export his revolution outside Hunan, or there would be dying and disorder everywhere.

Then he'd sign on with Second Squadron, which was flying newer Lincocks and OV-2s in Manchuria against the last great warlord, the military railroad master Chang Tso-lin, and a coalition of three other northern warlords named Feng, Yan and Wang.

These campaigns would have to be won so they could block any moves by the Japanese in the north and the Communists in the center. But he knew the big enemy was the Reds. Now he had a plan.

He felt the alarm of thirst, then smiled. He backed off the veranda and opened the high gate. He approached the fountain, running his fingers through the water. It was true: The little stone girl with the bucket, through which water coursed, looked a little like Da-tsien. He looked around; he was alone. Gently, he touched the statue's face.

Zee Zee opened the front door and walked in. He heard Chef Chu and his cooks working in the kitchen below. Zee Zee smelled the good food, and his stomach growled appreciatively. He saw his father-in-law napping in his chair, a book on the thick carpet where it had fallen from his lap. Mr. Tzu was sadly thinner.

Zee Zee wondered where Singh was; no one should be able to walk in the door unchallenged. He smelled women's sweet perfume and had an unbidden image of Da-tsien putting on makeup in front of a mirror in the honeymoon cottage in Soochow. He loved the soft curve of her back, the long sweep of her beautiful hair, and he realized that he missed her.

The mustached majordomo thought he had heard the door and came upstairs from the kitchen. It was the Young Master standing in the entryway! He ran to secure the young man's military duffel bags.

"Your wife and baby are upstairs," he whispered. "It's very good to see you, *Sow yeh*, Young Master. We need you in these hard times. Sir, you timed it most correctly. Before there were a thousand women here from missions and churches, and Amitabha knows where else to see your wife and baby."

Zee Zee thanked him. He walked up the stairs. The bedroom door was open. Da-tsien lay in a new bed under a brilliant vermillion coverlet, the color of imperial ink. Above her was a small national flag; she was covering all the political bases for the future of their newborn daughter. Amulets, crosses, small Buddhas and Taoist incense answered to the many possibilities of heaven. A tiny pink bundle lay asleep in her arms.

He tiptoed in and sat gently on the chair by his wife. She looked tired, pale and gorgeous. He looked at her. This was his child, their baby, and his wife loved the baby, even though it was his. His heart filled with weight. He sat there, clenching and resisting and closing his eyes, but still, tears ran down his face without his understanding their cause or why he couldn't stop them. He misunderstood what was happening inside himself and was as perplexed as if he were spontaneously sprouting breasts. Desperately, he flexed his arms and clenched his fists, but the tears wouldn't stop. Humiliated, he hoped that if he remained silent, this effeminacy, this powerful burst of *yin*, would stop its torment. He wiped his face with a rough cloth he used to clean condensation and grease from his cockpit windshield. He vowed not to think about this weakness. It would be a secret.

Da-tsien awoke to see Zee Zee in front of her. He looked so handsome in his uniform. She closed her eyes and opened them again to prove that she wasn't dreaming, which she did so frequently and deeply when he was gone. She felt her baby girl by her side, and now her young husband was here with grease smudges on his face. She felt an enveloping peace. Her eyes soft and tender, she smiled gloriously at him, holding nothing back.

"Oh, Zee Zee, isn't she beautiful? Isn't she the most beautiful baby in the whole world? Isn't she the most gorgeous baby born since the beginning of time in Eden?" Her voice carried all the magic of Soochow and the hopes of lonely men who yearned for love on silken sheets.

"She's cute," he said, his mind on a fog-shrouded mountain in western Hunan. He grimaced. "I didn't kill Mao. But someone will."

"Oh. Lovely," said Da-tsien. "Do you think you could please give some attention to your beautiful daughter, who's so perfect, instead of dwelling on that other subject, which is so much bad luck that I can hardly think? Oh, quick, say a good word from your heart, to cancel out the bad thoughts. Say it now! You have to! Don't wait another second!"

He waved a hand. "You're so damn superstitious."

"Do it! Quick! Now! This moment! Save her life! No curses!"

"Christ!"

"Oh, yes, good! Zee Zee, sometimes you scare me. Here, hold her, feel her warmth. Feel her little heart. Play with her tiny little toes."

Reluctantly, Zee Zee took the baby. She was full and round, but also small, fragile, soft, almost no bones. He held her, and she fussed and began to cry. Afraid, he handed her back, breathing quickly, tense even as Da-tsien cradled the infant. He smoothed his hair, which had thinned lately under the tugs of a tight leather flight helmet.

Da-tsien comforted Ah-wu with her soft Soochow voice. "Oh, Little One, Little Precious . . . you're so adorable . . . so wonderful! Your baba is here! And he loves you so much and is so proud of you, and of course, he's too brave and big and strong to be afraid of you. Yes, I swear! Oh, is it true, Zee Zee, that you can hear everything that people say?"

He frowned. "What?"

"You know what I mean," she said with a return frown. "You always pretend my questions are dense and hard to understand. It's true, right? When you're flying in an airplane, you hear what people on earth say."

Zee Zee breathed to calm himself. "No, I can't."

"Don't lie! You can tell me. It's not a secret anymore. Everyone knows. Shh, shh, *Shiaobaobee*, Little Precious One."

He covered his face, exhaled and shook his head. "This is what cripples China. It's superstition, Da-tsien. Not scientific fact."

"Well, it's scientific fact that you're mean and you left me but act like *you're* the one who's been hurt!" She managed to say this without disturbing her daughter, who was clutching her and falling asleep, already full of the wet nurse's carefully guarded milk. "Tell me, Zee Zee, why you're so angry. You went off to do what you wanted. To fly an airplane. To live away from me and hardly write. Are you upset because you didn't do *you-know-what* to *you-know-who?*"

He clenched his jaw and nodded.

"So, can you hear what people say on earth?"

"No, no. I really can't."

She was totally deflated. "Oh, I said you could. I told everyone." If he could hear what people said while he flew, well, *that* was something practical. Everyone needed information, right? It would be one benefit that came from flying. She'd wanted to ask him what her p'o-p'o really said about her when she was conferring with Ying-oh.

He saw her disappointment. Women were so strange. He opened his palms. Sometimes, flying into the maelstrom of the Kiangsi Mountains, the wind would croon through the wires and the struts of the Corsair's wings. It sounded like a singsong girl strumming a *p'i-p'a* in one of Pan's red-pillow good-time houses, and he would remember T.A. studying the Bible while the madam played bitter tunes on old pianos.

"Maybe I don't listen, and that's why I haven't heard anything."

She looked at him to see if he was kidding; he wasn't.

"Oh, Zee Zee! Thank you! I *knew* it was true! I don't have to tell anyone I was wrong, and I'm wrong so often, all the time now. Oh, I'm so happy you're home! Our clan is complete, our family isn't fractured and divided! And before long, we can sleep together and have spring."

"That's good," he said. "Very good." A deep breath. "*Very* good!"

"You know, we're never supposed to sleep apart. Or you get tense!"

"Such talk!" he said, blushing and looking around.

"Zee Zee, husbands and wives are an old tradition, even in this house where Baba has gotten so much criticism. Oh, listen, I have good news to follow wonderful news, helpful news to follow Ah-wu's birth. You look so skeptical! T. A. Soong came by, Zee Zee. He gave us this bed! Isn't it beautiful and wonderful and soft? Here, sit gently, feel it!"

Zee Zee gingerly lowered his weight onto the bed. It felt like sitting on a cloud, maybe lighter. He had been sleeping on a wood board for a year, and had appreciated it over sleeping on rock and dirt. Uncomfortably, he associated soft beds with a soft life. "Very nice," he said, knowing it would be a problem for him.

"T.A. has offered you a job," she said happily. "He'll pay you fifteen hundred dollars a month! You have to take it. My mother's threatening to leave the house again because Baba can't work and the food and utility bills get bigger, and your money will keep us together.

"Oh, and don't worry, he talked to some soldiers, and now you're on indefinite leave from the KMT army, or something funny like that." She sensed his withdrawal and rushed on. "Honey, T.A.'s going to make a million in the stock market. He tried to explain it to me, but I don't understand, and I don't think I even want to understand, because it involves deals of hundreds of gazillions of dollars, not all of it Shanghai money, but also from America and Europe and Rio de Janiero, and I know you're so smart and you'll figure it out, and darling, with your earnings, can we go back to Soochow with our darling little girl, and with our son, just for a visit?"

"*Son?*" For a moment he was afraid that in her rush to have a boy, she'd adopted a son of a servant or a maid. It was frequently done.

"Yes, silly! Our son! The son you owe me!" She smiled wickedly at him, and he grinned and drew his finger down his cheek, the Shanghai way of saying, *Shame on you.* She giggled and caressed his cheeks.

"Zee Zee, how did you get grease on your face? And your eyes are so red! Sweet honey, are you all right? Now you have to talk to me and tell me exactly how you're going to pray and how much spirit money you'll give to Hsi Wang Mu, Mother of the Western Skies, and to Guan Yin herself, to buy us our own son so I don't have to put up with Ying-oh and your mother and my mah-mee giving me those evil looks!"

For a decade, T.A. had tried to teach Zee Zee how to bargain, a process he neither admired nor coveted. Now he had a thought.

"See here," he said. "If you don't say bad words about my flying, I'll pray to Guan Yin and every great mother god in the western skies. And the eastern skies." She made a face. "I'll even go to the foreign church with you. And give *real* money to the Jesus God."

She wasn't yelling or hitting him. He pushed on.

"I'll think thoughts about male babies. Yes, I will, every night, like you asked. I'll go to the Temple of Incense and the City God and I'll pray to the old fertility stones of the Taoists in Pudong. I'll—"

"You miss flying so much?" she asked. His offers had made her voice small. She found herself holding Ah-wu closer as he nodded. "Will you have to kill people? You see, when you try to kill people, it hurts my heart and my faith, and it ruins your *chigong* and I know you can't make sons, so why even waste time with our spring activity?"

He shook his head. "By God, you're impossible."

She laughed. "*I'm* impossible? You're crazy, Zee Zee! I don't leave you! I don't turn down good banking jobs. I don't try to kill people. We have a Christian marriage. So please, no more killing. You don't have to kill, do you?"

He exhaled loudly. "No, no, I don't. But I have to finish the work in Hunan. After that, I'll ask for small assignments in Shanghai, out of Hongchiao Airport. Small sorties. Test flights, shuttle, courier runs. No guns or bombs. Boring jobs, but I'll be flying." He had wanted to fly in the north as soon as Mao was killed. Well, that, as Smithson would say, was now blown all to hell.

"And you'll stop when I have my son? Why do I say this? Because it's terrible, awful, bad luck to fly when you have a son."

Zee Zee's short lifespan had already been mortgaged; there would be no son. He was lifted by hope. "When you have our son, I'll stop flying."

"Oh, Zee Zee!"

He was flying again in August, when Hunanese thermals allowed him to soar to the Chingkanshan.

A *di-ren* dirt farmer had come to the airfield, asking for Handsome Man. Kitchen staff remembered that was Cook Soo's nickname for Lee.

"Cook Soo is dead," the farmer told Zee Zee nervously.

"What? How?" asked Zee Zee.

"He kept coming up the mountain to ask where some people slept at night. Some of those people got nervous, so Cook Soo died."

"Of what?" asked Zee Zee.

"Of being shot in the head. His cousin, too. I used to work in the kitchen with him. I don't think Soo or his cousin meant any harm, but it was time for me to run. Soo liked you. I thought you ought to know."

"I am in your debt. Have you eaten? Can we offer you a place?"

"I'll take food, but I'm not staying. All of Hunan stinks of death. Yet it's interesting seeing these big metal birds so close. I want nothing to do with them. By the way, Mao's no longer on the Chingkanshan. I don't know where he went, but he's gone. Hoy! My words upset you!"

Zee Zee sought comfort in the clouds. He loved the scent of fine blue engine smoke and the rudder-driven S-turns on takeoff; he could see the runway and clear his blind spots. He took comfort from the sight of control cables running on the floor of the open cockpit, the sharp window sections of his oil-spattered windscreen. He loved pumping the throttle with high-octane gas, the contact as the chief turned the prop and the engine roared and spat and coughed throatily like a Long River pirate, the great Wasp radial engine vibrating keenly, as anxious as he to escape the sluggishness and the tiredness of earth.

He flew bombing missions on the mountains and on the salt plains. But he flew bitterly, and he let a cold rage build in his heart for what he considered to be the injustices of life. He was good enough to control manifold pressure with his left hand, the joystick in his right; release his bombs and still throw out a twenty-pound Cooper side-explosive bomb by hand and then shoot his Colt automatic at Red troops who were shooting at him, the occasional round making deadly clangs on his cowling.

Periodically, Zee Zee flew home to honor his promise to give his wife a son. As often as he could, he took Da-tsien to the airport west of Shanghai. He introduced her to Anderson the pilot, whom she charmed.

"Why would your husband ever leave you?" he asked.

"I think, Mr. Anderson, that if I could grow a propeller from my nose, you would never see him again."

Zee Zee urged her to sit behind him in any number of air force biplanes. "It'll top our Soochow honeymoon! Fly with me!"

She quailed and turned pale and felt ill.

"Step on this stool. I'll lift you in."

"You're trying to kill me. Stop! Say no more!"

"Remember riding through Hongkew on the Harley? You loved it!"

"I hated it. I was sick for weeks. It gave me too much *yin*, and now I have only *daughters*!"

"God, Da-tsien! Airplanes are *yang*! Fly and have your son!"

"Zee Zee, I can't! It'd kill him! Stop it!" And she began to cry.

The next time he came home and mentioned Hongchiao Airport, Da-tsien brought her amah, little Ah-wu's wet nurse and Ah-wu. She saw the plane's tiny hole in which he wanted her to fit, and didn't think her demented husband would try to pack all of them in there. He had to know that taking the wet nurse, Fong, up in a plane would sour her milk and destroy their baby's brain. Da-tsien disliked the airport and detested airplanes, which she associated with Amah's fear of everything.

"Let's take a picture," said Zee Zee, who loved airports.

"No, no pictures here," Da-tsien said. "All this noise! It's so bad for our baby. I don't want a picture to remember her fear and my distress."

"Here," he said, giving his camera to one of the mechanics who had been serving the Fokker Trimotor transport. A nearby tea merchant in a gown, a homburg and black slippers studied the airplane that would return him to the Pearl River. He didn't like military pilots, who had precedence for gasoline and takeoffs, so instead of smiling at the camera along with the family, which would have been very Chinese, he turned his back.

Zee Zee took his daughter from Wet Nurse Fong and smiled as he pulled Da-tsien close to him. Two-year-old Elinor Ah-wu was worried. Just before the shutter clicked, an airplane flew overhead, and Da-tsien leaned away and hid her smile, praying that the god inside the camera would honor her requests and not allow a picture to result. She knew her husband wasn't praying, so she was certain all would turn out well.

When the picture was developed, she narrowed her eyes. "How did you do this?" she demanded.

He lifted his palms. "I used a camera?"

"I don't understand how you do these things. Your magic defeats my gods. Get dressed for church," she said.

"Christ, you sound like my mother," he groaned.

"Oh, I sound *much* better than your mother!" And Da-tsien lowered her voice while rolling up her sleeves to show off her skin, saying, in the cadence of P'o-p'o, "Da-tsien, do silly little Soochow tarts go to church dressed like Mongolian monkeys? Don't forget your Common Book of Prayer! Don't forget your donation! Don't forget to wipe your nose! Did you change your socks? Look, look now, at my lovely skin, how smooth!"

Zee Zee slapped his thighs and roared, and Da-tsien cried with relief, for her husband truly understood. He really, really understood, and she lowered her head to rest on his laughing chest, averting her eyes from the bad-luck picture of her and her daughter in front of an airplane.

forty-one

Betty Ying

Purchasing on margin leverages optimized returns. If you have performed a penetrating analysis about the levels of risk within each market segment, you can amortize the exposure against a possible call—"

T.A. glanced over his shoulder. Zee Zee was totally vacant.

"Zee Zee!"

He jerked. "Yeah! Every word!"

"The world market has crashed—even great America is falling apart in the Depression. But the Shanghai Stock Exchange is making millions! You have no fear of principals, professors, fathers—the Ts'ao Ts'ao bigger-than-life demons of life—but you fear small risks, even with my money. Zee Zee, I am in the fight of my life. I *must* make more money!"

"You have more money than two Han emperors!" said Zee Zee.

"But my siblings own the treasury of the T'ang Dynasty! I am being judged, this moment, by our deceased father, our mother, by the clan. See here, I have great fears! Constantly! I admit that your brother is a pain in the stomach. But *my* siblings would like to wipe me out.

"If we invest in the market—me, with the corpus, with caution, and you, with small portions, with daring—we could beat my brothers!"

Zee Zee exhaled. He had tried many arguments. Soong had cause to distrust others; the family's wealth was almost a curse. People wanted more from them. T.A. needed someone he could trust, and he trusted Zee Zee. He was as stupid as a rock with money, but he kept his word.

Long ago, the best *wu* fortune-teller on the Long River had said that the two of them would be friends, troubled only by a woman. T.A. had sworn before the altar of his ancestors and in two great Christian churches that he would let his friend have this mystery woman, whoever the heck she was. God had given T.A. intellect, money and status; the gods had given his friend Zee Zee good looks, honesty and no judgment.

"Know how I feel about money? Know that feeling, T.A., when you walk into an exam and you're not prepared?"

"No, I do not."

"You know when you walk in a restaurant, and you can tell by the bad smells that the food's going to be just awful?"

"No."

"You ever been disappointed?"

"Only by you. When you flunked out of St. John's. And now, when you refuse to help your best *pungyoh* in the struggle of his life."

"*Scheiße*," said Zee Zee.

"Now, I know what that word means! Zee Zee. Da-tsien came to see me at the bank. Her intent was to have me change your lifelong resistance to making money. She said that little Elinor will go to college in America, and that this would require much cash."

Zee Zee groaned.

"You groan. I wish I had such a wife! Zee Zee, she cares for you, and she's beautiful, and you are my friend."

"I have to finish what I'm doing. That's *important*."

"Supporting your family is *not* important?"

"Protecting China is more important!"

"The blood, the distress, the tragedy of war does not upset you."

"Not if the blood belongs to the Reds."

"You are wrong on many accounts. You have a wife and child and must produce sons." T.A. waved a hand, for him a big gesture. "Flying is for men without families of note."

A long silence.

"I will pay you more than enough to support your family. Okay?"

Zee Zee said nothing.

"I have intelligence sources that say the Japanese will attack Manchuria and Shanghai. The War Party in Tokyo—mostly the Japanese army—is assassinating the Peace Party ministers. So war is coming. The Japanese are a huge threat, and you should be here to protect your family and to provide security for me and my money."

Zee Zee could only nod.

"When you come back, you cannot ride motorcycles again with Pan. Please do not frown. If you work for me, you must look like a banker and not a fugitive from executioners. Agreed? No answer is assent, yes?

"I know Pan asked your help on an opium deal. He needed your intervention, and you gave it because you have this notion that the three of us swore a Peach Orchard oath like the heroes in the Three Kingdoms story. I swore no such oath to Pan. Nor did you; nor can you bind me to him. I must ask you, Zee Zee, to decline Pan's requests, for the sake of the bank. And please, stay away from Hongkew?"

"Christ, T.A., Pan's my friend."

"And I am not?"

Zee Zee rubbed his face. "You're friend and kinsman. If you call for help, I answer."

"Remember, Zee Zee, I ask for legitimate help for legal causes. Pan sometimes does not. And Da-tsien did not ask me to say this. She asked me to pray that your next child will be a son."

Zee Zee nodded. "You understand that she prays to doorknobs."

"No harm in that."

"She doesn't wake you up to make you pray. I'll help you. But I have to finish my business in Hunan first."

MANCHURIA WAS RICH in natural resources. Japan wanted those resources to fuel the conquest of Asia. In 1931 the Japanese Army dynamited the powerful Manchurian warlord's train, killing him. Then their troops invaded Manchuria.

In early 1932 the Japanese attacked the city of Shanghai, bombing and shelling the city.

Da-tsien wrote to Zee Zee, begging him to come home. She was about to deliver another baby, and she thought the bombs would scare off a son, an idea that made no sense to her husband. But the Fourth Squadron let him go—without an airplane—so he returned by train and military convoy. He arrived in the city as the Chinese Nineteenth Route Army, which had put up a heroic defense against larger Japanese forces, was being withdrawn because Chiang Kai-shek wasn't convinced of the commander's loyalty. This allowed the Japanese to establish a large military presence in the city.

The Japanese bombing had destroyed most of the Chapei district, which lay north of the Whangpu. Thousands of Shanghainese had been killed and wounded.

"I HAVE A bad feeling," said Da-tsien. "The bombs were terrible! I cried constantly. Why didn't you come sooner?"

The next child was a girl. She was as beautiful as Elinor, but she seemed even more female than her older sister, because she bore twice the responsibility for not being a son. A pall sat on both houses.

Da-tsien wept and wept, partially from the difficult and painful labor, and partially from the trauma of the war inside the city, but mostly from the gender of the baby.

"Go pray now!" she cried to Ah Tsui, who, perhaps more than anyone, had been responsible for making Da-tsien believe in every god and deity she had ever met. "To Guan Yin, who completely let me down! To Chong Kui, who lets every female ghost into my body when I'm pregnant! To the Masters of the Four Directions, who keep pushing the female master into this bad-luck house! To the Kitchen God and the Door Gods who found no good fortune here! Amah, we need more Five Lucky Symbols in my room, now! Oh, yes— and Nine Dragons! Ask the monks if I'm having girls because I'm in my house instead of Zee Zee's." She quickly added several other gods.

"Yes, yes, Mistress," said her amah. "Now, relax and rest! I know all the male symbols and all the gods and monks and will do as you say."

Ah Tsui heard Da-tsien's sister-in-law enter the house. "Prepare yourself— it's Ying-oh," she whispered.

They heard the tiny little footfalls on the stairs. It would take Ying-oh about five days to reach the second floor. Da-tsien shrank in her bed.

"All that prayer," said Ying-oh, entering the room with her son, fanning herself against the heat. She displayed the boy as if he were an imperial banner, manipulating his arms up and down in order to allow several viewings of him by all. "And still you produced a baby girl. At least she's very healthy and very pretty! Look, Lon-lon," she said to her four-year-old son, a handsome and quiet boy, "meet your new female cousin. Auntie's *second* baby girl! Now, don't stare at Dasonai, Auntie, just because she's so pale and weak and lost so much blood. She's not a very strong lady, very fragile!"

Ying-oh wasn't naturally cruel. She was learning the art in the House of Lee across the street. The longer she lived with Gee, the easier she found tormenting the one adult she outranked—Second Son's wife, Da-tsien.

"Can I get you anything? A cold cloth? Tea? Some big slippers? No? Well, good seeing you, Little Sister. P'o-p'o will send her special maternity chicken soup to you tomorrow. She's at church, praying for another grandson! I'll light incense for both of you. Sweet baby girl! Bye-bye."

"Next time," Da-tsien hissed to Ah Tsui, "tell her that I'm out."

"Don't think that'll work. Ignore her. Gee picks on her all the time. Mistress, he hits and bruises her. Even on her earrings, so it hurts more. He pinches her where it hurts. Oh, he's terrible, terrible man!"

"I can't accept that!" Servants knew everything, but this was unbelievable. "Why do you want me to pity her?"

"Aiy, Ying-oh deserves pity. What Buddhist or Taoist could not pray for her? She's a smart, beautiful girl! A little on the puny side—she needs more food—but she doesn't eat because she's very sad. Just like little Auntie Gao when she was married. Same thing!"

"Is this really true, Amah? How do you know?"

Amah was taken aback. "Oh, you spend all your time in the bedroom of your husband. You're not paying attention anymore! The servants of our two houses are intermixed. We share kitchens, right? Help on feast days, right? Chu helps Sesame Face cook crab. That's why we had such a spectacular Eight Heavens Lantern Festival banquet. We couldn't do that alone—we mixed kitchens. Young Missy," she said, using the old endearment, "we talk. Gee's old amah, who hasn't been able to sleep since the death of the Empress Dowager, tells me everything. *Everything!*"

And so Da-tsien knew that her amah had told the other servants everything as well. She hid her blushing face.

"Tsa! I don't tell everything on you and Zee Zee! They have no right. You're almost happy, you two. Oh, you fight, but then you hold your breath and turn red, and he gives in as he should. But *them!*" She hitched her head toward the Lee house. "They have sickness. His old amah has to talk, or she keeps the sickness inside and her eyeballs will fall out. And she can't talk to Zee Zee's amah because, well, it's the same house."

"There's a difference, Amah, between gossiping and listening."

Ah Tsui's face colored, and she bowed to her girl's knowledge.

"But I don't want this new baby girl. Oh, Amah, I'm so lost!" Da-tsien cried hard. Many women cried after giving birth. For nine months, the gods had accumulated fluids in their bodies, and after release, there were tears of surrender. Tears for survival, tears for terrible pain in so many private parts of the body, tears of gratitude for sons born, tears of loss for sons not delivered.

Amah held her own Little Missy as if she had fallen on her big feet and scraped her knees, and Da-tsien held her baby, crying. Ah Tsui took the darling little girl and carried her to the wet nurse, a small cheerful, low-voiced woman from Lo Chuen, Snail Creek village. She was from the old river community of Lee Shui-feng. No one remembers her name now, but she was always delighted to take the baby from the Mistress, and never refused the little girl anything. She sang to her baby girl so beautifully that Da-tsien was moved to take a dramatic step.

She asked Amah to invite her mother, Taitai, to visit.

Taitai came almost immediately, which surprised her daughter. Da-tsien didn't even have time to go downstairs; Taitai climbed the stairs on her tiny, deformed feet, helped by Deaf Man Fu, whom she could no longer tolerate unless he did some work.

"You look good, Da-zee," Taitai said, fighting for breath.

"Thank you, Mah-mee! I'm so sorry you climb—"

"Say nothing! I want to hear the singing! Show me the baby girl."

The wet nurse arrived, humming in a low voice. She bowed and showed the little infant to her maternal grandmother.

"Oh, she's beautiful, quite beautiful! Look at the eyes, the cheekbones! Yes, a beauty who'll garner a fine, rich husband."

"Oh, yes, Mah-mee, yes!" Da-tsien cried easily now, so she wept while smiling and reminding Amah to get tea for the Taitai.

"So, tell me, Da-zee. Why does the girl counselor of Shanghai want to see her unremarkable mother?"

They laughed over that.

"Mah-mee, I'm having a terrible time with my sister-in-law. Ying-oh lords over me all the time. It's bad enough getting it from P'o-p'o."

"Da-zee, Ying-oh has had more schooling than you. She had more money in her family," Taitai added pointedly. "And she has tiny feet."

Da-tsien waved away the remark. "I knew that part. What would you think of our naming your new granddaughter after her?" The women could discuss naming mere girls; patriarchs only named the boys.

Taitai scratched the back of her hand, thinking. The wet nurse remained in the difficult posture of leaning forward to show the infant to Taitai, who finally noticed and waved her away.

"A rare stratagem, for sure. To manipulate kindness?"

"A Christian gesture, to offer harmony."

"Hm, better. You always think like that. What does Zee Zee think?"

"I asked you first. I don't think he'll argue with our decision."

"He trusts you so much?"

Da-tsien shrugged. "He's good to me, but he likes to fly. He keeps going to Hongchiao Airport to find an airplane, even though T.A. waits to make him rich."

Taitai put up her hands as if ghosts were in the room. "What *is* it about men?" she asked, facing the wall, as if the answers were hiding in the paneling. "My husband chose reading and fishing over work. Your father-in-law chose opium and concubines. Brother Da-shing likes cars. Lao Fu sleeps, Chef Chu overseasons and Zee Zee flies *airplanes*!"

"YOUR NAME, LITTLE Precious," whispered the wet nurse from Lo Chuen to the infant, "do you know what it is? Oh, you don't! I'll tell you! It's *Ying*! Isn't that a pretty good-luck name? Won't that draw wisdom and wealth and longevity and a kind husband into your path? I'm so happy for you, little baby! And that's not all! Your mah-mee has given you a magical foreign name as well. It's . . . Beh-ti! Named for a very famous movie actress! Some day, Ying Beh-ti, we'll go to a movie, okay? Oh, I'd like that! I hear they're magic and the food is so good and we'll smell the food and watch the magic!"

"BABA, WHY HAVEN'T I had a son?"

"Hoy! What a question! Aren't your girls the most beautiful since you were a little one?"

"Of course they are. But I need a son! I'll have no honor until then."

"This is old-fashioned thinking," said Baba. "Try a new view. If Da-shing had never been born, I would not have loved you less."

"But you're a man! I'm a *da-jiao* girl married to a Second Son!"

"Can't you be happy with two beautiful, happy, smart daughters?"

"No, not possibly, Baba!"

"I must say this to you, because your mother won't. She's pretty traditional, too, as you may have noticed. The doctors say that having more children could be risky for you. You bleed too much, and you're heavy with *yin*, so the blood is out of balance. The details about the spheres and the sectors and the flowing of *chi* is somewhat beyond me."

"I can't stop, Father. Guan Yin and Zee Zee promised me a son."

"There are many ways to have sons. Many of the children you help in the foreign-god orphanage, aren't they your children, too?"

IN DISTRESS, DA-TSIEN sought out Tai Yueh, the girl with the beautiful name who had failed out of St. Mary's. Tai Yueh and her friend Lucy Kwok Lu were the funniest pair Da-tsien knew. Their friendly, unassuming, self-deprecating manners allowed them into many circles of Shanghai social life. They had gone to dinner with Communists who had studied in Paris, had lunch with American naval officers and enjoyed tea parties with mahjong associations that bet high stakes on high points.

As a Christian, Da-tsien did not frequent fortune-tellers, but she knew that Tai and Lucy were big fans of *ba-kua* prophecy.

Da-tsien met Tai Yueh at a teashop on Bubbling Well Road. Tai was working for Jardine Matheson, the same *taipan* organization that Da-tsien's father had served for a total period of about two weeks.

Tai hugged Da-tsien and gushed over the news of the baby girls. They both cried, missing Grace Sun, who had been murdered during the White Terror in 1927. Grace's close friend Elaine Yu had gone to college at Tsinghua in Peking, and only Da-tsien had maintained correspondence with her, being smart enough to never mention politics. Elaine had accused Grace and Da-tsien of being radicals, which they hadn't been, but she had been right about the danger. They also talked about humorous Lucy Kwok Lu, who had become a very fancy dresser.

"How about you?" asked Da-tsien.

"Don't you know?" asked Tai rather seriously.

"Oh, don't tell me I missed something in your life!"

"You didn't know. God, I wouldn't have believed it! Oh, listen—no, let the surprise arrive! So tell me what you need. I'm your dearest friend."

Da-tsien said that she wanted to consult a *ba-kua wu*, a fortune-teller who knew magic, but didn't know where to turn. Her Christian p'o-p'o used one frequently, but she could never possibly seek the same seer.

"Ask Lady Du," said Tai. "Zee Zee knows her. She reads the dark better than anyone. Then, for seeing the good, see Madame Joo. Both are best, and they both work in the Settlement." Tai twitched in excitement and kept looking at the door.

"Da-tsien, here's Zee Zee's best pal!"

Pooh Pan came up to their table. He wore a fine Western suit and smoked a cigarette. He put it out, bowed while exhaling smoke, smiled roguishly, took Da-tsien's hand and shook it.

"Lee Taitai, you are flowers in spring," he said. "What's my wife telling you? Nothing about my business, I hope!"

"Your wife! Oh, sweet heavens, you're married? Tai, Mr. Pan! Oh, I'm so happy for you! When did you marry? How'd we miss this? I'm so happy for you and so ashamed for myself! Forget my shame! Tell me of your joy!"

Tai clasped her hands together, looking up at her husband. "We married two years ago this New Year's," she said. "Pooh was so funny—he celebrated too hard at your wedding, if you remember, and had a little trouble walking. He was so funny that night! His eyes were so bright! Oh, Da-tsien, soon after he secretly hired a *chih huo* to find me, and so we were set up by a real match-maker, just like in the old days.

"Da-tsien, it was a beautiful wedding. I wanted to look like you in your wedding gown, but we did it all Chinese, nothing Western. His father's very traditional and thinks wearing white at a wedding is asking for trouble. But what a wonderful honeymoon!"

Da-tsien nodded. "Zee Zee was in Hunan, flying airplanes and trying to kill some very nice people. And I was pregnant. But that didn't matter—I apologize most deeply for missing your happiest day!"

Tai didn't say that invitations had been sent to Zee Zee in Changsha and to T. A. Soong in the French Concession. It was T.A. who had sent the message that neither he nor Zee Zee would be able to attend. T.A. had sent a check and beautiful flowers. He had prayed for Pan to change his ways, and Pan had not. So he had drawn a line against the old friendships of youth.

DA-TSIEN VISITED LADY Du and Madame Joo, as Tai had suggested.

Lady Du was quite beautiful and regal in a death-white dress. Da-tsien's palms said that she would have a son. They also said that she would die young. After the reading, Da-tsien identified herself as Lee Zeu-zee's wife.

"I knew already," said Lady Du. "You are House of Tzu, a *jia* of caps and gowns, bringing honor to the House of Lee."

"But I will have a son."

"Yes, Lady, assuredly."

"Lady Du, an excellent *chih huo* once read my palms and said I would have only girls because I had too much *yin*."

"She was partially right. Your *yin* is very overbalanced. You are a very passionate person. And you live in the house of your own parents. This is strong *yin*. You have two daughters, more *yin*. Your mother is perhaps stronger and more vocal than your father, *yin* again." Du stilled her face and flattened her voice. "Do you boss around your husband? No? Then that is good. That's *yang*."

Da-tsien didn't discuss the matter of an early death, quickly going to the tiny shop of Madame Joo. Joo was light and jovial and made plenty of jokes. She made Da-tsien laugh and shriek by juggling tangerines and then teacups and a melon.

"You will have many sons," she said. "Of many different ages."

"I'd have to live long to do that," said Da-tsien.

"Oh, you will live long, Lady," said Madame Joo. "You should have hope."

"Can an imbalance of *yin* kill me?" asked Da-tsien.

"What a question! An imbalance of anything can kill."

"You know Lady Du? She says I will die young, too much *yin*."

"She's a street *sven ming*, what does she know?" Joo asked, lighting a smoke and laughing as she escorted Da-tsien to the door.

On the way home to her babies, Da-tsien tried to assess what each woman had told her. This was her best chance. At home, with the babies and two wet nurses, thinking was a remote luxury.

"Ah Tsui, I want you to get ready to move back into the House of Lee. But don't move anything until I talk to Baba and then Mah-mee. And I want Ying's wet nurse to spend all her time with her from now on. The baby shouldn't sleep in my room. I don't want to see Ying. She has too much *yin* for my blood."

It was in these days that Da-tsien began to hate awakening, for she would find herself alone except for the knowledge that she had borne daughters. She hated not having Zee Zee in her bed and would sometimes rumple the sheets on his side and throw his pillow on the floor. Her foul mood would last for hours, and young Elinor learned to keep Ying far away.

Da-tsien began dreaming that she was surrounded by sons who put on her slippers and silently reached out to her. She would awaken and find real children ringing her bed. Rubbing her eyes, she saw Lon-lon, Chin and Lu-lu, the son and daughters of her sister-in-law, Ying-oh. There was Elinor, her own daughter, wearing her slippers.

"Tell us a story," said Elinor. "Tell us the one about the girl who almost fell down the well."

"No, no," said Lon-lon. "I want to hear a story about a soldier!"

"A princess!" said Chin.

"Yes, a princess!" agreed Lu-lu.

"Well," said Da-tsien, putting on her storyteller's voice, which made the children giggle and cover their mouths in happiness, "I don't remember any such story!"

Her daughter and nephew and nieces would scream out their favorite parts until she had to hush them.

Da-tsien would then pretend to struggle to remember while the kids held their breath. Slowly, she told a story that involved a princess with the courage of a warrior, who wandered too close to a well. The children would listen with large eyes and open mouths, and she would end the morning's episode with the girl in great danger.

In the following mornings, there were children from the House of Tzu, and later, from other houses as well, and the stories grew to include a larger cast of characters, always children facing unseen dangers. Da-tsien's audience would jump up and down and scream warnings to the child in trouble, just as she would do with actresses in jeopardy on the American silver screen.

forty-two

Katharine Houghton Hepburn

A BILL OF DIVORCEMENT began showing in Shanghai around the point when Da-tsien feared she was no longer a magical girl. The good *foo chi* that had been hers since the day Baba had rescued her from foot binding had become a daily grind of repetitive tasks. Her gentrification had been replaced by motherhood.

She was fatigued by her daughters, distressed by an inattentive husband, worried about the Japanese and frightened by the ongoing Chinese civil war. But she was mostly anxious because P'o-p'o and Ying-oh welcomed her return to the House of Lee as if she were bringing the plague and twenty hungry beggars. Naming her second daughter after her critical, ranking sister-in-law had brought no advantage whatsoever.

"You'd better keep her out of sight," suggested Ying-oh, who always wore long sleeves to hide bruising. "If my husband knows there's *another* Ying in the house, she'll be in trouble."

Da-tsien was not physically strong. She wasn't like Zee Zee, whom the gods had given boundless energy. He jumped out of bed, bathed in minutes and was out the door before she could lift her head from the pillow. They spent most of their married relationship in bed. As a result, she seemed unable to focus until midmorning tea, a point at which she was already in trouble with the senior females for being tragically behind in her many duties. She tried to help her slow amah supervise the two wet nurses, who tended to argue with each other because they were at the very bottom of the household's social order.

Deaf Man Fu would wander up the stairs and gesture at Da-tsien, pointing downstairs. This meant Sesame Face Wong wanted her help doing something impossible involving hatchets, knives, slimy seafood or dead chickens. Da-tsien would send Amah down to explain the delay caused by the things that babies do to adults, which was something Amah had to fix, but now Amah was in the kitchen, which Da-tsien found endlessly perplexing each time it occurred. More and more strands of Da-tsien's hair would fall into disarray.

Sesame Face would wait in the kitchen like a great cat sitting in a tree. The moment Ah Tsui wandered in, hoping to be able to snipe a taste of lunch while explaining her mistress's absence, she was jumped by Sesame Face and put to work. This left Da-tsien to deal with two feuding wet nurses and one amah who had been reluctantly hired, in these hard times, to serve both baby girls. Da-tsien would send this amah down to find Ah Tsui, and of course, Sesame Face would press-gang her as well.

Meanwhile, Ying-oh and P'o-p'o would offer their counsel.

"Da-tsien, did your mother teach you nothing?"

"You call this sewing? Monkeys do better with melons!"

"Why haven't you collected the fish buckets? I thought your father knew all about fish! At your wedding, he said you used to set bait!"

The more Da-tsien endured their petty tortures, the more she found relief in the movies. She had begun reading *Shanghai Hollywood*, a lowbrow publi-cation on American movie stars. She loved reading about Greta Garbo, Janet Gaynor, Norma Talmadge, Sylvia Sidney or her favorite, Lillian Gish. Like many stylish mothers of that era, she took her babies, their wet nurses and the amahs to the movies. In the summer of 1932, for a higher price, they could go to air-conditioned theaters with fewer country people present, and family groups could often sit together. Da-tsien was enchanted by the notion of air-conditioning, which she had experienced once in an ice factory, but she really couldn't afford the tickets.

When she discovered that Zee Zee could get free movie passes because he was a KMT officer, she was nearly ecstatic.

"Zee Zee, you can get them *free?*"

"Sure! I've been going with the pilots for weeks. Want some?"

"Oh gracious, yes! But you have to come with us."

"That's only for before marriage."

"You are so crazy! It's hot, Zee Zee, take us now."

"You tell those actresses up on the screen what to do without me."

"But it's not fun without you. I didn't know you were going to the movies. Take me now!" She had learned to grab his arm and push him when she wanted something, such as help in reaching a tall shelf, opening a difficult compact or brushing her hair.

Zee Zee had asked Lady Du if women became clumsy after childbirth. "It's like she has two left hands," he said.

Lady Du asked him for a cigarette. He lit it for her.

"It happens," she said, exhaling. It seemed to her that clumsiness would be a small price for a healthy child. She didn't tell him that she had met his wife and that she, too, would die young. "Is she a delicate lady? Sometimes such ladies lose so much blood, so much *yang*, that they get weaker. This can come out in clumsiness."

"That sounds scientific. Now tell me why I'm still alive."

"It isn't for me to say the reasons. I see only the results of you defying fate."

ON HOT DAYS that summer, Zee Zee left the airfield to take his wife and daughters and their retinue to the movies, a few of which were now talkies. Da-tsien's favorite was the Da Gua Ming, the Grant Theater opposite the race-course. It seated two thousand and had the coldest air-conditioning in Asia.

Zee Zee would rock his shoulders and tense, helping Douglas Fairbanks fight villains and jump from rooftops. His favorite film was *Wings*, about the world war aviators and their private lives. He could tell that the airplanes were models, but he didn't care.

He didn't like women's movies, and was prepared to hate A *Bill of Divorcement* before he showed his free pass.

Da-tsien disliked film characters such as Sydney Fairfield, who was unorthodox, so trying to coach her through the plot points with emphatic orders from a theater seat was a challenge. Of course, she found the actress who played Miss Fairfield unappealing. Da-tsien liked small, dainty, soft-voiced women, and this girl was a tall and arrogant amazon with a jarring voice. She remembered reading that the actress playing Miss Fairfield had been fired from a stage play for being insubordinate.

"You listen to me," warned Da-tsien.

Zee Zee was dozing, almost soothed by his wife's impassioned instructions to Miss Fairfield. Then it happened—a silence—she fell into an unsettling quiet. Quickly, he sat up. *Is Da-tsien sick?*

She was sitting on the edge of her seat, lips parted, barely breathing, ignoring Ah Tsui's complaints about this and that and Ying's fussiness.

Zee Zee followed Da-tsien's gaze. On the screen, a tall, high-cheekboned woman with an arrowlike nose, sharp chin and long flowing hair was talking like a man. *Harumph*, he thought, closing his eyes and going back to sleep. Da-tsien began shaking and slapping him.

"What?" he said, bolting upright again.

"Zee Zee! She's an American and can do what she wants, but she loves her father so much that she's giving up her own life and her loves for him!" And she burst into tears, sobbing on his shoulder.

Sighing, he put his arms around his wife, comforting her. Like most Shanghainese, he didn't notice the open conversation of the other theatergoers as they discussed and debated the actions on the screen.

We ought to avoid this actress, he thought.

"What's her name?"

He always remembered trivia. "Katharine Hepburn. I don't know what her name means. She's not pretty, and she has a strange voice."

"But she's so brave! So strong! Promise that you'll take me to *every* Hepburn movie! Oh, the three of us will have such a good time!"

"Us and Ah Tsui?"

"No, silly! You, Katharine Hepburn and I. She's the perfect, perfect actress. She's polite but always wins! Oh, she's going to be my model in every conversation I have with your mother and Ying-oh!"

STUDIOS ONCE MADE movies as if they were waffles, and Zee Zee thought that Katharine Hepburn was Hollywood's only batter, appearing in sequential movies that year. She played Eva Lovelace, a stagestruck actress, in *Morning Glory*, in which she had to compete against a stable of starlets to win a role. Da-tsien rooted for her as if Eva were competing against a houseful of rival sisters-in-law. Zee Zee was slapped and pinched and plucked into groaning wakefulness to see what would be Hepburn's first Oscar performance.

He tried to avoid the unpromisingly titled *Christopher Strong*. Zee Zee had already noticed that Hepburn wore pants. But when she appeared in a form-fitting silver lamé flying outfit—to fly an airplane—he sat up. The idea of a woman flying was so profoundly offensive to him that he could hardly swallow. Da-tsien was convinced that the flying would make Zee Zee love Miss Hepburn, until her character, Lady Cynthia Darrington, began courting a married man.

"Very bad," said Zee Zee, thinking about his baba's concubines.

"It's just a movie!" said Da-tsien. "It's not totally real."

"I thought she did what *you* told her to do."

"Oh, I tried, but Zee Zee, she's too strong and her decisions are so interesting that I can't be angry at her. I didn't know women could fly!"

"They can't! Women can't fly! It's just a movie."

ZEE ZEE WAS flying silver bullion to Peking to fund Chiang Kai-shek's campaign against the northern warlords. He wore a leather hat, goggles, a long, heavy, fur-lined leather coat, thick sheepskin boots and gloves and two heavy scarves. He carried four handguns. His Lincock fighter had two forward-firing Lewis .303 machine guns. He imagined bombing the Japanese warships anchored in the Whangpu, wishing that they'd fire on him so he'd have an excuse to attack.

Increasing numbers of Chinese domestics were acting disrespectfully to their white masters, so the European powers liked the idea of the Japanese shooting up Shanghai to punish the Chinese people. But the Chinese knew that the Japanese would be incredibly cruel to everyone, particularly the Westerners.

As the sun rose over the Pacific, Zee Zee found himself thinking about a sharp-nosed girl with long red hair, wearing goggles, soaring into a sunlit sky in a foreign land where the sun set on the ocean and girls wore pants and brazenly decided their own fates.

He wanted to see *Christopher Strong* again, though Peking's movie theaters couldn't compete with Shanghai's. But Peking was the portal to the Gobi. He traveled to North Gate and watched fresh camel caravans plod for Shandan-miao and the Kashmir. He ate barbecued lamb with Moslem pullers until a military expedition padded tiredly into the capital.

"Anyone know Dieter, Boxer of Camels?" Zee Zee bellowed. "The foreign-country man with no hair?" He then asked each string in the caravan.

"He went back to Germany, Lieutenant," said a Chinese sergeant. "A new group of German generals came in and softened the training. That pissed him off, so he quit. He said he missed his women."

Zee Zee missed the Fourth Squadron. He also missed Cook Soo, but he felt no responsibility for the man's death. It was war. He even missed Joghinder Singh, a thing that confused him because he didn't believe that a Chinese person could miss someone who wasn't a *Han ren*.

"WHAT DO YOU think, Dieter, am I a stupid, superstitious peasant for thinking I'm going to die young just because a fortune-teller said so? A fortune-teller, I have to tell you, who has no family name at all." Zee Zee had talked to an imaginary Dieter, and to himself, since that year in the desert.

He thought Dieter would say, "Of course you're not."

"I'm still modern, right?"

"Absolutely, *faehnrich*. Very, very modern."

"Of course, Da-tsien will miss me when I'm dead." This thought had a romantic ring. Like the mist-shrouded name Chingkanshan.

"Unbelievably. She'll grieve for you all her long days."

"My daughters will always remember me."

"With incredible respect. With back-breaking awe."

Zee Zee spat. "Dieter, I didn't kill that bastard Mao."

"Bad luck, *faehnrich*. But it's hard to kill from the air. Easier on the ground, when you can put the bayonet into the throat, *nein*?"

Zee Zee was flying back to Shanghai, following the coastline for the refuel at Tsingtao when he confessed to Dieter. "Katharine Hepburn, that's a romantic sound, too."

"Of course it is, *faehnrich*. Very romantic. She'd probably fall in love with you. Give up her life for you. Too bad you can't fly to America, heh?"

"Why do I keep thinking of her?"

"Ach, human nature. I think of Marlene Dietrich and her incredible legs. Katharine Hepburn, she'd be a piss-load of work, but she has passion, *nien*? Women with passion, that's very good stuff, *faehnrich*."

"Dieter, I'm a lieutenant. I'd be a captain if I hadn't screwed up."

"Ach, so, *Leutnant*! Just don't crash. Focus on your flying!"

"I keep thinking of her. But I don't want to be like my father, taking up with concubines."

"The one fricking advantage of being a Chinese man in a Western world is that you can have multiple wives. Me, I'm a Westerner—I can only have *one*! *You* can have as many as you can afford! If this Hepburn woman speaks to your heart, listen to her. Ach, I know, *Leutnant*. Ask: What makes *me* happy? The little *frau*, she's just for when you're with her. Soldiers glide on the wind!"

forty-three

Shiaobaobee

ᴸᴇᴇ Zᴇᴇ ᴀɴᴅ Da-tsien watched Katharine Hepburn play a spunky girl of the Ozarks in *Spitfire*.

"I told her to marry the doctor," cried Da-tsien, "and she's *going* to marry the doctor! Oh, Zee Zee, this girl can do anything!" She was happy because her husband really seemed to like Miss Hepburn, and delighted because she was pregnant again and would now finally deliver her long-awaited son. She would hold up little Lee Chien-sun and his little peanut and shout to her p'o-p'o and her sister-in-law, *My son is here!* And they could leave her be while she devoted her life to her precious boy.

Dᴀ-ᴛsɪᴇɴ ʙᴏʀᴇ ʜᴇʀ third child in the summer. A girl.

"Aiy, she's so beautiful!" cried Ah Tsui. "More beautiful than heaven! What will you name her?"

Da-tsien said nothing. As was her custom, she had hemorrhaged, and her slow clotting made doctors shower her in foreign and traditional remedies. These had the immediate effect of making her more ill.

She was surprised to find Mei-yi, her father-in-law's ghostlike concubine, wiping her fevered forehead with a hot cloth.

"No, Mistress, say nothing," whispered Mei-yi in her breathy Soochow voice. It sounded perfectly normal to Da-tsien's Soochow ears. "I'm not worth your lowest thought. I could never deserve hearing your voice. I'm here because Zee Zee's father, Master Lee the Patriarch, has heard that your third daughter is the most beautiful of all. He wants to see her. Could I possibly take her upstairs for a visit?"

"Aiyaaaaaaaa! No! Don't even ask!" cried Ah Tsui, barging into the room and making Da-tsien jerk in fear. "Get out! Now!"

"Yes, that's right! Run your stupid concubine bottom out of here!" This booming voice came from Tall Amah, the Shantung woman who had raised

Zee Zee. The bone disease had attacked her spine, and she was now bent over like a snail, but she still had her glass-shattering voice. She stood at the door, violently gesturing Mei-yi out of the room.

Da-tsien tried to stop the women from screaming at the poor fleeing concubine, but the damage was done.

"Don't say a word," ordered the round Ah Tsui. "Just listen."

"Mistress," said Tall Amah. "Did you know that there was a third Lee son? Ah, he was a beautiful boy, born between Gee and Zee Zee. Oh, he had the perfect face! The perfect organs! He would give the *jia* countless strong sons! No, shouldn't have said this. I'm so sorry. Oh, Mistress, don't cry! You'll have a son! Oh, your tears are daggers in my chest!"

Da-tsien stifled her thoughts about countless sons. It was so unfair! All Chinese girls begged for ten boys. She wanted only *one*.

"Well, this was back in Yangchow. Master Lee heard the women's excitement over this new baby boy. He sent his concubine—a woman of many curves—from his separate apartment to bring the baby to him for a viewing. The concubine did this, while Taitai screamed and cried to her Christian God to stop it. She didn't want her precious second son to be with her husband for even a single moment.

"The sad truth is that Master Lee never returned the boy."

"What?"

"It's true. He moved the wet nurse into his apartment. It overlooked the most beautiful garden, with a moon bridge and a— Anyway, he kept the baby with him so he could gaze at its face as he smoked his *ya-pien*, his black-peace opium."

Da-tsien forced herself to speak. "What happened? I never met this brother! Where is he?"

"Oh, Mistress, he's still in Yangchow, where he'll never leave!" Tall Amah suddenly sobbed and wept into her hands, shaking, bending even lower. Round Amah rubbed her back and arms to keep her *chi* from sinking into her feet and leaving her body. "He died! He breathed the black-crow opium smoke and caught the chest disease. He died the month after his Red Egg party. Oh, oh, what bitter days those were!"

Ah Tsui cried with Tall Amah, and Da-tsien joined them.

"I'm so sorry, so sorry," said Da-tsien. She realized that Tall Amah hadn't been hired to raise Zee Zee; her first baby was Zee Zee's second oldest brother, who had been beautiful, and who had died.

"Thank you, Tall Amah, for telling this story, and for stopping Master Lee from taking this baby."

Ah Tsui noticed that her mistress would neither name nor touch the baby. Her heart was broken over it being another girl.

Ah Tsui had the new wet nurse breast-feed the beautiful baby girl in the master bedroom so Da-tsien could see her gorgeous infant and send her the love and spiritual sustenance that babies need from their mothers. The na-ma, however, just a girl herself in these hard economic times, had no place to sleep in this room, and became increasingly fatigued.

So the three—Da-tsien, the na-ma and the new infant—were asleep that afternoon when Mei-yi stole silently into the room and gently took the baby from the na-ma's arms.

Tall Amah crept up the stairs and reported back that she could hear the little girl coughing inside Master Lee's private rooms. She confronted the man she felt to be her son.

"Zee Zee, you have to rescue your daughter from your father's rooms. Already she's coughing from the black-crow smoke. It's the same story as your second older brother all over again."

"No, can't do!" shouted Zee Zee. "No one can do this! He is the father! This is women's work!"

"No, it isn't! It's the work of men! Only you can talk to him!"

Unable to take her hard look, he turned and ran out the front door.

The beautiful baby girl was buried in a small plot with a tall stone in the family plot in the western cemetery at Hongya. It was an unusually hot June, when farmers throughout China celebrated the fertility of the earth, hoping that the heat did not mean a drout. She was never given a formal name, but Ah Tsui and Tall Amah always remembered her as *Shiaobaobee*, Little Precious.

DA-TSIEN WAS BROKEN by her third daughter's death. She sought sanctuary in the Methodist Episcopal Church, where she and Zee Zee had married.

Religion had been a way of life for her since Ah Tsui had introduced the fact that there were approximately five million gods who controlled everything you did, and that praying and appeasing each one of them was required to survive.

In the depths of Da-tsien's multilayered beliefs lay the conviction that she had killed her baby. If she had held and comforted the infant, the baby would have been startled by a stranger's touch and her subsequent kidnapping. But because she didn't know her mother's touch, she couldn't tell stranger from friend.

If she had simply named the baby girl, Master Lee couldn't have kept her in his room, because the baby's ability to know itself would have radiated onto him, defeating his selfish purposes.

If Da-tsien had loved the little girl, she wouldn't have been so despondent and unaware when the concubine had crept into the room.

Worst, in the depths of her soul, Da-tsien knew she had violated the Christian God's requirement that she love her children. Buddha could understand a little girl being returned to the karmic cycle, because girls were disfavored. Taoists accepted the mystery of life and event. Only the Christians placed on her the burden of loving God and loving all others, and the added responsibility of forgiving all others. Being forgiven was not Chinese. Blood fueds and ethnic enmities had been fostered for thousands of years and were actively encouraged through storytelling.

"God forgives me for killing my daughter?" she asked.

"He doesn't blame you," said Miss Roberts the American missionary. "Jesus died for all our sins."

"Oh, now that makes no sense! I've heard it a thousand times, and still it makes no sense at all!"

"Da-tsien, there is evil in the world. It's *real*. Like the bombing of Shanghai was evil, and the Boxer War and its beheadings were evil. God sent His only son as a ransom against that evil. If you don't see the evil, it's hard to see the ransom. If you don't believe the miracle of His life, then grace is hard to accept. But if you can see the evil without bending to it; if you can see the gift of Jesus' life without rejecting it; and if you believe in Christ's love and generosity, you are redeemed. Through Him."

"So I must do good deeds?"

"No, no. Jesus did them for you. He offers you a personal relationship. To be with you at all times, in all places, in all moods and emergencies. He forgives you every mistake, asking you simply to love Him, and to love all others, as consistently as you can."

"Aiy. This makes my head swim."

"Listen to this one part: Love Him and love all others. Experience your grief and weep, for that's life. But don't dwell on it. So many Chinese people never forgive or forget and are stuck in time. Husbands against wives, women against their p'o-p'os, clans against clans. Da-tsien, please don't be a part of that."

"But I killed my baby, my little *shiaobaobee*!"

"No, you did not. She died of tuberculosis, which kills millions in this land. It's very hard for a daughter-in-law to say no to her father-in-law. Don't blame yourself. Weep for her, and be prepared to move on."

"Oh, Miss Roberts! Will I have a son someday?"

"I don't know. I know that you have two daughters whom you should love. And a father-in-law you need to forgive, as God forgives you."

"So it *is* my fault!"

"We're all of us sinners and broken, in our own way. That's our fault. Jesus cleans us. The Holy Spirit supports us. God loves us."

"Oh, oh, I don't know what to think."

"I understand. Try praying to God, speaking to Jesus. We Christians believe He's still with us, walking among us, every day. And that if two or more are gathered in His name, He's present with us, showing us the way.

ELINOR AH-WA WAS five and had been reading for two years. She smiled so wonderfully that Ah Tsui was often stricken by the smile—it was like Da-tsien as a girl, returned—a golden child whose aura caused others to step more happily.

"Ah-wu, Ah Tiah wants to see you," said Madame Lee.

Elinor was incredibly bright, but she didn't know who Ah Tiah was.

"Oh, of course, you never heard. Ah Tiah is Master Lee, your *gung-gung*, paternal grandfather. He's heard how smart you are and wants to see you. *Kwala, kwala*, hurry, hurry, let's get you dressed for your visit!"

Elinor smiled as the servants bathed, dressed and groomed her. It was like going to church, except it was upstairs. She wore a navy blue dress with white stockings and tiny white gloves. Her hair was in pigtails, and she made a face as her amah pinched her cheeks to make them rosier. The amah walked her upstairs; both fell silent as they went higher.

"Remember your manners," whispered the amah. Elinor nodded.

"*Master Lee, ching-ah, ni sun nu*," said the amah, who then fled.

Elinor stood at the door. Eventually, it opened. A woman with a very pretty face motioned her into the room.

Master Lee lay on his teakwood *k'ang,* smoking a pipe. Many years later, Elinor would see Walt Disney's *Alice in Wonderland* and experience a jolt of recollection as she watched the caterpillar smoke its pipe.

Elinor walked in and knelt, kowtowing to her grandfather.

"They say you're a very smart girl," he said.

"I study very, very hard," she said into the floor.

"*Ho,* better than your father, yes? Stand up so I can see you."

She stood. "Baba's very smart," she said.

He laughed bitterly. "Yeah, sure, sure. Hey, you are beautiful! Good bones! That's from me. So what else do you know?"

"I know *san gang, wu lun,* first analects of doing, of welcoming far friends, of being unbothered by being ignored and the Four Virtues. I know the English alphabet. I can play 'Mary Had a Little Lamb' on the piano. I can also skip. I know that painting starts from plain white silk, and I can recite Confucius' story of the Ji family."

"Truly? Aiyaa, what a remarkable little girl you are. Now, I want you to come here." He beckoned, extending and waggling his hand.

Elinor approached his *k'ang,* blinking at the acrid smoke.

A ghostly hand approached. Bravely, she extended her hand. He put something in it.

She tried to bow, but the woman was pushing her out. She descended the stairs, smelling like a bad fire. At the bottom, the amahs, cooks and servants were waiting.

"See, she's alive!" "He didn't bite her!" "Look, she still breathes!"

"What did he give you, Little Missy?"

She opened her palm. In it was a tiny jar of English marmalade. The crowd made a huge fuss, making Elinor look at it again in case she had mistaken its contents. But she was happy because everyone was so gay. She gave the tiny jar to her amah, and this made everyone happier.

She wanted to show it to her mah-mee, but she was still recovering from not having a son. She thought about her baba, but he was in Tibet.

forty-four

Tibet

ORDON ENDERS WAS an American who had grown up in India. It was his lifelong dream to visit the mysterious hermit kingdom of Tibet and meet the Dalai Lama, the spiritual leader of the land of heavens.

Political strife had split the Dalai Lama from the political chieftain, the Panchen Lama. He had been exiled by civil war and Chinese military aggression to Tashilhunpo, a great castle in Peilingmiao, Mongolia, where he was almost equally revered as the Dalai Lama in Tibet.

Gordon was trying to talk a fellow expatriate, the lanky Mr. Anderson, into giving him free flying lessons. Anderson suggested he ask a Chinese pilot named Lee who lived right here in Shanghai.

"I want to go to Tibet and Mongolia," Enders said to Zee Zee.

Zee Zee laughed. "I fly single-engine fighters. You need a multiengine transport and a Himilayan pilot who's a top navigator."

"I know. You speak English. Want to be a translator and a bodyguard? Can you take pictures? The pay would be excellent."

The flight over the Himalayas to Dacca in India was spectacular. The flight to New Delhi and the road journey through Meerut to Almora were relaxing and enjoyable, for there were few bandits.

Zee Zee found the yak trek to Tibet oddly familiar and yet new. Yaks smelled worse than camels, and their tongues were like metal files. But they carried heavy loads at altitudes over eight thousand feet and were surefooted.

It was not a short journey from Tibet to Mongolia and Tashilhunpo. There they found the Panchen Lama to be a short, charismatic man who wore a loose purple sleeveless robe with the blue silk scarf of sacred Laman rank. He had a drooping mustache, a short haircut, a high forehead, a quick smile, muscular arms and pointed felt shoes.

This was a land of spectacular views, soaring temples, mournful religious music and very little oxygen. What Zee Zee found interesting in the highest country in the world was a fellow Chinese.

Colonel Tseng-tse Wong of the Kuomintang army had attended West Point as a foreign cadet, graduating third in the class of 1922. He had been trying to leave the Chinese army ever since the 1927 massacre of Red students and labor organizers in Shanghai.

"My flight instructor went there," said Zee Zee, "but didn't graduate."

"That happens to a lot of people," said Colonel Wong.

"What was it like, being a Chinese in that place?"

"Think of it! No Chinese food or Chinese people. I was very lonely. Athletics were hard; I'm southern and short. Everyone else was like a northern Chinese—tall. Luckily, academics were not that difficult."

"If you had a son, would you send him to West Point?"

"It's a very good school," said Wong after a long silence.

Zee Zee crammed Tibetan, Mongol and Indian words into his Chinese and English vocabulary and managed to avoid an international incident. The Lama spoke very good *Han-yu* Mandarin, so the most important work went smoothly.

DA-TSIEN, AH TSUI and the two girls had moved back to the House of Lee because its stronger *yang* spirit promised a son. But here Da-tsien smelled sticky opium, whether it was there or not. She began obsessively brushing and cleaning her clothes. She suspected money was a carrier of germs and death and religiously washed paper money and coins. She felt she was fighting an unending war against opium smoke, pestilence and death. The more she did this, the more P'o-p'o and Ying-oh avoided her, so it became a habit with two purposes.

"ZEE ZEE, WHAT should we do?" She had just opened the pretty boxes of clothing he had bought for her in Peking.

"Try them on," he said, inhaling steaming noodles, vegetables and pork.

"We're doing something very wrong. We have two daughters and a dead baby girl, and no sons and not enough money, so we're always poor. I've not said anything to you, but both our homes are dying."

"Nonsense! I don't want to hear this. Mustard greens and pork."

She passed him the dish. His mother had always served him. He paused, realizing that Da-tsien was being independent, and served himself.

"We're like a dying centipede, Zee Zee. The back end goes first, but the head has no idea."

He chewed and swallowed. "You're supposed to put me in a good mood, not a bad one! These words are very bad for my digestion."

Gently, she kissed him. "There," she said. "How was Tibet?"

"Very cold," he said. "The air's thin. Not good for flying. Nice kiss."

"Was the American a good man?"

"Mm-hmm. Great guy. More rice."

"How do the women dress?" she asked.

He had to think, which let him take another bite and swallow. "They look like the pictures we've seen of Inca and Aztec women. Long braids dangling with gold and silver. Brightly colored heavy woolen clothes, lots of red. They wear Chinese robes and striped, colorful wraparound skirts. Very long earrings. They like Chinese silk."

"Oh, Zee Zee, were the women beautiful?"

"The mountains were beautiful. Potola, the huge monastery in Lhasa, that was beautiful. It took my breath away." He took a huge bite. "And eating good food, that's beautiful. Oh, and you, too. It's good to see you."

"You're not making me feel like spring," she said with a frown.

He took her hand and led her to a soft chair. He stood behind her and gently caressed her forehead and her scalp. He loved her smile.

forty-five

See Me to the Next World

MEI-YI THE CONCUBINE crept through the house. When she saw Ying-oh, she quickly flattened herself against the wall, looking away. When Ying-oh left, Mei-yi resumed her tiny steps until she found each grown son. Whispering, Mei-yi told them that their father wanted to see them.

Zee Zee wandered into the bedroom.

"What's wrong?" asked Da-tsien.

"I think my father's dying. He asked to see Gee and me."

"O Zee Zee, that's wonderful!"

"Wonderful?"

"He wants to see you! He's going to give you the gift of his life." His blessing. "I know it'll be good," she said, rubbing his hands. "Go be with him. Focus on him, Zee Zee. Be present with him."

"I'M DYING," SAID Master Lee. He sat in a chair in a room that was soaked in the rich, dark gases of the opium poppy. It was the first time that Gee and Zee Zee had seen their father out of his hardwood opium *k'ang*. The great artwork that once populated the room was gone. In their stead were two bamboo nightingale cages.

Master Lee held a blue-steel Browning .32 automatic. Trembling, he hefted it, aiming it at random targets in the smoky room.

"How does this look in my hand? Good?"

"It looks very good," said Gee, his voice thick with emotion.

"How good?" asked Master Lee.

"Great," said Zee Zee, who saw that the magazine well was empty and that the safety was on.

"You must help me reach the next world in a good casket. Hear?"

"I will, Father," said Gee, bowing.

"Yes," said Zee Zee, also bowing.

"I want a good Yunnanese *nai moh* hardwood casket with copper and brass fittings and those swirly, confusing scrolls to keep bad spirits from finding the joints, so they don't open it and take me out and leave my soul to wander away, lost for eternity. Hear? Both of you, write good Confucian scriptures for me and put them in the casket to keep me from the eighteenth layer of Buddhist hell." He frowned. "Or the nineteenth. Scorpions! I shouldn't have said that." The upper levels of hell involved pain. The last one was pain and solitude—the ultimate in Chinese punishment. To mention it was *ji hui*, inauspicious talk, and increased its likelihood.

"And you two use good calligraphy for once! Show your education that I paid so much for." He shuddered. "Amitabha, I'm afraid of death . . . dammit, I can't stand pain! I can't stand fear! Why is life so hard?"

"You won't go down there," said Gee. "Your life has been good—"

"*My life has been hell!*" cried Master Lee. "You hate me and disrespect me and never ask my counsel, all these long years!"

"Father, you never—"

"*Shut up, Gee!* Zee Zee's smart enough to keep his stupid yap shut! *I* knew how to shut up, too! When my father, the *great* salt-tax administrator, chose to acknowledge me, the son of his *syau lao po*, his concubine, a *syau lao po* with French blood in her veins—I knew to be silent as I kowtowed deep to him!"

French blood? Zee Zee wondered. *Are we not pure Han?*

The hooded nightingale sang, trying to change the mood.

"Goddamn bird, shut up!" Master Lee tried to aim the gun at the cage, but he was too tired. "Gee, I don't even like your posture. How you stand!" He fought for breath. "Oh, my father was a *great* man, admired by all. He was married to the Bravest Wife! What crap! All crap! What did he give *me*? A big house—and no money! All his connections went to my half brothers, born of his Taitai! Oh, she was *special*, the woman who replaced the Bravest Wife. Not my mother, a half-foreign pretty face. For all I know, my father threw the Bravest Wife down the well so he could escape the Taipings! Ever think of that? I think about it, you know why? Because he threw *me* down a well, too!"

"Father, you should rest, you vex—"

"*SHUT UP, GEE!*" Master Lee fumbled with the pistol, trying to aim and cock it, and Gee cringed and backed up as Zee Zee stepped forward. He picked up the automatic after his father dropped it in a tangle of fingers.

"I should teach you something before I die. I'm not political. I had money—who needs politics? But I liked Kang Yu-wei and Prince Chun."

Kang was a *chien shih* scholar who advocated reform but held that the Manchus had the right to rule China. Prince Chun was another reformer who had failed.

"Pray to Buddha that I don't come back in the next life as a damn woman. Pray to Tao I don't come back as some screwed-up spirit." Master Lee gathered himself. "Under *no* conditions should your mother give money to the foreign Jesu-god! Understand? Nothing to that god!"

They understood.

"Zee Zee, you're a soldier, talk to the American marines next door. Make them play music for me. I want to hear that as I die. Not your voices. Not birds! I need Western music in my mind when I go to the next world. Or I will fear the other noises that I hear at night." He clenched his jaw. "You are both *tsong hwai*, spoiled rotten. I was too soft on you both. The proof is, you don't make any money. Where's my tribute? Am I not the father? Am I not the lord of this house? Will no one tremble at my voice? Oh, I'll blame you both, and hound you in your lives if I don't get a really good place in Yellow Springs. You know me. I mean what I say! I was hard on you when you were little, but I'll be the meanest dog-cur demon in your guts if you screw this up for me! Get me music, and make sure I get a good place in the Springs, helped by the sincere wailings of all those who loved me!"

ZEE ZEE POLISHED his shoes and put on his best KMT uniform. He had seen the ribbon-bedecked marine uniforms and wished he had gotten at least one medal for his hundreds of combat sorties.

He called on the Fourth U.S. Marines band director, who said they didn't perform individual requests. The director didn't like Chinese troops; some had been hostile to Americans and American business interests. He couldn't tell one from the other except for the Nationalists, whose twelve-pointed sun symbol he called the "Gearwheels." This lieutenant was a damn Gearwheel, so he blew him off.

Had Zee Zee remembered his U.S. history lessons, he could have spared himself the visit. He had called on the marines on July 3, 1934. The next day was America's birthday. The band played for nearly five hours. Zee Zee crept into his father's room, startling Mei-yi, to crank open long-shut windows. Military and national songs floated in. Most were Souza marches. Zee Zee sat near his dying father as the music bathed the room, and he smiled when he saw the pleasure on the old man's face.

He noticed that the second nightingale was no longer in its cage. He checked the floor and the corners. Without exactly knowing why, he wrapped the first dead bird and buried it in the courtyard.

While he covered the small grave, the band played "The Stars and Stripes Forever," and Master Lee, the son of the noble Lee Shui-feng of Snail Creek village, passed away.

Master Lee's small, drug-confused concubine wept for her uncertain future while his sons lowered their faces. Gee would have to order a fine Yunnanese casket. Zee Zee hoped that the second songbird had somehow escaped.

forty-six

Yi Kao

I WILL LEAD THE grand procession," said Gee. "My younger brother, Zee Zee, will follow in my footsteps. We will honor our father."

Gee's young son and daughter, Lon-lon and Chin, nodded.

"I have to find eight pallbearers," Gee said quietly to himself.

"Ask Uncle," suggested Lon-lon. Uncle could do everything. He flew airplanes and rode motorcycles and did tricks with string.

"You ask," said Gee. "You ask Uncle."

ZEE ZEE SELECTED his St. John's classmates T. A. Soong and F. C. Fong; Uncle Chu Lin-da, the textiles engineer who had married little Auntie Gao; his tall, handsome brother-in-law, Tzu Da-shing, who was selling automotive parts; his elegant flight leader, Captain Joghinder Singh of the Chinese Nationalist Air Force; and, after a heated debate with T.A., C. C. "Pooh" Tze-jih Pan, who was still active in the *Chingbang* underworld.

Zee Zee also selected Old Deaf Man Lao Fu, who was his father-in-law's manservant and the only *nu li* slave in the two households of Lee and Tzu. He was a symbol of *goo dai*, the old days, and it would imply that Master Lee was a lord who could make others tremble in his presence.

Zee Zee reserved the eighth spot for himself. He hadn't served his father very well during his lifetime, so he didn't think he deserved to walk behind the bier as an honoring son. He would carry the weight of his father's casket and give the spotlight to his older brother.

"Not a good idea, Zee Zee," said T.A. "A man's greatness is measured by the number of his sons who follow him. Your father had two sons. By carrying the casket, you cut the number in half."

"I think by helping to carry him, I multiply it by two."

T.A. frowned. "Mathematics is still not your field."

"But I know my father. He did everything backwards. Instead of making a fortune, he spent one. Instead of modeling rectitude, he supported the vices. He lived not so well, but I'm going to bury him well. Please review the Confucian scriptures that I wrote out for him. You see this one, about changing the self? Good, huh?"

FROM HONGCHIAO FIELD, Zee Zee assembled a raggedly detail of Kuomintang maintenance troops and trained them in Germanic close-order drill. He recruited Barrel Man Him Man Yao and thin Fen and stout Hwa to provide vehicles and crowd control. From St. John's he culled students—whose status most Chinese still revered—to walk behind Gee as putative sons. Zee Zee implored his devout mother to bring worshipers from Moore's Christian Church. He asked Da-tsien to invite all the American missionaries she knew. From the Salt and Tea Tax Administration, he cajoled their motorcycle patrol and taught them how to ride in formation.

"What about your father's friends?" asked Da-tsien.

Zee Zee scratched his head. "I don't think he had any."

"All men have friends," she said. "Didn't he go to the Spinoza?"

Da-tsien introduced herself to the Spinoza's proprietor. He was German and spoke bad English. He remembered the frail man who smelled like opium and took coffee with a concubine who had tiny feet.

"Ach, *ja*, she also smell like opium."

"That gentleman was my father-in-law," she said in English. "He just passed away. I wonder if you or any of your patrons would like to pay respects and attend his funeral."

"Nah," said the man, wiping down his tables. He perspired freely. He had big, rough hands and exuded stress signs she recognized.

"You were a soldier, weren't you?" she asked.

He puffed out his chest. "*Ja*, that I was."

"My husband was trained by the German army in the Gobi Desert," she said. "He was a *faehnrich* and a favorite of the middle soldiers."

"Your husband is German?"

"He's Chinese. But he's a German soldier," she said, showing teeth.

"*Gott in Himmel! A kamerad chinesisch!* This I must see!"

THE CORTEGE BEGAN at 44 Burkill with a KMT maintenance-crew honor guard smartly presenting arms as the eight pallbearers carried the $800 U.S. brass and copper Yunnanese hardwood coffin down the steps. Inside was a man who had died too young, covered in scripture that might have been too late. They adjusted the coffin, crossed the street and raggedly returned to the house while members of the Mourners Guild wept and wailed and ripped cheap clothing. The casket was quickly slid into a rented black Buick hearse before T. A. Soong expired from the ordeal.

Because his father liked Western music, Zee Zee had a bugler from the Shanghai Volunteer Corps' Chinese Company blow taps. Zee Zee thought the rendition was perfect. The volunteer corps had been created by Shanghai's foreign businesses to protect them from angry Chinese laborers. Barrel Man Yao's underground Green Gang *liumang* were also in the back pocket of the foreign businesses, so they clapped when the bugler finished.

The students, on the other hand, were on the side of the workers, and they frowned and murmured darkly at the bugler and the gangsters. The Mourners Guild made money from most social classes, and they tended to like everyone.

The salt-tax motorcycle patrol was in the vanguard. The honor guard performed facing movements to exit the stairs and flank the lead car. In front of the lead car and behind the motorcycles stood Deaf Man Fu, holding a gold-framed portrait of Master Lee when he was young.

Barrel Man Yao stood on the driver's running board of the lead car—a customized bullet-proof '33 black Dodge sedan—while Hwa and Fen stood on the passenger side. At the wheel was one of Shanghai's top getaway drivers, a notorious man named Kan.

At Zee Zee's signal, the motorcycles led off, and Lao Fu began walking at his leisurely pace, the car rolling behind him, followed by two American *jao-wei* missionaries who came for free, and a Taoist monk who had come for what he considered a modest fee. Following them was the hearse, and then Gee, the St. John's students, the big-bellied German owner of the Spinoza and a number of his red-faced staff and foreign patrons, the women of two clans, and the very loud Mourners Guild.

It was a three-mile march to the Hongya graveyard. Zee Zee had started the ceremony early, but it was July, and by the time the hearse rolled into the cemetery, various parts of the procession were straggling wetly while others had simply quit.

One of those was Da-tsien. The heat had simply eradicated her will to continue. Ah Tsui pulled her into a Bubbling Well café and fanned her while forcing her to take small sips of hot tea to cool her.

The Taoist monk was a thorough Chinese and read from the teachings of Lao Tzu and the ideas of Wen, father of Wu and king of Chou. *Earth and sky meet, wind and rain unite,* yin *and* yang *are in harmony.* The monk recited sutras of Buddha Saykamuni and the Confucian *Li Ji* rites as incense paste and perfume sticks burned to heaven.

The missionaries read from the *The Order for the Burial of the Dead. I am the resurrection and the life . . .* Master Lee, a dead hedonist of the first water, was being blessed by holy men he had always ignored.

Deaf Man Fu couldn't hear the foreign words, but carrying the portrait had exhausted him. His own master, Baba the kind fisherman, had never made him walk so far or so long. For the first time, Fu showed his age by trembling before the grave of a man he had never met. His legs were shaking, and Zee Zee found himself hoping that his father could see this sign of respect.

"Why are we here, Zee Zee?" asked Uncle Chu Lin-da. Next to him Auntie Gao, exhausted by the funeral, massaged the poor circulation in her bad foot. Other members of the House of Lee took chairs in the *ting* sitting room and removed shoes or picked their teeth.

"I'm sorry," said Zee Zee. "Traditionally, Gee should talk to each of you alone, to save face, but I don't have time, and I want all of us to reach agreements now. Uncle Chu, you lived in Europe. Foreigners hold meetings openly, right? I saw the same thing with the Germans in the Gobi and the Americans at Hongchiao.

"Here's the truth: We're out of money. We've borrowed past our limits. We owe every pawnshop owner in the city. Our father's death now frees us, however, from continuing debt." He paused to let everyone gasp. The debt was understood; talking about it was unheard of.

He glanced at his mother. "I've discussed this with Taitai. First, we're selling the house. Second, we have to release staff. Third, we'll use the house proceeds to buy small housing. You can all stay with us until you find better. Of course, the amahs are attached forever. Tall Amah, we still need you to care for our children, yes?"

"Yes, Young Master," she said in her still-strong voice.

"Mei-yi, as my father's *syau lao pu*, small wife and concubine, you have rights. But first, you sold all his paintings and artwork, right?"

She nodded, weeping, embarrassed to be pointed out publicly.

"You can stay with us, but on one condition: No more *ya-pien*, no more black-crow peace." No opium. "You stay, we'll care for you for the rest of your life. Go, you'll get small cash, but you leave. We all—"

"How can you say this to me?" she wailed. Hearing emotion from her was a shock, particularly because her face remained almost unchanged as tears ran down it, though her makeup was ruined.

"I was the most beautiful woman in this house!" she said, stamping her tiny foot. "Rich men offered me everything to share their beds, but I stayed with your father. I smoked *ya-pien* with him for *his* pleasure. I mixed all his inks. I cleaned up after him. He wasn't easy to please, I tell you! Now, you asking me about the *paintings*! He made me sell them! I loved them even more than life itself— Oh, I saw him make them. *They were my children.* But I sold them for *him*!" She wept bitterly.

No one breathed. A concubine taking center stage on the death of the Patriarch! Zee Zee looked down and cleared his throat. Da-tsien walked to her husband and stood near him. She wanted to touch him, to encourage him through this difficult moment.

"Little Mother," said Da-tsien, "you've served this house well. Won't you stay with us and choose a brighter path? You've earned some rest."

Mei-yi nodded gratefully. She dried her tears. But when she looked up, she saw angry, resentful faces that were still calculating how those paintings could have settled debts and bought meals. It wasn't her fault, but it was impossible to blame Master Lee, so they blamed her.

"Thank you, Little Daughter," she said respectfully. "But I am a worthless woman who doesn't deserve your kindness." She turned and walked slowly away.

Da-tsien looked at Zee Zee, who understood and gave her his cash. Da-tsien caught up with Mei-yi's tiny steps. Away from the clan, she gave her the money.

"May God bless you and all your days, Little Mother," said Da-tsien. When she returned, Zee Zee was back at work.

"Miss Wong Fu-lu, honored tutor, your home is always with us, but we'll understand if you choose to leave for better circumstances. My brother and I will always owe you our futures."

"You won't leave me, Young Master?" asked Skinny Wu the seamstress, who had no family.

"Of course not, Mother Wu," said Zee Zee. "You stay with us."

Da-tsien tried to contain her crying. Seeing the concubine's tears had been too much. This was her home, the *jia* of her husband, but it was just like leaving Soochow and their house staff when she was ten years old. She wanted to stay to honor her in-laws, and to not lose face in front of P'o-p'o and Ying-oh. She was proud of Zee Zee's near-Christian compassion, but the pain of loss was too great. She missed her baba and even her mah-mee, and she quietly left the room.

"Wong Mah-tze," Sesame Face, "we can't fill your rice bowls, but we'll always owe you for good service. The Taitai has recommended you to the Soongs, and we'll hear more about that in a few days."

Sesame Face kowtowed, his face to the floor. Being commended to the Soongs was like being referred to the emperor.

"Majordomo," said Zee Zee, "we've found a job for you in Hongkew. It's not a good one, nor is it safe, but it pays well. Do you want?"

"I want, Young Master," he said. "A thousand appreciations."

And so the House of Lee closed in the City of Shanghai with its servants released not one by one and face-to-face, as in the style of the Han, but collectively, in the manner of the West, and, as it would prove, in the manner of the Communists.

Uncle Chu sat down with Zee Zee.

"This is of course very sad. But I never thought the House of Lee would sell the great Yangchow mansion. Do you remember it?"

"Very well," said Zee Zee. He laughed. "Mostly the garden, where I used to run and climb trees and do a lot of jumping."

"I want to say two things to you. First is money. You're kinsman with the Soongs and can earn more than me. But you'd have to quit the army and really work at it. I am lending you five hundred dollars. If not for yourself, then take it as coming from my wife to yours. Little Gao simply adores your Da-tsien and will do anything for her. I'm only a few years older than you, but I'm your *dababa*, and I urge you to quit soldiering and work for money."

"I hear your words, Uncle." Zee Zee took a deep breath. "Right now China needs soldiers more than bankers." He didn't say: *And I don't have many years remaining.*

"Second, I remember the New Year in Yangchow, when your wet nurse disappeared and men ran about with old swords and pikes, looking for her. You were five years old. No, please listen. You lost someone important that night. You know, Nephew, I never forgot that.

"I've been to Africa, America, Europe. Ho, ho, your eyes light up! Passing Hong Kong, I looked for your na-ma. Zee Zee, I found her. She's in her forties now. I took her picture. She is still a very beautiful woman. Would you like to see her?"

Zee Zee had a checklist of two hundred tasks, most of them concerning opium debts and pawnshop transactions. He always wanted to be a man who refused to look back. He wanted to see the face of his na-ma, and he wanted to forget she ever existed.

He shook his head. "No, Uncle. That was history. I was just a baby. I'm a man now. So you found Sweet Plum Fu."

Chu frowned. "Who's that?"

"Sweet Plum Fu, my wet nurse."

"No, no. Her name is Fan Ju-wen, married into the Low family."

"Uncle, Tall Amah knew my na-ma. They worked together as servants. Amah said her name was Fu Mi-mei. And wasn't beautiful."

Uncle Chu shook his head. "Fan Ju-men says she remembers you very well. Maybe she changed her name. Or maybe we just don't know what happened. So the world's really upside down, is it?"

Zee Zee had flown that way over the Chingkanshan.

"Yes. Heaven's now below earth. The world changes. We adjust. I'll pay you this money back. No, don't leave the photo. Take it with you."

"I'm very afraid, Baba."

"No need, Little One," he said. "By the way, have you seen my glasses?"

She saw them on a table and gave them to him.

"No, the other ones."

"The other ones broke, Baba. They're gone."

"They are? So strange! I don't remember that."

"Baba, what will we do? The House of Lee is no more. They're selling the property, and they'll have to sell this one, too. It's their rental."

"I always liked Tsingtao. A nice port. Good fishing. Did I ever take you there? No, I think not."

"Baba, I'm sick of having to depend on things I can't control. I just wish we didn't have to worry about money or war or rent or electricity bills or the cost of green tea. I wish I didn't have to charge those poor women who seek advice."

"Yes, yes. Being *yi kao* is hard. Believe me, I know. I remember thinking that happiness is not having to *yi kao*."

"Yes, Baba, yes! That's so true."

"Oh, you think? Of course it's not. Being *yi kao* is life. We should depend on each other. We worry about money all the time, right? But if we had all the money in the world, then we'd worry about love. As someone who's had both worries, I'd rather be concerned about money."

"Well, I don't want to *yi kao*. Then I'll worry about love."

Her father laughed. "How I love hearing your voice! Do you know how lonely it's been without you? And you are living just across the street! Imagine how hard it'll be to hear your sweet words when we're flung to the winds! Did you know that I was once a pretty good writer? Yes, I was. We'll have to write letters, Little One." He looked down at his big hands, making fists. "I can still handle a pen. Strange how the fingers started hurting after I stopped fishing. Do you think we'll have to let the house staff go again? I'd hate to lose the domo, and Horseman Yip, and Chef Chu, and Singh. Of course, Lao Fu's a *nu li* slave, so he has to stay, right? What will become of your mother and me? Da-shing will do fine. He's strong and smart." He took a breath. "Talking too much. I don't get to see you enough, so it all comes out at once."

Suddenly weary, he put his head down and fell asleep.

"Oh, Baba," she whispered. "I'm so sorry to trouble you with my worries! I have to start taking care of you instead of asking you for help. I know it's Da-shing's job, but he's busy, so I'll take care of you, Baba, I promise. I really, really will. I owe you so much!"

forty-seven

Long Marches

"LEE ZEE," SAID Joghinder Singh, "Air Force HQ ignored your letter. They did not care that you had a plan to kill Mao."

"So, I bet you're going to tell me that Mao Tse-tung's broken out from Chiang's encirclement."

"He and his whole army are now running southwest out of Kiangsi Province. We do not know their destination."

"And I bet we're going to bomb them. In winter. Without supplies."

"Yes."

"Crap! I bet HQ hasn't set up advanced fields for us, so we'll land on rocks and wait for fuel and bombs and ammo to show up by magic. We'll grind down our engines and wreck our planes. But first, we'll stupidly bomb where the Reds used to be."

"You have obviously studied the operational order."

"We have to kill Mao, Joghinder."

"We will be lucky to avoid death by food poisoning. *Sir.*"

"Ah, force of habit. I talk to you, you know, even when you're not around. I call you by your first name. It's easier. *Sir.*"

"Really? That is extraordinary. Zee Zee, did you hear that the *Dong Tang,*"

Chiang's gestapo, captured Mao's wife, Kai-hui, and tortured her to death? Mao is in mourning. His star may fall. You are still the only one in the air force who would rather kill a political thinker instead of the general. Their army is called *Chu-Mao*; Chu's name is first for a reason."

Zee Zee shook his head. "That's very wrong, killing wives. But Mao likes women too much. That bastard'll recover and remarry."

"It will be an arduous campaign, regardless of which one we target. Any other lieutenant, I could simply order around, but you have the Soongs' red family seal on all your orders. Will you come?"

"Know what I'll have to do if I don't?"

"Yes, banking. We have to be in Hangyeng by dusk Friday. We leave in pairs. I want you to fly with me. We have to carry our own fuel, water, food. I suggest you presume, Zee Zee, that we will not kill Mao or Chu."

"Horse crap. It's the only reason I'm going."

"What about banking?"

"Two reasons for going."

"MY HUSBAND HAS abandoned me in front of everyone," said Da-tsien, who was surrounded by the entire Lee clan in a tiny apartment on Nanking Road.

"Baba will come back," said Elinor as she brushed Ying's hair.

Ying knew better than to say anything. She could never please their mother.

Da-tsien looked out the window. She wasn't alone. Also at the window were P'o-p'o, Ying-oh and Skinny Wu, who fortunately took up a very narrow space. It was a small window that looked down on the road. Below their two-bedroom apartment was the Hang Ah department store. On the avenue were mobs of shoppers and street merchants and altogether too many soldiers.

"How do you know he's coming back?"

"He always does, Mah-mee. He just doesn't stay."

Da-tsien laughed, and Elinor smiled. Ying had learned not to react. She once laughed when others did, but it drew her mother's criticism.

"Not funny, Ying?" asked her mother.

Ying didn't know what to say, so she shrugged.

"You stupid girl," said Da-tsien, thoughtlessly.

Elinor cried, "Mah-mee, tell us the gypsy story again! Please! Please!" She talked like a machine gun that by now everyone in Shanghai had heard.

"Really? Okay, you ready?" asked their mother.

"Ready!" cried Elinor, protecting Ying with her voice and her body.

"Well, you know, Elinor, who gypsies are, don't you?"

"No!" shouted Elinor. *No,* mouthed Ying silently.

"Gypsies are mean, cruel people who live in trees and steal babies and suck out their spirits and sell the spirits to the devil!"

Elinor shuddered and covered her eyes with one hand and Ying's with the other.

"We can't see gypsies because they crawl in the night like *wupo,* white-haired, red-eyed demon ghosts, and you only know they're here when you feel their breath on your eyelids!"

The girls clutched each other and closed their eyes. When their mother softly blew on their faces, they screamed.

"You know Amah—always looking for ghosts and yelling when she sees one, right? One day Amah—my true and best guardian against ghosts and gypsies—left to buy tea. I was too tired to go. This was in our grand mansion on Burkill, when we had money and didn't *yi kao.*

"Singh the house guard had taken your grandfather, my baba, to the doctor. Old Deaf Man Fu was with them. Taitai, my mother, was playing mahjong with guild friends, far away. All the cooks were at market."

She covered her face, whispering, "I was all alone in the big house." Her daughters stopped breathing. *Rap. Rap. Rap!* Da-tsien struck the floor, making the girls jump.

"It was a knock on the door. Not an ordinary knock. I was afraid to answer it. I was afraid *not* to answer it.

"Should I open the door or not?"

"Not!" cried Elinor. Ying anxiously shook her head.

Rap. Rap. Rap! "Again the knock! I went to the door."

The girls' eyes stretched wide.

"Very delicately, I touched the doorknob . . . it was so cold. A sure sign of *wupo*! I turned the knob . . . my fingers were freezing. I opened the door . . . and then I saw it! Oh, what do you think I saw?"

Elinor bit her lip and pinched Ying's finger to keep her quiet. Both girls shook their heads.

"On the porch sat a wicker basket, like Chef Chu used to use, remember? It was covered with a blanket. I lifted it. What was there?"

Their little mouths were open.

"Two baby girls!" Da-tsien placed her hands along her cheeks and opened her eyes wide, clapped her hands. "Two very dirty little girls!"

Elinor knew how the story would turn out, but it didn't matter—she was hooked. Mah-mee would use voice and animation and *so wu tzu tao*, hand dancing, to paint a vivid, expanding picture in their minds.

"Of course, I had to clean these babies. Not so easy."

Both girls nodded, having no clue that theirs was the only mother in Shanghai who obsessively washed all the money that she owned.

"Underneath layers and layers of dirt, I found . . . you two."

"Oh, Mah-mee!" they both cried. So amazing! So incredible! The girls burst into tears. "Don't stop! What happened next?"

What had happened next was killing Da-tsien.

Zee Zee had been gone over a year with hardly a letter. He was still trying to murder that fine man, Mao Tse-tung, as the entire Red bandit army had fled the Nationalists through southern and central China and then turned north to the Great Wall and Yenan in Shensi Province.

Shanghai workers said the Red army had walked over seven thousand miles and lost half their people—including women—but despite being bombed and outnumbered, they had survived.

While Da-tsien waited for Zee Zee to return, Japan had invaded Shanghai. This wasn't like the battle in 1931, which involved parts of the Japanese and Chinese armies.

This time the Japanese first conquered Manchuria and swept through Peking while bringing twenty-one warships up the Whangpu River to Shanghai. They shelled Chinese army positions in Hongkew and Chapei, raining enormous destruction on the city and shocking its durable citizens with the eradication of entire neighborhoods, industries, schools and businesses. Shanghai burned. Worse, Kuomintang pilots tried to hit the Japanese warships and instead dropped high-explosive bombs on the Palace Hotel, Sassoon's showpiece Cathay Hotel and the Great World, the cornucopia of entertainment and risk where Da-tsien and Zee Zee had danced while the gangster leader Big Ears Tu waltzed with movie stars. Tragically, the Great World had become home to thousands of refugees from the earlier shelling, and so even more were killed and injured as thousands fled a city that had once drawn refugees from every corner of the planet.

It was the summer of 1937. Only the Japanese military government knew that World War II had just begun. The Japanese flooded North China with two hundred and fifty thousand troops. The dual targets were Shanghai and Nanking, the financial and political capitals of Chiang Kai-shek's Nationalist government.

Every day the women looked out the window onto Nanking Road, hoping to see Zee Zee.

"Zee Zee will be able to fix the plumbing," said his mother.

"I just know he'll bring us great food," said Ying-oh, who was now the family's cook. She was a very smart but not particularly handy person who competed with four other families for room to prepare the family meals in a downstairs public restroom. Her husband had a job working for city utilities, but no one had been paid since the beginning of the war.

"Uncle will chase the Japanese out of Shanghai," said Lon-lon, who was thirteen. "And bring us great toys."

"He'll give me my son," said Da-tsien hopefully.

"And then he'll leave," said Elinor, who was eight.

Ying nodded, safely saying nothing.

"His being gone pains me," said their mother. "You be sure to marry men who don't leave you."

"What did you say to him in your letters?" asked Madame Lee. "If you don't say things the right way to my son, he doesn't do what you want."

"I promised him a son," said Da-tsien. "That should be enough."

TAITAI WRUNG HER hands as she paced with tiny steps.

"We sell our goods," said Baba, "and use the proceeds to pay the debts and move into a small home in Soochow."

"There are no small homes in Soochow. And Soochow is just like Yang-chow—both cities sit on strategic waterways. The war will go there. Is there not a single job you're willing to do here in Shanghai?"

"I'm not very useful now," he said. "Too old."

"You weren't useful when you were young! If my father—"

"Please. You beat me with him like he was a threshing pole."

"—saw all this, he would be so ashamed!"

"So what will you do?" She always made the decisions.

"Sell our possessions. Dismiss the staff. I'll take my amah and move in with my brother again. If he'll still take me."

"He'll take you. I never saw a lonelier man."

"You take Deaf Man Fu. I'll find a small place for you. That leaves the majordomo, Horseman Yip, Chef Chu and his cooks. That's all. I dismissed everyone else already. I expect *you* to dismiss them this time, not me. You understand? Not fair, making me do it twice, when it's you who won't work! Believe me, Husband, if I could get a man's job and a man's wages, I'd do it."

"We won't be together, then."

"We're not together now."

"It's a sad day when a man looks forward to being criticized by his wife, but I miss you, and miss your voice, even when you're angry at me."

They looked at each other. Long, silent moments passed as the European wall clock ticked. Both of them were losing their hair. A slight crook had developed in Taitai's back, and the pains that once inhabited her broken feet and tired ankles had migrated northward into many parts of her body. She had age spots on the backs of her hand, and no amount of scratching could diminish them.

"I will not miss being angry at you," she said. "Before, I did. No more."

"Maybe I'll go to Tsingtao. I hear the fishing is good there."

"That's a very long journey. You'll need many soft pillows and all your water remedies. Better you stay here. This is a city of doctors."

"Zee Zee has taken long journeys," said Baba.

"Zee Zee is a young man with red fire in his belly. You're a water-sign man. Everything you do is cool. Stay here by the Whangpu."

"Will you miss me, Wife, even a little?" He tried a brave smile.

She could have said *Yes*, to be polite. She should have said *Of course*, to be Confucian. She might have replied *Sometimes*, to be Buddhist. She could have lied, like a movie star, and said *Every day*.

"No," said Taitai. "I won't. I'm not going to think about you anymore."

ZEE ZEE CAME back to Japanese-occupied Shanghai in civilian clothes provided by T. A. Soong. He stiffened when Japanese sentries stopped him and studied his identity papers that revealed him to be an officer of Butterfield Swike, another British *taipan* shipping company and a major competitor of Jardine Matheson. T.A. figured that the Japanese, while wanting to conquer China, had no interest in antagonizing the navies of the Western powers, and would let Zee Zee into the city.

"Under no circumstances are you to bring Mr. Colt," wrote T.A. in the cover letter that accompanied the Butterfield identity packet. "I need you here, this moment, for crucial business with London. Hurry."

Zee Zee had needed a moment to identify Mr. Colt; T.A. was telling him not to bring his American automatic pistol. But to travel through China's bandits, warlords and Japanese troops unarmed was inconceivable. Pan had given him a number of holsters. Zee Zee chose the shoulder holster for its concealability; most gunmen carried pistols in their waistbands or on belts, and that was where cops always checked. Had the sentry opened Zee Zee's jacket, the vegetables, meat and toys that were intended for the small apartment on Nanking Road never would have been delivered. But the sentry, instructed to respect all foreign-business identity cards, waved Zee Zee into Shanghai.

Da-tsien had begged Zee Zee to return; she couldn't sleep with the machine guns clattering all through the night, the wailings of sirens and the unending parades of the wounded and dead. Nanking Road was Shanghai's Broadway, and the best thoroughfare to ten hospitals and the graveyards. Da-tsien hated to sleep alone now; she trembled, vulnerable and afraid, missing the warmth of her husband's body.

Zee Zee had been following the Red bandits on their overland trek across central China. It would come to be known as the *Chang Cheng*, the Long March, an epic six-thousand-mile journey across eight provinces, a hundred rivers and countless formidable mountain ranges. Zee Zee was exhausted from following them, and he was flying while they were walking.

He knew that below his bombs and guns walked old Shanghai acquaintances Chou En-lai and Teng Hsiao-peng, the pals of Uncle Chu.

He hadn't come home when Da-tsien asked. Nor had he responded to T.A.'s request. He came home because he had been grounded for disobeying orders.

Zee Zee had been a small cog in an international escadrille in which the dominant force was a Russian fighter squadron flying modern Yakelov monoplanes out of deep-desert bases in Mongolia. They had been hugely successful shooting down Japanese Type 3 fighter aircraft in North China. Next in the pecking order were Nationalist units flying American Northrop 2E monoplane fighters. Last was the collection of 1920s-vintage biplanes, which were used primarily for scouting.

Zee Zee disliked the restriction. To him, airplanes were to be used for attack. He bombed and strafed the Red bandits, which risked and then ruined his airplane. He was anxious to get a replacement.

"No, no more airplanes for you. You are on indefinite furlough," said Joghinder Singh. "The Reds started out with a hundred thousand men. They're down to five or six thousand. Go take care of your family."

Chiang Kai-shek was trying to organize China when the Japanese attacked Peking. It was July 1937. The next month, Japan assaulted Shanghai, a city the Nationalists couldn't afford to lose. Chiang lost nearly a quarter of a million troops in the city's defense as the Japanese army, navy and air force pounded his German-trained divisions. But he was outgunned and had to order a withdrawal towards his capital of Nanking. Some Chinese generals, such as Lee Chong-ren, lured the pursuing Japanese into classic double-envelopment traps, destroying more than thirty thousand crack Japanese troops. But overall, the retreat was a disgrace; KMT soldiers robbed and killed civilians for their clothing so they could escape the oncoming Japanese, while the military leadership in the capital proved to be neither military nor leaders.

The Japanese army entered Nanking in early December and subjected its inhabitants to rape, torture and murder. Japanese soldiers took pictures of their victims, of mothers being shot, of thousands of bound civilian prisoners being burned alive, of infants being bayoneted. They sent the film to Shanghai for development and later proudly mailed the prints home.

Zee Zee knew none of this as he traveled through central China. He backtracked to Shansi Province to catch a German transport flight to Chengchow in Henan. He rode Yellow River barges and walked the river roads to reach the Shantung Peninsula, then sailed to Shanghai.

Riding up the Whangpu was a shock. The Bund was untouched, but Pudong, Hongkew, Chapei and major parts of the International Concession were in ruins. The Great World tower was gone. The Cathay Hotel, where splendor was routine, had been wrecked. Smoke still rose from old fires. War had come to the city of sin.

He passed the remains of the *Da Shijie* amusement center. Huge craters had replaced buildings that he could no longer recollect. He had seen eight-inch howitzer impacts, but these were larger—maybe twelve- or even fourteen-inch naval shells. He had once thought that an eight-inch shell would be small, but the measurement was of the diameter, not the length; an eight-inch round could weight a hundred pounds. Coolies with face masks were still removing rubble and the dead. The more he saw, the greater his anger. *Screw it. I don't have to fly! I was trained in infantry! I'm going back to the army.*

He had been on the road for three months. As he stepped off the Nanking Road trolley, he saw that he had ruined his third pair of shoes, which were badly unshined. *A pair of shoes a month*, he thought.

His return, of course, was the cause of great celebration.

"Zee Zee!" cried his mother, nodding and standing near him. This was her right as the ranking elder. Clearly, she wanted to hug him, but the weight of propriety stopped her.

"Oh, how we missed you! I prayed for you so much! See how good the Christian God is, bringing you home! Now greet your older brother!"

"Brother," said Zee Zee obediently.

Gee waved halfheartedly from the apartment's only comfortable chair.

"Sister," said Zee Zee to Ying-oh, who gladly took his grocery bags filled with vegetables and small pieces of fish and chicken. The Japanese invasion had flowed up the Yangtze to Nanking. The Nationalists had throw two great booms across the Long River to halt the Japanese fleet. It had also blocked commerce into Shanghai. The city was being strangled.

"Hey, hey," Zee Zee said to his nephew Lon-lon and niece Chin, offering each of them little packaged toys he had purchased from street vendors. The children took them, looking up at him as if he were a god.

Elinor stood dutifully close, staring at her father. Ying, age five, couldn't wait any longer and ran to him, hugging his legs.

"Aiyaa! Stop!" cried Da-tsien. "Have you no manners? No judgment?"

Elinor pulled Ying from their father's legs and made her sit.

"I want a toy!" said Ying.

"Next time," said Zee Zee, rubbing her hair.

"Stupid girl!" said Da-tsien, unhappy that Zee Zee had not even acknowledged her. Ah Tsui scolded Ying to protect her. Zee Zee looked up for an instant at his wife.

A Chinese wife is the picture of acceptance; her status is secure as Taitai, bearer of sons. But Da-tsien's husband was a soldier of fortune, and she had no son and was living inside a small box with one window, in the same building as two hundred other people. Remembering Katharine Hepburn's films— *Alice Adams, Sylvia Scarlett* and *Mary, Queen of Scotland*—she approached Zee Zee, her head high, her long hair flowing, feeling every inch the verve of a social climber, the audacity of a girl masquerading as a boy, the majesty of a Scottish queen. She put her arm through her husband's and pulled him out the door while the remnants of the House of Lee dropped jaws and stared less they miss anything.

She shut the door. Placing her arms around his waist, she pressed her face against his chest, and he embraced her and kissed her long hair. She liked how he smelled, even though it was complicated by road dust, the mud of the Hwang Ho River and the salts of the sea.

"The city is occupied by Japanese troops," he said.

"Who cares! Zee Zee, you owe me a son!"

"I'm going back," he said, holding her tightly. "They need me."

She pushed him away. "What do you *mean*, you're going back! You *can't* go back!"

"Don't yell at me!" he growled, instinctively forming fists and then banging them together. "Don't raise your voice!"

"Oh, are you going to hit me now? How can you talk about yelling or saying anything after you say that you're *going back*? You *can't* go back! You just got here! Oh, be quiet? Okay, I'll be quiet! I won't even breathe!"

forty-eight

Be the Dragon

HOW CAN YOU sleep?" whispered Da-tsien.

Zee Zee blinked—he was awake. He looked at his German watch: two A.M. He remembered her question but didn't understand it. Sleep was sleep. With exacting silence, they had made love in a space occupied by his vain mother; his abusive brother and his lovely wife; the family's seamstress, who snored; a nephew, a niece and two daughters; and a portly amah who scratched herself and mumbled. The stress was enough to make him sleep for a week.

"Everyone's so close," she whispered. "I can hear everyone breathe! I didn't know Ah Tsui talked in her dreams."

"I used to sleep on rocks, with men on both sides and stinking camels tied to our wrists so they wouldn't run. Sometimes they spit on us."

She heard the words but didn't understand them. "Are you glad to be home?" she asked in his ear.

He saw the men, smelled the gagging food, felt the suction of endless mud on his boots. He was tired of fighting an enemy who wouldn't quit. Before leaving his squadron, he had thought of her, cleaning his hands with high-octane fuel until the skin was raw. He smelled like the earth now. He looked at his ruined airplane, shot full of holes. He had never been wounded, and his rear gunner had never been hit. He was lucky but didn't feel it. He missed the cough of his 450-horsepower Wasp, the thin blue smoke.

"Are you?" she whispered.

"Of course," he said.

IN THE MORNING, Madame Lee summoned her second daughter-in-law.

"I know I called you *jiang-nan* many times," she said. "Will you forgive me?"

"Of course, P'o-p'o," said Da-tsien. "Fact is, I am from south of the river, and I have that southern Soochow accent you don't like."

"But you know why, right? Because of my late husband's *syau lao po*. I tell you, by Jesus Christ our Lord, she spoke the truth that day. She *was* the most beautiful girl in all Shanghai." Madame Lee looked down at her pudgy hands. "She scared the wits out of me. She was stupid, but she was heart-attack mate-rial for men. And she had that breathy little voice that made them forget their promises and drop their pants. Me, I've always had the voice of a water buf-falo. Too big, too loud."

Da-tsien patted her mother-in-law's hand.

"Now, I ask you a favor. You see and hear how my Firstborn treats his wife and his children, yes? You know that it's very wrong, yes? I have an answer, but I've learned from you, Daughter. You always ask questions first. So let me pre-tend to be you: What would you do?"

"Oh, Mother, I would pray to Lord Jesus!"

"I did that, don't you know? What else? Don't name other gods."

Da-tsien closed her mouth. "I could raise them, Mother."

P'o-p'o smiled hugely, her gold teeth gleaming. "Yes! Excellent! Now I have to ask my son. Not your job! He'll say no, and I want him to say yes. When should I approach Zee Zee with this question?"

Da-tsien said a quick prayer, asking help from Jesus, then nodded and thanked Him. "Take a pedicab, Mother, and meet him for lunch at Japan Sugar cafeteria on Canton Road."

Madame Lee made a sour face. "Japan Sugar? No one goes there anymore! It's unpatriotic to give business to those people!"

"Exactly, Mother. No one will be there. You need privacy for this talk. Otherwise, if you go to Jar Fook or the Grand, you'll be interrupted. Everyone talks to Zee Zee because he works for T. A. Soong. Besides, the poor Japanese people need business now more than ever, yes?"

"So, WHAT DO you think, Zee Zee?" asked his mother.

"You have to be kidding, yes?" asked Zee Zee.

"I am *not* kidding! I am most serious. Gee's children love you. You take them for motorcycle rides. You teach little Lon-lon how to do magic tricks, and you're always giving horsie-back rides to little baby Chin. I think she loves you even more than the others! Of course," she added, "doing this occasionally with your own daughters will produce even bigger dividends than your work with your nephew and niece."

"See, Mah-mee, I don't have enough time for my own kids!"

"Because of Soong. He plays like you like a walnut."

"Hoy! You dislike the man who feeds us?"

"I distrust anyone who can control you so easily. Who reveres money over God."

"He doesn't control me! I agree to everything that happens."

"It's all my fault, you know," she said softly. "Your father had this anger. So quick to yell, so fast to blame, so much violent *yang* in defending what he did. I couldn't cure him of that. I tried really, really hard once. Oh, I prayed so much before! But he showed me. He went out and got a concubine. I tell you, the first one, she was almost a prostitute or a wild street peasant girl. He always picked them by their voices, not their faces or bodies. Well, you remember. He took your Chekiang na-ma, who could sing."

"I shouldn't raise my voice to you," he said.

"That's right. You shouldn't. And you should say yes to me, and take little Lon-lon and Chin off of Gee's hands before he hurts them."

"But Ying-oh's a good mother."

"Tsa tsa tsa! Doesn't matter. See, you don't know how we keep this family alive, do you? Ying-oh is selling our jewelry to buy foreign coffee and tea, and then she black-markets them to Russian retailers on Avenue Joffre. You think your paycheck from Soong can feed all our mouths and cover the debt service caused by your father?"

Zee Zee looked around. "I paid all his debts."

"So you thought," said Madame Lee "He borrowed from others. You never knew. He borrowed from people at the salt-tax office. He borrowed from the domo's family. Zee Zee, he borrowed from your wife's uncle, the brother of Taitai, Da-tsien's mother! You see, you're surprised, yes? Okay, will you take charge of your nephew and niece and save them?"

"Mah-mee, I can't. It's wrong. He's the Firstborn—"

"And he piddled it away, like you piddle yourself away on Soong!"

Zee Zee punched his right fist into his left palm. "I'm my own man. But I don't like children. Not even my own! I'd ignore them. At least you see the interest that Gee has in Lon-lon. It's more than I truly have."

"Oh, there you are," said S. Y. Shen, running into the shop, awkwardly bowing at the Japanese proprietor, who was bowing to him. "Zee Zee, T.A. wants you right now!"

"THANK YOU FOR coming back," said T. A. Soong. They were seated in the luxurious executive suite of the Bank of China branch on Yates and Bubbling Well. The Bank of China belonged to his brother-in-law, the gracious, easily smiling H. H. Kung, descendant of Confucius.

"I have a confession," said Zee Zee. "I came back because I got canned at Shinjiang in Shansi Province. For disobeying orders. For trying to kill Mao Tse-tung and wrecking my plane."

"Who is Mao Tse-tung?" asked T.A.

"A thinker. The KMT executed his wife. So now he's a very dangerous thinker who's going to kick our butt."

T.A. sighed. "Well, thank you for the truth. Factually, I need you. We have a grand market opportunity. This is the *Huang Jin Shidai*, the Golden Age of Business! Here, Zee Zee, in this time and place, the only immorality is poverty. See here, I need your help, but you frown. Be the dragon! Make decisions, shake earth! Next to you, you will find a banking binder. It is my master plan to acquire securities and common stock in combination with futures. It will take advantage of current market conditions. I wrote it with S. Y. Shen, who learned the American view of the market at Princeton. F. C. Fong also helped. Zee Zee, this way we acquire wealth to free us of *yi kao*."

"*Yi kao*. You're not *yi kao*!"

"Zee Zee—we all have *yi kao*. You dislike your version. I dislike mine." T.A. rang a small bell. A short servant, her hair in a tight bun, bowed and brought tea with three cups. She served, bowed and left. Then she returned, escorting another woman into the room. The woman was tall and beautifully gowned in shimmering silk. She had a perfect heart-shaped face that seemed illuminated from within, large eyes, a delicate nose and sculpted lips. She approached them with an impeccable and mesmerizing grace.

"Jih-iung, Lee Zeu-zee."

They shook hands.

"I've heard so much about you," she said. "I'm honored."

"The honor is mine," said Zee Zee. He looked at T.A. "No time for anything but banking, huh?"

"Will you help T.A. succeed, Zee Zee?" asked Jih-iung, laughing.

Thus, on typical impulse did Zee Zee become a stockbroker and a market speculator, following the order-and-sell instructions from T.A. and S.Y. They worked out of the Yates branch office and T.A.'s residence.

The first million they made was but a promise of more to come. T.A.'s plan was based on superior assessments made in the wake of the horrors of the Japanese invasion, and it was working flawlessly.

T.A. and his lieutenants, S. Y. Shen (balanced debentures), F. C. Fong (bonds and futures) and Zee Zee (high-risk arbitrage), sat in the paneled executive suite with Irish single-malt Scotch and Cuban cigars. S.Y. disliked alcohol and detested tobacco, and Zee Zee never drank, but they were contented. More importantly, each, except T.A., had at that moment a very relieved wife and a happy bank account.

"*Gambei*, empty cup," said T.A., lifting his glass.

"*Gambei!*" they intoned, drinking, or pretending to drink.

But T.A.'s brother-in-law H. H. Kung of the Bank of China saw no advantage to the Soongs siphoning money that was needed for the success of the Chinese Revolution. There were only so many hundreds of millions of dollars in Shanghai, and with the expensive war against Japan expanding, one could presume on less rather than more.

Chen Fu-chen, F. C. Fong, was a man of enormous cordiality. It was logical that he was the emissary of the bad news.

"Your brother-in-law sends you his regards," he said to T.A. only days after their celebration. "He tells you to bank your earnings in Zurich. And to leave Shanghai now."

T.A. sat immobile, his face like a Buddha's. The elegant, subdued lighting from wall sconces now made the suite seem funereal.

"Or what?" asked Zee Zee with a frown.

"Or he'll destroy you," said F.C.

"That won't be easy," said Zee Zee, planting his feet.

"No," said T.A. "He won't use guns. He'll empty my accounts."

"I apologize for delivering such bad words. But you know he just beat your brother, T.V., by succeeding him as the minister of finance—"

"That's a bad job," said Zee Zee. "Tax the poor and let the Blue Gown Gestapo, the *Dong Tang*, kidnap the top businessmen of Shanghai until they pay a ransom into the Kuomintang treasury."

"Now, that is not a fair statement!" said F. C. Fong. "These are desperate times, and I hear that the only men placed in these circumstances are collaborators with the Japanese army."

"Horseshit," said Zee Zee, proving why he hadn't been invited by H. H. Kung to deliver the message to T.A. "I can name you fifteen guys who paid ransoms to the treasury, and no way are they collaborators! They just have money. Hell, they're even sniffing after my father-in-law, and he's not a collaborator or even someone with petty cash!"

"Please," said T.A. "I cannot plan with such noise." He put down his drink and stubbed out his cigar. He closed his eyes a moment, then gazed about the luxurious office suite. In a corner stood a rank of tuxedoed Hainan waiters who could not understand the Songhai dialect.

"S.Y., transfer the money to Switzerland. Geneva, not Zurich. F.C., please tell my brother-in-law that as his junior, I obey his directions. Zee Zee, use the travel account and book passage to Hong Kong for all our families. Spend whatever you need to spend, but get us there safely. A ship and no airplanes, please. I depend on you to make sure no one in my family is harmed. I have never condoned the use of violence, but now I have enemies everywhere."

"You can depend on me," said Zee Zee. "I'll have to visit Pan to get more weapons," he added, rubbing in T.A.'s dislike of their childhood pal.

"Please also order a banquet at a random restaurant. I think it best if we do not eat tonight from my brother-in-law's kitchen."

Zee Zee left to make phone calls. In his absence, T.A. asked the other men if they would pray with him, and they did, as the Hainan waiters stood rigidly with stoic and unblinking faces.

DA-TSIEN COULDN'T BELIEVE her ears when Zee Zee told her they were going to Hong Kong.

"All of us?" she asked.

"Just us and our girls."

"What if we want to go, too?" asked Ying-oh.

"Better you stay here, your husband has a job," said Zee Zee.

"But they don't pay—"

"Shanghai's going to fall, right?" asked Gee. "And they're going to kill us, aren't they?"

"Soong has to leave for family reasons, and he wants me with him. God knows why—I know more about nursing babies than I do about banking." Zee Zee rubbed his face. "I can't fly anymore, but you'll have more room in this apartment without us."

"Help me pack," said Da-tsien.

They were alone. She packed and talked. He crossed his arms and leaned on the wall, thinking about how to repair his shot-up Corsair.

"Zee Zee, you're not listening! Okay, I'll say it again—when do we leave? Where will we live? What will be expected of me? How long will we stay? And please tell me that we're not flying there!"

He laughed. "We go by ship. We live with the Soongs. They have a big place in Kowloon. Servants and everything. You'll rest. No more churches. You work too hard here."

"Oh, Zee Zee! I never wanted to leave, but now I do! Will it be scary, going by boat? Can we bring your mother and your brother's family with us?"

"Christ, why would you want to do that?" He thought of hearing Gee slap and hound his small wife and terrify his kids. It was inconceivable that a younger brother could ask the Firstborn to act justly, and equally unimaginable to invite him to accompany them. Unspoken was the knowledge that traveling during the Japanese occupation of Shanghai would be exceptionally risky.

"Ying-oh," Da-tsien said, "isn't going to take more bad treatment. I think she's going to do something drastic."

Zee Zee sat on his mother's bed. "For the length of our marriage, Ying-oh's been a pain in the ass. She torments you. Criticizes you! I know why she does it, but why should you give a damn about her?"

"Oh, Zee Zee, you don't understand! Jesus loves me so I can love others. If I can love all, especially my enemies, he'll give me my son!"

Zee Zee rubbed the top of his head. "You know, you really are plain nuts."

She pushed him. "It bothers you that I love Jesus more than you."

His mouth dropped. "You *what?*"

"I do! He's my lord—"

"*I'm* your lord!"

"You're my husband on earth. Jesus is lord of all, everywhere else." She stopped folding clothes and sat on P'o-p'o's bed, facing him. "When you were scared, flying and fighting, didn't you pray?"

He frowned. "I think not."

"Were you ever scared?"

He nodded. "Many times. For good reason." He was always terrified of losing his airplane, of wrecking it, of losing control.

"And never prayed?"

"Never, never."

"I pray if I think I might run out of soap! I pray for hours, for every person I know. You have no idea how many hours I prayed for you this last year."

"God, Da-tsien, that's not living! That's being a nun!"

She laughed and hit him. "I was no nun last night!"

He blushed and scratched his ear. "Then pray for Ying-oh. But they can't come."

"Then talk to Gee before we go." She covered her face. Muffled, she said, "I forgot Baba. I have to say goodbye to him and wish him peace. I'll go now."

ZEE ZEE WALKED with Gee to his office in the Shanghai Utilities District. Gee had a tentative gait that always frustrated his brother, while Zee Zee's unrelenting stride always angered Gee.

"Here," said Zee Zee. "Please take it."

"A loan, only," said Gee.

"Of course. From Soong. Anything I can give you?"

"I want our father's pistol."

"Why?" asked Zee Zee.

"For safety. And for nostalgia. It was Baba's."

"Only if you let me show you how to use it."

His brother nodded. They furtively glanced up and down Citroen Road, seeing thousands of strangers but no Japanese soldiers. From the back of his waistband, Zee Zee withdrew the small Browning automatic that their father had loved. Shielding his hands with his back, Zee Zee showed his brother how to load, unload, safety and shoot. It wasn't a powerful handgun, but it was lethal. A *little like our father*, he thought. A *little like Gee*. A *little like me*. He passed the handgun to his brother, along with the extra magazine. He told him where he could acquire extra rounds if necessary.

"You still have your own, right?" Gee asked, running after Zee Zee, who wore Pan's heavy Colt .45 in a shoulder holster.

When they reached the office, Gee, slight of build and short, looked away rather than up at his younger brother. Centuries of ancient, unspoken words stood between them.

"Goodbye," said Zee Zee, looking past his brother at the city he kept leaving.

From the storefront window, Gee watched Zee Zee stride down the crowded street until he disappeared from sight.

forty-nine

Don't Let Them Hang You

PAN LOOKED AT his old pal from a thinner face devoid of mirth. He used to laugh when he was in trouble, and in those days, his trouble radiated from his ratty clothing like camphor from an old sea chest. Now he sat in the foreman's office of a bombed-out Hongkew warehouse. The office was neat, well lit and furnished in a modern, industrial way with metal furniture, but everything stank of fire and smoke and death. The warehouse floor was rubble and rock, courtesy of the Japanese navy and its marines, who had killed everyone they found. Bodies were still buried beneath hundreds of collapsed factories and tenements.

Next to him sat Angel San-t'ien, the *wünu* dance-hall girl with the heavenly face. She looked older, and Zee Zee realized that they all were. Christ, he was thirty years old, an age he had never expected to see.

"You both look good," said Zee Zee. "How's your wife?"

"Hey, Zee Zee," Pan replied, nervously snapping fingers. "Amazing, huh, that we're still alive."

"Lady Du told you her prediction about my death?"

"No, no, she was always protective about you. But every time we heard you were still flying airplanes out west or north, or that your wife had another girl, I saw her surprise. So I knew. Anyway, old friend, we still have our dicks and can drink *jinboi* like young men."

Zee Zee snorted. "I feel like I've been trying to score ten thousand points in a mahjong game with twelve ladies who know math." That was his new expression to describe his futile attempt to kill Mao Tse-tung.

"Lady Du said you'd die young?" asked Angel.

"I think my wife paid her to say that so I'd stay close. How's work?" he asked Pan.

"Barrel Man Yao has arthritis in every joint. He's losing weight. Hwa and Fen are still trying to get rich and build their own gangs so they can surpass me, and there's a new Mafia using the old name, *Hwang Jing Yong*, Yellow Golden Glory, that's causing me fits.

"Angel has fallen for the Japanese army because they're paying her in Mexican pesos, which they stole from me. Lady Du, I think, still hopes that she'll find a man for her old age. Hey, have a son yet? No? Too bad. I feel sorry for your wife. What do you need? Guns?"

Zee Zee passed him an equipment list and an envelope of money.

Pan made teeth as he stowed the envelope in his pocket. "Tommy guns? Have you heard? There are half a million goddamned Japanese soldiers in China, and most of them are here in Shanghai. You know, don't you, that they're going to attack the Western Powers."

"You have more guns than America. No way—Japan's strong, but they can't take England, France, Germany—"

"Angel, *she* knows something. Lady Du, *she* knows something. Japanese generals are such cocky bastards! They look down on us, *us*, the Chinese, who taught those assholes everything! I tried to sell the information to the British police—I know the French don't give a damn—but no one trusts it. So now I give it to you free: The Japanese are going to attack the Brits and Yankees. A huge naval operation—Singapore, Manila, Hong Kong—*bing, bing, bing,* one after the other, very fast." He snapped his fingers.

With his right hand, Zee Zee made the Chinese chopping gesture across the chest: *Rubbish.*

"The world is going to shit, Zee Zee, and the Japanese are going to be the big *ma-fen,* manure, salesmen of the world. Now they're going to get a partner—Nazi Germany. Yes! It's true! Angel got it from those fat little Tokyo generals. They diddle her and then babble like they're her babies and she's their *na-ma!* I just hope they don't kill her."

"They love me too much," said Angel. "I'm safe."

Zee Zee hadn't thought about political science since he left St. John's. But the logic of Pan's words wouldn't go away. The essence of warfare was intelligence, and in every war, leaders spilled secrets in bedchambers. He himself never said anything to Da-tsien or anyone, but he knew it happened. If Tokyo and Berlin united, the Japanese fleet could make surprise attacks on the West just as it had done to China in Manchuria, Peking, Shanghai, Nanking. Chiang Kai-shek had fled to Chungking. So Hong Kong was a target, not a haven.

He had to tell Soong. "No hurry. Take five minutes."

"Same old Run-Run Lee. I was going to give you the dodge, but you're in a rush." Pan picked up a crowbar and told him to follow.

They walked between mountains of stone rubble, Zee Zee pushing the pace from behind. The air was cool but foul with the underscent of rotting flesh.

They climbed over downed concrete pylons and climbed a rock pile that slipped like mountain scree. Under cleverly concealed tarps were boxes labeled in English stencils, CHINA CENTRAL MISSION BIBLES. Pan found the Bible box he wanted and pried it open with the crowbar. He removed a Thompson submachine gun, packed in cosmoline and oily, stiff brown industrial packing paper. He handed it to his pal, with empty magazines and .45 ammo boxes. Zee Zee ripped open the paper to check the gun's action, locking in a magazine and dry-firing it once.

"Same old Run-Run! You rush making love, too?"

Zee Zee laughed. "I live with my whole family. What do *you* think?"

They laughed like boys.

"What about Soong the monk? Think he even knows how to screw?"

Zee Zee fell silent. "Don't joke about him. He keeps my family alive. Christ, he's been doing it since we were in high school." He looked far away. "He honored my father better than I did." The rocks they were standing on slipped. Zee Zee balanced himself, looking at the machine gun.

"I don't joke about you, Pooh. I honor your wife. Tai Yueh is my wife's friend. You gave me a home, a place to become myself. You shared Barrel Man Yao, let me take more lessons than you. I never taught you calligraphy, hardly helped you read. You graduated from St. John's! I didn't." Zee Zee remembered the diploma above Pan's desk. "I owe you a deep debt. You're like my brother. But so is Soong."

Pan nodded. "I hear your words." He was suddenly nervous, as though he had heard something. He began descending. Zee Zee put the wrapping in the box, closed it, covered it with the tarp and picked up the crowbar.

Pan was talking, his back to him. "Hey, I graduated from St. John's because of your tutoring. It was all reading, like you said." He laughed. "I'm just a dumb bandit, aren't I?"

"You're a good friend," said Zee Zee. "I will always honor you."

"Thank you, Zee Zee. But who will I honor? I have to make a name for myself first! You're famous because you fly airplanes and you hang out with one of the richest guys in China." He looked about. "What about me? Will they tell proverbs about me?" They were at the bottom of the rock pile. "*Wan shih liu fang?* For ten thousand years?"

"They'll remember you for ten thousand years," said Zee Zee. "Let's be men together. Remember saying that so long ago?"

"I don't remember that one, but I remember that we three promised we'd never break up and never marry. It's a funny world, Zee Zee, and I'll miss you."

Zee Zee handed him the crowbar, not knowing when he'd see Pan again.

"Make some money now, Lee," said Pan.

"Don't let them hang you," said Zee Zee.

fifty

Hong Kong

LATER, DA-TSIEN COULDN'T remember what she loved more—the boat ride down the China coast, entering the Soong mansion or living with her aunt. All three helped mitigate the distance from her aging baba.

The boat ride was violent and choppy, but she had Zee Zee to herself in a private steerage room. She could give him her hands, which he always held, and look into his eyes, which sometimes looked into hers. She could love him and feel in their connection the promise of her only son.

In those glorious moments on the vessel, she forgot the tummy-churning anxieties that came from failing to deliver a boy, failing in the only Chinese duty assigned to her by destiny, history and culture.

Ah Tsui and the formidable Christian fundamentalist Miss Wu kept Elinor and Ying entertained while Da-tsien lingered over her husband and even fought her way across a pitching deck to bring crackers back to the bed. She tried hot tea once and screamed as the ship yawed and the teapot and cups flew off the tray.

She never wanted the journey to end, but it was over in two days. She insisted that the journey had taken a week, or perhaps two.

Zee Zee felt guilty. He would have loved a hard trek full of hardship and danger to make him feel worthy and alive. Sailing down the China coast in a soft bed with his loving wife made him feel decadent. In the field, he seldom thought of his family; now that he was cruising to Hong Kong to make money, he worried about his mother, his unhappy sister-in-law, his bright nephew Lon-lon and his lovely niece Chin.

Zee Zee told T.A. Pan's information—that the Japanese were going to attack throughout the Pacific Rim. T.A. was unfazed because he feared his own family more than Japanese soldiers.

Zee Zee had executed a military embarkation at the Bund quay as they left Shanghai. Without authority, he lined up the first-class crew of the small Italian liner, the *Conte Rosso*, and frisked each one for weapons. He checked the estate rooms for stowaways, kidnappers or assassins. He inspected the initial food stores as they were loaded.

He stood on the dock with a harbor official and his Thompson under his overcoat as the amahs, cooks, servants and the inevitable Bible-toting Miss Wu boarded. Last was Sesame Face Wong and his assistant, whom the Soongs had hired on a provisional basis.

Elinor, Zee Zee's firstborn daughter, had smiled and grabbed his arm as she stepped on the boarding plank. Ying had looked at him with equal measures of hope and fear, so he touched her face and marveled as her entire spirit seemed to illuminate the early-morning dock.

I shouldn't have such power, he thought. *It's wrong.*

Two Japanese marine sentries approached. The *k'u-li* porters saw them. Some froze; others began working faster.

"Softly. No rush," said Zee Zee, casually stepping between the workers and the sentries, motioning the official to follow him. He switched off the safety of the machine gun.

The sentries saw the Chinese businessman and the comprador. The businessman wore an overcoat and a very big gun.

The comprador anxiously displayed the harbor *hoppo*, supervisor stamps, and the expensively purchased seal of Japanese authority.

The Japanese marine corporal gestured for the gun.

Zee Zee maintained eye contact with him but ignored the pantomimed request.

"*Baka,*" idiot, spat the sentry, reaching for the coat.

Zee Zee stepped back. The harbor official's hands were shaking. He backed up, too. Zee Zee felt a cold rage. Japan was powerful, China was weak. He prayed to the Bravest Wife. Not for courage but for vengeance.

The other marine was afraid. Both Japanese had their Nambu 7mm rifles at sling arms. Neither had a sidearm. Their bayonets were sheathed. This Chinese man with a .45-caliber machine gun could kill them four times over before they could act. Zee Zee backed up more, negating a rush.

"*Dzai jen,* see you later," said Zee Zee.

It was in these moments that he was most alive. "I have the heart of a German guard dog," he told Da-tsien while they were in bed. "Too often, I end up being a little shih tzu. It makes me crazy. Here we are, fighting Japan, and I'm lounging on a boat!"

"Isn't it wonderful? We're free from that war! We're not caught up in it anymore, and it's all for our son!"

As THEY APPROACHED Hong Kong, T.A. made a rare speech. "I have good memories of Fragrance Harbor, Hong Kong," he said to Zee Zee and Da-tsien on a windy deck as they passed the rugged coastline under a southwest breeze.

Hong Kong is an east-west island, fifteen *li*, five miles, long. It shrinks in the middle to two miles in width. Victoria Peak is the high point. It was a simple fishing village under the Manchus. But the British saw the port opportunities in the narrow passage between the island and the mainland, in the wide east channel, in the harbor, in the fresh sea breezes that give Hong Kong its name.

"I hope you enjoy Hong Kong as I have. Sailing into the harbor from the east is most impressive." He turned and went to his cabin.

They entered the gap at the Eastern Channel at Li Yue Mun, Carp Gate, flanked on both sides by menacing and imposing cliffs. Zee Zee smiled, for he saw that the British could defend this harbor against the entire Japanese fleet. A mottled green British monoplane, the eight-gun Hawker Hurricane, flew cover in and out of lacey clouds.

In Hong Kong, an army of uniformed servants bowed as T.A., S.Y., F. C. Fong and Zee Zee passed through the covered entryway and stood in a marble entry hall. Valets removed their coats. Following at a respectful distance were F. C. Fong's son, the wives, the amahs, the servant corps, and Sesame Face, whose seasick helper brought up the rear.

The mansion faced North Point and Victoria Peak and overlooked the bay. Later, Da-tsien would have trouble describing the architecture, but she remembered many windows and a sense of being in the clouds, as well as an initial nervousness when looking down the steep cliffs to the water. There was a surplus of capable servants. This was the Soochow life she remembered, and it brought a deep sense of comfort.

Her favorite moments were on the balcony facing the opposing promontory. She could watch the ferries run from Pointed Sandy Beak. On Sunday afternoons, she would force Zee Zee to sit with her to take tea. The kitchen would serve dim sum, the Cantonese delicacies that involved artistically wrapped pieces of meat and fish—*small pieces of heart*. Ah Tsui insisted on holding her silk umbrella over Da-tsien's head, chasing away the servants who wished to install a more sensible table umbrella. Ah Tsui was getting older, so holding the umbrella was easier than watching Elinor and Ying, even if Elinor did most of the watching.

"Sweet honey, look at the little boats! The big ships! Look, is that the one we took from Shanghai? Oh, it was so spectacular! Do you think this will make our son a sailor? Here, try this one, Zee Zee! It has shrimp. They're delicious! Amah, did they make enough for Elinor, too?"

"Mistress, they made enough for everyone! I'm getting so round again!"

In the mansion packed with loyal servants, Zee Zee had no security worries. The machine gun was unloaded and stored in a high place that children couldn't reach.

The house was enormous, but even mansions have a finite number of rooms. The Japanese had committed two hundred and fifty thousand troops to the conquest of China. But the strong resistance of the Nationalists and the surviving Communist movement had made Tokyo double the number of troops, and then double it again. Many of the new regiments were even more poorly disciplined than the ones that had savaged Nanking.

China now knew of the Rape of Nanking. The Japanese army had maintained its cruelty, its arbitrary violence, its hatred of the Chinese population. Japanese troops were ordered to kill all refugees, an order that authorized the execution of a hundred million people. Anyone who could escape from northern China was doing so. The Soongs' relatives were coming to Hong Kong to flee the Japanese invasion, so the Lees had to move out. The farewells were brief and efficient, since there would be many subsequent visits.

Da-tsien had Tzu relatives in the New Territories of Hong Kong, so they called on Auntie Tzu, who was smart; she caught everything at first glance.

"Oh, look at you! You are exquisite! A beautiful girl! Oh, my father, who was your grandfather's brother, would be so happy to see you.

"So, introduce me to your husband, ah, tall, strong, big nose to smell the wind, likes to leave all the time, yes? Oh, good, two beautiful daughters, one quick one needing more love, eyah? Look, look, this is my daughter and two sons, Margaret, William and David—yes, go play!

"Ah, and a portly amah who sits a great deal but pretends at hard work. Ah, yes, Miss Wu, the great seamstress, I'm honored. Well, well, come in, come in, there's no more room if you wait!

"Ching-ah! Make tea, more crackers! Lots of hungry mouths here! They've been eating off Soong tables, and they're going to be disappointed, so serve them quickly and they won't notice!"

It was a lovely home built in conformity to boulders and oaks. It was rich in shade and thick with kindness, with a hard-working husband, a big-spirited wife and three happy children. Da-tsien knew she could live here always, except that the new quarters were almost as badly cramped as the Nanking Road apartment in Shanghai.

In the morning, Da-tsien pulled her husband into the kitchen for privacy. It was vacant nearly an hour a day.

"Zee Zee, feel here, see? I'm pregnant! And it happened up there," she said, pointing at the Kowloon hills, "where our son enjoyed the view and loved the dim sum and a grand kitchen and so many kind servants. I have a great sense of *ho-chi*, of harmony, about our boy, and now you're making money for him! Aren't you, really, so happy?"

"Of course."

She was looking in his eyes. They were vacant, so she hit his chest and wept. She knew he'd tell her to be quiet, so she tried to stop.

"Let it out!" urged Zee Zee. "Don't hold it in!"

She was sick of his loving airplanes and the army more than her, and she was sick of taking orders and sick of his controlling ways.

Zee Zee was afraid she was going to burst. "Do something!" he yelled. "You're angry, hit me!"

She angrily shook her head, turning an interesting purple. Zee Zee grabbed a plate and put it in her hand. "Throw it!" he commanded, and she threw it and it shattered on the floor, and he gave her another one and she hurled that, striking a glass cabinet and breaking it. Finally, she had to breathe, whooping for air, gasping, and he caught her before she fell.

"From now on, throw something when you get angry!" he said. "You're such a crazy person!"

She pursed her lips, clenched her fists and stopped breathing. He handed her a plate and she threw it, and then another.

"Okay, you songbirds!" said Auntie Tzu, stepping into the kitchen, light reflecting brightly from her rather severe spectacles. "What, you don't like our plates? Designs not that pleasing? You don't like our glass kitchen cabinets! How about arguing in another room?

"I know why you do this. After fighting, you two always go to bed. You think we don't know what's going on? We hear everything! And you, pregnant already! I don't know why you blush, Da-tsien! You get to have springtime! I'm the one who's embarrassed!"

A FEW DAYS LATER, Zee Zee got a telegram promoting him to major. The pay was not much better.

"You would be a colonel now," said T.A., "if you had only joined the party." The Kuomintang, Nationalist Party, of Chiang Kai-shek. "Why not join, Zee Zee? It would help our cause if you were higher in rank. I think, sooner or later, America will be in this war against Japan. If you were a colonel, or a general, that would be very good."

Zee Zee felt like spitting. "I don't like the Communists. You know that. But I don't like the Nationalists, either. We call the Reds *tu-fei*, bandits. Well, *both* sides are *tu-fei*."

ON A SATURDAY IN the spring of 1939, after another epic battle between their parents, Elinor and Ying were surprised when their father put them into a motorcycle's sidecar and drove them to a park. They played catch with a rubber ball, petted dogs, laughed on a swing set and ate ice cream. He even carried them on his shoulders, and they delighted in pulling on his ears. Later, Da-tsien loved hearing about the girls' pleasure with their baba.

In the morning, Auntie Tzu prepared a *congi tseuh* rice gruel and vegetables for the children. Da-tsien sensed that something was different.

Where was Zee Zee? She went upstairs and looked in the closet; his uniforms were gone. He had kept his guns in a case on an upper shelf in the attic. With great effort, she climbed up and looked: no guns.

"Looking for this?" Auntie slid a note to her. It said he loved her, that she should kiss the girls and that he was going to fight the Japanese. She looked for a plate to throw, but Auntie stopped her.

"He has a big nose, good for smelling winds to take him away. He's full of fire and light, right? Very exciting, great to play with in spring but full of pain in winter, right? Here, here, cry out your aches, yes, that's right. Children, eat in the other room. That's good, Young Missy, yes, and your baby's on the way. No, can't tell if it's a boy or a girl yet," she lied.

fifty-one

Mary Ming

D A-TSIEN PREPARED FOR the delivery of her son like Sun Tzu prepared kings for war. She planned, she schemed, she marshaled and she organized.

"Elinor and Ying, wash everything in this house! Now! Twice! Five times! Especially the money! Wash everyone's money."

"Why do you need money?" asked Auntie.

"So I can wash it," said Elinor, now ten. "For my baby brother," she added. It had become the coda to everything.

"Ah-wu, I don't understand," said Auntie. "Say that again."

Ying was seven and had become adept at washing coins. She had done less well washing paper money and had gotten in big trouble.

"Amah, I want mosquito netting to protect my son from any type of insect. No, don't get mosquito netting—get everything-netting."

"Auntie, the nursery has to be perfectly clean for my son. No germs. No visitors. No workmen. No fishermen. Absolutely no soldiers."

"Okay to let air inside the room?" Auntie Tzu asked dryly.

Da-tsien thought. "No, no air, either. Very, very clean!"

Da-tsien approached Uncle Tzu carefully. "Uncle, have you heard the new medical reports? They say smoking is bad for breathing."

"Uh, no," he said guardedly, lighting a smoke.

"And that it interferes with your sex life?"

He choked out the smoke. "No, I didn't hear that one."

"Or that it smells up your clothes and makes children sick?"

"Da-tsien, are you asking me to stop smoking for your new baby?"

"Oh, *Dababa*, you're so good! My son thanks you from baby lungs."

"Ching-ah," said Da-tsien, "wash all vegetables and fish and meat at least three times from now on. Hot, hot water! Kill all germs!"

Ching-ah didn't speak Songhai, but she nodded emphatically.

In Cantonese, Elinor told Ching-ah what her mother had directed.

"But why, Young Missy?" asked the cook. "Hot water will ruin the leafy vegetables and take away much of the food value."

"Mah-mee doesn't like germs," she replied.

"Well, no one likes germs. That's why we cook the food!"

"Maybe you can wash everything twice, cold water?"

"Shanghai people are so strange! I've heard her speak Cantonese, *say-yep*, *sam-yep*, even *Toisan*. Why doesn't she speak Cantonese to me?"

"She hasn't spoken Cantonese for a couple of months. She doesn't want my baby brother to be confused by too many dialects."

Ching-ah studied the beautiful girl. "You believe all that rot?"

"I don't have to. Mah-mee's the one who's pregnant."

"You sound like her daughter."

"I'm not her son. When he comes, he won't have to do any work."

Mary, named for Mary, mother of Jesus and Mary, queen of Scotland as played so glowingly by Katharine Hepburn, arrived in May of the world's last peaceful spring for six years. Like all the Lee children, she was healthy and lovely and very female.

Da-tsien was inconsolable. She had prayed and lived righteously, had endured unfair criticism from judgmental women, abandonment by her husband and geographical dislocations, and it all would have been worth it had this fourth child simply had one minor appendage. She decided to cope by using all the skills and maturity she could muster. She would simply cry for the rest of her life.

Ah Tsui tried to tell her the truth: "Your next child will be a boy." This inspired accusations of blatant lying and deeper sobs.

Elinor tried to lie. "We heard Baba's coming home," to which Da-tsien replied, "I can't face him without my son!"

Auntie successfully tried a little of each. "Hey, Da-zee, you look pretty good for a woman who just bled for three days. Now, collect your brains. Little Tail has a fever and will need your loving care. Wet nurse is good, but mother's touch is the best medicine." Little Tail was the nickname for the last-born. Auntie was hinting that Da-tsien's childbearing had come to its natural end.

Ignoring the hint but heeding the warning, Da-tsien remembered little Shiaobaobee, her dead baby daughter. She began issuing orders. Everyone had to wash everything all over again. The house could have no visitors and no one except her, the na-ma and Ah Tsui were to have any contact with Mary. Da-tsien would personally be in charge of the na-ma's diet, and there could be no yelling or loud noises. Family could not pass the nursery door unless it was closed.

In a radical move motivated by religious exhaustion, Da-tsien focused on Jesus and dropped the other ninety-three faiths. She was particularly peeved at Guan Yin, giver of baby boys, Crosses were hung in the nursery, and no one, not even Ah Tsui, was authorized to utter a single word to any god but the Christian God.

Da-tsien was free of her depression. As she monitored the wet nurse's diet, so would she later monitor Mary's input and output, both of which were carefully assessed. Evil influences were parried. Christian ideas were advanced. Money was laundered.

"*Yasu tiahng nu, wah see ching* . . ." she sang to little Mary. *Jesus loves me, this I know, for the Good Book tells me so* . . .

Now that her baby was out and was not a boy, Da-tsien freely used her Soochow, Songhai, Mandarin and Cantonese language skills, with emphasis on the latter, to find the best pharmaceutical houses in Hong Kong. She spent, overspent, bargained, cajoled and persuaded, getting the herbal doctors to surrender their best medicines for a baby girl who was, in fact, as healthy as a Mongol war pony.

WHEN IT WAS clear that Mary would outlive Abraham, Da-tsien thanked the pharmacists who had saved her against no odds.

She took the girls to see her favorite actress, Katharine Hepburn, with Cary Grant in *The Philadelphia Story*. Hepburn's character, Tracy Lord, took excellent stage direction from Da-tsien, and Hepburn was in her glory. Da-tsien identified with the lovely, misunderstood rich girl—a headstrong wife, a lonely divorcée, a once again loyal daughter, a woman who would love her husband and speak her mind when she wished. Da-tsien loved Hepburn's undeniable independence. Hepburn wasn't *yi kao*.

Elinor thought Tracy Lord was silly and superficial. Ying thought Cary Grant was dreamy. Mary loved sleeping in Mah-mee's arms and learned to survive her jumping about and yelling orders at Hepburn, whom she grew up thinking was a member of the Lee family.

Da-tsien gathered her daughters, their collective two amahs and one wet nurse—two-thirds of the assets belonging to Mary.

"Remember, you have a father. He's like Uncle, but he works far away. I don't know where he is. But I know he loves you all very much, and if he didn't have such a hard job—they don't even have ink in the army—he'd write to you. And, you should know, he's a major!"

"What's a major, Mah-mee?" asked Elinor.

"I don't know! Oh, your mah-mee's a silly woman. I saw this coming when I was a girl, but I married him anyway because he was so handsome."

Elinor rubbed her sobbing Mah-mee's back. Ying, who had developed an enormous empathy for people, cried with her.

"I'd never know if he was going to hold me or leave me forever!" wailed their mother.

"What happened next, Mah-mee?" cried Elinor.

fifty-two

Hubei

LEE ZEE WAS angry to be back in the army; it wasn't what he'd expected. He could take the division of the country—by 1939 China had become four nations: a Japanese region in northeastern China; a KMT nation in the south; a Chinese Communist Party, CCP, area in the northwest; and a Western colony inside Japanese-occupied Shanghai. He couldn't take his own government.

Instead of fighting the Japanese—the dominant threat—Chiang's KMT army kept chasing Reds, who actually were fighting the Japanese.

Burning Wuhan had fallen when Zee Zee arrived at the collapsing front line in western Hubei. He came not in a fresh regiment in a winning cause, but in his customary solo fashion. He walked through waist-high spike grass and millet fields, brushing away the flesh-eating flies that had blossomed to eat the dead. He stepped on guns, knapsacks, body parts. Hubei was rancid with defeat.

Chiang, after a million casualties, was ignoring the Japanese and withdrawing west to save his army for the civil war with the Reds. He and Madame Chiang Kai-shek had fled to remote Chungking, Szechuan, where they were beyond the Japanese army's ability to pursue.

The local army commander needed a rear-guard action to delay the Japanese pursuit. Zee Zee and a young captain who had also been trained by the German cadre volunteered. The captain, though wounded, was tough, schooled by the new Germans of General Hans van Seeckt. He limpingly led his decimated company to the northern roads. Zee Zee would find his unit at a replacement depot near a protected stream; he was to harass the enemy on the southern roads. The two men would defend an area that required a regiment.

A ragged line of emaciated, barefoot, bleeding men approached, roped by their abraded necks. Tougher ones were bound by their wrists; docile ones carried grain bags and water for the guard detail. The rope had been tied and retied to release the dead. Zee Zee didn't like restraints.

The middle guard had no rifle; his weapon was a rope that he used as a whip. He stopped the column, and the men didn't collapse but stood dumbly, gasping slowly looking for water.

"Deserters?" asked Zee Zee, blowing a fly off his mouth.

The guard spat. "Replacement troops," he said. "Already toughened!"

"Why are they roped?"

"Get them here, right? Think they jumped to join up?" He laughed a Chinese laugh.

"They don't look trained. They look like prisoners."

"Basic training in Taiyuan." They had marched from Shansi Province, seven hundred miles to the north.

"I'll take their papers."

"Papers?" The guard laughed. "No goddamn papers. These are fucking dirt peasants. You pay me a *yuan* per twenty. That's two *yuan* and a *yuan* for the fifty asshole dirt-men who dropped out and went to the next world."

"They say we were all dirt farmers once," said Zee Zee.

"That's before I got rich in the army, Major," he said, his bloody palm open. Villages were near. Cash would mean food instead of watered soup.

"You had them roped," said Zee Zee. "No need to hit them, too."

The man counted his money. "Don't whip 'em and they'd slit my precious throat, and then you wouldn't have any troops, would you?"

Zee Zee cut the ropes and told the men to follow him to the stream. They were terrified to move without orders, so he ordered them to drink. He let them gorge and throw up and drink again; he had done that once at a brown-water desert well as a teenage trainee.

He bought them food. From their ranks, he chose acting middle soldiers not based on leadership skills but on their ability to understand him. The acting sergeants made sure no one gorged on the rice porridge and the few fragments of old and tough bamboo shoots.

Zee Zee was given a variety of ancient German and Russian weapons. One was a Takarev Model 40 submachine gun; there was no ammo for it, so it became a club. The men didn't know Mandarin, Songhai or Cantonese. They were Shansi, Kansu and Ningshia men, with a few Mongols, Manchus, Moslems and angry Koreans. Some of the rural men thought they had been snatched to become *nu li* slaves for a warlord or a foreign-devil factory.

"Why they strip off our muscle before we work?" asked one.

The few urban men knew that a new republican government had kidnapped them to kill other Chinese. In China a regiment is named after its commander, so this was Lee's Company. If they beat the Japanese, he would give them his name and they would be his sons. Many warrior leaders of antiquity had been named Lee and Wong, which is why these names, out of the Honorable One Hundred, are so prevalent today.

Zee Zee showed them how to set and spring a simple rear-shoe ambush. He had enough rounds to let each of his men fire once at a haystack. The weak scrunched their faces and rubbed ringing ears and aching shoulders. No one tried to shoot him.

"The noise of a rifle," Zee Zee said, "chases away ghosts. But before we shoot the Japanese, we must have total silence! Like you're chasing quail, right?

"I will shout 'Shi shen tao ti!' Attack! You with rifles, shoot over here." He gave detailed instructions about timing and rally points to the rifle team, the weapon-recovery team and the ammo-gathering team. They would kill a few and then bravely scavenge before fleeing. Later, with more weapons, they'd begin seriously harassing the enemy.

"Don't shoot each other! It's bad for digestion!"

There were a few laughs but no time. They filled water bags and hurried to the roads, reciting the sequence and rally points. Zee Zee picked a good site with cover where a patrol might relax. A sliver moon slowly brightened.

"Hoi! Snakes in grass!" cried a soldier, starting to run.

"Quiet," said Zee Zee. "They're not poisonous. Later we'll catch and cook them, just like the enemy." He lay his .45 close by, at his boots.

But the Japanese who were coming had already been bloodied by the Communists, masters of ambush. They sent multiple point men in wedges instead of a single-file recon patrol.

Japanese infantrymen in the left wing of the wedge heard the untrained Chinese men. They froze as someone in Zee Zee's group whispered, urinated or scared a snake. The scouts halted, sized up the ambush party and back-tracked to alert their main body. Mortars and machine guns were set up. Japanese squads crawled forward; each member had several grenades. They took positions and inundated the Chinese rear with grenades. A Japanese grenade makes a small cough; forty or so sound like howitzers, and then the mortar rounds fell and machine guns opened up. The wounded screamed and the dead tripped those who could run.

"Fuck!" shouted Zee Zee. "Rally point! Rally point!" He emptied his Thompson at the machine guns, silencing one. He reloaded, firing in short, tight bursts towards another automatic weapon, offering defiance as his survivors fled. The mortar fire was rolling as the enemy withdrew, and Zee Zee ran like a track star.

There were a handful of wounded men at the rally point. One was a country herb doctor who squeezed shrapnel from bleeding bodies. There were no dressings and no sulfa, and of course not even a thought about morphine. German and U.S. field stations had nurses. The wounded quietly ground their teeth, waiting for death. Zee Zee was using torn cloth to bind wounds when he realized that he had left his wonderful .45 automatic in the kill zone. He remembered how many times men had offered to buy it from him in Shanghai, at any price. He cursed and felt an enormous depression.

They passed through the depot, relieved that the Japanese were not pursuing them, and perturbed that these valiant, starving farmers represented such a *de minimis* threat to the enemy that they were being ignored. Zee Zee wanted to set another ambush, but he couldn't use half-starved, untrained men to do it. *Dammit, they're farmers.* Tsou goh wan bah dan! He cursed fate.

He was the first to awaken. Even without roosters, he could sense dawn and open his eyes with complete alertness. He stood and stretched and counted his men. Some of his wounded had begun a seven-hundred-mile trek home. It was a sign of respect that they had not slit his throat and taken his Tommy gun. *We started yesterday. Japan started in 1895 and in 1905, when they beat Russia. Half a century's lead. Damn. They'll kill us all.*

fifty-three

Pearl and Margaret

T.A. HAD AUTHORED Zee Zee's army orders so he could recall him for tasks that superseded war, such as banking and the survival of clans. When Zee Zee was still seeking an effective role in the disastrous Hubei campaign against Japan, T.A. recalled him.

"I have to move gold certificates to America. Please help."

"Will I be gone long?" asked Zee Zee, thinking of the Japanese.

"You will be back with your wife in mere weeks," said T.A.

"I HAVE THREE daughters and a son on the way," Da-tsien announced to the ladies of various mahjong clubs. Mahjong requires the ability to remember points in scales of sixteen, and in about three minutes, Da-tsien would be playing according to rules no one else at the table understood. She was there to recruit mission workers. But the relative indolence of Hong Kong life meant that while few volunteered, her workload dropped.

This almost compelled her to raise the two daughters she liked and to make a ragged sort of peace with the one she resented.

"Oh, I know she's done nothing wrong, and she's perfectly beautiful, but why did she have to be a girl? Well, of course, Mary's a girl, too, I know. But she was born with a terrible, terrible illness, and I had to save her life. So Mary's different. Ying, she was born perfectly healthy!"

Zee Zee came home periodically for jobs that scared the other members of T.A.'s staff—transporting gold, flying overseas in noisy airplanes and carrying a gun.

"Why are you sad?" asked T.A.

"I think we're going to lose," said Zee Zee.

"Defeatist thinking is like cancer. What would make you feel better?" asked T.A.

"Training. Leadership. Generals who care about their men. Even generals who know something about war."

ZEE ZEE DELIVERED the gold certificates to the Bank of Canton in San Francisco. It was November 1941, and T.A., who was now chairman of that bank, had also asked Zee Zee to inspect a Studebaker truck plant in South Bend, Indiana, and a San Francisco Kaiser Steel plant with whom Chiang Kai-shek had fashioned contracts.

"What am I looking for in the plants?" Zee Zee asked.

"You know machinery," said T.A. "See if all is right and if they are making our trucks correctly. Two other requests. You have had bad luck. You did not graduate from St. John's. You tried to kill Mr. Mao in Hunan but failed, and that pained you. I think you are still angry, yes? Da-tsien needs a son, you have daughters. I offer to make you wealthy, you defy me. I suggest we alter your fortunes. Let us change your name."

An old Chinese tradition to change bad luck. Though Chinese had fixed family and generational names, informal names could be altered as easily as Charles wanting to be called Charlie instead of Chuck.

"How about 'Tsung-chi,' Second Luck? 'Tee Cee,' not Zee Zee. You would be New Fortune, not Merciful Longevity. You would be *Lucky*."

Zee Zee wasn't sure. Tee Cee didn't sound like him. It didn't sound like anyone. But Second Luck had a great sound. His old name, Zee Zee, "Longevity" and "Mercy," was a joke. He was supposed to die young, and here he was over thirty years old. Mercy was a religious concept. He laughed.

T.A. offered a dark wooden box. "Please. Open it."

Inside lay a gleaming deep blue Colt Super .38 automatic pistol on a .45 automatic 1911A1 chassis. This was a lighter and far more accurate gun than the .45. There were times in combat that Zee Zee thought the .45 automatic worked better as a hammer than as a gun. He hefted the .38. It was cool and solid, perfectly balanced. It felt wonderful. A smooth and tight action, the recoil spring a piece of magic.

Zee Zee put the gun in the case. "I like this gun, T.A. I also like my new name. Thank you."

"Take them both to America, Mr. Lucky," said T.A. "Guard the gold."

ZEE ZEE HAD two escorts in the United States, one Chinese and one American. Major Fan was a military attaché to the Chinese Embassy in Washington, D.C.; his job was to guard Zee Zee from San Francisco Airport to the Bank of Canton at the foot of Chinatown.

"You flew from Washington to drive me, what, ten miles?"

"I come to Frisco every chance I get. Only place you can get *chow fun* and *gai lan.*" Fan drove expertly up the road from the airport, watching for trailing vehicles. *Chow fun* is a delicious flat rice noodle usually prepared in a rich dark gravy with beef and often spiced with black bean sauce; *gai lan* is Chinese broccoli, chewy, tasty and rich in vitamins and fiber, cooked best in oyster sauce.

They exchanged biographies. The attaché was from Sian, where, five years ago, Chiang Kai-shek had been kidnapped by the Young Marshal, son of Manchuria's warlord, the man the Japanese had blown up on his train. The son tried to force Chiang to fight the Japanese—his father's assassins—instead of the Chinese Reds, who were fighting the Japanese invaders. Fan had been there during the kidnapping, and Zee Zee was fascinated by his personal account of the adventure, which had stolen all of China's headlines for two months. In the end, it was Chou En-lai who persuaded the Young Marshal to free Chiang. Chaing had then jailed the Young Marshal and renewed his efforts to kill Chou En-lai and all Reds.

"Been here four years," said the attaché. "I've become a real overseas man. It happens. I married a new wife. Left five children, two sons, in China. Hope their mother's doing okay. Hey, you look so serious. You're not Christian, are you? Good! I say a man is measured by his wives."

Zee Zee's American escort, arranged by the Chinese consulate in San Francisco, was Mrs. Margaret McAtee. She was a lively, head-turning blonde in a tight green dress, married to a Hollywood actor named Ben. He was stocky and slow of speech and lived in L.A. when he had work. She was the tallest woman Zee Zee had ever met, and her voice was bigger than Taitai's. But it was a *nan-jiang* voice, south of the river, husky, sexy and low, like Da-tsien's.

"Well, now, Major Lee, aren't you the handsomest Chinese man I've ever seen!"

Zee Zee concentrated on the question. "I do not know."

"Well, gracious sakes, you are! Now, I'm just gonna have to kiss you, Major, because you're so handsome and you've been fighting those damn hateful Japs. Major, this one comes from every decent red-blooded American gal who wishes our British and Chinese allies goodwill!" She kissed him on the cheek, leaving a red mark that she then wiped away. Major Lee stood as still as a schoolboy while all of this happened.

"I surely hope y'all can take my being so tall. Now, I know I'm supposed to be stiff as starch, but if I can't have a little fun in a steel plant, why the *heck* am I here? Now, just wait till Ben meets you! Some of his best friends in Hollywood are Chinese. Ben, he's not so tall, either, but he's a stand-up gentleman, and as he says, he's as friendly as hell!"

Zee Zee pulled out his notepad and recorded this expression. "*Friendly as hell*. Does this mean very friendly, or very unfriendly?"

She laughed wonderfully. "It means friendly. My, I *love* that uniform! Isn't it just absolutely glorious? I'm gonna have to fight the girls away!"

Zee Zee looked at his uniform with its high collar and smart Sam Brown belt. America was safe, so he wasn't wearing his Smith & Wesson .38 police-special revolver in the outside holster. But he carried key documents and huge wealth belonging to others, so he wore the slim, fully loaded Super .38 Colt in his shoulder holster.

The steel plant was impressive. Later, Zee Zee realized that their working on a Sunday was unusual; they were fulfilling urgent ship and truck requirements for Great Britain under Lend-Lease. World War Two had begun in Europe in the fall of 1939, and Germany had just tried to bomb England into submission, destroying major parts of London.

"A penny for your thoughts, Major," Mrs. McAtee said as she applied lipstick, opening her mouth seductively.

He knew that expression from film. "China needs steel plants."

"Hmm. That's a good idea. Are you ready? I'm your escort all day, Major, and wherever you want to go, Mrs. M. McAtee is taking you."

"I want to return to the Bank of Canton. Verify everything."

"Again? My, you're as thorough-goin' a detail man as Mr. Thomas Dewey! Okay, honey, let's go. Tell me, Major, does that bank of yours ever close?"

"No," he said, studying gray U.S. Navy vessels at Treasure Island. The Chinese worked seven days a week. Didn't everyone? Wasn't it possible for someone in the bank to abscond with the gold certificates and to lie on the books? That was why he made three visits.

It was early afternoon as they returned to the City in light Sunday traffic. Zee Zee's blood raced in America, for everything was startling. The prosperity, the cleanliness, the industry, the unbelievable number of cars, the soaring buildings, the blue skies over the Great Sea, the huge farms of the Midwest, the absence of hordes of beggars and orphans. The perfection of the Studebaker plant in South Bend had broken his heart; nothing in China could compare to it.

It had been wrong of the KMT attaché to leave his family. On the bridge, T.C. saw how it had happened. America could make you forget the world.

America also made him acutely aware of being Chinese. He was surprised by how few Chinese he saw; San Francisco reputedly had a large overseas Chinese community. But even the Bank of Canton's all-Chinese staff had stared at him with an American curiosity.

Everything at the Bank of Canton was in order. T.A. trusted America with his funds more than he trusted Switzerland.

"Where to now, Major?" Mrs. McAtee asked.

"Strange, I have no work. Perhaps I'll go back to my apartment?"

The bank maintained a corporate apartment on California Street, next to family restaurants, cleaners and the clanging cable car.

"Major, if you're out of things to go do, then I'm plainly obligated to show you the City of San Francisco!"

She took his arm and escorted him from the bank; there wasn't an employee who didn't stare. Later, she showed him the grand lobby of the elegant Mark Hopkins Hotel. Suddenly she put a hand on his arm, stopping him. "Something's happened. Now hush so we can listen."

The bell captain and the guests stood transfixed, mouths open, clutching luggage. The lobby was silent but for a radio broadcast.

". . . NBC News, with Station KFU in Honolulu. People in the listening audience, let me repeat what we have heard. The Japanese have attacked the U.S. naval base in Pearl Harbor, Hawaii. There are reports that several of our ships have been hit. Smoke is rising from many points in the harbor. Japanese planes are bombing Hawaii. There is great concern for loss of life. Every report we have received has confirmed this as real. It is not a drill. The Japanese have attacked Pearl Harbor. Let me . . ."

Zee Zee remembered what the Japanese had done to Nanking and Shanghai. He thought of the troops who were chewing up Chinese conscript armies in Hubei. He saw the Japanese marines on the Bund docks, three years ago, before Mary was born, before they had made the money in Hong Kong, just after the first Shanghai million. The Japanese corporal had called him a *baka*, a fool, and Zee Zee had his finger not on the trigger guard of the Tommy gun but on the trigger itself. He had killed his last Japanese soldiers in August, before returning to Hong Kong. The radio report continued. Japan had attacked America. Big, robust, industrial America! He turned to Mrs. McAtee, who was crying.

"We're going to win," he said. "Now we're going to win."

She threw her arms around him and wept. "Oh my God! Oh, my dear sweet God! They attacked us, the dirty, dirty bastards!"

"Hey, leggo a her, you goddamn fucking Jap!" Someone grabbed Zee Zee, and he put a half-elbow blow into the man's throat. The man choked as Zee Zee widened his stance, ready.

"Stop it!" screamed Mrs. McAtee. "This is Major Lee of the Chinese army! He was fighting Japs when you guys were still picking your noses! Don't you *dare* do anything but salute this man and be ashamed of yourselves. You hear me—now salute 'im right now, mister!"

The man was gagging, trying to recover his wind, his short tie bulging over a large gut. Very poorly, eyes popping, he saluted.

Zee Zee, amused, returned the salute.

"Now y'all go about your business, go on now," Mrs. McAtee said.

"Are all American women like you?" asked Zee Zee.

"Oh, heavens no. I'm outlandish. Just like my mama, always standin' up for the underdog, which, in Georgia, took some doin'."

He was thinking. "In the Far East, it's still December sixth. If the Japanese hit Pearl Harbor, they'll hit the Philippines and the British. Singapore, Malaya, Hong Kong." Just like Pan had said. He exhaled. "My family's in Hong Kong. I have to get back before the Japanese get there. I need a phone."

Mrs. McAtee hadn't called Ben, but she led him to the pay phones, dialed the Bank of Canton for him and was told that all circuits were busy. She marched him to the manager's office, where they gave him a line. She and the Hopkins staff listened as he spoke Chinese into the mouthpiece. The impossibility of that language made him seem even more interesting.

"How does he do that?" asked a clerk.

"I don't know, honey, but I think I'm always gonna know this man."

The clerk let her dial Ben next and she cried as they discussed the end of innocence in America. She told Ben she loved him and kissed him through the phone. The clerks were weeping again, so they all reapplied their makeup while Zee Zee, T.C., tried to figure out how to get home.

"Can't fly Pan Am China Clipper aircraft to Hawaii, Midway, Manila and Hong Kong. Only twenty-one hours to Honolulu. Have to go the long way, to the east, through Africa." He would fly to New York to Caracas, Caracas to Casablanca, Casablanca to Cairo, Cairo to Baghdad, Baghdad to New Delhi, New Delhi to Hanoi, Hanoi to Hong Kong. He had to beat the Japanese to Hong Kong and move his family.

He was thinking of how America would advance across the Pacific against Japan and thinking about where he should fight. America was in shock and he was joyous. He wanted to grab a mike and lead cheers for the U.S.A. As surely as Americans made steel, Japan would be whipped. American arms would flow into China, and Americans would march into Tokyo, put the military leaders against a wall and shoot them in the head.

Margaret insisted that they continue their tour of the city. He loved the views from Twin Peaks, Coit Tower and the Cliff House, but he kept staring at the ranks of office buildings and neat homes. He marveled at the Golden Gate Bridge and was amused by the garish artificiality of Chinatown's architecture. He sensed the isolation of its residents.

He had seen Shanghai, Peking, Yangchow, Soochow, Hong Kong, Canton, New Delhi, Lhasa, Shandanmiao, Cairo, Casablanca and South Bend, but he had fallen in love with the waters of San Francisco. The cool sea air soothed him.

At the Presidio, he saluted American officers and received their return recognition. His heart was softened by so many Americans who stopped him and tearfully thanked him for fighting the Japanese, stating that now they were in the war, with him, too. He was left speechless by common Americans who were willing to protect the world from evil.

He came to attention and saluted as the color guard sounded retreat and pulled down the half-masted American flag. On U.S. military installations around the globe, military personnel faced the flag and saluted. Zee Zee never forgot the sounds of weeping as the bugler played retreat and the flag came down. Some of the tears were his own.

He saw how Americans were unified where Chinese were not. But he was lucky and had a new name. He felt at peace in America.

He flew out of the San Francisco airport. The fog had cleared. Margaret wore a red dress, a white scarf and a white hat. Zee Zee wore military black, with a matching cap and a neatly concealed automatic.

"Promise we'll always be friends. I swear, after those stories you told last night, I'm half in love with you and totally in love with your wife!"

"Yes, Mrs. McAtee," he said.

"Can I call you something besides Major? And I'm Margaret. Mrs. McAtee's my mother-in-law."

"Margaret," he said. "I'm T.C. It means Second Luck. A good name." He laughed. "Maybe I don't answer when you say it. It's new even to me."

She whispered, "Well, bless your heart, taking on a new name as a spy, or whatever you're doing. I just know we're going to beat those Japs with you on our side! Now, T.C., is there anything I can do for you?"

"Actually, yes. Can you introduce me to Katharine Hepburn?"

"My God, she's tougher to reach than the queen of Sheba. Hepburn is the biggest movie actress in the world. I offered the world, T.C., but you just asked for the moon."

"It's not important. Thank you."

She saw his disappointment. "Do you promise to come back and visit me so I can really show you the town and introduce you to Ben? He'll just love you and you him. Doggone, are you good people!"

T.C. had a Chinese smile, bright with secrets. "Not so sure. Nice of you to say."

"T.C., you're top drawer. It's so cute how you write down what I say! Yes sir, you're the cat's pajamas, the swingin' best. Any other man, the way I acted so outrageously with you, would be trying to read the labels on my underwear, and you've been a doll. You come back to the U.S.A., now, hear? Now, I can't help myself—I just have to kiss you!"

She did, reading his resistance and just missing his mouth. The normally decisive T. C. Lee didn't push her away, and he wondered why.

He flew over the United States, gazing out the window at an impossibly blessed land. China and America were equal in size—a shade over three million square miles each. But most of China was unarable mountains; most of America was fertile plain. What an ally to have in war! He stopped breathing as they flew over New York City. He wanted to thank the heavens, but that was ridiculous, so he stopped himself.

fifty-four

America Has the Answers

T. C. LEE DISEMBARKED at the Hong Kong airport. He was hopping mad, and he hugged Da-tsien so hard that she squealed.

He had shared the flight with Kuomintang generals and colonels who were war profiteers. When they had realized somewhere over Vietnam that he spoke English, they pressed him to join them.

"We need your English skills! With America in the war, we can make millions and millions! Much better than the old days in Shanghai, when we had to kidnap rich businessmen for ransoms."

These men hadn't been trained in the military—they were Yangtze businessmen who got uniforms to exploit the poor. Chiang had needed the Mafia and big business to defeat the Old Order and the Reds. Now he was paying the freight.

These men were black-marketing military materiel. T.C. had thought the idea merely repugnant until they explained that the highest profit returns came from stealing grain at gunpoint from starving peasants and selling it behind enemy lines to the Japanese army. They sold even their weapons to the Japanese, who then used them to kill the Chinese troops who were following the stupid orders of the black-marketers.

T.C. had suspected a form of this kind of activity in the field but had disbelieved it. Confronted with its reality, he had thrown a fit, screaming, throwing papers and hitting the bulkhead, causing the generals' bodyguards to attack him. This resulted in an ugly brawl. When the guards got tired of being hit, they quit, sitting sullenly in the back. T.C. had resumed his seat, glowering at the men and cursing aloud all the way across the Gulf of Tonkin.

It wasn't even a good fight; he had given into rage instead of adhering to his training. It had been chicken fighting. He felt like biting the airplane. Worse, he was flying to Hong Kong with Chinese traitors to evacuate his family, all of them running from the Japanese. More retreat, more defeat, more bitterness in the mouth and in the gut. Thinking murder while glaring at huffy senior officers on the flight, he was ashamed to be Chinese.

T.C. organized the family for movement without knowing the new objective. Fight Japan? Fight the Reds? Make money with T.A.? Go to America and meet Katharine Hepburn? He had to hurry; the Japanese were coming.

He was taken aback by the passionate reception from his daughters. The girls, far from the *jia* and its weighty conventions, and being raised by an eccentric Christian woman who loved passion, ran to him and threw their arms around him. T.C. worried that his daughters were in some way defective.

Of course, honorable Chinese husbands didn't kiss American blondes, either. Or think about the kiss while flying around the globe.

Da-tsien still called him Zee Zee, which he liked. He'd be Lucky T.C. to the world and Zee Zee, Merciful Longevity, to his wife.

Her plans were unwavering: Make a son. She disliked his anger, which was not propitious for her purposes. She smiled enigmatically when he gave orders about what to pack. She would fill a suitcase and realize she had forgotten something, then empty her luggage and begin again.

Elinor saw this and helped her pack so she'd move forward instead of back. Ying tried to imitate everything Mah-mee did, which proved unproductive. Mary ran around the house; Da-tsien had recently allowed her youngest daughter to interact with other people.

"WHERE IS IT safest to go?" asked T.A.

"India," said T.C. "Big British army presence there, and any military action would require so many Japanese troops that they probably wouldn't invade."

"What about Singapore?" asked T.A., who had no holdings in India.

"The Japanese will attack it. We know not to underestimate them."

"You are sure we cannot stay here in Hong Kong?"

T.C. knew the reports. "The Japanese are massing ground and naval forces. They mean to take this harbor. It's key for them."

"I need to return to Shanghai."

"If you pay the Japanese, you can live there." T.C. shook his head. "But it's living in the mouth of the tiger."

"We must be flexible, T.C. Shanghai will be the base, because my main business remains there. But we have to be prepared to go all the way to Chungking, the new seat of government."

The return voyage to Shanghai was trouble from the beginning.

"I don't feel good about this," said Da-tsien. "See how the wind moves against us? All those Japanese soldiers waiting for us. I don't understand why we couldn't stay in Hong Kong. It was so lovely." She looked wistfully at the foaming wake of the vessel as it headed north along the coast on a cold December day in southern China.

"Lovely, but they're going to take Hong Kong," said Zee Zee.

"You said the British could defend the harbor, with those big cliffs."

"The Japanese won't come by sea. They'll come by land."

"Oh, I don't understand any of it! I'd rather move Baba here, where the Japanese aren't, than take our girls to Shanghai—where they are!"

"We just have to be very sharp, very clever." He looked at her, and his heart softened. She was lovely, her hair awry, her eyes large and knowing. All his life he had tried to subdue himself; while she wore all her emotions, which dramatically outnumbered his, on her supple face. Even after four children, she was a pampered princess. He sent the girls to their cabin with their amah and Ah Tsui.

"Da-tsien, can I talk to you alone?" he asked. "Really talk to you?"

She turned to face him, smiling with a touch of wonder and intrigue. "Honey, that's what I live for. What do you mean?"

"I want to train you. For Shanghai. Please, just say *shr*, okay."

"*Shr*." She smiled, but he was deadly serious.

"Da-zee, walk there." He pointed at the wall lined with orange life preservers.

"You move indecisively, leisurely, right? Slowly? I want you to move fast."

"Why, Zee Zee? It's not ladylike, and it makes my feet look big."

He looked in her eyes, which grew wide under his scrutiny. "Because of the Japanese, and *jun-fa* soldiers, and *tu-fei* bandits. Because of deserters and robbers. Because of the things they do to women. Think of Grace's fear of having her guts pulled out and being strangled by her intestines."

Horrified, she covered her mouth. "Oh, Zee Zee! Don't speak of it!"

"Not talking about it won't make it go away. Forget the old superstitions! This isn't *ji hui*. This is *surviving*! It's not thinking, it's *doing*!"

"You see all these sad, bad things coming, don't you?"

"It's going to be very bad. You must *be* fast. *Walk* fast. Have urgency. When you walk fast, you think fast. You can see two, three, even four moves ahead. In war, surprise is everything. *Everything*. If you're fast, you surprise *them*."

"Like you surprise others?"

"Yes." He shooed away people who had gathered to hear. They took affront. *How dare he close us out of an interesting talk?*

Da-tsien smiled at them to smooth their feelings.

"Walk again," he said. "Faster. No, not halfhearted. Full. Da-zee, walk like Hepburn! She takes big steps, like a man!" She did. She wore pants and had a long *da-jiao* stride.

Da-tsien laughed. "Oh, my. Is that why I love her so much?"

He laughed, too. "Probably." He closed his mind to a series of rampant images of the actress in an airplane. "Do it again."

In her mind's eye, Da-tsien saw Katharine Hepburn on-screen, and she lifted her head. Throwing her hair, she strode across the deck, excusing herself after bumping into people as they stared. She rubbed her arms. "I hit my elbow."

He grabbed her arms. "But you moved! You were fantastic!"

"Was I, Zee Zee? Was I really?" She was delirious with his praise.

"Yes! Do it again!"

He made her walk until she was exhausted. He rubbed her scalp and feet to revive her. That afternoon he repeated the drill. When the weather cleared, she even practiced on deck, despite earlier fears of being swept overboard.

In the morning she was her old self—slow. Had she been a peasant learning to establish a defensive position, he would have been patient. But she was a woman, so he went off by himself and smoked.

Later, composed, he taught her to play walnuts—a game of snatching a nut from the table. "Now!" she'd cry, and their hands would race. She was very bad at the game, as if her brain prohibited fast action. Each time he let her win, he rewarded her with a head massage. When he won, she had to look about the room, close her eyes and report what she had seen.

"Be observant. You see emotion and friends, but never danger. Must see danger—a man who stares at you then looks away. Men who bump into you to take your money. Men who look at the girls with hunger. No, don't cry. Not helpful to cry. Here, here, it's okay."

"It's *not* okay! All of what you say is hateful and wrong and unchristian, and just saying it can make it happen! *Ji hui!*"

"Crap on Christians and your mixed-up religion! This is war!"

When they docked in Japanese-occupied Shanghai, Zee Zee forced himself to ignore the enemy sentries who liked to fondle women, torment men and kill children. T.A. put the Lee family into an apartment on Moulming Road. It was small but attractive. He paid the rent; the Lees' contribution was to take in the zealous Miss Wu, who felt she had more ministry opportunities in the Lee apartment than in the Soong mansion.

Miss Wu was utterly devoted to Da-tsien and her daughters while praying fervently for Zee Zee, T.C., and his secular ways. She was ecstatic about the coming of Christmas and enlisted Elinor and Ying in decorating the apartment for baby Jesus' birthday. T.C. wearily endured their work.

T.A. sat with T.C. in his great study.

"What does China need most from America?" asked T.A.

"Airplanes," said T.C. "Lots of airplanes. Bombers to hit Tokyo."

T.A. impatiently shook his head. "Think larger. We need money. Millions and millions of American dollars. To stabilize our economy. To make the *yuan* worth something, to build our industry." It had devalued by approximately 4,000 percent. "To buy equipment for the army, including airplanes and bombers, but mostly artillery and tanks."

"I don't agree," said T.C. "But we certainly need money, too."

"T.C., I am being sent to America by Chungking. To ask for money. To acquire Lend-Lease funds. Washington is giving a *billion* dollars to the British to fight Hitler; they may give us *fifty million* to fight Tojo. Peanuts!

"I do not enjoy public speaking. Talking privately with Henry Hopkins, Sumner Welles or President Roosevelt, I can do this ably. But toasts are required." He gulped. "Speeches are required. Come to America with me, T.C. Give the speeches. Make the toasts."

"To get money from them."

"Actually, no. We are supposed to fail."

"You're kidding."

"Family politics. My brothers, T.V. and T.L., jockey for position. Roosevelt will give money only to Chiang or an emissary. I am not one. I have a new organization, China Defense Mission—not Lend-Lease. I go and ask so they can say no. Later, they will say yes to my brothers."

"That's a pretty lousy assignment," said T.C.

"Yes, and I need your help so it will succeed."

"By failing." T.C. shook his head. He hated missions that didn't succeed, much less those destined to fail.

"I cannot go to America without you. You are the adventurer. I would feel unsafe without you. What would induce you to say yes?"

T.A. had taught him how to bargain.

"I want to go to an American military school."

"Like West Point?"

"No, a field school, for weeks, not years. I researched them when I was in Indiana. The best is Fort Benning, their infantry school."

"That can be arranged."

"I also want to meet Katharine Hepburn."

"Who is Katharine Hepburn?"

"A movie actress."

"Goodness. Why?"

"She's the most beautiful woman in the world."

T.A. crossed his legs. "Next to Da-tsien, yes? I know nothing about actresses. Why be curious about a person who is below society?"

"In America, actors are above professors. You know this."

T.A. raised his hand. "Yet the difference is, I would not say it."

"Arrange it, and I'll go to America with you."

"This is not virtuous, you bargaining with me."

"I'm not virtuous. I've been killing the wrong men."

"What do you mean?"

"I've been killing Reds and Japanese. I should be shooting our own generals."

"No!" he hissed. "Do not say this, even to me! It is wrong because it is dangerous. KMT Blue Robes have ears. I am being watched, so *you* are being watched. Guard your words to protect your family, if not me."

"Dammit, T.A., I'm not a tea-sipping courier! We're buying new planes. I could transition to the new fighters. You could order me to go to America again. But you know that asking me to do this shit detail in Washington isn't fair. It's not what I'm good at. You keep using me for the wrong jobs. I'm a guard dog, not a lap dog!

"Oh yeah—I also want you to find me a guard dog to help protect Da-tsien and the girls here in Shanghai."

"You are more likely to know the people with such dogs."

"But your money allows you to acquire all things."

T.A. smiled. "Almost. T.C., I have another purpose in America."

"Holy gods, T.A., are you going to marry?"

He nodded. "It has been arranged. You met her."

"Jih-iung," said T.C., remembering the beautiful woman T.A. had introduced him to not long ago.

T.A. smiled happily, which lifted T.C.'s spirits. "Have you ever seen a more exquisite person, other than your own Da-tsien?"

"I wish you great and double happiness and many sons! Our wives are beautiful." For a moment, T.C. saw an American actress who, in his imagination, had flown with him above the blood-red skies of Hunan.

"T.C."

"Yes, T.A."

"How does one use a bathroom in a plane? Does it have a restroom?"

"Military planes have a piss tube and a can. The airplanes that take us to America are palaces. Bathrooms and even beds. Which is good, because it's going to take us a week."

T.A. sucked in his breath. "You know I do not like travel."

"You'll like America. America has about twenty restrooms for every person, and blond women who are not *yeh ji* wild-peasant prostitutes, who kiss your face in public because you're fighting the Japanese and they think you're cute. They have roads and factories and smokestacks to make you weep. I tell you, T.A., America has the answers. America makes China look like a sick old man."

"Hm. This reminds me. What to give my betrothed? She's Christian, and Christmas is coming."

"What sorts of things does she like?"

T.A. shrugged. "I do not know. Amah asked her amah. No answers."

"I would give food," said T.C.

"America has more food than the rest of the world combined. That would be like sending coals to Newcastle."

T.C. pulled out his notepad and recorded the expression.

"Newcastle mines coal," said T.A.

T.C. snapped his fingers. "Gold and diamonds!"

"I already did that."

"A poem. Write it yourself."

S. Y. Shen appeared. "Aha, Merry Christmas." He smiled. "And, of course, Happy New Year. I'm sorry to tell you that Hong Kong just fell to the Japanese."

fifty-five

Angel

TZE-JIH PAN HADN'T run this hard since fleeing Metro cops as a boy. His lack of conditioning produced side stitches. Behind lagged thin Fen and round Hwa, opium smokers. To them, running was like suicide. Old Barrel Man Yao was nowhere to be seen. They ran because driving during military curfew would draw the fire of Japanese motorized patrols.

Lady Du had not foreseen this event. She had knocked on Pan's Hongkew apartment door to breathlessly tell him that the Japanese had just arrested Angel San-t'ien, the *wünu* dance-hall girl whose face all men wanted on their pillows.

"How many Japanese? Officers or soldiers?" asked Pan, throwing on his clothes and rousting his bodyguards while his wife struggled to awaken. Their English clock said it was three in the morning.

"One very fat man," said Lady Du, pointing towards the Japanese garrison. "Oh, Pan, I was so scared! I thought we were dead, but the soldier just gagged Angel and took her."

"Pooh, she's just a dancer," tried his wife, to no avail. Pan cursed as he stuck a Colt .45 in his waistband and began running.

It was early, and the streets were wet, narrow and quiet. Thin dawn-shift laborers shuffled dumbly to twelve-hour factory stints under sadistic Japanese overseers.

The Japanese garrison was about ten blocks away, and now Pan walked, winded, almost stumbling. He heard a scuffle and a woman's voice that could have been Angel's. He ran and turned in to a dark, slimy alley. Under the faint illumination of a distant streetlight, Pan saw a fat Japanese soldier on his knees, shaking his head. Angel, wearing a short set of silk pajamas, was trying to crawl away.

The soldier held a pistol. Pan shot him, the roar of the gun echoing as the man collapsed. Dogs barked and rats scurried. Pan pointed the muzzle at the soldier's head, fanned his left hand next to the barrel and squeezed the trigger just as Zee Zee had taught him. The big automatic jumped and roared. Pan wiped his wet left palm on the soldier's pants leg. He looked around—he should have brought a smaller-caliber pistol. A curious fool opened a window. Pan safetied the gun and slipped it in his waistband. He lifted Angel, who moaned; her face was bruised. He jumped as machine guns racketed on Tsepoo, and he piled Angel into a doorway, trying to merge with the woodwork. A car engine started, and lights shot down the street. Two cars approached from opposite ends. Pan was illuminated.

"Do not move." Mandarin with a Japanese accent.

Better to die in a gunfight. Better for Angel. He moved for his gun, but something hit his arm, and his gun clattered uselessly on the street.

A Japanese officer pushed him on the shoulder with a swagger stick as one of the soldiers frisked him.

"You executed one of our officers in front of us. Guerrilla action against the Japanese Kwantung army leads first to painful death and then very painful deaths for all in your *bao-jia* collective-responsibility group—wife, parents, children, grandparents, uncles, aunts, cousins, coworkers." He looked at Angel. "Allow us to offer you tea."

Pan and Angel were seated in a military patrol vehicle. As the car backed out, Pan saw bodies lying red in Tsepoo Road. Hwa and Fen.

Inside the garrison, once a Manchu Bannerman barracks, Pan was offered a chair in the officers' dining room. No food. No Angel.

"You are a distinguished man, no? Pan Tze-jih, also known as C.C. Pan and Pooh Pan, a college graduate and an underworld figure, you can cooperate. Or watch us rape your wife and girlfriend until they beg for death, but they will be raped until they *are* dead. Want a cigarette?"

Pan took the smoke. He was having trouble using his right arm.

"Then we rape and cut up your relatives. Shoulder, hamstring and Achilles heel so they can't walk, crawl, lift or eat. They will die, of course. We'll take a month to kill you. We will slice off parts of your body and make you eat them. Does your arm hurt?"

Pan looked at his arm, and there was a whirring sound as the officer drew his sword and slashed. Pan's arm bore a short cut that went to the bone. The medic quickly bound the wound. The pain was unbelievable.

Pan remembered Lady Du's prediction that he would die hard. He sipped the tea with his left hand, hoping it was poisoned.

"The sword is a wonderful tool. In Nanking—well, I bore you. Your wife, Tai Yueh, is a lovely lady. She deserves a car, a driver, safety, money, fur coats, no? Your little *Chingbang* element of thieves and smugglers, they need new clothes, fine offices, better pay, no?"

Pan felt a stirring of hope.

"Pan, I can kill you or appoint you the police chief of Shanghai. Want to be the top cop and give me the traitors, the ones who oppose the Japanese empire . . . or eat your wife's ears?"

The door opened. Angel trembled as if she were cold.

"Here is your friend, all cleaned up. A beautiful girl, huh? Imagine her skin being used as a raincoat for my driver! Your wife, I hear, is also beautiful, with a sense of humor. What would make her laugh, eh? Want to laugh, Pan-*san*, or cry bitter tears? Your choice."

fifty-six

Japanese Shanghai

Da-tsien was trying to mend donated clothing at the Presbyterian mission, when Angel San-t'ien arrived wearing a sleek Vichy Parisian outfit with a white hat and high pumps.

Da-stien was pinpricked but cheerful. She had done good things for sad people. She saw the fancy lady and hoped for a hefty donation to God and His deeds. The public executions of patriots had brought more visitors to Shanghai's churches.

"I'm a friend of Pan's," said the lady. "My name is San-t'ien. I went to the movies with Zee Zee when he was single. No, don't frown, he was good. Oh, have you seen *Gone With the Wind*? I got to see it! Aren't I lucky?"

Gone With the Wind was a sensation in Shanghai, Atlanta and Los Angeles. It had been released in Asia before Pearl Harbor. "Is it as wonderful as all the papers say?"

"Clark Gable has big ears and a huge nose, but when he smiles you love him!"

"Was Vivian Leigh good? You know, Katharine Hepburn was supposed to get the lead role—I can't imagine why they didn't pick her!"

"Aiyaa, Vivian's great! The perfect lady. Very self-centered. But Pooh wanted me to tell you the Japanese are going to come for your father."

"Hurry, Baba. Go downstairs. Zee Zee will take you to our place."

"Where did you learn to rush like this? I don't know this behavior."

"It's war, Baba. The Japanese are coming. You must go!" She opened drawers, closed them, opened a suitcase, sat on the bed and wept.

T.C. appeared and emptied the underwear and socks drawer into the suitcase, threw in some outfits, walking shoes and toiletries. He latched the case, gathered his wife and father-in-law and walked them down the stairs.

"It seems wrong to leave," said Baba.

"Being questioned by the Kampetei is not pleasant." said T.C.

"I can't leave," said Baba. "What about the majordomo? Horseman Yip? Where's Deaf Man Fu? Chef Chu? Little Auntie Gao and Cousin Miao-miao? My son?"

"They're all safe, Baba," said Da-tsien. "Please get in the car!"

Baba entered the taxi, and Da-tsien and T.C. got in beside him. T.C. expected to see a Kampetei sedan as they drove north, but all was normal.

Japanese military dragnets had swept up hundreds of KMT officers—like T.C.—from their homes. The captives were taken to Hongkew and executed. T.C.'s presence endangered his family, so he was relieved when T.A. said they were going to Washington. T.C. was afraid of Da-tsien's anger, so he told her nothing.

T.C. taught his nephew Lon-lon to care for the German shepherd Soong had purchased. Da-tsien didn't like the dog, which ate as much as a person. Elinor and Ying helped walk the dog, running as the shepherd pulled them where it wished to go, growling at anything it considered a threat.

Elinor wanted to name him, but T.C. insisted on calling it *ch'uan*. Dog. Before he left, he gave Da-tsien all his money, which was more than enough to live on for two months.

"You're going back to America," she said.

"Don't cry," he said.

"I don't have a son! I'm not even pregnant. You can't go! Not now!"

"Must. It's how I earn a living."

"*Mai gi sho syau Soong!*" she said. Soong plays you like a walnut.

He cursed. "That walnut pays our rent and fills rice bowls."

"Oh, Zee Zee, I'm so sick of being *yi kao*! Isn't there another way?"

"Life is being *yi kao*. My grandfather had money, and *he* was *yi kao*. No one's free from being dependent."

"I wouldn't mind being *yi kao* like your grandfather!"

"If you have trouble, see Soong." A rueful smile. "Go to the Walnut Palace. The one thing they have is money. See S. Y. Shen, first. If he's not available, ask for a man named Poon. Your last resort is Pan. Send Amah to see his wife and your friend Tai Yueh."

"I'll send Ying," she said.

"No, don't send children. He's too unpredictable."

"You talk as if you're not coming back."

"I just want you to be safe."

"Then stay with us," she said, her eyes large and wet.

He shook his head. "Must go. *Yi kao*."

"Then don't sleep tonight, all night, no sleep, please!"

She awoke in the morning in an empty bed. She shifted over to his side, absorbing his residual *yang* energy, and remained in bed all day, letting Elinor serve her.

She and Zee Zee had practiced the spring rites to produce a son, following ancient prescriptions of waiting and holding and resuming. She knew a son would result. She disciplined herself from crying so the baby boy inside her would know no sorrow.

In Chinese homes, social interaction is the reward for work, and dinner is the highlight of the day. In the safety of family, each person can smack lips, inhale rich aromas, savor the good tastes and celebrate the survival of yet another day. It is time to eat, talk and drop the strict social restrains of society. In the Lee apartment on Moulming, meals had been shrunk by the cessation of trade on the Yangtze River.

P'o-p'o the paternal mother-in-law, was the senior elder. Gee was the ranking male. Ying-oh was the second ranking female, and their children—including the clan's only son, Lon-lon—outranked their three girl cousins. The last ranking male was a bright and handsome cousin named Li Hau, who occasionally visited for meals.

The third ranking female was Da-tsien. The fourth was Miss Wong; fifth was Miss Wu. At the bottom of this small ladder were Skinny Wu, Tall Amah and Ah Tsui. The other amahs and wet nurses had been shed long ago in sequential economizing moves.

"Why does Miss Wu stay with us?" asked Tall Amah. "When she's part of the Soongs, and they have money and we don't."

"She wants to convert us," said Da-tsien.

"I thought we were already Christian," said Elinor, expressing Ying's opinion, which couldn't be safely aired in front of her mother.

"We are, Ah-wu. Just not as Christian as she'd like."

Two places were set for absent people. One was for Baba, which she demanded. The other was for her husband, which P'o-p'o required.

Baba had evaded the Japanese and returned to the Burkill house, where he and Deaf Man Fu lived. The House of Lee had sold the property at a loss to a Japanese land consortium. The two old men hadn't yet been evicted, but they ate best when Da-tsien brought food that was increasingly precious to her in-laws.

No one knew Zee Zee's whereabouts. Da-tsien said he was in America. There were rumors that he was in Chungking.

"We don't have to save a place for Baba," said Elinor, age thirteen. "He's not coming back."

"Aiyaa, Ah-wa!" cried her mah-mee. "*Ji hui*, don't say that!"

"I agree with Ah-wa," said Ying, who was ten.

"You be quiet!" cried Da-tsien. She ran to the bathroom and returned with a handful of toilet paper, which she stuffed into Ying's mouth to absorb her bad words.

"You—you should do that to me," said Elinor. "I—I said it." She hurried so fast to assuage Mah-mee's anger that she had developed a stutter.

"Hush! Ying, you stop bad words before they leave your mouth."

Ying wept, panicked by her inability to breathe and red-faced that her *jia* was witnessing her humiliation.

"She's a good girl," said Ying-oh. "She only repeats what her older sister says."

"I didn't like what Elinor said. Ying should have seen that Elinor was already hurting my feelings." Da-tsien hated her anger that stormed on her hapless middle daughter. It was reminiscent of Zee Zee's rages. Her anger had cowed Ying into silence, it was making Elinor anxious, and Mary was becoming detached, but Da-tsien couldn't change her ways.

"Come, *Sun nu*, Granddaughter," said P'o-p'o. Ying looked for approval from her mah-mee, who reluctantly nodded. Ying went to Madame Lee, who removed the tissues from her mouth, patted her gently and gestured for the girl to return to her seat.

P'o-p'o wished she could say something to Gee. He smoked while others ate and ate when the table was empty. He still abused his wife and dragged Lon-lon to dance halls, pretending the young man was his pal instead of his son.

"Don't tell the girls you're my son, okay?" he asked.

"I agree," said Lon-lon.

At least Gee had graduated from college, even though it took him eight years. He finished at the age of twenty-seven; his three children attended his graduation. Ying-oh silently and dutifully offered him food as he actively ignored her and puffed cigarette after cigarette.

He had a job that paid, but the money seemed to disappear before it could be placed in the grocery-funds bowl. Soon Da-tsien could afford to bring only potatoes and gruel to her father and his slave.

Da-tsien went to visit the Soongs in the French Concession. Da-tsien hadn't been to the Soong mansion since Chiang Kai-shek's wedding to Mei-ling Soong fifteen years earlier. The house of twenty servants was strangely quiet. She rang the bell.

S. Y Shen opened the door, shocking her. Normally impeccable, he was unshaven and unbathed. He didn't recognize her.

"S.Y., it's me, Da-tsien."

"Oh, oh, of course, come in, a thousand pardons."

The mansion was empty; his bed was the living room sofa.

S.Y. threw water in his face and apologized for his condition. "Pan—you remember him, yes, Pooh Pan, Pan Tze-jih—warned me that the Soongs had better go. Told me to stay. I told the Soongs. They went to Chungking, I can tell you that. I stayed, terrified to go, afraid to stay." He sat, trembling. He took off his glasses and rubbed his face.

"They took my wife. They took her off the train at North Station, and I can't find her. The Japanese government claims to not have her. I visited Pan, now called Pan-da, Big Pan. Very important man now.

"I begged for her. He said he didn't have her. I promised anything! Aiy, I'm so stupid! I always thought she'd take care of me." He began to cry. "I didn't take care of her. They didn't do it on purpose. Japanese are violent by whim, by mood. Most dangerous, so unpredictable. Bank staff at North Station said that the Kampetei took ten or fifteen people off that train. She was one of them.

"I offered him all. He said he was sorry but there was nothing he could do. The chief of police, helpless. Funny, huh? This is what it means to be a Shanghainese."

"S.Y., I am so sorry. What can we do to help you?"

"Find my wife. Save her from pain. She's not a strong person."

"I'll do what I can." She was a woman of faith.

"Thank you."

Da-tsien took a breath. "We need to contact the Soongs, to borrow money. What do you suggest we do?"

"Money? You need money? Is that all?" He laughed. "Da-tsien, we're bankers!" He gave her a wad of bills. "Here, take it all!" They were lower-denomination bills, worth little.

"We thank you," she said. "Do you have an address for them?"

"No, no address. They couldn't tell me, or the Kampetei would bleed it from me."

"Come home with me, S.Y. Let us feed you and care for you."

He blinked. "Ah. Can I do that? Can she find me at your place? Here, I'll leave a note!"

He came home with her and sat at the table and ate ravenously, the Lees politely letting him eat their food while Da-tsien quietly returned his money to his pockets. Later, S.Y. waved for a pedicab to return him to the empty Soong home.

"Did I ever tell you, Da-tsien, that my grandfather and Zee Zee's grandfather were peers? Yes, they were prisoners of the Taipings in Nanking, both accountants who helped recover the salt-tax industry to rebuild the Empire. Well, good luck. If you need more money, please feel free to contact me, okay? And thank you for looking for my wife."

In the morning, Da-tsien opened her jewelry box. She fixed her long, beautiful hair as Elinor touched up her mah-mee's makeup and the two cautiously left to barter silver for vegetables.

"I can do it next time by myself," said Elinor. "Let me, Mah-mee." In negotiations, Mah-mee often forgot who had the greatest need.

In the afternoon, Da-tsien went to the Japanese occupational government buildings across the Garden Bridge. After Pearl Harbor, the Japanese had taken the best buildings and residences from the Europeans and the Americans, displacing them into the hotels and streets. The Bund was now a Tokyo skyline. She used her charismatic ways to successfully interrogate the Japanese clerk. She could make rocks speak. He found Mrs. Shen's name; she had been executed in Hongkew.

Conveying news about death in a land as troubled as China was tempered by the welcome comforts of dishonesty.

"The Japanese sent her to Tokyo to be a teacher," Da-tsien told S.Y. "At least she's alive. But don't expect to see her until the war is over."

He thanked her and kissed her hands, crying with relief.

fifty-seven

Pan-da

D A-TSIEN WAS ALWAYS tired. She would press the back of her hand to her forehead and collapse on the bed, staying there for hours. She let Elinor brush her hair and open the impossible compact to dab rouge on her cheeks.

Elinor asked Ying-oh for help with the next batch of jewelry. Auntie was good with numbers and had years of experience black-marketing for groceries. Elinor insisted on accompanying her because Auntie had bound feet and was a good robbery and harassment target. Elinor always planned two moves ahead and had a rock for the common defense.

She watched Auntie change earrings into gold into American dollars into Mexican pesos into meat. She traded meat for large rations of produce. Earrings had purchased food for thirteen souls for a week.

On one foray, Auntie left her in a pawnshop with one of Da-tsien's necklaces. The pawnshop man gave a figure and returned the necklace. Elinor made sure it was the same one, thanked the man with a smile and stepped outside. She didn't see Auntie, so she walked about, looking. Inside a teashop sat a man and a woman, holding hands and speaking with great warmth and passion. It was Auntie and her cousin Li Hau.

By June 1942, Da-tsien had donated most of her jewelry except her Christian wedding ring, a gold cross given to her by Miss Roberts and her King James Bible, which she considered indispensable to life. She tried to be gay about losing her baubles, including heirlooms that Taitai had reluctantly given her.

There were new rumors that the Americans had destroyed the entire Japanese fleet at a place called Midway. But Da-tsien looked out the window to see that Japan still ruled, so the rumors were false.

Tsao the Moulming property landlord lived above the Lees. He approached Da-tsien on her slow walk to mission work, where she fed the poor and got food for her clan. Elinor had skipped school to help her.

"Lee Taitai, *shia an*, Summer Peace to you. Hot day! Bad news. Soongs aren't paying anymore. You owe rent. You know how much, right?"

"Oh, I'm not sure. Five thousand?"

He looked at her carefully to see if she was kidding.

"Two hundred a month," said Elinor.

"The hell it is! Who the hell are you, kid?" he snapped.

"I am the unworthy daughter of Lee Taitai and Major Lee, who always carries a gun and has a big temper. Rent is two hundred."

"Yes, two hundred," said Da-tsien. "I remember."

"You and I can discuss rent, madam, without your daughter."

"Speak to my husband, Tsao," she said. "He'd enjoy talking to you."

"I've never seen a husband, with a uniform or a gun or a temper."

Later, Elinor said, "It's bad enough that Baba sends no money. He's why we're in trouble. P'o-p'o picking on you, Ying-oh being depressed, out of money, out of food, having to scrounge, worrying about Mr. Tsao—it's because Baba doesn't send letters or money or give any help."

Da-tsien wept. Elinor patted her mother's back. Soon Ying was crying. Ah Tsui joined in, and then Chin and Lu-Lu.

It was then that Zee Zee walked in the door.

"Hey, hey, I'm home!" He was round and full of luck and wore a Western suit with a fedora. "Why's everyone crying?"

"Remember, Mah-mee, it's all his fault," whispered Elinor.

Da-tsien flew into her husband's arms, kissing and touching him, rubbing his back to make sure it was truly him and that he was alive and the Japanese or Soongs or Americans hadn't consumed him.

Elinor watched Ying and Mary run to their father, followed by Madame Lee and Chin and Lu-lu. She thought: *Men are pretty scary people.*

With his Soong paychecks, Zee Zee paid off the bills, bought a larder full of food and took everyone out to a lavish banquet.

He was disappointed to learn that Da-tsien wasn't pregnant. He didn't want a son, but he was tired of his wife hounding him for one.

Elinor told her father about Mr. Tsao.

"Tsao, I'm Major Lee, Kuomintang. If you approach my wife or my family again, or if you raise rent, you will die."

"Yes, yes, a minor misunderstand—"

"Shut lips! Understand me? Nod. Good. Remember this, and live."

Zee Zee visited several banks. He slept with his wife. He ran with the dog and played with his daughters. He worried about Elinor, who seemed to resent him. He worried about Ying, who was obviously being mistreated. He frowned at Mary, who kept hugging and kissing him.

He said he'd leave lots of cash when Da-tsien told him that Pooh Pan was chief of police under the Japanese occupational government.

Zee Zee cursed. "Unbelievable. You hear about Wang Ching-wei, Sun Yat-sen's deputy? We thought he'd be president after Sun died? He's head of the Japanese puppet government—in Nanking, where the Japanese slaughtered. Maybe it's a different Pan."

She was going to ask if it was safe to see Pan, then meant to ask him to send money regularly. She forgot when he turned out the light.

He was gone in the morning. She did not know where.

"I don't think he's coming back," said Elinor.

By Christmas 1942, Da-tsien believed her daughter.

"You have to see Pan-da," she said.

"I can't, Mah-mee. He's a traitor. He kills the best of us."

"I can't hear that kind of talk! I can't! Mary's hungry and you're too thin. Ah-wu, please, you're my Firstborn. You have to go!"

"Why can't Uncle Gee go? He's a man, and he knew Pan when he and Baba rode motorcycles together. You're friends with Mrs. Pan!"

"I can't go. I'm not strong enough. You're strong. You go."

"Mah-mee, I can't! Pan-da executed my friends from St. Mary's!"

"Then I'll die with you. We need food. Ask him for money."

"How much?"

"A thousand? A million? I don't know."

Elinor conferred with Auntie Ying-oh. The house absolutely needed $800 Shanghai. They could use twelve hundred.

Instead of going to the main police station of the Japanese government, Elinor found the Pan residence. She would approach Pan Taitai, not Pan-da.

A Japanese sentry stopped her.

"I am Lee Ah-wu, daughter of Lee Da-tsien. Da-tsien and Mrs. Pan were childhood friends. I have a message for her."

"You give me message," demanded the sentry.

"It's verbal and only for Pan Taitai." Elinor closed her eyes when she thought the man was going to kill her for being a Chinese patriot.

Tai Yueh was in the bathroom when Elinor was ushered upstairs.

"Have you eaten?" she called. "Sorry I'm indisposed. What does your sweet mother want? It's so wonderful you're here! With everything going on, we don't get many visitors. Are you well, child?"

Elinor introduced herself and explained that they needed a loan.

"Open my purse, dear. Take all you want. Take it all! We have lots, but hardly any friends! At least not until they need something."

There was about six thousand dollars. Elinor counted out twelve hundred. She thanked Pan Taitai and left. She closed her eyes and breathed in scents of sizzling beef, wok-stirred onions and prawns, wild ginger and soy sauce, and an array of terrific scents she couldn't identify. To deepen the aromas, she stood on her toes. The butler opened the door, and she thanked him and left. She had smelled enough.

Ignoring the sentry, she walked smartly by. In a courtyard of sycamores and oaks, and out of sight of the Japanese soldier, Elinor bent over and wept.

fifty-eight

Spencer Tracy

THE FIRST MEETING with Katharine Hepburn did not proceed according to plan. T.C. had purchased a new suit and had asked nearly everyone, "How do I look?" It was Christmas 1941, and the present of the year was time alone with Miss Hepburn. Miss Hepburn, however, did not appear.

T.C. left the MGM lot with an enormous sense of disappointment. T.A. and his bride, Jih-iung, were waiting for him at curbside.

"What did you think of her?" asked Jih-iung.

"She didn't show," said T.C. "I think nothing of her."

"I am sorry," said T.A. "We now go to *another* studio."

The Warner Bros. lot was immense. The young publicist moved VIPs faster because of the war; the country needed patriotic movies. The Soongs met with studio executives, and T.C. got the tour.

On an enormous sound stage full of American bunting, T.C. met Cantonese cinematographer James Wong Howe, who would later win two Oscars. Then he met James Cagney, who was making *Yankee Doodle Dandy*, which would earn him an Oscar. On another stage, T.C. met Lana Turner, whom he thought more beautiful in person than in film. In a hallway, the publicist stopped Bob Hope to introduce T.C.

"Merry Christmas, Major," said Mr. Hope. "I can't tell you how much I admire pilots. I like flying except that part about throwing up."

T.C. met Anne Sheridan and posed for pictures with her. On the way out, he was introduced to an unknown actor named Danny Kaye, a brilliant man who struck T.C. as being fascinated by everything.

The Soongs caught up with T.C. on the set of *Tortilla Flat*. Victor Fleming, of *Gone With the Wind*, was directing. Tall and patrician, he worried about this movie, which would fail critically and financially. It starred Spencer Tracy, whom Fleming had cast in *Jekyll and Hyde*. T.C. was impressed by Tracy, whom he had liked in *Captains Courageous* and an obscure 1933 film called *Shanghai Madness*.

Everything about Tracy was a surprise. The star was so naturally friendly and magnetic that T.C. snapped out of his dismay over not meeting Hepburn. Tracy's head was enormous and boulderlike. His rugged facial features made him appear even tougher in person, less handsome. Nor was he as tall.

"I'm playing a pilot in Fleming's next film," said Tracy. "It's *A Guy Named Joe*. The blurb on you says you're a fighter pilot. That true?"

T.C. waved his hand at an angle—half yes, half no. "I flew a scout plane that was used as a fighter-bomber." He wrote down, *Blurb?*

Perhaps to be polite, Spencer Tracy asked T.C. about how to play a pilot. What does a pilot worry about? The toughest thing about combat flying? Any advice? The actor was a great listener.

T.C. smiled. "Flying isn't tough. Crashing is tough."

Tracy laughed warmly.

John Garfield, who would make war movies, *The Postman Always Rings Twice* and *Gentleman's Agreement*, appeared as required. He sat in a director's chair and focused on Mrs. Soong. T.C. found him relaxed and clever.

"You have your uniform here, Major?" asked the publicist.

"No," said T.C. It was in the hotel.

The publicist, frustrated that he had a Chinese officer in a civilian suit, nonetheless posed the group to show Hollywood supporting the war effort.

When asked to smile, T.A. assumed a face of stone and did not pretend to be involved with actors; T.C., however, smiled, on request, and kept giving Spencer Tracy tips on flying.

The Soongs returned to San Francisco. Jih-iung loved Hollywood and the attention of the movie community, but T.A. was depressed. He thought of his homes in Hong Kong and Shanghai—both, like so much of Asia, now under Japanese rule.

T.A. was grateful to T.C. for moving him from Hong Kong. But he couldn't understand how his friend could be so happy to be with foreign actors while evil dominated the Chinese people.

During the flight from Los Angeles to Atlanta, T.C. felt the letdown that follows emotional highs. His disappointment at not meeting Katharine Hepburn persisted for the two days that it took to reach Fort Benning, Georgia.

He had expected the fall of Hong Kong. The British had been arrogant for too long. The Americans had also been cocky but were kinder and more humorous.

The U.S. Army had orders from the War Department, courtesy of the China Defense Mission, to admit Major T. C. Lee to the Infantry School Company Officer's Course, a program designed for twenty-two-year-old American males who had undergone basic military training in U.S. military doctrine and weapons. Following that, he could attend the relatively new Parachute School, if he wished.

Fort Benning had never encountered a Chinese soldier who had been trained by the German army and had the one thing all others lacked—combat experience against the Japanese. He was assigned to Company T, Basic 206, First Training Regiment (Officers). It was already a curious unit. Because of Pearl Harbor, new training companies were being formed at breakneck speed. Company T included black American officers commissioned in Negro college ROTC programs, a radical move in a segregated army, a segregated U.S. and a segregated American South.

T.C. presumed that this was how America worked. Black and white officers treated him as a hero, a curiosity and a source of anxiety. The Infantry and Parachute schools worried that he would fail or be injured or be killed, any one of which would produce a great deal of paperwork.

T.C. had been inspired by Hollywood but was enchanted by Fort Benning.

He enjoyed the processes that intimidated and alienated most Americans: being issued standard uniforms and weapons, sleeping in barracks on cots; lining up for chow; exercising en masse before dawn; being coached with screams and shouts; being hardened for war.

He remembered the KMT captive enlistees in Hubei and relished the discipline and professionalism of the U.S. Army. If they wanted him to do push-ups in the mud and run with a rifle for a few hours up steep hills with American Indian names, that was fine. If they had ordered an equivalent of the Charge of the Light Brigade, he would have executed it without complaint. The foundation for their enterprise was moral. All men make mistakes, and none can defy fate.

The training at Fort Benning was at times brutal. Officer candidates would soon lead young, inexperienced troops against seasoned Fascist armies that had already defeated Poland, France, the Low Countries, Scandinavia, Belgium, Czechoslovakia, Manchuria, northern China and Hong Kong and were about to occupy the Philippines, Malaya, Singapore, Indochina and all of the South Pacific.

The post commander was responsible for Major Lee's welfare. General Leven Allen summoned T.C.

"Major, this pass gives you run of post and grants all privileges on the installation. If you want to go inside a parachute hangar, a rigger shop, a weapons room, the officers' club or the Airborne Corps commanding general's bedroom, this pass will admit you. It's my privilege to give it to you. We all send you our best wishes for successful completion of the course, and we're damned honored to work with you. We hope we can give you something to help in the war against the Japs."

Few Chinese generals of T.C.'s era would utter such kindnesses. "I tried not to get choked up," he would later say.

T.C. still wrote no letters home. He was guilty about the amount and the quality of the food he was consuming, but wanted to tell someone that his bowels were working fantastically.

"My digestion is very good," he said to Lieutenant Ed Schenk.

"That mean it wasn't so hot before?"

"What does 'hot digestion' mean?" T.C. asked, writing it down.

"'Hot' means good."

"Digestion terrible in the Gobi. Got very sick! You like the training?"

Schenk was a tall, muscular man from the Tennessee hills. "I don't exactly *like* it. I'd say I was toleratin' it. I'd rather be huntin' possum."

"Schenk. Am I doing okay? How do I look on marches, on obstacle courses, the rifle range? Grenades? Night exercise? Defensive-position prep?"

Schenk laughed. "Hey, you know all this stuff as well as the damn sergeants. Can I ask you something? How come you cuss in German?"

"I was trained by German sergeants in China." T.C. rubbed the top of his head. "I swore when I was with them. Now I swear again. Sorry."

"No need to apologize. Lee, you want a tip? A tip is a piece of friendly advice. You sure, now? Some of the guys think you're a little extreme on the military stuff. I mean, you do facin' movements like you was a Nazi. You stamp your boots. That's just plain un-American. You do attention and parade rest like a toy soldier. No offense. I understand the Germans did that, but they're gone and started the war and we're gonna have to kill 'em."

T.C. heard the truth. "Thank you, Schenk. You are a good friend."

"Don't mention it. One of these days I'm gonna get good and tired of some fifty-mile hike and ask you to take my rifle and pack."

It never happened. Schenk was mostly muscle and bone. He did most of the carrying of other men's equipment. It was a lesson for T.C., who had believed that a man's physical burdens were his alone.

He was surprised to see that while some of the white officers were going on to the parachute school with him, none of the black officers were.

"Negroes aren't allowed in," said Lieutenant Pierce, who was black.

"Why not?" asked T.C.

"They say our bone density is too great." He shook his head. "They don't have segregation in China? One group shut off from others?"

"Moslems are separated. The Hakka, the guest people, Chinese who migrated north to south. Europeans shut us out of Shanghai."

"Still the Tower of Babel," said Lieutenant Pierce.

T.A. wrote long missives, detailing his plans for T.C.'s future.

. . . *Concentrate on learning artillery, which is critical to China's future. You will be the artillery expert in the Chinese army. You will be liaison to the U.S. Army mission in China. The commander is a General Joseph Stilwell, who was with the U.S. Army in Tientsin and speaks fluent Mandarin and is beloved by his troops. Is this important? I thought gen-*

erals gave orders. Stilwell went to that school that fascinates you, West Point.

His chief of artillery is Colonel George Sliney, also of West Point. A bright man. He will be your staff counterpart. They are setting up American HQ in Kunming.

Please do not waste your time in Georgia shooting guns. I know you must do some of this. Please elect classes in artillery instead of marching.

Jih-iung says it is hot in Georgia now. It is foggy and cold in San Francisco. I worry about China. Thank you for shifting funds to the U.S. Whatever happens, our clans are safe.

Study hard, T.C. Not like you did before.

T.A.

P.S. You will return to S.F. through Los Angeles. You will be met by a man belonging to the Chinese consul-general. Do what he says.

T.C. had told T.A. that he was going to the Infantry School, which was in Georgia. The Artillery School was in Oklahoma, a completely different science. T.C. began spending weekends in the post library, reading the technical and field manuals on field artillery.

T.C. found jumping out of airplanes interesting, but he disliked the painful landings. He disliked jump school because it signaled his graduation and separation from the Infantry School, a place and time that he would miss for the rest of his life. America had a democratic spirit to its military, and he loved it.

Ed Schenk was the honor graduate. Lieutenant Pierce was a candidate, but a Negro couldn't win. T.C. was an honorable mention honor graduate, a title concocted for a short, older Chinese man who relished the grunt work that younger men had grown to endure.

T.C. was proud to have finished. Pierce and Schenk weren't. Pierce was going to drive trucks. Schenk had gotten boats.

"You'd think they'd send an honor grad to a prime infantry post. They assigned me to a damn *boat* company! Can you imagine me in a *boat*? Biggest damn war in human history, they need field leaders like beans in a fart war and they send me to go sail a damn *yacht*."

T.C. laughed. "It's the army. If you're big, they give you a carbine. If you're small, you get the mortar tube and base plate."

"I didn't think a sane man could love the friggin' army like you. I'll miss you, Lee. I'll pray you make it through the war." They shook.

During outprocessing, T.C. was informed he could keep anything he wanted. He told the supply sergeant that he wanted to keep it all, including the all-privileges pass that the post com had issued.

"Hell, Major, that's fine. Just sign here."

fifty-nine

Hepburn

THE ORIGINAL DERBY faced the Ambassador Hotel and was the strangest restaurant T.C. had ever seen. It was shaped like a brown hat. A circular bar and counter sat in the center of the circular floor plan. The perimeter's small numbered booths each featured a wall lamp in the shape of a derby.

T.C.'s uniform caused the normal jitters, but he shouted, "Don't worry, I'm a Chinese officer," drawing smiles of relief. He and the driver sat at a booth and smoked Lucky Strikes. Three of those powerful, unfiltered cigarettes came with every individual C-ration field meal, along with cocoa, sugar, toilet paper and salt. T.C. loved America.

Above each booth was a caricature of an actor. The one above theirs was Gary Cooper. "Who am I meeting?" T.C. asked.

"I don't know, sir."

The maître d' brought a telephone. "Mr. Chang? Call for you." Driver Chang spoke and hung up. "I'm taking you to MGM Studios, okay?"

At the studio, T.C. was seated in a conference room filled with art for upcoming film projects. He smoked and looked at his watch. Coffee arrived, and he asked for tea. He pulled out his notepad and reviewed English words he was trying to learn. "Wacko," crazy. "Geezed up," drunk. "Brodie," a failure. "Skids," on the decline. He reviewed his travel expenses for the Defense Mission. He reviewed the organization of division artillery in the standard U.S. Army table of organization and equipment, preparing for T.A.'s oral exam.

Someone was in the room.

He opened his eyes wide and burned himself with his cigarette.

"Miss Hepburn, I am T.C. Lee. I am honored to meet you."

He had rehearsed his English pronunciation for the December meeting that had never occurred. Now he hoped his high military tunic collar was snapped and his fly was closed. She wore a white cashmere sweater and tan slacks.

She offered her hand. They shook, she with strong and fine fingers.

"Major, the honor is utterly mine." *That voice!* "Please have a seat. I am so sorry I'm late. It's quite unlike me. I'm the martinet on the set, insisting on everyone being absolutely punctual, hitting marks and knowing lines. I'm making a movie, which is perhaps redundant to say since we're on a lot, but they do treat us like dumb beasts. And I just moved, which has proved more complicated than I imagined. But truthfully, my fine discipline failed me. I apologize abjectly. Will you forgive me?"

T.C. always had good posture; now he stood taller. Margaret McAtee said Miss Hepburn was nearly five feet seven, so T.C. had put lifts in his Class A dress shoes to boost his narrow one-inch advantage. The actress's billowing red hair made her seem even taller.

"Of course. Nothing to forgive."

He had heard her high-toned voice in movie theaters since 1932. Now it hit him like a breeze in spring. Her ash-gray eyes were startling in their aware-ness. Her cheekbones could support armies. Without makeup, her skin was lovely but surprisingly covered in freckles.

She was more alluring than beautiful, more charismatic than sensual, and he laughed, put out his cigarette, gestured to her and sat only after she had found a chair and crossed her legs.

"What movie are you making?" he asked.

"*Keeper of the Flame*; George Cukor's directing. We're trying to make it patriotic"—she made a fist and swept it partially upward—"but I have a bad feeling about it. Have you seen *Woman of the Year*? Oh, you really should, Spencer's simply wonderful. People loved it, you see, it was funny and fairly quick and had poignancy, but this one, this one has heart, though you couldn't find a laugh in it if it starred the Marx Brothers, and I fear we'll have set Spencer—Spencer Tracy—back with this one."

He didn't like hearing about Spencer Tracy. He wanted to ask which her favorite movie was, but he knew that would be trite. "Hard to believe, you wor-rying about—about popularity."

She smiled. "You have no idea how many times my career has been declared dead on arrival. Oh, I've been irrevocably written off, box-office poison, *finis!* And wait until this new one is released—I'll be pilloried and called sharp and unlikable and strident, you watch!" She said it lightly, but like a boy saying that his wet nurse didn't matter.

"I cannot believe that," said T.C. "You act for pleasure. Not approval! I'm the same. It's not honorable to be a soldier in China. Even now, with a million Japanese in our country. Always better to be a scholar in Chinese society. But I believe in being a soldier."

She leaned forward, her chin on her hand. "My goodness, don't stop! They said you've been fighting the Japanese." Her eyes searched his face, which had an electric effect on him. "Can you tell me anything about that without violating military secrets?"

He tapped a cigarette out of the pack and played with it, then thought of his father and his opium pipe and put it down. *Speak well*, he thought.

"Our army needs help. Japan wants to kill the fighters and make slaves out of the rest. They are unbelievably cruel." He took a breath. "You didn't ask, but I liked *Christopher Strong*. Because you flew a plane. Nice flying outfit, too. It made the audience go wacko."

She laughed, and her laughter had glory, full of nuances that had nothing to do with mirth, the kind of laugh that T.C. knew well. He moved closer to her. He was with the woman of his most secret dreams.

"Major, that movie was of another time! It just seems that everything that happened before December seven—before Pearl Harbor—was part of a totally different life. An innocent life. Don't you think? Does it have the same effect for you? The world's so troubled now. Social justice is in great jeopardy. But back then, I just really wanted to fly."

She had said *Don't you think?* like Da-tsien. It jolted him.

Her intelligence was a burning, penetrating thing. To her, the entire world mattered, and he was humbled that an actress could emanate such leadership. Her gaze reminded him of a line from *Gone With the Wind:* "*He looks at you like he knows what you look like under your petticoat.*" Could she see his feelings?

She smiled, "Major Lee, you're a different sort of beast than I'm accustomed to meeting. Not only are you not in the business, you're not even from this country! I'm from Connecticut, and the people who manage us come from wherever one raises surly little pigs, but you are truly from the other side of the world."

"But I've read a lot about Hollywood—"

"No, don't misunderstand me. I think it's positively marvelous that you're not from the industry. You see, Major, as soon as we wrap *Flame*, I'm going on the road to do a small thing onstage called *Without Love*, by Elliot Nugent, but if it's at all successful, they'll ruin it by rewriting it a hundred million times and turning it into a film. Hollywood!" She spoke breathlessly, like Da-tsien.

"What I'm trying to say, rather unartfully, is that I love not having to *worry* about you. You're not going to sell the story of seeing me to a confidential magazine or do a radio interview that will simply shock my family. And that's a very fine realization, believe me! So, the fact of the matter is, I love your company. Now, please, tell me about yourself."

"I'm no one," he said, his humility a surprise. "My grandfather, *he* was someone. Had great adventures! Escaped death many times. Became very powerful and had many wives. He built a beautiful garden."

She leaned on the conference table. "Many wives, huh? Well, you've seen adventures, too. It's registered in your very interesting face. What have you done that I haven't even seen? Tell me. I'm interested."

He sighed. For her, Greeks might launch a thousand ships; a Chinese man focused on the future could grant a backwards glance.

"I saw sunrises in the Gobi Desert. Colors, so many colors, colors you can't find in movies. I saw a purple and a gold that were so strong, I dreamed of them. I saw the tallest mountains in the world—the Himalayas." He said it the Tibetan way—Him-*mal*-yas. "I saw sunburned monks in bright, sunlike yellow robes blowing on trumpets twenty-five feet long, calling to heaven; that was so close, maybe, for them, it was only one more mountain range away. Snows so white.

"A field in Hubei covered by the dead. Like a harvest of wheat, but they were bodies. Black crows trying to clean up the entire field.

"I saw a mountain in a province called Hunan. Hunan is our Texas— everything's huge. They have the braggards and rebels of China, the spiciest foods. Parts of Hunan are still in the Bronze Age. The mountain was from a fairy tale. Covered in mist and tiny fires, each representing an enemy platoon. We fly up the mountain, fighting winds, guns . . ."

"They didn't tell me that you're a pilot."

"I flew a biplane called the Corsair. Funny little plane, now, compared to Japanese Zeros and Flying Tiger Curtis Tomahawks." He didn't say: *I had a plan to change Chinese history and kill Mao, a man who'll kick our butts. But the asshole in charge* tsa quo, *he blew it.*

"So, when will you learn to fly?" he asked.

A modest smile. "I already am a pilot. A pretty good one. Have you ever heard of Howard Hughes?" He shook his head, and she laughed. "How delicious that you haven't! Well, Mr. Hughes taught me how to fly. He used to land his airplane by our house at Fenwick, along a glittering sea, and he taught me stick and rudder and how to fishtail to see the clear path."

He laughed. "You fly! You have smelled the blue smoke."

"What a wonderful way to put it. And your surprise is a pleasure to behold! From what little I know of China—such a faraway place, isn't it—it's a pretty traditional culture. So I'm intrigued, Major. Why is a man from the oldest society in the world interested in meeting a woman who never wears skirts and has been accused of acting like a man?"

"My wife loves your films. You are her favorite. I'm from Shanghai. Until Pearl Harbor, we got all the first-run films."

"Really? I had no idea! You know, I was wondering if you had a wife. I notice the big college ring. Do Chinese men wear wedding bands?"

"Some do, some don't. I wore a wedding ring. But I just did aviation work with the American army, and they made me take it off." Da-tsien's whispered words in a distant Shanghai church. *Never lose this ring, because it contains my heart.*

"This ring is from the U.S. Army. Brand-new! How does it look?" He proudly held up his hand. He was with Katharine Hepburn, and parts of himself, once so deeply anchored, were shifting towards her.

"I think it looks fabulous." Hepburn must have recognized his common dose of celebrity adulation. She might have been surprised that this fan had come from China, and that he was a charmer and even a seducer. Her acute business mind knew that the blatant, easy sexuality of the Rita Hayworths, Betty Grables and Lana Turners would become more popular with men as the risks of war increased, while brainy Bryn Mawr graduates who covered their legs and knew Euripides and Shakespeare would find their careers at risk. This man, who had fought in the ghastly war that America had just joined, had picked her.

"I'd love to ask you about your wife, but that may be inappropriate. Is there anything I can answer for you?"

He gestured with a pointed index finger, showing his intensity. "There's an old Chinese story. Strangers meet in a tavern, each with a different past. The world is changing, so they see in each other not strangers but a common interest. Same destiny. They pledge to each other. They say, *We were born different days, but we die, same day.*"

He looked at her, enjoying this time, unaware that he was speaking English well not because of practice but because of inspiration.

She picked up his abandoned cigarette and put it between her lips. He lit it with a snap of the Zippo he had bought at the post exchange.

"I'm not one for pledges, Major. I'm an enthusiast for justice. Justice for all people, men, women, children and all races and creeds. May I call you by your first name? I'd like you to call me Kate."

"Kate." Perhaps he blushed as he said it. "I am T.C., but you can call me Lucky, which is what the name in Chinese means."

"I prefer T.C. Are you truly lucky, T.C.?"

He laughed a true laugh. "I'm in Hollywood talking to you. A few months ago, I met Spencer Tracy, Lana Turner, John Garfield. I'll meet the president of the United States. I just trained with the U.S. Army. I know the best soldiers in the world. They will fight to free men they don't even know.

"I have two close friends. One is the brother-in-law of Sun Yat-sen and Chiang Kai-shek. The other is the police chief of the largest city in the world. I have a beautiful wife. Three girls. Yes, I'm lucky. Are you? You lucky?"

She smiled. "Oh, I'd say I'm lucky. I come from quite a family, and they give me my luck. Yet they don't think much of my career choice, and they think an Oscar is a type of California cuisine. I love my family, T.C. They are my safety, my rock. In that way, I might even be a little Chinese. Now, tell me, what are your plans for the next couple of days? I'd love to see you again, not here, but at the Derby or Sardi's or Earl Carroll's, a place with character and food where I can get a good salad and men eat steak. Did you say you're going to meet President Roosevelt?"

He nodded as his heart lifted and perhaps even sang.

She looked at her watch. "Just remain seated. I have to digest lunch, and I had no idea I'd be with you so long—I'm not complaining, mind you—but I have to do this." She stood and lay flat on the floor, looking up at him. He felt he should stand but realized that would be completely stupid. She seemed incredibly beautiful and vulnerable, lying on the floor.

"I have five minutes to digest, and then I have to run back to Stage Seventeen and do George's bidding. George Cukor, a sweetheart of a man, a true genius and at times an enormous pain in the derriere. Oh, damn, I have to go." He stood as she did. Kate kissed him on the lips and left.

In the morning, T.C. was the first to appear at the studio gate. His name was on the list; he was admitted. His mind was aloft with wild thinking. He brought the silver airborne wings he had been awarded after Parachute School. They were a new element in army heraldry.

He planned to give them to a fellow pilot, a beautiful one with gray eyes, red hair and indescribable energy. He had brought along an army photographer he had conned out of Fort MacArthur. He would get a picture of him and Kate and have it for all time.

Kate Hepburn was late again. The photographer asked if he could use the latrine, and T.C. reluctantly let him go.

Kate appeared, apologizing—no time to take him to lunch, and as a consequence, they'd miss one of the great meals of their lives.

They sat in canvas directors' chairs on a sound stage occupied by carpenters and electricians. She questioned him about his history, about China, its religions, dialects and women, mostly Da-tsien.

He answered smoothly, happily, missing the damn photographer.

She was acquiring an analytic picture of his wife. Was she gauging the competition? He imagined her luminescent face in a photo, even on a pillow. That she was interested was undeniable, but he feared to hope.

A runner pulled her back. She had insisted on a partial rewrite of a key scene that was about to be shot.

"Wait here, T.C.," she said, "I'll be right back. Fifteen, twenty minutes." She asked the runner to bring the major anything he wanted.

T.C. wanted his photographer. "He's easy to find. He's in uniform. American army. Corporal. Bring him here!"

Instead, he got Spencer Tracy.

"Mr. Tracy," said T.C., standing.

"Major, have a seat." They shook hands. A tough, wide grip.

Tracy sat after T.C. He leaned forward, like a pal. "Listen, bub. There's something you ought to know. Kate, she's spoken for."

Over the years, T.C. had carefully studied Hepburn's biography in the international Hollywood press. He knew she had married an aristocratic blue-blood years before and divorced him amicably. He knew she was now unmarried and not seeing anyone.

"But she's divorced. And single."

"That don't mean she's not spoken for."

He got it. "Oh, you mean she takes care of her father. She loves her father and takes care of him, yes?" A Confucian projection.

"No, chowderhead. She takes care of *me*."

T.C. recoiled. "But you're married. Your wife, she's big in Hollywood society. Leads charities. And you have a son, and you are Catholic."

"Jeez. Gotta hand it to you. You been here fifteen minutes, and you figured out how to hit a guy below the belt. What the hell are *you* doing chasing a movie star? I read your bio. It was sent to us from your embassy. You got a wife and three daughters back in China. You look to me to be the black kettle, my friend." He paused because the major was writing something in his notepad.

"Hey, I bet you're a swell guy. If you didn't have it in for Kate and me, we could go have a drink and tell lies and pour our pasts out as new piss. But since you *do* have it in for my relationship, you can buzz off."

"She and I are friends now. Nothing to do with you."

"Bullshit!" An angry persona was emerging. T.C. recognized it instantly. "Bub, why do you think Kate's been grilling you about your wife? 'Cuz she wants her in the same sewing circle? Don't be an idiot, my friend. Kate's going to make an MGM movie called *Dragon Seed*. Based on a book by Pearl Buck, bet you heard of her. About a Chinese woman fighting the Japs. In China. They're buildin' the set in the Valley.

"When you told Kate your wife was an independent thinker, well, that was it—she had to know all about her. It didn't have anything to do with you. Even less to do with you and *her*. It's about Kate and her role. She's a pro. No one outworks her. No one's better, not by a long shot. She was doing research. Is that bourbon?"

"Tea."

"Too bad. Was going to join you. You look like you need it more than me. Sorry I had to give you the lowdown. Look, when Kate comes back, don't let on we talked or I'll get in trouble. I don't need that. Got it? Look, good luck in the war. I'd go, but I got bad kidneys and they say I'm too old. You know, I'm proud of you for fighting those lousy Japs, even if you are otherwise quite the genuine guinea asshole for crashing my party."

He put out his hand. T.C. shook it. Spencer Tracy lumbered off.

The carpenters and electricians glanced over and kept working.

When Katharine Hepburn returned, T.C. answered all her questions.

"Are you feeling okay?" she asked. "You're so subdued."

"You have a beau," he said.

"A beau. Ah, yes. You've heard the talk. The rumors. This town. Well, are you disappointed in me, seeing a married man?"

"No, of course not," he lied. "Not my business. I wish you good luck. Hard situations. I have a sister-in-law who thinks about doing what you're doing." He looked at her face, memorizing her. It was who he was, a water-sign man who watched the women in his life leave on the next tide. He had already lost her. He would not look back.

"For you." He gave her the airborne wings.

"You're a paratrooper? You jumped out of airplanes?"

"China has no paratroops, but I qualified to jump with the Americans. When you think of it, not too logical that I jumped."

"You should give this to your wonderful, beautiful wife."

"She wouldn't like it. You're a pilot. Means more to you."

"Will I see you again, T.C.? I'd like to hear from you. To know that you're well, and safe." Her eyes burned with sincerity, but not with love.

"I'm going to be busy." He wanted to take her in his arms and carry her away, to kiss her, to splay her hair on a pillow. Crazy thoughts. "Thank you, Katharine." He offered his hand. She shook it with both of hers, her eyes glistening, the metal airborne wings sharp in both of their palms.

He left the set building, blinking in the bright California sun. The army photographer was waiting for him, smoking a cigarette.

He felt like strangling the corporal. Instead, he pulled out his notepad. "Corporal, the word 'bub.' Is that a good word or bad word?"

THE FULLER IMPACT of meeting Katharine Hepburn struck him after he reported to Washington, D.C. He had been hit by shrapnel once and hadn't felt the wound until hours later, when adrenaline and fear had dissipated. In his second jump at Benning, he had landed badly but felt great—until the next day, when his back felt broken. Hepburn hit him as if she had been Planet Earth.

She had awakened in him a deep sense of T'ang romanticism, ancient, fabled and sad. The encounter left him feeling empty and tragic, for he had committed adultery in his heart and, in a critical way, had abandoned Da-tsien and his daughters. He felt as if he were in one of Hepburn's movies, and not one of the better ones. He had always admired the he-men of Hollywood, and now he felt like Leslie Howard, the weak Ashley Wilkes who wasn't much of a man.

Instead of feeling lucky for having trained at Benning and hosted in Hollywood, he felt unworthy because a woman he didn't know preferred to be faithful to the soul mate of her life. That the soul mate was a short, boulder-headed man who boozed and was as tough a curmudgeon as himself was galling. How could someone so unglamorous win her?

An isolated contact had catastrophically tainted his marriage. Hepburn had been intoxicating—her independence, her emotion, her vibrance, her strange vulnerability, for such a famous woman. He thought of her instead of his wife, the way a man who has stared directly into the sun focuses on the interesting spots in his eyes.

He hadn't wanted to tell Da-tsien about his military adventures because she was hostile to what he loved. Now, under the shadow of Katharine, the idea of writing to Da-tsien seemed impossible.

T.C. forgot that his family needed money more than letters. He didn't think life in Shanghai would be difficult; the Soongs had money and property and influence, and he was their adopted kinsman. In a pinch, there was always Pooh Pan. Further, the House of Tzu had endless resources, including the rich walleyed uncle in the French Concession.

TZU TAITAI LOOKED OUT her brother's window to see an impossible sight: Japanese soldiers were using bayonets and rifle butts to herd the untouchable Europeans and Americans into trucks. Guiding the troops were Chinese turn-coat cops and French inspectors and detectives. They had interrogated the house staffs until the servants revealed how many foreigners were in each house. Obstinate butlers were shot. Some foreigners had been ignored. They had bribed the cops for their freedom and would live in limbo as collaborators.

The turncoat cops and the French collaborationist detectives worked for Pan-da, the chief of police.

Taitai had planned for trouble; it was her life. "Brother, I'll be back. If the Japanese come, don't fight them!" An unnecessary admonition.

Taitai had trouble locating the Lee apartment on Moulming. She looked at the *bao-jia,* collective responsibility, placard, announcing that the neigh-borhood was safe and righteous, behaving in accord with law.

"Lee Taitai," said Tzu Taitai, "I beg your indulgence. May I borrow my worthless daughter and her eldest daughters for the day? That way they will not be available to poison you with their bad cooking."

Tall Lee Taitai could not deny Tzu Taitai. Deep inside herself, she wished she were small and pleasantly angled like Da-tsien's mother, or like Da-tsien herself, or like Ying-oh. For the trim body she'd owned as a girl, she'd trade her fine skin.

"Of course, Honored Sister. I wish you well in these hard times. *Even if you are growing your hair longer, pretending to be young.*

Tzu Taitai thanked her. "You are indeed too kind. Blessings on you," she added insincerely, because Madame Lee had swallowed the foreign faith.

"Come," said Taitai to Da-tsien. "Bring Ah-wa and Ying and as much clothing as you can carry. Summer and winter clothes. Hurry!"

Their rickshaw pullers passed smoke-spewing convoys of Japanese trucks packed with the white foreigners who had ruled the city and lorded over its inhabitants. Many Chinese domestic workers were inwardly happy. It didn't matter that the Japanese might also kill them; they had hated being treated like slaves by white men, women, and children. Confucius had directed that one should not feel anger when wronged; the best these domestics could do was to conceal their joy.

Taitai placed Da-tsien and the girls at the dining room table. She divided the clothes into four stacks. Her brother had given her a jewelry box, and she passed out necklaces, brooches, bracelets, rings and gemstones.

"These are from my brother. We don't deserve them, but they are our safety. He kept them in a bank, but he no longer trusts banks." She then gave them jewelry pliers and picks.

"Pry out the stones without scratching them. Open the hems of the garments. Put stones in the hem, sew them closed. Put the stones in joined hems to hide them better. My brother will break up and paint the gold pieces, and we'll hide them inside ginger and ginseng and roots in the big pantry. Move fast, but make no mistakes."

They cracked the jewelry like walnuts and began sewing. Their uncle trembled as he nervously used a chisel and hammer on the gold.

Da-tsien worked steadily but without much skill, and she kept pricking herself and crying. Elinor worked twice as fast so she could do the clothes in her mother's pile.

Ying worked steadily and silently. When she and Elinor were alone, she chatted wonderfully and spoke sympathetically of their mother. "She's just under a lot of pressure with Baba gone and no money."

"Mah-mee shouldn't pick on you," said Elinor. "It's n-not r-right."

"Don't blame her, Ah-wa. She's not very strong. She sleeps all the time now, and still looks tired."

The sewing took days. The girls enjoyed the work because they got full meals. Taitai gave her daughter six garments—a potential fortune.

The Lee women returned to Moulming; Da-tsien and Elinor collapsed, relieved by a sense of some independence. Ying stayed awake, remembering the food in Taitai's home.

The following week, Japanese soldiers made a random raid on the house of Taitai's brother. They knocked him to the floor, terrorized his wife, ransacked the house, seized the deeds that represented his wealth. They took his beloved artwork, his stores of canned beef, leaving behind bags of ginger. They didn't find his gold coins, which Taitai had hidden inside her hair bun. She had grown it for two years, anticipating this day.

Her brother had been bruised and traumatized by the raid. He withdrew deeper into himself and no longer bathed or shaved. Taitai and her brother's wife took care of him as if he were just another ineffective man.

As SHANGHAI SETTLED into a continuous cycle of abuse, terror and executions, Taitai's hair grew gray and then white, while her daughter, Da-tsien, stayed in bed longer each morning. When she awoke, she wrote long letters to Zee Zee begging him for money and sent them via an expensive courier system that supposedly ran through Nepal and India.

She cried all day when a dozen of her letters were returned to her by a dusty courier who demanded to be paid for his valuable service.

Diamonds

T.C. HAD BECOME an adventurer. Later, when recounting the war years, he would offer different levels of detail. The sparsest accounts covered his 1943 European journeys before the Allied invasions of Sicily and Italy. He flew from Brazil to Tunisia to reach neutral Spain and entered Nazi-occupied France to do unknown things with unidentified banks. He disguised himself as a Japanese courier, a ruse supported by his Germanic demeanor and Chinese moods. In subsequent years, he avoided details about this period of time.

In the fall of 1943, T.C. was in North Africa with diamonds. He deposited most in the Cairo vault of the Bank of England and cashed in lesser stones to buy weapons and bodyguards for Chiang Kai-shek.

Cairo was beautiful that fall. Before the arrival of heads of state and their retinues for the secret Cairo Conference, T.C. sailed up the Nile to Luxor and Thebes. He admired the Nile and loved Karnak, where he slept, his tunic his pillow while his camel puller rested nearby, his wrist swaying with the reins as the camels nattered. He didn't like Middle Eastern camels, which seemed naked without their Asian beards.

He visited the Cairo Opera House on Jazirah Island, a Nile suburb, admiring the women who were classic results of Ptolemaic Egypt's Macedonian officers and Old Kingdom women.

My father was born in the high-water sign on the fifth day after the tenth full moon of the Year of the Horse, the same year as Henry Pu-yi, the last emperor of China. Dynastically, he was born in the thirty-second year in the reign of the ninth emperor, Kuang-hsu. Kuang-hsu would recommend reforms, which would cause his aunt, the Empress Dowager, to murder him. My father and Emperor Pu-yi would cross paths but never meet.

My father had spent formative years in Yangchow, a city flanked by the great Yangtze River and the Grand Canal. He had spent more years in Shanghai by the Whangpu, and he had lived a memorable year in the desert. Here, in Cairo, *Al-Qahira*, which means victory, T.C. felt a harmonic peace.

He was in Cairo for a war-planning conference between the Great Powers, which, for the first time, included China.

Franklin D. Roosevelt, Winston Churchill and Chiang Kai-shek would meet to plan the defeat of Japan. Later, Roosevelt and Churchill would fly to Tehran and meet with Josef Stalin to discuss the defeat of Germany. The Soviet Union had not declared war on Japan, so Stalin did not come to Cairo. China had not declared war on Germany—a salute to the country that had sent so many military advisers to Peking—and hence, Chiang Kai-shek was not welcome in Tehran.

T.C. was made a liaison officer to Allied Headquarters in China—a political move to protect T. A. Soong's political and financial interests from eradication by his siblings or in-laws. T.C. wanted a more meaningful assignment, but he was ideally suited for the jobs that T.A. gave him: secret missions requiring language skills, imagination, the willingness to use violence in order to protect assets, and honesty with funds.

T.C. toured downtown Cairo, admiring mosques while questioning, as was his habit, the rationale for religion. He trusted in British military assistance at the airport but was worried about Chiang's security everywhere else. In the end, he recruited Chinese Embassy staff, trained them in the use of Sten submachine guns and heavy British Webley revolvers and deployed them around Mena House Hotel near the desert and the pyramids of Giza. Security at the Mena was excellent, and Chiang was unlikely to wander around the city, so T.C. presumed any assassination attempts would come from the inside. He spent part of his preparation familiarizing his five-man security detail with the hotel, and most of his time interviewing the hotel staff with his curious blend of German-American-Chinese-fractured, pidgin-modified English.

General Joseph Stilwell landed early, three days before Thanksgiving. T.C. had met him in Kunming, China. Stilwell returned T.C.'s salute with care; the general knew the major was a political officer and Soong ally and could be presumed worthless as a soldier. T.C. had made a point to describe his tactical observations of the Japanese army in Hubei, which Stilwell appreciated, but T.C.'s accounts about trying to kill Mao Tse-tung left the general unimpressed.

"The Communists are fighting the Japs," said Stilwell, *unlike you Nationalists, ignoring the Japs and fighting fellow Chinese.*

The only fact that impressed Stilwell about T. C. Lee was that he had never joined the Kuomintang.

"*Wei shen mo*, why not?" asked Stilwell in excellent Mandarin.

"They're bandits," said T.C. in his curious English. He desperately wanted Stilwell's respect as a soldier but was never to get it. Despite T.C.'s radical statement, Stilwell had probably wondered, How can one gauge a person if not by his friends?

If Chiang Kai-shek recognized Major Lee in Cairo, he concealed it.

President Franklin D. Roosevelt said, "Good to see you, Major," with a warm and engaging smile. He was happy to be in Cairo, which was now secure from Rommel's aborted drive for the Suez, and happy to be with Winston Churchill, his great wartime ally. He was also delighted to advance the notion of China being an equal power, and his prodigious memory allowed him to remember the Chinese delegation that had come to the White House asking for money.

"Major, how is my good friend T. A. Soong?"

"Very well, sir," said T.C. He was then ushered away from the president, who was preparing for an outdoor photo session with Churchill, Chiang and Madame Chiang. T.C. stood to the side, looking for security threats.

Behind him, the four appeared to converse, even though Chiang spoke no English; Roosevelt and Churchill spoke no Chinese; and Churchill disliked Chiang and was suspicious of his wife.

In late 1942 T.A. and T.C. had presented their Lend-Lease applications to the American government and were introduced to Secretary of War Henry Stimson and Roosevelt's personal all-purpose agent, Harry Hopkins. But Lauchlin Currie, Lend-Lease administrator for China, made it clear that Soong's China Defense Mission would have no further independent access to the Washington inner circle; henceforth, all contact would be through T.A.'s older brother T.V. Soong. T.A. was disappointed but not surprised. H. H. Kung had beaten T.A. in the Shanghai stock market, and now T.V. had beaten him in America—all as planned.

The most enjoyable meeting was with President and Mrs. Eleanor Roosevelt, who were friendly and charming and spoke of the Delano mercantile connections to the China trade and to the *cohongs*, the authorized merchants, of Canton. T.C. initially thought Mrs. Roosevelt unattractive. Then he listened to her and saw her smile.

A black steward served excellent coffee and tea. T.C. remembered to sip silently like a European, instead of loudly and gratefully expressing his appreciation of good tea.

T.A. spoke of the Chinese resolve and the miraculous movement of heavy industry from the coast into the interior, towards Chungking and away from the Japanese army.

"It is like an exodus," said T.A., "towards a promised land."

"Let us all pray for that day," said the president.

"We are so deeply honored," said the first lady, "that you took valuable time from your work to see us." She said it sincerely.

The Roosevelts reminded T.C. of old Mr. and Mrs. Tu-di, the kindly white-haired earth gods. Strangely, T.C., who disliked affairs of state, didn't want to leave.

THE CAIRO CONFERENCE was a fleeting victory for Chiang Kai-shek's China. The British promised a major amphibious landing on the Andaman Islands off the Burmese coast as a diversion to a Chinese invasion to free Burma from the Japanese. Chiang and Madame Chiang were photographed with the West's great leaders. But at the subsequent Tehran conference, Roosevelt and Churchill decided to shift the landing craft from Burma to the D-Day invasion of France, alleviating German pressure on Stalin's Russian armies in the eastern front.

Chiang Kai-shek, his entourage and Major Lee learned of this reversal when they returned to Chungking. Chiang was furious at Stilwell and Roosevelt.

"They're ditching us for the damn British again! To invade France—which surrendered to Hitler in thirty days! French troops in Hanoi and Saigon, all through Vietnam and Indochina, are working for the *Japanese*, shooting Vietnamese guerrillas. They're *traitors*! Who speaks English here?" T.C. raised his hand; T.A. didn't.

"Go to America! Demand a billion dollars for their treachery! The Japs are killing us, and they lie to me in Cairo and wait like cowards and have Stilwell tell me the truth when I return. The Japanese hold Shanghai and all our funds, and they're strangling us, and now America is too!"

"This is to our purposes," said T.A. later. "You must transport more diamonds. I want you to take any one of them, as payment, for Da-tsien." From his safe he withdrew a valise, giving them to T.C.

"I can't do that. They belong to the government."

"Look at the account books. These are ours. You insult me, T.C., on so many levels. Please! Take one of the diamonds."

"You remind me of that Bible thumper Miss Wu."

"You are a mule. Take one for Da-tsien's Christian wedding ring. For my feelings. I have not heard from anyone in Shanghai for months."

"Why a diamond for her ring?"

"You sound like Pan! You know why. Because of your attentions to that tall American actress."

"I don't need diamonds," said T.C. "Da-tsien doesn't, either."

T.A. selected one and put it in T.C.'s hand. "Do not argue."

EVERY DAY WITHOUT a letter diminished Da-tsien. Elinor considered faking a letter, but she didn't think she could capture his selfishness. Besides, there was no way to fake the money.

In the late fall of 1943, while T.C. was in Egypt with Chiang, Roosevelt and the Sphinx, Da-tsien decided to throw away boxes of her husband's keepsakes. First she had to dump them on the floor. Hollywood magazines cascaded across the faded rug. They had folded corners on certain pages. She turned to the first one and smiled: Katharine Hepburn, her heroine. The next folded corner led to another Hepburn photo, then another and another. Zee Zee had marked these pages for himself. Hepburn, again and again. In furs, showing her legs, with short hair, long hair, in berets, in outlandish hats, with Leslie Howard, standing in front of an airplane. An airplane. Da-tsien shook. Zee Zee had betrayed her.

She wept, prayed and wept some more. *Dear God, you know I really love you and truly adore you and I've prayed to you for money and food and a son for Zee Zee to love me and stay with me and now my husband whom I love so much . . . My husband whom I used to love has run away with an American movie actress . . . Lord, I had no idea . . . don't let them be together in any way! Make Zee Zee honor his pledge he made to me and You and the Holy Ghost and Jesus, to love only me. Oh God, I'm so sad, so brokenhearted! What to do? We're out of money and the Soongs are gone and I can't go to Tai Yeuh and Pan again for help! I can't! Oh, I can't stand him! But I can't give him up!*

A knock on the door. It was the landlord, demanding payment and peering around Elinor, trying to put his eyes on Da-tsien.

"Lee Taitai, you hear? New Japanese offensive in Hunan. Isn't your husband there? They say a million Chinese troops died! You have the rent? Hey, why hide from me? I own the building, so I own you, right? Hey, hey, your daughters are so pretty! How old are you, Young Missy?"

"I'm thirteen," said Elinor, "and you have to respect us, or my father will come back and shoot you."

"Ha ha! Your father's probably dead."

"I'm a *wu*. If you're not careful, I'll cast a spell on your organs."

"You should worry about the Japanese! They watch you even now!"

Elinor gathered her band—sister Ying and their cousins Lon-lon, Chin and Lu-lu. They were cousins in a *jia*—infused with Confucian politeness, culturally bonded, fed by common pots and joined at the hip. Chinese cousins are more like siblings. Further, they were closer because their intolerable fathers were brothers.

"What are we going to do about Landlord Tsao?"

"What do you mean? What can we do?" asked Lon-lon.

Lon-lon was rail-thin and razor-bright, the only male grandchild in two clans, so Taitai had redefined *tsong hwai*, spoiled. He had been colicky at birth, so she chewed all his food for him to ensure that his tender insides wouldn't have to work too hard. She forbade peaches, ice cream and hard foods. As a result, Taitai got rounder and Lon-lon became thinner. He and Elinor, the Firstborns, were the leaders, and although six years older, he recognized and accepted her leadership of their band.

"We could report him to someone," said Ying.

"Too dangerous," said Lon-lon.

"It's not right, his doing this to us," said Chin. Chin, whose American name was Jane, had been one of Da-tsien's favorites, reminding her of Katharine Hepburn, until the discovery of the magazines, while Lu-lu, the youngest, evoked memories of Lillian Gish.

"Deluge him with kindness and politeness," said Elinor. "I just tried to scare him off with a curse, and it didn't work."

Part Three
WATER

YING, AUNTIE YING-OH, ELINOR, DA-TSIEN, UNCLE GEE, LU-LU [back row], MARY, LEE TAITAI (BU-BU), LING-LING [front row], Shanghai, 1944, before the Run. Opium-smoking Master Lee and soldier-of-fortune Zee Zee are absent. Lee Taitai dislikes Da-tsien and favors Ying-oh, who loathes her husband, Gee. Da-tsien rejects her second daughter, Ying, whom Elinor protects.

DA-TSIEN, India, 1944. After the trauma of the Run, she worried about her looks.

ELINOR and YING, en route to Hong Kong, 1938. Elinor was Ying's guardian against a China in revolution, the ravages of World War Two and an angry mother.

YING, ELINOR, MARY, DA-TSIEN, T.C., Earl Carroll's Restaurant, Hollywood, 1945, not long after the family arrived in America from India to reunite with the man who abandoned them in war-torn China. As a rare favor to Da-tsien, T.C. is not wearing his uniform.

sixty-one

Goodbye, China

D A-TSIEN THOUGHT, BABA *will know what I'm supposed to do.*

Baba and Deaf Man Fu now lived in a tenement on Chung Wah Road at the edge of the Old Chinese City. They were old enough to have avoided the Japanese dragnets for slave labor.

Ah Tsui halted the tired rickshaw puller. Baba's tenement teemed with Japanese troops, who had cleared out the lower two floors for barracks. Baba and Fu were on the third floor. The Japanese troops clustered near the steps looked at Da-tsien; Ah Tsui instantly barked at the puller to turn around, fast!

Fighting panic, Da-tsien tried to ignore the ever increasing number of Japanese troops in the city.

"To the French Concession?" asked Ah Tsui. Da-tsien nodded.

"MAH-MEE, ARE YOU okay?" Taitai had opened the door herself. "Where are the servants? Where's Amah?"

"She died. My best soups couldn't save her." Da-tsien and Ah Tsui walked behind Taitai down the hall of the dark house.

"I'm sorry for your loss. You're limping, Mah-mee."

"No, no, my slippers are loose."

"How is Uncle?"

"Not good. His wife is sad, no sons. Well, you understand that complaint, right? Here, sit. Tell me your troubles."

435

"What if I had good news?"

She laughed. "Ah, Daughter, you dreamer! I could *smell* good news. The Japanese would leave. Brother would heal and read the papers. We would have our servants back to serve tea and food and wash clothes. Your gangster husband would get a job and give me my grandson."

Da-shing, Da-tsien's tall, broad-shouldered, handsome brother, had already produced two sons, but Da-tsien said nothing.

"I know your problems, Da-zee. You're out of money, and you don't want to sell the gems. Probably your landlord—I saw his evil eye—wants to do monkey business with you for the rent, right?"

"I think Tsao has a *chung liu*, a tumor in his brain."

"Well, something in his brain makes him want to do monkey business. It might as well be a tumor. And I'm sure you haven't heard from Zee Zee. And you have no son and you're losing weight. Even Old Tsui looks thin. Your daughters don't eat. What else?"

"That's enough, don't you think?"

"Sure, it's plenty. It's the Taipings all over again."

"Mah-mee, Zee Zee's in America. I'm sure. I want to follow him."

"To be *youmin*, refugees, people without roots or clan? Bah. Getting to America would be like flapping your arms to the moon. I won't take care of your girls. *You* were too much. Three is too many."

"Oh, I'd take them with me. At least Elinor and Mary."

"Tsa tsa, Da-zee! Ying is yours, too! Although leaving her would be better for her. You are still not a practical person, just like your father. Have you heard? The Japanese execute all *youmin*. This is after they do unspeakable tortures, particularly to women."

"I would plan our escape just like a business deal."

"Oh, I see. And when was the last time you made business?"

"Not that long ago. Five years?"

"More like twenty-five years ago. You were a girl. It was so long ago, Da-zee, that it was in those few days that your father worked."

"Will you give me your blessing, Mah-mee, if I go?"

Her mother looked at the back of her hands. "Impossible. Christian talk! You throw away your luck. You try to . . . to escape your fate. How can I bless your killing yourself *and* your precious girls?"

"I can't stay, Mah-mee. It's making me very bad crazy. My children are hungry. I can't sleep. Even Skinny Wu ran away."

"They'll kill her and cook her bones. You can't go. Too dangerous."

"Shanghai's killing me, just as both our clans have been dying for so many years. You know, like the centipede." Something secret and unknown was pushing on her from within. She, a fragile princess who could stumble walking across a room, was ready to encircle the globe. "Please bless me, Mah-mee, so I can go. Please!"

Ah Tsui turned crimson; no daughter could be so bold, and it was her fault: too much indulgence. Now Taitai would skin Da-tsien's body for her impertinence. Amah showed teeth.

"Yes, okay, Da-zee," said her mother, sighing deeply. "I give it to you now."

"Really? Not just words?"

"Da-zee, you're my only girl. If you leave, I will miss you. Now, I tell you this: You must start right in all endeavors. Use your brains for meeting people. I would use Elinor for knowing what to do. You don't want to get this wrong, since a small mistake in this area would mean the terrible death of all of you. Please, start correctly." Taitai lowered her head. Daughter and Amah turned aside to allow her to cry in dignity.

"*Manmanlai, Nu ehr*," she said. Go softly, Daughter.

She couldn't hug her mother, so Da-tsien stood and cried. Ah Tsui sobbed quietly. Also crying was the childless wife of Taitai's brother.

"God bless you," said the walleyed brother, trying to use words that would give comfort to his Christian niece.

"WE NEED MEN," said Elinor. "Good men."

"To carry things, right?" asked her mother.

"To keep us from being hurt," said Elinor.

"We need water, salt, peanuts for strength and medicine for Mary." Mary had never had a cold, but securing her medicine was a Lee tradition.

Da-tsien looked at her aging clothes. Was it possible that she'd once had beautiful Soochow silk gowns and dresses and cheongsams with gold braid and piping—all sold for vegetables and thin soup? "What else?"

"Our gems and a knife, and we need cigarettes and matches—"

"Cigarettes?"

"To sell for food. *Di Aiguo*, Great Patriots, are the best."

"How do you know this?"

"I've been to school."

"Did you say a knife?"

"In case we have to fight."

"Oh. Who will do the fighting?"

"The men, Mah-mee."

Da-tsien nodded with understanding, then put her head in her hands and wept. Elinor rubbed her back, which usually calmed her mother; she remembered doing this when she was nine or ten, when Zee Zee—she thought of him by his name instead of as Baba—had come home to mistreat Mah-mee, yelling at her, making her throw and break things. The fight involved Mah-mee's mistreatment by Auntie Ying-oh and Madame Lee, and Zee Zee had taken his mother's side against his wife.

"It's all your fault, being spoiled and independent!" he bellowed.

Mah-mee had grabbed Elinor and run from the house, weeping. They took a pedicab to the Hotel Plaza on Rue de Consulat. Without luggage or money, Da-tsien had taken a room. She sat on the bed weeping, while Elinor massaged her back, wondering why Mah-mee would expose her heart to a man who had no corresponding organ.

"I can't pay for the room!" she wailed. "I'll go to jail!"

"All taken care of," said Elinor, who had negotiated with the clerk. They returned the next day, trying to avoid Zee Zee and another fight.

Now they were planning an insane journey to find that man.

"Mah-mee, are you sure you want to risk losing Mary to the Japanese, just to find Baba so you can break more plates?" asked Elinor.

"He promised. He promised to me and to my parents and to the Christian God! In front of everybody! He promised, *only me*! Oh, Ah-wu, I can't imagine him with another woman. It just kills me!"

ELINOR WALKED BRISKLY towards the International Institute of China on Avenue Foch. She kept away from Japanese officers, who were sniper targets, and she avoided groups of Japanese soldiers, who were rapists. It was a long walk, but pullers were now charging hundreds of inflated dollars for a five-minute ride, and it cost thousands of dollars for an old, skinny stalk of *gai lan* with yellowed buds. She was so hungry that even she had begun to hope that a money envelope would arrive from Zee Zee, which she knew to be an impossibility.

At the Institute, she sat on a bench and studied the men around her looking for virtue. She dismissed anyone who stared or whistled, laughed too loud or was a showoff or prone to anger. She approached the top candidates.

"Sit next to me, here." said Da-tsien, placing Elinor by her side. Da-tsien brushed invisible lint from her dress. "Now see if we can form relationships with any of these people."

The first was tall and had a runny nose and kept wiping his hands on his trousers.

"Thank you," said Da-tsien. "You are kind to visit us."

The next said, bowing, "My honorable name is Ma. I am richer for your company. I ran track at Peking University. I had to care for my ailing father, so I couldn't go to Free China in 1941 with most of my classmates. My father has passed to the next world. If you let me join you, I'll try to protect you and your daughters." He smiled at Elinor. "I enjoyed meeting you, Miss Lee. You are well spoken for someone so young. I am Mohammedan. I do not eat pork. That will leave more for everyone else."

Elinor wrote down his name and address, and they arranged a method of leaving messages for each other in a bathroom at the Institute. They needed two men, had seen twenty and found one.

A young woman bowed. "My name is Kang. I have to leave Shanghai or I'll have *sang jing bin*, mind troubles, a nervous breakdown. I heard your daughter recruiting young men. Madam, excuse me for saying this, but I'm so terrified of being raped and then killed and having my intestines pulled out and wrapped around my neck. The Japanese chase me. I can't take it! You have to let me come with you. I'm not big, but I'll carry everything without complaint. I'm Buddhist, so I won't eat any meat."

Elinor was about to say, "Sorry," but Mah-mee asked about family.

"The Japanese killed my parents, and the Kuomintang kidnapped my brothers into the army. I've been living in the kitchen of a tenement."

"Thank you, Miss Kang. You will hear from me."

"Oh, thank you, madam! Thank you!" She wept and pressed her forehead against Da-tsien's hands.

The last man they interviewed was the second man they took. His name was Wu, and he was tall and broad-shouldered with a small waist, and he looked like he would be helpful when there was trouble. He had a deep voice and a kindly manner and was the son of a Pudong cotton family. Elinor had seen him carrying books for a student on crutches. He said he was also Buddhist.

"Any particular eating habits?" Elinor asked.

"I don't like peanuts," he said.

"We're eating peanuts. They're small and rich in protein," she said.

"I'll eat almonds, walnuts, cashews, pecans, Brazil nuts. Not peanuts."

It went without saying: These three people would rather risk death in trying to reach Chungking and Free China than remain in Shanghai, and they would have to rely on one another, like clan members, to survive.

"REMEMBER, AH-WU, DON'T tell anyone!" said Da-tsien.

"I won't, Mah-mee," said Elinor, running out the door. She knew how to race the clock. In an alleyway, a woman stopped her.

"Wait! Stop! Who are you? You look very interesting!"

She kept running. "I'm Lee Ah-wu, I'm late, sorry, goodbye!"

Kaiser Chang was a gentleman. He was entranced by fourteen-year-old Elinor, who had introduced herself to him when it became clear that her mother might want to get to Chungking. All this to stop an American actress.

"I am Lee Elinor Ah-wu. I need your help and am honored to meet you. How can a family get seats on a Shanghai train?"

It was a common question. His father was a senior manager at the Shanghai Railway Station, which the Japanese had bombed in 1937. Subsequently, it had been turned into an execution ground by the Japanese Kampetei, black-suited men who pulled suspected refugees, students, labor leaders and KMT soldiers and spies from trains to be shot or beheaded near the tracks.

Elinor had a unique personality and a magnetic aura. Kaiser Chang was quickly sympathetic to the teen's request. When she cut open her sleeve and offered him a gemstone, he was touched.

"Not necessary. You keep this. You'll need it to reach Free China. Do you have a father or a brother? A tough amah? Tough mother?"

She shook her head.

"Listen, this is a difficult process."

Elinor was directed to the Japanese military government transportation office in Broadway Mansions on the other side of Garden Bridge. She would have to be brave and able to endure Japanese soldiers touching her. She would proceed to a particular window in a particular office wing and wait in line for as long as a week to acquire the first set of identity papers. With those, she would begin another long wait to complete a transportation request, justifying the journey and convincing the Japanese that it would aid the Empire while not being a sham for flight. She would have to do this for every member in the party.

"If there are more than two of you, they'll issue identity papers but not rail tickets, because they'll figure you're trying to run away. Know what they'll do to you if they suspect you of running?"

Elinor nodded.

"How many in your party?"

"Seven."

"And you're the bravest of them all?"

"I'm the right age and height to get things done."

"If the Japanese don't kill you."

She nodded again.

"Getting everyone on the same train, same day, will be tough, there are so many of you. If you start now, you could leave perhaps in two months. Do you have the patience to do this? You will have to relieve yourself in line."

She nodded.

"Another problem is seats, even with tickets. Many get identity papers, because the Japanese gestapo welcomes information on us. Few, however, get tickets. Many of those with tickets don't get actual seats."

Elinor then began to live in long, angry, aggressive lines of panicked people trying to escape Shanghai.

On the day before departure, Baba and Deaf Man Fu arrived at the Moulming apartment.

"You are indeed being watched by Japanese gestapo," said Baba to Da-tsien. "We waited until the man who watches this building left for lunch. After you leave, we will walk in front of the windows, pretending to be the four of you."

Da-tsien was so happy to see her father but grief-stricken that she was leaving him.

"I will say goodbye for you to your brother Da-shing, and to the House of Tzu, such as it is. All will miss you for all their days."

She missed her handsome brother so much. She couldn't think of all the people they had already lost to bad economics. The memory of Soochow servants touching her cheek and making her bed on Sunday mornings when she was little made her cry.

"Will you come to America if I send money?" she asked brokenly.

"I like reading about far places. But I am Chinese." He looked at her, never doubting that she would reach safety with her girls.

"You won't die, Baba, not for a long, long time."

"Of course not," he agreed. "Now say your goodbyes to the Lees."

"I'm sorry," said Ah Tsui, "but did you not count me? With me, there are five who are leaving."

"You must stay, Amah," said Baba. "You're too old now."

Ah Tsui knew it was true but had prayed to the gods that no one would say it. Her job was to care for her girl until one of them died. It was her calling, her reason for being. She wept hot salty tears while Da-tsien patted her back and Elinor patted her mother's.

P'o-p'o intervened to alleviate the awkward situation.

"Do not say goodbye. We will see each other again," she said.

"Yes, Mother," Da-tsien replied. Now she seemed soft and kind instead of arbitrary and mean. Her beautiful skin glowed.

"Think of the reunions and go with God," Madame Lee said with great emotion, knowing that her clumsy daughter-in-law had but one chance in five hundred thousand of reaching Chungking. She was too pretty and too impractical—a nightingale among falcons and hawks. "Give my good wishes to Second Son. I miss him. I would even take his yelling at you now, just to hear him and to have him near."

That, thought Elinor and Ying, was going too far. The children gathered in the corner and sat in a circle. They had trouble looking at one another, for the pain of seeing someone they were about to lose was too great. War had taken the world, and as children, they were already too old.

Da-tsien asked her sister-in-law to join her in the bedroom.

"Ying-oh, I apologize for our disagreements," she said. "It was my doing. I'm a Christian, and I knew better, and I let anger get the better of me. You're my senior, but I let pride run my heart."

Ying-oh lowered her face. "Please don't say this. Don't be so kind. Let me shoulder responsibility. I was mean to you. It wasn't your fault."

"Can you love Gee?" asked Da-tsien. "Zee Zee drives me absolutely mad out of my mind. He's so controlling and angry, but he's the father of the girls and of the son he promised me. I promised to love only him on earth, and that's my responsibility, isn't it? I didn't say I'd love him only if he was good. I pray you and Gee can reunite."

Ying-oh shook her head. "I can't stand Gee. You're lucky. Zee Zee's impossible, but he's a man. He can be kind; I've seen it. I have never seen this in Gee. P'o-p'o spoiled him the worst, and Master Lee, when he was alive and smoking the pipe, beat Gee too many times in the head. It made him crazy. He chases *wūnu* dance-hall girls and comes back smelling of other women. I hate his bones. I wish I could go, too, but it's not possible."

Da-tsien said farewell to Deaf Man Fu, who nodded and wept, then she faced Tall Amah.

"You're too good for Zee Zee," said Tall Amah. "Remember us." She was like an auntie, and she hugged the three girls.

Da-tsien missed Auntie Gao and Miao-miao. The Japanese had confiscated Gao's husband's plant, and the fates of those three, like so many Shanghainese, were now unknown.

"You cannot leave as a group," said Baba. "Elinor and Ying go first. Wait at Henan Road. A puller will be there to take you to the station. Da-tsien and Mary will follow two hours later.

"Wait for the train. Students Ma, Kang and Wu will be there. Kaiser Chang will help you. You must get off in Soochow. Elinor, make sure! If you ride past your ticket, the Japanese will simply execute you.

"Horse Master Yip will try to meet you at the Soochow station, but you must presume that he won't make it. Do you know what to do if he's not?" His eyes softened. "I wish I could be with you and see Soochow."

"Come with us, Baba!" cried Da-tsien.

"Fu and I are now Shanghainese men. We stay. The air would chill my bones. You'd worry about me instead of pressing on. You must journey fifteen hundred miles on hard roads." He pulled out his foreign pocket watch, nervously winding it. "It's time for Elinor and Ying to go." He signaled, and the two girls stood. So did Lon-lon, Chin and Lu-lu.

"Well," said Lon-lon, "I guess this is it. Be careful. *Yongbao ni.*"

Share embraces. Chin and Lu-lu threw their arms around Elinor and Ying. Clutching one another, they cried.

Baba dramatically touched his two older granddaughters.

"You take good care of your mah-mee. Inside, you have the energy of your father and the people skills of your mother. You'll do fine."

The girls pressed their faces against his kind hands.

"We're now *youmin*, refugees, Grandfather," whispered Elinor. We are leaving the *jia*. We are leaving China. We have pulled out our roots."

Elinor thought like an adult and was a leader. A great political movement was under way at St. Mary's, and she had been part of it. In the morning, she would be marked absent for the rest of her life.

She was fourteen and couldn't believe that her mah-mee would choose to leave China. This was their nation, their country, and there was so much work to do; it was more important than finding one selfish man who had forgotten them. She needed to rebuild China. She couldn't do that from Hollywood.

sixty-two

The Run to the River

NORTH RAILWAY STATION near Hongkew was Shanghai in a small space. Terrified refugees pretended to be commuters fighting for toeholds on badly overcrowded French trains. Peddlers hawked rotting vegetables for mounds of mostly useless inflated cash as baby girls, once again, were abandoned in panic and desperate thieves and pickpockets struggled to take the possessions of others. Shanghai had become a spiritual abattoir.

A Japanese sergeant blowing a whistle and giving orders lost his temper and shot two pushy men. The crowd grew quiet, shifted to let the bodies fall, then resumed its screaming struggle.

Da-tsien and her girls were crushed as they fought their way to the car. They lost a bag before boarding, but Zee Zee had told her to move fast. She was trying to hold onto Mary and not go crazy from the screaming strangers. A man helped her up, apologizing for touching her. She turned to look at him and it was Singh, the house guard. When she and Mary were inside, she turned to find him, but she was jostled and pushed and he was gone. "Singh!" she cried.

"Ah-wu!" called a man who was waving at her.

Two other big men also waved while pushing the mob away from seats they were saving. They were yelling to her. She reached them and the man seated her and Mary and Elinor Ah-wu and then Ying.

"I'm Kaiser Chang, Taitai." He lifted the largest of their bags. "Too big!" he yelled. "Can't keep! Too dangerous! Take out only what you need!"

Da-tsien was paralyzed—it had taken hours to plan each bag. Decisively, Elinor extracted the garments with gems and gave the suitcase to Chang. The men stayed until the students—Mohammedan Mr. Ma, Miss Kang and the tall, handsome Buddhist Mr. Wu—arrived. They were rattled but smiling, thanking Da-tsien and Elinor and Chang with quick bows. They had small bags and they looked at each other with relief.

Da-tsien grasped Kaiser's wrists. "Thank you so much, bless you!"

Suddenly Chang and his men were gone. She said a prayer for them, thanking them and their kind spirits. She looked out the window for Singh, confused by the ghostlike reflection of her own face. Her heart jumped— there, on the platform, looking at her, round and full and older—was Mr. Tung. As she craned to see him more clearly, trying to wipe away her own reflection, she thought he waved at her. She raised her hand, and he was gone. She held her throat. Dear Mr. Tung. Had he somehow helped them? She realized that Tung would never have abandoned her in the manner of her husband. She tried not to think about leaving her own baba behind.

The train shifted to start and stopped with a jerk. Japanese soldiers using bayonets cleared a path through the packed car. Behind came Kempetai gestapo. The passengers fell silent; most looked down, many stopped breathing. The soldiers looked for refugees while the gestapo looked for victims.

"*Whose?*" asked a black-suited Japanese agent. He pointed at preposterously overstuffed suitcases in the overhead compartment. People raised hesitant hands and were taken from the train.

The agent studied a man, then him asked a question. The man answered bravely and the agent shot him. A woman screamed and the agent shot her. A boy cried and miraculously fell silent without a gunshot.

Da-tsien was trembling and crying. Elinor held onto her. "Pray, Mah-mee," she whispered. Mah-mee tightly scrunched her eyes shut and prayed. Elinor looked down, feeling the terror in the car. Guards were approaching. Footfalls stopped; they were looking at her mother.

"*Where you go?*" A terrible voice. A man answered hesitantly. The next gunshot triggered a panicked exit and many escaped the train to be shot down on the crowded platform by waiting soldiers, inspiring new flights that led to more shootings. Ying covered Mary's eyes.

Inside the car, the Japanese moved on. Ghostlike, head-down Chinese K'u-li laborers appeared to pull the corpses from their seats, absorbing the bad luck spirits of the dead. One of them was Mr. Wu. Standing passengers eagerly took empty, bloody seats. Elinor thought the train would leave, but Chinese rail agents, in the employ of the Japanese Occupying Forces, passed through the train to collect a *likin*-style surtax for the passengers' privilege of traveling with the Empire of Japan's Greater East Asian Coprosperity Sphere. Struggling with the amount, trying to breathe and trying not to cry, Da-tsien paid the tax. Young Mr. Wu was dead. The train rolled out of Shanghai. Da-tsien had never been more relieved to experience movement. They were heading northwest towards Soochow, where Da-tsien had been born.

So deep was her disappointment in God for allowing such unspeakable things to happen in front of her children that she flung away Elinor's efforts to comfort her. She was angry, angrier than ever before, and she had no idea what to do with her rage or her sense of betrayal. She knew why she had been exposed to such tragedy, however, and why she was now running: Her husband had lied to her and now she had a malign future.

To Da-tsien, God controlled everything, giving humans the capacity to do good and to follow the Law. She believed that while humans lacked many abilities, they could at least keep promises. She ground her teeth; she would keep her promise. In America.

The Japanese army stopped the train again to flush out spies, students, refugees, suspected refugees and attractive females. More passengers were removed. Often the train stopped without explanation and simply sat. Passengers alighted to relieve themselves in the fields and were left behind when the train pulled out quickly. Once, Japanese troops boarded and kicked out passengers without allowing them to collect their luggage or their children because they wanted seats. A day later, the train reached Soochow. Da-tsien's muscles had tensed for so long that she found it hard to stand. Elinor and Mr. Ma helped her down from the car. They were in Soochow, but it looked like Shanghai.

Through the milling fearful crowds and bullying Japanese soldiers who took whichever females and goods they wanted, Elinor dodged and darted, searching. She pulled a stiff, slow-footed Mah-mee with her. Ying followed.

Miss Kang, the small college student, carried four-year-old Mary. Mr. Ma carried the bags. They pretended they were not together.

Elinor approached a big man with a cart.

"Hello, Mr. Yip, how are you, have you eaten?" asked Elinor.

"Hello, Young Missey," he said, bowing graciously, as he had addressed her mother so many times. In the cart, whining with excitement and pleasure, pranced Dog, Zee Zee's German shepherd, who was so excited to see the girls and so fearful of big Yip that he peed on the boards. Yip cuffed him out of the cart and he landed, wagging his tail and urinating.

"He never did that before," said Yip, throwing dirt on the dog's water and using a brush to clean the boards. "It's the war. Changing all of us." He slapped his palms, wiped them on his trousers and bowed.

"Taitai, a pleasure for old eyes. Been watching Japs kill people all day. They're true bastards. They crawl like a damn anthill here. Upriver, they thin out. Excuse the horse. He shits like a storm."

In the cart bed was a water barrel, oat bags, tools, sacks of country potatoes and millet and an original small Soochow chest that the House of Tzu had employed in its sad move to Shanghai.

"Chest has stuff packed by your mah-mee," said Yip to Da-tsien. "Photos. Your wedding dress. She said it cost so much money that your daughters have to use it when they marry or she'll be so angry she'll come after you." He laughed from his gut and they laughed too, as Chinese people do even when their kin are slaughtered, their farms are burned and their memory tablets are shattered by marauders.

Mr. Ma loaded the cart. Da-tsien shaded her eyes in the morning sun, looking for the water gate that led to her old home. But the railway station was far from the canals. Her heart soared to be so close to her father's soul, but she knew that every moment put them farther apart.

"Where doggie sit?" asked Mary.

"Dog runs in front of us," said Yip. "Trained to smell bad men."

"There are no bad men," said Ying, comforting Mary.

"Of course there are bad men!" snapped Da-tsien, angry again.

"Mah-mee," said Elinor quickly, "where's the House of Tzu?"

Elinor feared what Mah-mee might do to Ying. Mah-mee wasn't strong and Elinor had heard her talk about leaving Ying behind.

Yip snapped the reins and they rocked away.

"Which way are we going?" asked Elinor, her voice vibrating.

"North," said Mr. Yip. Ahead was Free China. All around them were Japanese, brigands, bandits, disease, a lack of water, pain, death.

Before long, Da-tsien's mind went blank. She was a *youmin*, a refugee, a free-floating, disconnected human being without *jia* or roots. She and her girls had become ghosts who were fleeing the land and the duties that make people true and real. But she had yet to fulfill her purpose; she had yet to produce her son. To do that, she would have to find her disloyal husband.

She had freed herself from a hard mother-in-law and a sarcastic senior sister-in-law. *I'm free.* That thought made her smile, and she held onto it for nearly an hour.

"We will reach the Yangtze at Wushi. Avoid Nanking." The city the Japanese had raped had become their new capital. Smart charming Wang Ching-wei, Dr. Sun Yat-sen's deputy back in 1925, whom Da-tsien had enjoyed meeting in Shanghai, had committed a fabulous treason by accepting the presidency of Japan's puppet regime. Now, people spat at his name.

"Anyone going to Wushi by rail," Kaiser Chang had said, "clearly would be a refugee and would be shot. Wushi has become a huge execution grounds. Going by horse or foot is uncomfortable but safer, if you avoid the bandits and deserters and roaming remnants of the *jun-fa* warlord armies."

Yip was on a farm road that paralleled the Woosung watercourse. It would approach Wushi while avoiding Nanking.

"If a Jap patrol comes," he said, "everyone but Taitai and Mei-mei, get out. Hide in thrushes and swamps. Taitai, pretend to be my wife." He laughed. "Tell Zee Zee that! A Kwangtung horseman and a Soochow lady!" He slapped thighs and showed teeth and everyone laughed. Elinor thought Mr. Yip would be a good daddy. In the distance, she saw Dog.

After Soochow, Yip stopped and they stretched.

Yip pulled a vicious knife and waved it at Da-tsien. "You look like a *huaren* snob girl. Not good. Cut your hair. Girls', too. And female chests are sticking out. Better strap them down."

Da-tsien covered her mouth and blushed.

"No makeup." He squatted, rubbing dirt in his hands. "Put some of *this* on." He laughed, but this time, no one joined him.

Da-tsien, a delicate Soochow princess, pulled out her compact and looked at her pretty face in the small mirror. She checked her eyes, her eyebrows, her mouth. She patted her long luxurious hair. Far away, an airplane droned.

"No time, Taitai," growled Yip, offering her the knife.

Delicately, Da-tsien took it. Soochow ladies were famous for their beauty and their long hair, and Shanghai women were the most stylish. She gripped a handful of her hair and sliced it off. She began to cry and was unable to do it again. Elinor took the knife and finished the job. She then let Ying cut hers, and she cut Ying's and even little Mary's in a futile effort to make her less exquisite. Then she cut Miss Kang's hair, which was already bobbed in a revolutionary statement of patriotism.

"Now, we do look homeless, don't we?" sniffed Da-tsien, closing her eyes as Elinor brushed off her rouge and replaced it with dirt.

Yip was staring at them. "Do *di-ren* peasants wear *huaren* silk cheongsams? Not even on Buddha's birthday or *ching-ming*. They make people stare and wonder where you hid your gold. Time for you and me to piss," he said to Mr. Ma.

The two men left and the women changed clothes.

"Dress plain and old," called Yip, his back to them. "And dirty. Rub dirt in hands. And cut those long nails. Did your father tell you nothing?"

Yip returned and had them rub grit in their hands and roughen them with rocks. "Do this all time in cart. All time! Let's go."

Da-tsien didn't want to roughen her skin, but Yip scolded her into it. Elinor did it willingly and Ying followed her lead.

Dog came fast, tongue out and hair up; the Japanese were ahead. Da-tsien and Mary stayed with Yip on the cart. Yip pulled a machete and quickly cut millet, bound it with string and threw it in the cart, cursing himself for not doing it earlier. He gave sheaves of it to Mr. Ma and Miss Kang and put them on the road with Elinor. Now they were simply farmers and townfolk carrying millet, and not *youmin* in flight.

They heard the Japanese coming and pulled off the road.

It was thirty miles to Wushi and it took them three days because of Japanese patrols. Yip and Mr. Ma slept on the cold ground. The females slept on the cart bed under most of their clothing.

The horse was hobbled and Dog kept watch. In case Dog fell asleep, Elinor stayed awake. Ying sensed Elinor's wakefulness and also tried to keep her eyes open. Da-tsien and Miss Kang slept poorly, interrupted by the cold, Yip's snoring, and the unforgiving hardness of the cart's wooden slats. Da-tsien hated the dark and couldn't wait for dawn. A rooster crowed and it was still dark and she thought of Zee Zee's warm body and she missed him, missed his passion and his craziness. She remembered how she sang hymns to him as he fell asleep next to her on soft warm sheets and she began to cry. She fell asleep and in the next instant, she was being awakened.

"Time to go," said Yip, who smelled like a horse.

"I don't like it here," she tried to say with a thick tongue.

"I slept great, thanks. Lady, you look sleepy. Wake up!"

"That's not what I said. How much farther to Chungking? *Aiyaaa!*" she cried, recoiling and jumping. "A *bug!* With feelers! Did you know there was a bug in the cart? Oh, Mr. Yip, can we get a cleaner one?"

She was met with silence.

"Okay, so what time do we get to Free China?"

"This is April," said Mr. Ma, looking at the sky. "We hope to reach Chungking in June, before the new Japanese aerial bombing campaign."

"*June?*" said Da-tsien, counting the months on her fingers twice. "That's six, seven months? Why so long? Are we lost?"

"Taitai, June is only three months away and we have to cover five thousand *li*," said Miss Kang politely. Seventeen hundred miles.

"No one can travel that far," said Da-tsien. "Certainly, not me!"

"Three days, Mah-mee," said Elinor. "You can do that."

"Yes, three days," said Mr. Ma, "then we'll see where we are."

"I am ill," said Da-tsien. "I need a bath, a really good soak." She had a headache and she didn't have any hair to speak of and there was grit in everything.

"Food," said Yip, offering stale peanuts, wormy millet and old boiled water. Da-tsien walked unsteadily away from the group and bent over for a while.

"Potatoes for lunch, later. We're losing day. Let's go."

Wushi was a Japanese military headquarters, so Yip went alone into the city to fill the water barrel from a good communal well. They waited a day and Elinor worried while Da-tsien unsuccessfully tried to sleep. Yip returned with greens-filled *bao*, buns, and water. They feasted and drank water like camels. Mr. Ma made a fire, which was very risky, to brew tea. Da-tsien's spirits lifted for a moment until she realized that nothing had changed and then she cried bitterly.

"Next town is Chiangyin on the Long River. There, we'll have time to get fish. Remember," said Yip, "what a fisherman your father was."

Da-tsien smiled with the thought. "Oh, yes, Mr. Yip, he was!"

"I don't like fish," said Mary, and everyone laughed.

Near midday, not far from the *Da Yunhe*, the artificial tributary, the Grand Canal, they heard the mosquito buzzing of an airplane so they dismounted and dispersed. The plane did not come closer.

They continued onward. Elinor told Mary that hiding from the airplane was a game, and at first, she believed it.

"That could be Baba up there," said Ying to encourage Mary.

"Stupid!" said Da-tsien. "All planes here are Japanese." *Could Ying be right? How wonderful if Zee Zee were up there!* She didn't know for a fact that he was in America, courting the actress Katharine Hepburn, but she felt it in her bones.

"Zee Zee," she whispered just in case. "This is Da-zee! I know you can hear me. Can you also see me? I'm wearing the red scarf you bought for me in Peking. If that's you up there, be ashamed and come down now, please, so I don't have to walk anymore."

Da-tsien faced the irony that she had made Zee Zee notice Katharine Hepburn, the woman with fire and a beautiful face. Chinese cheekbones, burning eyes, precise eyebrows, perfect complexion, gorgeous hair. Da-tsien touched her short, dirty locks. She couldn't let Zee Zee see her like this. She covered her hair with her scarf. *Grow fast*, she urged, praying to God for a short journey and long hair and for her husband to come to her so she could stop the jarring ride. The cart ride was like a beating, so she stepped down.

Thinking of Hepburn, she pushed herself, making herself take a longer stride. *I thought you were beautiful, but you took Zee Zee.* When playing with these thoughts, no one had to tell her to hurry.

Chiangyin turned out to be another Japanese army outpost. Yip recommended against getting fish. The horse was strong and amply fed and the weather was good and he wanted to keep moving. Da-tsien's face was smudged with tears and her feet ached.

The river road was thick with people who were refugees, and therefore, targets, so Yip pulled off and tried another route and dead-ended at a swampy pond full of angry mosquitoes and small biting bugs. They tried another way, while avoiding the road, which drew strafing by a Japanese plane.

Da-tsien's ankles hurt and every step drove small knifelike pains into the balls of her feet and her heels. Yet the hard, spine-jarring cart was unendurable. She didn't appreciate the cool air that kept her from overheating or her ample feet that made the journey possible. She began to think of Soochow's canals and luxurious baths and Zee Zee rubbing her scalp and forehead and her neck and shoulders and she remembered the exact sensations of his massages. For a while these thoughts sustained her.

Long dusty days unfolded towards the river town of Chenchiang as the Yangtze Long River bent southwards and then to the west. Da-tsien couldn't think of her abandoned father without being overcome by guilt. It was easier to hate her short hair and her bound chest and her ugly clothes and the omnipresence of dirt and the dominion of bugs.

"This is good," said Yip. "Now we're headed in the right direction."

"We were lost before?" asked Da-tsien. "Is it June, yet?"

"No. We had to go south before we could go west."

"Soldiers," said Mr. Ma, who had the best eyes; he saw Dog racing to report the news. Miss Kang jumped too fast from the cart and fell, twisting an ankle. She limped to the fields away from the river. Mr. Ma took a machete and led the girls and Dog into the fields towards the river.

Da-tsien was bone tired. It was easy to remain seated next to Yip. She was too fatigued to carry fear and she smelled like the animal that clopped and pooped directly in front of her.

"Excellent!" said Yip. "Yes, good. Keep looking like that, dumb and tired. Take off your wedding band. Hide it."

The Japanese patrol was four mounted soldiers, approaching laconically in single file. Yip noticed the poor management of their nags. He imagined shooting each of them with quick bursts of fire.

He stopped the cart and smiled at them as stupidly as he could. He had a killing knife and a Mauser automatic self-loading pistol in his coat and an axe in the cart. He could kill all of them twice.

The patrol leader stopped to study the woman while his men watched the carter. The leader looked at her face and hair and then her body. He saw the big feet. But he also saw something beneath the dirt.

He reached down and grabbed her hands, feeling coarseness and roughness. The horse was perfect for its role, too, looking mangy even when groomed. It appeared small and bony but was strong and compact.

"Where live?" barked the officer, throwing away Da-tsien's hands.

"Town," said Yip, pointing forward.

"Name town!" said the officer, drawing his small automatic.

Yip cursed himself for not knowing. Refugees wouldn't know.

"Yentzufan," called Elinor from the reeds. "Hello, Yip *syensheng*, Yip

Taitai, how are you? Can you give a poor girl a ride home?" Elinor skipped to the cart and jumped in the back, smiling and waving at the officer.

"Nice horse," said Yip at the soldier's nag. "Bones on hooves." He spoke in Cantonese while smiling widely, "Defile your mother, Ugly One."

The officer nodded back. The patrol left. Yip snapped the reins and they began moving. Half an hour later, he stopped, pretending to check a loose wheel. The others regrouped and remounted the cart.

"Mr. Ma must always go ahead of us to get the name of the next village," said Elinor. "And learn what dialect they speak. I had trouble understanding the people in the last village—did you?"

"We're near Anhwei Province, now," said Miss Kang. "We should have thought of this before we left. This dialect problem."

"I thought of it," said Elinor. "Mr. Wu the Buddhist spoke Anhwei."

Miss Wang limped. "You need a doctor's ointment," said Elinor.

"Did you break it?" asked Yip.

Miss Kang knew that grooms killed horses that had suffered fractures. "No!" she said quickly. "Feels fine."

Thus began the process of pretending to be from the next village or the last. Mr. Ma returned, his hand full of stones that he threw at the earth god to ask for softer roads. "The next town is Chenchiang. We can get boats there. I think we're not alone, though. Looks like there are lots of other people also pretending to be villagers, trying to buy passage."

"Big boats? Like the Italian liner, *Conte Rosso?*" asked Da-tsien.

"Little ones, Taitai," said Mr. Ma. "One-paddle boats."

"Nighttime, right?" asked Mr. Ma.

Yip nodded.

"Then let's get as close as we can before dusk," said Miss Kang.

They clopped forward. Hearing noises, they pulled off the road and hid. A refugee mob moved noisily down the road, but they were headed towards the Japanese lines instead of away from them. Yip was puzzled. Then they heard a Japanese fighter plane, coming fast. The mob ran, showing its inexperience. These were beginners with little girls and big loads. They stayed on the road and ran faster, as if the airplane was an angry water buffalo they could outrun.

"*Get off the road!*" shouted Mr. Ma. "*Hide on the sides!*" No one listened. The scream of the accelerating fighter became unbearable and then came the *putta-putta-putta-putta* of its guns, churning the earth and turning people into pieces of meat, and no screams could be heard above the roar and monstrous whine of the aircraft as it thundered overhead, the prop blast flattening them as it pulled up, its bright red suns emblazoned on each green wing. People moaned and cried and others silently bled to death.

"Don't move!" cried Mr. Ma. "He comes back!" He recognized the airplane as a fast Mitsubishi A6M. The wounded tried to run away and fell as the green fighter strafed again, killing left and right.

Da-tsien buried her face in her hands, praying to God, apologizing for past sins and reciting the Twenty-third Psalm. When the shooting stopped, she had time to be horrified by the realization of what her husband had been doing when he flew airplanes. It made her so angry that Da-tsien defied Yip's orders and searched for a child whose wailing moved her.

"Stop! We have to run! Jap soldiers will come any minute now!"

"That's why we have to help these people!" she cried.

The crying little girl had been badly bruised when her mother had to drop her. "Mah-meeeeeeeee!" she cried.

Da-tsien looked about for the mother, but none of the wounded claimed her. Da-tsien was astounded to find four other perfectly healthy baby girls who had been discarded. The road was now cluttered with debris and abandoned goods and the dead.

Elinor scavenged for food, finding soy beans and chicken eggs and a bag of rice. While she was running back and forth to load the cart, Da-tsien put the five girls in the back. She wished she could find a goat to give milk, but, luckily, the babies were healthy; they were at the beginning of their journey.

It was another day to reach the village. Yip and Mr. Ma crept into Chenchiang at night to find an abandoned river village. All of the small fishing boats had been machine-gunned and the dead lined the roads and the quays. Somewhere, a baby weakly cried. Da-tsien looked for her but couldn't find her.

"Do you know how to patch a boat?" Mr. Ma asked Yip.

"No. They're ruined. Try another village. But cut south to get off the road and away from the damn planes." They reported this to the group.

"Better if we cross the Long River here," said Miss Kang. "I interviewed many people in Shanghai before we left. They said Anhwei is safer north of the river. Let's find boats on the opposite bank."

Yip rubbed his beard. "I can't get the cart over the river."

"Can you give up the cart?"

He thought. "Yes, but not the horse. It's a good horse. And Dog."

It took days of upriver travel to find a rickety ferry that had survived the Japanese raids. They awakened the proprietor, a toothless old pirate who barked at them like a dog until Dog barked back.

Elinor cut a precious stone from Ying's garment and offered it. They were down to six good gems. The man looked at it under a match, bit it and threw it in the river, making Da-tsien scream, the sound echoing across the water. Everyone froze.

No one killed them so he said something in a strange tongue. But the meaning was clear: That was worthless, what else you got?

Hating to do so, Elinor cut out a pearl. Five left.

The man motioned everyone, including the horse and dog, on the ferry. Skinny *k'u-li* laborers were kicked awake from their dirt beds. Instantly, they hauled mightily on the Hausers. The raft shook and leaked and soaked everyone, but it reached the north bank of the Yangtze. Then the old pirate returned to his side of the river. His coolies loaded the cart, and, with great effort, they moved it across the river.

For a small gemstone, they got a chicken and vegetables. Miss Kang snapped the chicken's neck and Elinor and Ying prepared it while Mr. Ma built a fire from wood gathered by the others. He constructed a spit and they feasted, talking like a Chinese clan under sparkling skies and a crackling fire, feeding their young and thinking of future sons. They made a crude broth, soaked cloth in it and let the babies suck the soup, but the babies cried for milk. The little girl who had lost her mother comforted one baby, and then the next. She could never get all four to be quiet at the same time.

They watched the girl trying to meet the challenge and debated her age— five or six?—when Dog raced back and they put out the fire and comforted the babies. A Japanese truck rumbled by, its searchlight probing for *youmin*. They tried to sleep, but the river wind bit into them and it was a bad night of mosquitos and Japanese motor patrols. Mary, whom Yip called Mei-mei, little sister, began to whimper as she tried to sleep; the friendly airplane game had become something that had shaken her.

"To avoid airplanes. I think we ought to travel at night and stop when we see light," said Miss Kang.

Everyone agreed, especially Mei-mei. She loved to sleep, which is what they did for the next day.

In the dark, the horse stepped in a gopher hole and came out lame. The cart was emptied and Yip pulled the bridle, helping the animal limp forward. They plodded on, making short progress.

Dawn came and they were too tired to proceed. They dispersed and slept. Da-tsien didn't care about an airplane killing her; she feared serpents. She awoke in the cart, hungry and sore, and found insects in her clothing. Too tired to weep, she fell asleep and dreamed of airplanes and hawks chasing her.

Elinor shook her awake. "Mr. Yip says we have to go now."

"What will you do in Chungking, Mr. Yip?" asked Da-tsien. Talking was better than thinking about her feet, which were blistered and sore, or her aching legs, or her bottom, which couldn't bear the cart. It was a question that burned at her: *What will we do when we reach Chungking? How do we get to America and Hollywood and that Hepburn woman from Szechwan?*

"Chungking is far away, Taitai," he said.

The airplanes returned and they hid. Against her will, Da-tsien fell asleep in the reeds and the mud, with Mei-mei next to her.

Again, they were awakened. The horse was no better and probably wouldn't improve if he had to pull even a lightened cart. They stopped and got off the road as a mob of refugees, moving faster than they, passed them.

They plodded on. At dusk, they saw a hint of faint lights. They breathed when they realized that it wasn't a Japanese patrol; the lights weren't moving.

Yip pulled out his Mauser. "Wait here." They seemed to shiver when he was gone.

Da-tsien gathered her daughters about her and ordered them to pray for no airplanes and no Japanese and for a female goat.

He returned at false dawn. *"Jao wei,"* he said. Missionaries. "I think this time, Taitai goes with Elinor. Talk foreign god-talk, okay?"

It was an American Christian Mission, covered with trees and netting. There was glorious shade everywhere. The *jao wei* took the infants into a nursery filled with baby girls and attended by school-aged girls who had also been abandoned. There were no boy infants or boy attendants. Sons were passports into the uncertain future and daughters were disposable burdens.

Da-tsien watched as the missionaries gave goat milk to the babies. For that moment, the punishing travel had been worth it.

God, I killed my little baby, Shiaobaobee, with my bad thoughts and my weaknesses. But I saved five from the river road.

"Come share our poor food," said the Americans in excellent Chinese.

The food was good, the straw cots were blessings and the baths were the best. There was so much water that she constantly brushed her teeth. She fluffed her clean short hair and used scissors to shape it and studied herself in the mirror and saw the resemblance to the hair vogues of the Flapper Twenties, and thought it almost cute. To restore her sense of self, she played at the hairstyles and the hair dressings that the voguish women of Shanghai wore before the Japanese came, shuttering her eyes and remembering. Wusong, very traditional Ming with the hair in bun across the neck. She had tried the Montmorand, a Euro-Parisian hybrid that flowed down the back, rejecting the dual side-bun Manchu style, and preferring the tall Imperial hair pile that Na-bu had let her wear when she had turned fifteen. It was Zee Zee's favorite. She had worn it for him to the Paramount the night that he had proposed.

She soaked in the tub to rid herself of the hints of chest-binding and biting bugs and the cart's splintered floorboards. Her feet were a mess and her tender bottom hurt far worse than when she had fallen from Zee Zee's motorcycle.

Da-tsien slept for two solid days and conversed in English with the *jao wei*, who were tall, kind, moderately frantic and dramatically overworked. Singing vespers with them before dinner, she missed her days with the Methodist Presbyterian Church in Shanghai. The *jao wei* loved her sweet voice, smiling broadly as she carried high notes. They also noticed that Elinor sang well.

Most of the Chinese people in the mission weren't believers; they were here for water, food and shelter. It was clear that the missionaries wanted Da-tsien to stay and work.

"They say," said an American woman, "that the puppet Shanghai government's police chief—a Chinese man named Pan—imprisoned all the Americans and Europeans in the city. That they're suffering horribly in an open-air prison, where they die of starvation, sickness and beatings. Lee Taitai, is that possible? Is this true?"

Da-tsien had heard of this from her mother, who had witnessed it. So she gave the Chinese answer, which valued relationship over rumors, and legitimized family hope instead of clan misery.

"No. I'm sure all our friends are safe and well, don't you think?"

Elinor was silent, remembering her visit to Pan-da's house, of Tai Yueh letting her take money from her purse, of crying without letting the Japanese soldier hear her. Of a city taken over by all the evil people. She felt in her bones that they should've stayed, to outbalance the bad.

"What can we do for you, Taitai?" asked the missionary.

"Accept our heartfelt thanks. Take care of those baby girls."

"Of course. Are you a believer? Will you pray with us, for God's work, for the salvation of our Lord Jesus in everyone's lives?"

She would.

Yip paced and Elinor copied him.

"We have to go," said Yip, looking at the sun.

Da-tsien cut a fine ruby and a pearl from her clothing, and Elinor showed her teeth because they had only two gems remaining. Her mother pressed them into the hand of the *jao wei*. "For Him," she said.

The horse had healed, so they headed for the city of Heshian and its fleets of small boats. They traveled in long stretches with short breaks. They passed corpses whose throats had been slit.

"*Tu-fei*, bandits," said Yip.

Da-tsien sat next to Mei-mei and covered her eyes whenever they passed through another tragedy involving defiled women and murdered boys and ransacked goods. Little Elinor scavenged for food.

"The surviving men were enslaved, the women put into brothels," said Yip. "Make more money that way."

A brown wolf followed them. Later, he was replaced by a pack of thin and mangy wolves that seemed as stressed by the Japanese invasion as the humans. Da-tsien hated these animals because they resembled the fox and the evil fox spirit; Yip worried when they disappeared because something had chased them away.

When he was certain that they were being followed by men, he gave the reins to Elinor and left them, moving silently into the dark woods.

Elinor slowed the horse.

"*Tu-fei*," said Yip upon returning. Bandits. He grinned at Da-tsien, who was covering her mouth to hide her teeth and her emotion. "Lady, never let the *tu-fei* see your fear."

Mr. Ma caught glimpses of horsemen coming closer. He gripped the machete. The bandits saw the men and trotted away.

The next time, they were sized up by horsemen who boldly rose into their path. Yip stopped and stood. "Hey, assholes!" he shouted with a huge grin, his voice echoing in the woods. "Want to kiss the devil's ass? Bring your lips closer!" The *tu-fei* melted away.

He faced Da-tsien, pulled out his killing knife, stuck it in the seat and tied its scabbard to Da-tsien's left forearm. He slid the blade in and showed her how to pull it out.

"Careful. Don't pull it too fast or you cut yourself. Big veins here, don't want to do that."

She hated it and tried to pull the scabbard off her arm.

"No, Taitai, leave it."

"Why give the knife to me? Why not to Mr. Ma?"

"Ma has the machete."

Da-tsien kept thinking about those horsemen. In their eyes she could see no heart, no compassion.

She pulled the knife and almost cut herself. She tried it again, more slowly. She hated the knife; it represented everything wrong with the world and she wanted to cry.

"Mu-Lan, woman warrior!" said Yip, laughing.

The great riverboats at Heshian had also been machine-gunned by the Japanese, but the surviving sailors had patched a few. They were willing to transport the Lee party up the river for millions in cash.

Days were consumed by negotiation. Passage on the clipper junk would cost the remaining opal and diamond, with two more glass stones thrown in the river while Da-tsien bared her teeth.

Sailing upriver on the Yangtze is a skill and an art and based in no small part in faith in the gods of the river. The river flows with irresistible mastery to the Hwang Hai, the Yellow Sea, and to the Pacific Ocean; sailing against the current that feeds and supports a fifth of the population of China is a full-time, high-risk and dangerous job. These inland sailors were very good, but it became clear that they had never navigated as far upriver as Anching, much less to the distant tricities of Wuhan that would mark a third of the journey to Chungking.

The girls liked the boat's bright eyes painted on the prow.

"Eyes to look for fish, Young Missies," said the *laoban*, the boat's boss-captain. "Also to look for tricky currents that eat boats, even big ones like ours. See, you Shanghainese, look at the water! This is the Chiang Jiang! Clear water! Not muddy like the ugly Whangpu! Stay in center of boat. Big winds on river! Blow you overboard, you gone for good, and slimy river gods embrace your hair forever! By time I turn boat around to find you, you're dead and your body is in America!"

"Can we go to America by turning around?" asked Da-tsien.

"No, no can sail across ocean in this, Taitai, sorry."

"You're sure it's faster to go upriver?"

"Oh, yes, Taitai, for certain. Not to mention, go other way, run into about fifteen billion fucking Japanese soldiers!" He smiled toothlessly.

"Here, on river, all they do is bomb us. Not even come down and shoot guns. Winds too dangerous and they crash! I show you later, Jap airplanes, all burned. Very lovely sight. Make my bones happy."

"How often do they bomb?" asked Mr. Ma.

"Who knows?" said the *laoban*. "They're not like tides. They bomb when they feel like bombing."

His crew was preparing to set out and wanted to load the party. Yip was sitting by the bank, whittling a piece of wood. "Can you take a horse?"

"Dead horse, yes. Live horse, very bad idea. They trample you."

"Can you part with the horse?" asked Da-tsien.

"No need. I go back now. I promise your father to get you on the boat to Chungking. First, you reach Anching, then, Chiuchiang. Later, Wuhan. Then Dongting, then, after that, don't know. Later, Chungking. I have to watch my family, now. I have to hurry. It's a long way back. Taitai, you want my gun?"

She was stricken by the idea of not having the company of the resourceful Mr. Yip, but she managed to speak. "Oh, heavens no, Mr. Yip."

"Maybe I give it to Mr. Ma. He's a good man."

"No, you keep it. You're going back to danger. We're safe now."

"*Ji hui!* Don't say! Spit out, right now. Spit, Lady!" He looked up.

Da-tsien gingerly released saliva into a handkerchief.

He laughed, spitting ferociously for her and making her jump.

"Taitai, you'll be fine. No, you keep the knife. Mr. Ma, he keeps the machete. I have the axe and other knives. That one, on your arm, it's very sharp. Very good knife for very good woman!"

He put his hand on Elinor's shoulder. "You're good, Young Lady. Very smart, very brave. You get everybody through to Chungking, hear? And you help your older sister, Young Missey," he said to Ying. He rubbed their heads, waved to Miss Kang and bowed slightly to Mr. Ma.

"You ready to die for these women?" asked Yip.

"I think so," said Mr. Ma.

Yip spat. "Wrong answer."

"I hear you, Yip. Thank you. Yes, I am. I'll miss you. Good luck."

"Remember, most of fighting is not fighting. You put in your eye that you are ready to kill? Most men don't want to die, so they back off. Some men, very big mind trouble, see your killer eye, they try kill you right off! Trick—knowing who pays attention to your eye, and backs off, and who sees your eye and wants to slaughter everyone. Understand?"

They watched Mr. Yip unhobble his horse and lead it back on the road which had brought them so far from Shanghai. Reaching Heshian on the Yangtze River had been akin to climbing a mountain—going up the slope near Nanking and marching down the other side. They would do this three more times, and then, they would face the gorges of the Yangtze.

Above would be Japanese bombers. On the sides of the gorges were *hai tao*, river pirates, who waited to catch unskilled sailors so they could slit their throats, rape their women, take their goods and burn their boats to keep warm on windy nights. Below would be water *kwei*, river ghosts who waited to catch and devour the stubborn men who dared fifteen-knot currents while trying to tack upriver into violent and unpredictable winds.

"The *kwei*," said the *laoban*, "love to take us into their watery kingdom and eat our tasty eyeballs, cackling over their catch, paying us back for stealing their fish for thousands of years."

The sailors lived in a small natural harbor that allowed them to launch into the river with full sails. They loaded the Soochow chest, up-anchored and waved goodbye to a small mob of wives and children. With a popping of crimson quilted sateen sails, a beating of good-luck gongs to chase away ghosts and to warn the *kwei* and lyrical, rhythmic songs of burning rope and hot sweat, the stout clipper junk with the red prow and the great black eyeballs boldly challenged the Long River and offered itself to fate.

Da-tsien shaded her eyes, looking for Yip. He was a good Chinese man with a good heart. When she saw him, she waved and he waved back. She couldn't bear to watch him disappear into nothing, so she closed her eyes but kept waving and thanking God for the loyalty of a good man.

"Goodbye, Mr. Yip!" cried her girls. "Thank you, Mr. Yip! Sleep well under stars, Uncle!" They were weeping inconsolably, missing him already.

The river dwarfed everything. The sea breeze was exhilarating at first, but it became brisker, and then hard, whistling and screeching through the rigging as if it were angry. Da-tsien sought the protection of the lower cabin, where the three girls were huddled with Miss Kang and Mr. Ma. Mr. Ma did not like ships and regarded every creaking rope as a sign of imminent destruction.

They were not the only passengers. There were four other families and clean razorback hogs and crates of smelly chickens. Sitting by Mr. Ma was Dog; Yip had given them one final important present.

There was also fresh carp, which began arriving a few hours after they had launched. The fish were thrown down to them from above.

"Clean, chop up, for cook!" yelled the deckhand. The women refugees collectively recoiled as great forty-pound river fish fought for life on the pitching, sawdust-covered floor of the hold. Elinor waited until one was almost dead. She found a knife in a wall scabbard and cleaned it as a dozen more were tossed down, angry and wet and fighting for life. She worked carefully in the rocking hold so she didn't cut off one of her fingers. Her mah-mee couldn't even watch and tried not to inhale.

Later, when Da-tsien became seasick, Elinor stood by her on the railing. The *laoban* saw them, became alarmed and tied both of them to the boat. The sailors were happy and helpful and cheered Da-tsien after her episodes. They passed a great seagoing junk headed for the Yellow Sea; it carried no fewer than two hundred people and what appeared to be ten thousand ducks in crates. Only the captains and the children waved to each other as everyone else was too busy, too sick or too solemn for greetings.

Suddenly there was a cry of *"CHING PAO! CHING PAO! WARNING NEWS! AIR RAID!"* and everyone was herded below. Elinor had to look; she saw a large number of twin-engine green airplanes flying above them. One dropped small objects and she grabbed hold as the junk heeled violently into the wind. She watched the bombs explode in the river in the place where they would've been had the *laoban* not changed course.

"They're killing our fish," muttered a sailor standing on deck. "Defile your mother and your father upside down in Mongol teashop!" he cried, shaking a fist and cursing colorfully until he saw Elinor.

"Aiya, Young Missey, did I curse in front of your young face? Hope not! *Pabupa?* Afraid? No?" He laughed. "Look at your brave face! How can they beat us when we have children like you?"

They reached Anching in under a week. In two weeks and only a few near-miss bombings, they had reached Wuhan in Hubei Province. The Japanese had just been pushed out of the city by elements of the Eighth Route Army, which was a *Gungtsetang*, CCP, Communist, military force.

Wuhan is actually three cities—Hankow, Hanyang and, on the east side of the Yangtze, Wuchang. They passed the bombed-out Customs House and entered the Han Shui Channel.

Later, Da-tsien bathed in a half-destroyed hotel room while Elinor studied the Red troops and the workers of Wuhan. These soldiers were very different; they helped clear rubble, cooked meals, fed the elderly, played with children who were not their own and protected the civilians first when the bombers flew overhead.

Elinor volunteered to help and the Red Army soldiers welcomed her. She cooked and comforted the wounded.

The city was bombed twice before they set sail for Dongting Lake. The farther they traveled from Shanghai, the happier were Miss Kang and Mr. Ma, who were beginning to talk together more frequently.

"I don't think I'll be raped now!" said Miss Kang.

"I can't wait to see Free China," said Mr. Ma. "And eat lamb!"

Da-tsien was a *chih huo* matchmaker in her heart, and still bragged about putting little Auntie Gao together with Uncle Chu. She couldn't wait to give advice to this new couple, even if in their youth they violated *ji hui*.

If I'm so smart about love, she thought, *why did my husband leave me for an American actress? What if she likes him? Oh, dear God, please, no.*

s i x t y - t h r e e

Hunan Running

HUNGKING IN SZECHUAN Province is due west from Wuhan, but to reach it via the Yangtze, a strong-hulled *fan ch'uan* must sail due south into Hunan before the river turns up and due north. Later, it will eventually begin its westward course toward Tibet and the Himalayas.

Hunan was the land of big hills, great spices, huge meals, vicious bandits and fiery revolutionaries. It was the home of the great conqueror of the Taipings, Tseng Kuo-fan, and the revolutionary Communist thinker Mao Tse-tung. It was where Mao's wife was cruelly tortured and executed by the Kuomintang, and where Zee Zee had tried to kill Mao on the misty mountaintops of the Chingkanshan.

At Dongting Lake in Hunan, the junk captain was greeted by a clan elder, but the elder directed the *laoban* to return immediately to Heshian with a sick relative. The relative was bundled onboard and preparations were made to get underway.

There was no question that the boat would leave its passengers and turn around; Confucius had made clear that honoring the father was one of the three sacred *gang*, or bonds, of life. The other was to the emperor, who was far away on the best of days and now, of course, was gone forever. The last was the bond of wives to husbands. None of these bonds was reciprocal. It didn't matter if the father didn't honor you—you had to honor him.

Da-tsien understood this, because Miss Roberts had said that God and Jesus loved you whether you returned the favor or not. This was the great appeal of the foreign religion—even if one acted like a stupid and recalcitrant slug, the foreign god promised you love. Chinese gods had higher standards.

The Lee party stood with its bags and a Soochow chest and Dog on the shore of one of the great lakes of Asia as the great, red-sailed junk re-entered the river for a relatively easy return voyage with the fast current.

They found another boat and used half of their remaining, worthless glass stones for passage. Da-tsien still didn't understand the difference between true gems and fake ones, and only noticed that this crew was tougher than the one from Heshian. She kept her daughters close to her and below deck. This time they were surrounded by chickens and ducks, and Dog had a hard time with several banty roosters. He would circle his nap spot ten or fifteen times instead of his normal three or four because the roosters bothered his harmony.

They and two other families left Hunan and sailed north into Hubei once more. They were not even close to reaching the beginning of Three Gorges when their new crew dumped the families and baggage onshore and turned around, hooting and holding their privates as they enjoyed this catastrophic joke played on gullible people.

"You didn't even know!" yelled a sailor through cupped hands. "Our small boat can't navigate up there! You think we couldn't tell fake glass from diamonds?" They howled and slapped their thighs.

The Lee party decided to keep going. Da-tsien threw away all the non-essentials, but kept her wedding dress and the family photographs. These were distributed into separate bags; Mr. Ma carried the cruelly rolled-up dress in his pack.

"That's pirate and bandit country up ahead," the other families had said to them before turning back. "Four families and one male, on the road? No guns? No horses. Even if you were all men, it wouldn't be safe."

At first, they were encouraged; Dog didn't rush back with bad news, and when they encountered troops, they were Kuomintang. These men were polite and friendly, sharing food and good water and giving fresh socks—U.S. Army issue—to Da-tsien, Miss Kang and Mr. Ma. In the course of one month, they had been hosted by the Communists and the Nationalists and now they both seemed equally inviting.

These soldiers wore the same uniform as Zee Zee. Da-tsien enjoyed their admiration of her and her girls and she forced herself to forgive them their unforgivable sins of 1927, when Grace Sun and many Shanghai students were murdered by this army's troops.

Following the course of the Yangtze, which would eventually reach Chungking, they found a small, clean village with a tiny hotel that had been painted black to camouflage it from air attacks. They booked one room and slept communally.

In a few days of rugged hiking they entered what seemed to be a new country. The land had flattened out into a low plain.

"It's the great basin of the Ch'iang Jiang," said Mr. Ma. "Here, they call the Long River the Yangtze."

"The road's ended," said Elinor. "Now it's just a path."

The next village was very small and had no hotel. There was no electricity—only tung oil lamps. The few buildings had been bombed and people stared at them.

Over the next few days, they found no villages at all. They were running out of civilization. They slept in farm sheds offered to them by kindly women while suspicious men glared. Da-tsien had lost track of time. She wanted to fall off the road into the ditch to the right, so she could stop hiking, but she didn't want to fall off the cliff to the left, dropping about four hundred miles straight down into the frothy, angry river. The heights terrified her and left her numb. She had trouble feeling anything except pain.

"One step after the other," suggested Elinor.

"I can't," she breathed back, but Elinor helped her to keep moving, as Da-tsien thought aimlessly of soft beds, feather fans and the Soochow estate. There used to be a servant who did nothing but carry groceries from the market. *What a soft job*, she thought.

There were no more hotels or theaters or even tung oil lamps; the people they encountered used Japanese pressure lamps, which were cheaper, or they used nothing. Here, people went to sleep when the sun went down.

At a small, ramshackle abandoned farm, Miss Kang gave up and said she couldn't go any farther. They decided to rest and wait a day. Meanwhile Mr. Ma found a brackish well and they drank deeply, only to become ill within hours. Miss Kang refused to continue, so Mr. Ma had to decide what to do. Even ill, Da-tsien was still a strong advocate of true love.

"If you love her, Mr. Ma, stay."

"If you love her," said Elinor, "get us to Chungking and then come back for her. You promised. Look, we have to find water, and we can't leave Miss Kang here, so let's go now and find water before anything else."

They trudged on. Da-tsien began crying and when Elinor pointed out that she couldn't afford to lose teardrops, it only made Da-tsien cry harder. She remembered P'o-p'o praising the Bravest Wife, goading her to be a martyr, if necessary, and die for the Lee clan. With that memory, Da-tsien got angry.

"I'm not going to die for those unkind women," she muttered.

The river road had become steeper, rockier and thick with scree that caused all of them, at various points, to lose their balance and fall.

Da-tsien hated pain and wanted to throw a tantrum at God. She remembered Miss Roberts telling her that God was prevenient, offering help before you even needed it.

"Oh, yes?" she asked in a mumbling ramble. "Where are you now? How could you let those evil men just shoot those poor people in front of my children at the Shanghai Railway Station? Or let Zee Zee abandon me! What kind of God are you, anyway? Do you know how much my feet hurt?"

In a delirium, she saw her unborn son and she was ecstatic that finally her wish had been fulfilled. She couldn't wait to shave his little newborn head to encourage a thick, luxurious growth of hair and to watch Zee Zee write their son's name in the memory book of the House of Lee while her fine, smart nephew Lon-lon tolled the generational bell to inform all ancestors. She had a son, and they could honor the rites, and he would take care of her in her old age.

The bombs fell later that day, killing many in a refugee group ahead of them. Da-tsien cried and felt better. So many bombs, and they were still alive.

"Okay, God, I'll make you a deal. You make sure my son doesn't hear any more bombs or explosions, and you make sure he isn't born on this terrible road, and you get my daughters through this, and you save Miss Kang and Mr. Ma, and let them get married and have many sons, and save this stupid dog that now makes me feel guilty because it got sick on the bad water, too, and you give me my son after letting me catch up with my husband, and you keep Katharine Hepburn from making springtime with Zee Zee, and I'll give the boy a Christian name and of course, give you anything you want. Yes. Anything. What do you want?" She reflected on what she had. "You can have my life," she said, gleefully. "I give it to you! I don't like it so much anymore, anyway, because my feet hurt!"

She thought she was at the head of the column, but then realized that she was sitting. Everyone else was ahead, looking over their shoulders at her. Even Miss Kang had gone farther. Da-tsien's mouth was so parched that all she could think about was water, and more water.

"You okay, Mah-mee?" asked Elinor. They were gaining elevation.

Mr. Ma ran back and helped Da-tsien to her feet.

"Can we rest?" she asked him.

"No, we have to find water. Come, let's go, one foot at a time. Funny. I hate water. Never thought I'd miss being on a river."

Walking slowly, they came to a bombed-out village.

"Japanese bombers, so cruel," said Mr. Ma.

"They bomb," gasped Da-tsien, "because they hear what you say."

"What?" said Miss Kang, who had come back to join them.

"The pilots can hear what you say up there. Yes, true, my husband told me. That's why so silly to paint things black to hide it. They hear your voices, so it doesn't matter what color you paint a building."

Mr. Ma seemed confused and then he fainted. Elinor and Miss Kang pulled him into the shade.

Elinor remembered baggage coolies huddling against hot buildings in August on the Bund, fighting for inches of shade. Shanghai seemed like another lifetime ago. She was fourteen, but she forced herself to look for a well. She found several, all dry and some reeking from bodies that had been dropped in them. She had trouble walking and she stumbled toward shade, panting in the relative cool of indirect sunlight, and passed out. She awoke to a strange sound. She had trouble moving, but she felt water filling her mouth. It was a delicious dream. No, the sound was her own gagging; she was taking small sips of water that hit her like torrents, choking her.

A Chinese woman was dripping water on Elinor's lips and speaking, but Elinor could hear nothing. Then she heard the woman's words: *Slowly, child, slowly. Don't get sick.*

"My mah-mee, sisters," said Elinor, gasping, lightheaded.

"Yes, we know, we found them."

"Who are you?"

"*Youmin*, like you. But we have a truck. Do you want a ride?"

MR. MA PUT his hands on the fender, on the side mirror, touching them as if they were of another world. "Truck," he said.

"Yes, sir, that's a truck."

"Has gas, good tires?"

"You bet."

"Going to Chungking?"

"Hope so!"

"Has battery?"

"Certainly, yes. But it's dead. We have to push."

"God is great!"

The driver had considerately stopped his vehicle facing a soft decline. There were thirty or forty people and clusters of children and they began pushing the rear of the truck as if it were a water buffalo. Some of the children asked permission of the truck before they put their hands on its bottom. They pushed and grunted and the driver got up to speed and let out the clutch and the engine coughed and caught and exploded foul exhaust plumes as it found its ignition sequence. The crowd erupted in cheers as the driver stabilized the RPMs with the choke. He braked and some of the men boarded the truck bed and took the children who were lifted up to them by other men. Then the women were lifted up, and the last men hauled themselves up. Ropes were stretched across the back, then someone thumped on the roof of the cab and off they went.

The journey was never to be forgotten. The truck bounced and the people in the bed bounced up and down with exaggerated effect.

Mr. Ma held onto Mei-mei, and Da-tsien held onto him and everyone was holding a friend or a sibling or a total stranger. In this way, laughing and shrieking with happiness and misery, they covered the miles.

"Ah-wu!" cried Mah-wee. "We forgot Dog!"

Jumping up and down, Elinor moaned and covered her mouth in shame. They tried to look back, but taller people blocked their view. Hours passed. In this manner, they reached the outskirts of Ichang and the beginning of the Yangtze River gorges.

"What can I pay you?" asked Da-tsien, her head spinning.

"Be kind to other travelers," said the driver, who was knocking dust from his clothing. "I get gas from the government. My wife and I drive the fields between here and Yachueling and find poor people who are dying of thirst. There's a well here and food stalls not far away." He saw Da-tsien's gold cross. "Pray for our work. Pray that we keep our strength. Pray that fear can end in our land."

The Lee party slept under the stars to an orchestra of singing cicadas, owls and night monkeys. They drank water and recited poetry about water and sang river songs that the Heshian boat crew had chanted to the river *kwei* when they left harbor, the girls hitting thighs as if they were gongs and drums. They removed some of their clothing and bathed from the well, laughing and enjoying life. They ate peanuts and millet and bought hot vegetables in vinegar sauce. The missionaries were going to give them waterskins and foodstores and they felt as if life had become sublime.

"How can water taste so wonderful?" marveled Da-tsien. "They must have better streams than in the East." She smiled when everyone laughed, knowing she had said something which delighted others.

"Thank you for not letting me quit back there," said Miss Kang. "I'm very embarrassed."

"Hey, I was bartering my life for a sip of water," said Mr. Ma.

Da-tsien reflected on her promise on the road: her life for the lives of others. It had been a good trade. She smiled at the young couple, encouraging them with her goodwill. That night, Da-tsien prayed for the people on the river and for the Good Samaritans of Ichang and the American missionaries in Anhwei. She counted the bumps in their hems and thought they had four good stones left, perhaps twenty less than they'd need to reach and establish themselves in Chungking. She didn't know that they had run out of good stones weeks earlier.

She freed a worthless glass gem and cried a little, thinking of Zee Zee. That night she dreamed of him. He wanted to have springtime with her and she was too dirty and had to go to the bathroom first and she kept finding twigs and toilet paper in her hair, then she awoke.

Dog was licking her; he had chased them and found them. She smiled and hugged him and let him lick her hands, then rooted in her bag for the last crumbs of food. She also gave him peanuts, which he choked on, waking up the others.

"Dog!" cried Ying, hugging him.

Miss Kang smiled perfunctorily and went back to sleep as Mr. Ma watched over her.

The other families had left. Da-tsien wanted to wait for the Samaritans so she could ask them if there were trucks to Chungking, but after two days, they hadn't returned. Rested, provisioned and well-fed, their feet in the best shape since they began, they set out on the final leg to the capital of Free China, a circular route to the north and then to the south that took them away from the Japanese bombers.

The country was less rocky. They found berries and small peaches and apples, which improved their spirits. They conserved their precious water and hiked from dawn to dark, sleeping soundly after their now-routine road work. The dried corn, the millet, the waterskins, the goat cheese, were their treasures.

One night, alarmed, Mr. Ma awakened Elinor. "Dog is back from his search."

Elinor didn't understand at first, nodding, and then she bolted up. Bad men. Japanese? *Tu-fei?* The sky was inching towards false dawn.

They listened, hearing many men in the distance. Too many for Mr. Ma to fight. They awakened the others.

Slowly, they crept away, avoiding crackling leaves and walking single-file on the softest earth they could find. They walked carefully but urgently, hearts in their throats, tears in their eyes. The sun rose. They came to a village that was half-deserted. They found an empty two-story building and hid inside. When they heard nothing but the sounds of villagers, they took separate rooms and fell asleep.

Suddenly Dog alerted Elinor to intruders and she froze.

A Japanese patrol entered the house. The soldiers were tired, dirty and demoralized, reacting flatly when they saw the refugees. The officer studied the group. Elinor hoped that they looked too healthy to be *youmin*, but the group also had the look of people who didn't live in the house. The officer kept staring at her.

"What do here?" he demanded.

"Our house," said Da-tsien, who had already hidden her gold wedding band.

The officer gestured for everyone to follow. Elinor shook Ying awake but was pulled away by an angry soldier. The Lee party was gathered in the street while their food was ransacked. A soldier used a bayonet to tear open some of their clothing, but he found nothing.

Elinor calmed Dog. The angry soldier realized that one of the girls was missing. He ran inside to find a girl still asleep. He yelled at her to move, and other soldiers threatened Da-tsien with long-knife bayonets as she instinctively moved to help her daughter.

Inside the house, the soldier prodded Ying with his boot and she stirred. He yelled again and she quickly sat up, startling the soldier who thrust his bayonet at her, the point cutting her throat. Ying was terrified and speechless. The soldier gestured, but she couldn't move. He was going to shoot her when Da-tsien yelled, "Ying, come here! *Kwala, kwala,* hurry!"

Her throat bleeding, Ying stumbled to her mother.

"Stay with me," said Mah-mee, putting her arms around her. "You okay?"

Ying couldn't answer; a roar louder than an airplane had filled her ears and her tongue wouldn't move.

Mr. Ma was hoping that the Japanese would kill them quickly, without torturing the girls.

The officer studied the women and saw nothing he wanted. Nanking had been better; the women had been clean city girls.

The soldiers took all the food and waterskins and moved on. In a few minutes, the Japanese were out of sight.

They were alive but in trouble. Go back and resupply? Or go on?

"What do you think?" asked Da-tsien.

"We need water," said Miss Kang.

"We should keep going," said Elinor. "Fast. We're in a bad place. It's no better back where we came from."

Mr. Ma agreed.

"Okay, let's go, then. Look for water and berries and fruit."

Da-tsien had been shaken and wanted to slow down and let her mind gain control. She remembered Zee Zee telling her to think, to be observant, to see everything.

Ying had been slow and she, Da-tsien, has sensed nothing, and this had almost killed her daughter. They had lingered outside Ichang and the result was a collision with a Japanese patrol.

"We have to hurry," she said, and they stepped up the pace. "Ying, you hear me?"

Ying had shrunk within herself. Elinor held one hand and Mah-mee occasionally took the other.

"You okay, Ying?" asked Elinor.

Ying didn't respond.

They were entering the Three Gorges, a place of such historical import that no equivalent exists in America. It is as if the *Iliad,* the *Odyssey,* Beowulf, Camelot, Valley Forge, Gettysburg, Pearl Harbor and Normandy were located within a challenging one-hundred-mile stretch of the Mississippi. In China, this is the region of the Three Gorges.

The area above the first gorge, Hsi-ling, was made up of limestone quarry and unstable shale. Landslides into the gorge below are common, and Mr. Ma found this encouraging.

"Too tough here for horses. We'll be safe from humans. We just need water." He tasted the air and liked it—they were high but it was humid, as if spring showers were near. They found a mud stream and soaked their clothing in it and then squeezed water from the clothing into their mouths. They walked hard and fast until light failed. They found a clearing and went to sleep. Ying lay down like the others, but she didn't close her eyes. She constantly touched the clotted wound on her throat.

At dawn, Mr. Ma showed them how to collect moisture from the tops of leaves. "My father was a farmer," he said.

Dog had not appeared and they walked as fast as they could on a sustained basis. The problem was Mei-mei, who had small legs but was hard to carry. Elinor and Miss Kang tore up clothing and created a harness which, if Mr. Ma gripped it, allowed Mary to be carried above his backpack. The other problem was food; they found cherries that made them ill and everyone was sick of the berries. They could find no true fruit trees, so they settled on *tseng,* a thorny tree that bore small, lovely citruses that offered tiny amounts of extremely bitter fruit and juice.

"We used to receive these as gifts," said Miss Kang. "Now I know why we never ate them and just used them for decoration. I can't believe how awful they taste."

With the webbed contraption for Mei-mei, the pace could be dramatically increased. They were in limestone quarries framed by jagged talus piles and spirelike peaks so high that they blocked the sun. Mist was at their feet. Here, heaven not earth and the towers of Illium defied time.

"We're above Wu-hsia, Witches Gorge," said Mr. Ma. "Look carefully. If we see Shen-nu feng, Goddess Peak, through the mist, it's good luck!"

Da-tsien wasn't thinking about goddesses. She was thinking about how thirty, hungry, tired and dirty she was. She was keeping up a rambling conversation with God when Mr. Ma stopped. He was listening and frowning. All Da-tsien could hear was the roar of the river through the granite narrows.

"Nothing," he said, but he extracted the machete from his blanket roll, and they continued on. Occasionally, he called out the names of the mountains— Wise Man Springs, Congregated Immortals, but he didn't say the name of the good luck mountain, Goddess Peak.

At the next stop, Mr. Ma pulled aside Da-tsien, Miss Kang and Elinor.

"This is bandit country. Poor farmers fight tigers up here with spears. It's the hard land that produces heroes and victims. Remember Mr. Yip telling me to know the difference between someone who'll kill us and someone who won't? I think bandits up here would kill us. My father told me the old fables we all heard as kids, but he wanted me to believe them. Yangtze gorge bandits eat the livers of brave victims, to capture their courage inside themselves.

"So if we see tu-fei, we need to be brave, but not too brave. Brave enough to keep them away. Not too brave to make them want to eat us."

They were trudging forward. Da-tsien and Mr. Ma were falling behind when Da-tsien heard the jingle of a bridle.

A man on horseback was studying them. Behind him were many men and there was no escape. Some of their lean, bony horses snorted. The bandits were mangy and mean and heavily armed. They were tu-fei assessing their victims, and they were hungry men looking at a banquet of hot dishes.

"You have to pay a tax for using my road," said the man. "Put down the machete and give us your knives or we shoot you right now."

Mr. Ma carefully placed the machete on the ground.

Da-tsien was instantly sobered by Mr. Ma's restraint. She had expected him to fly around like Pi-hsia the Cloud Princess, and stun them with celestial power and make them run away, just like he was Zee Zee. But all he did was submissively surrender his machete. A fear unlike any she had ever experienced ran through her. Had the bandits seen her girls and Miss Kang?

If they had, she would get to see her girls defiled and killed in front of her. She remembered the horrible stories whispered by girls in lavatories—bandits and soldiers violated you, cut out your intestines and tied you up with them, laughing as they cut out the livers of the braver girls.

Da-tsien knew it was *yeh*, karma, for her sins of disappointing her mother, abandoning her father, and killing her little Shiaobaobee. She prayed for mercy for her daughters and that her unborn son would not feel the pain transmitted through her own heart. She prayed for something she could never have imagined: their common quick deaths.

"Come on, we know you have knives in your clothes," said the *tu-fei*. "Give 'em up or we'll cut them off of you!"

With a start, she remembered the knife on her arm. She hated it and was glad to give it up. She pulled it from the scabbard to give it to them, but it made a sharp, threatening, metallic *zing* and the bandits flinched, studying her with sudden surprise and interest. She was about to drop the knife for them when she saw that they were staring at her arm. She was bleeding—she had cut the meaty base of her thumb with the incredibly sharp blade and blood pumped from the wound. *Ai-yaaa! I'm so clumsy! So awkward and stupid! I'm bleeding in front of men! I am humiliated! It hurts! Does he see my wedding ring? Can I take it off now?*

In the long silence she tried to throw the knife out of her hand, but she couldn't get her cramped, terrified fingers to work. Again, she tried to drop it, without success.

"Okay, okay!" said the man, smiling, holding up his hands in a gesture of mock surrender. "We give up! Don't threaten us or cut yourself anymore or frown so hard! We won't fight a killer like *you!*"

He looked at her, showing his teeth. Laughing from deep in his chest and shaking his head, he pulled reins and dug heels. His horse clattered away across the hard rocks, and his bandits followed them.

They were gone. Mr. Ma turned; Da-tsien was lying on the ground. He tore off strips of his shirt and bound her wound, elevating the blood-drenched hand above her heart.

Ch'u-tang was the last gorge. They were dwarfed by a range of rounded-boulder mountains. The great junks below looked like toys, and Da-tsien felt as if she were a magic woman, full of *mo-li*, blessed by the gods and placed into a special status among the clouds.

God, don't let my son know what happened back there. Take the story out of my blood so it doesn't go inside his little heart.

"Do not tell the girls about the *tu-fei*," she had told Mr. Ma. "It's a story only for my husband, when I see him, which will be shortly."

In Chinese culture, a daughter with a dying mother is expected to cut skin from her own body and add it to a medicinal soup that will heal her parent. Da-tsien, ever since her father had stopped her foot binding, had been an upside-down girl. Her feet were too big, her contrariness too great, her liver too large, and she could never perform as her mother expected or as tradition required. It was logical that her blood would not help Taitai, but save her daughters. But it was an embarrassing story, and it was all Zee Zee's fault, so only he should know it.

They heard the familiar noise of Japanese bombers and felt the vibrations, dispersing to hide under sheltering *tseng* trees while avoiding their thorns.

Miss Kang pulled out the guidebook that students had used in Shanghai to plan the Northern Route escape. She spoke mostly to Ying.

"After the gorges comes Wushan, then Yunyang. Then we'll see the Feng-tushan mountains. On the other side is Chungking."

s i x t y - f o u r

Free China

CHUNGKING SITS ON a peninsula girdled by the Yangtze and the Chialing Channel. For all *youmin*, it is the end of the flight from the Japanese and the worst horrors of World War Two. For the Lee females, it was a way station en route to Hollywood. Black smoke billowed and sirens wailed as fire companies fought the fires of the last air raid.

Mr. Ma and Miss Kang bowed. "It was an honor to accompany you and your daughters," they said in small voices, one after the other. "You have given our families a thousand precious memories." This was ridiculous, so they laughed, showing their teeth.

"You made our safety possible," said Da-tsien, giving them stones, unaware of their worth. "I am so grateful! Now, will you two get married and have many sons?"

They blushed and bowed their heads.

"*Tsai jen, syesyeni*," said Elinor, shaking their hands.

"You're a terrific girl," said Mr. Ma. "You're like Mu-Lan!"

"Strong heart," said Miss Kang to Ying, kneeling to look into her averted eyes. "You are very brave! Can you say goodbye to me? No? Well, let me hug you, sweet girl."

Ying absorbed the hug. Gingerly, she patted Miss Kang.

With wet eyes they pinched Mei-mei's cheek and walked away.

Da-tsien smiled happily; in the distance, the two students reached out to hold hands.

Da-tsien didn't love Chungking, an unattractive city whose looks hadn't been improved by bombing, but she loved the sense of a Chinese pastoral life that she had forgotten since her Soochow childhood.

"You can talk, Ying, it's safe now," she said. "See there? A *chun-ya* tea seller. Remember *chun-ya*, so good as an additive in morning tea? Look how clean everyone's clothes are! And there, a duckling salesman. Here, hold the little duckling, so cute! And there, a toy seller with so many things. There, see him across the street? A birdcage merchant with a lovely round sun hat! Oh, hot rice cakes and *chiao-tze*! See, everyone buying, bargaining, arguing over price!" She clapped her hands. "It's just like China, again! What do you want to eat?"

The Soongs had a big house in Chungking. You could tell by looking that there were servants whose only job was to carry groceries.

Elinor knocked on the door. Chef Chu, the former Tzu House cook, opened the door.

"Aiyaaaa!" He covered his face and bowed, overcome by emotion as other servants joined them, and he fought to find his words for all.

"It's Lee Taitai and her daughters from Shanghai!"

With bowing and weeping, Da-tsien and her daughters entered the home. They stood still in the entry, which was strangely cool and they realized that they were inside an actual house with intact walls and true floors. The servants stepped back and bowed continuously, lowering their heads again and again and crying, giving full vent to their emotions to allow their guests and kinswomen to gather senses and to thank the gods. Somewhere, far away, airplanes droned and bombs exploded.

Da-tsien accepted cups of welcome home hot tea and warm water, drinking politely. Her daughters drank like horses, sucking the fluids with understandable ardor, then they watched as Dog drank from a puddle of water. She watched the girls eat, cautioning them to go slowly. She saw herself in a mirror and blanched. Quickly, she left her girls and the Soong servants to find what she needed most: a good hairdresser.

She walked into a top beauty salon looking like a lady who had fallen from an airplane, sat and gave rapid directions to the stylist.

"Use *pau-hua-mo*," a natural wood-jelly product renowned for growing darker, thicker hair. "None of that modern material."

"We can't get modern stuff here, Lady," said the girl.

"And cut it so it grows faster, but not *Hsin-tzu* style, no shaving! And please massage my neck muscles. They're so tender! You'd better do my nails—they're ruined, ruined, so terrible. You have no idea what the wilderness does to your skin. Make me look like the most beautiful cinema actress in the world and hold nothing back! I'm going to see my husband and he'll have seen all the best hairstyles in all of America and I can't afford to look like I just spent two years walking here from Shanghai."

Hours later, the stylist stopped Da-tsien as she was leaving.

"You have to pay, please, Lady," she said.

"Bill the Soongs, please," she said.

"The Big Soongs?"

"Yes, the Big Soongs."

Elinor bathed for days and Ying imitated her. It was strange having amahs to help them again and Elinor resisted, liking her independence. Ying declined with hand gestures because she didn't feel worthy.

With her hair cleaned and styled, Da-tsien took a bath. She wept in the tub when she realized that carrying her son had been only a dream instilled by mountain spirits.

Later she and Elinor went to the square, where two pretty country girls in peach silk gowns and pants danced and sang. Each held a white cloth and a long bamboo pole with holes drilled to hold coins. As the girls sang and danced and twirled in unison, they delicately tapped the bamboo staffs on their feet or shoulders, their hips and opposing hands to make the musical sound, *jing jing jing.* They sang of love and steady hearts, of absent men and loyal women, and it was then that Elinor tried to introduce Da-tsien to a very presentable tall officer with wonderful manners. He was very interested in her and, at first, Da-tsien thought that he wanted or needed something and that she was expected to help. When she realized that her daughter was attempting to introduce her to a potential husband, she blushed and excused herself.

"But, Mah-mee," said Elinor later, "he's such a nice man!"

"Darling, he could be Confucius himself! I'm married, or didn't you know?"

"You were married," said Elinor.

A lovely little girl in a colorful silk outfit beat a flower drum with small drumsticks, throwing them in the air and catching them as she sang. Her brother hit a gong, singing her chorus.

It was the *Feng-yang* song that Da-tsien had heard as a girl in Soochow, the tune wafting up to her window.

The little girl laments that her husband only plays the drum, and the boy sings that his wife has huge, unbound feet. It is a bittersweet song, a country song, a Chinese lament of humor and pathos, and it left Da-tsien feeling a deep melancholy for her childhood and a sadness about her mother that would not go away. She hugged Elinor to her and thanked her for her good wishes.

"I promised your father my life, Ah-wu," she said. "I can't control the weather or the size of my feet or the Japanese or if we eat or live or die. But I honor my promises, and I expect your baba to honor his. I can't marry another. So if I want to be married, then I have to find him."

Avoiding air raids, she and Elinor began to scout out the routes to America. Consistent with her pledge on the river road, Da-tsien volunteered in the hospital and began to read the Bible, waiting for God to take her life for the good deal she had negotiated above the gorges.

SHE TRIED TO buy clothes with her last stones and was told that they were worthless. This couldn't be believed—Taitai was too smart to send her daughter into the wilderness with glass—but Elinor reminded her that the gems were Uncle's, and that he had poor vision and could have accumulated pretty glass stones along with valuable gems.

Using the Soong's generosity, Da-tsien bought the best clothes she could find. Because many KMT officers actively blackmarketed, she was well attired in a New York–fashioned dress and shoes when she walked into KMT head-quarters. She found the head of the travel directorate *yamen*, identified herself as the wife of Major T. C. Lee and the friend of T. A. Soong and requested air transportation to India and passage from India to Hollywood. She did this as if she were ordering two cups of tea.

The officer shrugged and had trouble looking her in the eye. Da-tsien then brought in her daughters. The man looked at her and looked at them and knew that somehow, he would get them out of the war.

T.C. WAS IN Buenos Aires when he received a telegram from S. Y. Shen informing him that Da-tsien and the girls were in India.

The telegram said that a special KMT passage fee of $467 would be required to move one woman, two teenage girls and a five-year-old girl from Calcutta to the United States of America via a U.S. naval vessel.

The telegram asked, "Shall I send $?"

T.C. was chasing German asset collateral for Bank of Canton loans while simultaneously attempting to sell Chinese tungsten, which is an essential ele-ment in high-explosives manufacturing. He disliked both jobs, and would've welcomed any distraction except the telegram.

He was not an indecisive person. Yet he was in South America, captured in indecision and swayed by an attachment to a tall, unavailable American woman with incredible cheekbones and a sharp mind who had used him to prepare for a movie.

He sipped coffee and smoked a Lucky in the Plaza de Mayo. He missed Da-tsien, but he felt an immobility, a strange, exotic form of paralysis when it came to either sending money, which he was sure would never reach her, or sending sentiments, which seemed to have been overcome by his meeting a woman named Hepburn.

He exhaled and saw himself: *I love adventure. I love movement. I can't stand doing the same thing over and over again. I wish I could fly again. God, they have great airplanes, now.*

It was June of 1944; the Allies had landed in France and the Germans had stalled badly in the Eastern Front against Russia. The Americans were push-ing the Japanese back all over the Pacific, from Saipan to Kwajalein, and would be in the Phillipines by October. Americans were flying P-51 Mustangs, P-47 Thunderbolts and P-38 Lightnings and they were blowing the Germans out of the air.

American bombers were now hitting Japan from China. A new American Vought fighter, also called the Corsair, was killing Japanese Zeros. Another year or two, and the Empire of the Sun would be crushed. Then what? Then the civil war in China, between Chiang and Mao, would begin in earnest. *They should've let me kill that man,* he thought.

He wanted the war to go on, but he was reluctant to support Chiang Kai-shek, who had surrounded himself with thugs. He knew the Communists were too dangerous. *So I'll fight the Reds. America will help. We'll win.* That part was simple.

I'll send the money to Da-tsien. If they make it to America, I'll set them up, and then I'll go fight the Communists. Equally simple.

NOT SO SIMPLE for his wife and daughters had been flying over the Himalayas, which was one of the riskiest flights of the war. Japan had blocked access to China except for its use of a back door—a five-hundred-mile flight across the Santsung Range that connected China to Tibet, India and Assam.

"You tell them," the KMT transportation officer had said to her, "that you're in danger in China and will be supporting the war effort in India."

"That would not be a lie," Da-tsien had replied, "except for the second part. I do not support war in any form."

"You will support the morale of your husband, a National Chinese Army officer, right?"

Da-tsien had nodded.

"Then it's not a lie."

The flight over fifteen-thousand-foot passes in treacherous winds involved a series of violent near crashes. Elinor comforted Da-tsien. Ying stayed awake; Mary slept. Elinor was worried about Ying, who had said nothing since the incident with the Japanese at the gorges. If Da-tsien had known that Zee Zee had "flown the Hump" a dozen times and loved it, she would've screamed.

"You okay?" yelled Elinor above the roar of the engines.

"I'm okay," said Ying, and Elinor yelped and hugged her.

"Ying spoke!" yelled Elinor to their mah-mee, who curtly nodded.

"Good," she said. There was a thunderstorm outside and she was trying to curl up within herself, clutching her Bible. She didn't know that the winds were exceeding a hundred miles an hour, and that below, five hundred crashed American aircraft littered the craggy, unforgiving mountains.

They landed in Assam, gasping—they had given up breathing for much of the journey and had been at high altitude. The American aircrew gave them chocolates and put them on another cargo aircraft that landed at Dum Dum Airport, Calcutta, India.

Entering the streets of Calcutta rendered them speechless. The city was clean and orderly. People walked about and spoke and shopped without fear or looking skyward. There were no raped girls, no men with slit throats, no mounds of the dead. Elinor hugged Ying and they danced happily, laughing, almost shrieking, delight in every gesture.

"Oh, can China ever be this good again?"

There was no war in India. Unknown to the girls, the catastrophic famine of 1943–44 had just struck Western and Eastern Asia, killing millions. In China, the landowning minority was oppressing the peasants as rigorously as the Japanese. In Calcutta, half a million starving and suppurating beggars had died and had been cleared from the streets, giving the appearance of a city without suffering.

Da-tsien and her daughters lived in India for nearly six months, waiting for Zee Zee to send the money for their transit across the sea. Every morning when they sat down to eat, served by Indian amahs, was a sensuous experience, tasting food, experiencing safe textures, drinking tea and water and iced tea and sugared water, chewing food, feeling it on their tongues and teeth; they bit themselves in their haste and laughed. They laughed all morning, and then began thinking of the pleasure of the next meal.

Part Four

WIND

DA-TSIEN, GUS, Berkeley, 1946. San Francisco was often foggy, and Mah-mee liked the sun in Berkeley and Burlingame.

T.C., San Francisco, 1952. Dad never went anywhere without speeding. Here, he wishes he were back in the army, instead of hustling in the Financial District.

GUS, SANTA, MARY, San Francisco, 1949. Mary was always very smart and Gus has no idea what is happening.

T.C., YING, ELINOR [back row], DA-TSIEN, MARY [center], GUS [front], Yosemite, 1949. Dad liked to make everyone visit national parks. Because of his combative style of driving and his angry presence, few wanted to go. Mah-mee's health is already in decline.

AUNTIE TZU, YING, ELINOR [standing], San Francisco, 1950. This generous relative opened her Hong Kong home to Da-tsien and her three girls during the war.

sixty-five

America

T. C. LEE STOOD on the windy dock at San Pedro, California. He adjusted his high, tight military collar. He had gained weight in America. Even though he always wore a gun, he didn't feel secure.

The U.S.S. *George Randall* was a Liberty ship, a massive, durable and ingeniously designed cargo vessel that could be assembled from prefabricated parts in less than two months. Earlier, it had sailed from San Pedro bearing trucks, bombers, fighters and ordnance for Stilwell's offensive in Burma. Seven days ago, empty of stores, it had sailed smoothly down the Mooghli River from Calcutta into the mouth of the Ganges to cross the great blue swells of the Pacific Ocean.

Onboard were badly injured soldiers from the China-Burma-India Theater, a compliment of serving nurses and two Chinese Nationalist families. The families had been kept primarily in their rooms for the voyage.

"It's for your own good, ladies," said the officer. "Our crew's a good group, but you don't want to tempt them."

The voyage had been wonderful except for their confinement and the difficulty of government-issue (GI) chocolates, which had been designed to survive transit through the tropics. Elinor had tried to eat one for several days, but couldn't get it to dissolve in her mouth.

The women were allowed on deck an hour a day. Da-tsien enjoyed the sea air, but her stomach told her that she was leaving China, and her father and mother, far behind.

As the ship approached the coastline of America, Da-tsien wasn't sure how to feel. Even prayer did not offer its customary comforts. Sobered by their survival, anxious about the fate of everyone she knew in China and angry at her husband, she struggled with God to find the one true emotion that could be genuine and admirable.

She decided on forgiveness.

Above the gorges of the Yangtze, God had forgiven her for her deficiencies as a daughter and a mother. He had held her life and the lives of her daughters in his hand so many times, and each time, had shown compassion and loyalty. She had promised her life to Him. That had made her feel almost like a *seng* monk, a *ni-ku* nun. She shuddered. She knew that if she fulfilled her promise to God, He would surely grant her greatest wish. She only hoped she could be courageous enough to do so.

"YOU MUST BE excited, huh, Major?" asked the Chinese Consulate driver who, two years earlier, had taken Major Zee Zee Lee to meet Katharine Hepburn in nearby Hollywood. "Hey, does your wife know you're friends with movie stars?"

Dragon Seed had just been released. This was the movie in which Katharine Hepburn played Jade, a Chinese women of great independence and personal verve who courageously resisted the Japanese and undertook a run to Free China.

T.C. had seen it with Ben and Margaret McAtee. He watched with amazement and horror as Katharine Hepburn seemed to imitate his own wife. Audiences loved it, and they cheered T.C. in the theater when Margaret had stood up to announce who he was. He normally enjoyed accolades, but seeing the movie reminded him of his failure to win Hepburn.

Now, as he stood on the docks in the steady Pacific winds, he remembered Da-tsien's face. He did the math; Elinor would be fifteen, Ying twelve and Mary Mei-mei just six. His wife was in her late thirties. So was he.

They were coming to America, where all the answers lived.

A BAND PLAYED as the wounded were carried off on stretchers and troops on leave flooded down the gangway to hug and kiss waiting wives and sweethearts. He wasn't a patient man and he paced, wondering if Da-tsien was even on this vessel. He remembered that she was always slow and awkward; she had probably missed the sailing time.

A woman was coming down the gangway. Her movements were steady and graceful and for a moment, he didn't recognize her. He wanted to remain rooted where he was, to not show emotion, but all he saw was her and he ran to the gangway, ready to take her in his arms. She stopped him, offering her hands, which he took and rather flamboyantly kissed, suddenly grateful that she was here, amazed that she was alive. He was also amazed that he was full of affection for this impossible, lovely woman who had made his pure, clean military life so difficult.

He thought she was beautiful, her hair piled atop her head like a Sung princess. He saw his daughters.

Elinor, tall and round cheeked, had been eating aggressively, compensating for years of privation. She was cool and distant. Ying was lovely and guarded. She had exercised on the ship, running on deck late at night. Mary Mei-mei was irresistibly cute and looked at him with curiosity.

T.C. put his arms around his girls and hugged them; they did not hug back.

There is a photograph that was taken that night in Earl Carroll's, a ritzy, stylishly raunchy Los Angeles tinseltown nightclub with dynamic floorshows, undressed dancing girls, overpriced food and extravagant bar charges. The Chinese Consul General and his wife appear relaxed. Da-tsien and T.C. sit at opposite ends of the table. Elinor is looking up at the ceiling. Ying is casting a suspicious look at the photographer. Only Mary looks truly happy.

DA-TSIEN WALKED UP the seven granite steps to the new apartment that her husband's employer, the Bank of Canton, had found for them in a blue-collar, shipbuilding neighborhood called the Panhandle in San Francisco. Zee Zee opened the door and she climbed the staircase. Straight ahead was the kitchen; to the right was a living room; to the left were bedrooms. It was very small but nicely furnished. A great soft chair sat in the living room, reminding her of Baba.

"You like it?" asked Zee Zee.

"Where is the nursery where our son will sleep?" she asked.

Her husband was handsome and strong. But she had seen him pose at the docks and had smelled his self-centered focus, knowing the sad measure of his heart. She didn't want him, but couldn't imagine losing him. He remained forty million miles away from the husband she deserved. He had used her for his pleasure. She would rely on him for her future.

s i x t y - s i x

Hongkew

.A. WAS VERY solemn. "You must return to China to empty the Bank of Canton's Shanghai and Chungking accounts. Most critically, you must put Miss Wu on a military airplane to wherever she wishes to travel. She is staying at my sister-in-law's former residence in the French Concession."

"So even you think the Kuomintang's going to fall," said T.C.

"I cannot believe that. Yet the Japanese are collapsing faster than we thought. And what we hold in China can be taken by either side. I know it's hard for you to go back now, with Da-tsien here. But this trip is essential."

That was because it involved Miss Wu, T.A.'s four-foot-tall, frizzy white–haired, Bible-thumping godmother.

"It will be dangerous, that is without question. The Japanese army still holds Shanghai. But they are tottering. Russia is about to declare war on Tokyo, because it wants to rush its armies to Peking to control the new government and to Shanghai to take its money. In any event, Miss Wu is in great danger. So are our holdings.

"No one here understands the *Huang Jing Yong* mafia, the *Chingbang*, Green Gang, the various KMT army elements and the Japanese Kwantung army better than you. You are comfortable in the street and you can get an old Christian woman on an American airplane; it is the kind of thing you do. You like adventure." He said it accusingly, defensively, gratefully. "It is the last favor I will ask." T.A. could not know that this was not true.

"I KNOW YOU'RE going to say I can't do this, but remember that Soong pays our bills. He gives us free rent. He gives me a *chi tz* car."

"Which I can't drive." Da-tsien sat at the breakfast table because a tiny sliver of light came through the window in the afternoon. She thought of it as her visitor and her friend. The girls were in school all day, and she had begun to read books about how to produce sons, which is to say that she was studying artbooks. Inside the books were photos of statuary of men with exposed male organs. She was convinced that if she studied the organs, a boy would be encouraged to grow inside her.

"I offered to teach you; you always say no."

"It's because of the way you teach. Inside, you're angry and impatient and I feel that and it makes me incredibly nervous!"

"Please don't raise your voice!"

"Aiyaa, I'm not! You're the one with the big voice! Not me!"

"Okay, okay! I have to go. Must go. Have to rescue Miss Wu out of Shang-hai." He grimaced.

"*Rescue* Miss Wu? So it *is* dangerous, very dangerous!"

"No, no. I'll be flying in with the American army. Incredibly safe."

"You always say that, but it turns out to be only a few men and an airplane! You can't go, Zee Zee! You simply can't! What if you get killed and I have no son? Why do you never think of that?"

"But Soong got you here!"

"NO! *I* got us here! *God* got us here! *Your daughter got us here!* I just used Soong's name in Chungking and his servants fed us! And bought some clothes. I'm not ungrateful, but we women did it, not you or Soong. Horse master Yip helped."

"I paid for the ship's passage!"

"I would've sold my gold wedding band and my cross for that!"

It was true; the wedding band held a Soong diamond worth the transit from Calcutta to California.

"I have to go. Now lower your voice!"

"You have to give me a son!"

"Okay, okay, you know I agree to that part." He looked at his watch. "We have time."

Outside their room, Elinor covered her face. For years she had highlighted her father's deficient moral character to Mah-mee. Mah-mee would agree, saying, *Yes, yes, Ah-wu, you're right, you're right.* Then T.C. would drop from the sky and Mah-mee would think dreamily about her missing son, forgiving her husband as if he were a loyal and ethical man. Then they would make springtime like newlyweds, without thinking, driving their daughters from the house.

THE AMERICAN AIR Transport Command pilot called T.C. up to the cockpit of the war-painted C-46 Commando cargo craft.

"They're denying landing permission at Hongchiao," he said. "They say that Jap snipers are still in control of the field. Will you talk to the tower and get us a landing strip?"

T.C. shook his head. "North of Hongchiao is a training field, Shienchiao. I trained there. You land from the east and have two thousand feet of runway but no lights. Plenty of light if we do it now."

The landing was uneventful. Ten heavily armed American OSS officers, Office of Special Services, and their Chinese translators jumped out before the aircraft stopped, and T.C. was right behind them. The aircraft turned, revved up and took off, waggling its wings. T.C., carrying a briefcase, ran for cover behind maintenance sheds. The plane would be back in twenty-four hours to pick up T.C. and his party. The OSS group would try to take Hongchiao field. The American airplane droned into the distance.

Sharp machine gun fire sounded from every point of the compass. Japanese Nambus and American Brownings. Citizens were hiding and the criminal element was grabbing all it could before the Kuomintang or the Communists took control. The Japanese would be slaughtering witnesses, burning records and fleeing. Killers would be settling scores, clans would be performing vendettas, and even more bandits would be entering the city. In other words, Shanghai would be its usual dangerous self.

Two days earlier, an American B-29 had dropped an atomic bomb on Nagasaki. Two days before that, Hiroshima had been eradicated by the first A-bomb. Russia had quickly declared war on Japan and was rushing troops into Manchuria to grab as much territory as possible for themselves and for the Chinese Communist armies. Meanwhile, American aircraft were desperately attempting to shuttle Chiang Kai-shek's Nationalist armies into the Northeast to seize Peking from the Japanese, who were now attempting to escape the country they had so aggressively invaded. The old colonial powers were gone and China was fighting itself again in its century-old civil war between the rich and the poor, with foreign powers picking different sides.

Despite the chaos, T.C. found a taxi driver who took him to the Bund. Using Soong's signature authority and matching stone chop imprint, he was able to compete successfully with panicked businessmen to withdraw Soong's assets and place them in his bag. He had to hurry.

The taxi then took him to the French Concession.

Little Miss Wu answered the door, saw T.C. and fell to her knees and thanked God. Moving Miss Wu and her baggage and a maid to Shienchao field was not difficult; keeping them alive until the plane returned was the challenge.

He had found an old barracks and placed the two women inside. There were plenty of cots and no linens, but they had brought quilts.

"You'll stay here?" asked Miss Wu, "and pray with us?"

"Yes," he said, trying not to grimace.

That evening, a Metro cop tried to roust the women for their goods.

"They're under the care of the Chinese government," said T.C., his hand-gun out. "Who are you working for now?"

The man shrugged. "Mostly myself. You going to kill me?"

T.C. studied him. "What's become of Pan?"

"Pan-da?" The man spat. "Your people already have him. They're torturing the shit out of him."

"Where?"

"The old imperial execution grounds. In Hongkew."

Major Lee's black KMT officer uniform was an imposing outfit. It could not be afforded by most field officers and its very color suggested high author-ity. The advantage within the KMT was that his orders would usually be obeyed; the disadvantage was that the uniform drew sniper fire from at least two other armies. To free his hands, he had left the bank vault assets with Miss Wu, who had quickly dealt with his decision to leave her and her amah at the airfield with a round of violent prayer that would probably bring more rascals, rowdies and killers.

T.C. pushed his driver to go faster. Dead Japanese troops littered the streets. There were no Japanese flags anywhere. The city clattered with sharp or muffled gunfire. As he approached the Railway Station, KMT troops became denser. Soon, they stopped the taxi and required T.C. to dismount. Trying to look more military, they checked his identification.

"No taxis allowed, Major. You can walk, but we still have Jap snipers, and they'd love to shoot a KMT officer in a black uniform and then we'd have a disabled taxi in the road. We have to keep the roads clear for our troops, whenever the hell they get here."

T.C. walked to the annex; no shots. Great black overturned locomotives burned from American airstrikes. Nationalist troops loitered, smoking and resting and cleaning weapons, many of which were good American M-1 Garands. They looked like good troops, probably trained by the Germans or by Stilwell. In one corner were the dead, awaiting burial. The wounded awaited transport in a large railcar area. T.C. was gratified to see qualified medics tending them. The landscape was different because the Japanese had constructed new barracks and defensive positions. The police annex building was a new structure.

It was late afternoon and fires burned all over the city as looting and pillage began to replace subjugation and terror. The dull thump of distant artillery and the sound of bombs exploding in the Whangpu merged with the unhappy wail of fire sirens. The annex had an inner compound with Jeeps and trucks from several armies and not far away, a broken wall led to a larger wall against which sagged the bodies of many Japanese officers and Chinese turncoat cops who had been executed and left where they fell. Smoke filled the area. He inspected the long ranks of the dead, hoping that Pan was not in this sad lineup.

The KMT was in control and was executing the enemy and all traitors, and certainly the friends of traitors.

With a tight jaw, he walked into Laoda Annex as if he belonged there. The interrogation rooms were below in a wet, hot, leaking basement—the water table in Shanghai was always high. They were illuminated by good electrical lights and Japanese pressure lamps. Blood from many victims stained the floors. Prisoners were crying out, but they were Chinese, so no one cried for mercy, only death.

Chinese live by rank; firstborns always trump others and elders outrank all. It was T.C.'s good fortune that the highest ranking officer in the basement room in which Pooh Pan was screaming was a captain.

Pan was suspended by his thumbs and was being simultaneously beaten with bamboo rods, burned by cigarettes and shocked by naked high-voltage wires. He had never been a particularly fit individual, and his slack muscles didn't have the toughening that would've allowed him to at least flex against the pain.

His torturers were KMT troops and they were working very hard. They didn't want information from Pan; they only wanted to hurt him for as long as possible. Awaiting him, like dessert, was a medieval display of knives, swords, cudgels, pliers and probes. It took T.C. moments to be enraged at the torturers for their cruelty, at Pan for not taking his advice, at Soong for sending him back to Shanghai at a time like this and at the Japanese for having advanced the science of torture.

He drew his automatic and unsafetied it, leaving the holster flap out to show that it was drawn, and placed the weapon behind his back.

"T'ing!" shouted T.C. *Stop.* "Get out. I have questions to ask."

"Can't leave," said the captain. "This is Pan-da!"

"Get the fuck out and take your monkeys with you! Keep mouths shut. Go eat so you can come back and work with excellence."

They looked at each other. The major wasn't going to leave and he was armed while they had Middle Age tools. Reluctantly, the men dropped their sticks and cables, stuck their cigarettes between their lips, grabbed tunics, shirts and, in some cases, trousers and left.

"Dammit, didn't I tell you not to let them hang you? *Didn't I?*"

"Shit," gasped Pan, "I'm police chief . . . never hang the chief."

T.C. disconnected the array of industrial batteries, cut the ropes, picked him up and sat Pan against the wall. His crotch was still smoking. Pan's arm bled from an old wound. T.C. found a warm teacup, thought of drinking it himself, but dribbled it in Pan's mouth. Pan spat it out.

"Gaak! Poison . . . they already gave it to me . . . don't want more. . . ."

"They don't poison people, Pan," said T.C. "Kills you too soon."

"Never heard of slow poison, asshole?" he gasped.

T.C. threw the cup away. "They really hate you. Can you walk?"

Pan laughed and struggled to talk, spitting, gasping, grimacing. "You're so crazy. Kill me. You'll kill me, right, Old Friend? You ditched Soong to come back to save me from pain, right?"

T.C. nodded. "That's right. Come on. You have to stand."

"Just kill me, okay? Can't stand. I hurt so bad. I think they'll kill me with a thousand cuts."

He draped Pan over his shoulder and hauled him upstairs. T.C. was in good shape but Pan was dead weight. T.C. had to rest at the top of the stairs, looking outside for a way to reach the vehicles. The compound crawled with officers and troops. Some listened to radios for news of the Japanese collapse. Others watched the sky; there was a rumor that American paratroopers were coming to capture the airfields.

"Hey," gasped Pan, "remember Yan Fe Loo, the street packed with all those cute drum flower girls, the ones that loved me so much?"

T.C. nodded. Time was racing; the interrogators hadn't left to get food—they'd gone to get reinforcements and guns. Luckily, there were too embarrassed to ask for help from their own units in the courtyard. To save face, they were looking for outside help.

"Ah, those bastards killed Angel San-t'ien," moaned Pan. "*Woyo tsi hue*. All my fault. They raped her first, of course, in front of me. Ah, Zee Zee, I fucking walked the crooked way. I served the Ming and fought the Ch'ing, but I never could tell the goddamn difference between Ching and Wei." The old Chinese expression of weighing pro's and con's. It was a true statement. Pan was resourceful, but he had no judgment.

T.C. started to lift Pan again. "Come on, Pooh, let's go."

"No, goddammit, I'm not going anywhere! I move and it's a thousand cuts . . . let me die here, asshole! Full of big ideas. Get rid of the foreigners. China for the Chinese. Well, Brother, everything under Heaven is totally fucked!"

Outside were hundreds of troops and a motor pool worth of vehicles. He could get Pan on the American air transport to Kunming more easily than he could get him a doctor in Shanghai. He'd give him an emetic at the airfield and hope for the best.

"Have you lost your brains, Major?"

T.C. turned to face a man in a blue gown. Dong Tang, the *Li Tsu Su*, Kuomintang secret police. Behind him, a mob of armed men in blue.

"I have questions, then you can have him," said T.C.

"Take him downstairs," said the Blue Gown.

"Five minutes," said T.C. He lowered his eyes to hide his anger.

The Blue Gown shook his head. "Risking yourself for a defiled son of a loose street bitch. Know how many skulls he turned into cups? He beheaded patriots and made drinking gourds from their heads! He drowned this city in good blood! He turned our troops over to the Japs for torture! We're going to impale his rectum with a hot bamboo stake, and burn him, then put out the fire. Then, Pan-da will eat his own ears, his own fingers and thumbs. He'll eat his own private parts and then, then, we will start to hurt him seriously in the gut, so he feels true pain. Nothing will stop us and I'd put Sun Yat-sen's widow in prison first."

T.C. counted the guns against him, and he knew Pan was dead.

"I don't care what you do to him. I want five minutes."

"Major, you don't understand. Shanghai's out of control and beyond command. You could be beheaded. No one would know."

"Don't eat your own bullshit. I came with Americans. Five minutes."

There was a long silence, filled with hope. Perhaps the man moved or blinked; suddenly, several guns were pointed at him. The chief removed T.C.'s sidearm. "Put your prisoner down."

T.C. COMPLIED AND was searched. They took his wallet, watch, passport, wedding band and ammunition clips.

Without permission, he lifted Pan and took him outside.

Silently he begged the Japanese to take a shot. A shot rang out and he thought *Yes!* Pan grunted as he took a sniper bullet, but it was in one of his dead legs and not mortal and troops in the courtyard snapped into action, taking cover and returning heavy fire into every building near them in a frenzy of explosions. Machine guns did the heavy work, blasting stucco and bricks and shattering windows as officers screamed directions to coordinate the wild fire. T.C. was running to the far wall and he sat Pan against it in a pandemonium of noise.

"Now be a man," said T.C., echoing the words his father had written to him a quarter of a century earlier after he had taken Zee Zee's wet nurse as his concubine.

"Will they tell proverbs about us for ten thousand years?" asked Pan. "Hey, Brother, thank you. Hear my words?"

"*Wan shih liu fang*, Pan. I'll try to get the *Dong Jen Fu An Tong* to put you in a good casket for the next world. See you later, Old Friend." He said, *Tsai jen*, and not *Tsai hui*, goodbye.

T.C. grabbed soldiers from their firing positions, put them in a ragged firing line, and ordered them to aim at the prisoner. He took a breath, saw his rifle squad flinching from fear of incoming rounds, knew he had only seconds, showed his teeth and gave the order to shoot.

The ragged gunfire of the impromptu firing squad was lost in the firefight.

He and Pan had been *pungyoh*, Chinese friends bound by ancient traditions and laws. So much is intuitively understood in China that moments outweigh words.

He looked up at heaven. "Fuck you," he said.

T.C. marched across the compound. He brushed past the infuriated Blue Gowns, found a bottle of yellow *ko-liang* sorghum whiskey, poured it into teacups and offered them to his own gestapo while gunfire rattled at distant walls and windows.

"Every man can do one thing well," said T.C., holding up the cup. "I executed my childhood pal. Come toast the death of the traitor Pan-da. *Gambei*, empty cup." T.C. downed the bitter liquid. "My sidearm."

The Blue Gown pointed at the pile of personal effects.

"Will you call the Benevolents to put Pan in a good casket?"

The Blue Gown smashed his teacup and spat on its shards.

As T.C. left Hongkew in search of a taxi, he looked straight ahead. The word had passed that Pan-da was dead and troops and civilians were running for the chance to spit on his body.

"His head should be put on a spear as a warning to all!" cried one.

"Skin him as revenge for thousands," muttered another.

T.C. stopped and waved at a battered, bullet-ridden taxi cab. He wasn't a man of backward glances, but he turned and saw that Pan was lying near the wall of the BMEA factory, where, so many years ago, he and Soong and Pan had hung KMT posters for Dr. Sun Yat-sen.

"Where to, Major?" asked the driver.

"Find me a Buddhist monk of the *Dong Jen*," said T.C., who realized that someone had pocketed most of his cash and his wedding band.

Only Son

"PAN KEPT US alive in Shanghai," said Da-tsien.

"He killed students and wiped out your friends," stormed T.C. "He worked for the Japanese! He executed good soldiers and patriots!"

"Tai Yueh was my friend and she gave us money for food! Now you've made her a widow! If we can't forgive people, then the world will become a place where we can't live! I forgave you for leaving us and not supporting us and chasing after Katharine Hepburn!"

He could never say anything after that. Nor could he look up; the walls were filled with pictures of artwork. Statues of David, of Moses, of Achilles and Hector and little bronze boys in fountains and they all had their male members exposed. It was enough to drive him crazy.

"Show me in the Bible where it says displaying the penis makes sons. Show me where it makes sense to have our daughters walk in here covering their eyes, bumping into furniture, hitting their shins. I'll be arrested if anyone outside the family sees this crazy stuff!"

"In the Book of Mark," she said, "James and John are called the Sons of Thunder, and you always say your male part is Thunder."

He struggled to speak.

"Thunder," she continued, "stands out." She smiled patiently. "You understand now. No more arguments about our son. And would I have to do this if your mother had made *lien-tzu* lotus seed cakes and soup for me on our wedding day, or sewed the Same-Hearts embroidery for our bedroom pillow? Of course not. If P'o-p'o had done these things, I'd already have my son, but he would've been exposed to the war and to the Run, and I promised God on the road above the Yangtze River to give him a Christian name, which was all because of your leaving us. So now you have no right to criticize me or make fun of my commitment to our boy. I swear, Zee Zee, every time you argue, or travel for T.A., or kill our friends, you use up your *yang* power. That's why we only have daughters. Now, I'm too distressed by criticism to play springtime with you, and it's windy, so you might as well drive me to the beach so I can talk to Baba."

She loved Sunset Beach, the closest point in San Francisco to Shanghai. She made Zee Zee drive her there on windy days. He sat in the car and read the paper as she ran down the beach to the surf, kicked off her cloth shoes and felt the sand between her toes, rinsing them clean in the frigid waters of the Pacific.

"Oh, Baba, how are you? Do you hear my voice, carried to you by the winds? Do you feel my love for you, my respect for you, my gratitude for your good heart? I'm so glad the Japanese aren't tormenting you anymore! Zee Zee sends money to you and to his brother, Gee, and P'o-p'o, and he heard that everybody's okay! I want to come back and see you and rub your sore shoulders, but Zee Zee says it's too dangerous, with the Communists and the Nationalists killing each other.

"I know you won't come to America, but I wish you would. There's no culture here and no clans, only individuals, but America's at peace. Baba, I value peace now, above all else.

"Did you know Lucy Kwok and Miao-miao were killed by bombs? But we're lucky, because you're alive and Mah-mee's alive and Uncle Tzu is okay and I think everyone will pull out fine, don't you?

"Zee Zee is angry as ever. He had to kill Pan, his old friend. Did you hear that the traitor Wang Chi-wei died in Tokyo? The Kuomintang army wants Zee Zee to kill the Reds again, but I've kept him here in America with his family. He hates banking and misses bombing people, but it's better to have him angry than gone, don't you think?

"You knew, Baba. You knew it would be the Taipings again, with women having to run with their children. You gave me my feet so I could do it. You told me to marry a man who loves his girls, so he could protect us. Well, I wasn't perfect, not ten out of ten, was I? I was five out of ten."

ELINOR TURNED SEVENTEEN a month before Japan's surrender ended World War Two in August 1945. Ying was fourteen, Mary was eight and Da-tsien and Zee Zee were in their early forties.

They lived in a walk-up apartment for shipyard workers who had built Liberty ships and submarines for the war against the Japanese Empire.

Where Shanghai sprawled like a drunken sailor, San Francisco was small and behaved and looked kindly upon a pretty Chinese woman who walked in the sun with a parasol, turning to talk to the amah who was no longer there.

At first, Da-tsien had attempted to care for all of her girls, but she couldn't manage it and no one required it. She was flummoxed by the multiple tasks of running a household of five persons. She still feared matches and had to wait for Elinor to come home to light the gas stove so she could then struggle with cooking, an activity that required management of simultaneous tasks, any one of which was enough to undo her. She often burned herself because the hot and cold water faucet handles appeared identical, and she forgot that hot pots conveyed heat. She cooked all day Saturday so she could honor the sabbath by not working.

Da-tsien spent her happiest moments in Chinatown's True Sunshine Episcopal Church, where she volunteered with Chinese Christian women who reminded her of the best people she had met in her life.

"I never knew their names," she said. "But some ran a mission in Anhwei. Others drove a truck near Ichang, just before the Yangtze gorges. They saved my girls and my son."

No bombs were being dropped in California, but she was involved in constant combat with her husband. The selfishness that is planted so easily in the sons of the rich had been mitigated in Zee Zee by war, for when, at times, he had been able to act selflessly. But in peacetime, he recovered his self-centeredness.

He made Elinor dress provocatively and required her to accompany him downtown, where he used her as visual bait to lure off-duty sailors into the car. While they ogled his daughter, he asked for stories about the American military, soaking up the camaraderie. When the sailors realized the setup, they left, and he would troll for another set of victims. T.C. was trying to recapture the war the way Master Lee tried to suck the last draw of *ta-yen* big smoke opium out of a broken pipe.

T.C. required his daughters to submit to his abusive and angry tutoring in math and history. These sessions inevitably conflicted with what they had already learned and often left Ying and Mary in tears, torn between rage and Euclid. He dealt with their frustrations with towering rages that induced Ying to stop eating while Mary experimented with overeating. Elinor, worrying about saving herself, found it increasingly difficult to protect Ying from his emotional swings.

He would return angry from the drudgery of civilian work, complete the bridge game in the paper and study the entertainment section.

"We go to movies, now," he declared.

"Can't," called Elinor from the kitchen table, "I have homework. I really can't afford the time to go to movies every night, Baba."

"Me neither," said Ying hopefully, who was sitting opposite Elinor.

"I don't feel like it," said Da-tsien from the sofa.

"I'll go, Baba," said Mary, proud of her independent ways.

"We all go now! Every night same!" yelled T.C.

"No! I didn't walk twenty million miles to America and give up my father to have the worst of China back in my nose!" cried Da-tsien. "Don't push me! Zee Zee, stop, this isn't fair! Stop pushing me!"

"I can't stand war movies!" cried Ying. "It isn't fair!" She blurted this out against the risks and the odds, for T.C. had learned how to focus on rebellion and create war from small sparks of resistance.

"DON'T ARGUE WITH ME! GET IN CAR! WHY ARE YOU SO STU-PID? YOU WANT MOVIES IN SHANGHAI, NO CAN GO, NOW CAN!"

T.C. began to hate his daughters' voices; they argued in elegant English accents, which they had absorbed in Shanghai, learned in Hong Kong and practiced in India. English accents reminded T.C. of China's colonial days, when colonial Englishmen barred Chinese people from the grand parks of Shanghai. It galled him that his own children used those class-conscious tones while speaking English far better than he.

"What movie, Baba?" asked Mary.

"Don't call me *Baba*. Call me *Dad*. We're in America."

Forcing them to watch war films was his lonely triumph. He wasn't discomforted by their silent resentments; he was encouraged by their miserable compliance. He had seen the results of a lack of order in China's wars, and swore that his family would survive the next through its rigorous exercise of Teutonic disciplines.

The movies were cultural training films. Attending them was mandatory. Later, he would ask them questions to make sure they had been paying attention, with scorn and criticism for wrong answers.

Like a traitor to the cause of her girls, Da-tsien quickly forgot her anger at Zee Zee as the film rolled. She was a storyteller and in these male-dominated screenplays, she could find one isolated female window-dressing character who was onscreen for at least a few minutes. Da-tsien would quickly advise her about how to keep herself and her man alive and to reach a happy ending.

She thought that the movies were good for Zee Zee; he was calm during and after them. Film tranquilized him and gave him a better personality. She understood that movies were a way for her angry husband to deal with his *gan-jin*, feelings, better than the opium ways of his father and the violent ways of his brother. She made sure, however, that she sat next to her girls and not Zee Zee, since she didn't want his bad moods leaking into her son, whom she believed to be in her tummy.

T.C. took his family on interminable trips to state parks and tourist sites throughout California. The sites were spectacular, but their beauty was negated by the oppression of T.C.'s projective will and his authoritarian control of what they could say and how they should express appreciation for all that he was doing for them. He had spent his adolescence running through the streets of Hongkew and now he could not permit his own children the slightest measure of independence from him. The three girls sat in the back of the Ford and closed their eyes to the world. When he resented their silence, he drove recklessly and suicidally against opposing traffic to make them scream and pay closer attention.

Da-tsien would close her eyes and pray. Later, she would advise her girls not to react. "The screams remind him of war. He has a devil inside him, and instead of fighting it, he feeds it."

Even under the duress of being far from home in a strange land with a controlling and troubled husband, Da-tsien kept her word to God; she didn't pray to other deities for her boy; she prayed to them only for small favors.

Protestant Christians understood the concept of Grace—that good deeds do not trigger compensation from Heaven—but Da-tsien worked hard in the poor communities of San Francisco. Her husband worked for Soong and earned money and status; she worked for her Lord Jesus and for her only son, who would bear a Christian name. She accepted Grace, but believed in putting good deeds in the celestial bank.

I was born in the summer of 1946. Mah-mee was pleased with her work, grateful to God and contented in a way that only a Chinese woman born in the beginning of the Twentieth Century could understand. Sons were a Confucian woman's proof of validity in a social system older than the Great Wall. With her son finally in the physical world, Da-tsien felt invulnerable to the habits of her selfish husband and the capriciousness of an unstable world. Her son would always stand by her, and remain ever faithful, in this world and in the next. She would shape his heart to be warm and open, and he would never be a soldier.

I was to be named Samuel Chien-sun Lee—Lee for the clan; Samuel for my mother's God; Chien-sun, or Healthy Grandson, for Master Lee, whose right it was to name his grandsons. This was clear.

Father asked the advice of the delivery nurses at the University of California hospital.

"Is there an American name for being born in August?" he asked.

"I thought you and your wife already picked a name," said one.

"Augustus is sort of related to this month," said another.

"Doesn't sound American. Must have American name."

"Name him Augustus and call him Gus for short. Like Charlie for Charles or Liz for Elizabeth. Gus is a real American name."

It was true. T.C. had seen American movies in which the guy delivering newspapers and driving trucks was named Gus.

"He's now Augustus Lee, no Chinese names," he said to Mah-mee.

"Are you *crazy?!* He's *my* son. I carried him, not you! He *has* to have a Christian name! I promised this to God above the river! And you promised your father to give him his Chinese name and his generational name! How can you finally have your only son and only give him one name? You're impossible! He has to be named *Samuel!*" She began to cry.

"Okay, okay, okay! Name him whatever you want! I don't care! Who the hell was Samuel?"

She wept and shook her head. Samuel was the prophet who had been loved throughout Israel for his obedience to God, for he had been promised to God's service long before he was even born to Hannah, an infertile woman. Samuel brought Israel its first king and helped establish the royal house of David. "He was a great man, bigger than Augustus!"

"Augustus was the first emperor of Rome!" said T.C. proudly. "The title of all the emperors to follow him."

"Male tyrants who crucified Jesus!" blurted Mah-mee, who won most of her arguments by highlighting the weaknesses of the men who opposed her.

My father didn't want any Chinese traditions, which my sisters, in their eagerness to avoid the social embarrassments of Old World ways, found oddly encouraging.

Mah-mee was horrified. When T.C. left on his next trip for T.A., she shaved my head to encourage a heavy growth of returning hair and surrounded me with chrysanthemums, which are admired for their hardiness and their ability to blossom even in spring snowstorms. She rubbed the flowers on my skin so I would take on their nature. She wrote T'ang poetry on bright red banners and read her Chinese Bible to me.

To preserve her youthful complexion, she washed her face in egg whites mixed with ginseng and a variety of things that were cooked in the kitchen, and shared this concoction with my face when I was bathed.

She pointed out to me the lesser gods of the house—the Door Gods who kept us safe, as if we still had a Spirit Screen and stone guard dogs; the Toaster God, who devoured bread and ejected it as toast; the General Electric God, who let students work late; the Door Bell God, who rang a bell just like a good boy in a good clan calling to ancestors, but who was so generous that it also rang its bell for mere visitors. Yet she made it clear that these were small fry compared to Jesus, who had saved us in China.

An amah was needed because Mah-mee had experienced some pain during nursing. The amah was a departure from tradition, for she was a busty Scandinavian-American woman from Minnesota with brilliant blond hair. She was a fundamentalist in the Miss Wu Bible-thumping tradition, and may have viewed the job as a missionary position without the discomforts of having to travel to China.

She was a pleasant woman with a good voice and apparently I was fond of her.

Mah-mee wanted a traditional Chinese birthday for my first year, but T.C. was going to be home instead of traveling, and this complicated her plans. So before my birthday, Mah-mee took me to *Chung Hwa Sin Gung Wei*, the True Sunshine Episcopal Church on Clay Street near Hang Ah, one of the best *dim sum* restaurants in the city. With her Chinese Christian women friends in attendance, she gave me a traditional *cha-chou*, Grasping Ceremony. In this, the little boy must bow to his ancestors and select one object from an array of small objects, each representing a future possible profession. The one he grasps is the one he will follow. It is a very impressive rite with perhaps a 5 percent rate of accuracy.

A brush represented a scholar; an ink stone represented a teacher; a seal, an official; a sword, a judge and a piece of ginseng, a doctor. There were no icons for bus drivers or steelworkers. *"Chu ch'i! Chu ch'i!"* cried Mah-mee. "Propitious writing, my son!"

Despite my mother's animated attempts to model the right behavior, I failed to bow to Master Lee and Baba and the Before Borns, who of course were not present corporeally and were probably too traditional to show up in a Christian church. Later, it would be discovered that I was very myopic, so I like to think that I was merely unaware instead of being contrary. Then I was placed on a small table surrounded by twelve representational objects. I faced a tiny Bible, a hymnal, a Book of Common Prayer, a cross, a votive candle and other symbols of the faith; all twelve dealt with God. I don't know which one I picked, but my mother was happy with my decision to be a Christian.

"Little Gus Samuel," she said. "Prophet and servant of the Lord!" Her friends applauded and apparently I showed my appreciation by crying.

Soon, I was taken to propaganda movies. It became a race between Da-tsien pushing Christianity and T.C. advocating war.

Father was at the bank during the day and I could be imprinted with theology in his absence. At the movies, Mah-mee held me in her lap and covered my eyes during scary scenes while simultaneously being able to deliver a narrative to explain her view of the film, which I couldn't see, because my eyes were too weak, and couldn't understand, because I was a baby and didn't speak English.

Father compensated by throwing destructive tantrums. He was like a typhoon and a volcano combined, full of supersonic winds and hot lava. Soon there was hardly a plate left in the apartment.

One day Mah-mee and Elinor took me to a hotel, where Elinor rubbed Mah-mee's back because she was crying. There was prayer and peace, and then we went back and the fights resumed.

sixty-eight

Remember Me

ELINOR BEGAN COLLEGE at Berkeley, but our father maintained his demands—she had to attend a movie every night with the family across the Bay in San Francisco and she had to join the trips to Sacramento, Modesto and Yosemite on his whim. Meanwhile, the Panhandle was being transformed by peace. The end of the war had closed the shipyards and the workers had drifted south to find jobs. In their stead came black families fleeing the injustices of the segregated American South. They were *youmin* refugees, and they were Christian, and Mah-mee liked them enormously.

Elinor, trying to surmount the academic pressure that Father created for her and the social embarrassment he engineered, found herself considering superior options to his company, such as marriage, suicide or a nunnery. Mah-mee was the volunteer success story at *Chung Hwa Sin Gung Wei* and Elinor Ah-wu regarded men with suspicion; that left the nunnery.

The grounds of Ohio's Convent of Transfiguration were beautiful, the Mother Superior was young, the food was incredibly good and everyone naturally suspected that this spectacularly beautiful Chinese girl was pregnant. The discovery of her chastity was cause for celebration.

"What are you fleeing, Elinor?" asked the Mother Superior.

Elinor considered a Chinese social lie, but she knew that the rules in Ohio were different. "My father doesn't harm me physically, but he makes me think about killing myself."

"The devil seeks our allegiance through our vulnerabilities. Do you feel safe here, child? Then, you are most welcome for as long as you wish. Now, you can't become a nun until you're twenty-one, but we'll send you to the University of Cincinnati whenever you elect to do so. While here, you must study religion for one hour a day and help us three hours a day with the seventy-five children who are housed in separate cottages by age, about ten children in each. You may stay in the guest house, which is quite lovely. We expect daily prayer, with genuine rigor."

Ying, about to graduate from Lowell High, phoned Elinor at the convent and left a message that she had questions about men. Elinor felt unprepared, so she in turn first called a friend of Mah-mee's.

"What advice can you give me about men?" asked Elinor.

"Do you know about the birds and the bees?" asked the friend.

"No," said Elinor, mystified.

"Well, it's quite simple. When you feel like sleeping with a man, you're in love!"

Elinor couldn't believe it could be that simple, but she remembered how angry Mah-mee would be at their father—and then they would sleep together and Mah-mee would forgive him. Elinor was in a convent, committed to Christian faith, love, hope and forgiveness, and she vowed to never let sex control her mind. Living in a convent, she phoned Ying to discuss men. "What sort of men do you like?"

"Hmm, *yishen*, men with nice clothes and sports cars," said Ying.

"Oh, Ying, I hope not." Elinor hadn't really liked men at Cal, but the types she found least disagreeable were threadbare intellectuals.

"Elinor, are you okay out there? Do they have Chinese food?"

Elinor laughed. "No, they don't, but the food is excellent. Oh, Ying, it's heaven here. I feel so free. How badly is Dad torturing you?"

Elinor would've loved staying at the convent and later going to school in Cincinnati in preparation for her vows, but she received a telegram from Mah-mee.

Dear Ah-wu I have cancer can you return Love, Mah-mee. STOP.

Elinor wanted to ask the nuns to help her pray, but there was no time. She had to send a telegram herself and pack.

Dad I'll come home to help Mah-mee, but you have to leave me alone and let me live in Berkeley and study. Elinor. STOP.

Grumpily, T.C. agreed.

Mah-mee required a mastectomy, which she accepted without resistance or complaint. Dad was not too helpful in these matters and it fell to Elinor and Ying to do most of the work in tending to our mother and us.

Mah-mee's friends from the church and neighborhood jammed into the small hospital room. Black Christian women from the Panhandle and Chinese Christian women from Chinatown looked at one another uneasily until Mah-mee made introductions. A careful fellowship, involving warm exchanges of Georgia collard greens and ribs and Cantonese barbecued pork buns and good-luck noodles, resulted.

Elinor was worried about Mah-mee and exhausted by sleepless nights and homework, but she was at least more frequently in Berkeley. She was also too polite to refuse a visit from a Cal classmate named Edwin Elliott, a friend since high school. He was tall, pale, handsome, brilliant, faultlessly polite and very foreign. Elinor had gone on dates, but only with Chinese men. Inevitably, one of them would say a word or exhibit a gesture that in some remote fashion reminded her of her father, and she would never see him again. Elinor liked Edwin because no matter how hard she tried, she couldn't find any resonance with T.C.

She went with him to Schnabel's, a Berkeley soda fountain and dessert shop. He carried the conversation, looking into her eyes with great ardor. Dad would look at her as if he were judging a horse. She closed her tired eyes; fatigue and worry about her mother laced every thought.

"You are so smart. I love how complete strangers stop you and ask who you are, and how you understand history and politics and the world. I think you're the most beautiful girl in the world."

Luxuriously, she stretched, pretending she was in bed. "I think I'm the sleepiest girl in the world."

"What do you think of when you're not sleepy?"

"My mah-mee. My father. They have huge personalities. They seem to control all my free thoughts when I'm not thinking about chem or calculus." She was grateful to her father for one thing—his torments kept her from descending into the guilt that flooded her after the *Bola*, the Run, out of China. She had bitterly blamed her father for ditching them in China without a cent, but just as certainly, she had abandoned her country when it was in desperate trouble. She was a young Chinese woman with advantages; it was her job to help find the answers.

"What if I asked your father if I can marry you?" asked Edwin.

Elinor desperately wanted to sleep and was hallucinating about a long journey on foot above a roaring river. She was with this young man who liked her, and she *really* wanted to go to bed. She remembered what Mah-mee's friend had said: If you feel like sleeping with a man, it's love. *Good God, does this mean I'm in love? With Edwin?* She sat up straighter.

"What if," she asked, "my father asked you to join him for a drive to Sacramento, to go to an air show? Would you go?"

"Would you want me to?"

"Oh, God, no!"

"Then I wouldn't."

"What if he insisted and gave you no choice?"

"I wouldn't be rude, but I still wouldn't go."

"What if he got really angry and threw things at you and threatened to throw you out the window if you didn't go?"

Edwin gulped. "He'd have to throw me out the window, then."

Elinor beamed. "Then I think you should ask my father for my hand. But now you have to take me home so I can sleep."

"ZEE ZEE, YOU must send more money to your mother and brother," said Da-tsien. "And, if you can, to my father."

"I will, I will," said T.C, who hated the task, for it required *hsing hui*, bribery through middlemen, a process he loathed. He had a habit of throwing money on the ground in front of officials who required squeeze.

"Zee Zee, please ask the doctor for medicines. You still shout in your sleep. You shout out to Pan, telling him to run away."

He waved his hand, ignoring the comment. "You're not going to die, you know."

"I know. But do you notice that you only pay attention to me when I'm in bed?" She smiled at him. "I like you like this. Almost sad and quiet. When you're like this, I can see you. You were like this when I sent you to say good-bye to your father, and secure his blessing for your life. No, don't put on that face. I like the sweet parts of you. Let me talk about important things for a change. Do you know that I'm very proud of you? You gave up your army for me. I'm very grateful, Zee Zee."

He was going to say that it was no sacrifice, but something told him to still his tongue. He was sick of his KMT army. The top brass couldn't be trusted. He was ashamed of how good farmers had been roped away from their fields to die stupid deaths under uncaring generals. He hated the top management for exploiting the poorest people. The Reds were no better; they were inciting the poor peasants to slaughter the rich, and they worshipped Communism, which sapped individual initiative almost as much as Confucianism.

What he missed was the American army. He had used T.A.'s influence to enter the U.S. army, but after the war, there was no place for a foreign officer in his late thirties, even one with a remarkable military background.

"I feel like a man without two countries," he said. "The one I gave up I don't want; the one I want doesn't need me."

"Oh, Zee Zee, your family needs you. The next windy day, take little Gus to the beach, and let him run on the sand, as if I were with him. Let him get his feet wet and talk to China, his words on the winds. Encourage him to talk to his Na-gung. Let him tell his grandfather about a life without war and bombs, without Nationalists or Reds. Tell Grandfather that he, little Chien-sun, is his strong and healthy grandson and that he'll eat thousand year eggs so he makes sons."

"You see, up there?" Mah-mee asked.

I looked up and saw various layers of darkness.

"That's the Literacy Arc, from there to there. That's *Bei Dou*, Great Bear, and his seven stars. They play chess with the Immortal of the South Pole god for our *yeh*, our fates. Of course, it's just a game, because Lord Jesus owns all the stars, isn't that true?"

"Yes, Mah-mee."

"Now, the bright one in the center is the brilliant Wen-ch'ang, the hard-working god of literature. He is your special friend! He rides the four stars of his chariot, helped by the homely K'uei-hsing, who gives the grades. Inside the chariot is little Chu-i, the deity for the inept and the lazy. But you can't see him, because Lord Jesus doesn't allow poor, lazy Chu-i to be even seen by humans. That's what happens when you get bad grades! You get lost among the brighter lights.

"Your father learned to navigate by the stars when he lived in the desert with the Germans. He taught them to me when we sailed to Hong Kong on a lovely Italian liner. We lay on deck lounges at night and he taught me the night sky, because he was trying to prepare me to be a woman warrior. I watched *Bei Dou* and called him my uncle during the *Bola*, the Run, even on cloudy nights when I couldn't see his bearish shape. He tells you the direction *bei*, north, which didn't matter, because I just followed Mr. Yip or the Old River.

"I'd lie awake at night, and even though it was very cold, I kept watch over your sisters and kept looking up at the stars and praying to Jesus for your soul. Yes, my Only Son, I prayed for you before you were ever born. It was a night like this, in October, with the quarter moon, when I remembered in Soochow that my mother, your taitai, told me that each of us has a star in the sky, and that we should sacrifice to it every year. So Chinese sailors navigate not by stars, but by people. But because we're Christian, and because I promised God everything for your life above the gorges, I don't do sacrifice to any other gods, anymore.

"Who is the god of scholarship?"

"Wen-ch'ang, Mah-mee."

"And who is Lord over all?"

"Jesus God, not Door Bell God."

"Yes, my son, the Jesus God. You see, as a girl, I was selfish, *tsong hwai*, spoiled rotten, full of the fox spirit and contrary, always angering Taitai, my mother, but God changed me so I could give you your life.

"Oh, Little Gus, a very sad thing has happened. We found out today that the Communists have won. They beat the Nationalists. This is very bad for your Na-gung and your taitai, who are my parents, and it's bad for Madame Lee, who is your father's mother. I never thought the Reds would win, but they have. Your father said they would. He was always better at politics than me, but I was always better at knowing people. At relationships which contain truth. It means, my son, that we can't go back to China." She began to cry, so I held her hand.

"It means my baba is in very big trouble, and it's all my fault!" She wiped her tears and tried to straighten her makeup.

"Oh, Lee Chien-sun, I hope you remember me. I hope you always remember your mah-mee, who loves you so very much. Let me kiss your nose, to keep it very small so it can't smell the winds that would take you away from me, and let's go inside before the god of frost takes our bones. I get cold so quickly now, which is so strange, because my love for you is like a huge bonfire that I hope my baba can see all the way from China. Oh, I wish I could send you like a little wind sprite across the Great Sea so Baba could see your face, and laugh to know my happiness."

sixty-nine

Korea

JUNE 25, 1950, found my mother, Mary and me at True Sunshine Episcopal Church, Elinor with Edwin, Ying in college at Cal, and Dad deliriously talking on the telephone.

Herman Flax, perhaps his closest postwar friend, had called to say that the Communist North Koreans, with Soviet support, had crossed the 38th Parallel to invade South Korea, which was supported by America, and that war was inevitable.

"Do you think?" said T.C. hopefully.

"Yes," said Herman, owner of Flax's Artgoods, the best artists' shop in the city. "Maybe they'll call you up, T.C. But better that you stay out and raise your children." Herman had always been kind to T.C.'s children, and had even coached Ying out of Dad's mad-hatter academic tutoring into a series of A's. Mr. Flax was a good businessman and he loved his wife and children and the children of his friends.

"Uh huh, sure, sure," said T.C. "Thanks for the great news!"

DAD NEVER CONFIRMED to Da-tsien the extent of his deep feelings for Katharine Hepburn. My mother interpreted his avoidance of her films after the war as a sign of consideration for her. She never knew that Hepburn had broken his heart. The only other person who probably could guess at that fact was Spencer Tracy, and fortunately, he didn't know Da-tsien, or she surely would have squeezed the information out of him.

Dad said, "We go Katharine Hepburn movie," and Da-tsien immediately asked Elinor to help fix her hair.

Sitting before the dresser, Da-tsien looked at herself from several angles. She had looked like a thirty year old when she had delivered her last child, but the cancer and the constant concern over the plight of her father and her mother had taken a toll; she now looked her age. This frustrated her, and she kept changing her orders.

"Ah-wu, make me look like Elizabeth Taylor, very glamorous."

Elinor built out the hair to emphasize its length and fullness.

"No, no, more like *A Place in the Sun*, not *Father of the Bride!*" Then, "No, no, Elinor—brush my hair so it looks as if I'm standing on the beach, facing China, the wind blowing it with the sunlight behind!"

The new Hepburn movie was *The African Queen*. Da-tsien enjoyed seeing Hepburn in a totally unglamorous role. In contrast, Mah-mee felt radiantly gorgeous.

It had been nine years since T.C. had seen Katharine Hepburn. Still, he could feel her incredible life force, the way she asked him, *Don't you think?* Her bright, shining eyes. Her high-toned voice, her interest in him.

"Yes, Rose Sayer," said Da-tsien to the screen. "Throw away all the gin bottles, every one! Don't give in to man's baser nature!"

"Shh!" scolded another viewer.

"I have to help her, don't I?" whispered Da-tsien.

T.C. wanted to speak to the screen, too. He wanted to tell Hepburn that he missed her, even after all this time.

Later, he sat in his office on Montgomery Street at the border of China-town and the Financial District, as runners arrived with stock news and gossip. Few of them bothered T.C., whose job was international communications, so he was surprised when S. Y. Shen appeared breathlessly.

S.Y. had become pals with Da-tsien, who was using him to help imprint Chinese culture on me.

This bothered Dad because he could never understand how Mah-mee could appreciate a man who couldn't protect her in war. He also regarded Uncle Shim's Confucian ideas as ethnic pollution. Uncle had the mind of a scholar, the wardrobe of an actor and the slow and tentative affect of a Mr. McGoo. He was awkward with my sisters, adored Mah-mee, admired T.A.'s financial genius and worried about T.C., whom he approached like a man about to pet a cobra.

"Ah ha, T.C., ah ha. I have interesting news. A man is here to see you. A government man. He claims he is from the Defense Department and—"

The man was from the government. "Major Lee," he said. T.C.'s heart sang to hear his old rank spoken aloud.

The official gave a snapshot synopsis of the war and asked for an estimate of the Chinese order of battle and the name of the senior commander.

"That would be Peng Du-huai, but his operations father, his spiritual father in fighting, would be Chu Teh." *Who I failed to kill in 1928.*

"Which army groups would that be?"

"I would think Fourth Field Army. Easiest to move to Korea from Manchuria. I'd be surprised if they used another one yet. They keep that in reserve."

The man nodded. "Major, the Central Intelligence Agency got caught chasing monkeys instead of tigers. We said the Chinese wouldn't come in. So they sent a million troops. We blew it and we've lost face. Now we need Chinese advisors at the strategic level and Chinese interrogators to question PLA prisoners at the tactical level. Can you help? We could compensate you quite fairly."

T.C. beamed. "Of course I can! But I'm no good strategically. I could be an interrogator. I probably know some of your prisoners. Tell me, will I be in the American army?"

"You'll be in the agency. The CIA. In Korea, you'll wear the uniform of an American army major, but otherwise, you'll be in mufti."

"Yes, excellent, excellent!"

"Uh, we notice, Major, that you're not a citizen. Are you planning—"

"Yes, I know. Embarrassing, but I haven't been studying—"

"Sir, we'll get you a tutor and you'll have no problem, I assure you. We're approaching a new winter offensive. How soon could you join us?"

He thought of his wife. "I need a month to close my affairs."

"Yes, sir. On behalf of a grateful nation, thank you. My card."

"Thank you, sir! Thank you! If I can ask, how did you find my name?"

"Madame Chiang Kai-shek. She remembers you from Shanghai but she also appreciates your providing security when she visits San Francisco. Madame Chiang sends her best wishes for your success in Korea."

DAD SHOPPED AT the Army-Navy Surplus store on Market Street and packed for Manchuria. Mah-mee asked him what he was doing, because he was making disturbing throat sounds. She was surprised to learn that he was humming, or trying to hum, military tunes.

"Why so many heavy clothes? Are you going to Manchuria?"

"How did you know?" he asked. "Who told you? Supposed to be secret!"

Mah-mee collapsed in a chair. Living with Zee Zee, she had developed a flair for the dramatic. "Manchuria," she whispered in disbelief. Manchuria was three million miles away.

"I don't go for another month," he said. "Time to practice northern dialects. I'm going to need notepads. Lots of pens. Clean socks."

"How long will you be gone?"

"I don't know, Da-zee. Awhile, I think."

She was silent for a long time. "Did Soong do this? No? What will you tell him?"

"Already told him. I was so excited!"

"I hope you didn't hurt his feelings."

"No, no, of course not. And I think S.Y.'s relieved. He'll watch after you while I'm gone. He keeps trying to teach Gus the classics and calligraphy and all that rot! You be sure to not let him! Gus is an American boy!"

"Oh? When did this happen? When I saw him a few minutes ago, he looked very much like a good Chinese son. How has he been replaced by an American boy? Did we put him in a toaster, to transform him? I asked S.Y. to teach Little Gus some of his culture. And don't get angry! You're so happy that you're going to war that I don't want to disturb your sense of *ho-chi*, your harmony."

Dad pulled out his automatic pistol and stormed out of the room.

Mah-mee found him teaching me how to field-strip a Colt Super .38 automatic. I was four and slow on the uptake, so Dad yelled a little louder until I started to cry, and then he cursed and left me alone.

"I'm going to have this pistol in Korea! How will he learn how to use it when I'm gone?"

"Zee Zee, no one teaches a little boy such things!"

"Oh, no? My father taught me when I was *three!*"

"Your father was crazy!"

"*No!* You can't say this about him! He was my *idol!*"

"Your idol? You didn't even like him!"

"BE QUIET! Don't make me stuff hankies in your mouth and lock you in the closet like happened to Ying!"

Mah-mee held her heart and went to bed. In the morning, she held me close as she lay paging aimlessly through movie magazines and the Bible. Like Miss Wu of the House of Soong, she randomly selected passages out of the New Testament and read them to me, searching for answers to her life.

"Your father makes great thunder but has no brains. Little Gus, he doesn't know me. Oh, I pray you will be a man who knows his mother and, later, his wife, just by the sound of her footsteps, by the sigh of the wind in her hair."

"I always try to *chung yong chi dao,* keep to the middle, to see all needs; he's always extreme, *yu pu chi,* always to one side, playing to his needs. He wants you to be a killer, but good iron is not used to make nails.

"Ah, well, I have so many stories to tell you, about your Na-gung, my baba, and his kind ways. About your Na-bu, grandmother, and her clever mind, but I also will tell you about the loyal Liang Shan-po and the beautiful Tzu Ying-tai, the most famous lovers of China. Not because of romance, but because of *chong,* loyalty. I am a loyal woman, like Tzu Ying-tai. Your father follows the wind. Confucius says you must follow the father at all costs. Lord Jesus says you must follow God. Your father dislikes Confucius *and* God. Oh, Little Gus, who will you be? Which one will you follow?"

It was in these days that Mah-mee, a woman of an earlier age, put me in the car and tried to drive the gas vehicle herself. She had never taken lessons, which was her husband's fault, and so had never been licensed, which was understandable. She regarded the three control pedals as separate deities, each of which had its own mind and would follow its independent dictates regardless of her entreaties.

Driving west to the ocean on Geary and making a turn to the north on the Great Highway to reach Mah-mee's favorite beach below the Cliff House is a simple matter. But the confusion between gas, clutch and brake, not to mention the traffic, resulted in my agreeing with Mah-mee that demons and ghosts were in control of the *chi tz* as it made its jerking, jolting and independent way to the west under a barrage of angry car horns.

I ran along the beach. She didn't. I spoke to the waves, the *shui*, which were in front of me, not knowing that I was supposed to be speaking to the wind, the *feng*, which carries words to China and the Before Borns.

Later, she put me on her lap and told me the true story of handsome Liang Shan-po and the beautiful Tzu Ying-tai. The wind blew her hair around and made us blink.

"Little Gus, parents are older and wiser, so they arrange the marriages of their children for the success of the *jia*, the clan. Of course, I was a different girl, and followed another path. . . .

"There was much competition from matchmakers for both children, because each came from a good and prosperous family, and the Liang boy and the Tzu girl were beautiful to behold and had excellent manners that accompanied a sense of self.

"One unusual day, the Tzu girl was allowed to leave her family compound with her amah, when she saw the members of the great House of Liang making a wedding journey. Riding a pony near the front was a boy, the honored Firstborn Son, just like you! The Tzu girl saw this boy only for an instant. What do you think happened in that moment? Oh, yes, she fell deeply in love with the boy on the pony. Without her will, her heart flew out of her body to go to him. Of course, she had to follow her heart, didn't she? As the boy rode away, she followed. But a girl couldn't spend time with a boy. What could she do?"

I was pulled by Mah-mee's passion and warmth, but I didn't know what the girl could do, and said so.

"The little Tzu girl was so smart! She pretended to be a boy. She wore boy's clothes and walked like a boy and bowed like a boy and was admitted by a great miracle into the Liang boy's studies with his tutor. For three years, the disguised girl studied alongside the smart Liang boy. He suspected there was something different about his classmate. Oh, how many times did the little girl hint to the boy that she was more than she seemed, but the boy, being a boy, never got it.

"Then the girl invited the boy to her house. Come meet my sister," she said cleverly, and he visited with his amah.

"Of course, the Tzu amah introduced the boy to the Tzu daughter, Ying-tai, who was dressed that day as herself. Liang Shan-po was so surprised! He saw that his friend and classmate was a beautiful and intelligent girl who loved him with all her heart.

"They spoke of books and poets, of birds and butterflies, of paintings and the stories of their clans. Unspoken was their desire to spend the rest of their lives together.

"The boy's amah saw what was happening, and broke the spell by telling both young people that the Liang *jia* had already brokered the marriage of Shan-po to a wonderful daughter of a fine clan. She said it was wrong for them, given the contract, to visit this way. With deep apologies, the amah pulled the boy from the Tzu house.

"The boy showed little emotion, and was polite when he met the lovely girl he was to marry. But he stopped eating." Mah-mee's voice broke and she began to cry. "He died, he died of a broken heart, for he had two hearts in his soul, his and little Ying-tai's, and the misery of two broken hearts took his life.

"Meanwhile, the House of Tzu—the same name as my original family— arranged Ying-tai's marriage to another. En route to her wedding, riding in a red palanquin carried by four men—just as I rode to my wedding to your father—her face veiled, something secret and unknown made Ying-tai look outside her curtains. Perhaps it was the darkening sky. Perhaps it was something else.

"What she saw, Little Gus, chilled her bones. There was Shan-po's amah, wailing at a grave, surrounded by the Liang clan, and Ying-tai cried and covered her mouth, for she knew that her beloved had died.

"There was brilliant lightning and cracking thunder, followed by a great quake that opened the earth. Little Ying-tai jumped out of her sedan and threw herself into the opening of the earth, to be with Shan-po, the holder of her heart.

"In the morning, the skies cleared and the winds died and a great and beautifully brilliant rainbow graced the sky. Rainbows symbolize God's covenant with his people.

"God in Heaven was moved by these pure young people's love for each other, and by their respect for their parents, whom God tells us to honor in the Fifth Commandment in the twelfth verse of the twentieth chapter of the Book of Exodus. So he turned the boy and girl into butterflies. Every spring, now, in China, the Tzu and the Liang butterflies flit together in green fields, and Ying-tai is reunited with Shan-po. They can fly together happily, without the worries of humans, without the pains of the past, gilded by God and graced by Heaven."

She wiped her eyes, "A mother always loves her children this way. I haven't been so good at this. I let Elinor take care of me. I let Ying feel my anger and my weaknesses. Only with Mary Mei-mei and with you, Little Gus, with God's help, have I done a little better. Now, I think I feel storm clouds coming. I feel the earth shake. If I have to go to the next world, Little Gus, I want you to remember God each time you see a rainbow. When you see a butterfly, know it is me, reaching out to you, reaching out to all my children, reaching out to my husband, and to my baba, and to my mother, to my amah, to my *jia*. I won't be reaching for God, because I'll be with my Lord. I know that, and it takes away my fear. I just pray that Mary will be a good Christian *chieh chieh*, older sister for you. God was good, because she's seven years older than you and she loves you and she knows Jesus loves her. She can care for you before she marries. I pray your father will remarry a Christian lady who will love you as much as I, for you are my *shinkan*, heart and liver. Is not life wonderful?"

She had always thought that having a son would resolve all of her life's issues. At first, she thought that the lack of global impact from my arrival was due to the obvious fact that it had occurred a million or two miles away from the warm approval of her mother and her baba, far from Ah Tsui's adoring gaze and far removed from Auntie Gao's joy. Then she blamed American culture, which, in the name of democracy, valued little girls almost as much as little boys.

But she realized that having a son who would honor her all her days was not as rewarding as having a husband who would listen to her. She had reached the conclusion that Zee Zee was bedeviled. He was insensitive to her. He charted his own course and never consulted with her or had heart for her feelings.

Chinese springs have a carnal connotation; Chinese autumns bear the notion of death. In the fall of 1951, Dad sent several hundred dollars to his brother and his mother through the old underground world of the syndicates. The couriers apologized and bowed low as the news returned: Gee, Dad's older brother, had died in Communist custody, and Baba, Mah-mee's kind, book-reading baba, had died. My father contained his reaction. My mother wept inconsolably, and her health visibly failed.

IT WAS AFTER Thanksgiving that Mah-mee went to the hospital with a sense of resignation and of knowing her fate. The spread of cancer wasn't necessarily terminal, but she believed that God was calling her.

Many of her friends in the True Sunshine church, from Grace Cathedral and from the neighborhood argued with her about this view. Her minister, Reverend Lee, told her that life was precious, and that God, unlike the devil, didn't make deals for people's lives. "God gives life. He doesn't bargain. He gives it with Grace, not for merit."

Mah-mee knew better. She had helped kill a daughter and her father, and women's lives had always been bargained.

MARY MEI-MEI LED me upstairs into the apartment attic so we could be closer to God as we prayed for the life of our mother. Mei-mei was incredibly confident, because Mah-mee had stored a million good wishes into Heaven's bank, and now, we were redeeming them.

seventy

The Christmas Present

YING SAT BY the bed. She closed her eyes to staunch her tears, but it didn't work. She put her head down and wept, her shoulders shaking.

"Oh, Ying, don't cry," said Mah-mee. She reached out to pat her daughter, but she sat too far away. The distance that had never been enough to protect her from her mother's anger and disapproval was now too great to allow a touch of fingers on a daughter's arm.

"You know, you're such a beautiful girl. Everyone says Elinor is beautiful, and, of course, she is. But you have *ren*, benevolence, kindness, love, love like Old Mo Tzu, who loved all people, honored all people. This is more important. My unkindness to you has made you vulnerable to others. You are my soft daughter, my good daughter. My prayer for you, Ying, is to marry a kind man who won't take advantage of your kindness." She began to cry.

"It seems that's what we do together, isn't it? Cry. I've put so many tears in your eyes and all I can ask now is for your forgiveness and for you not to think as badly of me as I treated you when you were young. You have a strong heart and *ren* and God will always love you."

"MEI-MEI, YOU KNOW how much I love you, yes? Now, remember, you're such a beautiful girl—don't worry yourself about school! Just marry a man with a kind heart and have lots of sons!"

"I'll take care of Little Gussie, Mah-mee, but I won't have to do it alone, because you're coming home and I'll cook for you and do the laundry, like I'm doing now, and you can just rest and read the Bible."

"Remember the story about Liang and Tzu, Mei-mei?"

Mary nodded.

"The rainbow is God. Butterflies, that's me. Now pray with me, Mei-mei, for our family, for your father's heart, for Little Gus's health."

"I'M DYING, AH-WU, because I have cancer. Because I was a little princess who had to walk out of China, using up all my *chigong*. It's not because I got pregnant and had a baby son. Now, how is your marriage?"

Elinor exhaled. "It's fine, Mah-mee. Edwin is a kind-hearted man."

"Do you love him, Lily?"

Elinor smiled. "You haven't called me that in a long time. It seems China is so far away. It's easy here in America. I know a girl at Cal who cheats on tests, and it really offends me. Being in America is almost like cheating. It's too easy."

"*Wong gut so yu ahr*," you look right and left, said Mah-mee. "So you're not that happy with a kind-hearted man. It's my fault. As I age, I think about old kind Mr. Tung. I was betrothed to him, but I didn't marry him because he was a little corpulent and had a mole on his face. I wonder now what became of him. I turned him down for the handsome boy across the street. What misery that brought! Ah-wu, are you the same? Are you not content with kind men? Do you need danger and risk?"

Elinor shook her head. "I don't miss danger." She shuddered. "I miss China, Mah-mee. I feel like a traitor, living soft here while Lon-lon, Jane Chin and Lu-lu and Uncle and Auntie Ying and Na-bu suffer. I think of all the household people. I worry about our amahs and Mr. Yip. I'm like a child stuffing her face in a warm restaurant while beggars die outside the window. But I can't go back to China now. I'm married."

Da-tsien closed her eyes with the thought of her father. "Lily. Will you take care of the family? Better than I did?"

She nodded. She was the Firstborn. She had led the way out of China, and would lead the family in America. Mah-mee was looking at her with her heart in her eyes, and Lily cried and hugged her, weeping as if she were just a girl.

MAH-MEE HELD HER husband's hand. It was strong and muscular, a Chinese farmer's hand.

"How soon do you leave?" she asked.

He looked at his watch, his foot pumping. He took it off and wound the stem. "Four days."

"I want you to get me a present. For Christmas."

"Of course." He smiled. "I always get you things that you probably don't like that much." He rubbed his head. "What would you like for Christmas, Da-zee?"

"I want you to stay with me until I die."

He recoiled. "You're not going to die!"

"Yes, I am, Zee Zee. Don't argue. It hurts my heart."

He gritted his teeth. "The doctors say you have—"

"They can't know truly what's inside me. God knows. Jesus is in this room with me, here, this very moment. Earlier, He sat with me and talked with me."

T.C. looked about uneasily.

"Elinor Ah-wu is ready. I apologized to Ying and asked forgiveness. I have commissioned Mary to be a Young Mother for Little Gus.

"The only thing left to do is to deal with you. To get you to love me and pay attention to me. To be kind to me as my true Christian husband. Just until I leave for the next world."

T.C. put his head down, trying not to cry.

"Zee Zee, we made five children. We lived like royalty. We have seen things and done things that most people will never know. But I know you. You're a man caught between two worlds. Part of you is Confucian, part of you is modern. Don't you see? The woman you romanticized, Katharine Hepburn, is just an American version of me. Zee Zee, stay with me, love me, the way you promised you would. Nothing held back. Don't go to Korea.

"In America, people pay a great deal of attention to Christmas wishes, because it's all done in the name of our Lord, Jesus Christ. God knew that people needed help, so he gave them the big Christmas present, his son. Zee Zee, do you think God uses Yellow Springs for the dead? Is Yellow Springs heaven?"

Comments like this always dried my father's tears.

"I don't know. It's all wild superstition."

"It doesn't matter, I guess. I'd rather go back to Peach Blossom Spring, along the Soochow canals where we honeymooned, where Mr. Five Willow Tree recited *shi* poetry for us, under a perfectly round moon."

"I remember that," whispered Zee Zee.

"I still pray for you to accept God."

"You waste your breath."

"I fear for your soul."

"Bah! Fear cancer! Fear bad doctors! Don't talk of this! Makes me so angry!"

She smiled and caressed his hand. "It was all decided, long ago. You know, I tore my wedding dress the day we married. It meant someone would die. I never thought it would be little Shiaobaobee. I knew on the river road, then, that it'd be me. Christmas is about giving. It's about the pleasure of giving. I have given you my life."

"You gave it to the foreign God," he said.

"Yes, I did. I gave Him my soul. Yet my soul mate is you. There were other men who looked at me. I never saw them. That's because I promised myself to you, in front of God and my parents and clan. I can't control if I live or die, but I can control my promises. I promised to love you always, and so I will. I promised to love my children, and so I will. It doesn't matter whether we're in China, or Soochow, or Shanghai, or in California or a million miles away in Yellow Springs or if I make it to Peach Blossom Spring. You can't see love and you can't see God, but both are most real. Do you see?"

He forced himself to nod, to take her truths, just once. It was very hard to say the next words. "You're very wise. All those women in Shanghai knew it, getting your advice." He had secretly desired wisdom, but it had remained elusive. Few asked his counsel; now the Americans needed him in Korea, and he sat in a hospital room in America.

A long silence. He smiled and rubbed her scalp, then her neck and shoulders as he always had. She closed her eyes, breathing softly.

"Hold me, Zee Zee. Make it my Christmas present, and tell me you'll stay with me until I die."

seventy-one

Colma

MAH-MEE WAS BURIED on a high hill in the Woodlawn Cemetery in the city of Colma, outside San Francisco International Airport. Her casket had hints of good-luck red and she was interred with the recitation of her favorite prayers. The Lord's Prayer from the Sermon on the Mount was for forgiveness; the Twenty-third Psalm was for salvation along the Yangtze and Paul's letter to Thessalonica, an eschaton, for the end of this time and the beginning of the new. No one clapped hands to gain the attention of the gods, no incense was burned, no saffron-robed monks chanted for an improved reincarnation cycle, and no one wore good-luck Taoist bags around their necks; Da-tsien had kept the promise to God she had made in Szechuan to honor only Him.

My family wept. My sisters avoided looking at Dad, whom they secretly blamed for this sad day. The cancer god hadn't taken Mah-mee; the killers had been his anger, selfishness and imposed will. It was his abandoning her and disturbing her sense of harmony by forcing a delicate indoor girl to walk out of China. Finally, it was his impairing her fragile health through a final pregnancy. She was forty when I was born.

The black women hummed and softly sang Mah-mee's favorite hymn, "Amazing Grace."

Da-tsien's death was a not a pebble dropped in a pond, but the collapse of a dam. Her unique blend of faiths was gone, and the bonds that connected us to our Chinese past had been broken.

My three brilliant, beautiful sisters would suffer divorces and untold hardships in which the anger of their father would be visited upon them by men they had married.

Dad returned to his German Gobi roots by quickly marrying an angry Pennsylvania Dutch woman who hated God and disliked Mary and me. Quickly, Edith Swinehart would evict Mary for her continued fealty to our dead mother and for attempting to fulfill her promise to our mah-mee to bind me to the Christian faith.

Dad's marriage to Edith caused a sensation in Chinatown, where she inspired controversy and jealousy in her tight, form-fitting, high-necked cheongsams. She had entered an inner Chinese society. Without intention, her outspoken ways offended too many people.

"T.C.," said T.A. Soong. "We can't tolerate your new wife. We know she married you to be close to our money. We will give her fifty thousand dollars to leave. No, no, don't get angry. Please. Contain yourself."

Thus did Dad end his lifelong friendship with T.A., fulfilling the *sven ming's* prophecy at Dongting Lake that Zee Zee and T.A. would fight each other over a woman. Dad, Edith and I would spend the next fifteen years in painful economic and spiritual poverty.

Mary, who had become my putative mother after Mah-mee's death, went to live in Minneapolis with Elinor and her second husband. Mary and I would not see each other again until we were both adults.

I would imitate my father's weaknesses in academics and judgment.

Mah-mee's life had meant different things to each of us, but her death had been devastating to the family that we had been.

Each of us would undertake a new Run, a new *Bola*, from her death in 1952, to accomplish a recovery of the values that she had sought to represent.

Elinor found a wonderful husband and created a new life. Ying would become politically prominent and successful, and then she would find her independence. Mary would find her career in medicine. Each would produce admirable children. I found a wonderful wife whose spirit and faith reminded me of someone I had lost when I was five.

Lost in all of this was the fact that Dad had been invited by the Central Intelligence Agency to undertake a great adventure along the 38th Parallel in the Republic of Korea. He would've loved being an employee of the CIA, authorized to wear the uniform of an American army officer, to travel on military transports, to associate with the men he admired the most in the world, and to eat in U.S. Army mess halls, which he alone considered to be a privilege.

He had given up this chance because his wife asked it.

I do not know what the two of them discussed in her final days. I like to think that she thanked him for freeing her from being *yi kao* dependent on anything.

Her greatest wish was to have a Christian husband who truly loved her. In April 1952, for at least a few days, that wish was fulfilled.

MY SISTERS HAD given me stories about Mah-mee, and they led to my first book. But there was no agreement as to where she was buried, except to say that her grave was in Colma. Colma is a city of cemeteries, and I painfully began searching Chinese burial sites, without success.

On Mother's Day 1991, my wife, Diane, announced to us that the present she wanted that Sunday was to find my mother's grave.

"If there's one gift we can't give you, it's probably that. Let's not."

It was interesting watching my children, Jena and Eric, carrying home-cut flowers and running gaily through Woodlawn Cemetery. We were looking for a lonely marker in an endless profusion of tombstones. I focused in the area heavy with 1952 markers, but I walked as if in a daze, as if I were a small boy.

Diane focused on the high ground that faced China and the sea. In minutes, she had found the gravestone. It was in the shape of a Bible, its lettering faded and stained, its black marble mottled and befouled. Under the dirt was a once-white cross and our engraved family name.

LEE

DA-TSIEN TZU

APRIL 26, 1906

APRIL 19, 1952

BORN IN CHINA

Diane had brought solvents and sponges. We cleaned the stone and weeded the area. The grave sat under a great sycamore. Jena and Eric placed the flowers. It was a moment of richness and sadness, of inestimable loss and of essential completion.

"I imagined where Elinor would've placed your mother," said Diane. "It's a place like I would've picked, high on a hill, with a view, so I came here."

I marveled at her, as I often do.

"Come, kids," said Diane. "Let Daddy be alone with his mother."

I knelt at the marker. "Hello, Mah-mee." I was forty-five and had a sense of returning home to a space I did not know. I had never spoken easily to the dead.

As the wind blew softly toward China, I imagined her voice, which was similar to Elinor and Ying's, with a slight hint of an English accent, but higher in tone, dusted as it was in the melodics of a Soochow accent. I said, *"Man-manlai,* go softly." Or perhaps I only thought the words in my imagination.

seventy-two

Ching Jinlai

IN 1975, AFTER a sweet-and-sour twenty-year marriage, Edith Swinehart Lee passed away. She died from the painful consequences of undiagnosed senile diabetes. She suffered enormously in her last year. Her death struck Dad more forcefully than Mah-mee's passing after their twenty-seven tempestuous years of marriage and separation. He had begun dating not long after Mah-mee's funeral, but he didn't begin his search for a third wife until some years had elapsed after Edith's death.

He then dated a number of women: an elegant descendant of Li Hung-chang, who had been one of the great generals during the Taiping Rebellion; an aristocratic Chinese opera diva with a classic voice; a head-turning auburn-haired flight attendant the age of his grandchildren; and a gifted young sculptor named Elinor.

Dad's last love, when in his mid-eighties, was the remarkable mother of one of the world's great authors. The mother's name was Daisy; her daughter is Amy Tan. Dad lived with Daisy. The two had the passions and arguments of young people.

"We do things," Daisy said to Amy, "that you haven't even heard of!"

T.C. and Daisy went to China to watch her daughter make a movie of her first great novel.

While they were in China, I received a phone call from my cousin Lon-lon in Shanghai. I had remet him only a few years before, when we discovered that we were both still alive.

"Cousin, Cousin, so exciting! Great news! Uncle is married!"

My father's married?

"Yes, so exciting! Cousin Gus, we're so happy for Uncle! His new bride is so beautiful and now you have a new mother! Congratulations!"

I bought an extravagant bouquet of long-stemmed roses and met the entourage at the airport when they returned from China. I kissed Daisy delicately on the cheek and offered her the flowers.

"What for?" she asked.

"To honor my new mother," I said, smiling like a good son.

"What you mean, *mother?*"

"I heard you got married in China," I said slowly.

"Bah!" cried Dad. "Ignore what you hear from China! China's run by damn Communists! We had to say we were married so we could sleep in same room! They check everything!"

T.C. and Daisy would share brief appearances in the resulting movie, *The Joy Luck Club*, in which both are forever young.

In time, despite the urgent counsel of his son, T.C.'s infamous anger got the better of his last opportunity at happiness. He and Daisy fortunately separated before his hard ways killed her. He would spend his final years bitterly ruminating about this last woman in his life.

When he was younger, only sixty-two, he had found his best civilian employment with a top engineering firm—John A. Blume and Associates, which became URS/Blume. He was eighty-two when he retired.

After retirement, he pursued ladies and traveled. His most significant trip was a final sentimental journey to Fort Benning, where he paid homage to his favorite place in America. A general he had never met welcomed him home and gave him the run of post.

Financially sound after years of economic hardship, he nonetheless remained a victim of unmanaged emotions. He spent much of his last decade raging about politics, Mao Tse-tung, Communism, Democrats, his disappointing family and the world.

I met my soul mate, Diane, in 1978. We married and the army sent me on many journeys. But after losing our first child, Jessica, to heart disease, I left the service, and we were later blessed with a healthy daughter, Jena, and a healthy son, Eric.

In 1993, after completing my second novel, I quit my day job and became a writer and a family man. I have never been happier.

The next year, Diane's mother, Maralyn Elliott, gave her the family's copy of *Harvest from the Front* (China Inland Mission, 1946). It had been written by their cousin, Margaret Crossett, and described the demanding lives of American missionaries in China. Margaret wrote that during World War Two, she and her husband, Vincent, had cared for countless refugees fleeing the Japanese on the northern escape route to Free China. They focused on saving female infants and girls. Their mission was located on the escape route, in Anhwei.

By Christmas 1996, when he turned ninety, relations between Dad and my sisters had reached a new nadir. Totally exhausted by his moods, his profanity for the world and his anger at his grandchildren for not dedicating their lives to him, my sisters resigned themselves to two facts: Dad would never change; and his failure to change, after nearly seven decades, was no longer endurable.

My infrequent telephone conversations with him revealed that he was growing deaf. I visited him during business trips from Colorado to California and saw that he could hardly walk. He had always been well-dressed in formal bow ties; now he was unkempt.

Diane and I celebrated Christmas in California that year so we could include Dad. My sisters politely declined, and so Diane, Jena, Eric, Max, Ying's son, and I drove to Mountain View, where Dad's independent-living residence was located.

Dad was so happy to see Max that he wept. Earlier, Dad had looked at Jena while we ate at a restaurant, and he had begun crying. I looked at my beautiful daughter, who was then fourteen, and realized how closely she resembled the pictures of my mother.

"She looks like Da-tsien?" I asked Dad quietly.

"Yes," he said, crying. That day, he unearthed his portrait of my mother, and displayed it, while removing his picture of Edith. It was a huge concession to his son and his youngest daughter.

"Dad, don't do that for me. They were both your wives."

"Better for your kids, they see your mother, not stepmother."

I nodded, unable to speak. I didn't want to bury Edith, but I simply did not want my mother forgotten.

"We have to move him to us so we can take care of him," said Diane. "It doesn't matter that he's resisted the idea. He needs help now."

I agreed.

Incredibly, Dad also agreed. Max and I packed up his apartment, moving vans hauled his goods to the Rockies and Dad and I flew to Colorado Springs. He was fascinated by the mountains. He liked looking out the window of his new, fully-assisted senior residence at the mountains, smiling and remembering. I thought he'd love Cheyenne Mountain, but his favorite was Pikes Peak.

"Ah, that reminds me of the Hump," he said, smiling. "Flying over the Himilayas in a C-46. You know, on one of those flights, that's where I met James Montgomery Flagg, who painted the famous *I Want You, Uncle Sam* poster. He drew my picture, my portrait, see?" He held it out. It was signed, *To my friend Major Lee, James Montgomery Flagg.*

Diane had arranged and decorated his room until his own furniture arrived. She had found for him a physician, a dentist, an audiologist, a masseuse and a practical nurse.

I would spend long hours with him every day, and someone from the family had a meal with him. He was one of the few men in the residence, and he caused celebrity-level inhalations when he greeted a tableful of women by saying, "Ladies, I would be honored to join such a beautiful group, but I will not blame you if you would rather remain without male company."

The women clasped hands, swooned or blushed and begged him to join them. He had found new dinner companions, and before long, he was regaling them with tales of China that I had never heard.

In his room, he sat comfortably in his great gray reclining chair.

"I told stories like that when flying the Hump, yelling over the roar of the engines. I never thought the airplane would crash. Our family has made many journeys. My grandfather walked and sailed from Snail Creek village to Nanking. Then he was carried to Yangchow. I've been on every continent on the planet. Your mother, she walked out of China. But, ah, the Bravest Wife! She killed herself to save her husband, so sad."

He began using different voices and rich gestures, waving his arms and rasping points of emphasis. He had become a father I had never known, with a personality he had reserved for others. I had a hint of how people outside of our family might have seen him.

"You see, fortune teller said I'd die young. So when war come, I think I die. Didn't think I have to stick around for consequences. You know, I was always faithful to your stepmother."

"In wartime, relationships happen. Sometimes, you break someone else's heart. Sometimes, they break yours. Then, Spencer Tracy tell me that Kate was spoken for. First time, man break my heart!"

"Kate?"

"Sure, Kate Hepburn! She used me to make a movie. You know it— *Dragon Seed*. So let me set stage for you. . . ."

After a lifetime of silence, he was telling me his stories and those of our clan. I was a writer and my office was his apartment, his coffee breaks were with ladies who wore makeup to breakfast.

His stories were told in his unique fashion, with more attention paid to mood and emotion than to chronology or a sense of completion. He wouldn't always end his stories, and I happily accepted whatever he described. Sometimes, he would loop back and close a chapter. Other times, he wouldn't.

In mid-February, he began slowing. He was recounting fewer anecdotes and sleeping longer during the day. It struck me for the first time that he might die—an incredible thought, because Dad had always seemed to me to be virtually immortal.

In an effort to keep his mind sharp, he began reciting T'ang poetry and a Winston Churchill speech he had memorized. He stopped sleeping in his bed, using instead his great reclining chair, where I would find him in the morning before breakfast.

His memories represent the greatest gift he could have left his family. By casually abandoning his wife and children, and by unintentionally provoking Da-tsien to chase him, we had become an American family.

BEFORE DAWN ON March 4, 1997, I was awakened by a phone call from his residence on-duty nurse. Dad was having a heart attack. As they wheeled him to surgery for an angioplasty, he grabbed my arms.

"Be prepared! May not go as planned," he said, a soldier once again. In other words, don't be surprised.

"I will be, Dad. You be sure to come out of surgery. Be the tough soldier. I'll see you soon."

The procedure went smoothly. He slept in recovery as the sun rose on a beautiful morning in the Rockies. He had a strong heartbeat.

"Nothing is certain. We're still waiting on the lab results," said the nurse. Later, I would realize that she was preparing me, as well.

After Diane got the kids to school, she joined me in the CICU, greeting the nursing staff whom she already knew.

We held hands while we considered the mystery of the generations. Dad was ninety-one and looked seven-five and had lower blood pressure than I did.

He opened his eyes, blinking, disoriented. He saw grand, snow-capped Pikes Peak. Then he saw us. He nodded, smiling, and then closed his eyes.

Later, Diane and I were quietly talking when I realized that Dad was sitting up.

"*Shr, shr, ching jinlai, ching jinlai,*" he said. Yes, yes, please come in, please come in. He smiled grandly, charismatically, magnetically, beatifically, the upturned corners of his mouth moving continents as only fathers can do, using an expression which I had always imagined he possessed. He was lifting gloom and changing the light in the room. His eyes were closed.

There was no one else with us. I stood. So did Diane. The nurse watched in wonder.

"Ah ha, *cha, cha.*" Tea, tea. He was interacting with someone we couldn't see. Slowly and methodically, like a Chinese gentleman, he went through the elaborate motions of pouring tea into two cups, offering the second, more deeply steeped cup to his invisible guest. He said something under his breath, laughing, then sipped, making the polite Chinese sibilance of drawing in a valued liquid, nodding as he heard his guest echo the social sound.

He began speaking Songhai, which I hadn't spoken since the death of my mother. But he said, "Da-tsien," and his eyes grew moist, and he was nodding, listening and acknowledging in a considerate way, as if he were a true husband who regarded his wife as the most important person in the world. He canted his head, then nodded again. There was a rattle of quick conversation, as if they were making arrangements.

With little transition, he turned to face the foot of his bed instead of the side, where he had addressed my mother. He chuckled and nodded, smiling with old familiarity. "Ah ha, T.A., T.A. *Ching jinlai, ching jinlai.*"

He poured tea for T. A. Soong, and sipped with equal gusto and ritual. Dad spoke. In dialogue with visible people, he seldom listened, charging ahead with his ideas, which he always considered more beautiful than anyone else's. In breathless moments on a bright, sunlit morning, Dad paused to listen deeply like a sage, nodding like a *lao-shr*, a teacher, and only occasionally would he answer, everything on his face reflecting pleasure, accord and hopeful anticipation.

Finally, a third person arrived. Dad stiffened. I wondered if it was Gung-gung, Master Lee, his opium-addicted father, and I prepared for the loss of a magical mood.

"Ah ha, C.C., Lao Pooh, *Ching jinlai, ching jinlai.*"

Pooh Pan was in the room, and Dad was pouring him tea. This time, he held the cup up, cocking it slightly and nodding before sipping loudly and truly, as if his *pungyoh* who had so wildly walked the crooked path had touched cups and cried out with his familiar gusto, *Gambei!* It seemed that his old friend had forgiven him, and now they could speculate and joke if people would tell proverbs about them for ten thousand years. Dad was now only speaking to the dead.

My father put out his hands as if he were touching someone, and then he reclined, his chest heaving, resting. I looked at his bed and the floor, half-expecting to see the teacups.

The doctors informed us that the angioplasty dye had put him in critical renal failure, and that it would take high-risk heroics to create a marginal extension of life. Much earlier, he had told me that he didn't want to be a vegetable.

"Too embarrassing, no way to live," he said. "You a lawyer. You decide for me."

And so I did.

Solemnly and with a sense of wonder, I welcomed the chance to spend a last night with him. I asked Diane to bring me his two favorite books, *Anthony Adverse* and Keegan's *Six Armies in Normandy.* I sat near his good ear and read to him from both books. I also read from books that were my favorites, which I, as his son, thought appropriate to the passing of a man of history. I did so sparingly and with great care. When I grew tired, I rested, gently placing my hand on his.

I asked staff from the church to join us, and we strove to make the time sacred. Steadily, his vital functions began to deteriorate.

The sun rose that spring morning on a man who had been born to the light of tung oil lamps. He had followed the path of his father's departure from an opium-filled room, and had moved to the next world. Dad looked peaceful. A man with so much rage and so much *t'i-mien*, life force, couldn't really be dead, but I cried as a Chinese son should cry for his father, expressing *shiao*, filial piety, the rock that I could never put my arms around, the rock I could never lift, the rock I could never drop.

When a parent dies, something within us dies as well. Yet we have the power to make choices in these matters by deciding what parts of our parents we will honor and give life to through our own behaviors.

In the end, Zee Zee Lee, a rogue and a self-centered man, was *yi kao*, dependent, upon his wife and upon the kindnesses of his family.

In the end, a man who had driven others mad and had chased Hepburn, had turned to his first wife for harmony and intimacy, giving her, for a few moments, all that she had ever truly wanted.